ALCOHOLISM

TEACH YOURSELF BOOKS

To the ex-patients of the Alcoholic Units at Warlingham Park Hospital and St Bernard's Hospital, and to the memories of E M Jellinek and Lord Rosenheim.

ALCOHOLISM

Max Glatt

MD, DSc., FRCP, FRCPsych., DPM

Hon. Consultant Physician, Department of Psychological Medicine, University College Hospital, and Hon. Senior Lecturer, U.C.H. Medical School, London; Member, Medical College, St Bartholomew's Hospital, London; Visiting Psychotherapist, Wormwood Scrubs; Medical Director, Jellinek Unit (Charter Clinic), London; Vice-Chairman, Medical Council on Alcoholism.

Foreword by
The late **Lord Rosenheim**
KBE, MD, FRCP, FRS

Emeritus Professor of Medicine in the University of London and Past President of the Royal College of Physicians Formerly Chairman of the Medical Council on Alcoholism

TEACH YOURSELF BOOKS
Hodder and Stoughton

First printed 1982

British Library Cataloguing in Publication Data

Glatt, Max
Alcoholism. – (Teach yourself books)
1. Alcohol – Physiological effect
I. Title
616.86′1   RC565
ISBN 0 340 26817 4

Printed and bound in Great Britain
for Hodder and Stoughton Educational, a division of
Hodder and Stoughton Ltd, Mill Road, Dunton Green,
Sevenoaks, Kent by Richard Clay
(The Chaucer Press) Ltd, Bungay, Suffolk.
Photoset by Rowland Phototypesetting Ltd,
Bury St Edmunds, Suffolk.

Contents

Foreword

The Late **Lord Rosenheim**
KBE, MD, FRCP, FRS

When Dr Max Glatt's book was first added to the Priory Care and Welfare titles in 1970, I said that I regarded it as an honour and a privilege to have been invited to contribute to the book. I also said that I was confident that the message in this excellent book would reach many students, young doctors and workers in related disciplines as well as the lay public itself.

Such has, indeed, proved to be true. The first impression of Dr Glatt's book was published in two sections and the first of these (for the general reader) was sold out in little over a year! Part II (treatment) followed this pattern in a matter of months. The reason for such success is not hard to find.

At the time I wrote the first Foreword, I said that I recognised Dr Glatt not only as one of the world's outstanding experts on alcoholism, but also as a man whose humanity and understanding had rehabilitated many patients who would formerly have been regarded as beyond hope, doomed to follow a downhill path to death. It was then, as is now, Dr Glatt's attitude to his patients, his personality and his use of group therapy that have gained so great a reputation for his unit at St Bernard's Hospital – and gained world-wide acclaim for his book.

We are fortunately emerging from the era in which the chronic alcoholic was rejected by public and doctors alike. The medical profession, the Department of Health and Social Security and many members of the public are coming to appreciate that alcoholism is a disease, a disease that can be prevented and cured. Dr Glatt outlines the various forms that this disease may take – the insidious onset, the developing dependence and the varied physical and psychological complications that may occur. He

stresses the social aspects of alcoholism, drawing special attention
to its incidence among business executives and professional men
who, starting with the daily round of drinks, fall victim to the drug,
losing efficiency and satisfaction in their work with eventual financial crisis and disaster.

While the newspapers in this and other countries are full of
articles on the recent epidemic of drug dependence, the problems
of alcoholism, which have been with us for so much longer, evoke
relatively little publicity. Yet, since alcoholism affects the middle-
aged more than the young, those with social responsibilities rather
than the irresponsible, and since it is one of the outstanding causes
of marital disharmony, broken homes and psychologically disturbed children, it is one of the major diseases of our time.

With the newer understanding of the background of this condition has come the appreciation of the need for its prevention as
well as treatment.

Medical students still receive too little instruction on the many
problems of the alcoholic and the general practitioner still often
fails to respond to, or even to appreciate, the call for help and the
urgent need to institute treatment. Proper health education of the
public is also sadly deficient. Dr Glatt stresses the value of special
units for the treatment of alcoholics, both as out-patients and in
hospital, the need to treat each sufferer with patience, sympathy,
understanding and firmness, and the necessity for the after-care of
the apparently cured.

The new outlook on the condition is emphasised by the
establishment of the National Council on Alcoholism and the
more recently founded Medical Council on Alcoholism which
have begun to spread information and to support research. The
establishment of further special units and hostels for after-care is
being actively encouraged by the Department of Health and Social
Security.

We are very fortunate at University College Hospital Medical
School in having Dr Glatt to discuss these problems with our
students. Supported by a generous grant from the City Parochial
Foundation, he takes groups of students to his special clinic, to the
St Bernard's Hospital Unit and to the Out-patient Clinic and
Halfway Houses attached to it, demonstrating the physical and
mental problems of the alcoholic and the achievements of modern
treatment.

Many people – patients and their relatives, as well as doctors
and ancillary workers – will welcome the decision to make Dr

Glatt's book available in a new format to an even larger readership in this country and overseas. One comment from among many when the book was first reviewed can, I think, be fittingly repeated now on the occasion of the second edition: 'Dr Glatt's experience, scholarship, and compassionate insight give his book breadth, weight and value that it would be hard to match' (vide the *British Journal of Psychiatry*, November 1971). There seems little doubt that this is a book which will, for a long time to come, continue to engender a new outlook and interest in alcoholism as a widespread social disease.

Emeritus Professor of Medicine in the   Rosenheim
University of London and Past President   *April 1972*
of the Royal College of Physicians
Formerly Chairman of the Medical Council
on Alcoholism

Preface to 1982 edition

My original intention was to update the 1975 edition of this book. However, during the 1970s, there has been an 'explosion' not only of the apparent numbers of problem drinkers but certainly of articles and books written about the subject. To do justice to this development has entailed much effort and time; and the result is virtually a new book whose aim is to present an up-to-date account of the problems of alcohol misuse, including alcoholism.

Max Glatt, London 1982

Acknowledgements

For their kind permission to republish my own material which over the past three decades has been published in journals and books I am very grateful to the editors and publishers of the following:

Journals: *Acta Psychiatrica Scandinavica*
Age and Ageing
Alcoholism (Zagreb)
British Journal of Addiction
British Journal of Alcohol and Alcoholism
British Journal of Delinquency
British Journal of Hospital Medicine
British Journal of Psychiatry (Journal of Mental Science)
British Medical Journal
Doctor
General Practitioner
Geriatrics
The Health Education Journal
Health Trends
Hospital Life
Journal of the Irish Medical Association
Journal of Social Psychiatry
The Lancet
Medical World
Midwife and Health Visitor
Modern Medicine
Monatsschrift für Psychiatrie und Neurologie
Narcotics Bulletin (UN)
Nursing Mirror
Nursing Times
On Call

Prevent
Proceedings of the Royal Society of Medicine
Public Health
Pulse
(Quarterly) Journal for the Study of Alcohol
World Health Organisation Chronicle
World Health

Books: *The Drug Scene in Great Britain* (1966), Arnold, London
Drug Addiction and its Treatment (1974), MTP, Lancaster
Drug Dependence: Current Issues and Problems (1977), MTP, Lancaster

Chapters in: *Alcohol and Road Traffic* (1962), Proceedings of the 3rd International Conference, BMA, London
Annual European and International Institutes on the Prevention and Treatment of Alcoholism, International Council on Alcohol and Addictions, Lausanne
International Conferences on Alcoholism, ICCA, Lausanne
New Aspects of Mental Health Services (1967), Pergamon Press, Oxford
Gradwohl's Medicine (2nd and 3rd editions, 1968, 1976), ed. F E Camps, John Wright, Bristol
Alcoholism: A Medical Profile (1973), 1st International Medical Conference, B Edsall, London
Notes on Alcohol and Alcoholism (1975), ed. S Caruana, Medical Council on Alcoholism, B Edsall, London
Progress in Clinical Medicine (6th edition 1971), Churchill Livingstone, London, Edinburgh
Dictionary of Medical Ethics (1981), Darton, Longman and Todd, London

I am also extremely grateful to the many authors and journals quoted in the text and references. I am greatly indebted to many medical, nursing and other professional colleagues, and to the secretarial staff, who over the years were associated with me in working with alcoholic patients and to my alcoholic patients – from all of whom I have learned a great deal.

It is also a pleasure to express my thanks to the publishers, and in particular to Ruth Kimber and Anne Alport for their unfailing courtesy and invaluable advice throughout our collaboration.

Charts and Tables

'Writing upon drinking is in one respect, I think, like drinking itself: one goes on imperceptibly, without knowing where to stop . . . Happy should I be, could I flatter myself that this paper will be received with as hearty satisfaction as is generally felt upon the opening of an additional bottle.'

(James Boswell, 'Boswell's Column, May 1780', (ed. M. Bailey), William Kimber Ltd, London 1951, p. 176.)

Introduction

'Doctors are good . . . drugs are bad' – whether they are or are not, and certainly not everyone would agree, that is their public image in Western Europe, according to the Deputy Editor, *British Medical Journal*, in the November 1980 issue [1]. How about alcohol? Is it – or its image – good or bad? Alcohol itself is of course a drug. It is a fairly simple chemical substance produced in nature by the fermentation of sugars. The alcohol taken in our alcoholic drinks, ethyl alcohol, ethanol, C_2H_5OH is a member of a family of alcohols (another one being the toxic methyl alcohol). Scientific textbooks describe it as a clear, colourless liquid with a characteristic weak odour and a strong burning taste, and with certain chemical and physiochemical properties. As such, alcohol is neither good nor bad, but what makes it, or its image, good or bad is the way in which beverage alcohol is used. The article quoted above points out that over the past twenty years public attitudes to drugs have changed from 'adulation to profound suspicion', and over the centuries the same process seems frequently to have occurred (as a two-way traffic) in regard to alcoholic drink.

Similarly, attitudes towards those who misuse alcohol have varied widely and wildly over the ages; 3000 years ago a Spartan king decreed that drunkards' legs be cut off; 1000 years later a Roman lawyer urged that such drinkers be treated as sick people [2] (a recommendation largely forgotten during the subsequent 2000 years, and again rejected by some in our days).

On the whole, however, the great majority of mankind who used ethanol, largely in moderation, have probably always regarded it, in general, as a pleasant enough and essentially 'good' thing!' What was wrong was not a feature of alcohol itself, but of the people who misused it in such a way that they came to grief or caused problems for others. The latter could then be dismissed as not being 'normal drinkers', whatever such a vague term may mean. Keller and McCormick's authoritative *Dictionary . . . about Alcohol* [4] starts off by calling the abnormal drinker 'one whose drinking is not normal in any of several possible senses'; and a problem drinker – a term employed frequently in recent years – is described in the *Dictionary* as 'an excessive drinker whose drinking causes private or public harm and who is seen to cause problems for himself or for others'. Of such 'problem drinkers' some become alcoholics, that is, they develop a state of dependence on the drug or suffer damage to their health from excessive drinking. Fortunately alcoholics and other problem drinkers form only a minority of users of beverage alcohol but as their numbers are increasing the world over, as more and more women and young people become involved, and because of the increasing severity of public health and socioeconomic problems caused by alcohol misuse to the whole community, the public image of alcoholic drink is perhaps also gradually undergoing a change. Even though prohibition is not a practical policy there is a need for society to abandon its *laissez faire* attitude vis-à-vis beverage alcohol because of its pharmacological nature as a drug. Used well, and on the whole not too unwisely, as it is by most people users derive, as the 1979 report of the Royal College of Psychiatrists (R.C.Psych) Special Committee [5] puts it, in rather too glowing terms, 'nothing but pleasure and benefit from it' (perhaps not undiluted pleasure, in view of the occasional hangovers and other risks). But, as the report continues, 'Alcohol is also a drug which can miserably wreck or destroy life, and which exacts these costs on a devastating scale'.

For thousands of years and all over the world, people have taken alcoholic drink. The great majority enjoyed it with impunity but there has always been a minority who had to pay heavily for the initial pleasure and to whom alcohol finally brought distress, social and economic decline, degradation, physical illness, insanity and death.

No wonder, then, that from ancient times on, attempts, often desperate in nature, have been made to prevent and combat alcohol-induced problems, including alcoholism. Countless treatises have been written about these conditions, and much progress has been made in our knowledge in this field, particularly since, in the past forty years, an objective, scientific approach towards 'alcoholics' (and 'problem drinkers') has begun to supersede the formerly prevalent emotionally-based, moralistic attitude towards the 'drunkard'.

In spite of all this research, much in the realm of alcohol problems still remains obscure, as regards such fundamental aspects as causation, prevention and treatment. On the other hand, a great deal is known that could help the professional worker, doctor, social worker, nurse and clergyman, as well as the problem drinker's family and friends, in their approach to the sufferer. But unfortunately available information has not become widely known to the professional or general public. In the past, in their training professional workers have learnt very little about problem drinking and alcoholism often knowing less about it than the patients they were supposed to treat. The late Dr John Y Dent, a pioneer of the apomorphine treatment in this country, and at the time Editor of the *British Journal of Addiction*, bitterly complained in an editorial: 'What is the doctor taught at medical school about the treatment of addiction? Little or nothing. What can he find in his medical textbooks on this prevalent disease? Almost nothing. Many patients nowadays know much more about it than he: they are beginning to be taught by Alcoholics Anonymous and the lay press. The doctor must catch up.'

Fortunately, in more recent years, doctors and others have begun to 'catch up'. Professionals, lay workers, family and friends can render a great deal of help by an understanding approach based on sound knowledge. The fact that there are many gaps left in our understanding and knowledge is not an adequate reason for standing idly by and doing nothing. As Sir Martin Roth said in his Preface to the 1979 Report of the Royal College of Psychiatrists, *Alcohol and Alcoholism* [6], 'incomplete evidence in no way justifies inaction in the face of an epidemic of that dimension'; and he quotes Sherrington that 'Science nobly can wait for an answer; commonsense pressed for time must act from acceptance'.

'Alcoholism [according to the opening paragraph of a DHSS Memorandum published in 1973 [7]] is difficult to define, difficult to describe and difficult to detect.' It is also difficult to prevent and difficult to treat. 'Yet [the Memorandum continued] its effects on the sufferer, on his family and on society are so serious that it is worth attempting to do so.'

Since that Memorandum was written, the prevalence and impact of alcoholism on sufferers, family and society have greatly increased, and what was important and was being attempted then has now become urgent. Alcoholism, as a leading article in the *British Medical Journal* [8] expressed in 1979, has become 'everyone's business'. Everyone should be informed about the basic facts of this disorder; not only professionals but also the public. Problem drinking is a matter of concern to the whole community.

Over the centuries many writers have extolled the virtues of alcoholic drink. 'Rum [as an American author put it half a century ago [9]] relieved the sorrowful and distressed, provided the soldier with courage, the traveller with endurance, the statesman with foresight, the preacher with inspiration, and sailor, plowman, trader and trapper alike with sustenance. By [alcoholic drink] were lighted the fires of revelry and devotion.' Yet it may be significant that the author, J A Krout, described all these qualities of alcohol in a book dealing with *The Origins of Prohibition* [9]. In the words of Keller [10], who quotes Krout's description, alcohol has always proved a 'double-dealer' in history. After centuries of heavy drinking Britain found itself, 250 years ago, in the grip of a severe gin epidemic [11], a state of affairs repeated 100 years later, in the nineteenth century, and, after a temporary improvement in the first half of this century, we now find ourselves at the start, or already within, a third wave of alcoholism [12].

In Britain, as in the rest of the world, problem drinking has greatly increased over the past twenty-five years [12], and in particular over the last decade. More and more money is spent on alcoholic drink – by men and women, the relatively young as well as older age groups, lower as well as higher income groups – and Canadian research workers have shown that there is a clear correlation between the extent of alcohol-induced harm to health in a given population and the *per capita* alcohol consumption [13]. Recent statistics found, for example, that over eight litres of pure alcohol were consumed per year per head of population; more than 100,000 cases of drunkenness yearly came before the courts; and drunkenness offences have increased by more than 50 per cent over the past ten years. Over the same period admissions to NHS hospitals for alcoholism have doubled and deaths from liver cirrhosis (a condition often taken as an indirect index of the prevalence of alcoholism) have increased by one third. Drinking and driving offences have more than doubled during this period, and more than one third of drivers (and some of the pedestrians) killed in road accidents had a blood alcohol level exceeding the legal limit of 80mg/100ml.

According to official statistics the average adult in the UK increased his intake of beer in the two decades 1955–77 by 47 per

Figure 1

Annual consumption of alcohol per person aged 15 and over in the United Kingdom (excluding home produced alcohol)

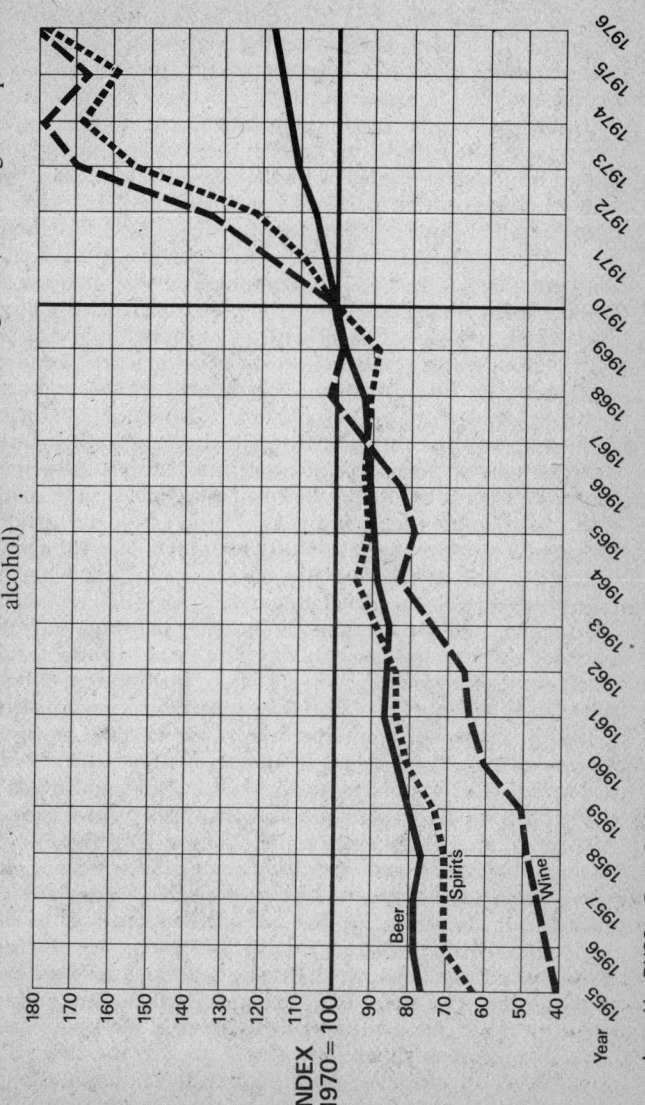

Issued by DHSS at Press Conference on
Advisory Committee on Alcoholism Reports.

cent, his intake of wine by 309 per cent, and his intake of spirits by 148 per cent. Or, if we just look at the increase in consumption of alcoholic drink that has taken place during the last decade, the average adult drank 14 per cent more beer in 1977 (as compared to 1970), 16.4 per cent more wine, and 54 per cent more spirits.

In view of the correlation between *per capita* consumption of alcohol and alcohol-related complications, such increase of alcohol consumption in the British population is likely to be accompanied by a rise in the various manifestations of alcoholism. No one knows the number of alcoholics in this country, but in 1979 a Government spokesman [16] mentioned an estimated rise from 490,000 alcoholics in 1957 to some 740,000 in 1977. Every alcoholic's drinking behaviour closely involves and affects other members of his family; thus several millions in this country are more or less directly affected by alcoholism. Clearly, however, alcoholism is by no means a disorder affecting only the individual drinker and his family but involves the whole of the community. It plays, for example, a disruptive role in industry (though this has largely been ignored), it contributes to crime and accidents on the road, at work and at home. Materially, society suffers from the number of working days lost by so many and the burden imposed upon the health and welfare services. Alcoholism is a liability – and a responsibility – of the whole community.

However, rather than thinking in this connection only of 'alcoholism' in the narrow sense of this term (see Chapter 1), one has to remember that alcoholism is no more than one example of a frightening and long list of problems caused by misuse of alcohol. In 1955 an Expert Committee of the World Health Organisation on *Alcohol and Alcoholism* [17] differentiated between 'Problems of Alcohol' and 'Problems of Alcoholism'; and similarly recent World Health Organisation publications speak of a wide range of 'Alcohol-related Problems' or 'Disabilities' [18], one of which (though obviously a very important one) is 'Dependence' on alcohol. Problems caused by misuse of alcohol – even in the absence of 'alcoholism' – are, for example, isolated occurrences of drunkenness, drink-related driving accidents, or violent behaviour under the influence of drink of a jealous husband, occurring in people who are usually moderate drinkers. Naturally such occurrences are much more likely to occur in 'alcoholics' than in casual roisterers but they may also happen in the absence of a 'dependence' on alcohol. Although often not appreciated, alcohol is a drug, a drug that, like narcotics or tranquillisers, depresses the nervous system, and it is this effect which is responsible for the various complications that may affect the drinker. The fact that alcohol has long become what Jellinek (the father of the scientific approach to alcoholism) has called a 'domesticated drug' [19] does not detract from its dangers; on the contrary, its ready availability and social acceptance only brings the risk within reach of many people who would not dream of misusing other potentially dangerous drugs. Similarly the fact that the use of alcohol is legitimate does not make it any less dangerous: nicotine – though legal – is now generally accepted to be a very dangerous substance, and the modern tranquillising drugs, though widely prescribed (and often over-prescribed) by medical practitioners, may lead to harmful consequences when taken in too high amounts or for too long periods.

Two or three decades ago, national councils on alcoholism in various countries usually proclaimed that their concern was with alcoholics but not with ordinary drinkers although it has probably always been realised by most of those interested in drink problems that there was no clear-cut demarcation line between 'excessive drinkers' and 'alcoholics', and that there was no uniform pre-alcoholic personality, i.e. a definite constellation of personality qualities that inevitably or commonly predisposes such an individual – once he has started to imbibe alcoholic drinks – to become an 'alcoholic'. The notion that it is mainly emotionally highly unstable and inadequate individuals who run the risk of developing alcoholism has long gone out of fashion. Under unfavourable circumstances it is likely that virtually everyone who takes drink frequently can in time develop 'alcoholism'; as Figure 3 indicates in the *Chart of Alcohol Dependence* (pp.74–5). Not only those individuals who drink for relief from internal or external problems but also others, who move in social or occupational 'subcultures' among whom regular drinking is rife or perhaps the 'order of every day', may in this way gradually develop tolerance and dependence. Certain occupations are high-risk groups; and this is only one example of how the drinking behaviour of individuals may have a profound effect on others who are in more or less close and regular contact with them. Similarly, the drinking behaviour of parents is likely to have a profound effect on their children and youngsters' own drinking patterns are likely to be closely influenced by the drinking habits of their peers. Wide social acceptance among increasingly younger age groups and women of rather heavy drinking as 'normal' and the 'done thing' is likely to lead in time to an increase of heavy drinking among these groups, who formerly tended to drink less than middle-aged men. Thus the heavy drinking habits of individuals are likely to influence those of some of their neighbours, associates and friends; such considerations may perhaps partly explain the recent findings of correlation between a population's average alcohol consumption and the incidence of alcohol-related damage to health. In a given individual the heavier the drinking the more likely the danger to his health. In recent years the notion of *safe* drinking limits (popularised a hundred years ago by the British physician and Editor of the London medical magazine *The Practitioner*, Robert Anstie) has again been taken up: the recent Report of the College of Psychiatrists [5], for example, mentions four pints of beer, or four double whiskies, or a bottle of wine per day as the maximum, and this obviously not to be taken every day. Such estimates are of course only tentative and no one knows for sure the 'safe' limits – respectively – as regards risks of development of dependence, or of harm to the various organs often affected by heavy drinking. Many individual factors are involved; women, for example, are more vulnerable to the development of cirrhosis of the liver as a consequence of regular drinking.

The figures quoted above probably come as an unpleasant shock – though a very timely reminder – to many who may have fondly regarded themselves as no more than ordinary or 'moderate' drinkers because they drank no more than the majority of their friends. The amount a person drinks – though not one of the factors mentioned in the widely quoted 1952 definition of alcoholism by the World Health Organisation [20] – is of significance as to whether he is more or less likely to develop dependence on alcohol or harm, although apart from the 'agent' alcohol other factors ('host' and 'environment') are obviously involved. There is certainly no clear-cut divide between the 'respectable', allegedly innocuous, regular drinker who night after night has his quota of several pints or 'shorts' in the company of his friends and the 'alcoholic': there is no definite fence separating those on the right side from those stigma-invested, 'irresponsible' and ostracised 'alcoholics' on the wrong side; or those who drink in moderation on most occasions from others who hardly ever do so. There are all kinds of gradations. There may be drinkers who show 'problems of alcohol' only rarely, or more or less intermittently, or more or less regularly. The latter may be called 'problem drinkers' by some, and such 'problem drinkers' may develop varying degrees of dependence upon alcohol, which in turn predisposes towards the development of other 'problems of alcoholism' or 'alcoholic-related disabilities'. But it may be significant that even advanced, clearly dependent alcoholics with 'loss (or lack) of control' [19] often can abstain ('go on the waggon') and at times may even be able to drink in moderation for shorter or (more rarely) longer periods.

That such dependent drinkers are occasionally able to exhibit a certain measure of control, naturally greatly contributes to their ability of deluding themselves that there is nothing really wrong with their drinking. Certainly even those who admit that they occasionally drink more than may be good for them manage, as a rule, to convince themselves that they are 'average social drinkers'. A National Opinion Poll (1979), analysed by the sociologist Laurie Taylor [21] showed 'heavy drinking' (i.e. a minimum of 6–8 pints or of six measures of spirits per day) as well as 'regular drinking' (i.e. at least twice a week) to be most prevalent among the age groups 18–34 years, although much regular and heavy drinking was found also in the age groups up to the mid-sixties. But even heavy drinkers had little difficulty in convincing themselves that their drinking was no more than 'average', by pointing to the abnormal secret drinking habits of groups such as solitary drinkers, drunken women and 'alcoholics'. They felt that their own drinking was 'poles apart' from the drinking patterns of these 'abnormal drinkers'.

The 'scapegoating' mechanism may also contribute to the phenomenon that it seems to take a surprisingly long time for myths to disappear, for example, that the 'typical' alcoholic is the skid-row homeless drunk rolling in the gutter, with whom the average ordinary drinker has nothing whatsoever in common. In reality, of course, in Britain and elsewhere, skid-row drinkers – while obviously in need of understanding and help – are no more than a very small proportion of the total population of problem drinkers and alcoholics, of whom the very great majority are probably living with their families, working more or less steadily, managing somehow to cope with the problems arising from their problem, and remaining largely unrecognised, undiagnosed and untreated. The minority, who are members of AA (Alcoholics Anonymous) or turn up in hospitals or Out-patient Clinics, are probably no more than the tip of the iceberg, and the extent to which such drinkers are representative of the majority of this country's 'problem drinkers' is unknown. But increasing *per capita* consumption of alcoholic drink among all age groups – men and women alike – reflects greater availability and social encouragement of drinking throughout the population, and under such circumstances more may be tempted gradually to increase their own consumption. Figures relating to problem drinking in this country may mean no more to most of us than nasty statistics and unpleasant reminders of what happens to others but are not of immediate personal interest and significance until 'it' hits someone nearer home; and the chances that this may happen unfortunately increase year by year. Under such circumstances many formerly popular notions can no longer be upheld, such as those of the majority of social drinkers who feel that they have no truck with the unfortunate few who because of 'bad character', lacking willpower, near-criminal negligence, etc., have become 'drunks' and deserve all that is coming to them: 'it surely could not happen to me'. The gulf between the 'social' drinker – and certainly the 'heavy' social drinker – and the dependent alcoholic has greatly narrowed, even though majority opinion would still tend to view those who become definitely dependent on alcohol as more than just the extreme variant of excessive drinkers. For example, psychological and/or as yet rather obscure physiological factors may predispose certain excessive drinkers towards developing dependence rather than other equally excessive drinkers.

Under such circumstances of increasing general alcohol consumption throughout the population, with the risk of increasing damage to health for many people, the alcohol problem may gradually assume a more significant personal meaning. This may be even more true of Scotland than of England, where the alcohol problem is estimated to be proportionately about four times greater than the English one. At least one in ten Scottish families has been estimated to have a member suffering from alcoholism. 120,000 Scots may have a drinking problem, with another half a million friends or relatives indirectly affected [22].

Fortunately, with the gradual worsening of the problems of alcohol and alcoholism, there has been an awakening of interest and activity by the State as well as by the professional and the public. The first edition of this book opened with a brief reference to 'August 1964 [when] London was the host city, and the British Medical Association House the venue, for the *Tenth European Institute on the Prevention and Treatment of Alcoholism*. Had such a congress [the First Edition continued] taken place in England only ten years earlier [i.e. in the early 1950s] – in itself something which no one could have imagined at the time – all that visitors from abroad could have been told was that there was then one small alcoholic unit working under the National Health Service, that there was not a single special ward or out-patient clinic anywhere in the country devoted entirely to the treatment of alcoholics, and that apart from the old established [in 1884] Society for the Study of Addiction, and a few private nursing homes and temperance societies, virtually no one cared about the alcoholic – nor for that matter seemed to be aware that he existed, except as a rare specimen. In fact, visitors from abroad were often told by the authorities that there was no alcoholic problem in this country [23]. A handbook on Health Education published by the Ministry of Education in 1956 devoted a mere one and a half pages to the subject of alcoholism and spoke complacently of 'a welcome and continuing reduction in the heavy drinking which at times in the eighteenth and nineteenth centuries caused great harm to our society'. And all this though clouds on the horizon were by no means absent. For example, a historical review of the English drink problem published by the present writer in 1958 [11] ended with a plea for vigilance, in view of the deteriorating statistics relating to the 'indirect indices' of alcoholism, such as public drunkenness, drunken driving and mortality from liver cirrhosis. All such 'indirect indices' have continued to reflect the worsening position ever since. For a period in the 1960s the gradually awakening interest in alcohol problems was overshadowed by the newly emerged problem of drug misuse and drug dependence among the young [24] but certainly the most widely used and misused drug (apart from nicotine) *is* alcohol, and the most widespread form of both psychological and physiological drug dependence is alcoholism.

This book is based, in the main, on personal experiences with many thousands of mainly British alcoholics observed during the past three decades in a great variety of settings: residential (such as NHS alcohol units – Warlingham Park Hospital and St Bernard's Hospital – or private nursing homes); the alcohol unit in Wormwood Scrubs; out-patient clinics (for example, Paddington Day Centre and University College Hospital); and during domiciliary visits to patients' homes. At the start of my interest in alcohol problems I greatly benefited from studying the writings of 'Bunky' Jellinek, founder of the modern scientific approach to alcoholism, and I am also extremely grateful for the opportunity of regular exchange of views and observations with international experts from all parts of the world at the regular institutes and conferences arranged by the International Council on Alcohol and Addictions (Lausanne) under its Executive Director, Mr Archer Tongue. Indeed, I have been privileged to count not only many recovered alcoholic ex-patients but also many international experts in the field of alcoholism among my personal friends and I have learnt a great deal from all of them. Likewise I have greatly profited, over the past thirty years, from the exchange of views following many talks and seminars both in Britain and abroad, and in particular from the stimulating contact following the regular discussions and demonstrations on alcoholism with medical students of four London Medical Schools (University College Hospital, St Bartholomew's Hospital, Middlesex Hospital, and Royal Free Hospital) over the past two decades. But I have to admit freely that what little I may have learnt about alcohol problems and alcoholics I have in the main obtained 'straight from the horse's mouth', from innumerable discussions with alcoholics, in particular during the often hectic, lively, exciting and always extremely stimulating and thought-provoking group therapy meetings.

Hand in hand with such clinical work and clinical research is, of course, the necessity to try to remain familiar with the ever-growing literature in the field and I have been helped in this task by having the pleasure and the honour to follow Dr John Y Dent in 1962 (until 1977) as the Honorary Editor of the *British Journal of Addiction* (now in the capable hands of Professor Griffith Edwards). No one doubts the necessity to validate clinical findings and to have, as far as is possible, in-built facilities for evaluation of newly-planned treatment programmes. But unfortunately in very recent years it has become difficult in this field to find a rational synthesis between the results of research work and the mass of clinical experience. 'We seem to be moving [states a 1980 editorial in the *British Journal of Addiction* [25] toward an era where there is a greater and greater divide between research worker and clinician . . . [There are] distinguished researchers in this field who have not for years seen an alcoholic, and they thus deny themselves access to the most important and fundamental experience for the research worker – listening to people talk.'

Alcoholism is a complex, and in many respects, a controversial subject. A reviewer of a recent book on the subject of Therapeutics [26] stated that: 'A wise teacher provides a simplified and dogmatic "party line" for students to grasp and plays down the controversy which is apt to confuse.' This book, however, is far from being a 'wise book' and will make no attempt to play down or to avoid mentioning the manifold controversies, or to provide simplified or dogmatic 'party lines'! Anyone active in such a field as alcoholism inevitably forms views of his own and has his own biases; but before presenting them, an attempt will be made to give the views of others which may be diametrically opposed, even though in this way some confusion may be unavoidable. At the same time such a presentation may stimulate the reader to try to discover why these views so often greatly differ. Controversies in this field are emotionally highly charged – as were the arguments between the 'wet' and the 'dry' – those in favour and against alcoholic drink respectively. In order to help the reader to get to know more about the topics of his choice, many references are given; and a chapter at the end of the book will indicate briefly the 'party line' of recent British books in this field.

As this book is largely based on personal experiences it is hoped that my frequent quotation of personal observations will be for-given. I first became interested in alcoholics and their problems in 1951, having just joined the staff of the very progressive Warling-ham Park Hospital in Surrey. I started to hold group therapy sessions with neurotic patients there, and found the occasional alcoholic patients who participated in these groups interesting; but they did not seem to fit well into the 'neurotics' groups, so in 1952 I started an experimental group for these patients only (of whom we then had four in the hospital) [27]. My main (and only) qualifica-tion then was that I had very little (or probably no) knowledge of alcoholism and, therefore, as I fondly deluded myself, no pre-conceived notions and no axe to grind. But it came almost im-mediately as a profound shock to me that the few notions I did have about alcoholics were utterly wrong and ridiculous. These patients were not 'layabouts' and 'n'er-do-wells', no weak-willed a social work-shy people who enjoyed their drinking so much that they did not want to give it up and who therefore had no time for, or interest in, anything else. How completely wrong I had been was also borne out by my first meeting soon afterwards with prominent members of Alcoholics Anonymous. Since then I have been privileged to work in close co-operation with members of that fellowship. Indeed there has been a very fruitful and stimulat-ing cross-fertilisation of ideas between AA and the many patients and ex-patients of the alcoholic units who joined AA and who have often played an active and leading role in various groups throughout the country.

Possibly even greater than the shock over my ignorance was the realisation that few other non-alcoholics were free from such gross misconceptions and completely erroneous notions about alcoholics, and that, with few exceptions, neither the general public nor the medical profession (including the [general and psychiatric] teaching hospitals) nor the State seemed to have the slightest interest in their welfare. However, my intention at the time to write a book about 'The alcoholic – the man whom the National Health Service has forgotten' which was to plead for a 'fair deal for the alcoholic', never materialised.

However, in spite of very little progress in the 1950s, signs of an improvement in the situation began to emerge in the sixties with the publication of a Memorandum (1961) by a Joint Committee of the British Medical Association and the Magistrates' Association [28]. This was followed, in 1962 [29] (and again in 1968) [30] by Memoranda of the Ministry of Health which recommended the formation of special Regional Alcoholic Units and which implied the acceptance by the State of alcoholism as an illness for which the NHS had to make provisions. Since then the State has taken an increasingly active interest (in particular since the 1970s) [31–35]; a number of voluntary and religious organisations have provided special hostels, crypts and shelters; many research papers on the subject have been published in leading medical journals, and the National Council and Medical Council on Alcoholism (both established in the 1960s) are making consistent efforts to keep the seriousness and the urgency of the problem in front of the general and medical public.

In spite of this though it is probably as true today as it was in previous decades that the average general practitioner knows of no more than two alcoholics out of possibly twenty to thirty in his practice; that no more than a small fraction of this country's total alcoholic population joins AA or comes to the attention of any professional or voluntary agencies interested in their welfare, and that, therefore, the great majority of alcoholics (and their families) continue to suffer in silence, loneliness and anonymity. This is the more tragic as, contrary to widespread misconceptions, alcoholics can very often be helped a great deal, once they want to get out of 'the mess' which their drinking career has landed them in, or once 'motivation' has been induced by a therapeutic team that befriends, understands and accepts them. It would of course be preferable to prevent the emergence of problem drinkers and alcoholics in the first place, and the recent emphasis on prevention of alcoholism [33–35] is very welcome. However successful such attempts may be, in a non-Utopian society there will, however, always be alcoholic casualties in need of special help. While all steps should be taken to encourage public understanding of and sympathy for alcoholics, it is equally necessary, in the interests of prevention, to foster public attitudes of strong disapproval of excessive drinking, drunkenness and drunken behaviour (irrespective of the need for research into, and attempts to alleviate, the psychosocial causes of such asocial and antisocial behaviour).

Clearly society suffers a great deal of damage from the behaviour of all drinkers and not just the 'dependent' or 'alcoholics'. Some recent publications therefore have dealt both with 'Alcohol and Alcoholism', such as the publication by the Royal College of Psychiatrists [5]. But in spite of much overlapping, there are also marked differences between the 'problems of alcohol' and 'problems of alcoholism', mainly arising from alcoholics' dependence on the drug which is missing in other drinkers. Whatever strategies may be best in the approach to non-dependent drinkers who drink occasionally to excess – for example, the casual roisterer who gets drunk and is involved in a brawl or driving accident, the drunken football hooligan, the antisocial individual whose activities also include occasional heavy drinking (i.e. the 'drinking criminal' in contrast to the 'criminal alcoholic' [36] – in all such cases the approaches required are, in the main, probably quite different from those that are helpful to the alcoholic. For such reasons this book is primarily concerned with the 'problems of alcoholism' rather than with the 'problems of alcohol' without minimising the great importance of the latter. There has been some criticism levelled in recent years at the fact that the interest of professionals in this field was concentrated in the past almost exclusively on alcoholics, to the exclusion and detriment of other drinkers with alcohol-related problems. There is probably a certain amount of justification in this reproach; but the gradual awakening of public interest in the plight of alcoholics has also paved the way for arousing interest in problems caused by behaviour of drinkers other than alcoholics. This would be similar to the welcome repercussions from the gradual acceptance the world over of alcoholism as an illness and of alcoholics as sufferers needing help, and also the extension of such understanding to addicts to drugs other than alcohol, in spite of a great deal of initial resistance [37].

Among important tasks still to be tackled is that of investigating the prevalence of problem drinking in industry both on the shop floor and in the Boardroom. In theory, industry has an excellent opportunity of establishing preventive and early diagnostic and rehabilitation programmes among employees whose past history would tend to indicate an essentially good or fair prognosis. In the past, there have been occasional reports indicating a relatively high number of problem drinkers – at least in certain industries – which, however, aroused no more than fleeting and rapidly forgotten interest followed by an approach characterised by masterly inactivity. Might one hope that some day in the near future it will no longer be necessary for the problems of alcoholism in industry, in general practice, in the Services, among doctors and other professional workers, etc., to have to be rediscovered every five years or so, and it no longer be the rule for such 'discoveries' to be greeted and commented on by the general and medical public with an air of somewhat indignant and incredulous surprise, only to be forgotten and laid aside rapidly? Industry – said an American speaker at an International Conference in Glasgow nearly ten years ago – cannot afford *not* to do something about the alcoholics in its midst, even for purely materialistic reasons. Industry cannot afford to do so, but obviously hitherto it has managed.

At present, though somewhat less than in the past, the fear of stigma, arising partly from lack of objective information and misunderstanding of the condition among the general public, is one of the main factors preventing problem drinkers coming forward much earlier, or even before dependence has set in.

In this book I have tried to concentrate in the main on those points which have cropped up most frequently in discussions on problem drinking with lay and professional groups. The purpose of this work will have been achieved if it can contribute a little, by assisting in the dissemination of some basic information, towards a better, more realistic appraisal and understanding of the difficulties confronting alcoholics and their families and thereby making their lot a more hopeful and less unhappy one. At the same time one might hope that greater awareness and appreciation by the general public of the risks attached to excessive drinking would, in time, have beneficial effects on general drinking habits, and thereby have a salutary effect in reducing the incidence of alcohol-related problems and damage to health. Politicians and

Government have the final responsibility for drafting the relevant laws, rules and regulations needed for the all-important legal and fiscal contribution to the task of prevention; but they will not be inclined to stick their necks out too far ahead of public opinion unless they feel supported, or indeed pushed along, by a well-informed and sufficiently motivated general and professional public [38].

Notes

1. Thirty years ago a meeting in London of the Hunterian Society rejected the motion 'that alcohol has contributed more to the happiness than the misery of mankind'; however 'from a large gathering not a single convinced teetotaller emerged to press his viewpoint', and various speakers talked, 'perhaps a little wistfully, of the days when gin was 3d (1½p) a glass'[3].

References

1 Smith, T (1980), *Brit. med. J.* 281, 1410
2 Pullar-Strecker, H M (1952), *The Lancet* i, 555
3 *The Lancet* (1949), ii, 1000
4 Keller, M and McCormick, M (1968), *A Dictionary of Words about Alcohol*, New Brunswick, NJ, Rutgers Center of Alcohol Studies
5 *Alcohol and Alcoholism* (1979), Report of a Special Committee of the Royal College of Psychiatrists, London, Tavistock
6 Roth, Sir Martin (1979), Foreword, *Alcohol and Alcoholism*, R. C. Psych. Report, vi
7 *Alcoholism* (1973), Standing Medical Advisory Committee, London, DHSS
8 *Brit. med. J.* (1979), 'Action on Alcohol' (Leading Article)
9 Krout, J A (1925), *The Origins of Prohibition*, New York, Knopf
10 Keller, M (1976) in *Alcohol and Alcohol Problems*, ed. Filstead, W J, Rossi, J R, and Keller, M, Cambridge, Mass., Ballinger, 5
11 Glatt, M M (1958), *Brit. J. Addict.* 54, 51
12 Glatt, M M, *Proc. Roy. Soc. Med.* 197
13 De Lint, J and Schmidt, W (1971), *Brit. J. Addict.* 66, 97
14 Jellinek, E M (1947), *Quart. J. Stud. Alcohol* 8, 1
15 Schmidt, W and Popham, R E (1980), *Brit. J. Addict.* 75, 363
16 Young, Sir George (31st October, 1978), *Hansard*
17 *World Health Organisation Expert Committee on Alcohol and Alcoholism* (1955), Wld Hlth Org. Techn. Rep. Ser. 48
18 Edwards, G *et al.* (1977), *Alcohol-Related Disabilities*, WHO Offset Publication, 32

18   *Alcoholism*

19   Jellinek, E M (1960), *The Disease Concept of Alcoholism*, New Haven, Hillhouse
20   World Health Organisation (1952), Alcoholism Subcommittee, World Hlth Techn. Rep. Ser., 48
21   Taylor, L (22 June, 1979), *New Statesman*, 906
22   *Brit. Med. Ass. News*, September 1979
23   Eriksson, A W E (1963), 59, 147
24   Glatt, M M, Pittman, D J, Gillespie, D G and Hills, D R (1968), *The Drugs Scene in Great Britain* (Revised Reprint), London, Edward Arnold
25   *Brit. J. Addict.* (1980), Editorial, 75, 1
26   Davies, E M (1980), 'Review of Controversies in Therapeutics', ed. Lassagna, L, *The Lancet* ii, 295
27   Glatt, M M (1955), *Brit. J. Addict.* 52, 55
28   British Medical Association and Magistrates Association, Joint Committee, *Brit. med. J.* (1961)
29   *Hospital Treatment of Alcoholism* (1962), Memorandum, Ministry of Health, 43
30   *Treatment of Alcoholism* (1968), Memorandum, Ministry of Health, 37
31   *Report of the Working Party on Drunken Offenders* (1971), Home Office, London, HMSO
32   DHSS (1973), *Community Services for Alcoholics*, Circular 21/73
33   DHSS (1978), *The Pattern and Range of Services for Problem Drinkers*, Report by the Advisory Committee on Alcoholism, London, HMSO
34   DHSS (1979), *Report on Prevention*, Advisory Committee on Alcoholism, London, HMSO
35   DHSS (1979), *Report on Education and Training*, Advisory Committee on Alcoholism, London, HMSO
36   Glatt, M M (1976) in *Gradwohl's Legal Medicine*, ed. Camps, F E, 3rd edition, Bristol, John Wright, 547–55
37   World Health Organisation Expert Committee (1966), 363
38   Glatt, M M (1979), *Brit. med. J.* 1, 684

Part I

Alcohol Dependence

I

Who is an Alcoholic (Who – Me?)

People have widely differing notions as to whom they would consider an 'alcoholic'. To some he is an individual who is practically always intoxicated or who can never leave drink alone, the person who is rolling drunk in the gutter, or the man who habitually beats up his wife once he has had a few drinks. Such individuals may or may not be 'alcoholics' but even if they are, they are no more than extreme examples of sufferers from an often long drawn out disorder; fortunately only relatively few reach such phases and only towards the end of their drinking career.

Such widely held misconceptions usually result in even very heavy drinkers not thinking of themselves as alcoholics because their behaviour does not match these beliefs. 'It never even dawned on me that I could possibly be an alcoholic – after all I have never been on "Skid Row", I have always been a conscientious, hard worker, I have never lost a job, and I have never fallen foul of the law,' is the type of comment one frequently hears, even from doctors who have finally realised that they belong to the fraternity of alcoholics. An alcoholic himself may label someone else an alcoholic only if that person's drinking history is decidedly worse than his own (a recent popular version is the 'definition' of an alcoholic as 'a person who drinks even more than his doctor'); and he will usually take good care that his own definition of an alcoholic excludes his own case.

Contrary to widespread belief, one cannot usually diagnose an alcoholic just by taking a brief look at him. 'I cannot define a psychopath,' replied a psychiatrist, a few years ago, when asked to give such a definition. 'Nor can I define an elephant. But I know an elephant when I see one.' However, it may be extremely difficult to recognise an alcoholic, and often it may be impossible without the help of people who know him intimately, such as his family. Only rarely will he give himself away by his appearance, and it is uncommon that one may apply such a simple 'ABC' as 'Alcoholism - Brandy Nose - Cirrhosis' [1]. Unlike the stereotype image, anyone may be (or may more or less readily become) an alcoholic: your respectable neighbour and his wife, the well established and highly esteemed professor, the unskilled building labourer, the chairman of the board; as well as the worker on the shop floor.

Due to general lack of information, 'budding' alcoholics themselves may have no idea that they are at risk; in particular when they are members of high-risk occupations where heavy social drinking is widely practised and accepted. 'I do not need to talk to the alcoholic patients in the wards,' said a radio-script writer engaged in writing a play on alcoholism twenty-five years ago, when visiting the alcohol unit at Warlingham Park Hospital. He had been advised by the medical staff that he would learn much more getting the information from the alcoholics themselves than second-hand from the doctors. Obviously he was frightened of getting too close to the unpredictable 'drunks' in the hospital. One or two hours later – although his discussion with the doctors was far from being at its end – he became extremely fidgety and restless: he had an urgent business appointment in town and unfortunately had to leave; he would have to come back another time to finish the discussion. In fact, the urgent appointment was a visit to the pub next to the hospital! A man behaving in this way may not yet be an 'alcoholic' but he may well be on the way towards becoming dependent on alcohol (*prodromal phase*) to the extent that he feels unable to function without it and tries to arrange 'appointments' in such a manner that they do not interfere with 'opening hours' (see Chapter 3).

The preceding discussion illustrates some of the difficulties surrounding the term 'alcoholic', and also other terms that have been suggested in an attempt to avoid the ambiguities attached to the various definitions of 'alcoholic' and 'alcoholism'. There is no dearth of such definitions, but the number alone shows that none of them is satisfactory or comprehensive.

In the past it has usually been accepted that, by itself, the amount a person drinks is not the factor deciding whether he is an alcoholic or not. Some men can drink a bottle of whisky a day without showing any obvious evidence of physical, mental or social harm. However, as Jellinek [2] pointed out, the frequent presence of such large amounts of alcohol in the organism may obviously interfere with its normal functioning and give rise to organic change. More recently, studies carried out by workers at the Ontario Research Foundation have suggested that the condition of patients admitted to alcoholism clinics tends to be associated with a range of drinking that exceeds a daily average intake of about 150 ml of absolute alcohol [3]. In view of such considerations, an old idea, proposed 100 years ago by a British physician [3a], has been taken up again – that is, the so-called 'safe limits' for drinking. The old 'Anstie's Limit' gave the upper safe limits of daily drinking as 3 oz of whisky, or half a bottle of table wine, or two pints of beer; the more generous amount proposed in 1979 by the Royal College of Psychiatrists' Working Party [4] was up to (but preferably less than) four doubles of spirits, or a standard-sized bottle of wine, or four pints of beer per day. The daily amounts regarded as 'safe' are somewhat lower for women drinkers who appear to be more vulnerable to the development of alcoholic liver cirrhosis than men. Suggestions as to the amounts of alcoholic drink which can be 'safely' taken by ordinary people can at present be regarded as no more than inspired guesses. The Swedish investigators, Rydberg and Skerfving [5], from a careful review of international data on dose-response relationships for ethanol on the various organs and systems, arrived at an estimate of a much lower 'acceptable daily intake of ethanol': i.e. 7g (0.1g ethanol/kg body weight) corresponding to:

> 20 ml distilled spirits
> or   40 ml dessert wines
> or 100 ml table wines
> or 250 ml beer

Not only the duration of exposure but also its distribution in time is of great importance (whether, for example, equal amounts are taken daily or once a week). Rydberg and Skerfving therefore give a tentative 'tolerable weekly intake':

> 0.7g ethanol/kg body weight, i.e.
> 150 ml hard liquor
> or 250 ml fortified wine
> or 700 ml table wine
> or 1.3 l of beer
> or 2.6 l of light beer per week

Rydberg [6], commenting on the safe levels suggested by the Royal College of Psychiatrists' Working Party, quite rightly emphasises the great importance of such questions and the need for very careful further studies in this area. However, one important aim of publishing such very preliminary and tentative data is to direct the attention of both the general and the professional public to this point as, by-and-large, a high proportion of drinkers, daily or frequently, consume amounts of alcohol which obviously carry a great deal of risk.

Some drinkers are more susceptible to the development of complications than others: there is a wide variation in susceptibility or tolerance. It is also important to remember that 'alcoholism' in some people undermines physical health only, leaving them in full possession of their mental faculties; in others only their relationship with other people may be affected and not their physical or mental health.

The reason why people drink, and under what conditions, may also be important regarding the question whether the label 'alcoholic' may be attributed to them by some observers but not by others. In certain heavy-drinking occupational or social groups, members will not readily call their friends 'alcoholics' in spite of the fact that their heavy drinking affects their behaviour or work performance, while 'outsiders' may take a different view. At a later phase 'alcoholics' may no longer drink for taste or pleasure; they may not necessarily drink because they like it but because they 'must'; they may drink because they feel that for a little while only alcohol helps them forget their problems, or assists them to cope with them, or to adjust to life in a better way. Alcoholics usually drink because of what they feel alcohol does *for* them, whereas their non-alcoholic relatives and friends only see what alcohol does *to* the alcoholic. This difference in viewpoint is an important reason for some of the misunderstandings between the alcoholic, his family and society. The alcoholic cannot take drink or (easily) leave it, like the ordinary drinker; he always finds a good reason for taking it, and when there is no good reason he has no difficulty in rationalising one which satisfies no one but himself. Drink for him has become a drug on which he has become more or less dependent, psychologically and/or physically; without its aid he may possibly feel able to exist and vegetate but hardly to 'live', even if, at the same time, he vaguely but increasingly realises that he cannot go on living *with* it either. But at this stage he no longer sees a way out of his dilemma, and therefore continues drinking.

All definitions of alcoholism have come under fire but, in spite of its age, probably the most widely quoted is the one given by the World Health Organisation (1952) [7]:

> Alcoholics are those excessive drinkers[1] whose dependence upon alcohol has attained such a degree that it shows a noticeable mental disturbance or an interference with their bodily or mental health, their interpersonal relations, and their smooth social and economic functioning; or who show the prodromal signs of such developments. They therefore require treatment. [8]

The WHO definition clearly stresses the central position of the phenomenon of 'dependence' upon the drug alcohol in 'alcoholics'; as well as the importance of the harm or damage which such a drinker can suffer in any sphere of his adjustment: mental, physical, social or economic. The definition seems to imply, however, that it is only in the presence of ('a degree of') dependence that harm may accrue from excessive drinking. Yet such harm may follow excessive drinking even in the absence of dependence. As we have seen, repeated heavy drinking, for whatever reason, may in time be followed by complications. A publican (and his wife) may consume large amounts of alcohol without necessarily being physically or mentally dependent (perhaps because taking drinks regularly offered to them by their customers is obviously good for business and increases their popularity); and the danger following such regular heavy drinking is reflected in the high mortality rate of liver cirrhosis both for publicans and (slightly less) their wives. Jellinek's Beta alcoholism [2] consists in the occurrence of 'such alcoholic complications as polyneuropathy, gastritis and cirrhosis of the liver . . . without either physical or psychological dependence upon alcohol – heavy drinking in such individuals for example being due to customs of certain social groups in conjunction with poor nutritional habits'.

The WHO definition clearly implies the position of alcoholism as a form of drug dependence so that alcoholics are no longer free agents who can stop drinking when they want to. At the same time, the definition implies that alcoholism is not an all-or-nothing affair and that it is a matter of degrees of severity or seriousness. The Chart of Alcohol Dependence (pp. 74–5) indicates a gradual development of the disorder: clearly the drinker is not one day a 'non-alcoholic' and an 'alcoholic' the next. Certainly for the benefit of newcomers, members of Alcoholics Anonymous have often tried to elucidate the alleged difference between an ordinary drinker and an 'alcoholic' by statements such as: 'You are either pregnant or not – you cannot be a little pregnant – and the same holds good for alcoholism!' But, as with various other slogans and explanations often heard at AA meetings, all such terms are couched in popular layman's language, designed to show the confused and bemused newcomer some daylight at the end of a long, dark tunnel. Many clinicians working closely with AA have for many years insisted that there is no such person as 'the alcoholic', that 'alcoholics' are individuals who (in spite of a common 'final path') may differ a great deal from each other; that in spite of a frequently heard statement that all alcoholics are just one drink away from disaster, in practice it still makes a great deal of difference whether an alcoholic has been sober for years (and has largely lost his preoccupation with drinking) or for a few days only (so that he may be much more readily tempted to have his first drink); that the differentiation in a given individual between 'heavy drinkers' and 'alcoholics' was often difficult or even impossible (for the time being); and that in spite of certain 'milestones' the regression of the drinker's career was a gradual one; and that even the most important milestone, the 'loss of control', constituted no sharp demarcation line, but a hazy and diffuse border area [9]; and was affected by many social and psychological as well as pharmacological variables [10] (see p. 87).

Clearly the emotionally fairly stable individual at the start of a career of heavy drinking may, under circumstances of stress, find the effects of alcoholic drink increasingly attractive; but his 'dependence' – initially nil, with his powers of control and his ability to stop drinking at will virtually unchallenged – will only gradually increase in intensity towards a much later phase where his dependence on the pharmacological effect of alcohol might have become virtually overwhelming. In between the beginning (no dependence) and the late, strong degree dependence stage there are the intermediate stages where, in spite of the progressively higher degree of dependence, the drinker at times may be able to withstand the 'lure' of the pharmacological effect of alcohol. This may happen, for example, in the case of an emotionally fairly stable personality and in spite of difficult environmental circumstances, but is possible even in a fairly inadequate personality because of strong social support by a still cohesive family or a stabilising and congenial job.

The 'anomalous' inclusion of 'prodromal symptoms' (see Chart, pp. 74–5) in the WHO (1952) definition of the syndrome itself (i.e.

alcoholism) has been criticised by Hore [11]; obviously no one knows at what stage dependence may begin to set in. Possibly this may be somewhere in the course of Jellinek's late 'pre-alcoholic' or prodromal phases [12]. At any rate, the 1952 WHO definition indicates that, contrary to recent criticism, the proponents of what in the 1940s to 1960s was called the new (or in Jellinek's formulation [2], the 'renewed') approach to alcoholism and now is sometimes described as 'traditional concepts or models'[13]* were to some extent fully aware of what is now sometimes hailed as new insights such as the realisation that there are degrees of dependence, and the vital importance of concentrating on the early, prodromal phases of alcoholism for diagnoses and institution of remedial measures, rather than waiting for the development of the firmly established picture of the late phases.

In view of the ambiguity of the terms 'alcoholism' and 'alcoholics', in 1977 a group of investigators, called together by the World Health Organisation, discarded the term 'alcoholism' in favour of the notion of 'Alcohol-related Disabilities', [16] a term meant to embrace the general range of alcohol-induced problems. The group suggested the substitution of the terms 'alcoholism' and 'alcohol addiction' by that of 'Alcohol Dependence Syndrome'. In line with these recommendations the World Health Organisation's *Ninth Revision of the International Classification of Diseases* dropped the term alcoholism, replacing it by the term 'Alcohol Dependence Syndrome'. The definition reads:

A state, psychic and usually physical, resulting from taking alcohol, characterized by behavioural and other responses that always includes a compulsion to take alcohol on a continuous or periodic basis in order to experience its psychic effects, and sometimes to avoid the discomfort of its absence; tolerance may or may not be present.

The description goes on to say that 'A person may be dependent on alcohol and other drugs . . . If dependence is associated with alcoholic psychosis or with physical complications, both should be coded'. While 'acute drunkenness in alcoholism', 'chronic alcoholism' and 'dipsomania' are listed under the alcohol dependence syndrome, the term excludes: 'alcoholic psychoses, drunkenness NOS (which is listed elsewhere under the general heading of "Non-dependent abuse of drugs") and physical com-

---

* In contrast to the 'Emerging Concepts' [13] the 'New Directives' [14] 'New Responses' [15], etc.

plications of alcohol, such as cirrhosis of the liver, epilepsy, gastritis'. In this connection, the meaning of 'Syndrome', according to Professor Griffith Edwards [15] (who chaired the group of WHO investigators in 1977), is 'an observable coincidence of phenomena' not all of which need always be present or present to the same degree. Whatever the usefulness of the term and the 'idea'[2] discussed by Edwards, one immediate difficulty arising when reading the new definition is the required presence (always) of a 'compulsion' to take alcohol continually or periodically. In this case the definition, for example, would exclude the already mentioned cases of the heavily-drinking publican and his wife whose regular drinking, often in the absence of compulsion but carried out for social or business (economic) reasons, often causes liver cirrhosis, the latter being expressly excluded from the term 'alcohol dependence syndrome'. Obviously certain alcohol-related disabilities can arise in the absence of compulsion and dependence. The newly proposed term thus does not fully replace the term 'alcoholism' (or 'alcoholics') as understood by the WHO 1952 definition [7], as this clearly included mental and physical drink-induced complications.

Quite apart from the notion of alcohol dependence syndrome, the plausible equation of 'alcoholism' with 'alcohol dependence' (or also as 'a drug dependency upon ethanol') [17] has recently been proposed by various observers; for example, the National Council on Alcoholism in the USA and the American Psychiatric Association [18] have adopted the definition of alcoholism as 'a pathological dependency on alcohol'. The publican, however, who even in the absence of dependence ultimately dies from liver cirrhosis as a complication of his heavy drinking, has surely acquired the right posthumously to be diagnosed as having been an alcoholic in his lifetime – even though he may have shown no clinical or other evidence. For such reasons not everyone might regard the substitution of 'alcoholism' by the 'alcohol dependence syndrome' as a completely satisfactory step. Moreover the term is clumsy; one might doubt whether drinkers or their families and friends in the future would really describe their state using this new term. A pointer in this direction may be seen for example, in the Royal College of Psychiatrists' Report (1979) on *Alcohol and Alcoholism* [4]: 'To have less recourse to this ponderous phrase [alcohol dependence syndrome] the Report will usually in context refer simply to "the syndrome" or "dependence".'

Although other disabilities or complications can also occur in the absence of 'dependence', the likelihood of such complications is obviously the higher, the greater the intensity of dependence. This correlation between state of dependence and likelihood of resulting harm probably explains the wording of the 1952 WHO definition. Possibly the higher the incidence and the more severe the intensity of such complications, the greater the likelihood of the presence of a considerable degree of dependence. Take, for example, the case of an intelligent, conscientious, emotionally stable individual who repeatedly drinks himself into a state of stupor or drives when intoxicated. In theory, of course, such a person may act in this way quite deliberately; much more likely, however, the repetition of such behaviour by otherwise mentally sound individuals and in spite of so many negative 'rewards' (ostracisation by family and society, or punishment by the law) may denote a considerable degree of dependence upon alcohol.

The extent to which the factors resulting in dependence overlap with those causing damage to the body is unknown, and the same may apply to the question whether alcohol amounts leading to dependence are larger or smaller than those causing harm to liver, brain or heart, though the Royal College of Psychiatrists' Report [4] clearly states that the levels of drink harmful to health are lower than those responsible for inducing dependence. With so many outstanding queries the question of which amounts are 'safe' becomes even more difficult to answer. Obviously the period over which the alcohol is being taken, whether it is taken regularly day after day or intermittently only, the adequacy or otherwise of nutritional intake, are all factors which may have a bearing.

Of the various other definitions proposed probably the most frequently quoted is that given by Jellinek (1960) [2]. In a deliberately broad sweep, Jellinek termed as 'alcoholism' 'any use of alcoholic beverages that causes any damage to the individual or society or both', and in view of the great number of types of alcoholism, he prefers to talk of the 'alcoholisms' rather than of alcoholism. He delineated a minimum of five types, only two of which he regarded as varieties of alcohol addiction (the Gamma- and Delta-varieties (see p. 104)) because of the presence of physical dependence. The term 'alcohol addict' was formerly often used for any type of alcoholic but it is obviously preferable to restrict the term 'addiction' (now replaced by the term 'dependence') to certain types only.

Jellinek's broad definition of alcoholisms includes the whole family of 'problems³ related to alcohol'. Some observers think it undesirable to include a host of so many varied conditions in the term. For example, a Report (1967) of the Co-operative Commission on the Study of Alcoholism (in the USA) [20] uses the term 'problem drinking' to describe much the same conditions included in Jellinek's definition: 'a repetitive use of the beverage alcohol causing physical, psychological or social harm to the drinker or others'. By the term 'alcoholism', on the other hand, the Commission understood: 'a condition in which an individual has lost control over his alcohol intake in the sense that he is consistently unable to refrain from drinking or to stop drinking before getting intoxicated.' It would, in fact, seem that the Commission's term 'problem drinking' refers to alcohol-induced harm,' and its term 'alcoholism' to dependence.

Again, it is only fair to mention that the term 'problem drinkers' too, has been employed by various writers in quite different ways and has become so ambiguous that it is important for anyone using it to indicate clearly what he means. Thanks are certainly due to Keller and McCormick's 'authoritative but not authoritarian' *Dictionary of Words about Alcohol* [19].

Taking a look at the operational definition one again finds both elements prominently represented of which one or the other or both figured largely in the previous definitions quoted – i.e. dependence and harm (or 'disability'). 'Alcoholism' they say is:

A chronic and usually progressive disease, or a symptom of an underlying psychological or physical disorder, characterised by dependence on alcohol (manifested by loss of control over drinking) for relief from psychological or physical distress or for gratification from alcohol intoxication itself, and by a consumption of alcoholic beverages sufficiently great and consistent to cause physical or mental or social or economic disability. Or a learned (or conditioned) dependence on alcohol which irresistibly activates resort to alcohol whenever a critical internal or environmental stimulus occurs.

Again, certain questions arise when looking at this definition. Thus

(i)   Alcoholism, though very frequently 'a progressive disease' in many drinkers intermittently or for very long periods, may come to an uneasy halt after reaching a certain phase, with or without the interference of a crisis; and the 'progression' or otherwise seems to depend on the interaction between 'agent, host, and environment'. (See p. 89.)

(ii) Alcoholism could also be a symptom of an underlying social situation or condition: peer group pressure, poverty, affluence, marital disharmony, etc. Often such 'reactive' or sociogenic' or 'situational' alcoholism may have a 'psychosocial' origin.

(iii)   As discussed above, should 'alcoholism' be regarded as present only when 'dependence' and 'disability' are present, or should it rather be 'dependence' and/or 'disability'?

(iv)   'Dependence' on alcohol may often manifest itself only by impairment or a relative lack of consistent control rather than a total 'loss of control'.

(v)   The 'learned [conditioned] dependence on alcohol may activate resort to alcohol' more or less strongly but not necessarily 'irresistibly' on occurrence of a critical stimulus. Many alcoholics can at times, temporarily, resist giving such a conditioned response – the ego (host) managing on such occasions to intervene between the stimulus and the conditioned response.

In spite of these criticisms all the quoted definitions have a lot of justification. It is much easier to criticise minor inaccuracies than propose one's own definitions. Nevertheless, as we have seen and is stressed by Hore [11], all these definitions emphasise either harm or dependence or both. Our own choice of a definition therefore would be: 'Alcoholics are those drinkers whose regular or recurrent heavy drinking has led to dependence (psychological and/or physical) and/or harm (physical, psychological, and/or socioeconomic).' This would closely resemble the definition proposed by D L Davies [21] who sees in alcoholism 'the intermittent or continual ingestion of alcohol leading to dependency [addiction] or harm.'

In attempting to give a definition of 'alcoholism'/'alcoholics' one must never ignore the complexity of the condition. As implied in Jellinek's term 'alcoholisms', there are many different types and subgroups which may vary a great deal from each other. It should be one of the main aims of future research to attempt to delineate more clearly such subgroups [22]. Possibly their origin may be different. Genetic factors, for example, may be relatively more prominent in some types than in others and the therapeutic needs may vary to some extent from type to type. One formerly popular division of alcoholics was into primary and secondary types of alcoholism. Jellinek (1960) [2] found this classification confusing but its use has been recommended again in recent years [22, 23,

24]. Ewing [23], for example, differentiates between primary or essential alcoholism and 'secondary' or 'symptomatic alcoholism': the primary alcoholics 'have an illness with an inborn constitutional component calling for total abstinence if health is to be maintained [whereas] secondary alcoholics [who started their drinking as a means of coping with underlying feelings of anxiety, depression or other emotional conflicts, might possibly] again become controlled drinkers . . . when [they] recover from the primary underlying disease'.[4] Among primary alcoholics (those without 'other manifestations of diagnosable psychopathology apart from alcoholism' [22] or 'without evidence of other major pre-existing psychiatric disorders' [25]), subgroups have been described who 'while not necessarily sociopaths [nevertheless] exhibit some definable disturbance prior to the onset of alcoholism', [22, 24], such as childhood hyperactivity (or 'minimal brain dysfunctions' as the condition is described in the USA). Alcoholism, supervening in psychopaths or depressives, would be an example of 'secondary alcoholism', though in clinical practice it may often be very difficult to determine what condition came first: drinking can frequently cause reactive depression, and the behaviour of severely dependent drinkers may often simulate that of psychopaths.

Similarly a subgrouping of alcoholics into those predominantly 'psychogenic' and those predominantly 'sociogenic', may often be of value. Those drinkers ('psychogenic') whose alcoholism arose mainly for psychological, emotional reasons may more often be 'bout' drinkers and Gamma types, and seem prone to misuse other drugs as well as alcohol. 'Sociogenic' alcoholics, who started their excessive drinking without gross emotional problems, and usually under the influence of their social peer groups or occupational groups, may be relatively often steady, daily drinkers of the Delta type, and more prone to the development of definite physical complications and possibly *delirium tremens*, but less inclined to the misuse of CNS-affecting drugs. The 'psychogenic' alcoholics may more readily develop psychological dependence and find themselves in special alcoholic units, whereas predominantly sociogenic alcoholics may more often require treatment in general hospitals for their physical damage. Thus this differentiation may to some extent correspond to the definition of alcoholics as people suffering from dependence or harm though of course alcoholics very often experience both complications.

As rightly stressed by Keller [26] what are needed are not

'terms' but 'delimited categories of behaviour to which significant degrees of risk of developing problems or illness . . . can be attributed'. He names certain *drinking 'behaviours'* (amounts or frequencies of drinking) together with the 'risks of social (including economic), or psychological, or somatic problems or illnesses' which they are thought to carry. He is at pains to stress that the amounts of alcoholic drink and the consequences are suggestive only and serve as basis for discussion but are not by any means exact criteria:

1   *Somatopathic drinking*: The intake of an average of the equivalent of 115 ml of absolute alcohol per day, or occasionally more. 115 ml is the quantity said to be necessary to induce tissue damage.
    This may lead to intoxication, hangover, or damages to tissues (such as gastritis, hepatitis, myopathy).
2   *Thymogenic drinking*: Frequent (at least twice a year) intake of 85 ml of absolute alcohol per occasion, in order to cope with problems of living, or to get along with people, or to avoid social discomfort or emotional pain.
3   *Dyssocial drinking*: Frequent (at least twice a year) intake of the quivalent of 70 ml of absolute alcohol (or more). This may result in legal troubles, or upset family and social relationships or the economic functioning.

Each of these drinking behaviours would also fall under the much more vague and much less specific term 'pathological drinking' or 'problem drinking'. Any of these three drinking behaviour patterns may, in Keller's view, be implicative of 'alcoholism', and carry a possible risk of irreversible damage.

4   *Thymosomatophathic* or *Dyssociosomatopathic drinking*: Inelegant terms, denoting a combination of drinking the amount (115 ml) mentioned in somatopathic drinking with the effects mentioned in the other forms. Either combination would be strongly implicative of alcoholism 'or at least of "pre-alcoholism" (i.e. a prodromal stage)'.

The presence of the combination of all three forms (somatopathic, thymogenic and dyssocial drinking), in Keller's view, warrants 'a confident diagnosis of alcoholism (alcohol addiction, or alcohol dependence syndrome)'.

Alcoholism 'at risk' register (R H Wilkins, 1974) [27]

The use of an 'at risk' register, as developed by Dr R H Wilkins at Manchester, has proved very helpful in the identification of problem drinkers and alcoholics by the medical practitioner. Wilkins' *Modified Alcoholic At Risk Register* consists of the following items (i.e. with the number of items reduced from the original 'research AARR', so as to make it more handy for the busy practitioner):

1 *Physical diseases* (cirrhosis of the liver, peptic ulcer, gastritis, epilepsy for first time at twenty-five years or over, from no apparent cause, obesity in men).
2 *Mental diseases* (anxiety, depression, attempted suicide).
3 *Alcoholic symptoms* ('shakes', 'blackouts', *delirium tremens*, alcoholic epilepsy).
4 *Occupations* (catering trade, publicans and others working in a pub or the drink industry, seamen).
5 *Work problems* (three or more jobs in year preceding consultation, three or more spells of absence off work in year preceding consultation for three days or less, patient requesting certificate for absence from work for conditions which are possibly not genuine).
6 *Accidents* (at work, at home, road traffic).
7 *Criminal offences*
   (i) drunk and disorderly/incapable, and/or drunken driving, and/or offence committed while under influence of drink;
   (ii) any other criminal offence.
8 *Family problems* (children suffering from neglect, family disharmony, children with mental or psychosomatic disease).
9 *Help asked for treatment of alcoholism by either*:
   (i) patient;
   (ii) a parent, or the spouse, or a sibling, or a child, or any other relative of suspected alcoholic;
   (iii) member of ancillary staff or social agency.
10 *Patient smelling of drink at consultation.*
11 *Marital status* (single, male, forty or over, married more than once, divorced, or separated).
12 *Living in a hostel for destitutes.*
13 *Known alcoholic* (confirmed by psychiatrist).
14 *Family history of abnormal drinking.*

To anyone with experience with problem drinkers the great majority of items on the Register make immediate sense. The list is not exhaustive: Wilkins' original Register, for example, also mentioned pancreatitis, peripheral neuritis, malnutrition etc., all pointers to the possibility of the presence of a drink problem; and there are obviously a number of high-risk occupations or groups. (All of these issues will be discussed in later chapters.) But, keeping these items in mind will considerably raise the practitioner's index of suspicion and encourage further inquiries. Some items have a much lower diagnostic value than others and may merely cause the practitioner to be alert to the possibility rather than the probability of the presence of a drinking problem.

A list of *Diagnostic Criteria of Alcoholism*, formulated by a Committee of the National Council on Alcoholism in the USA (1975) [28], like Wilkins' Register is very valuable in raising awareness and helps in the diagnosis of alcoholics. The Committee divides the criteria of alcoholism into two broad areas:

1   *Physiological and clinical* ('Track I')
Physiological symptoms include:

(a)   Physiological dependence (as indicated by withdrawal symptoms: gross tremors, hallucinations, or withdrawal seizures or DTs);
(b)   Tolerance to the effects of alcohol, as shown by a blood level of more than 150mg per 100ml without gross signs of intoxication;
(c)   Alcoholics' 'blackouts'.

Clinical: this would include the alcohol-associated illnesses.

2   *Behavioural, psychological and attitudinal* ('Track II')
'Major' Track II symptoms include, for example, drinking despite strong medical contradictions fully known to the patient and despite severe social disapproval.

Laboratory tests which are held to provide 'direct major evidence of alcoholism' are blood alcohol levels at any time of more than 300mg per 100ml or, in a routine examination, of more than 100mg per 100ml.

The Committee felt that only 10 per cent of those who drink develop the psychological and physiological dependency on alcohol that can be characterised as alcoholism. Isolated events, such as rare drunken episodes, are excluded from the definition but in the view of the Committee, as of the American Medical Association, 'it is appropriate to describe alcoholism (once it is established) as a disease and . . . it fits established definitions of disease'.

As regards 'Track II', the continuation of drinking by a (non-psychopathic) person who has been made fully aware of the serious medical dangers, and of the fears and objects expressed by family, friends or employers, denotes the likely presence of psychological dependence on alcohol which is strong enough to outweigh the patient's fears of physical consequences and social ostracisation.

As with all such generalised lists, any special circumstances have of course to be taken into consideration. Being capable of driving a car with a 300 mg/100 ml level would be impossible for an ordinary drinker, but the highly tolerant, chronic, heavy drinker may still 'manage it after a fashion' while exposing himself and other road users to the greatest danger. On the other hand, the condition of a car driver involved in an isolated accident after heavy drinking, would not fall under any of the accepted definitions of 'alcoholism'; nevertheless his case obviously needs examining, as it constitutes one of the many examples of problems associated with misuse of alcohol other than 'alcoholism' *per se*.

A patient presenting himself at a doctor's surgery with a highish blood alcohol level at any time may be significant although it is somewhat less ominous if the appointment had been made some time ahead and happens to coincide with a social event.

In an attempt to help a person decide whether he is an alcoholic or not, certain questionnaires have been used. One frequently employed is that devised by the late R V Seliger, one of the American pioneers in the treatment of alcoholism [29].

Alcoholism, I presume?
Questionnaire (warning signs) (Robert V Seliger)

1 Do you require a drink the next morning?
2 Do you prefer to drink alone?
3 Do you lose time from work due to drinking?
4 Is your drinking harming your family in any way?
5 Do you need a drink at a definite time daily?
6 Do you get the inner shakes unless you continue drinking?
7 Has drinking made you irritable?

8   Does it make you careless of your family's welfare?
9   Have you become jealous of your husband or wife since drinking?
10 Has drinking changed your personality?
11 Does it cause you body complaints?
12 Does it make you restless?
13 Does it cause you to have difficulty in sleeping?
14 Has it made you more impulsive?
15 Have you less self-control since drinking?
16 Has your initiative decreased?
17 Has your ambition decreased?
18 Do you lack perseverance in pursuing a goal since drinking?
19 Do you drink to obtain social ease? (in shy, timid, self-conscious individuals).
20 Do you drink for self-encouragement? (in persons with feelings of inferiority).
21 To relieve marked feelings of inadequacy?
22 Has your sexual potency suffered since drinking?
23 Do you have marked dislikes and hatreds?
24 Has your jealousy, in general, increased?
25 Do you show marked moodiness as a result of drinking?
26 Has your efficiency decreased?
27 Has your drinking made you more sensitive?
28 Are you harder to get along with?
29 Do you turn to an inferior environment while drinking?
30 Is drinking endangering your health?
31 Is it affecting your peace of mind?
32 Is it making your home life unhappy?
33 Is it jeopardising your business?
34 Is it clouding your reputation?
35 Is drinking disturbing the harmony of your life?

Every 'yes' answered to the above questionnaire is regarded as a red light warning to a drinker 'to put on the brakes'. Obviously, 'yes' to certain questions means only that the drinker begins to lean too heavily on alcohol for support, whereas other questions refer to a more advanced state with alcohol dominating the drinker's life[5] (this questionnaire should be read alongside the Chart of Alcoholism dependence and recovery on pp. 74–5).

Notes

[1]   In turn *excessive drinking* was defined by the same WHO Committee (1952) [8] as: 'any form of drinking which in its extent goes beyond the traditional and customary "dietary" use, or the ordinary compliance with the social drinking customs of the whole community concerned, irrespective of the aetiological factors leading to such behaviour and irrespective also of the extent to which such aetiological factors are dependent upon heredity, constitution, or acquired physiopathological and metabolic influences'.

Interestingly, neither the definition of excessive drinkers nor that of alcoholics mentions the possible significance of the absolute amounts of alcohol so much stressed nowadays. Excessive drinking is defined in relation to the drinker's community drinking patterns which of course vary a great deal. What may be regarded as 'excessive' amounts in Anglo-American communities or among non-conformist clergymen, might be socially completely acceptable and the norm in France or among merchant seamen.

[2]   Laying stress on the 'dependency syndrome' term, incidentally may have valuable effects in the education in this field for under- and post-graduate medical students. In the past what most medical students and doctors related to excessive drink was the physical harm, such as liver cirrhosis. Emphasis on the 'dependency' aspect may help to direct the attention to the importance of the underlying syndrome which, in so many cases, is responsible for the harm done. It would also help to explain why so often, in spite of everything done to treat the organic damage caused by drinking, and in spite of all warnings, such patients often return again and again.

Similar welcome effects may of course also be reflected in the understanding of other groups, such as magistrates, who so often experience the failure of their well-meant exhortations to the drinker in the dock.

[3]   The term *Problem Drinker* often proposed as an alternative to the ambiguous term 'alcoholic', appears much too imprecise to have any scientific connotation. It is certainly preferable in clinical practice when first meeting a person referred because of his drinking habits to avoid the term 'alcoholic' (which may only lead to indignant denials or useless semantic arguments) and instead to talk to such an individual about his 'drinking problems' or his problems caused by drink, which he could probably hardly deny. Mark Keller's *Lexicon of Disablements Related to Alcohol Consumption* states that 'The term "problem drinker" (problem drinking), even more than alcoholism, has lost all precision and appears useless in scientific discourses' [26]. Similarly the 1977 WHO Group of Investigators which proposed the term 'alcohol-related disabilities' and 'alcohol dependence syndrome', explained that their approach discards the notion of 'problem drinker' as a category with any certain meaning [16].

The present writer therefore apologises when in the present text the terms 'problem drinkers' and 'problem drinking' nevertheless may appear from time to time mainly in order to avoid the endless repetition of the same terms (such as excessive drinkers). On such occasions it will be used in an unspecific way, to denote people whose drinking repeatedly gives rise to problems without it being clear at the time whether they were alcohol-dependent or not.

4   What however, should not be overlooked is that in the majority of cases, problem drinkers, when first seen, insist that it is not alcohol misuse that is their basic problem but rather some underlying factors, such as depression, family problems, or factors which they themselves cannot identify but which they hope the therapist may help them discover. Often one is left with the feeling that such people may have a (possibly unconscious) vested interest in proving that it is not alcoholism that is their basic problem, so that they could continue drinking with a better conscience than at present with the family usually urging them 'to do something about your drinking'. They then hope that if some underlying factors can be uncovered and 'dealt with' or cured, the cause for their uncontrolled drinking would be removed and there would then be no further problems with their drinking. Often the greater a drinker's dependence the greater his 'denials' and hope for, and insistence on, the underlying cause to be detected. Yet even when there are important underlying emotional or social factors involved which originally precipitated excessive drinking, superimposed secondary changes during the cause of the drinking career may often raise serious obstacles to the desire for safe, controlled drinking even after removal of the factors originally responsible. Moreover, unlike other individuals who in spite of similar emotional or social problems manage to remain, on the whole, moderate drinkers, the development of 'secondary alcoholism' might indicate a degree of more than average 'vulnerability' or 'susceptibility' to the effects of alcohol which raises serious questions as to the possibility of safe, moderate drinking in probably a large proportion of such secondary alcoholics. A similar consideration might apply as in the case of alcoholics whose organs had suffered some harm due to heavy drinking but had improved after a period of abstinence. Would they be able to tolerate a resumption of 'controlled drinking' without risk, or might even some relatively slight impairment of functioning make them even more vulnerable or susceptible – as the initial impairment of the particular organ affected had thereby indicated some vulnerability to the effects of alcohol?

5   As indicated elsewhere, the time when the idea of taking a drink first thing in the morning, on an empty stomach, after 'the night before' begins to appeal to the drinker, rather than to appal him as hitherto, may be a significant pointer to a change in his approach to drinking.

References

1   *Aspects of Alcoholism* (1963), Philadelphia, J B Lippincott
2   Jellinek, E M (1960), *The Disease Concept of Alcoholism*, New Haven, Hillhouse
3   De Lint, J (1973) in *Alcoholism – a Medical Profile*, eds Kessel, N *et al.*, London, B Edsall, 77
3a Anstie, F E (1870), *Practitioner* 4, 219
4   *Alcohol and Alcoholism* (1979), R.C. Psych. Special Committee Report, London, Tavistock, 140
5   Rydberg, U and Skerfving, S (1977) in *Alcohol Intoxication and Withdrawal*, ed. Gross, M M, New York, London, Plenum Press, 403–15
6   Rydberg, U (1980), *Personal Communication*
7   World Health Organisation (1952), Wld Hlth Org. Techn. Rep. Ser. 48, 16
8   World Hlth Org. Techn. Rep. Ser. (1952) 48, 15
9   Glatt, M M (1972), ICAA International Congress on Alcoholism and Drug Dependence, Amsterdam
10 Glatt, M M (1967), *Brit. J. Addict.*, 62, 267
11 Hore, B D (1976), *Alcohol Dependence*, London, Butterworths, 1
12 Jellinek, E M (1952) in Wld Hlth Org. Techn. Rep. Ser. 48, 29
13 Pattison, E M, Sobell, M B and Sobell, L C (1977), *Emerging Concepts of Alcohol Dependence*, New York, Springer, 1–6
14 Filstead, W J (ed.) *et al.* (1973), *Alcohol and Alcohol Problems: New Thinking and New Directions*, Cambridge, Mass., Ballinger
15 Edwards, G E and Grant M (eds) (1977), *Alcoholism – New Knowledge and New Responses*, London, Croom Helm, 136–56
16 Edwards, G *et al.* (1977), *Alcohol-Related Disabilities*, WHO Offset Publication, 32
17 Kissin, B and Begleiter, H (eds) (1977), *The Biology of Alcoholism* (Vol. 3), New York, London, Plenum, 1
18 *Connect. Rev on Alcoholism* (February 1975), 24, 9
19 Keller, M and McCormick, M (1968), *A Dictionary of Words about Alcohol*, New Jersey, Rutgers
20 Co-operative Commission on the Study of Alcoholism (1967), *Alcohol Problems, A Report to the Nation*, prepared by T F A Plaut, New York, Oxford University Press
21 Davies, D L (1974) in *Alcoholism: A Medical Profile*, eds Kessel, N *et al.*, London, B Edsall, 13–22
22 Jaffe, J H (1980) in *Alcoholism Treatment in Transition*, eds Edwards, G and Grant, M, London, Croom Helm, 32–48
23 Ewing, J A, Internat. Confer. on Alcoholism, Bath, England (September 1980)
24 Tartar, R E *et al.* (1977), *Arch. Gen. Psychiat.*, 34, 761
25 Schuckitt, M A (1980) in *Alcoholism Treatment in Transition*, eds Edwards, G and Grant, M, London, Croom Helm, 59–69

26 Keller, M (1977) in *Alcohol-Related Disabilities* eds Edwards, G *et al.*, WHO Offset Publ., 32, 23–60
27 Wilkins, R H (1974), *The Hidden Alcoholic in General Practice*, London, Elek Science, 34–51, 140–1
28 Committee of the National Council on Alcoholism, *Diagnostic Criteria* (1975)
29 Seliger, R V (1954), *Alcohol Hygiene* (National Committee on Alcohol Hygiene), I, 5

2

What makes an Alcoholic (Why Me?)

In spite of an enormous amount of research work no definite answer to this question can be given. It is likely that there is a variety of factors at work. The presence of the 'agent' alcohol apart, other influences must be involved: alcohol is the causative 'agent' only in those who are, or become, susceptible. Perhaps the clearest way to illustrate the dynamic interaction between the various factors involved is to discuss the causation of the disorder in a manner analogous to the process in infectious diseases where the triad of host, environment and agent have to be considered [2]. Factors which initially have put an individual on the road to heavy drinking may possibly be different from those that create or maintain a state of dependence where biological and pharmacological factors might assume relatively greater importance. In Van Dyjk's formulation [3] dependence is not a separate entity but the later stages of a process which starts off with contact, experimentation and excessive use. In causation of dependence, he distinguishes between those factors that generate (e.g. the pharmacological effects of the drug, the user's personal attributes, the social meaning and value of a drug and of drug-taking and the influences of the environment on the user) and those that maintain the state (e.g. interacting vicious circles: a pharmacological, a cerebro-weakening, a psychological and a social vicious circle).

1 The pre-alcoholic make-up of the individual: 'host'

Corresponding to the 'host' in infectious diseases would be the role in alcoholism of the drinker's personality. The importance of the role of an individual's psychological make-up in the causation of alcoholism, at least in initiating his excessive drinking, is generally accepted. The role, on the other hand, of a predisposing physiological make-up, though widely postulated and the subject of intensive research, seems as yet not fully proved, although, in the past few years, increasing evidence has been put forward to indicate the role of genetic factors in (at least certain types of) alcoholism. Body and mind are too interwoven to be considered in separation but are better considered as different aspects of a 'psychosomatic' entity; and as yet little is known of a physical basis for higher mental functioning [4].

Psychological factors
It is difficult, if not impossible, to draw conclusions from the state of a long-established alcoholic as to his pre-alcoholic personality as many facets of such an outwardly often rather similar personality-façade may be products formed during the course of his long drawn out drinking career rather than pre-existing 'causes' for his drinking. Nevertheless, in many alcoholics one comes across certain common personality features such as emotional immaturity, inability to take unpleasant realities, low frustration tolerance, unwillingness or inability to endure and to cope with tension, or to stick for long to a given course of activity, etc. [2]. Individual alcoholics may talk of 'typical' alcoholic personalities: 'All alcoholics are perfectionists' is a statement often made by alcoholics. But nurses working in an alcohol unit would hardly agree that all their patients had been particularly meticulous, hard-working, excessively tidy or punctual. The astronaut 'Buzz' Aldrin, a self-confessed alcoholic, listed a number of personal traits which he felt were common to all alcoholics, including sensitivity, perfectionism, and a lack of feeling of being 'comfortable'; the drinker (Aldrin stated) assumes that 'normal' human beings possess such a feeling and hopes that he could possibly obtain it by drinking. Writing in a somewhat similar vein, the writer Constantine Fitzgibbon [6], himself an alcoholic, believes that the sensitivity of artistically inclined individuals may sometimes induce in them a greater need of the sedative qualities of alcohol. Certainly a heightened degree of sensitivity may be one of various factors leading to heavy drinking in creative artists. But while such traits are frequently noticed among alcoholics, they are by no means specific.

'Stupidity' and 'lack of willpower' are attributes commonly mentioned by alcoholics themselves as reasons for their relapses. 'I must be stupid to have resumed drinking in full knowledge of the consequences.' In fact such behaviour may often reveal the degree of psychological dependence on alcohol (see p. 109). But whatever other qualities the majority of alcoholics may have, stupidity is certainly not one of them. They may often lack staying power, may be impulsive, emotionally unstable or immature, but more often than not they are intelligent and in many ways very capable individuals, their achievements reached in spite of alcoholic drink, and not, as they believe because of it. Similar considerations also largely give the lie to the notion of alcoholics lacking willpower. When not drinking, this 'lack of willpower' seems more or less specific in resisting the lure of alcoholic drink, and does not commonly (in non-psychopathic alcoholics) extend to other areas of functioning. Again, many alcoholics in spite of their 'lack of control' manage, under certain conditions to discontinue their drinking long before reaching a state of utter oblivion. No particular strength of willpower is needed by people who are not dependent on alcohol (or on smoking) to refuse the offer of drinks or cigarettes; yet for people dependent on such drugs it may require an uncommon degree of willpower not to follow the dictates of their compulsion. When acting in line with the direction or the dictates of their compulsion many alcoholics often evince a great degree of obstinacy – for instance walking great distances to ensure their presence in good time in another part of the town where pubs open at unusual times – a feat which no ordinary non-alcoholic drinker would contemplate.

However, the choice of symptom (or escape route) in the individual who has a low tolerance for frustration often seems largely accidental, and determined less by qualities inherent in the personality but rather in the environment: for example, in the availability (or acceptance among the individual's social or occupational group) of a suitable escape route at the time when the individual feels in need of one. Nevertheless, it is still necessary, to a certain extent, for such a route to be acceptable to his personality, and not to run counter to his general outlook, values and attitudes. The finding that many alcoholics (in particular the psychogenic ones – see Chapter 15) also tend to misuse other drugs affecting the central nervous system [2] seems to speak against the hypothesis of a specific predisposition to alcoholism (at least in certain types). Rather this seems to point to a tendency among certain immature, unstable and emotionally vulnerable personalities to look for, and avail themselves of, various (and in particular chemical) ways of obtaining relief from discomfort and distress or, alternatively, to attain a higher degree of gratification than they have experienced in the past. The degree of emotional and physical discomfort, the individual's ability to tolerate it, and the strength of internal control of behaviour, are among factors of importance in the potential addict's personality and in the development of alcoholism or other types of drug dependence [5]. Individuals who are anxious, timid, or who feel socially inadequate are more likely to experience a 'rewarding' alleviation of such feelings after drinking, and are more likely to look for a repetition of such 'positive rewards' than basically more stable people. Behaviourists thus see in alcoholism a learned condition (that can be unlearned by retraining) in which both the principles of 'Pavlovian' or 'classical' conditioning, and of Skinner's 'operant' conditioning may have been at work.

The influence of the Pavlovian classic condition can be seen in the case of the drinker entering a pub or when meeting friends in whose company he has previously experienced euphoria when drinking. Associations had been formed so that entering the pub or meeting these friends may immediately arouse a desire for drink.

Apart from the preceding theories of personality make-up and those based on behaviour theory, many other hypotheses have been put forward. In psychoanalytic literature, dependence on drugs is frequently seen as a phenomenon resulting from 'oral fixation', or as aggression directed against oneself (gradual suicide). Repressed homosexuality was also mentioned in early psychoanalytic literature. Other psychological theories stress the role of parental or other dominant figures in the life of the very young by mental mechanisms such as imitation or identification. The finding that alcoholics frequently have heavily-drinking parents may, in theory, be due to nature and/or nurture, and the not uncommon occurrence of an alcoholic grandfather having a teetotal son whose child, in turn, then develops alcoholism, is no evidence either way. In a completely different way, followers of the school of transactional analysis regard alcoholism as a 'game' in which both the drinker and his family and friends join, in order to derive some advantage for themselves [7].

Summarising this discussion, it would seem unlikely that far-reaching, all-embracing hypotheses will explain the aetiology of such a complex condition. There is no such person as the typical alcoholic. Even in a relatively small sample of alcoholics, Jones [8] found as many as seven distinguishable states of mind (e.g. maternal dependence, social insecurity, escapism, unresolved

Oedipal conflicts and unconscious homosexuality). If alcoholics seem to resemble each other, it is largely due to the effects (mental, physical and socioeconomic) of their long-continued drinking on themselves, and of their relatives' and friends' reactions to their drinking. These, then, in turn lead to secondary (defensive-aggressive) counter-reactions in the alcoholic. It seems to make sense, however, that there may be in certain people a predisposing psychological make-up, so that the man or woman who is tense, anxious or beset by feelings of inadequacy and who has not developed satisfying ways to cope with internal or external stresses, or who has greater difficulties in establishing or maintaining satisfying social relationships, may be more inclined to rely on alcoholic drink as a quick, readily available, socially sanctioned and even encouraged morale booster. Such psychological predisposition might possibly consist, for example, in an inherent ill-defined unspecific instability of the central nervous system that may lead to a relatively low tolerance to endure frustration, or it might stem from early childhood experiences where lack of parental affection, acceptance or consistency may leave the individual in a state of emotional insecurity. The positive reward of anxiety relief or euphoria by drinking may reinforce the drinking pseudo-solution to problems, repeated drinking in time leading to tolerance and dependence.

Physiological, neurophysiological and biochemical factors
As regards the physical constitution of the (future) alcoholic, over the years many theories have been put forward in an attempt to explain his 'vulnerability', 'susceptibility' or 'predisposition'. Some of them have enjoyed a more or less fleeting popularity, such as theories of a heightened need for vitamins or of a primary dysfunction of the adrenal glands. However, in an alcoholic who has been drinking excessively for years it is very difficult or impossible to draw conclusions from his present state as to what he was like before he started his drinking career. Certain physical or biochemical abnormalities found in a long-standing alcoholic could just as (or in fact more) likely be consequences of his drinking as its cause.

Alcoholics, for example, habitually eat too little; often indeed, they act as if eating were a waste of valuable drinking time (and energy). They may develop vitamin deficiencies and may require vitamin supplements in treatment. But this by no means proves that such people needed additional vitamins *before* becoming alcoholics. Similarly, any changes in the adrenal glands found in a given alcoholic may more likely have been the result of stress induced by long-continued excessive drinking and not its cause.

Genetic influences

One of the first questions put by problem drinkers (or their families) is whether heredity plays a role in alcoholism. Alcoholics sometimes claim that they were born with the tendency to enjoy or benefit from drinking, because they found it difficult to stop drinking (or indeed did not want to do so) from virtually the very first occasion they had taken alcoholic drink. The finding that there are often a number of alcoholics in one family is often cited by alcoholics as 'evidence' that it was, after all, their ancestors' 'fault', and that they therefore could not really have escaped their fate.

By itself, the finding of a number of alcoholics in a sufferer's family does not prove 'inheritance'. In theory it could equally well result from early environmental influences. For example, the alcoholic parent's unstable and unpredictable behaviour could be responsible for the young son's emotional insecurity; and later in life such insecurity might predispose him, when faced by stress, towards escape to excessive drinking. The father's drinking may possibly act in such a case as a determinant of the 'choice of symptom' as unconsciously the alcoholic's son (or often also his daughter) may identify with him, despite his occasional undesirable, drunken behaviour. But one also comes across cases where the son of a teetotaller who was strongly biased against drink, may develop alcoholism – only for the grandson (in an example of 'reaction formation') to revert to teetotalism.

In the connection of our text, possibly a teetotaller coming from a family in which there were alcoholics, might unconsciously fear the presence of 'alcoholic' tendencies in himself, and guard against them by avoiding any risks, through abstinence.

One investigation often cited in the past as favouring the environmental origin of alcoholism among children of alcoholics was the study of Anne Roe (1941) [11]. Two groups of children, one of alcoholic and one of ordinary parents, were brought up by non-alcoholic foster-parents who were not related to them. Had such children been brought up by their alcoholic parents the expected incidence of alcoholism would have been between 20 and 30 per cent, and for the children of ordinary parents perhaps about 1 per cent. In the event, by the time these children had grown up to an age of about thirty years no significant differences were found between the two groups, and there were as many maladjusted individuals among the normal parentage group as among the group who had alcoholic parents. Roe therefore concluded that the reported high incidence of alcoholism (and psychosis) in the children of alcoholics could not be explained on the basis of heredity factors; and that, moreover, alcoholic parentage did not preclude good adjustment or (given reasonably adequate life circumstances) make it more difficult.

However, in complete contrast to this investigation, very similar recent research carried out by Goodwin on adopted children [12] points in exactly the opposite direction, and favours a hereditary causation. In his study carried out in Denmark, of the adopted sons (with an alcoholic parent) brought up by non-alcoholic foster-parents, 18 per cent developed drinking problems, as against 5 per cent among those adopted sons who came from biological non-alcoholic parents. The two groups had been matched for age, sex and time of adoption. One group consisted of fifty-five sons of an alcoholic father (85 per cent of cases) or an alcoholic mother, who had been hospitalised for alcoholism; the control group consisted of seventy-eight men who had no biological parent ever hospitalised for alcoholism. All these men had been separated from their biological parents in infancy (before they had reached an age of six weeks). As far as could be ascertained the adoptees subsequently had never met their alcoholic parents. Nevertheless it is only fair to mention that, like other similar studies, this one too has met with some criticism as fully discussed in Goodwin's book itself.

Like adoption studies, twin studies are another favourite method employed in investigating the possible influence of hereditary factors in psychiatric disorders and in alcoholism. The rationale underlying twin studies is the difference between identical (monozygotic) and familial (dizygotic) twins. Identical twins share all their genes whereas the familial (dizygotic) twins share only 50 per cent of their genes. Some of the results obtained from these studies were discussed by Schuckitt and his co-workers in 1972 [13]. There is a higher agreement of drinking habits between monozygotic than among dizygotic twins; and similar drinking habits have been found to occur among twins who were separated from each other and brought up in different environments. Schuckitt and his co-workers' own studies in children of alcoholic parents found that the rates of alcoholic dependence resemble each other a great deal, and it seemed to make little difference whether they were brought up by their alcoholic parents or by non-alcoholic foster parents.

In another type of approach, Schuckitt [14] carried out research among half-siblings of alcoholics. Such half-siblings have genetic material stemming from one of the alcoholic's parents (either the alcoholic or the non-alcoholic one), and it is possible to investigate the effect of upbringing with an alcoholic or non-alcoholic parent independent of the half-sibling's genetic make-up. Schuckitt interviewed ninety-eight half-siblings of forty-one alcoholics. Comparison of the effects of having an alcoholic parent, on the one hand, and on the other hand of the upbringing within a family with an alcoholic parent, indicated the greater significance of hereditary influences in the development of alcoholism.

A conclusion that hereditary factors may be significant as regards drinking behaviour and dependency on alcohol but not as far as the social consequences of drinking are concerned was drawn by investigators in Finland from a large-scale study on pairs of twins [15] in the 1960s. Heredity was of influence in questions of how frequently, and how much, was drunk, but not concerning the question of 'arrests for drunkenness'. As regards 'loss of control' – i.e. dependency and the ability to control one's consumption – hereditary factors were important in younger but not in older drinkers.

Animal studies are another technique used to investigate the influence of genetic factors in alcoholism. It has often been demonstrated that strains of rats and mice may have widely different rates of preferring or avoiding alcohol. The ability to metabolise acetaldehyde may be associated with some differences between such strains. Professor Jorge Mardones [16] in Chile, a pioneer in this type of research, emphasises the wide individual fluctuations in the normal 'physiological appetency' in the 'pharmacological appetency' (i.e. drinking for the effect of alcohol), pathological appetency' (characteristic of the loss-of-control and inability-to-abstain drinker), and in the susceptibility to medical complications. While such fluctuations might originate from environmental as well as from genetic influences, environmental factors act on everyone (accessibility to drink, cultural rules governing the use of alcoholic drink). The significant individual differences therefore, in Mardones' view, must result from genetic factors which influence the evolution of dependence. Mardones lists three examples where, in his view, genetic influences have been demonstrated:

1   The genetic origin of individual fluctuations in alcohol preferences of rats of alcohol solutions compared to water.

2   The existence of an atypical form of alcohol dehydrogenase (the enzyme responsible for the oxidation of 90 per cent of alcohol in the liver) of a six times higher activity than the typical one. (This was first demonstrated by von Wartburg [17] in 5–20 per cent of individuals, the proportion varying in different countries.)

3   The discovery (in Chile) of a significant correlation between colour blindness, liver cirrhosis, and alcoholism [18]. (Subsequently such correlation was, however, not confirmed by observers in other countries.)

Other studies carried out in order to elucidate the possible importance of genetic influences on alcohol dependence include those into the secretion (or rather its lack) of certain (AB) blood group substances in the saliva of alcoholics [19] and immune response investigations which point to possible genetic influences in the development of certain alcoholic complications, such as cirrhosis [20]. Of special interest has been the finding that, in comparison with Caucasians, in Orientals even small amounts of alcoholic drink can induce flushing [21]. Goodwin's [22] research in St Louis found such flushing in two-thirds of the Orientals he studied; this kind of 'endogenous Antabuse', he felt, was likely to protect them from the development of alcoholism.

In this connection one might also speculate as to possible constitutional differences in developing alcoholism between, for example, asthenic and pyknic individuals.[1] Some 'cerebrotonic' asthenics may often feel sick and have little tolerance for alcohol and are thus unlikely to obtain positive rewards from drinking. It would appear more likely that the immediate negative rewards would deter them from persisting with their drinking career long enough to develop increased tolerance and dependence. Pyknic, viscerotonic individuals, on the other hand, with an initially high tolerance for alcohol (a 'good head') may be thereby encouraged to continue drinking, the more so as the pyknic body type frequently goes with a gregarious, extravert temperament, leading to an enjoyment of social gatherings where drink is freely available. In fact some years ago, Sheldon [23] suggested that alcoholism was most likely to develop in certain types of body build (and temperament), and highly unlikely in certain other types. There is also the greater likelihood among extraverted, pyknic, sociable drinkers of more regular heavier social drinking, and among the more introverted of psychogenic 'relief' drinking, perhaps more often in bouts. Regular heavy drinking appears, for example, to be more deleterious to the liver than bout drinking interrupted by drink-free intervals. Theoretically – and all this is highly speculative – there might therefore be some connection between constitution and the likelihood or otherwise of development of alcohol-related harm, perhaps often with a greater risk of either dependence or harm in certain constitutional types.

There appears to be a certain correlation between the pyknic body build, and the possible development of a manic-depressive psychosis, and similarly between the asthenic and the athletic build and schizophrenia. Some manic-depressives tend to drink heavily, both in their depressive and manic phases. The frequent occurrence of such attacks may thus favour the development of tolerance and dependence on alcohol, in spite of the often lengthy free intervals. Genetic influences are therefore important contributory factors in the relatively infrequent instances where a 'symptomatic' or 'secondary' type of alcoholism develops in individuals suffering from manic-depressive psychosis either in its unipolar form (depressive periods only) or in its bipolar form (alternative depressive and manic phases); and also in illnesses such as schizophrenia, certain forms of mental subnormality and possibly psychopathy.

Insofar as nature as well as nurture may be involved in the make-up of anxious or obsessional types of personality, genetic factors play a certain contributory role in such individuals who, under stress, may start drinking in order to obtain relief. This is more likely when such people live in cultures or move in subcultures where regular drinking is common. These then would be examples where a possible genetic contribution interacts with environmental, sociocultural factors. In general the question as to the 'inheritance of alcoholism' is surely not whether alcoholism is inherited, but whether there is (and perhaps in certain individuals or certain types of the alcoholisms only) a genetic predisposition or susceptibility which makes individuals more vulnerable to the effects of the agent alcohol (and in some individuals also to related substances sedating the CNS) and this to a lesser or larger extent in the presence of certain environmental factors. There is also the question of genetic protective factors which could possibly minimise the likelihood of the development of dependence or harm to tissues. There is also the possibility of some genetic predisposition being present in varying individuals to a different (major or lesser) extent, thereby requiring the additional presence of other, environmental factors and circumstances, which would need to be more potent in some cases, less potent in others, in order to bring the latent predisposition to light. It is therefore by no means necessary to regard possible genetic and environmental influences in the development of alcoholism as excluding each other; on the contrary, it seems much more likely that they may interact with each other, to a varying extent of their mutual spheres of influence in the various subgroups and types of the 'alcoholisms'.

In general, most researchers into the relationship between heredity and alcoholism are cautious in drawing far-reaching conclusions from their (often preliminary) findings. In answer to the question whether alcoholics are born or 'made', earlier editions of this book (1970) stated that 'Majority opinion today is probably that, while a physical predisposition to alcoholism cannot be excluded, there is so far no definite evidence that it does exist, and the verdict as yet must be one of "not proven".' As a consequence of intensive research in this area in the intervening years there probably has been a certain shift in the majority view. Many nowadays might possibly agree with Madden's [26] summing-up: 'The studies on heredity and alcohol dependence are suggestive but not conclusive.'

Neurotransmitter changes in alcoholism
Much research in recent years has been concerned with the release and uptake of neurotransmitters in the brain [27]. These are chemical substances involved in the transmission of nerve impulses from one nerve to the other across the synapses situated between two neurons. Neurotransmitters are released on the arrival of the nerve impulse at the synapse and diffuse through the membrane of the first nerve to reach the cell-body of the second nerve setting up an impulse there. Some transmitters assist the transmission of nerve impulses, others (such as G-aminobutyric acid-Gaba) inhibit it. The best known among the transmitters is acetylcholine but several others have been closely studied, such as three monoaminergic neurotransmitters: serotonin, norepinephrin and dopamine. Increased secretion of such catecholamines may follow the consumption of alcohol; it has been said that the initial effects of alcohol felt to be 'stimulating' may be due to the release of the catecholamines, whereas the depressing effects are due to the directly depressing effects of alcohol [29]. Gaba transmission,

incidentally, according to a very recent hypothesis, may be involved in the action of diazepam. Action of alcohol, according to another recent claim, has been said to resemble to some extent, the action of this inhibitory neurotransmitter Gaba [28]. Other new discoveries are the neuropeptides, the endorphins and the encephalins. Several such endogenous (i.e. produced within the body) peptides have in recent years been isolated from the brain and other areas which possess opiate-like activity ('endogenous and opiate-like substances') and antagonists of opiates, such as naloxone, have been found to block the action of these endogenous peptides. It is obviously of great interest that recently naloxone has also been found to be an effective inhibitor of ethanol intoxication [30], and it has been suggested that certain central effects of alcohol may be mediated by opioid peptides [31, 32]. These peptides appear to be naturally occurring pain-killers although their ordinary physiological function is unknown. They normally act on specific opiate receptors – structures with a high capacity to bind opiates – and are situated mainly in the central nervous system. Endorphins have been tried in a number of psychiatric conditions without, as yet, any definite results, but they may turn out to be important for states of euphoria and drug dependence [27].

There are a number of similarities (as well as differences) between dependence on opiates and on alcohol [33]; in fact a WHO Expert Committee (1967) recommended approaching various forms of drug dependence, whether on alcohol or on 'other drugs', as fundamentally closely related problems [34]. So far, however, it has not been possible to demonstrate in a satisfactory way a direct chemical link between alcohol and opiate dependence[27]. There have been suggestions made since the 1970s that ethanol might react with the transmitter dopamine to produce a substance resembling a tetrahydropapaveroline compound which, in the opium poppy, is a chemical precursor of morphine. But there seems as yet no clear evidence that these tetrahydroisoquinolines, morphine-like derivatives of acetaldehyde and metabolites of catecholamines, play a role in dependence on alcohol although, in the view of Littleton [27] 'the possibility that these metabolites are produced at some site and play a role in ethanol dependence must not be ignored'. The question has also been raised whether there might possibly exist a defect of neurotransmission in certain types of alcoholism. It is clear that neurotransmitter research seems likely to become of great importance in alcoholism as in dependence on other drugs.

2   The environment

The possibility that a tense, anxious individual may happen to 'hit' on the drinking response, and after finding such response to be 'rewarded' by tension-reduction on the first few occasions, and be in a position to avail himself of the drinking response again and again, is of course very much greater when society and, in particular, the closer circle in which this individual moves ('subculture') tolerates, accepts, or even encourages regular drinking. The fact that in certain cultures, in contrast to others, alcohol is in widespread use, makes it much easier for such an individual to progress from using it socially or as a pleasant thirst-quencher, to increasingly employing alcoholic drink as a tranquilliser.

But attractive as psychological theories of the aetiology of alcoholism may sound, by themselves they cannot explain the whole story. The influence of environmental factors is clearly illustrated by the well known traditional (though gradually disappearing) differences in the numbers of male and female alcoholics. Women can hardly be regarded as being less beset by worries, anxieties and fears than men. Yet male alcoholics have always outnumbered female alcoholics. This example alone points to the great importance of environmental factors – in this case probably largely traditional and sociocultural in nature. In spite of emancipation, society still condemns a drunken woman much more than a drunken man (an attitude which, in general, exercises a restraining effect on heavy drinking among women). Up to a point (unfortunately) heavy drinking among men is even encouraged, a general societal attitude which probably greatly contributes to the relatively greater prevalence of alcoholism among men. On the other hand, a psychologically more 'vulnerable' woman under stress may be more inclined to take drugs [35] (formerly barbiturates, nowadays 'minor' tranquillisers) which do not betray the drug-taker by their smell and may be more easily carried in the handbag than a bottle, but which may produce similar desired effects as alcoholic drink. Nevertheless, recent years have witnessed everywhere an increasing incidence of heavier drinking and drinking problems among women; again probably largely a reflection of changing social conditions and psychosocial factors such as emancipation, greater independence, women going out to work and obtaining highly responsible positions, conflicts over identity and so on (see Chapter 6).

The finding of often widely varying proportions of male and

female alcoholics in different countries may, to some extent, be explained by the degree of acceptance and tolerance of women's regular drinking by society in the country concerned. In general one might assume that the hypothetical female alcoholic might have been a more 'vulnerable' type of person than the average male (pre)alcoholic, since in order to become an alcoholic, she has had to break many more social taboos than a man. This assumption may also partly explain why the outlook for the average female alcoholic has often been found to be less favourable than in her male counterpart [36].

These considerations are in line with Jellinek's 'vulnerability-acceptance theory' [37] which attempts to explain differences in character and prevalence of alcoholism in various countries. According to this theory, differences in the degree of national acceptance or rejection of drinking, may to some extent account for differences in the prevalence of alcoholism, the varying proportions of psychiatric and certain organic disorders among alcoholics, the predominant pattern in which alcohol is taken, and the occurrence and age of onset of the main symptoms of alcoholism. Jellinek's working hypothesis, for example, serves well to explain what type of person is most likely to become an alcoholic in a given country or society. In certain countries such as France heavy drinking is widespread and generally accepted. Most Frenchmen believe that wine improves health. Frenchmen drink more alcohol per head of the population, spend more money on alcoholic drinks, and have a higher mortality rate for liver cirrhosis than people in any other country. (Although it is only fair to say that in recent decades French authorities have made intensive and to a certain extent successful efforts to alter attitudes towards alcoholic drink and to try to reduce the amount of drinking.) Economic factors play a large role as a considerable part of the French population earns its living by producing wine. Under such socioeconomic circumstances of widely accepted heavy drinking, even relatively 'normal' (average) personalities may be exposed to the possibility of heavy drinking and with it the risk of alcoholism. In other countries, where heavy drinking and drunkenness are not readily tolerated or accepted (such as the USA), in the main psychologically vulnerable personalities will run the risk of being regarded as, or labelled, 'deviants'. 'Sociogenic' theories of the causation of alcoholism may therefore be more popular in countries such as France in view of the relatively greater importance of social factors in the genesis of alcoholism, and 'psychogenic' theories in countries disapproving of heavy drinking. Like all generalisations, however, one has to be careful in applying such theories too widely. In the UK excessive drinking is not generally widely tolerated or accepted yet many alcoholics appear to have no more 'abnormal' pre-alcoholic personalities than the average non-alcoholic. Similarly, among women alcoholics a relatively high proportion appear to have started their excessive drinking career at a period of abnormal external stress rather than as a consequence of high emotional instability.

To a large extent drinking, and the habit of heavy drinking, may be regarded as learned social activity. Heavy drinking (and thereby alcoholism) arises in individuals who initially started to drink socially before gradually drinking more and more, either to obtain emotional relief or in accordance with the drinking patterns of their peers or their socio-occupational 'subcultures'. Drinking fashions differ between members of different social strata: middle-class drinkers, by-and-large, prefer spirits; working-class drinkers, beer. Spirit drinking is relatively more common in Anglo-American culture, where drinking often takes place mainly in the evenings, rather than intermittently or continually throughout the day as among the French with their wine and 'plateau'-drinking. Spirit drinking, in Jellinek's hypothesis [37], is more likely to lead to bout drinking and the Gamma ('loss of control') type of alcoholism; wine (and beer) drinking to a more steady, continual or intermittent ('topping up') consumption of alcohol, with the risk of developing the Delta (or 'inability to abstain') type of alcoholism (and a higher risk of liver cirrhosis). If such hypotheses are valid, then drinking patterns 'learned' by individuals from their subculture may have important repercussions not only on their ordinary drinking but even on the type of alcoholism and the likelihood or otherwise of developing certain organic complications.

Another sociocultural factor said to play an important role in the development of alcoholism is the degree, or lack, of integration of drinking customs with the rest of the culture. Such sociological hypotheses state that, where drinking customs are not well integrated into the general cultural pattern of the group, conflicting attitudes towards drinking tend to develop as the heavy drinker may feel guilty. Where they are well integrated, the drinker is not worried by conflicting attitudes. Usually quoted in this connection, are the alleged low alcoholism rates of Jews and Italians in contrast to the high rates among the Irish [38, 39].

Irish-Americans are usually given as examples of a group with high rates of alcoholism. With them the purpose of drinking is to get drunk, but there is great variability of the drinking situations on different occasions, and of the degree of intoxication with which the drinker may hope to get away without punishment. The first drink ever [40] may have been taken away from the protecting atmosphere of home and under the influence of companions who egg the newcomer on.

Investigations of Italians and Italian-Americans have shown that while they drink very often, and start in childhood, they do not often suffer from alcoholism. One important reason may be the Italian dietary habits [41]. Italians drink wine with meals and their drinking habits are well integrated. This may explain to some extent the differences in rates of alcoholism between the French and the Italians. However, as so often with alcoholism, some of these earlier hypotheses have not been supported by later findings. More recent investigations, for example, have shown alcoholism to be by no means uncommon in the cities of Northern Italy.

As regards the alcoholism rates of Jews [39], they have been found to be very low, through the centuries and in various parts of the world, in spite of the finding that they have a very small proportion of total abstainers. In the sixteenth century, for example, a German writer [42] found inebriety common to all strata of the population, men and women alike, but absent among Jews. Among the various reasons given for the relative rarity of alcoholism among Jews most widely accepted, is that of sociocultural learning by Jewish youngsters of drinking patterns at home: for example, 'ritual' drinking at home, with drinking among the orthodox preceded and followed by a prayer, thus associating drinking with religion and a state of sobriety [38, 43], and the degree of orthodoxy influencing the amount of drinking and militating against drunkenness [43]. In the view of Charles R Snyder [43], the leading research worker in this field, 'through . . . cultural mechanisms, the religious Jew learned how to drink in a controlled manner, and also how not to drink'. It is of interest in this connection that in the UK, the USA [44] and Australia [44a] heavier drinking practices and alcoholism appear to have increased among Jews with the waning of orthodox religious practice. In London, for example, the present writer [44b] has noticed over the past fifteen years an increasing number of Jewish alcoholics (including women) though mainly men. Such cases however occurred as a rule among the more 'accultured' sections of the Jewish population, i.e. those following in this (and other) aspects the pattern of the majority culture. (In the view of Sargent [44a] this again reflects a social learning process.) The only case of alcoholism seen by this writer in an orthodox Jewish man was in an emotionally highly unstable individual in whom possibly the need for relief from 'unbearable' emotional pressures proved greater than the religious 'brake' against heavy drinking (which would be in line with the 'vulnerability-acceptance' hypothesis). Jewish 'ritual' drinking habits have often been contrasted with 'secular' or 'utilitarian' (producing pleasurable effects) drinking practices among the Irish [38]. Snyder's recent (1979) review of the subject [44] concludes that 'the weight of evidence favours a sociocultural rather than a biological explanation . . . of the relative rarity of alcoholism among Jews'; but he is at pains to point out that a genetic explanation cannot be ruled out altogether with other factors in individual cases. He ends his review with the plea (a familiar ending of any paper dealing with any aspect of the drink problem) for the 'need for more systematic research on Jewish alcoholics and alcoholism'.

The example of Jews running a greater risk of alcoholism when moving away from their religious and sociocultural controls reflects a wider social phenomenon – that the risk of alcoholism in populations undergoing rapid and intensive sociocultural changes increases with the breakdown of previously important and effective informal social controls. This may be one of the factors contributing to the increasing alcoholism problem in the developing countries. Once individuals under such circumstances have embarked on heavy drinking, the resulting societal reactions – censure, pressure and ostracisation – may lead to progressive alienation of the individual. In this way society's reaction may influence even the symptomatology, the course of, and the type of disability produced by, alcoholism. Such reactions by a rejecting society may provoke the erection of even more firmly entrenched defence mechanisms by the isolated individual which in turn may become new motivations for further excessive drinking, thus perpetuating a vicious circle.

The role of *economic factors* in the causation of alcohol problems is reflected in the very high incidence of alcoholism in France with its high production of wine and strong vested interests. Economic influences are also involved in today's 'affluence' alcoholism in some parts of the world, as they were in the 'misery' or 'poverty' alcoholism prevalent in the eighteenth and nineteenth centuries. During the time of the Industrial Revolution, for example, at a time when wages were low, work hard, the price of bread high, housing conditions appalling but drinking facilities cheap, plentiful and attractive, the temptation was great for the working man to take the 'quickest way out of Manchester', and to escape from poor sordid living conditions and the depressing home atmosphere to the warmth, light and companionship of beer houses and glamorous gin palaces [45].

The all-important factor of availability of alcohol is involved in the contribution of the relative price of alcohol to the prevalence of alcoholism and alcohol-related damage to health. Increased taxation with other restrictive and legislative measures may have contributed greatly to the marked reduction of problem drinking and its consequences towards the end of the First World War [45]. Various studies demonstrated a close, inverse relationship between changes in the relative price of alcohol and the consumption of alcoholic drink [46] and the association between such consumption and mortality rates from cirrhosis of the liver. The fact that in Great Britain the price of alcoholic drink in terms of disposable income has fallen in recent years has probably been one of the significant factors in the increase of alcohol consumption. According to statistics quoted by Sir Bernard Braine [47], chairman of the National Council on Alcoholism, in 1950 a male manual worker in Britain had to work 23 minutes for a pint of beer, or 6½ hours for a bottle of whisky. In 1976 though, it was 12 minutes for the pint of beer, and 2 hours for the whisky.

In recent years there has been increasing recognition of the relationship in a given population between *per capita* consumption of alcohol and the prevalence of alcohol-related problems, such as convictions for drunkenness, mortality rates for liver cirrhosis, and hospital admissions for alcoholism. Though hardly ever referred to nowadays, in the 1920s and 1930s Dr Rudolf Bandel [47a] in Nuremberg was probably among the first to point to, and statistically to illustrate, the association between the amount of alcohol consumption in a given population and the prevalence of alcohol-related damage. Dr Ledermann in France in the 1950s [48] described a 'quasi-mathematical connection between reasonable consumption of alcohol and unreasonable consumption [of alcohol]'. Extending such work on the probable influence of widespread drinking among a given population on the development of heavy drinking, with resulting alcohol-related complications among a minority, workers at the Ontario Research Foundation [46, 49], in more recent years, showed that alcoholism rates tended to rise and fall with the overall level of alcohol use in a given population, leading to an 'apparently fixed relationship between consumption averages and alcoholism prevalence'. Surveys indicated a log normal distribution, i.e. a smooth distribution of alcohol consumption with no discontinuities in the curve so that infrequent drinkers were most numerous in such a distribution, moderate drinkers less numerous, and heavy drinkers least numerous. An increase of *per capita* consumption is associated with an increase in the number of heavy drinkers carrying a risk of alcohol-related damage to their health; whereas a reduction of *per capita* alcohol consumption also diminishes the proportion of heavy drinkers. There has been some criticism by statisticians of the assumptions leading to such theories but the findings of a relationship between *per capita* use and frequency of alcohol-related complications obviously have an important bearing on prophylaxis and the type of preventive programmes (see Chapter 21).

The important role of environmental factors in the causation of alcoholism is well illustrated by the finding that members of certain occupational groups are prone to develop drink problems much more frequently than others. This is confirmed not only by the findings of many treatment agencies but also by the high rates of mortality from liver cirrhosis in some occupational groups. In the UK the Registrar General has, since 1911, regularly published liver cirrhosis mortality rates as seen in selected occupational groups – twenty occupations with the highest cirrhosis mortality rates being shown in the latest list – can be seen in the following table: (Mortality in the average population is taken as being 100.)

Publicans and innkeepers, as has been the rule over the past sixty years, head the list with a mortality rate sixteen times as high as the average. Company directors, who were found to have by far the highest mortality rates (2200) in the previous list, were not included on this occasion; the reasons for the high rates of alcohol problems among this group will be discussed later in Chapter 10.

Also not mentioned on this occasion, but included in past publications, are wives of publicans and innkeepers who also constitute a high-risk group as regards cirrhosis mortality, with rates five to six times the average. This would indicate the importance of easy access to, and ready availability of, alcohol; similarly to the finding over many years of a relatively high proportion of

Table 1
Standard mortality rates from liver cirrhosis
(England and Wales 1970–72)

Company directors	2200 (1961)*
Publicans, Innkeepers	1576 (773 in 1961)*
Deck, engineering officers and ship pilots	781
Barmen, barmaids	633
Deck and engine room ratings, barge and boatmen	628
Fishermen	595
Proprietors and managers of boarding houses and hotels	506
Finance, insurance brokers, financial agents	392
Restaurateurs	385
Lorry drivers' mates, van guards	377
Cooks	354
Shunters, pointsmen	323
Winders, reekers	319
Electrical engineers	319
Authors, journalists and related workers	314
Armed forces	350 (1961)*
Medical practitioners (qualified)	311 (350 in 1961)
Garage proprietors	294
Signalmen and crossing keepers (railways)	290
Maids, valets and related service workers	281
Tobacco preparers and product makers	269
Metallurgists	266

* The figures in brackets refer to the preceding publication of the Registrar General giving such mortality rates for 1961.

so-called 'professional addicts' to drugs other than alcohol among doctors, pharmacists and nurses [2], just as the finding of high cirrhosis mortality rates among occupational groups where drinking is widely accepted and expected, such as merchant seamen, journalists, certain sections of industry, and retired army and naval officers.

In some of the 'high risk' groups the question may arise as to what extent people attracted by the availability of drink may have chosen such jobs. A recent Scottish study carried out by Plant (1979) [50], comparing 150 male manual workers who had recently joined 'low risk' occupations, indicated that the workers in the brewing and distilling firms had often been heavier drinkers before taking up this occupation. However, follow-up over a 2–3 year period indicated that workers in the drink trade continued to drink much more heavily than those in low risk occupations, and developed much higher rates of alcohol-related problems. Workers leaving the drink trade for low-risk occupations tended to drink less heavily. The study indicated the importance of current occupation on drinking habits and the development of alcohol-related problems. The present writer's own inquiries similarly indicate the importance of environmental factors: for example, the great majority of alcoholic publicans who had entered this business after the Second World War had not been heavier drinkers than their fellow soldiers; they were mainly attracted to the publican trade as a promising way of using their gratuity to make a good living.

Ready availability of drink may also explain the high cirrhosis mortality rates among *proprietors and managers of boarding houses and hotels*, *restaurateurs* and *cooks* (the latter, however, frequently complain of the hot atmosphere in which they work and which makes them very thirsty). To have to work in hot or dusty or very cold and unpredictable climatic conditions, may be another environmental hazard in certain occupations encouraging habitual or frequent recourse to alcoholic drink. Having frequently to take shelter when heavy rain makes it impossible for them to continue work is a reason frequently given by *building workers* for the onset of their heavy drinking habits.

Opportunity to drink freely may be among the factors at work amongst *commercial travellers*, various interacting factors may also be involved: having to entertain potential customers, frequent separation from home and family, time spent in towns and hotels where they do not know anybody and where, feeling bored and lonely, they drift to the bar to find company. Frequently too, the psychological factor of having to overcome shyness in approaching strangers may also be very significant to this group.

Other professions with a high risk of cirrhosis mortality are medical practitioners [53] (whose wives, too, showed in the 1961 list a cirrhosis mortality rate twice the average population) and journalists. The case of alcoholic doctors will be discussed later (see Chapter 11). Alcoholic journalists [2] claimed that alcoholism was not merely an occupational hazard but almost an occupational necessity because of the many opportunities and socio-occupational pressures to drink. The newcomer, watching the seasoned journalist drinking heavily, begins to follow his example; and a great deal of time is spent in pubs which are the best place to obtain stories and information; and one may have to 'wine' rather than 'dine' the person from whom one hopes to get a good story;

again one is often in the company of heavy drinkers or alone, far from home and family.

Factors of importance among *merchant seamen* (as among other sailors and servicemen in general) may be the individual's feeling that on ship (or in the army) he is expected to drink like the great majority of his (often much older and much more alcohol-tolerant) colleagues. Away from the restraining influence of parents or wife, and having few alternative recreations for dispelling boredom and loneliness, may be additional reasons for falling in line with the pressures – real or imagined – of colleagues. Such reasons are frequently given for the onset of heavy drinking by former soldiers who, for example, had been serving in Germany (the SMR of members of UK Armed Forces was given by the 1961 General Registrar's list as 350, equalling that of doctors). Continually mixing with much older more seasoned drinkers and the desire to keep up with them was frequently mentioned both by merchant seamen and also many other alcoholic patients as an important reason for having started to drink heavily. Heavy drinking more commonly occurs among long-serving merchant seamen.

In many cases social and emotional factors are closely related, not only in the example of 'retired army officers' (found to have a high SMR for cirrhosis in a previous Registrar publication) but among the retired in general [54]. Loss of status and of former friends, social relationships and routine, feelings of uselessness, loneliness, boredom, frustration and similar factors may all be involved.

A recent review by Plant [55] lists eight reasons for high rates of drink problems in certain occupations. In addition to those discussed above he mentions collusion from colleagues, special strains and stresses, recruitment of 'predisposed' individuals to certain professions, and very high or low income levels.

Examples of the importance of separation from ordinary social or sexual relationships are servicemen and seamen, in any experience the high proportions of Irish and Scottish single male alcoholics in London seen in alcoholic units, too. Living in 'digs' on their own, the pub may be the best place for such lonely people to find company, and – often lacking inner or outer resources to spend leisure time in an enjoyable way – by taking sufficient drink to pluck up courage to ask a girl for a dance.

Collusion by colleagues is an important factor in the 'covering-up' regime so often at work in industry, protecting workmates who risk dismissal should their drinking habits be discovered (see Chapter 10). Special 'strains and stresses' may be at work not only in doctors, journalists, and in the 'job insecurity' of actors, for example, but also among retired army officers, the unemployed and the elderly who, to do some job or other, keep encountering insurmountable difficulties and endless frustration and disappointment in their search for work.

Climatic conditions may largely explain the differences between drinking patterns of the Northern Europeans' spirit drinking, and the Southern Europeans' wine drinking habits. Spirits, said James Boswell [51] 200 years ago, are 'a means to supply by art the want of that genial warmth of blood which the sun produces'. Rather surprisingly this point has recently become somewhat topical in a controversy as to whether Alexander the Great had been an alcoholic. This is by no means a novel theory but was taken up in an American magazine article in October 1980 according to which Alexander had been a drunkard whose death at a very young age was caused by acute alcohol withdrawal complicated by malaria. This statement was indignantly attacked by Greek scholars and officials who pointed out that the more northern Macedonians inevitably consumed wine that had a higher alcohol content than that of southern Greeks 'just as the Russians drink almost 100 per cent alcohol in order to keep warm'. In addition, the explanation added that stress of war 'also made drinking necessary' without this affecting the Macedonian leader's abilities. The Greeks received support from a French author of a book on Alexander the Great: 'Alexander an alcoholic? No. A good drinker, yes. But for heaven's sake, after so many victories the man deserved a drink' [52] – a charitable thought which perhaps could also be applied to Attila the Hun whose death is sometimes reported to have occurred in somewhat similar circumstances. (Incidentally, the vasodilation which by making the drinker feel warmer in a cold climate and thus encouraging him to drink, leads in the long run to dangerous loss of heat.)

3   The agent: the pharmacological nature of alcohol

Although the contribution of the various factors (physical, psychological, social, pharmacological) causing alcoholism is discussed here under separate headings, the previous discussion has shown that a clear delineation between various factors is not possible. As regards the pharmacological role of alcohol itself as an aetiological factor, it may be of interest to recall the division of drugs affecting the central nervous system into three classes, on the basis of interaction between the individual's make-up and the pharmacological nature of the drug, made by a WHO Addiction Subcommittee in 1952 [56]. Sometimes it is the pharmacological properties of a drug that are most important: for example, in the case of opiates, the majority of people using them even for a relatively short period (perhaps weeks only) may become psychologically and physically dependent, however stable their underlying personality and even though they may (initially) use small, therapeutic doses only. Among individuals misusing barbiturates a much smaller proportion (a minority of users) may become dependent, after consumption for a few months, in slightly above therapeutic dosage [35]. In the case of alcohol, an even smaller proportion of drinkers (usually perhaps 1–2 and possibly no more than 5–6 per cent) may develop dependence after grossly excessive drinking for several years. Thus, from the aspects of dosage, length of time of administration, and the proportion of users who develop dependence, alcohol would be a less serious dependence-producing agent than barbiturates, and these in turn less so than the opiates. From the point of damage to health, however, the physical complications following excessive drinking may be more dangerous than those occurring after misuse of barbiturates and opiates; and the dangers to life of acute alcohol or barbiturate withdrawal in very heavy drinkers and barbiturate addicts respectively may be greater than those from the withdrawal of the drug in opiate addicts.

According to the classification of the 1952 WHO Expert Committee [56] opiates would be an example of their first group of drugs where the pharmacological nature of the drug is paramount and the user's individual reactions no more than an adjunct; sooner or later 'addiction' will develop in the great majority of users. In a second group of drugs, pharmacological nature was described as playing no more than a subsidiary role, the drug user's psychological make-up being decisive; such drugs would never produce 'addiction' or an irresistible need for the drug but they could lead to 'habituation' (psychological or emotional dependence) in vulnerable personalities. Finally, with a third group of drugs, pharmacological action is intermediate in kind and degree between the 'addiction-producing' and the 'habit-forming' drugs: pharmacological role is significant but the predominant factor is the mental make-up, and 'addiction' might develop in vulnerable personalities. A few years later, two WHO Expert Committees (1954, 1955) [57, 58] concluded that alcohol was a drug with 'a pharmacological action intermediate in kind and degree between addiction-producing and habit-forming drugs so that compulsive craving and dependence can develop in those individuals whose make-up leads them to seek and find an escape in alcohol', personal make-up being the determining factor but the pharmacological action also being significant. It is interesting to note that the influence of environmental factors in interaction with personality and agent was not mentioned at all. Because of continuing semantic arguments and confusion, the WHO Expert Committee recommended (1964) [59], the use of the term 'dependence' in place of addiction and habituation, and later [60] alcohol was listed together with barbiturates in the alcohol-barbiturate type of drugs, as one of eight types of dependence-producing drugs. The place of alcohol as a sedative-tranquillising drug may explain the phenomenon of cross tolerance, the danger of possible potentiation (i.e. an effect greater than explainable by mere summation) when used simultaneously with such drugs, and the risk of substituting other types of dependence in place of alcoholism.

It is the effect of the drug alcohol on the brain that explains its role in inducing dependence. By its depressant effect on higher functions of the brain, it diminishes inhibitions, offers rapid relief from worries, tension and anxiety, and brings peace and comfort to the troubled mind, though by removing ordinary restraints it releases acting-out behaviour and aggression. Successively higher doses lead to confusion, stupor and death, usually at blood alcohol concentrations of, and above, 500 mg/100 ml.

The longing for the detachment from worry and anxiety and for relaxation and peace are the effects of drinking frequently mentioned by alcoholics as among the reasons for their resumption of drinking after a period of abstinence.

An attractive feature of alcohol for drinkers is the rapidity of its effects: it is quickly absorbed from the stomach and small intestine. (Presence of food in the stomach slows the absorption down an experience well heeded by alcoholics who usually avoid eating when engaged in serious drinking.) Alcohol enters the bloodstream within fifteen to twenty minutes and reaches peak level in the blood within one to one and a half hours, beginning to decline after two hours, and disappearing from the blood within twelve hours. It is the immediacy of its effects which is appreciated by the alcoholic who tends to remember the relief rather than the hangover the 'morning after' and the long-term painful and disastrous mental, physical and social effects; and it is probably this factor of very rapid relief that explains the drinker's 'learning' to appreciate the 'positive rewards' rather than the long-term 'negative' rewards.

Very little alcohol (up to 15 per cent) is excreted unaltered through lungs and kidneys (but enabling breathalysing and urine alcohol as well as blood alcohol determinations), while most is metabolised in the liver. The rate of metabolism of alcohol in the liver largely determines its length of action which therefore may be greatly different in the 'chronic alcoholic' suffering from advanced liver cirrhosis. The breakdown of alcohol* in the liver proceeds at a constant pace, with the help of the enzyme alcohol dehydrogenase. It is first metabolised to acetaldehyde, which in turn is further broken down, by the enzyme aldehyde dehydrogenase, to the harmless acetic acid. Acetaldehyde may be a more dangerous substance than ethyl alcohol, and may be responsible for some of its toxic effects. It is held by some to be responsible for myocardial damage occurring in some heavy drinkers. The interruption of the alcohol metabolism beyond the acetaldehyde stage, resulting from disulfiram administration, is the basis of treatment of alcoholics with alcohol deterrent drugs. The possibility has been discussed, but not proven, that acetaldehyde could be the cause of alcohol dependence in which case one could term such a condition 'acetaldehydism' rather than alcoholism [27].

In the view of Littleton 'there is little doubt that acetaldehyde plays some part in ethanol dependence' but it remains uncertain whether this is its main role [27]. As so well expressed by Mark Keller, alcoholics differ from each other as much as non-alcoholics. They all show, however, one common factor: they all take alcoholic drink. Therefore as regards the causation of alcoholism, in the past, the answer, for prohibitionists, was clear: the cause of alcoholism is alcohol. Obviously this cannot be the whole story as the great majority of drinkers do not develop dependence or suffer harm. On the other hand, a slogan that acquired popularity a few years ago and is still frequently heard, is also inaccurate – that alcoholism does not come in bottles, it comes in persons. In early phases of heavy drinking the future

* Unless otherwise specified, 'alcohol' in this book means ethyl alcohol, ethanol (CH_3 CH_2 OH) which is broken down in the liver to acetaldehyde (CH_3 CHO).

alcoholic may usually feel impelled to drink by personality (unless propelled by environmental factors) rather than compelled by alcohol. But the more the process continues the more important the role of alcohol.

If the term 'alcoholism' is taken to include not only dependence but also alcohol-related harm, the fact that alcohol, though a food, is a very inadequate foodstuff, is of great relevance. It provides calories but lacks essential vitamins, proteins and minerals. Alcoholics often try to satisfy all their food requirements by alcoholic drink, and the resulting deficiencies may often be largely responsible for certain complications, for example, in the CNS and the peripheral nerves. Liver complications are nowadays largely ascribed to the direct toxic action of alcohol itself [61].

Clearly a great deal remains obscure although research is gradually beginning to illuminate some of the dark areas. However, it seems highly unlikely that there is any such thing as 'the' cause of alcoholism; rather it would appear that in the various subtypes of what is collectively called 'alcoholism', or in the many different 'alcoholisms', host, environment, and agent are all involved in close dynamic interaction, perhaps in varying intensity of influence in the various types, and certainly in different individuals. Psychosocial factors are probably most important in inducing

Figure 2
Interaction between host, agent and environment

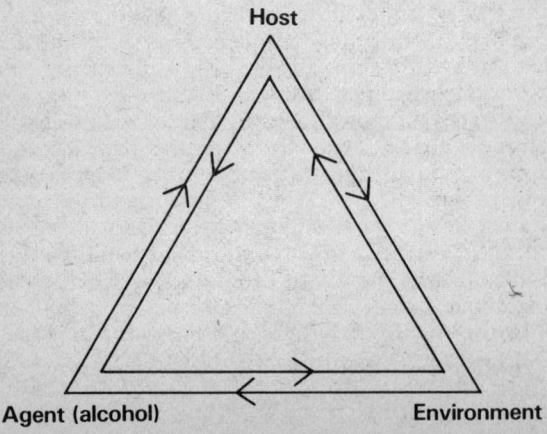

Host

Agent (alcohol)   Environment

heavy drinking, whereas the action of the agent may progressively become more significant the longer the drinking process continues. In trying to prevent or at least to minimise the rates of alcoholism, close attention must therefore be paid to all three areas, and should not concentrate exclusively on one or the other.

One important point to keep in mind is that it may be far more helpful to concentrate on analysing the reasons, and the factors responsible, for causing the relapses into drinking, rather than directing all one's attention to factors which may have caused the individual to embark on his drinking career in the first place. In day-to-day work with problem drinkers, while the factors (psychological and/or social in nature) that originally made such an individual take to heavy drinking might still be at work and may lend themselves to working through in therapeutic approaches, it is usually much easier to discover the reasons (or rationalisations) in the here-and-now and the internal and external cues that have triggered off recent relapses, and to try to motivate the drinker to do something about these.

Notes

[1] Sheldon [23] extended Kretschmer's original typology (developed in the 1920s) by his own researches into the varieties of constitution and temperament. He talked, instead of Kretschmer's [24] pyknic type, of physically 'endomorph' and temperamentally 'viscerotonic' types; instead of Kretschmer's athletic, of 'mesomorph' and 'somatotonic', and instead of Kretschmer's 'asthenic' of 'ectomorph', cerebrotonic types. For example, there is supposed to be a correlation between the temperamental quality of cerebrotonia and the physical constitution of ectomorphy, such individuals said to be lean and 'linear' are more often sensitive, and have difficulty in emotional expression and adaptation to their environment. Eysenck [25], however, is critical of Sheldon's research and conclusions.

References

1 Johnson, Samuel (1776) quoted from Beckett, A G *et al*. (1961), *Brit. med. J.*, 2, 1113

2 Glatt, M M (1974), *A Guide to Addiction and its Treatment – Drugs, Society and Man*, Lancaster, Med. Techn. Publ. Cy.

3 Van Dyjk, W K (1974) in *Alcoholism – a Medical Profile*, ed. Kessel, N *et al*., London, B Edsall, 133–42

4   *Brit. med. J.* (1978), Editorial, 2, 1569
5   Reichard, J D (1947), *Amer. J. Psychiat.*, 103, 72
6   Fitzgibbon, C (1980), *Drink*, London, Granada
7   Steiner, C (1971), *Games Alcoholics Play*, New York, Grove Press
8   Jones, Howard (1963), *Alcoholic Addiction*, London, Tavistock
9   *Encyclopedia of Psychiatry for GPs* (1972), Vol. Ph-Z, London, Roche, 352
10   Thakurdas, H and L (1979), *Dictionary of Psychiatry*, Lancaster, MTP, 39
11   Roe, A (1945) in *Alcohol, Science and Society*, New Haven, *Quart. J. Stud. Alc.*, 117
12   Goodwin, D (1976), *Is Alcoholism Hereditary?*, New York, Oxford University Press, 139
13   Schuckitt, M A *et al.* (1972), *Amer. J. Psychiat.*, 128, 1132
14   Schuckitt, M A (1972), *Ann. N. Y. Acad. Sci.*, 197, 121
15   Partanen, J *et al.* (1966), *Finnish Found. Alcohol Studies*, no. 14, Helsinki
16   Mardones, J (1970) in *A World Dialogue on Alcohol and Drug Dependence*, ed. Whitney, E D, Beacon Press, 367–88
17   Von Wartburg, J P *et al.* (1965), *Can. J. Biochem.*, 43, 889
18   Cruz-Coke, R (1965), *The Lancet*, i, 1131
19   Camps, F E and Dodd, B E (1967), *Brit. med. J.*, 1, 30
20   Bailey, R J *et al.* (1976), *Brit. med. J.*, 2, 727
21   Wolff, P H (1973), *Amer. J. of Human Genetics*, 25, 193
22   Goodwin, D (1975) quoted in *Brit. J. Hosp. Med.*, 19, 686
23   Sheldon, W (1942), *The Varieties of Temperament*, New York
24   Kretschmer, E (1925), *Physique and Character*, London
25   Eysenck, H J, Arnold, W J and Meili, R (eds) (1975), *Encyclopedia of Psychology*, Vol. 2, London, Fontana, Collins
26   Madden, J S (1979), *A Guide to Alcohol and Drug Dependence*, Bristol, John Wright and Sons, 16
27   Littleton, J M (1977) in *Alcoholism: New Knowledge and New Responses*, eds Edwards, G and Grant, M, London, Croom Helm, 107–116
28   *The Times*, Science Report (13 August, 1980)
29   Murphee, H B (1976) in *Alcohol and Alcohol Problems*, eds Gilstead, W J *et al.*, Cambridge, Mass., Ballinger, 135–65
30   Jefferys, D B *et al.* (1980), *The Lancet*, i, 308
31   Jeffcoate, W J *et al.* (1979), *The Lancet*, ii, 1157
32   Kiball, C D *et al.* (1980), *The Lancet*, ii, 418
33   Glatt, M M (1970) in *Under One Umbrella*, ed. Whitney, E D, Boston, Beaver Press, 311–66
34   World Health Organisation (1967), *Services for Prevention and Treatment of Dependence on Alcohol and Other Drugs*, Wld Hlth Org. Tech. Rep. Ser., 363
35   Glatt, M M (1962), *UN Bulletin on Narcotics*, 14, 20
36   Glatt, M M (1961), *Acta Psychiat. Scand.*, 37, 143

37 Jellinek, E M (1960), *The Disease Concept of Alcoholism*, New Haven, Hillhouse
38 Bales, R F (1946), *Quart. J. Stud. Alc.*, 6, 480
39 Snyder, C R (1962) in *Society, Culture and Drinking Patterns*, eds Pittman, D J and Snyder, C R, New York, John Wiley
40 Ullman, A D (1952), *Quart. J. Stud. Alc.*, 13, 602
41 Lolli, G *et al.* (1952), *Quart. J. Stud. Alc.*, 13, 27
42 Frank, Sebastian (1941), 'On the horrible vice of drunkenness', *Quart. J. Stud. Alc.*, ed. Jellinek, E M, 2, 391
43 Snyder, C R (1977), *Alcohol and the Jews*, Carbondale, Southern Illinois University Press (Reprinted edition)
44 Snyder, C R (1979) in *Diseases among Ashkenazi Jews*, eds Goodman, R M and Mohalsky, A G, New York, Raven Press
44a Sargent, M (1969), *Drinking and Alcoholism in Australia*, Melbourne, Longman
44b Glatt, M M (1970), *Brit. J. Addict.*, 64, 297
45 Glatt, M M (1958), *Brit. J. Addict.*, 54, 51
46 De Lint, J and Schmidt, W (1971), *Brit. J. Addict.*, 66, 97
47 Braine, Sir Bernard (February 1980) quoted from *Alliance News*
47a Bendel, R (1934), *Proc. 20th Internat. Congr. Alcoholism*, London, 74
48 Ledermann, S (1964), *Alcoole, Alcoolisme, Alcoolisation*, Paris, Inst. Nat. Etudes, Demographiques, Trav. et Doc. Cahier No. 41
49 De Lint, J (1977) in Madden, J S *et al.*, *Alcoholism and Drug Dependence: a Multidisciplinary Approach*, New York, Plenum, 425–50
50 Plant, M A (1979), *Drinking Careers*, London, Tavistock
51 Boswell, James, *Boswell's Column*, ed. Bailey (1951), London, William Kimber
52 *Internat. Her. Trib.* (18 October, 1980)
52a Rose, H K and Glatt, M M (1961), *J. Ment. Sci.*, 107, 18
53 Glatt, M M (1976), *Hospital Life*, 7
54 Rosin, A and Glatt M M (1971), *Quart. J. Stud. Alc.*
55 Plant, M A (1979), *Brit. J. Al. Am.*, 14 (3), 119
56 World Health Organisation (1952), *Expert Committee on Addiction-Producing Drugs*, Wld Hlth Org. Techn. Rep. Ser., 57
57 World Health Organisation (1954), Wld Hlth Org. Techn. Rep. Ser., 84
58 World Health Organisation (1955), Wld Hlth Org. Techn. Rep. Ser., 94
59 World Health Organisation (1964), Wld Hlth Org. Techn. Rep. Ser., 273, 9
60 Eddy, N B *et al.* (1965), *Bull. WHO*, 32, 721
61 Lieber, C S, and De Carli, L M (1977) in *Metabolic Aspects of Alcoholism*, ed. Lieber, C S, Lancaster, MTP, 32–79

3

The Road to Alcohol Dependence

One of the main difficulties in the treatment of alcoholism is that alcoholics all too often are not recognised until they have arrived at a late stage when they may have already developed serious or even irreversible mental or physical complications, and where, apart from custodial care, not much else can be done for them. (See Chapter 16.) Moreover, both the alcoholic and his family are on the defensive when it comes to recognising the existence of an alcoholic problem in the early stages. Thus, the alcoholic often does not acknowledge his alcoholism until many years' excessive drinking have brought misery not only to himself but also to those closest to him, and until he has been forced – unnecessarily and avoidably – to this crucial stage or an even later one. Yet for many years before he arrives at this late stage he will have shown a number of features which could have provided valuable clues to a much earlier diagnosis. The fact that the road to the final stages is so long – more often than not extending over many years – and often well signposted, should be of great assistance and a spur to earlier diagnostic and preventive action.

Jellinek's description of the average drinking history has already proved very valuable in directing the interest of professional workers and therapists to the importance of the 'drinking history' which, until then, in general had attracted interest only by members of AA. Formerly, psychiatrists were interested almost exclusively in pre-alcoholic aspects and not in the events occurring after the onset of heavy drinking. It is interesting that nearly thirty years after Jellinek's emphasis on the importance of the drinking history, in a recent issue of the *British Medical Journal* a consultant physician [1] regrets the failure of junior doctors to take an 'adequate drinking history', and of failing to record the alcohol consumption in the case notes in 39.1 per cent of 327 adult medical and surgical patients recently admitted to a large London Teaching Hospital.

The course of alcohol addiction was described by Jellinek [2] in 1952 on the basis of replies to a questionnaire which had been previously received from over 2000 American members of AA. This questionnaire had been extended and some questions reformulated after a smaller questionnaire sent by AA to a smaller number of members had shown the potentialities inherent in such a study. As the questionnaire was formulated on the basis of experiences in the USA, and the replies were given by American alcoholics and by that segment of them who were members of AA, it is essentially a description and progress of 'loss of control', Gamma alcoholism. However, as our investigations at Warlingham Park [3] in the late 1950s have shown, Jellinek's description holds good for English middle-class alcoholics too. Our subsequent experiences with large samples and various types of drinkers coming from all social strata of the British population have indicated that, on the whole, such features in roughly a similar order also occur in their drinking history – though naturally aspects of the personality, of the sociocultural situation, the way in which drink is usually taken in the drinker's culture or subculture, the type of drink taken, outside events and emotional experiences which the drinker might encounter or undergo either without, or (often) after meeting up with Alcoholics Anonymous or professional therapists, may exert a considerable modifying influence on the course of his disorder.

Other studies have also confirmed those features in the drinking history of alcoholics as described by Jellinek, in other countries [4, 5]. Jellinek's *Chart of Alcohol Dependence and Recovery* (pp. 74–5) distinguishes four phases. Each of these enumerates a number of more or less characteristic symptoms shown by a great majority of alcoholics, though certainly not by all, and where these characteristics do occur they are not necessarily, or regularly, in the sequence depicted and described here. The Chart, therefore, merely depicts the average trend, and Jellinek's concept of 'phases' obviously does not imply any sharp demarcation line between the various phases.

1 Pre-alcoholic symptomatic phase

Having started to drink for social reasons, the drinker discovers in alcohol easy means of allaying tension and worries, so much so

Figure 3
Chart of alcohol dependence and recovery

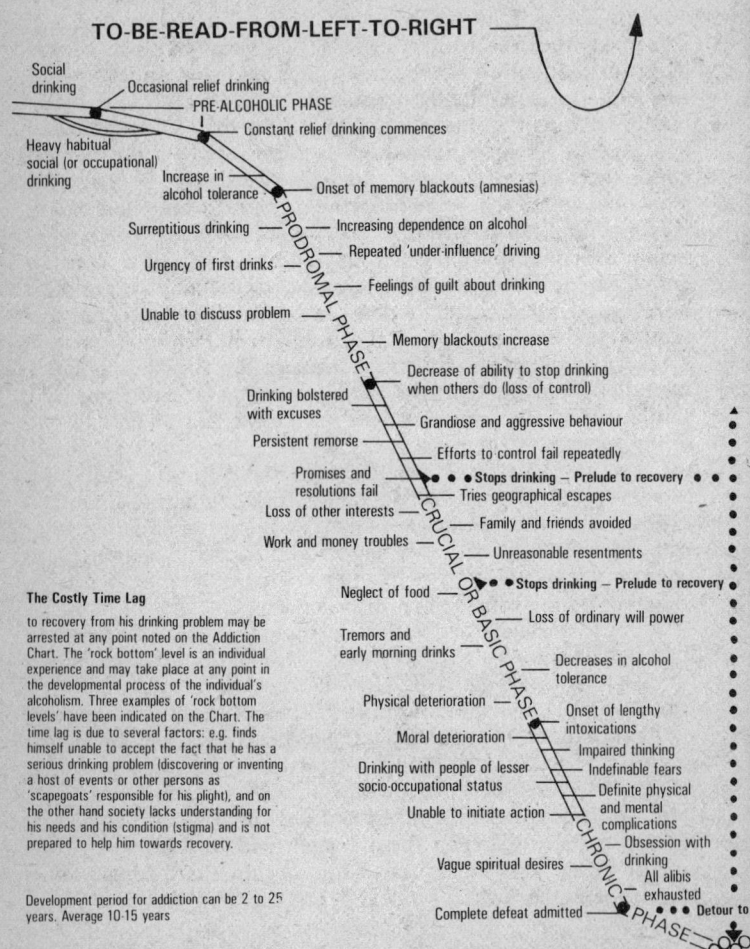

TO-BE-READ-FROM-LEFT-TO-RIGHT

Social drinking

Occasional relief drinking

PRE-ALCOHOLIC PHASE

Constant relief drinking commences

Heavy habitual social (or occupational) drinking

Increase in alcohol tolerance

Onset of memory blackouts (amnesias)

PRODROMAL PHASE

Surreptitious drinking — Increasing dependence on alcohol

Urgency of first drinks — Repeated 'under-influence' driving

— Feelings of guilt about drinking

Unable to discuss problem

— Memory blackouts increase

— Decrease of ability to stop drinking when others do (loss of control)

Drinking bolstered with excuses

— Grandiose and aggressive behaviour

Persistent remorse

— Efforts to control fail repeatedly

Promises and resolutions fail — ● ● ● Stops drinking – Prelude to recovery ● ● ●

— Tries geographical escapes

Loss of other interests — Family and friends avoided

Work and money troubles — Unreasonable resentments

CRUCIAL OR BASIC PHASE

Neglect of food — ● ● Stops drinking – Prelude to recovery ●

— Loss of ordinary will power

Tremors and early morning drinks

— Decreases in alcohol tolerance

Physical deterioration — Onset of lengthy intoxications

Moral deterioration — Impaired thinking

Drinking with people of lesser socio-occupational status — Indefinable fears

— Definite physical and mental complications

Unable to initiate action — Obsession with drinking

Vague spiritual desires — All alibis exhausted

CHRONIC PHASE

Complete defeat admitted — ● ● ● Detour to

OR OBSESSIVE DRINKING

(possibly to point of no recovery —

The Costly Time Lag

to recovery from his drinking problem may be arrested at any point noted on the Addiction Chart. The 'rock bottom' level is an individual experience and may take place at any point in the developmental process of the individual's alcoholism. Three examples of 'rock bottom levels' have been indicated on the Chart. The time lag is due to several factors: e.g. finds himself unable to accept the fact that he has a serious drinking problem (discovering or inventing a host of events or other persons as 'scapegoats' responsible for his plight), and on the other hand society lacks understanding for his needs and his condition (stigma) and is not prepared to help him towards recovery.

Development period for addiction can be 2 to 25 years. Average 10-15 years

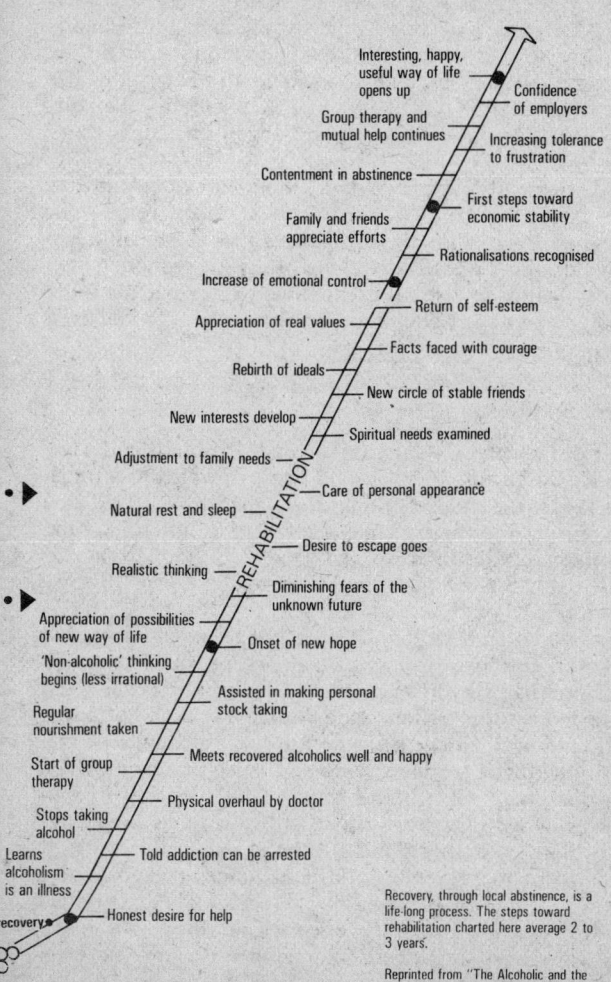

Interesting, happy, useful way of life opens up

Confidence of employers

Group therapy and mutual help continues

Increasing tolerance to frustration

Contentment in abstinence

First steps toward economic stability

Family and friends appreciate efforts

Rationalisations recognised

Increase of emotional control

Return of self-esteem

Appreciation of real values

Facts faced with courage

Rebirth of ideals

New circle of stable friends

New interests develop

Spiritual needs examined

Adjustment to family needs

REHABILITATION

Care of personal appearance

Natural rest and sleep

Desire to escape goes

Realistic thinking

Diminishing fears of the unknown future

Appreciation of possibilities of new way of life

Onset of new hope

'Non-alcoholic' thinking begins (less irrational)

Assisted in making personal stock taking

Regular nourishment taken

Meets recovered alcoholics well and happy

Start of group therapy

Physical overhaul by doctor

Stops taking alcohol

Told addiction can be arrested

Learns alcoholism is an illness

recovery

Honest desire for help

Recovery, through local abstinence, is a life-long process. The steps toward rehabilitation charted here average 2 to 3 years.

Reprinted from "The Alcoholic and the Help He Needs", M.M. Glatt, 2nd Edition, 1972 (Copyright Reserved)

CONTINUES IN VICIOUS CIRCLES

(irreversible mental or physical deterioration)

that he gradually takes to the bottle more and more often and, later on, whenever he wants 'relief'. In this way, gradually, his willingness or readiness to face reality and his ability to bear tension and frustration decrease, but his tolerance for alcoholic drink increases so that he requires more and more to obtain the effect he desires. While 'learning' to use alcohol whenever he has to face any stress or difficulty he fails to grow in emotional maturity as he fails to use difficulties as a challenge or a spur to extra efforts.

While Jellinek only described the 'emotional' route towards heavier drinking there is, of course, an alternate route – for example, when living within a socio-occupational subculture in which heavy drinking is the 'done thing'. Like the predominantly 'psychogenic' route, so also his predominantly 'sociogenic' route can gradually lead to an acquired increase of tolerance and even heavier drinking.

2 Prodromal phase

After a period, which may vary between a few months and a few years, the alcoholic enters the second phase in which prodromal signs foreshadow the shape of things to come. Such features may thus help bring the prospective alcoholic to attention and treatment much earlier than is usually the case. Formerly it was often held that the alcoholic would have to slip down to 'rock-bottom' before he would be ready for treatment. Fortunately, this has been proved utterly wrong. The alcoholic can learn from the examples of other, more advanced alcoholics, provided he can be made to realise that, should he continue drinking the way he does, he will quite likely suffer a similar fate. Moreover, 'rock-bottom' is not a static point meaning the same for every alcoholic. It is a personal, individual experience, and an unpleasant event which one individual may take in his stride, and may be able to rationalise away without great effort, but which may be a shattering body blow to another. Thus the first serious traffic accident, the first admission to a psychiatric hospital, or the first appearance in court may for some people be sufficient to ask for help. In others it may not have such salutary effects, and there are many alcoholics who have remained frequently recurrent, or even 'perpetual skidders' in spite of repeated psychiatric hospital admissions or prison sentences. In such cases familiarity with such initially possibly 'punishing' experiences has obviously bred contempt, and care should, therefore, be taken to convince the excessive drinker of the need for taking a close look at himself and his drinking habits on as early an occasion as possible when his drinking has clearly been responsible for such untoward consequences.

The pre-monitory signs enumerated by Jellinek as occurring in the prodromal period are:

(a) *Alcoholic amnesias (blackouts)*

These experiences do not consist of loss of consciousness, but of the inability of the drinker clearly to remember the events during last evening's drinking. As Jellinek states, and as confirmed by a few of the moderate drinkers questioned by us such amnesia can also occur in the ordinary drinker as a symptom of severe intoxication. What Jellinek felt was characteristic of the amnesias of alcoholics was

(i)   Its occurrence after relatively moderate drinking;
(ii) The absence of features of intoxication at the time (so that friends notice nothing extraordinary in the drinker); and
(iii) Its increasing frequency.

Thus the drinker is unable to remember where he had been the previous evening, to whom he talked, or what he said. Not uncommonly, alcoholics state that they had no idea next morning where they had left their car, only to find that they had apparently managed to drive it home and into the garage. Sometimes hair-raising stories are told about exploits during 'blackouts' – for example, the driver who drove his car to Scotland from London and back. However, ulterior motives were probably present when two of our alcoholic patients claimed to have married while in a 'blackout'. In each case the patient maintained that on waking up next morning with a girl by his side (in one instance having spent the previous day in Ireland and finding himself the next morning in a hotel in London), he had no idea who the girl was! But then a well known journalist reputedly advised his colleagues 'always order the local paper so you know which town you're in when you wake up' [6].

Clearly these alcoholic amnesias can be of great medico-legal importance; among alcoholics seen at WPH, of the men three in four, and of the women, two in three, stated in a questionnaire reply that they had experienced alcoholic 'blackouts'. In evaluat-

Table 2
Drinking history of 192 male alcoholics
(Warlingham Park Hospital 1952–6)
(Events arranged in order of frequency of occurrence)
Frequency of occurrence of certain events (i.e. percentage
of patients reporting them). Average age at *first*
occurrence of these events.

Event (or experience)	Frequency of Occurrence %	Average Age at first occurrence years	Standard Deviation years
First drink	100.0	17.6	3.09
Getting drunk	100.0	20.1	6.28
Drink helping to mix with people	98.4	27.0	8.92
Reaching lowest point	93.8	41.7	8.99
Neglect of food	87.5	37.0	9.20
Loss of control	85.9	34.4	9.17
Morning drinks	85.9	35.3	8.67
Persistent remorse	84.9	38.4	9.56
Periods of abstinence ('going on the waggon')	80.7	36.2	8.71
Admitting defeat to oneself	78.1	40.7	8.37
First amnesia	77.6	30.1	9.27
Alibis for drinking to excess	77.1	36.1	8.99
Periods of despondency	77.1	35.5	11.19
Increase in tolerance to alcohol	76.6	31.3	8.55
Feeling more efficient when drinking	75.5	30.7	8.86
Uncontrollable tremors	75.0	37.2	8.92
Drunk in daytime (but without being drunk the next day)	74.5	32.4	9.01
Solitary drinking	74.5	34.3	10.06
Drinks before party to ensure against shortage	73.9	30.9	9.38
Financial extravagance	73.9	34.3	9.82
Gulping drinks	72.9	30.8	8.79
Prolonged intoxications ('benders')	70.8	34.9	8.53
Sleeplessness	70.8	36.4	10.08
Vague fears	70.8	36.8	9.94
Drinking once a month at least, sometimes drunk	68.7	24.3	6.70
Voluntarily sought psychiatric advice to stop drinking	68.2	39.4	8.44
Sneaking drinks	67.7	31.9	9.55
Drinking interfering with recreation and interests	67.2	35.0	8.67

Table 2 (continued)

Event (or experience)	Frequency of Occurrence %	Average Age at first occurrence years	Standard Deviation years
Drinking once a week at least, sometimes drunk	66.6	24.0	8.20
Drinking more than once a week, sometimes drunk (but no hangover)	65.1	25.0	7.40
Unreasonable resentment	64.1	35.7	8.29
Hospitalised due to acute intoxication	63.5	40.2	10.06
Contemplating geographical escape	63.0	36.8	8.76
Reproach by wife	62.5	34.1	7.78
Drinking once a week at least without getting drunk	60.9	22.0	7.51
Thought people were showing contempt	60.9	36.1	8.84
Frequent amnesias ('blackouts')	60.9	32.7	7.92
Decrease in tolerance to alcohol	59.8	38.3	8.08
Seeking psychiatric advice on stopping drinking because of family pressure	58.8	39.1	8.39
Losing time from work due to drinking	57.8	33.3	9.17
Drinking once a month at least, without getting drunk	57.2	20.3	5.13
Admitting defeat to others	57.2	41.3	8.65
Indifferent to brands of liquor	56.2	33.6	8.33
Seeking medical advice for bodily ailment due to drinking	55.2	39.3	9.05
Protecting supply of drink	54.7	37.4	9.05
Drinking more than once a week, getting mildly drunk on most occasions	52.1	25.2	8.06
Self-pity	52.1	35.0	9.78
Losing job due to drinking	51.5	36.3	8.94
Walking out on jobs	50.5	35.0	8.92
Thinking best solution would be to be dead	50.5	37.1	9.70
Seeking psychiatric advice because of fears and anxieties	50.5	40.0	8.85
Adopting 'What is the use?' attitude	50.0	38.9	9.04
Feeling religious needs	48.4	35.7	9.54
Staying drunk over weekends but (fairly) fit on Monday	47.9	27.5	8.26
Refusing to talk about drinking	47.9	32.1	9.87
Acting aggressively, dangerous to oneself or to others	47.3	33.6	8.63
Abandoning efforts to control drinking	45.3	40.7	9.63

Table 2 (continued)

Event (or experience)	Frequency of Occurrence %	Average Age at first occurrence years	Standard Deviation years
Friends walking out	44.2	34.5	8.33
Diminishing sex potency	44.2	40.3	8.17
Unemployed for more than 3 months	42.7	37.0	8.46
Changing pattern of drinking	42.7	35.6	8.78
Contemplating suicide	41.1	35.7	10.47
Seeking aid of a go-between to straighten out matters with family etc	39.5	39.3	8.36
Walking out on friends	37.5	33.4	7.82
Afraid that alcohol would cease to give satisfaction	31.2	37.8	8.66
Thinking friends were 'stuffed shirts'	29.7	34.1	8.82
Family changing their habits due to husband's drinking.................................	28.6	36.2	7.86
Feeling that family lacks consideration	28.6	34.9	6.73
Feeling people were 'sitting on' one	27.2	35.5	9.18
Hospitalised for physical illness due to drinking..	25.5	40.8	9.31
In trouble because of driving when drunk...	22.9	32.0	7.66
Jealous of wife or girl friend....................	21.8	33.2	9.06
Rationalising one's neglect of family	20.8	36.9	7.42
Convulsion following after a drinking bout .	19.2	38.6	9.58
Methylated spirit etc. drinking 'in emergencies'	17.7	35.8	6.66

ing such statements one has to take notice of their unreliability (see p. 91), although once they have started to collaborate with treatment they become much more reliable. Apart from outright lies and genuine amnesia, a great obstacle to accepting alcoholics' statements about themselves consists in unconscious defence mechanisms helping them to explain away uncomfortable experiences (see below). However, while in hospital, as opposed (e.g.) to court appearances, these alcoholics had no motive to exaggerate the number of amnesias. In fact, regular checks with relatives have made it very clear that the percentages of remembered events are much too low.

The origin of such alcoholic amnesias is obscure. Jellinek felt that they might signify a heightened susceptibility to alcohol in the prospective alcoholic, psychological or physical in origin. It has been suggested that many amnesias occur relatively earlier and more frequently in the 'loss of control' than in the 'inability to abstain' alcoholic, possibly because the first type of alcoholic tends to drink spirits and in bouts; thus the blood alcohol level may change rapidly, which might precipitate the 'blackout' (the term under which such amnesias are known in AA).

To the drinker the first occurrence of such amnestic periods ('palimpsets') is naturally an alarming experience. For some it may be enough to induce them to review their drinking habits. In others however, such amnesias – though they keep on recurring with increasing frequency – are shrugged off as an unfortunate side-effect. He has to 'accommodate' them as by now he no longer enjoys drinking like the ordinary social drinker but increasingly needs alcohol. This is shown by the other changes in his drinking behaviour which occur in this period whilst amnesias come with increasing frequency.

(b) Surreptitious drinking
At parties, meetings or business conferences he excuses himself under some pretext to 'sneak' a few drinks on the quiet. Or he may make the generous and gladly accepted offer to serve as bartender so that he may have three drinks for every one he is serving to guests.

(c) Preoccupation with drinking
When considering whether to accept invitations for parties his decision depends on the likelihood or otherwise of sufficient drinks being available. He makes sure, at any rate, that he will not go short by drinking in anticipation of a possible shortage. He arranges his business appointments in such a way that drinking facilities are close at hand, and that his discussions will not interfere with opening times. This behaviour naturally does not increase his interest, efficiency, or punctuality at work and does not contribute to his popularity with business associates or employer. (See also p. 493.)

(d) Rapid gulping down of drink
His 'thirst for the effect' of alcohol is so great that he hastily gulps down the first few drinks, making sure at the same time that he has already ordered the next ones. He cannot understand what his companions have come to the bar for as they drink 'so slowly' and waste precious time. ('Why don't they drink?!')

(e)   *Guilt feelings about his drinking*

As he still has some measure of insight he has by now realised that in some way or other his manner of drinking is not the same as that of his friends. He thus begins to drink more by himself in order not to arouse suspicion.

(f)   *Avoids referring to drinking*

He avoids referring to drinking in ordinary conversation. He covers up, and now plays down the amount he drinks – whereas in the beginning of his drinking career he may have boasted of his capacity to hold drink, and may have tried to impress others in order to find popularity and acceptance by his peers, by overt heavy drinking.

To these drinking behaviours enumerated by Jellinek should be added:

(g)   *Frequent or regular driving of a motor car while in an alcohol-impaired condition*

In our experience this is a regular occurrence in alcoholic drivers and begins to happen relatively early in their drinking career [7]. It is continued throughout the course of their 'active' alcoholism and involves not only the alcoholic in great risks, but also his family and other road users. Often, already at this early stage, the drinker's wife is frightened of going into the car with him, or asks him to stop and let her out. She begins to worry and to wonder whether he will be all right or has met with an accident when he is late home.

Unfortunately occasional alcohol-impaired driving can also occur in drivers who are not 'alcoholics'. But its increasingly regular occurrence in individuals who are basically not psychopathic (or not mentally subnormal or disturbed) personalities can be regarded as denoting the beginning of dependency on the effects of alcohol and constitutes a very early diagnostic feature. It may serve as a fairly 'objective' – i.e. noticeable also to people other than the alcoholic himself – prodromal, warning signal, at a relatively early stage when the drinker may still have sufficient insight and a degree of control left that enables him not to get drunk in public on important occasions or to arouse suspicion by his heavy-drinking behaviour which then may still be restricted to evenings.

No excuse is offered for giving so much space to this phase in the alcoholic's life and drinking career because from the diagnostic point of view it is, or should be, the most important one. In

Table 3
Drinking history of 77 female alcoholics
(Warlingham Park Hospital 1952–6)
(Events arranged in order of frequency of occurrence)
Frequency of occurrence of certain events (i.e. percentage
of patients reporting them). Average age at *first*
occurrence of these events.

Event (or experience)	Frequency of Occurrence %	Average Age at first occurrence years	Standard Deviation years
First drink	100.0	19.7	6.42
Getting drunk	100.0	30.9	11.11
Reaching lowest point	88.3	46.3	10.44
Loss of control	85.9	41.7	10.56
Solitary drinking	85.7	39.2	9.69
Periods of despondency	85.7	38.9	9.63
Persistent remorse	84.4	42.1	9.45
Morning drinks	83.1	38.8	9.60
Feeling more efficient when drinking	81.8	36.9	11.75
Alibis for drinking to excess	79.2	41.1	9.27
Admitting defeat to oneself	76.6	45.7	7.83
Sleeplessness	74.0	38.1	11.48
Drink helping to mix with people	72.7	34.3	12.11
Neglect of food	72.7	41.5	9.25
Thought people were showing contempt	72.7	42.1	8.80
Increase in tolerance to alcohol	71.4	38.1	9.91
Vague fears	71.4	40.3	9.67
Admitting defeat to others	71.4	45.4	8.99
Sneaking drinks	70.1	38.2	10.08
Periods of abstinence ('going on the wagon')	70.1	40.5	9.72
Voluntarily sought psychiatric advice to stop drinking	66.2	45.6	8.53
First amnesia	64.9	37.8	9.84
Drink interfering with recreation and interests	64.9	40.7	10.04
Protecting supply of drink	64.9	40.2	8.62
Drinking once a week at least without getting drunk	63.6	25.9	6.63
Drinking once a week at least, sometimes drunk	63.6	34.5	9.88
Uncontrollable tremors	63.6	42.1	8.31
Drinking once a month at least, without getting drunk	62.3	24.9	7.31

Table 3 (continued)

Event (or experience)	Frequency of Occurrence %	Average Age at first occurrence years	Standard Deviation years
Hospitalised due to acute intoxication	62.3	43.3	9.69
Drinking once a month at least, sometimes drunk	61.0	30.5	9.01
Drunk in daytime (but without being drunk the next day)	61.0	38.5	10.40
Reproach by husband.............................	59.7	36.5	9.31
Drinks before party to ensure against shortage..	59.7	36.2	9.19
Gulping drinks	58.4	38.1	11.04
Contemplating geographical escape..........	58.4	39.9	9.24
Refusing to talk about drinking	57.1	37.2	10.01
Indifferent to brands of liquor	57.1	38.9	9.63
Drinking more than once a week, sometimes drunk, but no hangover..............	55.8	32.2	9.51
Decrease in tolerance to alcohol	55.8	43.1	8.83
Changing pattern of drinking	55.5	46.4	11.31
Drinking more than once a week, getting mildly drunk on most occasions	54.5	34.4	9.75
Adopting 'What is the use?' attitude	54.5	40.5	8.95
Seeking medical advice for bodily ailment due to drinking	54.5	42.8	10.04
Thinking best solution would be to be dead...	51.9	39.1	10.35
Frequent amnesias ('blackouts')	50.6	37.9	9.51
Financial extravagance	49.3	37.3	8.89
Seeking psychiatric advice on stopping drinking because of family pressure	49.3	46.3	11.00
Feeling religious needs	48.0	38.7	9.33
Seeking psychiatric advice because of fears and anxieties	46.7	41.9	8.74
Unreasonable resentment	46.5	40.3	9.52
Prolonged intoxications ('benders')	45.4	39.2	9.72
Abandoning efforts to control drinking	44.2	41.3	8.07
Self-pity...	44.1	37.9	9.18
Seeking aid of a go-between to straighten out matters with family etc.	41.5	41.0	10.01
Feeling that family lacks consideration	40.2	40.8	8.36
Staying drunk over weekends but (fairly) fit on Monday....................................	39.0	32.4	9.63
Friends walking out	35.0	36.7	8.06

Table 3 (continued)

Event (or experience)	Frequency of Occurrence %	Average Age at first occurrence years	Standard Deviation years
Acting aggressively, dangerous to oneself or to others	33.7	40.1	9.32
Contemplating suicide	33.7	39.1	9.13
Rationalising one's neglect of family	31.1	48.6	8.81
Afraid that alcohol would cease to give satisfaction	29.8	44.2	6.98
Family changing their habits due to wife's drinking	27.2	43.2	10.12
Losing time from work due to drinking	27.2	36.0	7.81
Walking out on friends	27.2	35.1	7.81
Jealous of husband or boy friends	24.6	37.4	11.23
Unemployed for more than 3 months	22.2	39.8	6.73
Walking out on jobs	20.8	38.4	6.66
Feeling people were 'sitting on' one	20.8	37.8	5.63
Hospitalised for physical illness due to drinking	20.7	47.4	8.38
Losing job due to drinking	19.4	41.0	6.99
Thinking friends were 'stuffed shirts'	19.4	37.3	6.71
Methylated spirit etc. drinking 'in emergencies'	12.9	35.3	4.78
In trouble because of driving when drunk	11.7	43.0	5.99
Convulsion following after a drinking bout	10.4	42.8	5.26

teaching on alcoholism, professional training should lay comparatively less emphasis than hitherto on the relatively infrequent and late 'complications' of chronic alcoholism, and in its place teach more about the prodromal features which occur almost universally among future alcoholics [8].

In order to achieve the goal of early diagnosis, it is absolutely necessary that the future doctor's and other professional workers' image of the 'alcoholic' changes; that they stop equating 'alcoholism' with its complications; and that the doctor starts thinking of alcoholism as a possible diagnosis long before a man presents him with liver cirrhosis, peripheral neuropathy or alcoholic dementia.

At this stage the alcoholic 'in the making' still has some insight and control so that outside influences – family, friends – still have a considerable 'braking' influence. Gradually such 'brakes' become less effective but even in the later stages, they may yet exercise some effect even if only intermittently [9] (see Chapter 9); depending on such environmental factors and the drinker's personality make-up, the length of the prodromal period may vary from a length of one or two to six months to as many years.

3   Crucial phase

This phase is initiated in the Gamma alcoholic by gradually increasing 'lack' or 'loss of control' which obviously does not occur in all excessive drinkers, and not even in all alcoholics: it is absent in the Delta alcoholic and in what Jellinek called the Beta alcoholic – the excessive drinker who may develop liver damage without necessarily being dependent on alcohol.

According to Jellinek's original description (but later revised by him – [17, 18] 'loss of control' means that 'as soon as any small quantity of alcohol enters the organism a demand for alcohol is set up which is felt as a physical demand by the drinker, but could possibly be a conversion syndrome'. The drinker, now lacking control over drinking within a given bout, thus *may* continue drinking on some occasions until he is either too drunk to go on, or until his stomach refuses to keep any more alcohol down (although on other occasions he may feel he had 'enough' long before passing out). The stage has now been reached when, as AA members put it, 'one drink is too much, and one thousand not enough'. From now on, the alcoholic still has a clear choice as to whether he has the first drink or not; once, however, he has resumed drinking – whether accidentally,[1] by choice, because of emotional 'needs', because of a 'pathological desire' born out of psychological dependency, because of social pressure or 'contagious infection' by his group, or because of psychological or social conditioning – he may find it difficult to stop at will. What he can more easily achieve (and often does later on) is to go 'on the waggon', i.e. abstain altogether for longer or shorter periods. But during these 'dry' periods he is not happy; what keeps his morale up is the knowledge and the hope that 'D (drinking) day will come'.

'Loss of control' was regarded by Jellinek as the hallmark of addiction (or physical dependence) in the Gamma alcoholic [14]. The drinking bout, which on sudden alcohol withdrawal may produce severe physical abstinence manifestations, is often carried on because the fear of the severe abstinence symptoms provokes the drinker. Similarly, it may be the fear of (the less severe and more gradually increasing) withdrawal symptoms in the intermittent 'plateau' drinking of the Delta or 'inability to abstain' type of alcoholic, that may induce him to top up, but not immediately after a drink or two (as is the case with the Gamma alcoholic). In the view of Jellinek (and still today in that of the great majority of observers) loss of control implies that alcoholics cannot ever hope to become *safe* 'social drinkers'. At the present state of knowledge, they should remain lifelong abstainers, even though AA rightly 'sugars' this initially very bitter pill by its 'twenty-four-hours' programme: 'I shall remain sober today.' (A few alcoholics seem to have managed successfully with a somewhat risky variant of the AA version, promising themselves: 'I shall be drinking tomorrow, but today I will remain sober.' This latter method cannot be recommended as ideal, but because of its importance, and of several controversial factors, some additional comment seems necessary to the subject 'loss of control' (see also Chapter 4).)

'Loss of control' does not mean, as is often thought, that the alcohol addict ends up drunk on each occasion that he drinks. What it does imply is that the alcoholic can never be quite certain whether he will be able to call a halt once he has started [9, 10]. The course of events may be as follows: the alcoholic has abstained successfully – perhaps even without much effort – for some time. Gradually (or suddenly) he feels that it might not do him much harm if he just has a drink or two. He makes the attempt – feeling somewhat guilty and often very much afraid – and 'succeeds' much better than he had hoped; he feels no craving whatsoever for a second drink and goes home feeling very pleased with himself. Next day he might feel the need for a further drink, but more often he feels pleased that he still has no craving. He therefore decides that as he felt so well (or got on so well) after one drink he might just as well have two now. Probably he will get away with that too, but sooner or later, he will revert to his original, uncontrolled drinking pattern.

'Lack of control' is not a static event, but seems rather to be a variable, dynamic phenomenon that does not set in overnight but develops and increases gradually in degree, remaining, during its existence, subject to modification by the influence of psychological, psychosomatic, psychopharmacological, physiological and environmental factors. Possibly with increasing duration of 'dependence' and with increasing intensity of drinking, the range of blood alcohol levels at which 'lack of control' begins to manifest

Table 4

Drinking history of 192 male and 77 female alcoholics (WPH 1952–6)
Average age at *first* occurrence of selected events
(arranged in order of first occurrence in males)

Event	Average Age (years)		
	Males	(Jellinek) (U.S.A. men) (1946)	Females
First drink	17.6		19.7
First drunk	20.1	(18.8)	30.9
Drinking at least once a week, without getting drunk	22.0		25.9
Drinking more than once a week, sometimes drunk	25.0		32.2
First amnesia	30.1	(25.2)	37.8
Drinking before party to ensure against shortage	30.9		36.2
Increase in tolerance to alcohol	31.3		38.1
Sneaking drinks	31.9	(25.9)	38.2
Daytime drinks	32.4	(31.0)	38.5
Frequent amnesias	32.7		37.9
Solitary drinking	34.3	(31.2)	39.2
Loss of control over drinking	34.4	(27.6)	41.7
Friends walking out	34.5	(29.7)	36.7
Prolonged intoxications ('Benders')	34.9	(31.8)	39.2
Early morning drinking	35.3	(29.9)	38.8
Attempting to drink in a different manner	35.6	(32.7)	46.4
Unreasonably resentful behaviour	35.7	(33.0)	40.3
Contemplating suicide	35.7		39.1
Alibis for drinking to excess	36.1	(29.2)	41.1
Periods of abstinence ('going on the waggon')	36.2	(30.7)	40.5
Neglect of food	37.0		41.5
Uncontrollable tremors	37.2	(32.7)	42.1
Protecting supply of drink	37.4	(32.5)	40.2
Decrease in tolerance to alcohol	38.3		43.1
Seeking medical advice for physical illness due to drink	39.3		42.8
First hospitalisation connected with drinking	40.2	(36.8)	43.3
Abandoning voluntary efforts to control drinking	40.7		41.3
Admitting defeat to oneself	40.7	(38.1)	45.7
Reaching one's 'lowest point'	41.7	(40.7)	46.3

itself[9] – and which may vary from individual to individual – may decrease so that in time 'loss of control' may exert its influence more regularly and more immediately after the alcoholic has had his first few drinks. It will then tend to become less of a 'relative' lack of control and more of an absolute 'loss of control', but probably only in a minority even of Gamma alcoholics will it ever become completely 'absolute' in the sense of leading to drunkenness on each occasion when the genuine alcoholic has taken one drink.

The rapidity of the progress of the alcoholic's drinking process is determined by various factors: by his psychological (and probably also physiological) make-up or predisposition; and by social and pharmacological factors i.e. our familiar triad: host, environment and agent.

During a drinking career, gradually, but to a varying extent in individual alcoholics, the forces acting as counter-pressures and brakes within the personality itself, including conscience ('the "super-ego" is the part of the mind which is first dissolved in alcohol') weaken, and the drinker may find himself more and more at the mercy of his instinctual impulses without taking notice of his obligations to family and society. In some psychopaths – often younger people – but also among some non-psychopathic young drinkers the whole process of alcohol dependence runs its course much more rapidly than in the hypothetical 'average' alcoholic (see Chapter 7). In alcoholics with originally little 'susceptibility' or predisposition (or with a high degree of resistance, all of course very vague hypothetical concepts) the process may take a very long time and sometimes comes to an uneasy lull for some reason or another. Such considerations, as we have seen, may also influence the length of the prodromal period; clearly the influence of such psychological tendencies does not cease overnight resulting in a sudden outbreak of 'loss of control'. On the other hand, with the gradually increasing intensity of 'lack of control', it seems that, to a certain extent, processes leading to physical dependency have now entered the picture with pharmacological and biochemical processes joining the previously present psychosocial factors. But the latter factors, some of which may have delayed and prevented a much more rapid progress to the crucial period, still continue to exercise their influence on the 'loss of control' phenomenon itself.

Thus, from time to time, one may come across the following types of case [15]. (In all such events one can, of course, not accept the word of the practising alcoholic who is very much an interested party, but all the events to be described now have been checked carefully with relatives or close friends, who had no interest in putting his drinking in a rosy light.) The alcoholic is able to limit himself to a few drinks only when in a café and taking drinks with his spouse; or when he is in the company of friends; or when he is taking his drinks with a meal. Alternatively, during the day, when he is at work, he slips out in the morning and has a few drinks, and the same thing happens at lunchtime; this may go on day-in day-out for weeks, and he has little difficulty in stopping drinking on these occasions; but every evening after work he starts drinking and cannot stop, and more often than not ends up drunk. Others may manage to drink in moderation in the evenings during working days, but at weekends get drunk on every drinking occasion. Such people often get drunk when they drink alone. (Women alcoholics frequently say that when they go to parties with their husbands they have no difficulty in stopping after a few drinks, adding: 'I couldn't let myself, or my husband, down in public.' But as soon as possible after getting home they rush to get intoxicated. Likewise they may end up drunk when they start taking drink without food.) A male alcoholic may not have many difficulties with drinking if his wife is at home but if she goes away for a few days, he is unable to stop. Motivation may play an important role. Alcoholics often worry about what might happen if, for example, they inadvertently eat a food dish baked with a little wine. Occasionally one comes across alcoholics who have taken a little alcohol in this way who have no difficulties in not drinking. But, as stated previously, while the risk should not be minimised, it is probably fair to say that such a really unintentional 'sip' is not quite so dangerous as an intentional or private 'research-motivated' first drink. It is perhaps important to mention this because one often hears alcoholics argue: 'I've had the fatal first drink anyway, now I can just as well go to town with it!' Mood is claimed to make a great difference by many alcoholics who maintain that they can drink quite safely as long as they are happy and contented; but their drinking soon gets out of hand once they start drinking if they are worried or depressed.

A favourite escape mechanism of the alcoholic is changing his drinking pattern from one drink to another – usually without much avail, although one does meet alcoholics who are able to hang on (albeit with grim determination, and desperately unhappily) to this method for some weeks or so. And some alcoholics manage to persist for a while with such a method of 'diluted' drinks (beer or wine) more or less successfully. Sooner or later, however, they will find that these drinks do not give them what they want from alcohol, and they revert to spirits, ending up in uncontrolled drinking within a few days. Contrary to popular fallacy it must be stressed that there are many alcoholics who have been exclusively (or predominantly) beer, cider or wine drinkers although such drinkers probably had to work harder, longer, and with greater dedication at their excessive drinking before developing dependence.

Alcoholics, when asked whether they could have stopped drinking on a given occasion after a drink or two, usually say that they could have done so, but add that they did not feel like it or did not see any necessity for it, or that they were unwilling to go home to a reproachful spouse. These may clearly be excuses but at the same time it is often very difficult for an alcoholic to say truthfully whether he could have stopped after the first or second drink or not 'if I had really tried'. ('I do not know whether I could have stopped – all I know is that I *did* not stop,' is a statement often made by such drinkers.) Sometimes they claim that they went on drinking because as the first drink had made them feel well they then wanted to feel even better although even at the time they were aware from previous experience that they would never reach what they were looking for: a goal that remained elusive until they had overshot it anyway and were drunk. Psychosomatic processes may often be important in such cases and on many occasions where 'lack of control' contributed to the drinker overstepping the 'mark' there may not have been a clear demarcation line between the 'cannot' and the 'will not'. Clearly psychological, psychosomatic, psychosocial, economic and physiological factors[2] strongly affect the working and the intensity of lack of control.

The crucial stage often witnesses a gradual deterioration in many spheres of the alcoholic's life, though not in all of them at the same time and to the same degree. He gradually starts to drink earlier in the day and is often drunk by the evening. His inability to control his drinking becomes obvious to his family, friends and workmates. Thus, the drinker has to produce no end of ingenious excuses and alibis to explain away his 'lack of control'. He comes to rely more and more on his favourite mental defence-mechanism: outright conscious denial, repression, rationalisations and projections, i.e. ascribing one's own defects to others. Thus, everything and everybody is wrong (especially the members of his family who may become enemy no. 1! at a time when friends still think of the drinker as a decent and reasonable person).

For some time the family will have tried to reason and to keep the 'skeleton in the cupboard', feeling both ashamed and vaguely guilty themselves. But gradually they detach themselves from the alcoholic and begin to build up a life as if he were not there: the wife assumes the duties, responsibilities and the rights of the householder. The home atmosphere may become very bitter; there are continual quarrels and mutual recriminations. Matters are not helped by the alcoholic's jealousy, arising largely from diminution of his sexual potency and of his extra-marital adventures. These, quite apart from other complications, may also carry the risk of catching VD. Reproaches by family and friends only serve to increase bitterness, resentment and self-pity, and feelings of isolation and of being misunderstood. Frequent feelings of remorse and guilt only serve as further motivation to even heavier drinking, and he compensates for his inwardly-felt misgivings and often intense guilt by bombastic, grandiose or aggressive behaviour. Periods of abstinence, with which he may try to reassure himself, or changing his drinking pattern (see above) fail to bring more than a temporary respite. He may anticipate and forestall rejection by his friends and the threat of losing his job (which he has jeopardised by turning up late or not at all; by his inability to concentrate when he did turn up; and by being rude to the foreman etc.), by his deliberately dropping his friends and by resigning the day before he expects to be sacked. He may also change his domicile – the 'geographic escape' – but he soon realises that he has taken his problems with him, and he cannot rid himself of them as easily as his wife, friends and work.

An alcoholic's wife may tolerate considerable hardship, and sometimes seems to be a veritable glutton for punishment. Her attempts to assist only lead to more quarrels and sometimes to blows if she tries to cope with the problem of 'hidden bottles' by finding them in the latest ingenious hide-out and pouring the contents down the sink. (Hiding bottles is another one of the alcoholic's desperate but favourite efforts to 'protect supplies', but it has happened that an alcoholic woke in the morning only to find to his horror that he had hidden the bottle so well, that he had forgotten where he had put it!) Equally pathetic is the case of a married couple of alcoholics each of whom is anxious to protect his or her own supplies from the alcoholic spouse.

Gradually the drinker becomes more and more isolated even

Table 5
Drinking habits of moderate drinkers (men and women) 1955
Frequency of occurrence of certain events

	Men		Women	
	No.	%	No.	%
First drink	80	100.0	35	100.0
Drunk	49	61.3	9	25.7
Drink helping to mix with other people	29	36.3	10	28.6
'Decrease in tolerance' to alcohol.............	13	16.3	5	14.3
'Amnesia'...	8	10.0	0	0
Needing more drink to get the same effect..	7	8.8	2	5.7
Feeling more efficient when drinking	6	7.5	2	5.7
Early morning drink	6	7.5	0	0
Solitary drinking	3	3.8	1	2.3
Gulping drink..	3	3.8	0	0

(This table is based on the replies of individuals reporting occurrence of the event without giving their ages at that time, in addition to those individuals giving their ages.)

though he may have started to drink as a passport to popularity and acceptance. His friends may also feel that they mean no more to him than providers of drinks. Alcoholics often state that having no money is no bar against drinking – but this seems true only to a very limited degree.

Many alcoholics, in spite of great compulsion to drink, would not commit any antisocial actions to obtain it. One does not help an alcoholic by lending or giving him money which he will only drink away: a meal, a railway ticket or something similar, is a much more constructive way to help.

Many alcoholics ultimately find themselves with huge debts. There are several more serious and more immediate dangers. Alcoholics often suffer from insomnia, and once an alcoholic has taken to drugs, he may become dependent on them as well, and run a risk of accidental over-dosage. He may feel utterly alone and may try a suicide attempt in a vain bid to attract help; if something goes wrong he may only be found after it is too late. Although alcoholics are relatively more commonly represented among the 'failed suicides', a fatal outcome is a very real danger. In some cases alcoholism may represent a symbolic and gradual form of suicide, as suggested by Menninger; in other cases it may have been an (unconscious) attempt at adjustment – by means of which the alcoholic may have hoped to stave off the necessity of suicide. But when he realises that alcoholism has failed to bring about the required solution he may see no other way out – in particular when a certain amount of drunkenness has diminished his fears of the act; nevertheless his intoxication, interfering with the performance, increase his chances to survive. These, and his tendency to get involved in accidents at home, work or on the road, may now bring him to hospital for the first time – though usually not for the last.

By now drunken episodes in the evening are responsible for severe hangover states the morning after. Alcoholics often state contemptuously that non-alcoholics have no right to call the nausea and vomiting which they (the non-alcoholics) experience after an occasional drinking session, a 'hangover'; their (i.e. the alcoholics') hangover is both qualitatively and quantitatively a much more shattering experience which necessitates rapid relief by the 'hair of the dog' first thing in the morning. Ordinary drinkers may feel bad enough the morning after but as a rule they would feel even worse at the mere thought of starting the day with another drink. The first time this thought begins to appeal to a drinker, may in fact be a very significant landmark on the road to alcohol dependence. Such morning drinks appears not only to stop the morning 'shakes' (probably caused by the blood alcohol fall during the night) by appeasing physical withdrawal symptoms, but also give some peace to the painful head and rumbling stomach.

By now the alcoholic may have arrived at a stage where he can hardly start the day without an 'eye opener', and increasingly he begins to drink throughout the day.

4   Chronic phase

Whereas many alcoholics may cling to a precarious foothold within their social circle, others may now be rapidly losing their last links with their social group and family. The last residue of physical and mental resistance is dwindling away and, more and more demoralised, such a drinker is reaching the last, 'chronic' phase. Obligations to family, employers, society, no longer matter. He now lives solely for drink; but as he can no longer handle the same quantities as before – the former acquired increase in tolerance now having been replaced by a decrease – he gets drunk much more readily and rapidly, the more so as he rarely eats anything. He may now be drunk throughout the day, either drinking by himself or, having excluded himself (or having been thrown out) from his own social circle and his usual drinking haunts, he may move to another end of town and drink with people far below his former social status where he may still feel accepted and 'at home' to a point. Having run out of money he may now have to make do with surgical spirit, boot polish, etc. He may spend several days in a state of prolonged intoxication (*benders*) or even in a prolonged stupor, risking death by starvation, from infections, or from an accident (burns after smoking or being run over as a drunken pedestrian in a traffic accident). He may also have developed liver illness, peripheral polyneuropathy, or other physical or mental complications (see Chapters 14 and 15). His capacity to think and to reason rationally and to make proper unbiased judgements have long been impaired and he may also develop a definite alcoholic psychosis. He is unable to carry out even very simple acts without alcohol and may need help in getting the glass containing the first drink of the day to his lips. He drinks obsessively and compulsively. At this stage as described by Bacon [16]: 'He is no more a drinker than a kleptomaniac is a customer, or a pyromaniac is a campfire girl. Alcoholics may consume alcohol. They do not drink.'

The drinker has now arrived at the end of his tether. This may bring him to treatment or, as sometimes happens in these late phases, vague religious hopes and wishes have arisen as there seemed to be no way out, which (rarely) may make him ripe for a 'conversion'. Thus, he may receive help from AA or medical, religious, social and other agencies. If he does not (and although the alcoholic's life sometimes seems to be a charmed one – as for example when one hears of his drunken-driving exploits) intercurrent infections, helped along by starvation and low resistance, accidents in traffic, at work, at home, by drug overdose, suicide, physical complications of alcoholism, all take their toll.

The whole process from first drink to dependence and later degradation varies greatly in length from individual to individual, from a few to a great many years. By the time the alcoholic has reached the final phase, as many as 15–20 years may have passed since his first 'blackout', and demonstrated to others by his behaviour that he was lacking in control over alcohol (see Tables 2, 4, 7–10). The hypothetical average *male alcoholic* patient had taken his first drink as a youth, had first got drunk 2½ years later,

Table 6
Drinking habits of moderate drinkers (men and women) 1955
Average age at *first* occurrence of certain events

First Occurrence of Event	Average Age at Occurrence of Event	
	Men	Women
First drink	16.8 years (66)	18.5 years (27)
Drink helping to mix with other people	20.8 ,, (26)	23.9 ,, (7)
Getting drunk	21.0 ,, (48)	28.4 ,, (9)
Needing more drink to get the same effect	21.0 ,, (5)	22.0 ,, (1)
Feeling more efficient when drinking	21.3 ,, (5)	29.0 ,, (2)
'Amnesia'	24.0 ,, (8)	(0)
Early morning drink	24.7 ,, (6)	(0)
Solitary drinking..........................	25.1 ,, (3)	30.0 ,, (1)
'Decrease in tolerance' to alcohol	33.5 ,, (11)	32.8 ,, (5)

Total number of individuals questioned: 80 men, 35 women.
Figures in brackets indicate the number of individuals who not only ticked off occurrence of the event but also gave their ages at that time.
Average age of individuals questioned: approximately 40 years.

Social Class (Occupational Distribution) of the 80 Males questioned:

Class........................	I	II	III	IV	V
Number of Individuals ..	21	32	20	7	0

and had become a regular drinker in his mid-twenties. Signs foreshadowing the development of dependence appeared first in his early thirties and 'lack of control' in his mid-thirties. Not until the age of forty was he first admitted to hospital for some manifestation arising from his drinking, and he did not enter an alcoholic unit until aged forty-five years, i.e. not until 10–15 years had elapsed since first showing definite signs of alcoholism.

Of course, when looking at the ages depicted in these tables one has to keep in mind that nowadays both men and women often start at a considerably younger age so that the average ages of first occurrence of the events of the drinking history would now be several years lower than they were 25–30 years ago. However, having followed the drinking histories of male and female alcoholics in this country continually throughout the intervening years (mainly – though not exclusively – those treated at the alcohol unit at St Bernard's Hospital from 1958–77) it is clear that in principle the course of events in and experience of, alcoholics as described in the case of those seen some time ago also characterises many of today's alcoholics – unless they take such lessons to heart and come forward early on in their drinking career.

Further comments on 'the road to dependence'

Several paths may lead to alcohol misuse and from there to dependence. Obviously under certain social conditions favouring heavy drinking, even mature and 'adequate' personalities may start drinking to excess although the emotionally insecure and immature will reach a state of dependency more rapidly in such a situation. The more rapid development of alcohol misuse and dependence in young drinkers may be explained by a combination of psychological and social factors (as well as from a possibly greater biological vulnerability of an immature CNS): the need to be accepted by the subculture, a feeling of increased self-confidence and acceptance by the group; with the resulting heavier drinking leading to increased tolerance and the pharmacological-biological need to further increase their drinking. By then the superimposed process of operant pharmacological conditioning – the avoidance, and the suppression, of abstinence symptoms by further drinking – has been added to the earlier process of social conditioning, the youngster becoming more popular with his group by falling in with their drinking habits.

Alcoholism is frequently described by AA members as a 'progressive illness'. The reason might be the finding that alcoholics, who had abstained for years and then resumed drinking, may experience a rapid onset of severe intoxication and a general decline which may set in much more quickly than in their previous drinking career. A possible partial explanation for this may be the loss, during their sober years, of their previously acquired tolerance. At any rate there is indeed in many alcoholics a progressive decline, punctuated and interrupted temporarily by episodes of escalation or intermissions with relative improvement – the latter perhaps following a decrease of environmental stress, or an emotional shock following a serious car accident, or being breathalysed, a period of remorse and guilt following a realisation of particularly obnoxious behaviour towards the wife, and intervention by family. Factors of host, environment and agent all influence the pace of progress of the disorder.

Fortunately it is only in a minority of alcoholics that the intermittently downhill progress of the disorder may lead to an absolute 'rock bottom' (or even to the 'chronic phase') as indicated in the Chart (p. 74–5) by the horizontal lines crossing over directly from the downward path on the left to the upward path on the right. Without the alcoholic having to experience the painful features shown towards the bottom of the Chart, the downhill progress can temporarily or permanently come to an end at any time or at any stage, either spontaneously or as the result of therapeutic intervention. The Chart, therefore, does *not*, as is sometimes alleged [11] denote an inevitable, 'inexorable' decline, but, on the contrary, depicts, by the arrowed horizontal lines, the feasibility and utmost desirability of stopping the *threatening* decline long before the absolute 'rock bottom', and of inducing the missing motivation in drinkers long before they might be 'ready' to do something about their drinking habits if they are left totally to their own devices.

Fortunately many drinkers stop far short of the later stages, and clearly both the downward and the upward paths are not rigid lines; there are numerous, unforeseeable ups-and-downs, and there are many fits and starts, with shorter or longer interruptions in the direction in which the alcoholic may be travelling. He may at times 'go on the waggon' or even drink moderately, but all too often this may prove to have been a temporary lull only. Similarly, after a spell of detoxification in hospital, the drinker and his family may be convinced that this means the end of all their troubles – only to find that this was no more than the first step on a long, difficult ladder, and to stop there may only mean a great risk of falling off the 'ladder of hope' altogether, because of the spurious feeling of security and 'control' the first step has engendered.

The spontaneous occurrence of remissions and exacerbations of drinking in problem drinkers' careers attracted the attention of a number of American research workers. Cahalan and Room [12] found that 72 per cent of a sample of male drinkers interviewed had experienced at least one serious type of drinking problem. In spite of or because of such experiences, and possibly because they were sometimes heeded as warning signals, these men had modified their drinking habits. These authors saw such occurrences as demonstrating the existence of 'a remission phenomenon in problem drinking'. A similar phenomenon was described by Straus [13] as the 'in and out' pattern: people drinking in a problematical way for years, interrupted by years of sobriety. In Straus's view, such

Table 7
Percentage of 192 male alcoholics reporting occurrence of
selected events (WPH 1952–6)

	Percentage
More sociable after drinks	98.4
Neglected food	87.5
Morning drinks	85.9
Loss of control	85.9
Persistent remorse	84.9
Attempted control by water waggon	80.7
Amnesia	77.6
Period of despondency	77.1
Rationalisation	77.1
Increased tolerance to drink	76.6
Felt more efficient after drinks	75.5
Persistent tremors	75.0
Solitary drinking	74.5
Daytime drinks	74.5
Ensured against shortage of drink	73.9
Insomnia	70.8
Felt fear	70.8
'Benders'	70.8
Sneaked drinks	67.7
Behaved in a resentful manner	64.7
Thought people showed contempt	60.9
Decreased tolerance to drink	59.8
Lost time from job	57.8
Protected supply	54.7
Acted in an aggressive manner	47.3
Contemplated suicide	41.1
Lost job	51.3

intermittent problem drinking is usually associated with social stress, and improves when the social situation improves. Straus mentions, in this connection, the example of young people who may experience a remission when finding satisfaction at work or in marriage but who nevertheless 'may be vulnerable to a return to problem drinking in the face of future stress'. This example closely resembles the present author's concept of a 'relative lack of control' (see pp. 125–9) which may often manifest itself under some forms of stress only, but not when the going is good. Straus speaks of 'situational dependency' related, for example, to such areas as work, sex and leisure, all of which provide great opportunities for satisfaction and happiness, but also for great disappointments.

Experiences similar to those described by Cahalan and Room had been noted in the history of a small minority of moderate drinkers studied by the author in the 1950s [3] (see Tables 5 and 6). As noted at the time (1961): 'interesting points . . . are the occurrence of increase and later of decrease of tolerance to alcohol, of early morning and of solitary drinking (and of alcoholic amnesias) in the history of a small percentage of the "moderate" drinkers'. The periods of excessive drinking in these men and women had occurred mainly during stress periods – for example when the men were serving abroad during the Second World War and the women were left at home. Apart from stress there was then also ample opportunity for drinking. Apparently after the war and return to more normal and stable home and peace conditions the personalities of these men and women proved sufficiently adequate to withstand temptations to drink to excess. Thus factors involving host and environment (apart from the agent) also seem of significance in such occurrences of moving 'in and out' of drinking and 'situational dependency'.

It would seem that there may be many intermediate grades between the occasional and the dependent heavy drinkers. For example, 'average' types of personality may occasionally drink to excess mainly at times of stress but perhaps not long or heavily enough to develop tolerance and dependence: this group might form an intermediate grade between those drinkers who have never shown a drink-related problem (and who, according to an American study [12] among men, formed a minority of no more than 28 per cent) and the group of drinkers exhibiting a prolonged remission phenomenon; a further stage might be represented by drinkers who frequently move 'in and out' of excessive drinking; next would be drinkers exhibiting 'relative lack of control' with frequent episodes of uncontrolled drinking; and finally those exhibiting almost absolute 'loss of control'. Obviously these groups are not demarcated. But as Straus [13] rightly emphasises, much more longitudinal, long-term research is necessary in order to identify early problem drinkers and chart their progress, remissions and relapses, and the causes for them.

There are many other possible permutations of the possible course of alcoholism. For example, one comes across alcoholics who may have abstained from alcohol for a number of years and who, for some reason or other take a drink or two, followed several days later by further drinking, and who may then develop into 'intermittent skidders' every few weeks or months. Such people may often find it extremely difficult to return to their previous emotional 'wavelength'. In some such cases, a change in life-circumstances may have occurred some time before the resumption of their drinking but often there has been no clear-cut social change.* The complex interaction in such a long-drawn out process as the development of alcoholism, between so many different personalities and numerous environmental possibilities will always leave room for individuals or subgroups to deviate from the usual route taken by the majority of alcoholics.

However, the upward part of the Chart also indicates something else: that there is hope. The horizontal lines indicate it is preferable for the alcoholic to opt out of the dangerous journey at a time when he is still 'taking the drink' but when increasing tolerance, amnesias, reliance on and preoccupation with the subject of drink, etc. give strong hints that 'drink' is gradually beginning to make a 'take-over bid'. The matter has become even more urgent when, in the crucial phase, 'drink' frequently is dominating the drinking sessions. But having missed these warning signals, there is still time and hope – as will be apparent to any drinker from one glance at the Chart – however much in the grips of drink he may find himself, and however hopeless the future may seem. Clearly the message will not be lost on the drinker's family either.

The findings that some or perhaps many alcoholics can have spontaneous (though often only temporary) remissions and can move 'in and out' of alcoholism, in no way detracts from the important lesson which AA has learned many years ago. As the Chart shows, alcoholism, like many other illnesses, has a great number of characteristic symptoms. The fact that so many of them occur in the great majority of alcoholics, though in (slightly) varying combinations and order of appearance, is of the greatest importance not only diagnostically but also therapeutically: so similar is the drinking history in many problem drinkers that the alcoholic attending his first AA meeting or his first therapy session within a group of alcoholics may often feel that the speakers had previously been told his own story. This similarity of experiences and symptoms enables alcoholics to understand, and to identify with each other the world over and to help each other actively.

* Not uncommonly such 'intermittent skidding' may have gradually followed an attempt to achieve the aim of 'controlled drinking'.

Notes

1   A drink taken accidentally (a risk never fully avoidable but one that can be minimised for example by not unnecessarily going to pubs etc.) is much less risky from the 'lack of control' aspect than a drink taken deliberately. The drinker's intention and state of mind, play a great part in the activation of the 'lack of control' phenomenon [9] (see Chapter 4). Deliberately exposing oneself to the chance of such 'accidents', in the possible hope that someone might 'slip' alcohol into one's drink (so that no one was really responsible for it), is not an accident and much more likely to trigger off a bout (within a few days) than a genuine accident occurring without the drinker's conscious or unconscious forethought.

2   Recently, questions have been raised whether minor brain damage revealed by computer tomography (see Chapter 14) could contribute to LoC, relapses and unpredictable behaviour in alcoholics.

References

1   *Brit. med. J.* (1980)
2   Jellinek, E M (1952), Wld Hlth Org. Techn. Rep. Ser., 48, 26
3   Glatt, M M (1961), *Acta Psychiat. Scand.*, 37, 88
4   Park, P (1962), *Acta Psychiat. Scand.*, 38, 227
5   Park, P and Whitehead, P C (1973), *Quart. J. Stud. Alc.*, 34, 887
6   Cashin, Fergus (17 July, 1980), *Doctor*
7   Glatt, M M (1964), *The Lancet*, i, 161
8   Glatt, M M (1967), *Brit. J. Addict.*, 62, 267
9   Glatt, M M (1965), 11th Europ Inst. Prev. Trtmt. Alcoholism, *Brit. J. Addict.*, 62, 267
10 Keller, M (1958), *Ann. Am. Acad. Polit. Soc. Sci.*, 35, 1
11 Pattison, E M *et al.* (1977), *Emerging Concepts of Alcohol Dependence*, New York, Springer, 26
12 Cahalan, D and Room R (1973), *Problem Drinking among American Men*, New Brunswick, NJ, Rutgers Center of Alcohol Studies, Monogr. No. 7
13 Straus, R (1976) in *Alcohol and Alcohol Problems*, ed. Filstead, W J *et al.*, Cambridge, Mass., Ballinger, 29–56
14 Jellinek, E M (1960), *The Disease Concept of Alcoholism*, New Haven, Hillhouse
15 Glatt, M M (1980), *Brit. J. Alcoholism*, 15 (2), 48
16 Bacon, S D (1958), *Annals Amer. Academy Pol. and Soc. Sci.*, 315, 55

4

Alcoholism – an Illness?

What is alcoholism? The man in the street has usually regarded it as a weakness of character; the moralist sees it as a vice; the law representative as a crime; the psychiatrist as a symptom of underlying personality difficulties; the sociologist as a social problem; and possibly many a clergyman regards it as a sin. Alcoholics Anonymous approach it as a disease; behaviourists view it as learned behaviour.

Anyone seeing very large numbers of alcoholics will probably come to the conclusion that while there are a great many similarities among them there are also many differences. There is no such person as 'the' alcoholic. Likewise, there is not one type of alcoholism but many different types [1], and among one main type there may be various subgroups. In different types of subgroups or individual alcoholics some of the features stressed by the various hypotheses as being essential to the nature of alcoholism may simultaneously be involved to a varying degree. The recent College of Psychiatrists' Report on *Alcohol and Alcoholism* [2] rejects such explanations as 'extreme reactions' adopted by society in place of a needed balanced perspective. Such reactions enable the majority, who enjoy alcohol, to go on drinking with a less troubled conscience. It is only a minority of the population who regard all drinking as bad to both society and to individuals. Dr Lincoln Williams [3] one of the pioneers in the field of alcoholism in the UK, divided alcoholics into four categories: the 'normal'; the 'bad' (psychopaths); the 'sad' (neurotics) and the 'mad' (psychotics). The majority of drinkers were able to dismiss the self-indulgent, 'bad' drinkers, as their behaviour was self-inflicted and they had it coming to them; the psychotics and neurotics could be left to the mercies of the psychiatrist. The 'sick' model, so it has been claimed, also enabled the majority of ordinary drinkers to stop bothering about the problem because the problem could then be left to the doctors [2]. On the other hand, it can be argued that it was not the majority of ordinary drinkers who initially took up the disease notion of alcoholism, it was in the main the alcoholics themselves; and, like the great majority of doctors (at least until recent years), society in general did not consider alcoholism a disease nor alcoholics as sick people. Certainly the idea that the disease concept of alcoholism gives the ordinary drinker peace of mind as he is poles apart from the sick alcoholic, is immediately dispelled by even a very brief glance at the Chart of Alcohol Dependence (see pp. 74–5).

In his detailed analysis of the question 'Is alcoholism a disease?', Jellinek [1] named five common subspecies of the 'genus' alcoholism. Common to all alcoholisms are two features: drinking, and the damage it causes.

In *Alpha alcoholism* the individual drinks in order to free himself from mental or physical pain; the drinking is purely 'symptomatic', the dependence psychological.

Such Alpha alcoholism may progress to *Gamma alcoholism* but often it will only impair the drinker's interpersonal relationship or his work performance: withdrawal symptoms are absent. Alpha alcoholism is identical with 'symptomatic alcoholism' or 'secondary alcoholism' following such conditions as mental deficiency, psychoneurosis, or psychosis [4].

It is only fair to mention that some observers (such as Keller [5]) would not regard excessive drinking that is symptomatic of other underlying conditions as 'alcoholism'. Jellinek himself does not regard it pharmacologically as an 'addiction' or a 'disease' because of the absence of 'loss of control' or 'inability to abstain' (see below). This point is important because, at least in theory, excessive drinkers whose alcohol consumption has become excessive because of a temporary period of stress, may return to moderate drinking. They could thus be viewed as 'alcoholics' who have reverted to 'controlled' drinking – but then they never had suffered from 'loss of control' (characteristic of the Gamma alcoholic) in the first place.

Beta alcoholism results from the heavy drinking customs within the drinker's community, possibly coupled with poor nutritional habits; with or without liver damage and even in the absence of psychological and physical dependence and of withdrawal symptoms complications may follow, such as gastritis, polyneuropathy, or liver cirrhosis. The harm done may also affect working capacity, interpersonal relationships and may shorten life. Early brain damage was demonstrated in the last few years by Computerised Axial Tomography [6, 7] as occurring even in clinically 'normal' excessive drinkers, and could also be a manifestation of Beta alcoholism.

In theory, as in Alpha alcoholism, Beta alcoholics (who did not progress to Gamma or Delta alcoholism) might also resume 'controlled drinking' as they have never suffered loss of control or inability to abstain. In practice, however, medical specialists describing such alcoholic physical complications invariably stress the need for abstinence (see Chapter 16). Further, the development of such complications which occur in a minority only, might indicate the original presence of some 'susceptibility' or 'vulnerability' and makes it appear highly unwise to resume drinking after recovery.

Epsilon alcoholism is periodic alcoholism, formerly referred to as 'dipsomania'. Characteristically, such an individual exhibits drinking bouts separated by intervals of total abstinence. Patients suffering from depression or mania may exhibit a similar drinking pattern but are probably responsible for only relatively few instances of periodic alcoholism. More commonly one finds alcoholics who have abstained for some periods, then resumed 'controlled drinking', leading after a few days or weeks of 'moderate drinking' to a bout of excessive drinking. Clearly there are various, completely different subgroups among the Epsilon alcoholics.

The only two varieties among his alcoholisms which Jellinek considers strictly speaking to be 'diseases' are Gamma and Delta alcoholism, because in his view they are 'addictions' in the pharmacological sense: metabolism has become adapted to the presence of alcohol; physical dependence has developed so that sudden discontinuation (or too rapid reduction) of alcohol consumption may lead to drastic withdrawal (abstinence) symptoms.

In *Gamma alcoholism*, there is, according to Jellinek, an acquired increased tissue tolerance to alcohol, adaptive cell metabolism, withdrawal symptoms, craving (presumed to be due to physical dependence), and 'loss of control'. The drinker suffers from both psychological and physical dependence ('alcohol addiction'), and there may be considerable behavioural changes and physical and mental complications.

In *Delta alcoholism* there is, likewise, acquired increased tissue tolerance, altered (adaptive) cell metabolisms, withdrawal symptoms, and craving; but instead of the loss of control there is 'inability to abstain'. In Delta alcoholism cell metabolism has adapted to the presence of alcohol, conditioned by its continual presence, in contrast to the adaptation, in Gamma alcoholism, to the presence of alcohol, conditioned by the signal of the first drink.

The characteristic feature of Gamma alcoholism is thus the 'loss of control' over further intake of alcohol on a given occasion. Loss (or rather 'lack') of control drinkers are able to decide whether to have the first few drinks or not, but, as a rule, once they have resumed their drinking, they will, sooner or later, end up in uncontrolled drinking. Possibly the most common course of events is that such a drinker has abstained for weeks or months, he then begins to feel that, surely as a mature person who has now learned his lesson, he would now be able to have a drink or two (in particular as he has no particular 'craving' and therefore feels that there is no risk in taking a drink). At a party or with friends he then takes a drink, and discovers to his satisfaction that he has no compulsion to have a second. This proves to him that he had never lost control in the first place and that he was not really an 'alcoholic': two days later he may have two or three drinks, and within a matter of a week (or sometimes a month or more) he is back where he had so often been before: uncontrolled drinking.

On the other hand, the 'lack of control' alcoholic can often abstain altogether for weeks or months ('going on the waggon'); quite wrongly, many Gamma alcoholics proudly proclaim this as evidence that they are not alcoholics and are in full control of their drinking.

Delta alcoholics, as a rule, cannot go on the waggon; they drink day-in, day-out intermittently from morning to night. Whereas the Gamma alcoholic mainly drinks in bouts and often gets drunk, the Delta alcoholic drinks regularly each day but usually without getting drunk; what the latter needs is to achieve a certain 'plateau' of blood alcohol level. There are less psychological and social complications in Delta alcoholism – usually held to be the most common type of alcoholism in France and other wine drinking countries [1]. Gamma alcoholism is usually said to be the most common type in English-speaking countries – so much so that, as expressed by Jellinek, AA's image of the alcoholic originally was the Gamma alcoholic.

As a result, in the UK most published work has dealt with the Gamma alcoholic who is the type commonly seen in alcoholic units [9]. But undoubtedly there are also many Delta alcoholics who may possibly be relatively more common among 'sociogenic' alcoholics whose excessive drinking derives mainly from continual occupational exposure to drink, and among beer-drinking, working-class alcoholics.

In clinical practice it may often be very difficult to decide whether 'relief drinking' has already progressed to Alpha alcoholism with psychological dependency, or whether Alpha alcoholism has already merged into Gamma alcoholism; the latter difficulty arises because of the problem of deciding whether there is already evidence of 'lack of control' – the drinker in such cases claiming that he could have easily stopped drinking after the first few glasses had he really wanted to do so.

Jellinek and the WHO Expert Committee (1955) [10] drew a fairly clear-cut distinction between the Gamma and Delta types. Gamma alcoholism was more common in spirit-drinking countries, Delta in predominantly wine- and some of the beer-drinking countries. A hypothetical explanation was that the more sudden alterations in blood alcohol levels led to more rapid onset of withdrawal symptoms in spirit drinkers, with immediate onset of 'loss of control', necessitating a second drink immediately after the first. The slower blood alcohol level alterations after the (less concentrated) wine produced withdrawal symptoms relatively later, necessitating 'topping up' only every one or two hours. There may possibly be some connection here between the prevalence of spirit drinking and of Gamma alcoholism among the middle classes, on the one hand, and of the possibly higher prevalence of 'inability to abstain' alcoholism (or also non-dependent problem drinking) among the more beer-drinking working class, on the other hand. Yet Gamma alcoholism has been found to occur in as many as 50 per cent of chronic drunkenness offenders [11] who obviously constitute the lowest social class among alcholics. On the other hand, Delta alcoholism has been found to be as common among the whisky-drinking Scots as the Gamma type [12].

In our own experience, the difference between Gamma and Delta alcoholism appears much less clear-cut than generally described; in fact, they quite commonly coexist, manifesting themselves at different times [13, 14]. It would seem that, as in the case of the aetiology of alcoholism (see Chapter 2) and the pace of its downhill progression (see Chapter 3), so also the question whether on a particular occasion an individual drinker may manifest the Gamma or Delta type may be influenced by environmental and personality factors as well as, in Jellinek's hypothesis, by the nature and the concentration of the 'agent'. For example, the alcoholic who knows that his wife prefers him not to come home drunk might not finish his bottle in the pub, secure in the knowledge that he could do so later at home (i.e. Delta); if on the other hand, he knows that he will not be allowed any drink after having come home, he may tend to 'make hay while the sun shines' and finish the whole bottle while still in the pub (i.e. Gamma). The importance of the opportunity to drink later during the day and of the amount of drink taken earlier on on the pattern of drinking is very frequently stressed by alcoholics. If they know that they will have a chance to drink later on, they may be satisfied to drink less earlier on, and they rely on 'topping up' intermittently throughout the day or even waiting after the early morning drinks until the evening. If however there seems no chance of access to drink later on, they may tend to consume as much as possible (or often the minimum which they hope might see them through the rest of the working day) until they can resume drinking after finishing work in the evening. In such examples the main difference between the Gamma and the Delta types seems to be that in Gamma alcoholism the drinker has to proceed in a hurry because of the pressure of other commitments, and between his attention to work or other responsibilities; whereas in Delta alcoholism the drinker can proceed at leisure as he may have ample time or because social, occupational or domestic conditions allow him to drink whenever he wants to and without fear [5].

The 'host' factor may affect the manifestation of Gamma or Delta, for example, in that certain personalities may be able to withstand the pharmacological 'pull' of 'loss of control' much better than others: some alcoholics who feel like having a second or third drink immediately after the first, meekly give in to what they experience as an overwhelming craving, and end up drunk; others, who also wish to continue drinking, are sometimes able to muster the effort to return, e.g. after lunchtime drinking in the pub, to their offices. These examples demonstrate that loss of control is not an absolute, all-or-none phenomenon but consists of a relative 'lack of control', so that, at least on certain occasions, responsibilities such as work become more important than the craving to obey the dictates of the loss of control. Thus in many Gamma alcoholics this feeling often takes its place in a queue among other relative 'priorities' [14].

Another possible question arises in regard to Jellinek's adoption of a somaticist's view [15] in seeing diseases only in those varieties of alcoholism caused by physiopathological processes, i.e.

Gamma and Delta. It is true that it is physical dependence that is much more dangerous to life in the immediate post-intoxication phase because of the risk of severe abstinence symptoms (epileptiform fits, *delirium tremens*). But, long term, it is psychological dependence (or psychosocial factors) rather than physical dependence which may be more important in causing relapses after periods of sobriety; and it is psychological dependence rather than physical dependence which may encourage drinkers not only to relapse but also to go on with the more regular continual drinking day after day in spite of the danger of serious physical complications. Although such complications (Beta alcoholism) may also occur in the absence of dependence, the presence of the latter – encouraging more regular and heavier drinking, with increasing tolerance in turn necessitating further drinking – makes the occurrence of such complications more likely. Of course, physical dependence, inducing the drinker to continue drinking in order to avoid the feared abstinence features, may often be an important factor but probably less so in this connection than psychological dependence.

Psychological dependence (defined by Eddy *et al.* [16] in 1956 as 'a condition in which a drug produces a feeling of satisfaction and a psychic drive that require periodic or continuous administration of the drug to produce pleasure or to avoid discomfort') is probably the main feature that makes alcoholism and other forms of drug dependence so difficult to deal with [17]. Often, however, factors other than psychological dependence may precipitate a relapse after a period of sobriety, most often perhaps the drinker's belief that he may be once more in a fit state to achieve moderate or controlled drinking; but also social factors such as pressure (real or assumed) by his peers, subcultures, conditioning, or even the neurotic pre-alcoholic personality problems which may have been a significant factor in the individual starting to drink heavily in the first place.

Physical dependence (according to Eddy *et al.* [16] 'an adaptive state that manifests itself by intense physical disturbances when the administration of the drug is suspended . . . i.e. the withdrawal or abstinence syndromes') may be largely concerned in inducing the drinker to continue his alcohol intake within a given drinking bout, for fear of the onset of abstinence symptoms.

Thus, although in Jellinek's view, strictly speaking alcoholism becomes a physical 'addiction' and a 'disease' only after the inability to abstain has set in, psychological dependence too can be responsible for a great deal of suffering, strongly inducing the drinker to continue or to resume heavy drinking. Many laymen and professional people may still look at alcoholism as more or less wilful misconduct, but at what stage is it wilful [18]? Alcoholism is not synonymous with deliberate acute intoxication, for which a drinker is generally held responsible. It can hardly be regarded as wilful when the stage of physical dependence has been reached but a condition of psychological dependence, too, greatly interferes with the individual's volition. This is so although in most alcoholics pharmacological factors and their interplay with the personality are not fully in command, but interact with often powerful social, psychological and possibly physiological factors. The acceptance of the disease concept of alcoholism by no means excludes ethical considerations. In non-dependent problem drinkers too, ethical questions are obviously involved, for example in self-indulgent heavy drinking, possibly (or probably) in the heavy drinking of psychopaths, and in 'symptomatic excessive drinking' arising from underlying emotional states such as milder degrees of anxiety or depression. (The involvement of ethical considerations becomes more debatable though they clearly enter into the picture when very severe depression or extreme anxiety and panic attacks drive a person to heavy drinking.) In all such conditions, personality inadequacy or other problems may have greatly affected the individual's volition, control of, and full responsibility for, his heavy drinking. This is even more so after the development of a severe degree of psychological or physical dependence which greatly affects volition, control, and the issue of responsibility.

Yet even in the case of the hypothetical 'average' alcoholic – initially free from personality problems – it may be difficult to defend the view that alcoholism is a sin, crime or weakness of character. With a few important exceptions, religious and national laws do not condemn or prohibit moderate drinking, so that the average person may feel somewhat of an outsider if he refuses to partake in social drinking. Thus at an early stage when he could have cut down on his drinking, the drinker may see no need to do so, nor does anyone in his circle advise him to do so. Once he has reached the later phases, his drinking may have become more or less compulsive, physically or psychologically, and he can no longer easily reduce his intake without outside help.

Ethical and moral questions are certainly involved in the attitude of society towards alcoholism and its casualties [18]. It has failed to educate the public, and in particular the young and members of high-risk occupational groups, about the risks of heavy drinking. Moreoever society has hardly interfered with indiscriminate, sometimes unscrupulous advertising, whether carried out openly or in a more subliminal manner. Nor has society insisted that medical and other professional undergraduates receive a proper education in this field which would enable them to give a positive lead.

As an illness alcoholism certainly does not follow an inevitable pathological process and the finding that it is not the pathological process alone that determines the progression of alcoholism is of great practical and therapeutic significance. Alcoholics can be greatly helped by understanding two important points: first, that alcoholism is a dangerous illness with, very frequently, dangerous complications and a partial or general decline. And second, that the drinker is by no means a completely helpless victim, as psychosocial factors play such an important role. Thus even though such a drinker may, by mistake, have taken a drink on a given occasion, he need not fatalistically (and perhaps sometimes even gratefully) embark on a glorious 'bender' – it is still up to him to make the effort to call a halt, for example by asking for help from AA or others.

Preoccupation with the 'disease concept' of alcoholism has sometimes been alleged to have led to the neglect of problem drinkers other than 'alcoholics'. This risk must be kept in mind, and one has to remain aware of the need for concern with all types of problem drinking. On the other hand, one may wonder whether without the dedicated efforts of many thousands of AA members the world over, society would be prepared to concern itself greatly with the needs of any problem drinkers, dependent or otherwise. After all, it is usually the (problem) drinking behaviour and its manifestations that has brought the alcoholic to public and professional attention, and such manifestations occur in both dependent and non-dependent problem drinkers. In this sense the increasing acceptance of the disease concept of alcoholism may have indirectly contributed to creating a better understanding of problem drinkers other than 'alcoholics'.

At the same time, there may be a risk that by drawing the net indiscriminately, some of the understanding that has been engendered as to the plight of the 'sick' alcoholic, may gradually evaporate with old memories of the 'drunkard' coming to the fore again.

Some drinkers' ability to withstand the temptation to get hold of drink at any price may reflect either a lesser degree of dependence on alcohol, or alternatively a personality with a stronger ego or superego (conscience), or often presumably both. The same question arises quite frequently in regard to the drinking pattern of many alcoholics. Some alcoholics can go days or weeks without a drink, others 'never drink before midday' (even though they may suffer from more or less severe 'hangovers' or morning shakes denoting a certain degree of physical dependence); many make the (often very doubtful) claim that they have never been 'really drunk'. Such a statement may often reveal lack of insight or honesty, or a memory blackout, or it may point to the possibility in such a case of Delta rather than Gamma alcoholism being involved, but it may also reflect on the degree of dependence, or the 'host's resistance' in enduring the discomfort of withdrawal symptoms up to a certain point before having to have a drink.

Drinkers who always 'must have a drink' first thing in the morning, who gulp out of the bottle rather than 'wasting time' on pouring the drink into a glass, who have to secure supplies by hiding drinks, or have to have drinks before attending a party for fear of a possible shortage of supplies, or who always finish the bottle once it is open, may reflect the influence of various factors, including degree of dependence and certain 'host' factors. Some alcoholics appear satisfied once they have reached a certain blood alcohol level ('plateau') at least for a certain period, and this may happen not only in Delta drinkers but in others who in the main appear to be of the 'lack of control' type. Often such drinkers exhibit both Gamma and Delta patterns simultaneously: 'I could not stop until I had had five or six doubles [i.e. "lack of control"]; then I felt I had enough for two or three hours; I then needed a few more, and so on throughout the rest of the day [i.e. "inability to abstain"].' 'After coming home and having dinner, I had a large brandy, then another one and many more before going to bed [i.e. LoC].' On the other hand, there are many lack of control alcoholics who, more often than not, seem to have no great desire or need to continue drinking as long as they stick to a few half-pints or a few single whiskies, but once they have passed beyond the first few drinks they behave as if they have to go on suggesting the possible presence of a 'threshold' which may vary in the same individual from occasion to occasion. Often such alcoholics explain that they feel 'safe' in being able to stop until they begin to feel the effect of alcohol on themselves. At any rate, whether the reason for temporary ability to limit one's alcohol intake may be mainly due to 'ego strength' or to a lesser degree of dependence, in general such factors do more than give a fairer chance to 'survive' somewhat longer with an attempt at controlled drinking than other drinkers: they certainly do not guarantee success in that direction.

In this connection it may be interesting to mention some of the many reasons given by lack of control alcoholics for their continuing drinking after the first drink. Often the answer to the question: 'Did you have to go on?' or 'Did you not want to stop?' is: 'I do not know. All I know is that I usually go on, perhaps not always but nearly always.' Others may explain their behaviour by saying: 'I felt fine after a few drinks, so I hoped I would feel even better,' or: 'One or two drinks did not do anything for me, so I hoped I would feel better . . . . but of course one is never satisfied,' or: 'After the first few drinks I began to feel fed up with myself (guilty),' or: 'I knew my wife would be angry so I just carried on,' or: 'After the first few drinks I no longer cared, my conscience and determination went overboard with the first few drinks,' 'One is never concentrating on the drink that one is having at the moment, it is always the next drink that matters and that may bring whatever one may vaguely hope for it will bring.' And finally: 'Of course I could have stopped but my companions continued drinking, so I just followed suit.'

Naturally, the whole problem of excessive drinking is frequently seen as the wife's fault: 'She looks so reproachful when I come home and has not touched a drink herself over the past year that I just have to escape into drinking by myself, and then I do not stop.' Unfortunately, however, when the wife bravely tries to drink with her husband, it does not make the slightest difference as he is then forced to find other even more ingenious rationalisations to explain away his alcohol dependence. Certain other drinkers again, may see no necessity for rationalisations: among these there may be psychopaths or hedonists, and it may be difficult to determine to what extent one might label their drinking problems as belonging to the Gamma variety, or whether their uncontrolled drinking may be mainly symptomatic or secondary to their personality problem as they may be unable to exercise the necessary degree of self-discipline needed to attempt limiting the amount they drink to socially acceptable levels.

In Keller's view [5] loss of control occurs before the first drink, as the drinker often knows the likely consequences of his first drink from previous experiences. Semantic arguments may here enter the picture. The drinker having the first few drinks in 'cold blood' knowing full well the likely consequences, probably thereby often manifests psychological dependence but not LoC in the physiopathological sense as originally understood by Jellinek [1]. However, when understanding LoC in a multifactorial (psychosocial as well as in the physiopathological) sense [14], a lot could be said for Keller's view. Even before having the first drink such an individual may be haunted or attracted by the unforgotten lure of the bottle conjuring up memories of an 'elixir' making his mouth water, whenever he returns to his former drinking haunts and friends, or perhaps even when idle talk happens to drift to the subject of drink. Although the pharmacological factor has not entered into the picture at such a stage (before the first drink), nevertheless such a drinker obviously is not fully in control when for such psychosomatic reasons he feels impelled (or compelled?) to take the first drink. Accepting Keller's view would clearly extend the 'disease' concept even to the situation before the first drink. In the examples just given, however, such an individual often could not care less about the likely consequences. In other cases, psychosocial factors might prove stronger than the drinker's fear of the likely, long-term consequences: he may require his relief here-and-now whereas the untoward 'punishment' may not be due until tomorrow; or conditioning proves too powerful, such as the anticipation of immediate pleasant or tension-reducing effects following the first few drinks.

In view of the gradual development of lack of control and of a state of dependence, it is by no means always easy to differentiate quickly between 'the alcoholic' and the non-alcoholic heavy drinker or the 'wilful drunkard', although it is a question which often crops up. An answer often given is that the 'drunkard' could stop if he wanted to, whereas the 'alcoholic' cannot. As we have seen, however, in practice the matter is far more complex than this. A person is not a self-indulgent drinker one day, and a dependent 'alcoholic' the next; there are various degrees of dependence as implied in the widely quoted WHO definition (1952) [20] and much more strongly emphasised in their recent publications [21]. Loss of control alcoholics, as we have seen, often manage to stop or cut down their alcohol intake. In practice, quite commonly the loss of control alcoholic, when first seen, claims that he could have always discontinued if he had wanted to and certainly the therapist meeting him for the first time has no way of knowing whether such a claim is true. There are, thus, obvious difficulties in making, in practice, an easy distinction between an 'alcoholic' and a non-alcoholic 'drunkard'. There is, too, the semantic argument: the non-dependent, heavy drinker who day-after-day consumes five or six double whiskies may in time develop alcoholic cirrhosis which in the view of Jellinek (Beta alcoholism) and some other observers would label him 'alcoholic'.

Unfortunately the term 'dependence' has often been used indiscriminately to include, for example, people feeling put out if they cannot have their usual drink at 6 pm on their way home from the office. But as the report of the Royal College of Psychiatrists' Working Party [2] states, in spite of all gradations between ordinary and 'dependent' drinking, there is more than a merely quantitative difference involved: 'the reality of the alcohol dependence syndrome, its separateness from normal experience, and the force of its implications, must be insisted on unambiguously, and the clarity of its message must not be lost in any semantic confusions'. After a clear state of dependence has developed it becomes an autonomous process with its own momentum, superimposed upon the conditions which originally may have caused heavy drinking. Long-recovered alcoholics themselves, with the benefit of hindsight, are often convinced that they know when their drinking in the past had begun to take on the character of 'alcoholic' drinking, having become more compulsive, etc.

Over the past few decades the *disease concept of alcoholism* has gradually gained increasing (though often grudging) professional and public recognition, in large measure due to the practical successes of AA and the scientific work of Jellinek. However, in more recent years the disease concept, and with it the loss of control hypothesis and the so-called 'medical model', have come under fire, in the main (though not exclusively) from some sociologists and psychologists. It is generally accepted that the disease concept has been of great help towards gaining sympathy and understanding for the 'sick' alcoholic in contrast to the popular contempt felt in the past for the weak, spineless drunkard. In itself, however, this does not lend any scientific support to the applicability of the disease concept. Neither do criticisms in non-medical quarters that its acceptance carries the risk of a kind of medical 'take-over' bid, necessarily proving that alcoholism is not an 'illness' or a 'disease'. In fact, throughout the centuries, doctors as a rule have been singularly disinterested in problem drinkers. Yet both in Great Britain (Dr Thomas Trotter in Edinburgh) and in the USA (Dr Benjamin Rush in Philadelphia) doctors were among the first* to talk of alcoholism as a disease. In modern times, however, the disease concept was popularised by a non-medical professional man (Jellinek) and a non-professional fellowship (AA). Thus the controversy as to whether alcoholism is a 'disease', has certainly not followed strict professional 'party lines'.

If alcoholism is indeed an illness, what then is the essential element in it? This question is discussed in the Royal College of Psychiatrists' publication *Alcohol and Alcoholism* [2]. Is it dependence (physical or psychological)? Or physical or psychosocial harm? Or is it related mainly to factors associated with the 'agent' alcohol, such as the amount and the way in which it is consumed? And what role do associated factors play, such as neglect of nutrition? Does the illness set in only with, or after, the onset of drinking? Or were the foundations laid long before that? Among significant factors in the drinking history, is it the first occurrence of drinking or of 'intoxication'? Of drinking for relief? Of evidence of dependence?

There is now fairly general agreement that a number of factors, in dynamic interaction, are involved in the causation and in the development of alcoholism. Are alcoholics 'born' or 'made'? (see Chapter 2). No one really knows but as only a relatively small minority of drinkers become alcoholics the presence (in at least a proportion among them) of an initial *susceptibility* or *vulnerability* appears likely. Many factors may be involved in such a susceptibility: for example, genetic or acquired during (and perhaps as a reaction to) long-continued heavy drinking, factors that might be of chemical, neurophysiological, psychological or environmental origin.

If drugs that depress the central nervous system are taken frequently and regularly, the organism reacts by adaptation. Alcohol is no exception, and if increasing amounts of drink are ingested (for example, for psychological or social reasons) the body adapts to the effects of alcohol and *tolerance* develops; as defined by Seevers and Woods (1953) [22], 'a phenomenon of cellular adaptation to an alien chemical environment characterised by diminishing biological response'. Development of tolerance necessitates the drinking of larger amounts to achieve the effects previously obtained. Such tolerance may consist of both metabolic and cellular or tissue tolerance. Metabolic tolerance

* Early in the nineteenth and late in the eighteenth century respectively.

enables the body to detoxify and to get rid of the drug in question more rapidly, and thus to deal with larger amounts of alcoholic drink. Such increase of the metabolic rate (which has been ascribed by Lieber [23] to the microsomal enzyme system in the liver) is held to be of relatively minor significance only, compared with the more important tissue or cellular tolerance which enables central nervous system tissues, as a consequence of intra- or inter-cellular alterations and adaptation, to respond pharmacologically to previously toxic amounts of the drug [24].

Initially, some drinkers who may have found their drinking psychologically or socially rewarding tend to repeat this experience more and more frequently, thus 'learning' to drink (see Chapter 2). This deliberate heavy drinking leads to biological changes in the form of tolerance. Thus an increasingly important additional factor, organic in nature, provides another basically quite different reason for increasing the alcohol intake. On top of the original psychosocial reasons for his heavy drinking the drinker now has developed a biological need which drives him towards increasingly heavier alcohol intake (although much later on during his drinking career, usually many years later, his tolerance decreases so that he begins to get drunk on amounts which previously he had handled easily).

The phenomenon of tolerance, in the view of Kissin [24], is of the greatest importance in the development of *physical dependence*. Much larger amounts of alcoholic drink can now be consumed regularly so that the central nervous system becomes exposed for longish periods to sustained high concentrations of alcohol. Physical dependence has been defined (by Seevers and Deneau [25]) as 'a state of latent hyperexcitability of the CNS cells manifesting itself in the abstinence syndrome'.

At this stage, learning processes will again enter the picture, as the drinker may soon find that by renewed drinking he can successfully 'treat' the distressing abstinence syndrome; and possibly somewhat later he may discover that he can forestall and avoid (or at least greatly reduce) the onset of abstinence symptoms by not interrupting his drinking in the first place.

Many observers may regard the relationship between tolerance and development of dependence as unclear. While much of the discussion above, largely based on the account given by Kissin [24], at present awaits confirmation or correction by further research, it presents an attractive combined biological-psychological and social explanation of the dependence process; and a somewhat similar combined biological and learning theory explanation of dependence ('psychobiological dependence syndrome') has been presented by the Working Party of the Royal College of Psychiatrists [2].

The current debates about the alcoholism disease concept, 'medical model' and 'loss of control'[1]

In general the disease concept of alcoholism has been thought to stand and fall with the reality of the loss of control hypothesis. In the view of Jellinek [1], of his various 'alcoholisms' two types constitute diseases in the strict pharmacological sense because of the involvement of physiopathological changes: the Gamma (LoC) and the Delta varieties. The LoC notion led to the acceptance of total abstinence as the main, immediate therapeutic goal, as the means towards achieving contented sobriety, in line with the philosophy of AA.

As already mentioned, during the past decade it has become increasingly fashionable – chiefly (though not exclusively) in some sociological and psychological circles – to criticise the disease concept and with it the so-called 'medical model' of alcoholism and the 'loss of control' hypothesis [26]. To start with, these doubts and criticisms probably originated from a number of studies [27] which showed that a minority of alcoholics had reverted to 'controlled' or 'moderate drinking' (5.8 per cent of 3847 alcoholics in a number of studies reviewed by Emrick [28]). Secondly, certain experimental studies [29–31] have shown that small amounts of alcohol given to alcoholics do not necessarily lead to immediate loss of control and drunkenness; and thirdly, a number of therapists [29] have reported certain successes with therapy aimed at assisting alcoholics to become moderate drinkers. All this would indicate that LoC and alcoholism are by no means irreversible, so that it is no longer necessary to insist on total abstinence as the therapeutic goal for all alcoholics. On the contrary, in some quarters the abstinence goal soon came to be criticised because it was held to be 'counter-productive' in various aspects. Under the circumstances alternative therapeutic approaches were put forward, i.e. (behavioural) techniques aimed at teaching alcoholics to drink in moderation. Various techniques have been used in recent years of which some reported successes [29], while others ended in failure [32]. Some of the relevant issues have been discussed in previous chapters; the following attempts a critical (though still incomplete) review [14] of the so-called 'older' or 'conventional' (i.e. abstinence-oriented) and 'new' approaches.

1 The disease concept

To a large extent some objections to the disease concept of alcoholism seem to be based on semantic arguments, and how one defines the terms 'disease', 'medical' and 'alcoholism'. Many critics not only of the disease concept of alcoholism but also of the notion of mental illness in general [33], equate 'disease' and 'medical' with organic, physical changes only. If such narrow definitions were accepted there might be legitimate doubts as to the status of alcoholism as a 'disease', seeing that biochemical or constitutional causation, though often hypothesised, has not been proven; and of course the definite physical complications are only results of the disorder in relatively late phases. On the other hand, one should not overlook the occurrence of development of cellular and metabolic tolerance, or also of alcoholic amnesias and withdrawal symptoms, fairly early in the alcoholic's drinking career. But the wide divergence of views of the meaning of 'disease' can perhaps be well illustrated by quoting two leading British behaviour therapists (keeping in mind that some behaviour therapists are in the forefront of the critics of abstinence-oriented treatment), Meyer and Chesser [34]: 'Disease is an abstract concept, and can therefore be fashioned to one's choice. [In] the most simple model of a disease . . . a specific cause initiates a specific pattern of symptoms which follows a predictable course and is . . . associated with specific structural and functional changes in particular parts of the body.' Naturally, alcoholism would not conform to this 'most simple model': there is no specific cause but probably a number of unspecified predisposing and precipitating causative factors working in dynamic interaction with each other; the course is not definitely predictable (although in most cases it follows a very similar pattern and shows very similar symptoms), and specific structural changes in particular parts of the body occur in some alcoholics only, and then only relatively late in the process. Yet Meyer and Chesser continue: 'In practice, few diseases can be defined in this way because there is rarely such perfect correlation between cause, symptoms, course and demonstrable pathology. The causes are often uncertain and there may be no demonstrable somatic pathology.' They also state: 'The notion of "mental illness" and its differentiation from disorders and behaviour, variations of behaviour and variations of personality remains a contentious subject.' Statements made by Sainsbury [35] in the World Health Organisation magazine *World Health* in regard to 'mental illness' – its predisposition, precipitation, prevalence, course and outcome – certainly apply fully to alcoholism:

> Social factors are related to the occurrence of mental illness in a number of ways . . . Often . . . social events or conditions are largely responsible for precipitating a mental illness, while social conditions may combine with psychological or biological factors to predispose an individual to illness. Cultural environment and changes in it certainly affect the prevalence of mental illness in a community and in the social groups composing it. Social factors can also influence the course and outcome of mental illness, since the effectiveness of treatment will depend largely on the social context in which it is provided . . . Cultural attitudes and beliefs also play a part in defining who in a society is to be labelled mentally ill . . . recognized as needing treatment, . . . referred to the psychiatric services.

Among psychiatrists criticising the disease concept of alcoholism is Hershon [36] who feels that 'only two features of disease . . . are generally applicable and universally constant [i.e. the disease] should be seen to be related to an aetiologically relevant physical process which the person cannot choose not to have or will away'. Asking whether 'alcohol drinking, which at times seems to be out of control [is] a disease', he argues that as 'drinking was not demonstrated to be directly due to any physical process recognizable as a disease, and [because] as a behaviour it was subject to personal control . . . the drinking behaviour of alcoholics does not conform to proper notions of disease'. One does not know, however, who is to decide what is the 'proper' notion of 'disease' yet even if Hershon's 'proper notion of disease' is accepted, strictly speaking the absence or otherwise of a physical process at the start of the alcoholic's drinking behaviour (and possibly in only in certain types of the various 'alcoholisms') is still very much the subject of scientific research and current debate, and remains *sub judice*. If the views of certain researchers such as Goodwin [37], Mardones [38] or Littleton [39], are ultimately confirmed, Hershon's first point (referring to the relationship of alcoholism to an aetiologically relevant physical process) would no longer be valid. It may be of some interest in this connection to quote the recently expressed view of a medical specialist, Professor R F Mahler [40], who included alcoholism under the heading of 'metabolic disorders'. Among his 'good reasons' for this was his belief that 'addiction to drink, like addiction to drugs, and perhaps also to food, may develop from some metabolic change at receptor sites in the nervous system'.

The second point made by Hershon, that the alcoholic's drinking behaviour was subject to personal control and choice, is of course closely related to the LoC controversy. In the present author's view [14, 26, 41] in the very great majority of alcoholics, such personal control is severely restricted (lack of control), and, where it is present at all, it depends on many unpredictable internal and external cues and conditions. Hershon's conclusions are therefore very much open to question.

On the other hand, there are many observers who have little doubt as to the applicability of the disease concept to alcoholism. For example, the Australian psychiatrists Drew, Moon and Buchanan [42] argue that the view that a disease must always have a physical basis was derived from the false assumption that physical and psychological aspects of human life could be separated. In reality, however, behaviour and bodily function are inseparably related: every psychological event requires a physical mechanism and leaves a physical 'trace' in the brain. In reference to the above-named, restricted, purely organic definitions of 'disease' these authors name hypertension, arthritis, asthma and heart disease as examples of disorders which may have a number of causative (including psychologically poorly defined) factors, a variable course, and a varying outcome responding to various (including psychological) measures of intervention.

As discussed previously, the LoC hypothesis and the disease concept are, in the present author's view, by no means invalidated by the finding of an occasional return by alcoholics to moderate drinking, even though Jellinek himself based his 'disease' and 'loss of control' definitions on physiopathological processes. First, altered physiological or metabolic reactions to alcohol, acquired during the drinker's career, need not necessarily be irreversible [15]. Moreover 'lack' (rather than loss) of control over alcohol intake is, in the present author's view, essentially multifactorial in nature, depending on psychosocial as well as on pharmacological and phsyiophathological factors – certainly not exclusively on the latter as hypothesised by Jellinek.

Another frequently heard objection to the 'disease' concept – that it provides the drinker with a welcome alibi to continue drinking – is quite ridiculous. In the abstinence-oriented approaches, stress is laid on the necessity of keeping away from the first drink (and the great majority of alcoholics admit they do not really 'crave' alcohol until after they have had a few drinks and not usually before the first drink). Clearly therefore the therapeutic approaches based on the disease concept do not remove the alcoholic's overriding responsibility to avoid the first drink at all costs. The 'new' approaches (aiming at teaching certain alcoholics to drink in moderation), on the other hand, obviously remove the alcoholic's responsibility for taking the first drink, and shift the responsibility towards putting up resistance against having a third or fourth drink. Certainly, in our own experience with a great many alcoholics, the 'need' for alcohol becomes much greater and the ability to resist it much less the greater the alcohol intake on a given occasion [41]; possibly because of the existence of a critical range of blood alcohol levels^2 varying from individual to individual, and from time to time, depending on psychosocial and other circumstances, above which increasing 'lack of control' makes resistance to further drinking more and more difficult.

2   The medical model
If, as proposed by its critics, the 'medical model' is understood as a purely organic and physical one, its application to alcoholism is subject to similar considerations as discussed above for the 'disease concept'. But with few exceptions, such as Dr J Y Dent, the British protagonist of the apomorphine treatment [46], most doctors interested in alcoholism have always applied a comprehensive multidimensional approach combining drug treatments (which usually took a back seat) with psychosocial approaches. In the UK for example, where those drinkers requiring specialised hospital treatment have mostly been treated in alcohol units starting with the first unit (Warlingham Park Hospital) in 1952 [49], psychosocial therapy (therapeutic community, group therapy, 'collaboration with AA social aftercare') has always been regarded as the cornerstone of the units' therapeutic programmes, with drugs usually no more than an adjunct. Such therapeutic programmes – though, or perhaps rather because, they were introduced by medical men interested in the plight of alcoholics – have always dealt with host and environment as well as with the pharmacological agent.

Such an approach to the multidimensional nature of the 'medical model' is very much in line with the views expressed by many medical experts, such as those given at the First International Medical Conference on Alcoholism, organised by the Medical

Council on Alcoholism in London in 1973. As Professor Van Dijk [47] expressed it on that occasion: 'The medical model is a multidimensional construct . . . it takes into account the psychological and social, as well as the physical aspects of the afflicted person . . . The medical model is a general model to investigate some types of behaviour and experience, looking at the picture, aetiology and pathogenesis with a view to therapy and prevention.' In the present writer's view the acceptance of such a broadly understood medical model does not mean that in each treatment facility the doctor is necessarily the leader of the re-quired therapeutic team: experience, personal bent, attitude and aptitude, apart from local conditions, may often be more im-portant than such an individual's own professional discipline.

Surely few medical men would regard their role as being re-stricted to treating organic illness by means of drugs, to the exclu-sion of emotional and social factors and approaches – least of all, the great majority of psychiatrists? Few of them are likely, there-fore, to fall in with proposals put forward by the psychologist H J Eysenck [48]. While agreeing that the ancient split between body and mind is nowadays untenable, Eysenck believes in a dichotomy between two groups in psychiatry: the medical, organic group, concerned with the effects of physical conditions to be treated by physical or pharmacological means; these, Eysenck suggests, should be treated by psychiatrists. The second group dealing with the behavioural part of psychiatry, is concerned with disorders of behaviour largely acquired through learning, unlearning or failure to learn. Such behaviour disorders, in Eysenck's view, should be treated by behaviour therapists and psychologists alone who would have complete responsibility for their patients.

The extension of the disease concept to neurotic disorders and to alcoholism, in Eysenck's view, is 'completely unreasonable'. Presumably, he would also give behaviour therapists full re-sponsibility for treating alcoholics, apart from the treatment of abstinence symptoms and organic complications. Few, if any, would deny that in an overall comprehensive team approach to alcoholism, behaviour therapy has a very important part to play (for example, in training the alcoholic to be on the look out for and learning to cope with, likely 'cues' that might trigger relapses) just as have psychodynamic, social and other approaches. Few 'neu-tral' therapists and clinicians at this stage, however, are likely to put all their trust in the 'new' methods which hold out a promise of 'controlled drinking' for some Gamma alcoholics. The behavioural techniques that have in the past been employed in alcoholism – aiming at creating a conditioned aversion by classic (Pavlovian) method – have not, in the view of most observers, proved particularly successful, and probably by-and-large less so, than other methods. Surprisingly, good results have certainly been claimed by some protagonists of the new approaches, such as behavioural techniques aimed at fostering moderate drinking habits by positively rewarding patients who manage to keep their drinking down to acceptable amounts, and at discouraging excessive drinking by negative rewards ('punishment'). However, in a condition as complex as alcoholism, and with so many unpredictable internal and external 'cues' in innumerable permutations acting as possible triggers of relapses, it may be difficult, if not impossible, to 'immunise' the alcoholic against all possible contingencies. Moreover, in our experience, possibly the most common 'trigger' seems to be the alcoholic's insistent belief and hope that, in spite of it all, he could yet be a moderate drinker – so there is no need for a definite external cue to bring on this feeling. Also, even if most possible 'triggers' could have been successfully anticipated and provided for, there still remains the susceptible 'soil' on which alcoholism has arisen in the first place – perhaps a relatively greater susceptibility for the development of psychological dependence in the mainly psychogenic alcoholic, and a relatively greater vulnerability of certain organs to the harmful effects of alcohol in the mainly sociogenic alcoholic. Giving up excessive drinking is not the extensive therapeutic goal in alcoholism; the idea of reducing the danger of likely 'trigger' situations by behavioural techniques appears excellent (although one might feel they should in general be directed at training the Gamma alcoholic for abstinence and not for controlled drinking) but they would certainly require supplementary psychosocial approaches. It also seems very doubtful whether training in laboratories or hospitals could fairly adequately guard against similar contingencies in real life. There remains the final problem that all too often, and especially in psychiatry, good results achieved by enthusiastic initiators have not always stood the test of time when routinely used by other workers.

3   *Lack of control*

The extent to which *ad hoc* definitions have contributed to recent criticisms of the 'conventional' (i.e. abstinence-oriented) approaches is most evident in the case of the 'loss of control' hypothesis. As was well known to Jellinek himself [49] and to every clinician with practical experience of the drinking behaviour of alcoholics (probably most) Gamma alcoholics on many occasions do not end up drunk each time they have one or two drinks. Clearly LoC only implies that such a drinker can never be quite certain that he will always be able to stop on a given occasion once he has started to drink [44, 50, 51]. The idea that LoC means that an alcoholic who has one drink immediately and inevitably has to continue drinking, is, as Gillow rightly said [52], quite ludicrous; yet tests were carried out in hospitals in order to prove that alcoholics did not have to continue drinking after having been given alcoholic drink, and this result was then claimed to indicate that 'loss of control' was no more than a myth [30].

It is difficult and often risky to generalise from experimental hospital conditions to real-life situations. After all, the great majority of alcoholics have little difficulty in abstaining from alcohol during their hospital stay, even when allowed out regularly to go to local shops, or to visit friends. However, in our experience with certain alcoholic private patients who insisted that they were sure that they could drink in moderation, it turned out that, in fact, many managed to keep to a few drinks for several days, some for a few weeks, and a few for several months – before they reverted to uncontrolled drinking [26, 41, 51]. Almost all of these people were relatively stable personalities, living under good, stable socio-occupational conditions, i.e. individuals who in theory could perhaps have been expected to stand a fair chance of achieving their desired goal of safe controlled drinking, if more than very few alcoholics could do so.

Such experiences bear out the statements that the hypothesis of an irreversible metabolic, biochemical change as the basis of 'loss of control' (and applying to all the possible subgroups among the Gamma alcoholisms) seems untenable. This, however, by no means proves LoC to be a myth. Many hypotheses exist in regard to 'loss of control', and, as Edwards [15] has rightly stressed 'researching on alcoholism . . . will only be damagingly constrained if any of [the] very provisional hypotheses is prematurely accepted as the given law'. Nevertheless, in our view most consistent with present-day observations is a multidimensional concept of impairment or 'lack (rather than loss) of control' [14, 26], which differs from Jellinek's hypothesis that LoC is essentially a physiopathological phenomenon. In our multidimensional LoC concept there is not only dynamic interaction between the pharmacological 'agent' alcohol with the physiological and psychological make-up of the personality ('host') but psychological and social factors are also prominently involved.

Our own experience in the field of 'controlled drinking' in alcoholics is derived mainly from the method of using, since 1963, a 'Gentleman's Agreement' [51] with those newly-seen alcoholic patients who made it clear from the outset that under no circumstances would they be prepared to undergo treatment aimed at total abstinence without having first been given a chance to prove that they could become moderate drinkers. Such patients were told that there had indeed been a number of reliable reports of alcoholics having managed to revert to 'normal' drinking. The patient was asked to fix a daily maximum of alcoholic drinks; no matter what the circumstances, he was on no account to drink more than this amount. He was also advised about the circumstances which some of our patients in the past had found favourable to the (usually very short-lived) maintenance of moderate drinking. Whenever possible, the patient's spouse was kept in the picture. As a rule, while the alcoholic himself was enthusiastic, spouses were highly sceptical and often openly hostile to such arrangements, even though the drinkers had agreed that, should the 'Gentleman's Agreement' fail, they would accept such failure as evidence that they were not in control of alcohol but *vice versa*, and that they would then adopt the only possible alternative, i.e. to abstain.

Over the past seventeen years this approach was adopted by over 300 alcoholics. In the main, they were emotionally fairly stable and highly educated men, in their forties or fifties, often in high executive or equivalent positions, usually with a history of professional achievement and success, and still holding good positions, with their marriages intact, in spite of their wives' growing concern over their drinking. Their degree of dependence was often considerable, but there were the balancing factors of above average emotional and social stability, as evidenced by their ability to keep often highly responsible jobs and the affection of their families. They had usually tried to control their drinking in the past and failed, but all were more or less sober at the first interview, and confident that they would succeed. All of these patients by the end of one year had had quite a number of failures, but requested yet another chance to continue with the trial [26, 41, 51].

Such observations confirm of course that in many alcoholics the first drink does not immediately precipitate a bout, but sooner or later will. Factors influencing the drinker's ability to control his drinking, in our experience, appear to be associated not only with the activity of the agent alcohol (such as concentration and amount of drink and the rapidity with which it is taken) but also with environment and personality in dynamic interaction with each other. For example, moderate drinking was more likely as long as the drinkers:

1 Slowly sipped a relatively weak beverage (beer or wine), or, if it was spirits, one or two drinks only ('agent').
2 Drank in company ('environment').
3 (a) Drank with meals ('host': physiological aspects);
  (b) Drank when relaxed and cheerful ('host': psychological aspects).

The same patients usually relapsed into uncontrolled drinking:

1 When they gulped spirits ('agent').
2 When they drank alone, or in the company of heavy drinkers ('environment').
3 (a) When they drank on an empty stomach ('host': physiological aspects);
  (b) In particular, when they drank while depressed, tense, frustrated, resentful, tired, bored, upset ('host': psychological aspects).

Patients were often aware of some of these risks. Many replied in answer to the question whether they could drink in moderation, 'Well, it all depends,' and the factor mentioned most often in this connection was: state of mind. In fact, from the experiences of such patients it would almost seem that alcoholics could often drink moderately as long as they did not really 'need' it, but when they 'needed' it – for example, looking for the pharmacological effects of alcohol in order to find relief from tension or depression – they became unable to control their drinking. Paradoxically, therefore, alcoholics could more readily 'get away' with controlled drinking as long as they did not really care whether they had a drink or not but hardly ever when they really craved its medicinal effects.

Another interesting point was the statement by many alcoholics that they could stop drinking on a given occasion as long as they did not 'feel' the effects. Two possible hypotheses might account for this phenomenon:

(i)   The already mentioned possibility of a threshold, a critical range of blood alcohol levels (certainly not a fixed amount) above which LoC effects begin to set in.

(ii)   As a consequence of psychological or environmental (residential, occupational, domestic) changes the LoC drinker may learn a technique of disciplined and rationed drinking which enables him to remain, for shorter or longer periods, below the threshold range of LoC.

At any rate, our patients seemed to exhibit not an absolute 'loss of control' but a relative 'lack of control': not a static and absolute but a relative, variable, and in many cases, intermittently progressive phenomenon, occurring, in many patients with increasing frequency in later phases of alcoholism. Apparently – given some insight, a degree of emotional maturity, considerable effort and a good portion of luck – some alcoholics are able to manage to stick to relatively small amounts of drink as long as the 'going' remains good. Sooner or later, however, the constellation of required favourable factors in areas of host and environment may no longer pertain: the wife may start nagging once more, business may not prosper, the boss make unreasonable demands. In this way the precarious and uneasy balance between the opposing influences, i.e. between the 'pull' of the LoC on the one hand, and the psychosocial 'brakes' on the other, may once again be tipped towards a defeat of the controlling or disciplining factors [53].

In view of these theoretical considerations, it should cause little surprise if follow-up studies show a certain proportion of alcoholics who have become moderate drinkers and if successes have been reported by therapists using behavioural approaches in order to assist alcoholics to become moderate drinkers. At this juncture, however, no one knows beforehand who could possibly succeed in this direction. Obviously on the long road during the insidious process from social drinking to alcohol dependence (i.e. during Jellinek's pre-alcoholic and prodromal phases), there is a considerable period where budding alcoholics could take stock and revert to normal drinking. Obviously the earlier in his downward path the drinker is 'reached' (secondary prevention) the greater this possibility. Once the stage of even a slight degree of dependency has come, the possibility of safe controlled drinking may become more remote. Drinkers who misuse alcohol in the absence of chemical dependence (i.e. by deliberate choice rather than need) or because of socioenvironmental influences (drinking haunts and friends), excessive domestic or occupational stress (i.e. symptomatic or secondary excessive drinkers) should in theory have a relatively better chance to become safe moderate drinkers. Careful assessment of the stage at which the problem drinker presents himself, of the psychosocial factors contributing to his excessive drinking, and of presence and degree of his chemical dependence, is therefore very important. But as a rule it is just those drinkers with a long history of severe alcohol misuse and with clear evidence of dependence who are most vociferous in claiming that, in spite of all their previous failures, they could yet drink 'normally'.

Alcoholism – symptom or disease?

Is alcoholism a 'symptom' (a view often adopted by psychiatrists) or is it a 'disease' in its own right (the view of AA)? As in many other aspects of alcoholism the question here, too, may be one of and/or rather than either/or. In practice there can be little doubt that AA's approach of concentrating on the 'disease' aspect and on the patient's drinking habits has proved much more successful than the psychiatrists' search for factors underlying his drinking. There appears, however, no reason why one could not approach alcoholism from both angles at one and the same time: i.e. as a condition that frequently (though not necessarily so) may have started as symptomatic of underlying psychological or social malfunctioning but which, subsequently, has outgrown its purely symptomatic aspect, the excessive drinking itself secondarily producing complications in its own right. In time, with the development of lack (or loss) of control an independent disease process may have become superimposed which proceeds at its own momentum and which requires therapeutic attention in its own right, quite apart from treatment directed at the underlying psychosocial factors which may have been responsible for the individual's excessive drinking in the first place.

Notes

[1] Based in part on lectures given at the 21st International Institute on the Prevention and Treatment of Alcoholism in Helsinki, June 1975 (ICAA) [14] and at a meeting of the Irish Branch of the Royal College of Psychiatrists in Dublin (St. Patrick's Hospital), 1 November, 1979 [26] and reproduced here by kind permission of the respective organisers.

[2] Criticising this notion of a critical blood alcohol concentration, because various studies have demonstrated that 'persons repeatedly addicted to alcohol' can drink a great deal obtaining a high blood alcohol concentration 'without developing physical dependence', Paredes *et al.* [45] comment that 'it may well be the case that physical dependence is initiated by drinking over a sufficient length of time *and* maintaining a sufficiently high blood alcohol concentration'. Our hypothesis of a critical threshold-range of blood alcohol concentration refers to alcoholics who have become dependent after drinking heavily 'over a sufficient length of time'. We have seen a great many alcoholics who insist that they can safely interrupt drinking as long as they have, say, four or five pints, or two or three whiskies; once they pass such amounts, they find themselves in difficulty, and often they are convinced that having one or two drinks more, they have lost control. But here again, apart from the amount of drink, seemingly psychosocial factors also enter into the threshold range: e.g. when under great stress, the threshold seems to be lower. But our threshold-range hypothesis would apply only to those who are already clearly dependent.

References

1 Jellinek, E M (1960), *The Disease Concept of Alcoholism*, New Haven, Hillhouse
2 R.C.Psych. Working Party Report (1979), *Alcohol and Alcoholism*, 2, 7, 46
3 Williams, Lincoln (1960), *Tomorrow will be sober*, London, Cassell
4 Keller, M and McCormick, M (1968), *A Dictionary of Words about Alcohol*, New Brunswick, NY, 17, 20
5 Keller, M (1972), *Brit. J. Addict.*, 67, 153
6 Lishman, W A *et al.* (1980), in *Addiction and Brain Damage*, ed. Richter, D, London, Croom Helm, 215–27
7 Bergman, H *et al.*, *ibid*, 201–14
8 World Health Organisation (1964), Wld Hlth Org. Techn. Rep. Ser. 273, 9, Geneva, WHO
9 Glatt, M M (1955), *Brit. J. Addict.*, 52, 55
10 World Health Organisation (1955), Wld Hlth Org. Techn. Rep. Ser. 94, 7
11 Gath, D (1969) in *The Drunkenness Offence*, ed. Cole, T *et al.*, Oxford, London, Pergamon, 9
12 Ritson, B and Hassall, C (1970), *The Management of Alcoholism*, Edinburgh, London, Livingstone
13 Glatt, M M (1974), *A Guide to Addiction and its Treatment*, Lancaster, MTP
14 Glatt, M M (1978), *Brit. J. Addict.*, 71, 135

15 Edwards, G (1970) in *Modern Trends in Drug Dependence*, ed. Phillipson, R E, London, Butterworths, 140–63

16 Eddy, D *et al*. (1956), *Bull. World Health Organisation*, 32, 721

17 Glatt, M M (1977) in *Drug Dependence – Current Problems and Issues*, ed. Glatt, M M, Lancaster, MTP, 3

18 Glatt, M M (1977) in *Dictionary of Medical Ethics*, eds Duncan, A S *et al*., London, Darton, Longman and Todd, 9–13

19 Mello, N K (1976) in *Alcohol and Alcohol Problems*, ed. Filstead, W J, *et al*., Cambridge, Mass., Ballinger, 175

20 World Health Organisation (1952), Wld Hlth Org. Techn. Rep. Ser., 48

21 Edwards, G (ed.) *et al*. (1977), *Alcohol-Related Disabilities*, Geneva, WHO

22 Seevers, M H and Woods, L A (1953), *Amer. J. Med*., 14, 546

23 Lieber, C S (1973), *N. Engl. J. Med*., 288, 356

24 Kissin, B (1974), in *The Biology of Alcoholism*, Vol. 3, eds Kissin, B and Begleiter, H, New York, London, Plenum, 14, 141

25 Seevers, M H and Deneau, G A (1963) quoted from *Biology of Alcoholism*, Vol. 3, eds Kissin, B, and Begleiter, H (1974), 159

26 Glatt, M M (1980), *Brit. J. Alcohol and Alcoholism*, 15(2), 48

27 Davies, D L (1963), *Quart. J. Stud. Alc.*, 24, 109

28 Emrick, C D A (1974), *Quart. J. Stud. Alc*, 35, 523

29 Pattison, E M *et al*. (1977), *Emerging Concepts of Alcohol Dependence*, New York, Springer, 96–7

30 Merry, J (1966), *The Lancet*, i, 1257

31 Mello, N K and Mendelson, J H (1971), *Arch. Gen. Psychiat.*, 25, 527

32 Ewing, J A and Rowse, B A (1976), *Brit. J. Addict.*, 71, 123

33 Szasz, T S (1972), *The Myth of Mental Illness*, London, Paladin

34 Meyer, V and Chesser, E S (1970), *Behaviour Therapy in Clinical Practice*, Harmondsworth, Penguin

35 Sainsbury, P (1974), *World Health*, October 1974, 20–3

36 Hershon, H (1974), *Brit. J. Addict.*, 69, 123

37 Goodwin, D (1976), *Is Alcoholism Hereditary?*, New York, Oxford University Press

38 Mardones, J (1970) in *A World Dialogue of Alcoholics and Drug Dependence*, ed. Whitney, D E, Boston, Beacon, 367–83

39 Littleton, J M (1975), *Brit. J. Addict.*, 70, 99

40 Mahler, R (1975), *Medicine*, 13, 579

41 Glatt, M M (1974) in *Alcoholism – A Medical Profile*, eds Kessel, N *et al*., London, B Edsall, 122–32

42 Drew, H R *et al*. (1974), *Alcoholism – A Handbook*, London, Heinemann

43 Larkin, E J (1974), *The Treatment of Alcoholism*, Toronto, Addiction Research Found.

44 Glatt, M M (1965), *Quart. J. Stud. Alc.*, 26, 116

45 Paredes, A *et al*. (1977), in *Emerging Concepts of Alcohol Dependence*, ed. Pattison, E M *et al*., New York, Springer, 97–8

46   Dent, J Y (1955), *Anxiety and its Treatment*, London, Skeffington
47   Van Dijk, W K (1974) in *Alcoholism – a Medical Profile*, ed. Kessel, N *et al.*, London, B Edsall, 134–42
48   Eysenck, H J (1975), *The Future of Psychiatry*, London, Methuen
49   Jellinek, E M (1952), *Quart. J. Stud. Alc.*, 13, 673
50   Keller, M (1958), *Ann. Amer. Acad. Pol. Sci.*, 315, 1
51   Glatt, M M (1967), *Brit. J. Addict.*, 62, 267
52   Gillow, S E (1979), *Cancer Research*, 39, 2836
53   Glatt, M M (15 March, 1979), *Mimms Magazine*, 5–6

5

How many Alcoholics?

The sight of men sprawling drunk in the streets is now fortunately relatively rare, and, for example in London, limited to certain areas only. But the 'skid row' drinkers form only a very small proportion of the country's problem drinkers. Drunkenness is not synonymous with alcoholism. The very high blood alcohol concentrations observed sometimes in car drivers are hardly ever reached by non-dependent self-indulgent drinkers or all-night revellers and in the main only by seasoned highly alcohol-tolerant habitual excessive drinkers and alcoholics; the latter may often not show outward evidence of being drunk (although this does not detract from their being a menace at the steering wheel). Yet drunkenness is probably the main feature of alcoholism that has attracted public attention. It is probably the remarkable drop in public drunkenness after the 1914–18 period [1] compared with conditions prevailing in this country until the time of the First World War that may have been largely responsible for the lack of professional and lay attention to the alcohol problem in this country between the 1940s and the late 1960s and early 1970s. Yet in spite of views to the contrary, frequently expressed around the middle of this century, and in spite of the general attitude of apathy and indifference exhibited by State, professionals, workers and the general public, alcoholism in the UK has never been a thing of the past – even though this was the official position presented to foreign visitors between the 1950s and the mid-1960s. Now this country may be on the threshold of, or already well within, a 'wave of alcoholism' [2].

In 1951, England and Wales came last but one in a list of eleven countries ranked according to the prevalence of alcoholism by the World Health Organisation [3] with an estimated proportion of 100 alcoholics per 100,000 adults. Moreover, a questionnaire inquiry carried out by Parr [4] in 1957 found the number of alcoholics known to general practitioners in England and Wales to be about 35,000 (i.e. about one tenth of the WHO estimate). However, even then there was no ground for complacency. Apart from Parr's study there were no field investigations carried out to estimate the actual number of alcoholics. Then, as now, one had to make do with the so called 'indirect indices', such as figures for drunkenness convictions, deaths from liver cirrhosis, etc. It is obvious that by themselves none of them can be taken as a reliable indication of the prevalence of 'alcoholism' (though they clearly reflect the increase or otherwise of drink problems, serious enough whether or not they reflect the rates of 'alcoholism'). But it can still be assumed that they tell us something about the general trend provided that they all point in the same direction. And that indeed, appears to have been the case.

In a 1958 paper reviewing 'the past decade', the present author [1] cited four indirect indices:

1 A rise of drunkenness convictions from 20,000 in 1945 to 48,000 in 1950, and over 60,000 in 1956.
2 A rise in the number of deaths from liver cirrhosis from 816 in 1948 to 1157 in 1955. (The increase was especially marked in women.)

   Jellinek's estimate of 86,000 'chronic alcoholics' [3] – i.e. those with definite physical or mental complications – and, arising out of that, a total estimate of 350,000 alcoholics in the UK had been based on the liver cirrhosis mortality figures for 1948. It was clear that the estimated number of alcoholics was likely to have risen greatly in subsequent years, in accordance with the increasing cirrhosis mortality.
3 A rise in the number of alcohol-related driving accidents.
4 A rise in the national drink bill (i.e. the yearly personal expenditure on alcoholic drinks) from £700,000,000 in 1946 to £900,000,000 in 1956.

The conclusions drawn from these statistics at the time (1958) was that they failed to show 'any evidence that the downward trend of the drink problem which started in the first half of the century . . . continued into the present time; and that . . . even if nowadays drunken people are not sprawling on the streets any more, there is still need for research, vigilance, and public education in the complex phenomenon of alcoholism' [1].

Thus there were obvious shadows on the horizon in the 1950s but it was not until very clear evidence of the deterioration of the drink problem appeared in the late sixties and seventies that the State, professional bodies and the general public attempted to come to grips with it. It is only fair, however, to note that certain voluntary organisations, such as the Rowntree Trust, had given serious attention to the alcohol problem, as of course had the Society for the Study of Addictions and the various Temperance Organisations.

Studies and estimates in the 1950s and 1960s* [5]

On the basis of the Jellinek Formula – founded on the well known, though inconstant connection between alcoholism and liver cirrhosis – the World Health Organisation, in 1951, arrived at a 'probably reliable' estimate of 86,000 'chronic alcoholics' (i.e. those with definite physical or mental complications) in England and Wales; and at a 'guess' of a total of approximately 350,000 alcoholics (i.e. those with and without complications). If the assumption was correct, as in the USA, so also in this country, alcoholics without complications outnumbered those with complications by four to one. In spite of many theoretical objections to the use of the Jellinek Formula, in most cases where independent field surveys were carried out, the forecast based on the use of the Formula proved reasonably correct.

In this country a number of studies carried out in the 1950s and 1960s arrived at estimates which were all lower than the WHO figure. Thus a questionnaire enquiry by Dr Parr in 1957 [4] found the number of alcoholics known to general practitioners to be approximately 35,000, about one tenth of the WHO estimate (1.1/1000 as against 11/1000 adults). Another general practitioner estimate of alcoholics, based on a 1956 College of General Practitioner enquiry, gave an even lower figure, i.e. 0.2/1000 of the population, or less than 10,000 alcoholics.

Employing not general practitioners but health visitors and probation officers as informants or investigators in a 1961/1963 study carried out in five English cities, the Rowntree Social Service Trust [6] estimated the number of established alcoholics in this country as at least 70,000, and the total number of alcoholics

* This section is based on a talk given at the AGM of the Medical Council on Alcoholism, 29 July 1970, and reprinted here by kind permission of the Editor of its journal (*British Journal on Alcohol and Alcoholics*).

as probably several times this figure.

Naturally only a certain proportion of alcoholics come to the attention of any single agency, such as general practitioners, health visitors or probation officers. The broader the basis of a field survey, the greater, naturally, the likelihood of unearthing a higher proportion of the total alcoholic population. The only broad-basis investigation in this country aimed at finding the number of alcoholics was carried out in 1961–1964 by Moss and Beresford Davies [7] in Cambridgeshire, their sources of information including not only general practitioners, probation officers and the after-care services but also hospitals, hostel staff, clergymen, Alcoholics Anonymous, social and welfare agencies and the police. The estimate arrived at in this way was 6.2/1000 of the male population and 1.4/1000 of the female; and the authors themselves felt that for a number of reasons the incidence of alcoholism in most other parts of England was likely to be higher than in Cambridgeshire. In 1970 an estimate by the Office of Health Economics based on an extension of the Cambridgeshire findings to England and Wales, in the light of Parr's earlier findings of regional differences, arrived at a figure of 220,000 alcoholics in the country.

Indirect indices

Field studies such as the Cambridgeshire study are of course a much better, direct indicator of the prevalence of alcoholism than the *indirect indices* – such as drunkenness convictions etc. However, the latter possibly indicate the general trend, i.e. whether alcoholism is on the increase or the decrease. In fact, the trend indicated in this way is of a marked decrease of the problem in the first half of the century followed by a gradual increase during the 1950s and 1960s, i.e. since the time of the WHO estimate. For example, drunkenness convictions stood at about 200,000 at the turn of the century, 20,000 at the end of the Second World War, and 80,500 in 1969. During the 1960s there was a considerable rise in drunkenness convictions among the young (under twenty-one years of age): 6600 in 1959, 12,000 in 1968. There has, likewise, been a marked rise in convictions for being drunk-in-charge and similar offences, e.g. a doubling of prosecutions between 1959 (5700) and 1967 (12,000), followed by a steep rise in 1968 (20,000) after the introduction of the breathalyser (indicating that previous figures had only reflected the 'tip of the iceberg'). These figures are relevant to our present discussion, as, contrary to previous views, it is now recognised that alcoholics contribute much more than their fair share to drunken driving and traffic offences, and in particular to severe and fatal accidents, so that alcohol-impaired and drunken driving constitutes not only a 'problem of alcohol' but also of alcoholism.

Modern trends: 1970-8

1 *Deaths from liver cirrhosis*
Deaths from liver cirrhosis, like deaths from alcoholism, drunkenness convictions and spirit consumption figures, fell steadily in the first half of the twentieth century, from 4000 in 1901 to 800 during 1944-8. They rose again in the 1950s and early 1960s to remain fairly steady for a number of years, at a figure of about 1350 [5].

Between 1971-8, however, there was a considerable rise: in men by 36 per cent (i.e. per 100,000 of population in England and Wales from 3.14 to 4.28). Considerably greater was the proportionate rise among women over the same period, i.e. by 24 per cent (from 0.14 to 0.48) [8].

A similar picture emerges with regard to deaths from alcoholism. These increased in men from 2.60 in 1970 to 3.58 in 1978 (i.e. by 38 per cent); and in women again considerably more, from 0.1 to 0.23.

2 *Admissions of alcoholics to psychiatric hospitals and alcohol units*
In England and Wales these have steadily risen during the past three decades: 204 in 1952, 1900 in 1960, 5800 in 1967.

Again the pace quickened considerably in the 1970s. Between 1971-8 the increase of admissions among men mounted to 77 per cent from 23.3 to 41.4 per 100,000 of population. Women again showed a relatively much higher increase, by 137 per cent (from 6.8 to 16.1). The total number of alcoholic admissions in 1978 was 14,972.

3 *Drunkenness convictions*
These stood at about 200,000 at the turn of the century, 20,000 at the end of the Second World War, and 80,500 in 1969. Between 1971-8 proved drunkenness offences on adults over fourteen years increased, among men, from 409-522 (i.e. by 27 per cent). In women the rise was once again considerably greater, from 25-41, i.e. by 64 per cent.

Over the past twenty years drunkenness offences have doubled, so that there are now more than 100,000 convictions per year. (1979: 117,813 convictions out of 119,616 prosecutions.) One interesting point is that the number of female alcoholics is thought to be not much less than that of the men but in spite of the relatively much greater rise in the number of female drunkenness convictions, the numbers of hospital admissions and deaths from cirrhosis and alcoholics are nowhere near the corresponding figures for the men.

Drink-driving offences

Proceedings against motorists 1970–8
(note: not 'convictions')
There has been a gradual rise of proceedings, from 31,794 in 1970 to 64,816 in 1978. The highest figure – 70,394 – was reached in 1975, followed by falls to approximately 63,200 in 1976 and nearly 53,000 in 1977. The Christian Economic and Social Research Foundation [9] ascribes this fall to the reduced real incomes of 1976 and 1977 the effect of which manifested itself readily among motorists. With rising real incomes, drinking offences have begun to increase again. Based on the Chief Constables' reports, the Foundation forecasts for 1979 a 10 per cent increase over the 1969 figures, i.e. approximately 73,000.

As to the age distribution of drunken motorists, official Home Office statistics show a relative stability between 1976–9 of convictions. The Foundation, however, reviewing its statistics of proceedings against motorists for offences to do with drink or drugs, found a steadily changing pattern in the age distribution when considering a longer period (1962–79). Figures before and after the introduction of the breathalyser in 1967 are not comparable. However, after a stable period in the early and mid-1970s, there has been a continuing increase of proceedings against younger motorists; the percentages of the under twenty-ones gradually rose from 10 per cent in 1968 to 12 per cent in the 1972, 13 per cent in 1974 and 1976, and is expected to be 14 per cent in 1979; the 21–29 age group remained steady during the corresponding period at 39 per cent and is expected to be 38 per cent in 1979; the thirties-and-over age group was 51 per cent in 1968, 49 per cent in 1972, and has remained stable since then at 48 per cent. There has been a slightly above the proportionate rise in the younger drunken drivers group (in Scotland as well as in

England and Wales) during this period, when considered in relation to the population changes in the relevant age group which have largely remained unchanged during the last twenty years.

Regional variations
As in Scotland (see p. 143), heavy drinking and alcoholism are more prevalent in some parts of England than in others. This was indicated in a recent Report by the National Council on Alcoholism [10] based on a study of three indicators of excessive drinking: deaths from liver cirrhosis, drunkenness offences, and drink driving offences. Areas north of a line from the Severn to the Wash had the most serious drinking problems; the only region in the South with a severe problem was Greater London. The North of England, Wales and Greater London were most seriously affected. Liver cirrhosis was found to be most prevalent in the more affluent parts of the country, Cornwall, Devon, Somerset and Sussex all showing death rates from cirrhosis lying above the average. This association of liver cirrhosis with affluence is of interest as – contrary to previously held views – liver cirrhosis is nowadays attributed in the main to the toxic action of alcohol itself, rather than to nutritional defects.

Consumption figures of alcoholic beverages
These are another indirect index with a bearing on the prevalence of drinking problems. High, or increasing consumption, in theory, may be spread fairly uniformly throughout the population, or a relatively small proportion of very heavy drinkers (problem drinkers or alcoholics) might be responsible to a relatively less large extent. As discussed elsewhere (Chapter 2) recent Canadian work points to the likelihood of a high correlation between rise of *per capita* consumption and an increase in the numbers of problem drinkers and with them of the incidence of alcohol-related disabilities. Such a relationship is well illustrated by a table published in the R. C. Psych. Working Party Report [11]: annual *per capita* consumption of alcohol (given in gallons of proof spirit) in 1885–9 amounted to 3.8, alcohol-related mortality (given in terms of annual deaths from chronic alcoholism, DTs, or cirrhosis/per million living) in the same period, was 154. In the period 1900–04 the corresponding figures were 4.1 and 193 respectively, and during 1930, 1.6 and 42 respectively.

In more modern times, between 1949–50 and 1971–2 consumption of beer in Britain (per head of the adult population) rose from

24 to 30.8 gallons, i.e. by over 40 per cent; of wine from 0.30 to 1.32 gallons, i.e. by over 300 per cent; of spirits, from 0.25 proof gallons to 0.52, i.e. approximately 120 per cent. Putting such figures in a slightly different way [12], between 1950 and 1976 consumption of beer rose from 26 million bulk barrels to 41; of spirits from 10 million proof gallons to 36; of wine from 13 million gallons to 81.

Annual *per capita* consumption/per adult (over fifteen) between 1950–76 rose from 5.2 litres of absolute alcohol to 9.7. Both sets of figures indicate that, proportionately, the increase was greatest in the intake of wine.

Seen against the background of drinking in other countries, by 1961 the average Briton with a consumption (given in the table published by the R. C. Psych. Working Party Report [11]) of 7.1 litres (in terms of absolute alcohol) per year, trailed considerably behind the Frenchman (26.8), Italian (24), West German (11.5) and North American (8.2), but was ahead (again a rather doubtful distinction in this context) of the Dane (6.9) and the Swede (5.6) [13].

The rise in alcohol consumption appears to have affected all European countries, except the French who for several decades have been making strenuous efforts to reduce their alcohol intake. Between 1950–2 and 1968–70 [14], *per capita* consumption (in litres of absolute alcohol), increased in the UK from 4.9 to 6.2 (i.e. by 27 per cent). Apart from the French with their reduction of 9 per cent and the Belgians, whose drinking increased by 27 per cent, all other West European nations (with estimates presented) [15] showed an often much more marked rise in alcohol consumption. This mainly affected the West Germans (181 per cent) and the Dutch (179 per cent); Austrians and Finns increasing their drinking by 100 per cent and the Danes, Norwegians and Italians by 75 per cent, 67 per cent and 46 per cent respectively. In absolute amounts of drink taken, however, the French, in spite of their successful measures, still far outstrip other nations with a *per capita* consumption, in 1968–70, of 16.1 litres (absolute alcohol) (compared to 17.6 litres approximately twenty years earlier). The Italians are next (13.71 in 1968–70) followed by the Austrians (10.8) and the West Germans (10.1). The average Dutchman (5.3), the Finn, (4.4) and the Norwegian (3.5) during that period drank less than their British counterpart. Such figures from other European countries are of course much more significant nowadays, with the greater economic co-operation between the

EEC nations, the marked growth of travelling (and the possible learning of different drinking habits from neighbouring nations).

Increased alcohol consumption over the past decade throughout Europe – according to the Commission of European Communities [16] – has been causing harm to the social well-being, the economic functioning, and the health of the European population. This, the Report stated, required urgent action, both in the field of prevention and in the provision of treatment centres. Increases of more than 50 per cent in deaths among young car drivers were found in twenty-eight out of thirty countries investigated by Dr Havard's WHO survey [19], and in the USA the number of deaths nearly doubled in the fifteen year period between the late 1950s and the early 1970s. Likewise, the USA annual casualty rate of over 70,500 (of all age groups) killed in car accidents far surpassed that of any other country but only six countries had higher fatal casualties from car accidents than England and Wales. Of all drivers killed on the roads in England and Wales 40 per cent had a blood alcohol level above the legal limit. Alcohol misuse is nowadays considered to be the main factor responsible for the increase of car accidents throughout the world.

The UK's drinks 'bill' has increased enormously in recent years. The annual cost to industry has recently been estimated to amount to much more than £350 million and drunken driving has been said to cost the country possibly £100 million a year [21]. Alcoholism in the UK has been rated as the greatest killer after heart disease and cancer. Thus problem drinking affects not only the health of the individual but also has considerable harmful consequences on the functioning of family and society. It will cause little surprise, therefore, that voices have often been raised suggesting that some of the revenue obtained from drink should be used to support measures to reduce alcohol problems and assist alcoholics. Thus Lord Kimberley [22] himself a recovered alcoholic (who regularly calls the attention of the House of Lords to the dangers of problem drinking, as Sir Bernard Braine, chairman of the National Council on Alcoholism, does in the House of Commons), in a recent debate in the Lords pointed out that in 1978 British society had obtained £2585 million revenue from drink; and he urged that a proportion should be rechannelled towards minimising the damage done to society by alcohol.

There is no sign that the rise of the alcohol problem is beginning to slow down. According to a publication of the Christian Economic and Social Research Foundation (1979) [9] the conclusion drawn from an analysis of Chief Constables' Reports is that after a year's interruption, drinking offences were once more on the increase (which the Foundation felt was a result of rises of real income). Proved offences of drunkenness rose from just over 106,814 in 1978 to approximately 115,000 in 1979, and proceedings against motorists for drink-related offences increased from 64,816 in 1978 to about 73,000 in 1979.

Taken together, the total rise of all drink offences in England and Wales in 1979 amounted to 10 per cent. Similarly, after a reduction in the previous year, analysis of the Chief Constables' 1979 figures with regard to drunkenness convictions among the under-eighteens was expected to show a rise of about 6 per cent. The Foundation commented that the trend towards the relative increase of proportionately younger drivers for drinking and driving offences, after a period of stability during the early and mid-1970s, might be connected with the fact that, compared with the 1950s, during the 1960s and 1970s a larger number of young people became car owners.

In summary a brief glance at the indirect indices shows a progressive and worsening situation. The value of each of these indices as reflecting an increase in the number of alcoholics could be criticised. As to drunkenness convictions, for example, only a proportion of people found drunk in public are alcoholics although the latter are likely to contribute more than their fair share and may be found drunk repeatedly; there are great variations in the attitude of the police to 'drunks' in various regions, which also may change from time to time; many alcoholics (especially women) may get intoxicated relatively more often in their homes than in public; certain alcoholics (such as the Delta alcoholics) in contrast to Gamma alcoholics (with their bouts) may not get drunk very often, etc. As to liver cirrhosis deaths, these occur only in a relatively small proportion (perhaps 8 per cent) of alcoholics and there are other common causes of cirrhosis besides heavy drinking. Moreover, much depends on the verification of the clinical diagnosis by post-mortem examination. As to admission figures, the rising trend may to a certain extent reflect the establishment of a larger number of adequate facilities, a decrease in the stigma, an earlier diagnosis as people present themselves at an earlier phase (in particular women), and a greater awareness among doctors and other professionals of increasing incidence, and their greater familiarity with the features of the condition. There are some who doubt the relevance of consumption figures to changes in the trend of a rising or falling number of alcoholics, but clinical impression and the trend of all these indirect indices support the notion of a corresponding marked rise in the number of alcoholics. And it should be remembered that drinking problems are not caused by alcoholics alone; while they are responsible for an undue proportion, the much larger numbers of non-dependent, heavy drinkers are probably responsible – in absolute figures – for more alcohol problems than those caused by the one or two per cent of alcoholics in the population.

The fall in the 'real' price of alcohol, making alcoholic drink something in the nature of a 'bargain' [23], has probably encouraged its consumption. At the same time one should consider whether rising unemployment in the 1980s, with its psychosocial consequences – boredom, resentment, insecurity, etc. – may contribute to a rise of drinking problems among the unemployed, in spite of their fall in income. (However, no such rise was noted during the widespread unemployment of the 1930s.)

Scotland and Ireland

Our exposition so far referred in the main to England and Wales but a few figures relating to Scotland and Ireland may be of some interest. All available evidence indicates that the Scottish and Irish problems of alcoholism are proportionately greater than in England. This is well illustrated by a table compiled by Dr D Walsh [24] comparing the rates for first admissions and re-admissions for alcoholism and alcoholic psychosis to psychiatric facilities in the Republic of Ireland with those in Scotland [25] and England. His table shows that the Irish rates (per 100,000 population) – for the year 1964 – first admissions: 42.5 (men), 6.2 (women); readmissions: 52.7 (men), 9.6 (women) – were roughly twice the Scottish rates (referring to the year 1961) – first admissions: 20.6 (men), 3.3 (women); readmissions: 26.1 (men), 3.6 (women); and ten to twelve times the English rates (for the year 1959) – first admissions: 3.6 (men), 1.0 (women); readmissions: 3.7 (men) 1.0 (women). These difference are striking even when taking into account that the Irish figures refer to a later period (1964) than the Scottish (1961) and the English figures (1959), and remembering that there had been a steady increase in the number of admissions for alcoholism in English psychiatric hospitals in the 1950s and even more so in the 1960s. It is also interesting to note that the ratio between female and male admissions is far higher in

England than in Ireland and Scotland.

   Dr Walsh pointed out that the Irish rate of 24.5 per 100,000 of total population seems to be 'one of the highest of all national first admission rates for alcoholism, being surpassed only by first admission rate of 28.3 per 100,000 for France in 1964'. One seems to detect a slight note of relief that he was able to discover in the literature reports that certain 'more delimited areas' in various parts of the world had in fact even higher rates than the Irish, such as Helsinki (45.0 per 100,000 of population, in 1960), the Scottish Highland and Island catchment area of Craig Dunan Hospital (45.0 per 100,000), with even higher rates reported from the Virgin Islands. According to another table compiled in 1964 by Phillipson, who compared admissions for alcoholism and alcoholic psychosis in English, Scottish and Irish psychiatric hospitals, the rates per 1000 of total population were 0.08 (England and Wales), 0.299 (Scotland), 0.522 (N. Ireland) and 0.280 (Irish Republic), amounting to a percentage among total admissions to psychiatric hospitals of 5.3 and 0.6 (men and women respectively in England and Wales), 18.7 and 3.1 (men and women in Scotland), 11 (N. Ireland) and 5.4 (Irish Republic). For Northern Ireland, studies among general practitioners reported in 1962 gave an alcoholism rate of 191 per 100,000 adults in rural N. Ireland. This compares with Dr Parr's findings (1957) [4] of 110 per 100,000 adults in England and Wales and of 240 per 100,000 in Scotland.

   Many references to the seriousness of the Scottish alcoholic problem – and to its increase among the young and among women – were made in symposia held in Edinburgh and Glasgow in the late 1960s. The total number of alcoholics in Scotland was estimated to be 60,000 to 80,000 – clearly a much higher proportion of the population than in England – and it was said that 10 per cent of Britain's total alcoholic population resided in Glasgow, Paisley and Lanarkshire. Not much less than 1 in 5 of all admissions to Scottish psychiatric hospitals were due to alcohol. Dr H W Whittet [26], Physician Superintendent of Craig Dunan Hospital, Inverness, reported that a 1963 survey in the Highlands and Islands had found the in-patient admission rate for alcoholism to be about three times the Scottish average, and that in 1963–4 alcoholism accounted for 1 in 4.5 of the admissions to Craig Dunan Hospital. There may be some relationship between these findings and Dr Whittet's comparison of 'the "Gin and Jaguar" belt of England . . . the beer-drinking black-belted Midlands, northwards through the "half and half pint" Lowlands of Scotland and ever upwards over the Grampians to the Highlands and Islands, where alcohol is synonymous with whisky, and only whisky, for the rest is hogwash to be reckoned in terms of the soft stuff – the drink of the stranger'. Spirits, of course, are very popular in other parts of Northern Europe as well as in Scotland (much more so than in Southern Europe). Climatic conditions have probably aided and abetted the popularity of spirits, which were described by James Boswell 200 years ago as 'a means to supply by art the want of that genial warmth of blood which the sun produces'.

Figures relating to somewhat earlier periods indicate that the alcohol problem then, too, was greater in Scotland than in England [27]. Thus in 1954 the death rates from alcoholism in Scotland were 0.6 for men and 0.2 for women – as against 0.1 for both sexes in England – per 100,000 of population. In 1957 the death rate from liver cirrhosis in Scotland was 4.7 per 100,000, compared with 2.6 in England and Wales (1956), 2.3 in N. Ireland (1957), 2.1 in Eire (1957) – and 10.7 in the USA (1956). Convictions for offences against the Intoxicating Liquor Laws (i.e. chiefly for drunkenness) have always been proportionately much more frequent in Scotland than in England and Wales: e.g. per 100,000 of population in 1948, 140 in Scotland as against 76 in England and Wales, and in 1954, 233 as against 126. In the early 1960s the proportion of alcoholics was nearly one-fifth of the total male admissions to Scottish psychiatric hospitals, the corresponding figure in England and Wales was just above 1 in 20.

The relatively high estimates of the alcoholism problem in Ireland are in line with findings of high rates of alcoholism among Irish–Americans and the relatively high proportions of Irish admissions to the alcohol units in Warlingham Park Hospital in the 1950s [40] and St Bernard's in the 1960s. Similarly, of male drunkenness offenders in London courts and of females in Holloway Prison every second was found by Gath [28] and D'Orban [29] respectively to be of Scottish and Irish origin, and in our own experience, too, Scottish as well as Irish alcoholics contribute a relatively high proportion to the ranks of alcoholics seen in alcohol units and in prison. The fact that so many of these Scottish and Irish migrants are single and lonely obviously contributes greatly to their difficulties and thus probably also to their excess drinking [39].

From time to time Irishmen become sensitive about the Irish reputation for heavy drinking and try to show – by referring to comparative national statistics on alcohol consumption per head of population – that the Irish are, after all, a relatively sober nation. A report published a few years ago pointed out that the *per capita* consumption in Ireland was lower than in many other countries, including England. But this seems hardly a fair statement. After all, out of nearly two million adults in the Republic only 800,000 were then estimated to consume alcoholic drinks. The 'population at risk' is thus much smaller in Ireland than among other nations with their lesser proportion of teetotallers – and the average Irish drinker therefore consumes about double his share in order to keep the average *per capita* consumption of the Irish at levels not very different from those nations with a much higher proportion of drinkers. According to one estimate in 1969 [30] the number of alcohol-dependent drinkers in the Irish Republic was then about 60,000. This would give an Irish alcoholism rate of about 3 per cent out of 1,900,000 people aged fifteen and over, or over 7 per cent out of those taking alcoholic drink – percentages which are not only much higher than any English estimates but which would rank with the highest alcoholism rates anywhere in the world.

Despite the greater prevalence of alcoholism in Scotland and Ireland, the lack of professional and general interest and of planned treatment programmes was as much in evidence there as in England, and in those years no Scottish or Irish delegates ever seemed to turn up at international alcoholism meetings. However, in recent decades all this has now fortunately begun to change (e.g. a very active Irish National Council on Alcoholism was formed in 1966), and the increasing number of local and regional meetings as well as of international conferences on alcoholism – such as those held in Cardiff, Dublin and Glasgow as well as in London, Liverpool and Manchester – bears witness to the increase of interest in the problem in Wales, Ireland and Scotland as well as in England.

Modern trends in Scotland and Ireland

The rise in both Scotland and Ireland of drinking problems remains relatively greater than in England and Wales. In a recent survey (June 1980) the Secretary of State at the DHSS [31] estimated that if account were taken not only of the effect of alcohol misuse on the sufferer himself but also on his family and friends, 'something like 1 in 25 of the population in England, Wales, and much higher in Scotland and Northern Ireland, maybe 1 in 10 . . .

may be personally affected by severe alcohol-related problems
. . . [These were] . . . startling, indeed horrifying figures [adding
up] to an epidemic which deserves urgent attention'.

Scotland
The number of problem drinkers in Scotland was estimated, in
1975 by the Scottish Council on Alcoholism [32], to be between
75,000 and 112,000: they were mainly men. Between 1957 and
1977, according to a statement by the Under-Secretary of State for
Scotland [33] in December 1979, the number of alcoholics in
Scotland increased from 81,000 to 110,000. (These figures were
based on the number of deaths from cirrhosis of the liver and
adjusted to take account of the proportion of such deaths not
derived from alcohol.) Presumably therefore the term 'alcoholic'
as used in this context compares to the usual WHO estimates (such
as the ones made in 1951 [3]) which at the time led to the 'guess' of
350,000 alcoholics in England and Wales based on cirrhosis deaths
in 1948.

The indirect indices quoted by the Under-Secretary of State all
pointed to a marked increase in the problem, over the two decades
1957–77:

1 Deaths from liver cirrhosis rose by 45 per cent.
2 Established deaths from alcoholism rose eight times.
3 Admissions to Scottish hospitals for alcoholism and alcoholic
   psychosis rose by 102 per cent.
4 There was also a rise in the number of drunkenness offences
   and of drink-driving offences.

According to figures quoted in Parliament [34], blood levels of
over 80 mg/100 ml were found in over 40 per cent of patients
admitted with head injuries to the Western Infirmary, Glasgow in
1974. Prosecutions for drinking and driving in Scotland in 1975
were 789 per 100,000 licensed vehicles – as compared with an
average of 372 in Great Britain as a whole.

As in England there were regional variations in the size of the
problem [35]. In a distilling area, 10 per cent of the adult working
population had an alcohol problem. In Glasgow, in 1975, 25 per
cent of the acute male medical hospital admissions had an alcohol
problem; in 19 per cent such admission was either directly or
indirectly due to the effects of alcohol.

As regards death from cirrhosis the rate in the Shetlands is 34.3

per 100,000; in the Orkneys, 22.2; in the Highlands 16.9 and in Strathclyde 15.7 [36]. Hospital admissions for alcoholism in Strathclyde (37.2 per 100,000) are much less than half that of the Highlands, the admission rate in the Highlands [38] being ten times the highest in England (9.1).

As to the possible relationship between alcohol and murder, among 400 people charged with murder in the West of Scotland between 1953 and 1974, 58 per cent of the accused men and 30 per cent of the women were intoxicated at the time of the offence. Not only the killer but often also the victim in such cases had been drinking.

The loss to the community as a consequence of alcohol misuse, in the view of the Under-Secretary of State for Scotland [33], considering the ten-times smaller Scottish population, in terms of money and resources, was equally as large as the cost resulting from alcoholism in England and Wales, estimated as between £430 and £650 million.

One interesting finding repeatedly noted by the Christian Economic and Social Research Foundation [37] is that Scottish youths are less prone to be apprehended for drink-driving offences than those in England and Wales. To some extent the lower proportion of convictions for young motorists in Scotland might be related to higher unemployment figures in Scotland so that youngsters could not afford cars at the same early age as in England. Nevertheless the Foundation concluded that (even if considering the relative proportions of the populations in the relevant age groups) 'there has been a slightly more than proportionate increase in the younger offenders group (17–20 years)', in Scotland as in England and Wales. In Scotland the 17–20 years age group made up, in 1968, 9 per cent of the total of drunken drivers, the same in 1971, 10 per cent in 1974, 11 per cent in 1976, and 12 per cent in 1978.

94 per cent of the Scottish population over the age of seventeen take alcoholic drink [36] and, according to a survey published in 1979, nine out of ten children in Scotland have tasted alcohol by the age of fourteen years [38]. Of the 192 boys and 192 girls interviewed, one in five said they had been served alcoholic drinks on licensed premises but in most cases children had had their first sip in the parental home, often on a special occasion and given to them by their father. This Scottish Health Education Report nevertheless concluded that parents exercising very strict control over their children's drinking might thereby encourage them to-

wards secret drinking.

The Under-Secretary, while stressing the seriousness of the drink problem in Scotland, also had some positive things to say, pointing for example to the prevention efforts made by the Scottish Health Education Unit, the widespread counselling and active assistance provided by the twenty-three local councils of the Scottish Council on Alcoholism, and the treatment given by three special units (situated in general hospitals). Most of the residential treatment given to alcoholics takes place in the general wards of hospitals; for example, in 1976, 4096 people were admitted to hospitals for alcoholism or alcoholic psychosis. Voluntary organisations played their part, such as the Salvation Army, the Cyrenians and the Talbot Association. Scotland has twenty-three residential homes (with a total of 270 places) for recovering alcoholics; with one exception they have all been established by voluntary organisations [39].

Why has the alcohol problem in Scotland always been more acute than in England? Various reasons have been given and there is obviously not a single explanation. Tradition, the cultural image pertaining in Scotland to drink, the climate, the pride taken in, and the popularity of, whisky as the national drink etc. To close this brief section on Scotland, here is what Sir Archibald Geikie [41] had to say at the beginning of this century (1904):

The question is often asked why so much whisky should be consumed in Scotland. One explanation assigns as the reason the moist, chilly climate of the country and this cause may perhaps be allowed to have some considerable share in producing the national habit. No small proportion of the spirit, especially in the Highlands, is drunk by men who are certainly not all drunkards, and who can toss off their glasses without being any the worse for it, if indeed, they are not, as they themselves maintain, a good deal better. But it must be confessed that, especially among the working class in the Lowlands, tipsiness is a state of pleasure to be looked forward to with avidity, to be gained as rapidly and maintained as long as possible. To many it offers a transient escape from the miseries of life, and brings their only moments of comparative happiness [42].

Ireland

Ireland, like Great Britain, has experienced a marked rise of alcohol problems. This has been well illustrated by a number of statistics collected by the Irish National Council on Alcoholism [43].

1   *Consumption*: Gross national spirit consumption (approximately 965,000 gallons) in 1951–2, fell slightly in the 1950s, and gradually increased in the 1960s and 1970s. After a temporary slight fall in 1976, it rose again in 1977 to approximately 2,595,000 gallons.

Beer consumption showed a similar trend, slightly falling in the 1950s, and gradually increasing since the late sixties. The consumption in 1977 (1,608,500 gallons) is over one and a half times as great as that of 1951–2 (970,000).

Wine consumption – over 530,000 gallons in 1951–2 – remained static in the 1950s and then began a continuing rise throughout the sixties and seventies to arrive at the 1977 figure of over 2,150,000. Over the past twenty-five years consumption thus increased fourfold, spirit consumption over two and a half times, and beer consumption over one and a half times.

As to *per capita* consumption, in the International League Table of 1976, the Republic of Ireland is listed 23rd out of 31 'competitors'. The average Irishman imbibed during that year 7.0 litres of absolute alcohol (all beverages included), slightly more than the UK inhabitant (6.8) but far behind the leading European nations.

Compared with the UK, the average Irishman drank slightly more spirits (1.98 litres of absolute alcohol, compared to the UK drinker's 1.66) and slightly more beer (123 litres of bulk beer against the UK's 118.9) but less wine (3.09 litres of bulk wine against 5.64 in the UK). The highest *per capita* spirit intake in that year (calculated as given above) was achieved by the Canadians (3.24), highest beer intake by the Belgians (145.0) and highest wine intake by the French (101.31 litres of bulk wine) who however were only marginally ahead of the Italians and Portuguese.

But one should remember that the Irish Republic has a high proportion of abstainers so that the *per capita* consumption would be somewhat greater if drinkers only were included – compared to the smaller percentages of abstainers in the other countries.

The Irish Council points out that the 'relatively favourable position of Ireland in the League Table is misleading because the Republic contains a disproportionate number of young people. Compared with Great Britain where 23 per cent of the population (55.9 million) are no older than fifteen years, 34 per cent of the Irish population of 3.1 million are in that age group. Compared to Great Britain's beer consumption *per capita* of adults (over fifteen years of age) of 154.5 litres, the Republic's corresponding figure was 186.36 litres; *per capita* spirit consumption per adult in Great Britain 3.63 proof litres, in the Republic 5.25 proof litres; wine consumption in Great Britain (per adult) 7.32 litres, in the Republic of Ireland 4.68 litres. The adult Irishman's *per capita* absolute alcohol consumption of 10.6 litres was clearly greater than that of the British [45].

Looking at these figures and considering the correlation between *per capita* consumption of alcoholic drink and alcohol-related harm, such risk would seem definitely greater in Ireland than in Great Britain. Again, the relatively higher consumption of the more potent spirits (with the relatively greater potential for harm and for the lack-of-control type of dependence) might appear to increase the risk.

2 *Expenditure on alcoholic drink*: This reached a record level, ascribed in the main to the increases in cost. Gross expenditure on alcohol (in millions) at current market prices, was approximately £37.00 in 1958 with a steady rise to an estimated over £390.00 in 1977.

Customs and Excise duties rose gradually from approximately £55.700 (millions) in 1970 to £170.500 millions in 1977.

3 *Number of drinkers*: The very significant increase in consumption indicates a substantial rise in the number of drinkers. The number of drinkers (including moderate and infrequent drinkers) is estimated to number 1½ million.

4 *Number of alcoholics*: As elsewhere, there is no reliable information; on the basis of the WHO formula 'about 75,000 out of the estimated 1.5 million drinkers will in time develop alcoholism'. (The WHO estimates that up to 5 or 6 of every 100 drinkers may develop a dependence on alcohol.)

5 *First admissions for (the treatment of) alcoholism to psychiatric hospitals*: Such admissions showed a steady increase from 699 in 1965, to 1252 in 1970, 1697 in 1972, and 2105 in 1974.

Based on these figures and on the Census of population, the Medico-Social Research Board has calculated an alcoholism *disease expectancy rate* for the years 1972–4: of persons surviving to age sixty-five, in 1972 8.6 out of every 100 men (and 1.6 out of every 100 women) will have been admitted at least once for the treatment of alcoholism; in 1973, 9.9 men, 2.0 women, and in 1974, 10.1 men and 2.0 women.

6   *Drink-related offences*:   Between 1967–76, the number of total offences increased gradually: prosecutions from 7099 in 1967 to 13,570 in 1976; convictions from 6980 in 1971 to 10,778 in 1976. Among these, drunkenness prosecutions rose from 3339 in 1971, to 4540 in 1976; drunkenness convictions from 2731 in 1971, to 3599 in 1976.

7   *Drink-driving offences*:   Prosecutions which had risen from 1225 in 1967 to 4650 in 1974, fell in 1975 and again in 1976 (3147). Convictions which had risen from 1586 in 1971, to 2515 in 1974, afterwards fell to 1556 in 1976. According to the Irish Council, however, because of legal technicalities such figures give little indication of the extent of drunken driving as the drunken driver usually only attracts attention by careless or dangerous driving, and there is no random breath testing. Interestingly, among convictions 99 per cent involved men; and in regard to age groups, 94 per cent of convictions involved the twenty-one-and-overs.

An important comment made in this Report by the Irish Council is that the temporary halt in the steadily upward trend of consumption that occurred in 1976, was probably due to the significant budgetary increases in January 1976 and trade increases in the same year. Whereas the consumption of other alcoholic beverages decreased in 1976 due to imposition of the 'largest-ever price increases', the sales of cheap cider rose by 30 per cent. In 1977 when price rises on other beverages were small, there was a (small) reduction in the consumption of cider. Cider is a drink favoured by many teenagers as it is relatively cheap and potent: it is seen by the Council as a barometer of the effects of price increases on the consumption of alcoholic drink in general. When increases in price of other alcoholic beverages are small (as happened in 1970–3), cider consumption falls, whereas it tends to rise with large price increases of other beverages – as it did in 1974–6.

Such experiences obviously reflect the important role which the 'relative price' of alcoholic drink has on *per capita* consumption, and the possible significance of this relationship from the aspect of preventive measures.

The latest statistics about the Irish drink problem came from the Irish State-owned Medico-Social Research Board [44] in August 1980. The Irish are said to have become 'the heaviest drinkers in Europe, seeing that they now spend 13 per cent of their income on drink . . . more than any other European nation'. It is also reported there has been a great rise in the number of hospital admissions for alcoholism and alcohol insanity. There seems little reason to doubt the accuracy of the last statement which, after all, only confirms for Ireland what holds good in Great Britain, and probably most countries in Europe and elsewhere. But remembering the League Tables mentioned by the Irish Council, the Irish would have to break all records to even come within reach, let alone surpass, all those nations who only four years ago were so far ahead of them when it came to the intake of alcoholic drink.

As regards the contributing causative factors in the Irish drink problem, Irish attitudes to drinking have often been said to be an important factor. The Irish National Council in 1973 [45] summarised them under the following headings – pointing out that such attitudes are affected by economic, traditional and historical factors.

(a) The great importance to the national economy of the trade in alcoholic beverages, which is an important source of revenue to the State, and livelihood for a large section of the population.

    (i) 28,000–29,000 people are employed in the alcohol beverages industry;

    (ii) Income tax and profit taxes from such employees and firms contribute to State revenue;

    (iii) Turnover tax on liquor sales for the year 1970 came to £7 millions;

    (iv) Customs and Excise Duty, by far the greatest source of State revenue, on alcoholic beverages, in the year ending March 1972, amounted to £68.56 million.

(b) The ambivalent Irish attitude to drinking: often disapproving in private but tolerant in public. Drinking is part of the national scene and widely accepted. There is great tolerance of offenders against liquor laws (unless offences endanger lives) and pressures on people to drink. Interestingly, the Council does not mention the suggestion of integration of drinking customs into the socioeconomic structure; this suggestion is often mentioned by American sociologists [46] as an important factor in Irish drinking habits but was recently strongly criticised by Joyce O'Connor [47] who herself stresses the still prevailing influence of the once so strong Irish temperance movement.

(c)   The general apathy of the general public towards the drink
       problem.

Northern Ireland

According to a recent survey undertaken by Queen's University,
Belfast [48], and published in 1979, the province may have over
40,000 alcoholics (mainly men) and the total number of people
experiencing serious drinking problems may be five times as high
as the number of 'alcoholics'. The survey was based on questionnaire replies (obtained from 85 per cent of a random sample of
approximately 4000 people questioned) out of just over one
million electors.

   Alcohol abuse was greatest among the younger age groups,
aged 18–29, and among women in the 20–24 age bracket. Most
drinkers had started taking alcohol at about eighteen but 10 per
cent had begun to drink before the age of seventeen. The most
popular drink was spirits but among male beer drinkers nearly a
third tended to consume eight or more glasses in a session.

   The survey showed that a minute proportion of people with
drinking problems (10 out of 2350 individuals questioned) had
asked for assistance. The problem in Northern Ireland may in fact
be even more serious, as the proportion of life-long abstainers has
been estimated to be well above one third of the population. This
would mean that the less than two-thirds of the population who do
take drink do so fast enough to more than compensate for the
non-drinking of their countrymen.

References

1   Glatt, M M (1958), *Brit. J. Addict.* 54, 51
2   Glatt, M M (1977), *Proc. Roy. Soc. Med.*, 70(3), 202
3   World Health Organisation Expert Committee on Mental Health
     (1951), *Report on the First Session of the Alcoholism Sub-committee*,
     WHO Techn. Rep. Ser., 42
4   Parr, D (1957), *Brit. J. Addict.*, 54, 25
5   Glatt, M M (1970), *Brit. Journal Alcohol and Alcoholism*, 5(3), 86
6   Prys William, G and Glatt, M M (1966), *Brit. J. Addict.* 61, 257
7   Moss, E C and Beresford Davies, E (1967), *A Survey of Alcoholism
     in an English County*, Cambridge, Geigy (UK) Ltd
8   Sir George Young, Hansard, 25 July, 1980, 447–8
9   *Drink Offences*, Chief Constables' Reports (1979), London, Chris-
     tian Economic and Social Research Foundation
10 National Council on Alcoholism Report, July 1979, *The Last 20 Years*

11 Royal College of Psychiatrists' Special Committee, *Alcohol and Alcoholism* (1979), London, Tavistock, Tables 4, 5, 93–5

12 Sir George Young, quoted from *All. News* January, February 1980, 10

13 Robert, A (1966), 12th Europ. Institute Prev. and Treatment of Alcoholism, Prague.

14 Bruun, K *et al.* (1975), *Alcohol Control Policies in Public Health Perspective*, Helsinki, Finnish Foundation for Alcohol Studies

15 *International Statistics on Alcoholic Beverages, 1950–72* (1977), Finnish Found. Alc. Stud. and WHO Reg. Off. Europe, 209–22

16 Commission of European Communities, quoted from *Alliance News*, January, February 1980, 9

17 The Rt Hon P Jenkin (June 1980), 26th Internat. Institute Prev. Treatm. of Alcoholism, Cardiff

18 *Brewing Review* (Brewers' Society), July–September 1980, 10

19 Havard, J, quoted from *All. News*, January, February 1980, 4

20 Lord Soper, quoted from *All. News*, January, February 1980, 10

21 'Action on alcohol', *Brit. med. J.* (1979), Leading Article, 1, 361

22 Lord Kimberley, quoted from *All. News*, January, February 1980, 9

23 Quoted in *Brit. med. J.* (L.A.), 1979, 1, 361

24 Walsh, D (1969), *Brit. J. Psychiat.*, 115, 1021

25 Morrison, S L (1964), *Health Bull.*, 22, 1

26 Whittet, H W (1969), *Journal of Alcoholism*, 4, 153

27 Glatt, M M (1967), in *New Aspects of Mental Health Services*, ed. Freeman, H and Farndale, S, Oxford, Pergamon

28 Gath, D (1969), in *The Drunkenness Offence*, ed. Cook, T, Gath, D and Hensman, C, Oxford, Pergamon, 9

29 D'Orban, P (1969), *ibid*, 51

30 Percival, R (1969), *Journal of Alcoholism*, 4, 251

31 The Rt Hon. P. Jenkin, 26th Internat. Instit. Prev. Treatm. Alcoholism, Cardiff, June 1980 (quoted from *Brewery Review*, July, September 1980, 14–17)

32 Report of Scottish Council on Alcoholism (1975)

33 Under-Secretary of State of Scotland, Hansard, 21 December, 1979, 1138

34 Hamilton, W (1979), *ibid*, 1138

35 Scottish Council on Alcoholism, quoted by Hamilton, W (ref. 34)

36 Scottish Council on Alcoholism, quoted from Cashin, F, *Doctor*, 17 January, 1981

37 Differences between Scottish Drunkenness and Drunkenness in England and Wales (November 1977), London, Christian Economic and Social Research Foundation, (1979).

38 Scottish Health Education Unit (1979), *Ten-to-fourteen Year Olds and Alcohol*, London, HMSO

39 *Habitual Drunken Offenders*, Report of a Home Office Working Party, London, 1979

40 Sullivan, J D and Glatt, M M (1956), *J. Irish med. Assoc.*, 146

41   Sir Archibald Geikie (1904), quoted from Ritson, E B and Plant, M A (1977) in *Drug Dependence – Current Issues and Problems*, ed. Glatt, M M, Lancaster, MTP, 120

42   Ritson, E B and Plant, M A (1977), in *Drug Dependence – Current Issues and Problems*, ed. Glatt, M M, Lancaster, M T P, 119–45

43   Irish National Council on Alcoholism, 1978 Statistics, Dublin

44   Irish Medico-Social Research Board, August 1980, Dublin

45   Irish National Council on Alcoholism (1973), *Alcoholism*, Report to the Minister of Health, Dublin, 11–12

46   Bales, R F (1946), *Quart. J. Stud. Al.*, 6, 482

47   O'Connor, J (1978), *The Young Drinkers*, London, Tavistock

48   Queen's University, Belfast (1979), quoted from *Doctor*, 5 April, 1979

6

Women Alcoholics

Reference has already been made to certain special aspects of alcoholic women, as compared to men, in the discussion of the influence of sociocultural factors in the aetiology of alcoholism; and to evidence that problem drinking among women and the proportion of women alcoholics have greatly increased, as reflected for example in the disproportionate rise of the 'indirect indices' (deaths from cirrhosis and alcoholism, hospital admissions, drunkenness offences) among women (see Chapter 5). Figures presented later in this chapter based on our own experiences with alcoholics in the 1950s and 1960s indicate, however, that in the UK the proportion of female alcoholics was always relatively high; for example, in our experience (not only with the selected samples at Warlingham Park Hospital but also among out-patients) there was no less than one female to four male alcoholics [1]. Currently fashionable statements of an increase of female-male ratios of alcoholics from perhaps 1 woman to 7 or 8 men in the 1960s to, say 1 to 2 at present, in our experience greatly exaggerate the trend – although clearly there has been a marked increase of female alcoholism, possibly from approximately 1 in 4 in the 1950s and 1960s to more than 1 in 2 now. Such estimates about the numbers of female alcoholics in the 1960s seem based on experiences then gained in the new advice centres as established by voluntary (and highly efficient and understanding) workers and organisations within the community. It stands to reason that it might have taken women alcoholics in the 1960s (even more so than today) some time and considerable moral courage to present themselves at such centres, however sympathetically they were received (and their anonymity respected). There never was any dearth of alcoholic women applicants for admission to WPH in the 1950s and to the special female alcoholic ward in St Bernard's Hospital in the 1960s [2] although both were psychiatric hospitals and thus might not have been particularly attractive to women alcoholics. However, the feeling that in a special ward they would be understood by an experienced and sympathetic staff probably outweighed other considerations deterring women from entering such wards or units in psychiatric hospitals – anyhow women alcoholics were less averse to presenting themselves (at the time) at centres within the community which had only just been established.

To a certain extent the increased misuse of alcohol by women is probably related to their increased use of alcohol. A recent survey (1979) in the UK [3], estimated the number of regular women drinkers as 8½ millions. Marked differences were found between the sexes as to where they were buying drink. Only 7 per cent of the women, as against 14 per cent of the men, bought drink from public houses and public house off-licences, but slightly more often from ordinary off-licences (33 per cent) than men which sold drink to only 30 per cent of the men. The increased earning powers of women as well as their liking for alcoholic drink were apparently reflected in a greatly increased turnover in licensed supermarkets. One is not infrequently told by such women that they had no intention of buying drink when going into the super-market (to buy groceries) and that their attention was attracted by the displays of alcohol.

A rising proportion of female members has also been reported by AA; women are now reported (1980) to make up one third of AA members as against one fifth in 1972 [4].

Contrary to popular notions, misuse of alcohol by women is by no means a contemporary phenomen. 'A tendency that keeps cropping up in the writings of any period,' (says Keller [5]), is naïvely to blame the alcohol-related troubles on "modern", newly risen phenomena, such as the "new phenomenon" of alcoholism among women;' and he goes on to quote examples of female heavy drinking from many areas, such as Greece and Israel, Finland, and England in the fifteenth, sixteenth and eighteenth centuries. (Hogarth's famous 'Gin Lane' print shows a gin-sodden woman and the famous Virgin Mary Nursing Home for women suffering from alcoholism and other forms of drug dependence has just celebrated its centenary [6].)

Others, however, ascribe the recent increase largely to modern developments. Lowry, in her book *Guilt Cage* [7] believes that the 'heiresses of the suffragettes have gained an empire but do not always know how to lose a role'. Women's entry into the labour

Table 8
Drinking history of 77 female alcoholics (Warlingham Park Hospital 1952–6)
Average age of *first* occurrence of selected events

	Average age
First drink	19.7 yrs
First drunk	30.9 yrs
Ensured against shortage of drink	36.2 yrs
First amnesia	37.8 yrs
Frequent amnesia	37.9 yrs
Increased tolerance to drink	38.1 yrs
Sneaked drinks	38.2 yrs
Daytime drinks	38.5 yrs
Morning drinks	38.8 yrs
Solitary drinking	39.2 yrs
'Benders'	39.2 yrs
Attempted control by water waggon	40.5 yrs
Protected supply	40.2 yrs
Neglected food	41.5 yrs
Loss of control	41.7 yrs
Persistent tremors	42.1 yrs
Decreased tolerance to drink	43.1 yrs
First hospitalisation	43.3 yrs
Admitted defeat	45.4 yrs
Lowest point	46.3 yrs

force between 1951–76 has led to a situation where a quarter of the total work force consists of married women [8]. But despite their higher spending power women have often remained dependent on the husband's earnings because of greatly increased cost of living.

For some women being a housewife is not as fulfilling as they initially might have hoped. Middle-class female alcoholics in particular, often complain bitterly that they find housework boring and that they miss the satisfaction that they obtained prior to their marriage, from their creative and responsible jobs. They may feel that they have sacrificed a career in which they had not only found satisfaction but might also have achieved much more than their husband who has been able to continue his own career, often largely assisted by his wife who remains in the background. (As one such patient bitterly complained: 'My husband is professionally going from strength to strength while I am sitting at home, going from bottle to bottle.') The fact that the woman

Figure 4
Gin Lane (William Hogarth)

formerly had no chance of 'breaking out' into a job or profession may make some modern women perhaps more prey to regret and depression when she has chosen the traditional role of marriage instead of an exacting, responsible job.

However, women going out to work were shown to be more at risk from alcoholism than those who remain at home with their children, according to a study commissioned by the DHSS in 1977 [9]. Single women's heavier drinking was ascribed to the absence of responsibility for children, to increased spending power and increased opportunities. Women in the 34–54 age-bracket not going out to work but no longer having the responsibility of looking after children, were found to drink somewhat more heavily than those in the same age group not working but still looking after dependent children. This finding has been taken to indicate the importance of opportunity but it also is in line with statements made by many female alcoholic patients throughout the years that children leaving the home often leave their mothers with an emotional void as they no longer feel needed.

Another possible factor that may turn some women to drink has recently been put forward by the sociologist Shaw [10]; a lack of sexual identity and confusion as to her sex role arising from the recent sexual liberation of women. In view of persistent 'double standards' relating to promiscuous males and females, the woman will still often feel very guilty about sex (as she may be about her drinking). Again, nowadays many women may experience a feeling of being 'let down' or of being sexually inadequate or unfulfilled when listening to, or reading in, popular women's magazines, the currently fashionable preoccupation with, and a demand for, or the need for, enjoying sex and experiencing orgasm. This may possibly in some ways be a similar experience as that nowadays experienced by some men who may fear not coming up to modern girl's sex expectations and then turn to drink to appease their anxieties and fears.

Of some interest may be that the male sociologist's suggestion of doubts about sexual identity as a cause of female drinking, brought an immediate reply from a female sociologist [11]. There is nothing new, this lady wrote, in women having a lot of pressures on them, this has always been so. The pressures on one's grandmothers to make ends meet were very real indeed. Todays pressures are not greater, they are just different. Today's female alcoholics may not necessarily be career women but possibly, rather, housewives and mothers pressurised by an outside job,

Table 9
Percentage of 77 female alcoholics reporting occurrence of
selected events (WPH 1952–6)

	Percentage
Loss of control	85.9
Solitary drinking	85.7
Periods of despondency	85.7
Persistent remorse	84.4
Morning drinks	83.1
Felt more efficient after drinks	81.8
Rationalisation	79.2
Insomnia	74.0
Felt more sociable after drinks	72.7
Neglected food	72.7
Thought people showed contempt	72.7
Felt fear	71.4
Increased tolerance to drink	71.4
Sneaked drinks	70.1
Attempted control by water waggon	70.1
Amnesia	64.9
Protected supply	64.9
Persistent tremors	63.6
Daytime drinks	61.0
Ensured against shortage of drink	59.7
Decreased tolerance to drink	55.8
Behaved in a resentful manner	46.5
'Benders'	45.4
Acted in an aggressive manner	33.7
Contemplated suicide	33.7
Lost time from job	27.2
Lost job	19.4

who may find it easy to obtain relatively cheap alcoholic drink in
supermarkets and off-licences. Such women 'buying their booze
with the shopping' and drinking it (often secretly) at home are no
more 'liberated' than their grandmothers. They have just found
another-and-dangerous-way of trying to cope.

Many other factors may contribute to women's excessive
drinking, for example, premenstrual tension, dysmenorrhoea, or
menopausal depression; the wider acceptance of women's public
drinking, greater independence, economic freedom and spending
power, responsibility and status, all then often leading to worrying
identity conflict. In some lonely women it is the lack (or loss) of

husband that may be a reason for their drinking, in others it is dissatisfaction with, or boredom in, the marriage. As with male alcoholics, the married female drinker may often ascribe her drinking to marital unhappiness whereas the spouse, more often than not, blames the unhappy marriage on the partner's drinking. Initial failure to cope with problems in some cases will undoubtedly give rise to drinking which anaesthetises such a woman against her problems; on the other hand, in time, drink then reduces her coping ability even further, producing a progressive vicious circle. Nevertheless such a housewife may secretly drink for years without her husband finding out until she has reached a late phase of alcoholism.

The presence of constitutional factors in women's drinking may perhaps be reflected in the drinking during premenstrual tension, or menopause but possibly also in the finding that so often abstinence seems relatively easy to some women during pregnancy (an important issue in view of the risk of the 'alcohol foetal syndrome', see Chapter 14).

Again, women's tolerance to drink seems to be lower than that of men. This has led doctors, such as Roger Williams [12], head of the Liver Unit at King's College Hospital, London, to recommend strongly somewhat lower amounts of alcoholic drink to serve as safe upper limits in the case of regular women drinkers, compared to men: i.e. 3 double gins, or 3 pints of beer, or less than a bottle of wine. This would mean up to 60g of alcohol per day in place of 80g 'granted' to regular drinkers by the Royal College of Psychiatrists (see Introduction). There may thus be differences between the way the male and the female organism copes with alcohol: allowing for body weight the same dose may be more harmful to the woman drinker. Different immunological reactions have been thought to be a possible factor in the apparently greater vulnerability of heavily drinking women to the development of liver cirrhosis than of men.[1] This may become a progressively more important issue the more women take to regular drinking. According to a survey carried out in 1975 more than half the women were using pubs – and it is significant in this connection that in the period 1969–73 drunkenness convictions among young women (aged under thirty) nearly doubled. Regular drinking, perhaps partly for constitutional, immunological or hormonal reasons, may prove more damaging to the woman's health than equal amounts of alcohol would be for the man. It is important to think of possible liver damage even in those fairly heavily drinking

Table 10
Percentage of male and female alcoholics reporting certain
events among 192 male and 77 female alcoholic patients
(Warlingham Park Hospital 1952–6)

	Men	Women
Periods of despondency	77.1%	85.7%
Solitary drinking	74.5	85.7
Prolonged intoxications ('benders')	70.8	45.4
Sleeplessness	70.8	74.0
Contemplating geographical escape	63.0	58.4
Reproach by wife or husband resp.	62.5	59.7
Frequent amnesias ('blackouts')	60.9	50.6
Losing time from work due to drinking	57.8	27.2
Seeking medical advice for bodily ailment due to drinking	55.2	54.5
Losing job due to drinking	51.5	19.4
Walking out of jobs	50.5	20.8
Acting aggressively, dangerous to oneself or to others	47.3	33.7
Friends walking out	44.2	35.0
Contemplating suicide	41.1	33.7
Walking out on friends	37.5	27.2
Hospitalised for physical illness due to drinking	25.5	20.7
In trouble because of driving when drunk	22.9	11.7

women who are free from characteristic 'tell-tale' signs or fail to report any symptoms and who are not overtly drunk. Looking well groomed, and outwardly self-assured and contented is not a guarantee that such a woman may not be a heavy drinker. Inwardly she may feel hopeless, very guilty and even sinful about doing 'wrong' and, too ashamed to come clean, she may resort to the bottle even more. Awareness among doctors and other professional workers of situations such as these and tactful, discreet questioning might possibly encourage women to part with their guilty secret more readily and face up to the need to take constructive action.

Therapeutic and prognostic aspects in women alcoholics

For many hundreds of years, women, like men, have not only enjoyed drink but have often misused it. However, the criticism of a 'male dominated approach to science' [16] certainly seems to apply to the subject of alcoholism and its treatment, as practically all the general pronouncements in this area are derived from a consideration of male drinkers, and the findings rather uncritically generalised to women. The assumption that 'the' typical alcoholic is a 'he' has in recent years become increasingly incorrect, seeing that all over the world there has been a relatively greater rise in the proportion of female problem drinkers and alcoholics. National ratios of male and female alcoholics may be misleading in that there are great differences between subgroups, for example, this ratio having found to be 1:1 among private patients but eleven males for every one female in a prison population in recent American studies [17]. Male-female ratios of 'inebriety' quoted in the past now seem grossly out-of-date, as for example, those given in Jellinek's pioneering work *Alcohol Addiction and Chronic Alcoholism* (1942) [18], such as Norway 23:1, Switzerland 12:1 and USA 6:1. Estimates in the USA, for example, now talk of a ratio of approximately four men for every one woman [19]. In England it may be about 2:1 or even less. The numbers of women with a serious drink problem in the USA may now amount to possibly two million [20], and in the UK between 250,000–400,000. Surely the mere numerical size of the problem therefore has now reached such dimensions that the subject of female alcoholics has to be approached as an independent entity and not merely as a relatively insignificant appendage to their male counterparts.

The present position in this area has been well summed up in a contribution in a recent, excellent book *Alcoholism Problems in Women and Children* by Greenblatt and Schuckitt [21]: there is scant scientific literature related to women and alcohol because the preponderance of experimental studies related to acute and chronic effects of alcohol have evaluated only male counter-participants. Therefore the practitioner who is interested in understanding and treating women with alcohol problems has little scientific data on which to base treatment approaches.

Thus when discussing treatment of alcoholism in women one finds oneself in considerable difficulties. Under these circumstances there may perhaps be some excuse for relying not only on some relevant findings noted in the literature but also on one's own impressions and experiences in the treatment of several thousand female alcoholics in a wide variety of set-ups in the Greater London area: National Health Service and private patients seen in their own home; out-patient clinics; special

OP clinics for alcoholics, such as the St Marylebone Clinic and the Paddington Clinic; or the OP teaching clinic of a Teaching Hospital (University College Hospital); special alcohol units (Warlingham Park Hospital, St Bernard's Hospital); and the special Alcoholism and Drug Dependence Centre exclusively for women at Spelthorne St Mary; private nursing homes, including, in the main, patients treated individually at the Regent's Park Nursing Home or by therapeutic community and group therapy methods at a private alcoholic clinic, alcoholic women seen at Holloway Prison and subsequently treated in hospital; patients seen in consultation in various London teaching and non-teaching general hospitals, in hostels, etc. It goes without saying that these experiences have confirmed that, like male alcoholics, so also female alcoholics are a very heterogenous group. There is no such person as 'the' female alcoholic; quite different personalities with widely varying psychological and physical make-up who have taken alcoholic drinks of varying composition and concentration for different reasons under different conditions have become alcoholics [22]. Clearly therefore not only may there be important differences between male and female alcoholics but among the latter themselves there are not only many different individual personalities but possibly subgroups so different from each other that generalisations from one to the other may be as suspect as those made from male to female alcoholics. At any rate, as in male alcoholics, it seems extremely unlikely that one and the same treatment modality should be the best for all female alcoholics; it would seem more likely that the best approach at the present juncture should consist in assessment of the factors most significant in the given individual and then applying a combination of therapies best suited in her case [22]. As among men, a large number of factors such as age, social class, marital status, the degree of emotional and social stability, intelligence, the drinking pattern and the stage reached in her drinking career, psychological and physical condition, her living environment, use of other drugs, the type of help available locally, etc. may all have to be taken in consideration in the individual case when deciding on the type and venue of treatment.

Obviously all these factors are at work in men and women alcoholics. Are male and female alcoholics and their treatment requirements fundamentally very similar to each other or are they markedly different? Is there any definite evidence indicating that women drinkers as a group, or certain subgroups require a therapeutic approach different from men, or is it rather a difference between individuals independent of their sex? A search of the literature as well as our own experiences indicate quite a number of factors – psychological, social or biological factors, manifestations and complications of their drinking behaviours, etc. – which may be different in men and women alcoholics. Unfortunately, the experiences of various observers often vary a great deal from each but we would like to discuss some factors often found different in the case of male and female alcoholics, and therefore possibly having implications for treatment and prognosis.

Drinking history

The frequency of occurrence and the age of onset of certain features have often been found to be markedly different in male and female alcoholics. Tables 4 (p. 88) and 10 (p. 164) show some such differences as they were noted among 192 male and 77 female in-patients (predominantly middle-class) treated by us at the Warlingham Park Hospital Alcoholic Unit between 1952 and 1956 [24]. In general these early findings correspond to those related in the literature and to our own experience with patients treated in the 1960s and 1970s. A hypothetical average alcoholic woman had started to drink just before she had reached the age of twenty. Five years later she drank regularly in moderation but had begun to get drunk on occasions after the age of thirty-one. Another five years later premonitory signs of alcoholism had made their first appearance, such as surreptitious drinking, drinking 'in anticipation of a possible shortage', 'alcoholic amnesias'. These were very shortly afterwards followed by more obvious signs. Prolonged periods of intoxication occurred first at an average age of thirty-nine years, 'loss of control' at forty-two years of age. The rapid downhill path continued, and the first hospital admission for alcoholism occurred at that time, but the average female alcoholic did not reach her 'lowest point' and did not admit that her drinking was beyond control until she was in her mid-forties.

From the difference of nearly three years between the average onset of prolonged drinking bouts and of 'loss of control', it seems that quite a few women remained in a state of intoxication for days, despite the fact that they had not yet lost control within a particular drinking situation. Such behaviour in a woman, even more than in a man, means a violation of every social and moral code of conduct, and implies either the presence of a grossly disturbed 'pre-alcoholic' personality, or the demoralisation of a basically less disturbed personality by years of excessive drinking. The presence of such gross (primary or secondary) personality disturbances may be an important factor in the poorer response to treatment in certain women as compared to men.

While the symptomatology of male and female alcoholism in many respects may be 'quite similar', as indicated in several larger tables published in 1961 [23] (Tables 2, 3, 4 (pp. 78, 83, 88), there seem to be important differences. For example, in a 1977 review Edith S Gomberg [19] summed up various characteristics given in the literature as differing in men and female alcoholics (and largely corresponding to our own findings between 1952–78). Women started to drink later and had a later onset of alcohol problems; they had a lesser incidence of 'blackouts', but, in general, more suicide attempts. Women were more often solitary drinkers but experienced 'benders' less often than men.

Male alcoholics, who (Tables 2, 7, 10) showed aggressive drunken driving behaviour much more frequently than women, were more often arrested for alcohol-related action and also lost jobs and friends much more often than female drinkers. Thus the impact of female alcoholic behaviour, in contrast to that of the man, is exerted at home, within the family circle, rather than on general society: women alcoholics less often upset friends or come to the notice of employers, and less often fall foul of the law. Women alcoholics often drink secretly at home rather than in pubs or with friends (it may be noteworthy that in our experience even women alcoholics with undoubted 'loss of control' commonly manage to restrict their drinking – when dining out in their husband's company or that of friends – to one or two drinks [22, 25]. Under these circumstances outsiders will find it more difficult to spot a woman's drink problem early on, and the courts and industry will be in a less favourable position than in the case of male problem drinkers to initiate the therapeutic and rehabilitation process [22].

As clearly indicated in Table 4 and confirmed by many observers [19, 21] the course of alcoholism is much more telescoped in the female as compared to the male drinker. But though the downgrade path of the female alcoholic is much more rapid and theoretically should be much more noticeable to her husband, it is remarkable how often the husband relates that for years he did not suspect that his wife was drinking even if in retrospect he feels he could have done so. Reproach of the female alcoholic by her husband did not occur more frequently than that of the male drinker by his wife, in fact, it is often reported that such husbands for quite a while are much less keen on pressing their drinking wives into treatment than is the case of the wife of an alcoholic husband. Possibly the feeling of guilt and shame within a family may be even greater where the wife or mother is the alcoholic than when it is the husband or father – and thus the 'skeleton in the cupboard' remains hidden even longer from the public gaze.

At the same time – whether the acting-out behaviour of the female drinker may too be explosive, whether her goading tongue may be more hurtful than the male drinker's battering hand, or whether the male spouse is much less of a glutton for punishment and much less emotionally resilient than his female counterpart – the proportion of divorced alcoholic women has been found by many observers to be much higher than that of divorced alcoholic men and the same holds good, incidentally, for the proportions of alcoholic widows and widowers respectively. Among our WPH patients, there were 10.5 per cent divorced alcoholic males as against 23.5 per cent divorced women, 3 per cent widowers as against 17.7 per cent widows [23]. Among the women alcoholic patients only a few were spinsters but whereas of the originally married men the majority were still living with their wives, of the originally married women two-thirds had lost their husband by death, divorce or separation – a significantly higher proportion than among men. As noted in our report at the time, 'loneliness was among women a factor frequently given as a reason for excessive drinking and often proving an obstacle in the effort to maintain sobriety after discharge'.

Loneliness – like depression, which also according to literature and our experiences is a much more important factor in female as compared to male alcoholics – could of course be a consequence as well as one of the contributory causes of alcoholism. At any rate the relatively high incidence of loneliness [26] and depression [17] constitutes an important complicating factor in particular among female alcoholics and has to be carefully considered in any overall treatment plan. An often heard *crie-de-coeur* from middle-aged alcoholic (divorced or widowed) women is 'what is the point of my stopping drinking – nobody cares whether I am alive or not!'

The feeling of 'no longer being needed' is by no means confined to the divorced or widowed; it is also frequently given as the reason for the onset of heavy drinking by the woman whose children have grown-up and left home ('empty nest syndrome'). Often it may be accompanied by boredom – which again seems much more common in female than in male alcoholics. There is for example, as already mentioned, the plight of the wife left on her own at home for long stretches, either because the ambitious husband is 'married' to his job, or he is often away on assignments for days or weeks, etc. Emotional and sensitive (or also sex-starved) women who find that they cannot communicate to their 'cold' and less sensitive husbands, are in some aspects in a similar quandary (although of course one also comes across female alcoholics (perhaps somewhat frigid) who ascribe their heavy drinking to the 'insatiable demands' of their allegedly 'oversexed' husbands.

Many other examples clearly indicate that often merely helping the alcoholic to give up drinking is not enough, that the factors contributing to her drinking have to be considered and dealt with as far as possible (or the patient be helped to learn to live with those that cannot be altered), and in particular that, as in the case of the male alcoholic, treatment of the alcoholic is not complete unless the spouse (and often other family members) are brought into the course of treatment [22]. Especially in the case of the alcoholic woman there is also emotional neglect of children who may require help in their own right. In this connection the possibility of the (long neglected but recently resurrected) 'foetal alcohol syndrome' must not be overlooked when dealing with an alcoholic woman.

In view of alcoholism being an illness closely affecting the whole family certain aspects often mentioned in regard to the *husband of the female alcoholic* deserve mentioning. Female alcoholics much more often than male alcoholics are found to have an alcoholic spouse [26, 27, 28]. Thus James [27] found that in a group of female AA members 23 per cent had alcoholic husbands and 18 per cent had heavily drinking husbands; and in a Swedish sample reported by Dahlgren [28] 51 per cent of alcoholic women had an alcoholic spouse, as against only 13 per cent of the alcoholic men. In general, much less research has been carried out regarding the husband of the female alcoholic as compared to the male drinker's wife. Estes and Baker [29], in a recent review, mention only two studies [30, 31] in the literature with research focusing on the male spouse. Such a husband may use denial of his wife's drinking even more frequently than the wife of an alcoholic. This may reflect the double standard adopted by society towards female as compared to male heavy drinking. But the husband may later abandon his alcoholic wife, though some husbands – like wives of alcoholic men – may react like martyrs or try to control their wives' drinking. Clearly all such reactions on the part of the husband may all serve to accelerate the alcoholic's downward path. A study carried out by W Flintoff in [32] in the early 1960s among the husbands of our patients at the St Bernard's Hospital alcoholism unit showed three groups of husbands who had stuck to their alcoholic wives. Those who had married at a time when their wives were already heavy drinkers, usually had marked personality difficulties of their own: for instance they were neurotics, psychopaths, heavy drinkers, had physical disabilities or sex problems, etc. Among those husbands whose wives had become alcoholics only since their marriage, there were two main groups.

(a)   Some were a few or many years older than their wives and dominated them, the wives sometimes able to 'talk back' only with the help of 'Dutch courage'. These husbands may often be successful business men but insecure and anxious about their position; or they may themselves be heavy drinkers often treating their alcoholic wives like children.

(b)   The second group among husbands of women becoming alcoholics after marriage consisted of intelligent, but very rigid and obsessional men completely under the thumb of their wives whose acting-out they tolerated in a manner quite in contrast to their own inhibited behaviour.

Clearly, as among alcoholic women (and men) so also among their spouses there are many different personalities. Especially in those whose own personality problems preceded (and may sometimes even have precipitated) their marriage to a woman who was already by then a heavy drinker, the drinking female has little chance of marked permanent improvement if assistance is not also provided for her spouse.

   Of obvious implication for treatment is the common finding that habitual *misuse of drugs* other than alcohol seems relatively much more common in female than among male alcoholics. Among our WPH patients in the 1950s, of 200 men 24.5 per cent had misused other drugs, of seventy-seven women approximately 36 per cent [23]. In the 1950s and the early 1960s it was in the main barbiturates (and amphetamines) whereas, since the late 1960s and 1970s tranquillisers have started to play an increasing role. Higher rates

of drug misuse among women have also been noted in the literature [27, 28]. In our experience the risk of misuse of other drugs is
greater among those whose heavy drinking originally started for
mainly psychological reasons than among those in whom it was
mainly sociogenic (e.g. as members of a drink-prone occupation
or 'subculture' [22, 23]). Such habitual misuse of drugs apart from
alcohol in the given female patient, may thus indicate the importance of psychological factors and a greater need for (brief) psychotherapy. (Though, here too, the 'double standard' of society may
encourage such an alcoholic woman to take recourse to tablets
which can be more easily stored in the handbag than the whisky
bottle.) From the prophylactic angle, in view of the considerable
risk of superadded drug misuse and other drug dependence, especially in the case of alcoholic women, it is imperative that the
doctor, particularly in the case of 'vulnerable' women, be on his
guard and restrict the prescribing of psychoactive drugs to a
minimum. On the other hand, one cannot be a perfectionist and
especially in the alcohol withdrawal phase, drugs such as the
benzodiazepines, or in more severe cases, chlormethiazole [22],
will be necessary and helpful but should be stopped as soon as
possible.

As with the incidence and type of social consequences, differences have also been found among male and female alcoholics in
the incidence and severity of *medical complications*. By and large
they seem to be more serious in the case of women. DT has usually
been found to occur mainly among men (but not always – Sclare
[33] found it more common in Glasgow among female than male
alcoholics for example) but liver damage seems to affect the
female drinker much more frequently. Among our WPH alcoholics, Kay *et al*. [34] found a much higher percentage of
abnormal liver function tests among women than among men.
Women drinkers have also been found to suffer more often than
men from anaemia [35, 36] peripheral neuropathy [36] and to be
not only psychologically more disturbed but also more prone to
develop alcohol-related physical diseases in general and more
quickly [38], and to show an even higher excess mortality than
male alcoholics. In Sweden for example, Dahlgren [28] found that
after age and sex standardisation there was a statistically significantly higher mortality rate among female (5.6) than among
male (3.0) alcoholics.

Among factors often found to have some bearing on the
therapeutic approach and prognosis are age and social class. On

the basis of age groups most often affected female alcoholics have been classified by some observers [19, 39] into adolescent drinkers, drinkers in their early twenties and those in their late forties. Adolescent problem drinkers and alcoholics emotionally usually very immature, tending to act out, often also misusing other drugs, require a great deal of patience and tolerance from the therapist. As in the case of male problem drinkers and alcoholics so also among female alcoholics nowadays an increasingly higher proportion of younger people is being seen, mainly in their twenties. Of 268 male and female WPH alcoholics in the 1950s, 5.2 per cent were aged thirty years and younger, of our 745 male and female alcoholic patients admitted to the St Bernard's alcohol unit in the 1960s 8.5 per cent (a difference statistically significant at a level of 5–10 per cent). Similarly, the proportion of young female alcoholics (under thirty years) admitted to the Spelthorne St Mary Nursing Home rose from 3.4 per cent (thirteen out of a total of 379) in the 1950s to 4.3 per cent (fourteen out of a total of 327) in the 1960s. Nevertheless, even today most women alcoholics coming for treatment are probably still in their thirties or forties (twenty years ago the mean age of female alcoholics admitted to the WPH Unit was 48.2, that of male alcoholics 44.7 years) [23].

The middle-aged female alcoholic is the one usually described to be the most typical: lonely, often depressed; drinking on her own and, in contrast to men, not a member of a drinking group, though occasionally she may drink with her alcoholic husband or with another lonely female drinking companion. Her depression may be reactive (the fear of her life 'as a woman' coming to a close, may occasionally be a contributory factor) or involution (menopausal in origin). The finding that many women alcoholics ascribe the onset of their heavy drinking as coinciding with the period of premenstrual tension or the menopause reflects the importance of special biological factors in female alcoholics, alongside the more often described psychosocial ones, such as 'sex role confusion', economic factors etc.

One interesting and generally ignored group in our experience constitute *elderly* female problem drinkers and alcoholics, aged sixty-five to over eighty [40, 41]. In contrast to the usual sex ratio among alcoholics (in the 1960s and early 1970s approximately 2–3 M/1F), among elderly problem drinkers seen by us this ratio was reversed into 2M/3F, with widows being particularly common among them. Some of these elderly women had been heavy drinkers all their adult lives, in others experiences such as bereavement, or feelings of loneliness and boredom were involved in triggering off reactive excessive drinking in or after the mid-sixties. On the whole, personality factors were less important in the causation of problem drinking among the elderly than social factors, so that preventive measures (forestalling psychological and socio-economic strain and stress) and therapeutic intervention could frequently be of great help. In the other age groups too it is of course equally important to keep the predisposing and precipitating factors in mind when drawing up the treatment plan.

Similar considerations apply to *social class*. The middle-aged, middle-class housewife with a 'respectable' background, financially often quite secure even when divorced or widowed (the type often seen in private practice but also in some National Health Service Units) has usually a better prognosis than the somewhat younger woman often deprived in childhood and coming from a broken home. As among men, the high degree of emotional and social instability among these younger alcoholic women makes their outlook much more problematic than that of the middle-aged woman. A wide range of measures of long-lasting social and emotional support will be required – on top of direct treatment of their alcoholism – in this unfortunate group.

As regards prognosis, most observers have found it to be worse in women than men [24, 28, 35, 36]. A follow-up over an observation period of six months to 3½ years after discharge among our WPH patients in the 1950s showed among 150 men 68 per cent recovered or improved, among women only approximately 50 per cent. (In the 1960s and 1970s this appeared considerably higher.) There were a few studies however which did not show any difference in treatment outcome between men and women and one researcher [43] even found a significantly higher improvement rate among women.

In our discussion at the time it seemed the poorer treatment results with our female patients at WPH were possibly due to factors such as 'the possibly greater pre-alcoholic personality maladjustment in these women, the greater frequency of precipitating (environmental) stresses in female alcoholics, loneliness following marriage breakup more common in female alcoholics, or menopausal difficulties' [24]. The double standard attitude of society to heavy male and female drinkers respectively in the past probably meant that, in the main, it was emotionally unstable women or those with abnormal environmental stresses who exposed themselves to social censure by heavy drinking. The gradual erosion of such double standards may paradoxically make the prognosis of many of the alcoholic women seem relatively more favourable than in the past. On the one hand with women gradually moving out of the home and in the business and professional world assuming similar roles and rights as men, they may also expose themselves to extra responsibilities and anxieties, as well as temptations. This, as well as the finding that younger and younger girls in increasing numbers take to drinking, make it likely that in the future probably the number of female alcoholics will continue to increase. On the other hand, with increasing acceptance of public drinking by women, probably an increasing proportion of relatively stable women may expose themselves to the risk of becoming dependent on alcohol, mainly as a consequence of habitual heavy drinking. The likely higher proportion of relatively stable personalities among the higher numbers of female alcoholics in the future may consequently mean a relatively better prognosis for the hypothetical average female alcoholic of the future.

It could of course be argued that the usual finding of women alcoholics faring worse in treatment may in part be due to the fact (or artifact) of quite inadequate research in the field of female alcoholism and the failure to try to correlate research findings as regards background and personality factors of women drinkers with the provision of special treatment centres geared to their particular needs. There can of course be no doubt as to the need for research directed specially at problems which are particular to women alcoholics and problem drinkers, in view of the relative lack of such studies and the often conflicting results.

Would treatment results be better if separate facilities were to be made available for women or if female alcoholics would be mainly under the care of women therapists? It could after all be argued that so far women alcoholics have been treated mainly by male therapists in facilities designed primarily for male patients. Again there is little evidence at this juncture to answer such questions. Edith Gomberg's reply [44] to these questions is that, 'it is a matter of opinion, and it is my opinion that while some all-female residential units and all-female therapy groups should be available, segregation of therapy by sex seems unnecessary'.

Our own experiences as far as residential treatment and group therapy are concerned were gained mostly in units where the sexes were treated together. Though living in separate wards for male and female alcoholics respectively, the great majority of group therapy sessions were mixed though from time to time all-female groups were established. For what it is worth on the basis of these experiences our view would largely correspond to Gomberg's [44] with the proviso that more often than not segregation seems not only unnecessary but undesirable. Men and women alcoholics in the same group often seemed to act as mutual catalysts and cross-fertilisers of discussions; in particular women patients, with whom I often discussed this question, used to come out strongly in favour of mixed groups.

Similarly, as regards the importance of the therapist's sex, in twenty years' experiences of having both male and female doctors at various times in charge of the female alcoholic ward at St Bernard's Hospital, the more popular and successful ones predominantly happened to be the male therapists. What clearly seemed to matter most was the individual doctor's attitude and ability to establish a helping relationship to these female patients, and not his or her sex. What also may be of interest is the finding that on the whole the same therapist – whether male or female – proved either more or less popular with both male and female patients and male and female nursing staff alike.

Conclusion

Female alcoholics like their male counterparts form a very heterogeneous population obviously composed of various personalities and probably various subgroups. In view of the depth of research in the subject of female alcoholism it is at present impossible to say whether by and large female alcoholics require somewhat varying approaches from the males, or whether, as more likely on the basis of our own experiences, the difference is that between individuals, independent of their sex. While many features and symptoms are common to male and female alcoholics, in certain aspects there seem to be important differences – psychological, social and biological in origin – with likely implications on treatment planning. At present women alcoholics seem by and large to constitute a psychologically more unstable group and also to suffer from more medical complications than men. Nevertheless even today a great many women alcoholics can be helped by the available techniques; and many of our female patients have played a very active and leading role in organising after-care meetings, social reunions etc. With the progressive lessening of double standards and increasing emancipation of women, in future among the increasing numbers of women alcoholics one might paradoxically also expect a much higher proportion of relatively stable personalities among them, with correspondingly better prognosis than in the past. This likelihood that the typical alcoholic of the future may soon be a 'she' as frequently as a 'he' may have important implications for the planning of preventive and some aspects of the therapeutic programmes. Awareness of this fact should also raise the suspicion-level of doctors and other professionals and lead to earlier diagnosis and earlier institution of therapeutic measures.

Notes

[1] Seeing that women's livers are more vulnerable to alcohol than men's livers, and that spirits are more potent than beer, the finding of a study reported in a recent newspaper article [14] may add another important reason for the increase of women's alcoholism. Among men (frequenting pubs) almost 90 per cent favoured beer whereas half the female regular drinkers consumed spirits. Findings such as that of a rise in death rates for liver cirrhosis between 1970–8 of 243 per cent and 36 per cent among women and men respectively may thus be explainable in part due to the activity of the 'agent' as well as to features of 'host' (personality) and environment [15].

[2] Based on a paper read at a plenary session at the 24th ICAA institute, Zurich, June 1978, and reprinted here by kind permission of the ICAA.

References

1   Glatt, M M (1955), *Brit. J. Addict.*, 52, 55
2a Glatt, M M and Judge, C G (1961), *Med. J. Austral.* (22 April), 590
2b Glatt, M M (1967), *Brit. J. Addict.*, 62, 35
3   ITC Magazines' Survey (1979), reported in *All. News* January, February 1980
4   *All. News*, January, February 1980
5   Keller, M (1976) in *Alcohol and Alcohol Problems*, ed. Filstead W J, .5–28
6   Sister Mildred Rebecca (1970) in *Modern Trends in Drug Dependence and Alcoholism*, ed. Phillipson, R V, London, Butterworths, 206–22
7   Lowry, S (1980), *Guilt Cage*, London, Elm Tree Books
8   Cole, E, quoted from Lowry, S (ref. 7)
9   *Drinking in England and Wales* (1980), London, HMSO

10 Shaw, S (1980) in *Women and Alcohol*, Camberwell Ccl. on Alcoholism, Tavistock Foundation, London, NJ
11 Chappell, H, *Standard*, 14 October 1980
12 Saunders, J B, Davis, M and Williams, R (1981), *Brit. med. J.*, 282, 1140
13 *Brit. med. J.* (L.A.) 1977, 4, 1371
14 Quoted from Mary Kenny, *Sunday Telegraph*, 21 December 1980
15 Glatt, M M (1979), *Brit. J. Alcohol and Alcoholism*, 14 (2), 77
16 Jones, B M and Jones, M K (1976) in *Alcoholism Problems in Women and Children*, eds Greenblatt, M and Schuckitt, M A, NY, London, Grune and Stratton, 103
17 Schuckitt, M A and Morrissey, E R (1976), *ibid*, 5
18 Jellinek, E M (ed.) (1942), *Alcohol Addiction and Chronic Alcoholism*, New Haven, Yale University Press, 48
19 Gomberg, E S (1977) in *Alcoholism: Development, Consequences and Intervention*, eds Estes, N J and Heinemann, M E, St Louis, C V Mosby Cy, 174
20 Wilsnack, S C (1976) in *Alcoholism Problems in Women and Children* (ref. 167)
21 Greenblatt, M and Schuckitt, M A (1976), *Alcoholism Problems in Women and Children*, NY, London, Grune and Stratton
22 Glatt, M M (1974), *A Guide to Addiction and its Treatment – Drugs, Society and Man*, Med. and Techn. Publ., Lancaster
23 Glatt, M M (1961), *Acta Psych. Scand.*, 37, 88
24 Glatt, M M (1961), *Acta Psych. Scand.*, 37, 143
25 Glatt, M M (1976), *Brit. J. Addict.*, 71, 135
26 Mulford, H A (1977), *Quart. J. Stud. Alc.*, 38, 1624
27 James, J E (1975), *ibid*, 36, 1564
28 Dahlgren, L (1977), *Acta Psych. Scand.*, 56, 81
29 Estes, N J and Baker, J M (1977) in *Alcoholism: Development, Consequences and Interventions*, eds Estes, N J and Heinemann, ME, St Louis, C V Mosby Cy, 186
30 Busch, H, Kormencay, E and Feuerlein, W (1973), *Brit. J. Addict.*, 68, 179
31 Rimmer, J (1974), *Quart. J. Stud. Alc.*, 35, 281
32 Flintoff, W (1963), *Brit. J. Addict.*, 59, 81
33 Sclare, A B (1975), *Journal of Alcoholism*, 10, 134
34 Kay, W W, Murfitt, K C and Glatt, M M (1959), *J. Ment. Sci.*, 105, 748
35 Krasner, N, Davis, M, Portmann, B and Williams, R (1977), *Brit. med. J.*, i, 1497
36 Morgan, M Y and Sherlock, S (1977), *ibid*, i, 939
37 *The Lancet* (1977), Annotation, ii, 1015
38 Ashley, M J, Olin, J S, le Riche, W H, Kornassowski, A, Schmidt, W and Rankin, J G (1977), *Archs intern. Med.*, 137, 883
39 Cahalan, D, Cisin, I H and Crossley, J M (1969), *American Drinking Practices*, New Haven, College and University Press Services

40 Rosin, A J and Glatt, M M (1971), *Quart. J. Stud. Alc.*, 32, 53
41 Glatt, M M, Rosin, A J and Jauhar, P (1978), quoted from Glatt, M
    M, *Alcoholism: Clin. and Exper. Research*, 2, 23
42 Beckman, L J (1976) in *Alcoholism Problems in Women and
    Children*, eds Greenblatt, M and Schuckitt, M A (see ref. 16), 65
43 Davis, H G (1976) quoted from Beckman, L J (ref. 42), 75
44 Gomberg, E (1976) in *Alcoholism: Interdisciplinary Approaches to
    an Enduring Problem*, ed. Tarter, R E and Sugerman, A A, London,
    Amsterdam, Addison-Wesley Publ. Cy., 603
45 Jones, K L, Smith, D W, Ulleland, C N and Streissguth, A P (1973),
    The Lancet, i, 1267

7

Young Alcoholics

1 Young alcoholics

In the past the majority of alcoholics in clinics, hospitals and at Alcoholics Anonymous meetings were middle-aged men and women well into their forties. Such people had, however, often become alcoholics many years earlier; but they were able to go on functioning and to put up a struggle against total demoralisation and desocialisation for many years, until gradually their mental and physical resistance had become undermined.

Occasionally, one had already, in the past, seen people who had become alcoholics at a much younger age. Among the alcoholics seen at Warlingham Park Hospital about twenty-five years ago, already at the relatively early age of twenty-four, one-third of male alcoholics had experienced their first 'amnesia', nearly a quarter had frequent amnesias, about a fifth drank surreptitiously and were frequently drunk at daytime, or had by then 'lost control', had started morning or solitary drinking and behaved aggressively. More than one-tenth had at that age already experienced prolonged intoxication and had protected their drink supplies. In 7 per cent, excess drinking had led to hospital admission before the age of twenty-four years [1].

The appearance of symptoms of possibly grave portent at such an early age might very occasionally be a consequence of a more definite mental disorder or mental subnormality. At that time when, unlike today, heavy drinking was still rare among the young, more often it probably just denoted a serious degree of emotional instability as, for example, psychopathy. Such people, therefore, were either more vulnerable or seemed unable to bring into play internal resistance or assets which could inhibit the rapid progress of alcoholism once it had started.

In this minority, therefore, personality maladjustment may usually be primary and may have led secondarily to excessive drinking; whereas in the great majority of middle-aged and older patients it took long-continued heavy alcohol consumption to bring about the deterioration of personality and of social conduct. Such considerations would serve to explain that prognosis in the average young alcoholic in the past was generally worse than in the middle-aged. However, one occasionally also meets later-life alcoholics without any manifestations of psychopathy who feel they have been 'alcoholics' practically from the word go; almost as soon as they had started to drink they felt an extraordinary desire to continue ('primary alcoholics').

Another sign denoting the greater psychopathological deviations in yesterday's average young alcoholic may perhaps be seen in the findings that, whereas among *unselected* samples of individuals who attempt suicide older age groups preponderate, the relatively young age groups predominated among suicidal alcoholics at Warlingham Park Hospital in the 1950s [13].

Abuse of drugs, formerly the prerogative of (middle-aged) adults, had, during the 1960s, become widespread amongst youngsters [2]. Recently, however, it is mainly alcohol misuse and alcoholism that have greatly increased among younger age groups.

Coinciding with the emergence of the drug problem among the young there had been a temporary lull in 1963–4 in the steady increase of drunkenness offences of youngsters so that Prys Williams at the time raised the question whether juvenile drunkenness had improved only because drugs had emerged 'as alternative and substitute passports to Nirvana'. However, subsequently there followed an increase among the young both of drug abuse and of juvenile drunkenness offences. The evaluation of the figures is complicated by the 'bulge' in Britain's teenage population in the mid-sixties following the immediate post-war period birth increase, but the number of convictions of drunkenness among persons under twenty-one years of age has crept up gradually from over 5100 in 1956 to 7600 in 1960, 13,000 in 1970 and over 18,800 in 1975, in England and Wales; the corresponding rise among the Scottish under-age group, was from 347 (1956), 553 (1960), 1026 (1970) to 1420 (1975). There was also increasing drunkenness among the under-eighteen age group; and after a decrease between 1977 and 1978 a considerable increase (of about 6 per cent) seemed again likely between 1978 and 1979 [3]. Corresponding figures for girls aged under twenty-one in England and Wales were:

258 in 1956 (Scotland: 28)
303 in 1960 (Scotland: 22)
589 in 1970 (Scotland: 112)
1209 in 1975 (Scotland: 185)

The most recent survey carried out in 1980, interviewing a sample of 2000 men and women in England and Wales under the auspices of the DHSS, indicates that one man in eight (in the under twenty-five age group) and one woman in twenty-five [4] regularly consumes quantities of alcohol dangerous for their health, considering the safe limits suggested by the R.C. Psych. Report (see p. 8). Such dangerous drinking was twice as common among this younger age group than their father's generation. Regular drinking started at a much earlier age than in the past. Out of ten drinking young people, seven had had a drink in a pub before having reached the minimum legal age of eighteen. In contrast to the over fifty-five age group who remembered the onset of their drinking as having been over twenty years of age, the under-twenty-fives had started to drink when they were sixteen. Whereas among the older age groups, 6 per cent of the men and 1 per cent of the women drank more than the Royal College of Psychiatrists' 'safe limits', the corresponding percentages among the 18–24 year olds, were 13 per cent of the men and 4 per cent of the women.

This official study thus clearly confirms the onset and prevalence of dangerous drinking habits at an earlier age. The survey, for example, also found little respect for drink-driving laws: among the men, 25 per cent admitted having driven home during the preceding week after having taken enough drink to take them beyond the legal blood alcohol limit.

However, regarding the young drinkers, other investigations paint an even more disturbing picture. Commenting on the official survey, R F Kinden [5], Director of the Somerset Council on Alcoholism, reported on the findings of a Somerset survey in 1979 involving 5000 children. Of boys and girls aged 13–15, 78 per cent and 73 per cent respectively, and of those aged 16–19 years, 94 per cent (boys) and 92 per cent (girls) admitted to regular drinking, often in pubs. Of the 1800 drinkers 45 per cent had been drunk at least once in the previous six months, two-thirds of them more than once.

Quite frequently there are nowadays stories about lunchtime drinking among school children. According to a newspaper report in December 1980 Mr David Ennals [6], former Minister of Health (whose wife is a school teacher) told of school children unable to concentrate on their afternoon lessons after having had drinks at lunchtime.

Another point of interest in this connection is that more young-sters take alcoholic drink and begin to do so at an earlier age. For example, middle-aged alcoholics (and moderate drinkers) at Warlingham Park Hospital in the 1950s, and at St Bernard's Hospital in the 1960s, stated that they had taken their first drink way back in the 1930s at an average age between seventeen and nineteen years, which contrasts rather sharply with today's state of affairs of most youngsters having had experience with alcoholic drink by the age of fifteen. Thus a study of drinking habits of teenagers, aged fifteen to eighteen, carried out in 1960–1 by post-graduate students of the Public Health Department of the London School of Hygiene and Tropical Medicine showed that 6 per cent of the total (630 boys and 480 girls) had taken alcohol before the age of 10 and 90 per cent of both sexes had done so by the age of 15. This finding also is in contrast to the result of a study of ordinary adults' drinking habits obtained by the Hulton Readership Survey in 1950 when about one-third of persons *over* sixteen were found to be total abstainers, i.e. 40 per cent of the women and 20 per cent of the men.

On the other hand, similar findings to the English teenagers' study of 1960–1 were reported among North American high-school students by Maddox and McCall [7] (1964): of nearly 2000 teenagers, boys and girls, 92 per cent had tasted alcohol at some time; and Lennard Goldberg [8] (1968) reported from Sweden that in two Stockholm schools 60 per cent of approximately 300 school children (aged sixteen) had been intoxicated at some time. Over half of the English boys and one-third of the girls (aged eighteen) stated that at some time or other they had had 'too much to drink'; and 40 per cent of the boys and 18 per cent of the girls were by then 'regular' drinkers. More than 90 per cent of the parents knew about their children's drinking and apparently most of them approved of it [11].

Similar findings were obtained by a four-months survey of the social drinking habits of youngsters carried out during 1969 by the London Borough of Hammersmith's Health Education Service under the direction of Dr A D C S Cameron, the Hammersmith Medical Officer of Health. The average age at which young males under twenty-one had taken their first alcoholic drink was found to be 12.8 years, young females had done so at the age of 12.3

years. Occasionally drink was mixed with drugs in order to obtain a better 'kick'. The survey pointed to a lack of responsibility among parents, to a lack of understanding and trust between the young drinkers and the GP, to the lack of facilities for alcoholics and to the urgent need for research.

American sociologists have often claimed that it is in the main the surreptitious drinking of teenagers, unbeknown to the parents and in contrast to their wishes, that may prove dangerous in the long run. However, the hypothesis that early introduction of children to drinking in parents' homes to some extent 'immunises' them against the later risk of alcoholism can – at the present state of knowledge – by no means be regarded as proven. Generally speaking and other circumstances being equal, it might be expected that the greater number of regular drinkers in a community, the greater the risk of a higher rate of alcoholism a few years later. In line with the acceptance vulnerability hypothesis of Jellinek (p. 55) the example of the French shows that in a community where heavy drinking is widely accepted, even persons not emotionally vulnerable may drink heavily and thereby run the risk of becoming alcoholics. An increase in the number of regular drinkers coupled with the rise of juvenile drunkenness during the past decade might thus give rise to the fear of a possible rise in alcoholism in this country in the future, perhaps especially among younger age groups [9].

In fact there was some evidence of a recent increase of alcoholism among the young in this country in the 1960s, e.g. from a comparison of the proportion of young alcoholics (thirty years and under) admitted to the Warlingham Park Hospital alcoholic unit in the mid-1950s (1952–7) and to the St Bernard's Hospital unit ten years later (1963–7). In the 1950s, of 268 male and female alcoholics admitted to WPH 5.2 per cent were aged thirty years and under; in the 1960s, of 745 male and female alcoholic admissions to St Bernard's, 8.5 per cent. This difference is statistically significant at a level between 5 and 10 per cent. But then, because of the somewhat improved climate of opinion regarding the disease concept of alcoholism some alcoholics may present themselves for admission at an earlier stage and age. This consideration would also apply to the rise in the proportion of young female alcoholics (under thirty years of age) admitted to the Spelthorne St Mary Nursing Home in the 1960s: thirteen among a total of 379 alcoholics (3.4 per cent) between 1950 and 1959; fourteen young alcoholics out of a total of 327 alcoholics (4.3 per cent) between 1960 and 1967. But it is interesting that Carstairs (1965) [10] referred to an increase in the number of Scottish alcoholics in their twenties; and that two Milanese doctors in 1968 reported that they had noticed a greater frequency of *delirium tremens* cases in young alcoholics [17].

In the past, as we have seen, by and large the young alcoholics – though forming a heterogenous group comprising many types of personalities who may have started to drink for a variety of psychological, social, etc., reasons – were emotionally much more disturbed than the hypothetical average adult alcoholic. Often they seemed to have been more insecure from the beginning, not infrequently emotionally deprived, and to have started drinking in order to reduce anxiety, tension, feelings of inadequacy, etc. [11]. Not surprisingly, the most disturbed types of young alcoholics were observed by us in prison. Here one interesting finding was that more than half these men came from parts of the British Isles other than England, a point that touches on the problems which confront the migrant worker who finds himself friendless and lonely in an unfamiliar environment.

Largely because of the underlying personality inadequacy the decline of the young alcoholic was often rapid and his prognosis poor. Ritson and Hassall [12] spoke of the 'malignant nature of alcoholism in the young' and emphasised 'the need for awareness that alcohol addiction can and does exist in young men in their late teens and twenties'. Since 1970 there has been an increasing tendency of youngsters beginning to drink regularly at a progressively younger age, of a rise of drunkenness convictions among the young, of a shift of onset of the condition in the hypothetical 'average' alcoholic patient seen towards earlier age groups (such as perhaps the late twenties and thirties), of rising numbers of alcoholics seen in their late twenties and quite a few in their late teens. Paradoxically enough, the trend of widening social acceptance of drinking among the very young means that the onset of alcoholism in relatively young age groups no longer points to a poor prognosis: such wide social acceptance of drinking among the young means, on the one hand, that even average, non-neurotic youngsters may start to drink heavily and may thus develop alcoholism. On the other hand, however, it means that among such young alcoholics in the future there will be increasing numbers of fairly stable personalities with relatively much better prognosis than the often highly unstable young alcoholic of the 1950s [13].

All the same, very young people are more sensitive to the effects of alcoholic drink than others, and often the progress from heavy drinking to alcoholism proceeds at a much more rapid pace. It is therefore of great importance to warn the young drinker that – as among older age groups – an average degree of emotional stability and maturity by no means offers protection from the risk of alcoholism; and that the more they mix with a peer group of heavy drinkers, the greater the risk of development of dependence and of other harm to their health.

Justified concern with the drinking habits of the young should not make one overlook the drinking behaviour of those who are older. All too often one encounters the heavily drinking father who proudly proclaims 'Thank God, my daughter never smokes "pot", she only drinks!'

An interesting review of reasons for their drinking given by youngsters was recently given by Derek Rutherford [14], Director of the National Council on Alcoholism. The main reasons were parental and social influences, their friends' drinking, drinking in order to feel 'good', and, sometimes, the presence of serious emotional problems.

1   *Influence of parents*:   Surveys carried out in Scotland [19] and a London suburb [15] showed that a youngster's intake of alcoholic drink tended to rise with the frequency of drinking by father and mother. In general boys tended to follow their father's example, girls that of their mother. (However, in our own experience, in the case of alcoholic women, one finds not infrequently that they had alcoholic fathers, and that, apparently, they had identified with the father rather than with the 'nagging' mother.) In Rutherford's view, it is the life style of the parents which is the most significant single factor in determining whether a person decides to drink, and his pattern of drinking.

2   *Social influences*:   Young people's attitudes to drink may be affected by advertisements and the mass media. The latter may be in a position to foster norms for moderations and for the appropriate settings for drinking.

3   *Influence of peer group*:   In adolescence, when the parents' influence begins to wane, it seems that that of one's peers begins to have greater effect. A Scottish study indicates that adolescents tend to reject images of the teetotaller and the heavy drinker alike:

the teetotaller because he is regarded as lacking in sociability and manliness, the heavy drinker – though his 'manliness' is appreciated – because he too is unsociable. Drinking adolescents tend to have friends who drink, abstaining youngsters are friendly with other abstainers and with those interested in the Church.

4   *Drinking makes youngsters feel 'good'*:   Youngsters may also appreciate the pharmacological effect of the drug alcohol, which gives them feelings of well-being, euphoria, or of a 'kick'. It is of some interest that 10–15 years ago, when the drug wave in this country had hit youngsters, one often heard comments from them such as: 'We are not interested in alcohol or "sleepers" [barbiturates] which slow us down – they may be good for older people but not for us. What we want is drugs such as "pot" [cannabis], "acid" [LSD], "speed" [amphetamines] which extend our mental horizon and our "consciousness", or "pep us up".' [13] From this writer's observations at the time it seemed that whereas 'arty' students went over with flying colours to 'pot', most medical students, even at that time, kept faithful to 'booze'. During the 1970s alcohol once more has become the favourite drug with the young as well as with their elders. Nonetheless the situation of misuse of drugs other than alcohol has been worsening once more since the early seventies.

5   *Children from problem drinking homes*:   In Rutherford's estimate, there are at least 500,000 children under fourteen in the country with one or both their parents suffering from a drinking problem – an estimate based on the number of drinkers seen by the local councils attached to the National Council. He quotes an investigation by Margaret Cork [17] who found that almost all 115 children of alcoholic parents studied by her experienced difficulties in inter-personal relationships, school work suffered in 112 children and there were many emotional problems and sometimes also physical (or psychosomatic) effects. It is well known that many young alcoholics experienced a disturbed or deprived childhood. Not only verbal lashings by the drinking parent but child battering is by no means uncommon in such a home. 60 per cent of child cruelty cases – according to an estimate of the Council of Europe – may arise in alcoholic homes. The frequency of noisy, bitter arguments between parents does not contribute to a healthy home atmosphere. (See Chapter 9.)

The same theme – i.e. factors of importance in the development of drinking behaviour among the young – was studied in recent years by Joyce O'Connor [16], an Irish sociologist. Her investigations concerned two ethnic groups, English and Irish, as well as intermediate group of 'Anglo-Irish' (people born in England to Irish parents). The study comprised interviews with 774 young people, aged 18–21, as well as 613 fathers and 747 mothers. Previous investigations had highlighted the significance of four main factors in this connection: ethnic and cultural; parental; peer group; and social and personal influences. O'Connor's work ascribed the development of drinking behaviour among the young to four main variables: sex status (reflecting the fact that males were heavier type drinkers than females); peer group support for drinking (found to be 'the most explanatory variable of heavy and very heavy type drinking to emerge in all groups'); parental influences, in the main 'children's perceptions of father's attitudes to mixing drinks and drinking three or more drinks on one occasion'; and ethnic status which, though of no direct influence, had affected the fathers' attitudes. Influence of young peers was found to be stronger than that of the parents but much more important than the influence of a single factor was the interaction between the various factors, culture, parents, and peer group.

In our own experience [11] young alcoholics, when asked why they had started to drink, stated they had done so in order to behave like adults or their parents, but at other times, also to show independence or register a protest against their parents; or to fall in with the attitudes or behaviour of their peers or 'subculture'; to feel at ease and more relaxed in company (in particular, when mixing with the opposite sex); often such drinking behaviour had started when working alongside older colleagues (whom they wanted to impress with their own drinking prowess 'even if it was killing me'); sometimes because they were curious to find out what the experience of heavy drinking or intoxication would be like; or a 'consolation' type of drinking after a failed examination, a broken affair, etc. Naturally enough, among our patients, very often home atmosphere in such young alcoholics' homes had been very disturbed because of the behaviour of the drinking parent, as well as of the bitter reaction shown by the non-drinking parent.

Among our young alcoholics, alcohol was often used at an early stage for the effect it gave, and sometimes it was taken in solitude [11]. Often the development of an abnormal drinking pattern seemed to be an attempt at a short cut to an adult role, supplying a false feeling of omnipotence to a disturbed personality acting out his inadequacy.

Certain factors, which seemed to be significant in the histories of these patients [11, 13] included early emotional deprivation and the experience of physical or psychological trauma in childhood; heavy drinking by one parent and dominance by the other; unsatisfactory sexual adjustment; over-identification with a parent of the opposite (but at times also of the same) sex; over-compensation for feelings of inadequacy by anti-social behaviour or withdrawal from society; or a difficulty in accepting an adult role, with a confused attitude to their own children.

However, these impressions and observations refer to young alcoholics who grew up at a time when drinking by youngsters was not yet widely accepted as the 'done thing'. Clearly under 'modern' conditions the finding of a young alcoholic by no means implies a likelihood of a disturbed 'pre-alcoholic' personality, as often it may mainly reflect the type of company this individual had kept. There might then be the significant implications of whether he (or she) had initially freely searched out such company, or whether he quite accidentally had 'skidded' into a drink-oriented 'subculture', with the pharmacological effect of alcohol fairly soon getting the better of him and inducing a state of dependence.

Finally, two important factors which so far have hardly been mentioned in this chapter: one, the possible effect in the development of regular drinking habits in the young of the relative dearth of competing attractions and places to meet friends. Mary Kenny [18] in a recent newspaper article points out that nowadays the pub has become a focus of social life for the young, who spend much of their leisure time there complaining that there is nowhere else to go and socialise, and clamouring for bringing down the legal age limit for drinking in a pub from the present under-eighteen. The other factor possibly contributing to heavy drinking among some of today's youngsters – already touched upon in Chapter 2 – could be the spiritual void and disillusion with today's materialistic society, perhaps coupled with the lack of family cohesion at home; youngsters may therefore try to find other ways of obtaining some measure of satisfaction.

References

1 Glatt, M M (1961), *Acta Psychiat. Scand.*, 37 (1) 88
2 Glatt, M M, Pitman, D, Gillespie, J, and Hills, D R (1969), *The Drug Scene in Great Britain* (Revised Reprint), London, Edward Arnold

3   Christian Economic and Social Research Foundation (November 1979), Chief Constables' Report

4   DHSS (1980), *Drinking in England and Wales*, London, HMSO

5   Kinden, R F, quoted in *Daily Telegraph* (19 October, 1980)

6   Ennals, D, quoted in *Daily Telegraph* (13 December, 1980)

7   Maddox, G L and McCall, B C (1964), *Drinking among Teenagers*, New Brunswick, NJ, Rutgers Center of Alcohol Studies

8   Goldberg, L, quoted from Glatt M M and Hills, D R (1968), *Brit. J. Addict.*, 63, 183

9   Glatt, M M (1970), *The Alcoholic and the Help he Needs*, Royston, Herts., Priory Press, 60

10 Carstairs, G M, Foreword to Kessel, N and Walton, H (1965), *Alcoholism*, London, Penguin, 9

11 Glatt, M M and Hills, D R (1968), *Brit. J. Addict.*, 63, 183

12 Ritson, B and Hassall, C (1970), *The Management of Alcoholism*, Edinburgh and London, Livingstone

13 Glatt, M M (1974), *A Guide to Addiction and its Treatment*, Lancaster, MTP

14 Rutherford, D (March–April 1980), *UK Alliance News*, 11–14

15 Edwards, G et al. (1973), *Brit. J. Psychiat.*, 123, 169

16 O'Connor, J (1978), *The Young Drinkers*, London, Tavistock, 146–62

17 Cork, M (1969), *The Forgotten Children*, Ontario Gen. Pub. Co.

18 Kenny, M (December 1980), *Sunday Telegraph*

19 Dight, S E (1976), *Scottish Drinking Habits*, London, HMSO

8

Elderly Alcoholics[1]

Hundreds of years ago, among the Aztecs of Mexico, it was apparently only the old who were permitted to take alcoholic drink [1]. In our times, however, much attention is, rightly, given to the increasing misuse of alcohol by the young whereas the possibility of alcohol problems is generally overlooked in the elderly – although the existence of old-age alcoholism has been described in publications both in the USA [2, 3] and Europe [4, 5].

Among the sample of alcoholics seen at Warlingham Park Hospital in the 1950s (see Chapter 3), at the end of the scale opposite to the young described in the previous chapter, there was a relatively small number of people in whom symptoms of alcoholism did not appear until a relatively late age. Thus among the WHP male alcoholics 2 per cent were not admitted to hospital for some alcohol manifestation until they had reached an age of fifty years; and only at that age had 10 per cent 'lost control', and 7 to 8 per cent started early morning or solitary drinking or embarked on prolonged drinking bouts [6].

Usually such people had started drinking socially at a young age similar to the main body of future alcoholics. They then had gone through life as moderate drinkers coping fairly well with average stress and strain, without taking recourse to excessive drinking for many years. Often heavy drinking did not set in until after a situation of severe emotional stress, such as the loss of a wife. Late onset of alcoholism may thus often – the more likely, the more severe the precipitating factor – denote the presence of a personality better able to cope with internal or external stress than that of the younger alcoholic breaking down under ordinary situations without extraordinary, severe environmental stress. Again, this may help to explain the relatively better prognosis in the past in older than in the very young alcoholics [6].

Because the number of old alcoholics is so much less than that among the middle aged – a difference not fully explained by the (admittedly high) mortality rates of alcoholics – the concept of alcoholism as a self-limiting disease has been put forward [7], possibly due to spontaneous recovery later in life, reminding one of the 'maturing out' hypothesis in middle-aged heroin addicts (most heroin addicts are very young, only a few are middle-aged so that it is possible that quite a few recover in their late thirties). On the other hand, alcoholics in their late sixties are by no means as uncommon as often assumed, and they may find their way into the geriatric department of general hospitals, into psychiatric hospitals or into alcoholic units. From a joint investigation carried out a few years ago by the geriatric department of a London general hospital and the alcohol unit at St Bernard's Hospital [4] (a total of 103 patients), and confirmed by the findings of a 1976-7 investigation in ninety-two patients [5], it seems that elderly people who present themselves with drinking problems fall into two broad groups: those whose excess drinking is a continuation of heavy drinking which began at a much younger age (e.g. alcohol 'addicts' continuing to drink into old age); and a second group consisting of old people who were teetotallers or moderate drinkers until late in life when they took to heavy drinking after severe emotional stress, such as bereavement, an increasing feeling of social isolation, loss of socio-occupational status, etc. Personality problems were by and large more important in the first of these two groups, factors connected with the ageing process (physical, mental or environmental effects of ageing) in the second.

With advancing age, changing psychological, physiological, and socioeconomic conditions may affect the balance and dynamic interaction between 'host' (the drinker's personality), environment, and the pharmacological effect of alcohol on personality. Tolerance to alcohol may decrease, underlying personality problems and emotional conflicts which originally (possibly many years ago) may have been responsible for heavy drinking, may, in the course of time, have become less acute and less worrying, and there may also have been biochemical and nutritional changes [8]. Thus some drink less in old age, whereas in others amounts of drink which were formerly well tolerated, in old age may prove relatively too much and produce domestic, social, mental and physical complications. Not only may there be reduced pharmacological tolerance to the effects of alcohol but also an inability to cope with other stresses as well as in younger years (the more so as also in absolute terms such domestic, social and other stresses may often have increased unfortunately in man too). The 'straw which breaks the camel's back', may be a very small one when the camel is nearing the end of its journey [9].

The aged show a greater susceptibility to drugs in general, and not specifically to alcohol, so that there is a need for extra care in prescribing drugs for them. In particular in the elderly alcoholic there may not only be the delay in elimination, excretion and metabolism characteristic of the old but also an additional impaired ability of the liver, which is not only aged but also alcohol-affected, to metabolise alcohol and other drugs. However, chlormethiazole, our routine tranquilliser in the treatment of serious alcohol withdrawal stages (see Chapter 16), is in general well tolerated by elderly patients, and has proved very effective in the aged alcoholic, including a few cases of withdrawal DT.

Problem drinking among the elderly is often unsuspected. Elderly problem drinkers may come to light when old people are found suffering from malnutrition, social neglect and dementia. It seems more common among women than amongst men: e.g. 5 per cent of male alcoholics seen at Warlingham Park Hospital in the mid-1950s were in the age groups 51 to 60 as against 10 per cent of the female alcoholics, and similarly among alcoholics seen at St Bernard's Hospital in the early 1960s; 5 per cent of men were over sixty years of age as against 12 per cent of the women. Women also predominated numerically among the alcoholic elderly patients in investigations in the 1960s and 1970s. There were also relatively many more widows than widowers among the recent samples in proportion to the total of female and male alcoholics respectively [5]: twenty-four widows among seventy-seven female alcoholics (in the 1967–76 series) as against only five widowers among forty-five male alcoholics. However, such ratios do not differ very much from the national ratios of (numerically preponderant) elderly widows compared to widowers in the country's total population (slightly above 4:1). Anyhow, one ought to be aware of the risk of misuse of alcohol among elderly widows.

On the other hand, while keeping the possibility of alcoholism in mind nowadays among the elderly so other mental or physical conditions must not be overlooked just because a patient's breath occasionally smells of alcohol. Often, however, improvement in an elderly person's drink problem may make it much easier to deal with underlying conditions, such as, for example, affective disorders. But in the old, alcoholism is so often symptomatic of an underlying sociopsychobiological condition that often a wide set of measures is required, possibly including economic and housing improvements.

Compared to alcoholism in the young, with (often) a relative predominance in causation of personality factors, environmental circumstances are frequently of greater importance in causing excess drinking among the elderly. Decline of the desire for drinking as well as limitation of access to alcohol by progressive bodily and mental deterioration in old age may curtail drinking among old people; on the other hand, such waning of physical and mental prowess and agility may become causes of heavy drinking.

Occasionally one comes across elderly people who have not completely given up alcohol but have managed to cut down a great deal, for example from a high intake of spirits in middle age while working, to a few half-pints after retirement. Williamson [10] mentions cases of male pensioners in Edinburgh and Liverpool who had been heavy drinkers during their working life but who stopped entirely or reduced their drinking to low levels after retirement. In view of the greatly altered social, occupational, and personality circumstances and in the light of the relative 'lack of control' hypothesis (see Chapter 4) it would not seem difficult to understand such happenings.

Various explanations have been put forward in an attempt to explain factors at work in reducing drinking as people are getting older [8]:

1   Decrease of tolerance, either because of age or, possibly, also in a long-continued drinking career. Decreased tolerance after years of drinking is a common clinical observation but little research has been carried out in this area.
2   Originally present conflicts and anxieties, such as those connected with sexual aggressive feelings, have become much less worrying so that the need for this variant of 'escapist' or 'appeasement' drinking no longer exists.
3   Biochemical or nutritional factors – which, at least in theory, might initially have encouraged or maintained heavy drinking – may have changed in later years.
4   For some reason or other, the relative strength, within the commonly 'ambivalent' alcoholic of the voices for and against drinking may have altered in such a way as to finally maintain sobriety. This is, of course, often only a continuation of the struggle between opposing factions within the alcoholic that

may have precipitated exacerbations and also remissions from time to time in such a person's drinking career earlier in life (see Chapter 3).

5   To these factors one might add the environmental changes brought about in elderly drinkers by their retirement and its reduction in financial resources and opportunities for drinking, progressive restriction of physical capacity and mobility etc., all tending to limit severely the elderly person's consumption of alcoholic drink.

The relative importance of environmental factors in the causation of problem drinking among the elderly highlights the opportunity and the need for intensive social therapeutic measures. Programmes of preventive care such as regular health visiting, extension of social care and home nursing, day hospital care, transfer to a welfare home etc., may be of help in detecting alcoholism in the elderly in an early phase and in arresting the downward path.

At any rate, alcoholism as a possible cause of obscure symptoms must not simply be written off because the individual may seem either much too young or too old. Neither youth nor old age confers on its owner immunity from alcoholism.

Note

[1]   Based on lectures given at the 28th Internat. Copor. on Alcohol and Addiction, Washington DC, 1968, at the National Forum, National Council on Alcoholism, San Diego, 1977; and at a conference 'Disturbance in the Elderly', Jersey, CI, Dec. 1977.

References

1   Schlegel, A (November 1977), Internat. Symposium, *Jugend und Sucht*, Berlin
2   Bailey, M B *et al*. (1965), *Quart. J. Stud. Alc.*, 26, 19
3   Zimberg, S (1974), *Gerontol (St Louis)*, 14, 221
4   Rosin, A J and Glatt, M M (1971), *Quart. J. Stud. Alc.*, 32, 53
5   Glatt, M M *et al*. (1978), *Age and Ageing*, 7, Suppl., 64
6   Glatt, M M (1961), *Acta Psychiat. Scand.*, 37, (1), 88
7   Drew, L (1968), *Quart. J. Stud. Alc.*, 29, 956
8   Murphee, H N (1976) in *Alcohol and Alcohol Problems*, eds Filstead, W J *et al*., Cambridge, Mass., Ballinger, 135–66
9   Griffith, H R (1966), *Canad. Anaesthet. Soc. J.*, 13, 7
10 Williamson, J (1978), *Age and Ageing*, 7, Suppl., 68

Part II

Alcohol-Induced Harm and Complications (domestic/social/physical/ mental)

9

Alcoholism – a Family Illness

Possibly more than any other illness, alcoholism also closely affects the lives of the sick man's family. The alcoholic's inconsistent and sometimes aggressive behaviour necessarily, in time, leads to reactions from wife and children, with the development of a vicious circle of increasing mutual distrust, suspicion, resentment, bitterness and frustration. Wives and children are thus very much affected by the unpredictable behaviour of the alcoholic husband and father.

The American sociologist Joan K. Jackson [1] distinguished certain successive stages in the behaviour and reactions of a family with an alcoholic husband and father. An initial attempt to deny the existence of a problem altogether is followed by efforts designed to eliminate the problem. Lacking clear-cut guidance as to what to do in such a situation, and too ashamed to confide in any outsider, the wife tries everything possible to cope with the situation, including such widely varying methods as drinking with her husband at one time or pouring his bottles down the sink on other occasions; often she is extremely patient with him, only to nag him mercilessly at other times.

When, however, all these alternative methods fail to bring any long-lasting relief – short periods of hope always sooner or later being dashed by the alcoholic's relapse – family life becomes 'disorganised', as the alcoholic's wife 'gives up' in despair for a while, before attempting to find a way out and to reorganise family life in spite of the problem.

She may gradually assume the role of the father as well as of the mother; she becomes the master of the household and the alcoholic is often treated as if he were hardly a member of the family; he has, in fact, been 'written off'. The wife, having previously lost her confidence in herself, now regains some measure of self-confidence and self-respect in this new role. She organises

efforts to escape the problem, and may be successful in reorganis-
ing part of the family. Ultimately, if and when the alcoholic
recovers, a new – sometimes very difficult – reorganisation of the
whole family will become necessary.

Ultimately the alcoholic often loses not only his friends and job
but also his family. The wife, after trying desperately for years to
adjust herself to life with the alcoholic husband, may leave him –
taking the children with her.

Sometimes it is because the wife has left him, or has seriously
threatened to do so, that the alcoholic finally comes for treatment.
On the other hand, one often wonders how it is that wives of
alcoholics are able to bear so much for so long; they seem veritable
gluttons for punishment, to such an extent that one feels the
situation must often fulfil some unconscious need of their own.
Husbands of alcoholic wives, as a rule, leave home much earlier
than wives of alcoholic husbands.

In this whole process, the alcoholic's wife is naturally not just a
passive partner and her personality and behaviour play an important role in helping to shape the course of events.

In a certain proportion of alcoholics' marriages, the wife is older
than the alcoholic, she may be more masculine in attitude and
behaviour and may have dominated the husband from the start of
the marriage. Up to a point such a woman may 'enjoy' her domina-
tion just as the alcoholic, to a certain extent, may 'enjoy' his
dependence on such a wife (also in the not too uncommon cases
where the alcoholic has married a nurse), though both the wife and
the alcoholic may bitterly protest against such an interpretation.
She is often more mature and more stable than her possibly very
intelligent and capable, but emotionally very immature and unstable alcoholic husband. Very often such women knew when they
married the alcoholic of his excessive drinking; but they state that
at the time they hoped they would be able to help him to decrease
or give up his drinking.

As long as he is drinking such women naturally have to organise
the household, and in some ways they may treat their drinking
husbands like wayward children. These wives usually maintain
that they would have been glad to leave the master-of-the-house
role to the husband, but that his inability to fulfil this role forced
them to take over. This may be true in some cases, but in others it
is clear that to some extent such a wife enjoys this domineering
role. We have already referred to the corresponding cases where
marrying an alcoholic woman seems to satisfy some personality

needs of the husband's.

It may seem surprising, at first glance, to note that in a number of cases the wife of an alcoholic is herself the daughter of an alcoholic, and occasionally one meets a woman who, prior to marrying her present alcoholic husband, had been married to another alcoholic. Again, such a course of events points to the existence of certain personality needs of the woman concerned; for example, the alcoholic's daughter may have identified with her alcoholic father, this in spite of his unpredictable and often manifestly unfair behaviour towards her mother.

Analysts may see in this the working of the Oedipus complex in reverse (Electra complex), but anyway this illustrates the difficult situation in which the wife of an alcoholic may find herself. In trying to cope with her husband she may gradually become a nervous wreck herself and, because she is angry, anxious and bewildered, short-tempered towards the children, nagging her husband, her children's sympathies may often be more on the side of the drinking father.

This may be the more so as the alcoholic does not behave badly all the time, and in his intervening drink-free intervals he may go out of his way to make up, as far as he can, for his bad behaviour during his drinking period by showing a great deal of affection towards his children – and it is in such an 'over-compensating' role that they often later remember their alcoholic father, and side with him rather than with the mother. In fact, very often the alcoholic's wife, independent of what her emotional state was when she married the alcoholic, may later on be as much in need of skilled professional attention as her husband.

Four common personality types of wives of alcoholics, as observed in a family counselling agency in Texas, have been sketched by Thelma Whalen [2]. She calls them 'Suffering Susan' (whose need to be miserable is gratified by her marriage to an alcoholic); 'Controlling Catherine' (who marries a man whom she regards as somewhat inadequate or inferior to her); 'Wavering Winifred' (who herself is fearful and insecure, and feels secure in a relationship with a man only as long as she feels he cannot get along without her and needs her, but whose tolerance may wear thin when her husband's drinking gets too much out of control); and finally 'Punitive Polly' (whose relationship to her husband resembles that of a boa constrictor to a rabbit – the 'rabbit' sometimes likes being swallowed, though at other times he may rebel and go out to get drunk). In all such marriages the alcoholic's behaviour is only one factor in a family situation which produces emotional problems. Certainly such (and other) types of wives of alcoholics are seen quite often, but frequently they may all be temporary phases during a wife's desperate and long-drawn-out effort to detect – by a method of trial and error – how she can transform her husband (who has changed so completely since he started to drink to excess) back to the man he was at the time she married him.

Wives of heavy drinkers will often feel too ashamed to come out into the open – the more so as they may vaguely feel that the husband's drinking may really reflect on their (the wives') short-comings and inadequacies. This may be even more so in the frequent cases where such women had known before the marriage of their future husband's heavy drinking and had even been strongly warned against marrying him by anxious parents or friends. Such wives may conceal their suffering, or over-compensate for it by concentrating on looking after the children extremely well. They may also over-indulge their children or, on the other hand show rejection by being extremely harsh or irrit-able with them. Over-indulging the children may also be an attempt at atoning for deeply felt dissatisfaction with, or complete rejection of, the children. Such wives may often become ex-tremely nervous, anxious, even suicidal, and may frequently present themselves to their GP's surgery asking for tranquillisers or antidepressants, or producing a host of psychosomatic com-plaints without ever spontaneously mentioning their husband's drinking; they may take to drinking themselves with the possible development of 'conjugal alcoholism', the children being the main victims of an increasingly disturbed emotional home atmosphere. Wives may even become violent towards their drinking husband, but more commonly they withdraw emotionally and physically, sexual relationships becoming increasingly infrequent and often ceasing altogether – a problem that may extend far into the re-habilitation phase after the husband has given up drinking and keenly and sincerely may desire to make amends. Meanwhile his wife may herself have had short-lived affairs, and even though they may not have meant much to her, the husband's drinking behaviour may have left too many scars for her to regain her former affection. But here again quite a different outcome may yet be possible in spite of all bitterness and emotional alienation during the drinking time.

The finding that so often the wife of an alcoholic derives some fulfilment of her own personality needs in being married to a drinking husband explains to some extent the observation that not infrequently the husband's recovery from alcoholism is not immediately and naturally followed by a complete happiness of a united family. On the one hand, the alcoholic returning home from hospital often feels that he deserves the welcome reserved for a homecoming, conquering hero, whereas the wife may feel that, after all, he has done nothing more than she could reasonably have expected him to have achieved years ago by just 'pulling himself together' without inflicting years of suffering on her and the children.

Moreover, the wife and the family, having for years got used to regarding the alcoholic husband and father as completely unreliable, may not trust his newly won sobriety, and the wife may be afraid to hand over the mastery of the household to him. Clearly much readjustment will be necessary on both sides, and both may require a great deal of help during this period.

Not infrequently, the alcoholic's wife may be jealous of Alcoholics Anonymous which has achieved, possibly in a short time, what she has tried in vain to do in years. The 'AA widow', left at home for evening after evening while the husband is attending meetings, may not take too kindly to the notion that this is what is needed to stabilise and maintain his sobriety.

Great tolerance and patience are required from the alcoholic and his family alike, and both should try to look at this issue from the other's point of view. The alcoholic may try to heed the injunction which he heard from fellow AA members that at this stage 'your sobriety must come first' – he hopes that his family understands this and realises that this may be the best way to maintain his newly gained sobriety and sanity of outlook and behaviour. The family, however, may feel that all that has been happening is that he has exchanged his former obsession with drinking into a new obsession with talking and thinking about 'non-boozing' all day long, to the virtual exclusion of other interests and areas of concern; and family members may feel that he should remember that apart from doing something about the disease alcoholism, he also should begin to do his part in improving the lot of the 'sick family' whom he has wronged so much in the past. Failure to ventilate openly this vital area of mutual concern makes it the source of much bitter misunderstanding and indeed deeply hurtful conflicts that may endanger not only the alcoholic's peace of mind and sobriety but also undermine the shaky foundations on which the family harmony is to be rebuilt.

It is in this respect where so often Al-Anon (the family groups run by relatives of alcoholics) or psychotherapeutic groups for alcoholics' families have an important contribution to make. Al-Anon (see Chapter 16) may help the wife a great deal to understand her husband and herself better than in the past. 'I am so glad we kept together,' wrote an alcoholic's widow shortly after his death, 'and I now wish I would have been able to join Al-Anon decades ago, as I am positive the partner of a person suffering from the disease of alcoholism could help enormously if she knew that she had got to be steadier, stronger and a more helpful person than if she married a normal person. And I think it is often the more sensitive person who gets caught in the awful alcoholic-addiction trap.'

Emotional health and development of children growing up in an alcoholic household can naturally not remain uninfluenced by the inconsistent and unpredictable prevailing atmosphere. Emotional relationships between the child and his parents will be severely disturbed, forming a fertile breeding ground for insecurity and maladjustment. Children are torn in their loyalties between father and mother and are continually called upon to make fresh re-adjustments, in an atmosphere characterised by continual quarrels, emotional upheavals, mutual recrimination, threats of separation with temporary reconciliations, the emergence of hope from time to time, only to be followed by sad disappointments.

Many cases end in a completely 'broken home'. Of the alcoholic patients entering Warlingham Park Hospital, one-third of the men and nearly two-thirds of the women were divorced or separated. Conditions, however, are often just as bad when there is a virtually broken home, although parents still live together. In such households, consistency in parents' attitude as well as between the attitudes of both parents, genuine affection, the feeling of acceptance – prerequisites for allowing the child to gain emotional security – are missing [3]. Children may feel deprived and neglected, and the vicious circle described by Bowlby [4] may be set in motion – today's deprived, neglected children may grow up into tomorrow's psychopathic, neglectful, unstable parents who are again unable to provide a normal home life for their children.

The risks threatening the growing child's emotional development do not arise solely from the alcoholic's own attitude but also from the reactions of his wife. Bewildered, embittered, frustrated, angry or anxious, she may, for example, try to satisfy her own unsatisfied emotional needs by over-attaching her son to herself, and by over-indulging or over-protecting him; alternatively, her marital unhappiness may cause her overtly or unconsciously to 'reject' her child. Anyway, the alcoholic's drinking habits may often cause a fundamental disturbance of the marital relationship, with its chain of reactions exposing the children to the threat of emotional deprivation and neglect.

Outright physical cruelty to children in today's predominant variety of affluence alcoholism, might have been expected to be much less common than in the past days of poverty alcoholism, but, like wife battering, cases of physical *child abuse* in the alcoholic home are unfortunately by no means a thing of the past and may in fact be quite common. In the alcoholic family, child abuse may come both from the drunken father but occasionally also from the irritable, despairing wife who, not knowing where to turn to for help, may lose her temper and take it out on the children who may 'get on her nerves'. Naturally enough, she may often feel extremely guilty about it afterwards – as indeed her husband may be who may try to over-compensate for his having battered the children the previous evening by over-indulging them with material gifts the following day.

A report published in 1980 by the NSPCC pointed to factors producing family tension such as economic recession, unemployment, redundancy and crippling mortgages as often being responsible in cases of child abuse. However, physical neglect and ill-treatment of children have continued in spite of rising living standards, and although most known cases of child battering occur among poorer families, cases of battering have occurred 'upstairs' as well as 'downstairs'. There have been cases, as Dr A Gilmour, Director of the NSPCC put it, 'when we have gone to the front door of a stately home, not the back' [5]. Maybe those who are grateful for smaller mercies may see some progress reflected in reports that nowadays neglect and minor injuries appear to be more common than outright battering. Among the signs of such non-accidental injury [6] may be (most commonly) bruises, ecchymoses (loss of skin), lineas lesions from beating with a stick, loss of hair, cigarette-end burns, scalds, and skin lesions due to neglect; but there may be injuries elsewhere other than only skin lesions. The NSPCC has established several special treatment units, situated mainly in the larger cities. Their collaboration with families as well as with children and local authorities has often enabled early recognition of danger signs and careful monitoring, and with it the reduction of seriously injured children. There are obvious problem families in which the risk of physical child abuse may be suspected but certainly the families of heavily drinking, aggressive alcoholics must be high on the priority list of families who may need assistance in trying to prevent physical as well as emotional abuse. In view of the strong correlation of child abuse with unemployment, financial problems and alcoholism – all very much on the increase – a leading article in the BMJ in March 1980 [6] forecasts a 'steady increase' in the frequency of such injury and asks clinicians to be alert to the possibility of child abuse. Often, of course, physical and emotional abuse of the alcoholic's wife and child go hand in hand, such as in the case of a recently seen case where the wife, trying to prevent the child being hit by her husband, received some battering herself, with the crying six year old girl crying out: 'Mummy if this is marriage, I never want to get married!'

Under the inconsistent conditions so often prevailing in the alcoholic household it is difficult to imagine the children undergoing normal emotional and social development and acquiring the capacity to experience satisfactory emotional relationships. Rather could one expect among them reactions and difficulties manifesting themselves in, for example, the shape of neurotic symptoms, behaviour disorders, possibly delinquent acts. Father-child as well as mother-child relationships may often be disturbed in the alcoholic family so that the child may suffer from paternal as well as from maternal rejection, deprivation and inadequacy. The frequent 'intermissions' caused by the alcoholic's drinking-free intervals may not help a great deal in this connection and may, in fact, only serve to lead to more confused parental images [3].

It is thus little wonder that many investigations have shown alcoholism to be a relatively common occurrence among parents of neurotics, would-be suicides, alcoholics and delinquents. In children of alcoholics the incidence of mental and nervous disorder has been estimated to amount to 20 per cent, the incidence of alcoholism between 20 and 30 per cent.

That alcoholism is so common in children of alcoholics has often been taken as showing the influence of an hereditary factor (see Chapter 2). Roe [7] (1945) reported an interesting study in which two groups of children, one of alcoholic and one of normal parentage, were brought up by foster-parents who were not related to them. Had these children of alcoholic parentage been brought up at home, the expected incidence of alcoholism would have been between 20 and 30 per cent, and for the group of normal parentage perhaps about 1 per cent. In the event, after these children had grown up it turned out that there were no significant differences between the two groups, and there were as many seriously maladjusted people among the normal-parentage groups as among the group with alcoholic parents.

Roe therefore concluded that the reported high incidence of alcoholism (and psychosis) in the offspring of alcoholics could not be explained on the basis of any hereditary factor, and that alcoholic parentage does not, in fact, preclude good adjustment or, given reasonably adequate life circumstances, make it more difficult. This last point is, of course, borne out by the observation that, in spite of all such handicaps, one occasionally comes across children of alcoholics in their teens who seem to be remarkably mature for their age and who are a great help and support to their mother in trying to cope with the difficulties caused by the more or less perpetually drunken husband and father. In these children, increased strain and responsibilities seem to have acted as a challenge and spur towards earlier and more rapid emotional growth.

Investigations carried out during the last decade similar to the studies of Roe (such as Goodwin's [8] and Bohman's [9] investigations in Scandanavia and those by Cadoret [10] in the USA) have come to exactly the opposite conclusions from those drawn by Roe, and point to hereditary influences at least in certain cases. The point, however, that children of alcoholics can make good, and many do extremely well, is not contradicted by the recent studies. The relative influences of interacting genetic and environmental influences in the various alcoholisms is of course still very much a matter of research. How unclear and speculative the matter is at the moment is clear from comments in a recent Leading Article in the *British Medical Journal* [11]; 'it would be a gross oversimplification to say that male alcoholism is genetic and female [alcoholism] environmental'. This statement seems contradicted to a certain extent by a reference in the very next sentence to findings that 'Those women who are affected [by alcohol dependence] have a higher mortality rate and incidence of cirrhosis than men'. No one, however, would take issue with the concluding statement in the article, that 'Unfortunately, the most certain thing that we can now say about female alcoholism is that it is showing a new and deplorable rise – not, presumably, for genetic reasons'.

However, it is clear that children of alcoholic parents start off in life with many disadvantages and may often be in need of help and advice. Corresponding to Al-Anon, the Alateen Fellowship has been formed in which alcoholics' adolescent children try to help and support each other (see Chapter 16).

In general, the all-important early detection of emotional neglect of children is a very difficult task. The knowledge that it is so frequent an occurrence in families of alcoholics presents a challenge and an opportunity in the task of prevention of mental ill-health.

Over the past few years, fortunately, there has been a great deal of improvement in public and professional attitudes and willingness to render active assistance to the sick alcoholic. But as yet, few appreciate the plight of their families – whether they hold out in silence, or dare to come forward and ask for help. AA were the first to bring active assistance to the alcoholic himself but now professional and voluntary organisations have actively joined in. In the case of the alcoholic's family too – who are often at least as much in need of understanding and help as the drinker him- or herself – the whole burden cannot be shouldered by the self-help fellowship of Al-Anon, and much more needs to be done, and can be done, by professionals to assist Al-Anon and the alcoholic's family.

The wife's dilemma: 'To leave or not to leave, that is (my) question'

'. . . I do not want to waste your time,' – began a recent letter by a middle-aged wife of an alcoholic patient – 'by either letting off steam or by giving you details of the horror of living with an alcoholic which no doubt you have heard *ad nauseam* . . . as the same situation must arise over and over and over again with other alcoholics . . . Do you understand that he both drinks and takes sleeping pills together with the intention of making himself quickly very, very drunk? Every day in varying degrees . . . that he has often with no provocation been violent towards me? I do everything I can to avoid this particular situation but cannot always do so.

'. . . that he has recently become much worse even in public although I think, not at work, whereas in the past he has usually reserved his excesses for the privacy of his home. I do not mean that he is violent in public but that he is on occasion zombie-like and ataxic.

'. . . that he still functions, apparently, as far as I know, very efficiently at work but that is all – when he leaves work, it is a determined flight into oblivion. I do not know how long it can remain undetected at work or even if it has remained completely undetected but he can cover to a certain extent in front of people other than myself. Today was the first time I have ever seen him unsteady after eight hours in bed when he left for work at 7 a.m.

'IN THIS POSITION IS THERE ANYTHING I CAN DO?

'I have tried everything I can think of over the years but although it would be like chopping off both arms after marrying at eighteen, living with him for twenty-nine years and fighting this problem for probably fourteen of them, and although it would upset my children who are fifteen and fourteen and whom I managed until very recently to protect from everything but a slight awareness of the problem, it is becoming, I think, positively dangerous for me to persevere. (My daughter is at boarding school.)

'If you have nothing to suggest to me that I can do or say to alter things, I think I must now admit defeat and prepare to abandon the struggle even though I am certain that I shall be responsible for an even quicker deterioration than is taking place with me here. This weekend when, only for the second time in five years, he refused to come home . . ., I have never seen him as violent and ataxic as when I returned yesterday evening . . . Still, he may once again do an about-turn and come with me . . .'

The decision with which the wife of an alcoholic is so often confronted, whether to stay or to leave him, is often extremely agonising. Whichever way such a woman may want to turn, difficulties seem unsurmountable. Often, by sticking to him through thick and thin, she may only protect him from experiencing the consequences of his actions; shielding and cushioning him against physical and emotional injuries and pain, she may unwittingly enable him to continue with his drinking behaviour. Leaving him, on the other hand, without being able to make adequate precautions and provision for somebody else to keep an eye on him, may expose the husband to great if not deadly danger. Many alcoholic men separated from their wives, (even sometimes only for a few days) tend to drink much more during such a period. Moreover, the alcoholic's wife may also feel that she owes it to her children to stay with their father at least until they are grown up. Naturally, economic factors may enter into the question as to whether she could or should leave him, taking the children with her. The course commonly adopted by the wife – forever threatening her alcoholic husband of walking out on him without ever following it up, or after returning to him after a few days – is more than useless; it only assures the drinker that she will never really leave him in spite of all her threats.

On the other hand, while a great deal has been written on the consequences of a broken home on the children, less has been said about the effects of divorce. However, a few studies have shown that divorce (in non-alcoholic marriage) is not necessarily an unmixed blessing for the children. Physical separation from one parent – commonly the consequence of divorce – may mean an additional stress for the child [12] leading occasionally to depression, grief reactions, 'acting-out' behaviour, and aberrations of identification. The question whether, from the children's point of view, it is better to live with one divorced but possibly less unhappy parent than with two unhappily married parents, therefore, will have to be assessed separately in a given case. The comfortable doctrine of 'get on or get out' [13] certainly does not provide a ready-made and foolproof prescription for the spouse of the badly 'acting-out', drinking alcoholic. Compared, however, to other disrupted marriages, alcoholic marriages additionally carry the greatly increased physical risks to health of wife and children (culminating, not infrequently, in wife- and child-battering) which sometimes virtually takes the choice out of such a wife's hands.

The *battered wife* phenomenon has, in recent years, attracted considerable attention. It might perhaps be worth mentioning that frequently the drunken woman's goading, vicious, deeply hurtful tongue may be as traumatic to her partner as the battering fist of the intoxicated man – not that anything can be said in defence in either case. In clinical practice, neither the alcoholic nor his or her spouse seem very keen to mention spontaneously such incidents (perhaps they both feel ashamed and guilty). Probably the incidence of such happenings is therefore underestimated. Gayford [16] found in a recent study that out of a 100 battered wives who had been investigated, fifty-two stated that their husband was a heavy drinker. Similarly, social agencies and courts involved with problems of families or children report that, in a considerable proportion of their case load, problems are closely connected with heavy drinking.

A recent investigation of this subject, carried out by the sociologists Dr and R Dobash [17] for the Scottish Home and Health Department concluded that this problem was one of the most covered up and ignored social ills. In their view 'drink may be associated with it' but they are convinced that it does not constitute the 'fundamental cause'. Among 106 'typical' cases of wife-beating the husband's drink was the cause in 6 per cent. More common than drink were factors such as sexual jealousy (45 per cent), money troubles (17 per cent), and rows over 'issues' such as housework, the husband's meals etc. (16 per cent). Looking at these factors considered to be more frequently involved than drink, the observer may feel that they all occur probably relatively more often in the alcoholic than in the non-alcoholic marriage. Thus even where drink may not be the essential issue it may yet exercise an influence behind the scene which disturbs the atmosphere and contributes to flaring tempers, finally provoking the assault. These authors' findings, that a high proportion of beatings are endured in silence, undoubtedly also applies to drink-induced cases. In previous years such cases were only rarely noted by us; but since recent publicity directed our attention to it and we began to ask leading questions, such questions were often answered in the positive. Frequently such wives explained that although they were living in constant fear of repetition of previous beatings, they were even more afraid of what might happen to them if they were to report their plight: they were convinced that nothing effective could or would be done to stop their husband who, even more enraged would afterwards, within the privacy of their four walls, and unimpeded by outsiders, let fly with intensified vigour.

On the other hand (in contrast to those of wives of alcoholics), it is quite common to get cases of alcoholic women who present themselves with bruises and complain bitterly of terrible beatings which they had suffered at the hands of their husbands. Sometimes they may give that as the primary reason for their drinking. More frequently, however, it may turn out that the husband has tried almost everything else to stop his wife drinking before resorting to hitting the drinking wife, as by then he did not know of any other way of handling the increasingly desperate situation.

In the Scottish sociologists' view the most fundamental reason for continued wife-beating is the widespread acceptance of the assumption that the man has all the rights whereas the wife has to conform. Surely, however, in drink cases special factors are often involved? For example, alcohol removes the individual's usual inhibitions enabling him to give free expression to his aggressive instinct, and to 'act them out'. This leads to the 'Jekyll-and-Hyde' syndrome among alcoholics with Dr Jekyll, the morning after, bitterly regretting such behaviour or that part of it that he may happen to remember. Not infrequently, however, he may feel so disturbed or disgusted with himself that he may indignantly deny that he has been responsible; confronted with the evidence by his wife – such as bruises, a black eye, etc. – he may accuse her of fabricating all this, suggesting that she may be ill, and that she – the wife – should be the one to consult the psychiatrist: she was the one who was imagining things and was sick, he himself was feeling quite well and surely there was nothing wrong with a man occasionally having a few drinks! The statement 'my husband (or wife) is a veritable "Jekyll-and-Hyde" – a wonderful husband and father (or wife and mother) when sober – but quite the opposite when in his (or her) cups' is made so regularly by the spouses of alcoholics that it may serve as a useful diagnostic hint.

Some of the interacting reasons why so often battered wives suffer in silence and passivity are discussed elsewhere in this chapter (see, for example, 'Suffering Susie'). The Scottish authors reject the psychoanalytic hypothesis that masochistic wives obtain something from such situations. They believe instead that such wives have accepted the 'double standard' morality that dominating, forceful behaviour may be good for the gander, but subordinating behaviour more seemly for the goose. Frequently, however, in clinical practice one comes across much more realistic explanations, such as that often there is nowhere for the wife and children to go, or that they depend financially on the husband. Nevertheless, even the most submissive and meekest wives are driven to a pitch where they answer or scream back, or even fight back when at the end of their tether, although physically they are no match for the husband. In such cases the surprised husband may be taken aback momentarily, or even for a certain period of time. More often, unfortunately, the wife's answering back will provide the drinker with a good alibi confirming his view that it was the nagging by his wife that was at the heart of all the trouble and his occasional drinking.

Very occasionally the 'fighting-back' approach by the alcoholic's wife, may have somewhat startling consequences. In a recent case, a woman married to a physically overpowering husband had endured many beatings from him in his drunken rages, partly because 'when he was sober, one could not wish for a better husband'. Finally, however, on one such occasion, in desperation she picked up some ashtrays and threw them at her husband. In utter consternation, the flabbergasted husband in self-defence, picked up the telephone, announced himself as Dr X (he was a businessman with a PhD), and asked the hospital to send an ambulance immediately for an emergency case: his wife was mentally deranged. On arrival the ambulancemen immediately grasped the situation – the husband obviously still very much affected by drink – and in deference to his wishes took his 'mentally deranged', frightened wife with them. She was only too glad to leave the house with them; she proceeded to seek refuge with friends and, after all her previous wavering and vacillating, to leave the husband for good.

Unfortunately, the outcome in such situations is often left to chance; much more organised and planned constructive measures are needed to improve the lot of battered wives and families. Wives, by joining Al-Anon, often find that the method suggested there of detaching themselves from the alcohol problem though not from the alcoholic himself might often help them. At the 'being battered' stage such advice may usually come a bit late in the day. A constructive practical development in recent years has been the setting up of special homes for battered wives and their children. By September 1980, 150 organisations or groups were running refuges in England and Wales, with the average refuge providing places for six women and nine children [14] (see Appendix I).

Frequently, under the often utterly unpredictable situations so often present in alcoholic homes, insufficient time is left to make decisions in a cool, calm and collected manner. Alcoholic drinking behaviour often creates conditions of great and immediate urgency. Every professional worker with experience in the field of alcoholism will have come across incidents with a tragic outcome where alcoholics, whose requests for urgent attention (such as immediate admission), had to be turned down because of lack of accommodation, or who had threatened to take an overdose of tablets for the nth time, or where the drinker's family had requested that 'some' action had to be taken immediately but with the drinker adamantly refusing to co-operate with any action suggested. With alcohol leaving the drinker befuddled so that obviously he often has no idea what he is doing, and, on the other hand, an emotionally often highly charged atmosphere in the home and tempers frayed all round, unfortunately anything may be possible and sooner or later something is almost bound to happen and often does. The alcoholic woman, who on previous occasions had got away with taking some sleeping tablets while drinking, finally may end up taking a fatal overdose on top of half a bottle of vodka; the drinker, so often warned in the past about the dangers of alcohol-affected driving, managing to take the car out, when on one occasion his wife forgot to hide the car keys, and ended up in a fatal crash.

Fortunately a tragic outcome ending with the deaths of two alcoholics at the hands of their desperate children (sentenced to imprisonment), as reported in November 1980, is rare but it illustrates what might happen [14].

In the first case the mindless drinking, it was reported, of both parents drove their sixteen year old son, a very good pupil at the local grammar school, and hoping for a university place, into a state where he 'felt sick and helpless. There was no end to these bouts of drinking which occurred every night for as long as I could remember . . . Every day my father would purchase some form of alcohol – an average two bottles of port and other drinks'. The mother had become 'moody and unpredictable because of her drinking'. When one night again the father came home 'carrying the familiar brown paper bag containing alcohol', the boy could take it no longer: 'I was shaking and in a state of shock . . . [Taking a shotgun] I went into the living room and just pointed the gun and squeezed the trigger. I only wanted to stop her destroying my family home'. The defending barrister explained that for a long time the boy had 'sincerely believed that his mother hated him and he was convinced there was a serious drinking problem. He told of a sense of desperation, helplessness, and frustration. He did not intend to kill her but to frighten her. He thought she needed a shock'. Afterwards the boy ran to the police station to confess. He denied murder but admitted manslaughter and was sentenced to be detained for four years.

This happened not in the long forgotten, far-off miserable days of 'poverty' – induced gin epidemics of the eighteenth and nineteenth centuries but in our age of the affluent, sophisticated and technically so advanced society – November 1980. Fortunately most similar, and by no means atypical situations in an alcoholic home do not end up with quite so tragic an outcome. But the described 'sense of desperation, helplessness and frustration' pervades many such homes, and also grips the would-be helpers confronted with the urgent pleas 'to do something, as otherwise anything might happen'.

That indeed 'anything' can happen in the homes of drinking alcoholics was demonstrated again, within a matter of a few days, by another killing of a drunken parent – in a case that attracted widespread public attention in this country towards the end of 1980. Two sisters who killed their 'bullying, drunkard father' were each sent to prison for three years. Their fifty-year-old father had, during twenty-nine years of marriage 'inflicted terror' on his family, regularly beating his wife, his fits of temper often spilling over to his children. 'Police were called to the family's home countless times to restore order.' Because of his extremely drunken and violent behaviour the father had been barred from pubs near his home. But there was apparently no way in which the terrorised family could have him barred from the domestic home, where he drank too much when unable to frequent the pubs. 'I suffered many injuries [said the mother in court] at his hands, including bruises, cuts, broken fingers and head injuries, and on one occasion he was violent also towards the daughters. I was hurt almost every week . . . [but] until the night he died, the girls [aged 21 and 18] and I never offered him any violence . . . I thought he had gone completely mad. I had never seen him like that before.' He attacked first one daughter and then the other. 'I pleaded with him to stop. I heard screaming and shouting. He said he was going to kill the girls. I was never so frightened in my life. The older daughter was screaming "Please God, someone help me." The younger sister brought her a knife from the kitchen and the father was stabbed to death. The younger daughter went next door to call the police.' It was the first time the daughters had defended themselves after all the years of violence, said the mother; and they had never been in any trouble before. A plea of 'not guilty to murder but guilty of manslaughter' was accepted. On sentencing them to prison the judge told them: 'It is a very sad history. It is also a very sad duty I have to perform because you deliberately and unlawfully stabbed and killed your father. I bear in mind your suffering but the least sentences I can impose are of three years in prison for each of you.'

The judge agreed that the girls had acted under 'substantial provocation', and there was 'a growing campaign' for legal moves to have the girls freed, 'messages of support and sympathy' were pouring into their home 'businessmen, battered wives, young mothers and action groups, all pledging full support'. Impassionate pleas for release on humanitarian grounds were made, and the sentences were contrasted with a three-months' jail sentence given on the same day in another Court to a motorist (with nearly twice the legal limit of alcohol in his blood) for causing the death of two young girls by 'reckless driving'. 'Is this justice?,' asked the editorial of a national newspaper. The sentence on one girl was confirmed, the other's was reduced on appeal.

Newspaper reports pointed out that in several recent cases women, convicted of manslaughter after killing violent men under extreme provocation, had been put on probation but that it was the deliberateness of the killing, and the use of two knives in the case of the father's killing by his daughters, that made this case more severe. One wonders whether in view of such widespread concern *after* a (not quite unforeseeable) tragedy has happened, preventive ways and means could not be considered to try to minimise the likelihood of such occurrences.

An approach of 'constructive confrontation' (see Chapter 11) has been successfully used in American industry to motivate alcoholic employees to take a close look at their behaviour and to undergo treatment where indicated, *before* losing their job (and undermining their health). A somewhat similar approach has just now been worked out to motivate doctors in Britain to do something constructive about their drinking (and other) problems thus being given the chance to forestall and avoid actually having to appear before the General Medical Council (see Chapter 11). Possibly somewhat similar approaches might prove helpful in trying to forestall the repetition of tragedies like the two killings described above.

The alcoholic marriage: drink not the only significant factor

The fact that alcoholism is an illness of the whole family does not mean that all problems in a drinker's family are a consequence of his drinking. Yet, as Orford [15] has rightly pointed out, most studies concerned with the alcoholic family have concentrated on alcoholism and have often neglected the possible or likely contribution of *other factors*. It appears likely that during later phases of family disruption in an alcoholic's family the situation may be more or less dominated by the alcoholic's drinking behaviour and by his family's reactions to it. Clearly, however, many other factors must enter into the picture. For example, the drinker's pre-alcoholic personality may have to some extent contributed to his embarking on heavy drinking etc. (see Chapter 2), and feelings of insecurity may still interfere with his way of coping, or failing to do so, after his marriage, however much he may use drink to drown such unpleasant and distressing emotions. Often before marriage the alcoholic's personality problems interacted with environmental stresses in a way that was conducive to heavy drinking; since his marriage some of the former stresses may have gone into the background but many new, just as formidable ones, may have taken their place. For example, there is the need to adjust to another personality with her own attitudes and outlook (possibly quite different from his own), her emotional problems, the feeling of suddenly having been thrust into a position of responsibility for others (not only wife but also children), and of having taken on not only the role of husband but also of father. On top of a somewhat emotionally immature and unstable personality, whose problems drove him into the arms of alcohol even before marriage, such additional stresses must exercise a great burden. There is likely therefore to be all kinds of cross-fertilisation between the various 'host' personalities of drinker, spouse and children, with mutual interaction, and in response to a continually varying constellation of environmental situations and stresses. The children's immature personalities are likely to be affected by the unpredictable home atmosphere – the father's drinking, the mother's reactions, both coloured by the parent's pre-alcoholic personality make-up. All these factors make for numerous permutations quite apart from the admittedly very important one of the alcoholic's drinking. Under such circumstances the questions raised by Orford's criticism of the one-sided approach to the alcoholic marriage are fully justified: to what extent are the problems commonly seen in an alcoholic marriage predominantly due to alcohol, to what extent do they largely reflect difficulties also encountered in marriages disturbed for reasons other than drinking?

Events and experiences that may profoundly disrupt non-alcoholic marriages are naturally quite common in alcoholic marriages, too; frequently indeed they may occur relatively more often. In alcoholic marriages the problems become even more complex because the reaction of both the drinker and his spouse to a very traumatic event, such as the death of a close family member, may be coloured not only by the personality make-up itself but by the personality changes during the drinking career (and in the case of the wife, due to her reactions to her husband's drinking). Factors that might cause some disharmony in non-alcoholic marriages may do so even more in alcoholic marriages, and may in fact provide the drinker with another set of rationalisations enabling him to continue, or resume, his drinking with a diminished feeling of guilt. Economic problems and unemployment too, causes of problems in non-alcoholic families, could in an alcoholic family be cause and consequence of drinking and of relapses. Adultery, so often the cause of unhappy marriages, is probably much more common in alcoholic marriages; strangely enough, not infrequently, the drinker's wife seems to be able to console herself that this was merely one of the many possible manifestations of his drinking behaviour so that he was not really to blame: this may make her own position less intolerable and less painful. To some extent, this might slightly change the kind of interaction between the wife's own emotional problems (such as insecurity, intolerance of frustration, anxiety) and her reaction to the husband's unfaithfulness – or the alcoholic's wife might have 'given up' and resigned herself to such habitual behaviour of her husband, whereas the wife of a non-drinker might react furiously as it may have occurred quite unexpectedly. In other cases, however, possibly where the alcoholic still has a large degree of control over his behaviour, his wife's reactions may very much resemble that of the wife of the non-alcoholic – although she may be afraid that too open an expression of her resentment might provide her drinking husband with yet more ammunition justifying another drinking bout. Or, alternatively, she may blame her own 'unreasonably hostile over-reaction' to her husband's drinking for driving her husband to unfaithfulness, etc. etc.

Clearly in cases where unreasonable behaviour of the partner, or intense family upheaval, preceded and precipitated the spouse's alcoholism, such underlying factors themselves require attention. There are also the pathetic cases of hopeful wives coming along to ask for help for their 'alcoholic' husband – 'hopeful' because they have heard that alcoholics can be helped, but it quickly turns out that the so called alcoholic husband is in fact a heavy drinker but that clearly from the abused and battered wife's description his asocial behaviour has preceded his heavy drinking by years. He had never held a job before meeting his wife who is going out to work, looks after him and pays for his drinks – whereas he sits at home possibly entertaining girl friends. He appears, from her description, totally devoid of any feelings of remorse or guilt. True, his heavy drinking probably greatly exacerbates the situation and requires attention but such a marriage would seem doomed whether such a psychopathic personality has a superimposed drinking problem or not.

The importance of factors other than the drinking behaviour itself in problems within the alcoholic marriage, is obvious, for example in the case of the alcoholic woman who may have started to drink when feeling bored, lonely and no longer needed, because of her workoholic husband's concentration on his business, or being out with his cronies, his indifference to her emotional needs, the complete lack of communication, etc. Her alcoholism in time may become so obvious that it may penetrate the husband's indifference. For the husband merely to refer – as so often happens, in the case of alcoholic marriage – the drinking wife for treatment, obviously will not help. He will have to review his own life style, and not primarily that of his wife; in such an instance the wife's drinking may have been similar to the suicidal individual's 'cry for help'. In such an example the dynamic interaction between alcoholism and other factors, the absolute necessity for the spouse to review and try to alter his own attitudes rather than merely demanding that his alcoholic wife stops drinking, are clear. Sometimes indeed the emotional turmoil engendered by the drinker's behaviour – possibly as a result of familiarity having led to a boring routine of family life, and a completely 'taking each other for granted' attitude – may encourage both partners to take a long, close look at themselves and their relationship, and may even turn out to have been a blessing in disguise. In other cases, however, the disease aspect of alcoholism may have rendered drinking an autonomous process which cannot be arrested any more by removing any factors that in the past may have been causally important, or a similar process may have been at work in the drinker's spouse. For example, the wife may have become so embittered as to lose all feelings for her drinking husband. If he finally stops drinking, he may hope that removal of his drinking behaviour which had caused the family disruption, may undo all problems, only to find that his wife's attitude has by now become autonomous and quite independent of his drinking behaviour. Given patience and tolerance, this state of affairs may gradually improve but often it does not. This is yet another example illustrating the need to 'catch' a drinker early in his career and try to motivate him to do something while there is still time, not only for himself but also to keep his family together.

Just as the alcoholic's illness affects his family so, too, will his successful rehabilitation bring relief to several other people. Early detection and rehabilitation of alcoholics are important prophylactic measures in regard to the threatened maladjustment of the alcoholic's offspring. Not only the tragic case histories related above but also – though not making headlines – the influence of the alcoholic's conduct on the emotional development and mental health of his child should not be lost sight of when considering whether passive standing-by or active interference is the better course to follow in cases where the behaviour of the 'practising' alcoholic endangers the physical and emotional health of his family and when he seems unable to pull out of his drinking habits without outside aid, at the same time lacking the insight to ask for help. That appears to be one example where a great deal of invaluable preventative work and help can be rendered by professional community workers with access to people's homes, such as health visitors, district nurses, and community psychiatric nurses (see Chapter 18).

References

1   Jackson, J K (1954), *Quart. J. Stud. Alc.*, 15, 562
2   Whalen, T (1953), *Quart. J. Stud. Alc.*, 14, 632
3   Glatt, M M (1958), *Brit. J. Delinq.*, 9, 84
4   Bowlby, J (1951), *Maternal Care and Mental Health*, Geneva, WHO
5   Gilmour, A (1980), NSPCC Report, (quoted from *Sunday Times*, 4 May 1980)
6   *Brit. med. J.*, (L.A.) 1980, 1, 881
7   Roe, A (1945), *Alcohol, Science and Society*, New Haven, *Quart. J. Stud. Alc.*, 115
8   Goodwin, D W *et al.* (1974), *Arch. Gen. Psychiat.*, 31, 164
9   Bohman, M (1978), *Arch. Gen. Psychiat.*, 35, 269
10 Cadoret, R J (1980), *Arch. Gen. Psychiat.*, 37, 561
11 *Brit. med. J.* (L.A.) 1977, 4, 1371
12 McDermott, J F (1970), *Arch. Gen. Psychiat.*, 23, 421
13 *Brit. med. J.* (L.A.) 1971, 1, 302
14 Quoted from *Daily Telegraph*, 11 November, 1980
15a Orford, J and Edwards, G (1977), *Alcoholism*, Oxford, Oxford University Press, 73
15b Orford, J (1973), *Quart. J. Stud. Alc.*, 36, 1537
16 Gayford, J J (1975), *Brit. Med. J.*, 1, 194
17 Dobash, Russell and Dobash, Rebecca (1980), *Violence Against Wives*, London, Open Books Publ. Ltd.

10

Problem Drinking in Industry

The age groups affected by alcohol are economically the most productive ones. At present the average alcoholic coming to the attention of the helping agencies in this country – as things are, the very great majority (certainly far more than 90 per cent) of alcoholics do not come forward anyway – is in his late twenties to mid-forties. For five to fifteen years prior to that, he has worked at a level below his potential peak. Quite apart from absenteeism, when he did turn up for work he often worked at no more than half-speed, being present bodily but not fully in mind and 'spirit' and functioning as a 'half-man' only. His judgement, concentration, attention, skill, initiative, etc., have often been considerably below his potential best and he has been unable to profit from increased practice, training and experience.

Certainly alcoholics are found in all social classes and occupations, but in this country a considerable proportion of them are above the average in terms of intelligence, drive, initiative, ability and enterprising spirit (provided that their minds are not befuddled by alcohol), even though they sometimes are of a personality make-up that may lack stamina, perseverance and consistency. The loss to the community must be considerable if such potentially extremely valuable assets are squandered by unnoticed and unchecked drinking habits and turned into chronic liabilities requiring intermittent care by doctors and hospitals, or restraints by police, courts and prison, and if they and their dependants often become burdens to voluntary and state welfare agencies.

Twenty-four years ago the director of a large English business concern [1] attempted an inquiry among his business acquaintances and among managers and directors of English business concerns as to whether they were aware of a drinking problem in their businesses and factories.

His inquiry drew an almost complete blank. Most firms replied indignantly that they had no alcoholics working for them and, if there were any, they would still not present a problem as they would be dismissed immediately. It was clear, however, even at the time [2] (1957), that such negative replies did not denote the absence of a problem. Absenteeism caused by acute drunkenness may indeed be rare, though it may sometimes be hidden behind more 'legitimate' diagnoses presented as excuses for staying off work on Mondays; and few advanced alcoholics will manage to stay on in their jobs when indulging in frequent prolonged drinking bouts. But hidden heavy drinking of alcoholics continued for many years may yet be an undetected factor contributing to impaired factory output.

Industrial managers are obviously not unaffected by the popular misconception that the alcoholic is a more or less permanently drunk and incapacitated individual who either never finds a job or is very soon 'found out' and fired. If there is an alcoholic problem in industry it is caused not by the advanced alcoholic but by the much more frequently found type of man who is still in the early or middle stages of his drinking career. He will be found among all ranks of employees as well as among employers, and certainly to some extent also among the ranks of the higher executives, managers and the highly skilled, as is obvious from the wide range of occupations and professions among members of Alcoholics Anonymous and among those presenting themselves for treatment.

The combined wastage stemming from this source must be considerable. Factors such as faulty decision-making loss of efficiency, and production, absenteeism, accidents to themselves as well as responsibility for accidents to fellow employees, loss of years of training in preparation for a responsible position – all these must contribute to the cost of industry estimated in the UK to be at least £350 million a year [3].

Figures obtained at Warlingham Park Hospital in the 1950s showed that of approximately 200 male alcoholics of an average age range from forty to fifty years more than half had begun to lose time off work due to drinking many years beforehand, at an average age of thirty-three years, and had lost their jobs for the first time about three years later. They had thus worked below their potential peak level for about ten years before first losing their jobs, as their excessive drinking had started at an average age of twenty-five years. But not until they had sometimes lost several more jobs, and not until they reached an average age of thirty-nine years did these people first come under medical attention for their drinking habits [2].

A few had first gone to their family doctor for advice when threatened with the loss of their job; but at the time (approximately twenty-five years ago) hardly anyone among them had sought assistance at the direct advice of their employer. More recent impressions indicate that this picture has slightly improved. But even today a lot of 'covering-up' by alcoholic employees themselves and by their fellow workers is certain to go on for fear that if their affliction became known to the management they would be liable to instant dismissal.

Incidentally, in this country with its relatively high proportion of alcoholic women, problems may also arise from the behaviour of the alcoholic wife of, for example, business executives and managers. Sometimes such women blame their husbands' being 'married' to their jobs, never being at home, etc., for their drinking. At any rate the knowledge of his wife's alcoholic behaviour while he is at work, by creating anxiety and tension, affects his concentration at work and again he is not helped by the fact that he does not dare discuss his dilemma with anybody. Clearly this is a problem not limited to the business executive; army officers, civil servants, diplomats, etc. – whose wives have become alcoholics – may also find themselves in considerable difficulties if, on the one hand, they live in perpetual fear of what might be happening at home whilst they are at work and if, on the other hand, they fear for their position if their secret should leak out. But it is only fair to mention that for many years the military services as well as the Civil Service [5] have both adopted a constructive attitude by making available sick leave for treatment and by making arrangements for providing treatment.

A study carried out fifteen years ago on a sample of forty male alcoholics at St Bernard's Hospital [4] showed that 40 per cent had been drinking in excess for at least ten years and that thirty-four patients admitted having lost time off work due to their drinking, often over a period going back many years. Half these patients had realised for at least five years that they were in need of treatment but had nevertheless continued working though knowing quite well that they were not working efficiently.

Gradually many men had slipped down the socio-occupational scale: ten out of eighteen men who originally belonged to classes I and II (professional, managerial and 'intermediate' types of occupation) had now drifted into 'lower' occupations, and while originally none of these men had been an unskilled labourer (class V) by the time of admission to the hospital twelve had this type of occupation – if they were working at all! In terms of time lost from work (including hours lost despite turning up at work) these men averaged a loss of eighteen days per year. They themselves remarked frequently on the impression which they had gained in interviews with their employers that in view of their potential, or good work record in the past, they deserved another chance to 'pull their socks up' – but at the expense of some other company! Thus it came that quite a few men made many such 'voluntary' job changes.

Frequently alcoholics when first questioned about their work record maintain that they never received the 'sack' – only to admit a bit sheepishly later on that they often anticipated being thrown out by handing in their notice just in time to forestall dismissal.

The extent of 'problem drinking' (i.e. including people who still had some measure of control over their drinking) in British industry was investigated in 1967 by research workers at the Institute of Psychiatry [6]; a questionnaire enquiry addressed to the managing directors brought replies from 247 firms in a London borough. The rate of 'problem drinking' found was 3.54 per 1000 men, 0.09 per 1000 women employed at the time of the enquiry. From these findings the National Lifeline, a consortium formed by various Trusts, drew a number of 'rough and ready' conclusions. Thus the 'visible' rate obtained from the management was considered for obvious reasons not to reflect the true picture, and it was suggested that there were in the country at least 250,000 workers with a drinking problem, a cost in lost working days alone of £50 million to £75 million a year, and if items such as sickness benefit, social security and loss of efficiency were also taken into consideration, it was then thought that the cost to the country may amount of £250 million a year.

One welcome sign of a beginning change of attitudes could be mentioned here: in the past few years quite a number of alcoholic employees have been referred at the request of their firms for treatment rather than being sacked – formerly a very rare phenomenon.

In recent years both the National Council on Alcoholism and the Medical Council on Alcoholism in this country have rightly paid special attention to the problem of alcoholism in industry. At an Annual Conference of the National Council in the late 1960s, members of the Glasgow Council on Alcoholism reported the result of a field study carried out in a firm in Glasgow [14]. According to a review in a leading medical journal [21], a 'startling' fact emerged from this study, i.e. whereas the industrial managers had expected an alcoholism incidence of 4 per cent at the top level of industry, the actual incidence was found to be 14 per cent.

Alcoholism in other parts of Britain is likely to be considerably above its incidence in Glasgow; one may hope that this pioneer study will often be repeated elsewhere. But it must surely be amazing that such findings should be so unexpected and that indications that there is, after all, a problem in British industry should come as a startling surprise even to a leading medical journal [22].

Top executives are no more immune to the risks of alcoholism than other occupational groups. The ambitious, hard-working, worrying, up-and-coming businessman may often feel in need of a relaxant both during the time when he is trying to reach the top and later on when he has to work hard to stay there. Moreover, such a man moves in circles where drink is widely accepted as a social and business lubricant; under such circumstances even a personality who is emotionally fairly well adjusted, and psychologically not particularly 'vulnerable' may be tempted, and learn to drink heavily as a result of social pressures.

Thus personality make-up, environmental strain and stress, combined with accepted group customs, may make alcoholism something of an occupational hazard among top business executives. Fortunately, it is just this type of person – the man with a good, stable work record, good social stability and fairly good type of personality – who could be expected to do well with treatment.

In the United States in recent years much attention has been given to the problem of alcoholism in industry, but reliable figures are still scarce. American estimates made approximately thirty-five years ago included that of an annual loss of twenty-two working days by the employee in industry due to his excessive drinking, compared with six to ten days' absence of the average worker, and an accident rate twice as high as that of the ordinary worker. According to an often quoted estimate, problem drinking causes an annual cost to American industry of one billion dollars.

A valuable list of frequency signs of developing alcoholism as reported by supervisors of alcoholics and alcoholics themselves (in the USA) prepared by H M Trice was published in 1969 by the Christopher D Smithers Foundation, the most active American Foundation in the field [8].

Signs noticed

(a) Signs noticed *early* (and frequently thereafter) by the supervisors included: leaving the post temporarily, absenteeism, more unusual excuses for absences, lower quality of work, mood changes after lunch, and red or bleary eyes; at this stage the alcoholics themselves reported hangovers on the job, increased nervousness and hand tremors.

(b) Signs noticed *late* (but frequently thereafter) by the supervisors were: less even, more spasmodic work pace and hangovers on job; whereas the alcoholics at this stage noted red, bleary eyes, a more edgy feeling and an avoiding of the boss and associates.

(c) Signs noticed *fairly early* (but infrequently thereafter) by the supervisors were: loud talking, drinking at lunch time, longer lunch periods, and hand tremors; by the alcoholics: drinking in the mornings before work, at lunch time and during working hours; absenteeism, more unusual excuses for absences, leaving the post temporarily, arriving late at work and leaving early.

(d) Finally, signs noticed *late* (and infrequently thereafter) by the supervisors were: drinking during working hours, avoiding boss or associates, a flushed face and an increase in real minor illnesses; whereas the alcoholics themselves at this stage reported mood changes after lunch, longer lunch periods, the use of breath purifiers, and lower quality and quantity of work.

The decline of work efficiency appears to vary with the type of occupation. People employed in a higher-status job tended towards 'on-the-job absenteeism' – turning up for work despite hangover, fatigue and poor memory. Employees in lower-status jobs, on the other hand, were more inclined towards absenteeism but did a fairly good day's work whenever they did turn up.

There is, therefore, ample scope and need for a programme of research and education and for constructive company policies in the problem of alcoholism in industry. The company policy should be well defined and known to employees. Greater understanding of the problems would engender in employers and personnel managers a more sympathetic attitude and a wish to participate in the rehabilitation of their alcoholic employees. The knowledge that he would find assistance, not instant dismissal, would in turn encourage the alcoholic to ask for help at an earlier phase.

In the United States many companies have in recent years adopted some type of 'programme' for alcoholism. Four basic points of a positive company policy, as formulated by one corporation [9], are the defining by top management of alcoholism among its employees as a health problem requiring treatment, and towards which the company takes a treatment attitude and assists in securing therapy; it is made clear that if after reasonable opportunity for progress the employee does not show noticeable improvement at his work he will be dismissed; and this policy will be widely communicated by the officers of the company with their full approval.

In the experience of Dr L G Lederer [10], Corporate Medical Director of American Airlines, there are three main requirements for successful industrial programme for alcoholic employees:

1 Management and employee recognition of the problem.
2 Union co-operation and participation.
3 Adequate company insurance coverage for medical needs and sickness pay while rehabilitation is undertaken.

Government, management and unions, are, or should be, concerned in the drink problem in British industry. Like management, unions in this country, by and large, have hardly been active in this field until very recently. Among the exceptions is the Civil and Public Services Association, Britain's biggest civil service union. The union's national welfare officer, according to a recent newspaper report [11], stated in May 1980 that there were a lot of heavy drinkers in the civil services but he was at pains to emphasise – and he is surely right in this – that the drink problem was no lesser or greater in the civil service than elsewhere in the country. The union urged Government and employers to approach alcoholism as a medical condition and make treatment available, with special leave and pay or sick leave terms; and alcoholics, when voluntarily undergoing treatment, should not be subject to code of conduct and disciplinary rules.

A special risk group, singled out by the union's national welfare officer, were customs officers who, in the course of their duty, were exposed to special temptations. Such men were at risk when going aboard ships because of the skippers' generosity of offering them not just small drinks but 'half pints of whisky'. And drink was also at hand when custom officers were visiting bonded warehouses.

As regards the unions' interest in the problem of alcoholism in industry, encouraging signs can be seen not only in the attitude adopted by them when faced with problems among individual members but also in developments such as a proposition carried at a Post Office Employees' Union meeting [12] in August 1980. The Proposition was 'To negotiate as a matter of urgency an agreed procedure with the Post Office for the treatment and rehabilitation of members suffering from alcoholism'. Reference was made during the debate to the procedure adopted by the Post Office in Scotland that 'The employee while undergoing recognised treatment is considered to be on sick leave and entitled to the normal sickness benefits under Post Office rules. Every effort will be made to ensure that the employee, after treatment, is able to return to the same job. There will be no downgradings and retributions unless matters of discipline or inefficiency are involved'. There was an interesting discussion during the debate on the proposition which was on the whole on a very knowledgeable *niveau* and ranged over a wide field. One member considered alcoholism a 'curse' and referred to the possible benefits of acupuncture; another member echoed the view of radical sociologists that alcoholism was a product of the 'sick society', arising out of the 'stressful system we live under', involving work, everyday worries, 'the anxieties of capitalism': what was needed was 'trying to change the society we live in, not to deal piecemeal with every little [!] problem that arises within this society'. Other speakers were 'not absolutely convinced' that by changing society '. . . the problem of alcoholism would automatically go away'. A member of the National Executive Council talked about the difficulties encountered at the national level to get things moving but, the Post Office apart, '. . . significant sections of trade unions . . . feel that the problem [of alcoholism] is so delicate that they should not be tackling it'. He promised, however, in view of the seriousness of the problem, that the National Executive Council would be doing all in its power in the coming year to see the matter through. There was also a contribution from a Birmingham speaker who felt 'proud' that this union had this proposition on the order paper, and finished his brief talk with the statement: 'Delegates, the man who moved this proposition ought to be standing twelve feet tall'.

Problems that may be encountered in industrial programmes have recently been surveyed by Hore [13]. They may arise from the attitudes of the unions (who, for example, may object to the idea of medical snooping); attitudes of management (who may object to industrial programmes because they might be seen as reflecting inefficient management); the difficulties of establishing desirable joint union and management negotiations in occupational health programmes, rather than those being mainly directed by either management or unions; the selection of employees (there should ideally be no preference by companies in instituting rehabilitation programmes for blue collar workers rather than for high-status personnel); and the evaluation of such programmes.

Beginnings have certainly been made. For example, as recently described by Blacklaws [14], the Scottish and Newcastle Breweries Limited (S & NB) in the past few years developed a 'progressive' policy on drink-related problems within the company. The policy adopted was applicable to all employees. On recognising a potential problem, i.e. drinking that affects the employee's work performance, the manager sought the advice of personnel and medical departments who could start the treatment process when and where required. While undergoing treatment the employee was on 'sick leave', entitled to normal sickness benefit schemes, and he would return to his position after finishing treatment, unless he offended against the disciplinary code or it became clear that he was incapable of responding to treatment.

Blacklaw's review stresses that as the policy is only in its infancy, conclusions can only be tentative, but even so 'it is apparent that the majority of employees [with] conspicuous drinking problems can be helped to overcome these, at least in relation to their work performance. And that [Blacklaw concludes] must be good for them, for us, and for society'.

A valuable review of the subject, *Alcohol and Work*, was published four years ago by the National Council on Alcoholism [16]. It was estimated that there may be a minimum of two million people, from company directors to shop floor workers, whose drinking was costing Britain millions of pounds. There was, however, general reluctance to face the implications. The number of working days lost through strikes attracts general attention and creates widespread concern but compared to the six million days lost through strikes in 1975, it was estimated that such a loss was probably small compared to that incurred as a consequence of excessive drinking. Workers in general lose on average 16½ days a year but the average excessive drinker is now thought to lose five times as many days. (This up-to-date estimate is certainly much higher than the eighteen days' loss found in our own study among a sample of alcoholic employees fifteen years ago [4] and that of twenty-two days per year found by Jellinek [17] in 1947 among American alcoholic employees – then thought to be two to four times as high as the average loss among American employees in general [18].) A study carried out by the Information Centre of the National Council found that 88 per cent of their clients were drinking periodically before going to work; 62 per cent sometimes took a bottle to work – 12 per cent doing so every day, and 91 per cent sometimes drank throughout the day. The Council recommended that the Health and Safety Executive should investigate the cost of loss of production and earnings due to accidents, sickness and sub-standard work caused by excessive drinking; and that management and employee representatives should formulate a joint code of practice with the aim of helping employees with their drinking problems while at the same time safeguarding their jobs.

This theme was taken up again at a conference on alcoholism in industry in December 1980 [19] where a 'leading industrialist' blamed excessive drinking for sapping 'the life blood of business (i.e. creativity, positive thinking and enthusiasm)'. Nevertheless, it was said many industrialists saw alcoholism only as a disciplinary problem and failed to realise the financial gains that could be made by reducing its occurrence. The head of the TUC's industrial welfare department at the same meeting regretted that there was no specific general agreement for dealing with alcoholism problems; the TUC, he said, had been trying in vain to get together with the CBI about coming to such an agreement.

There has been a recent study as regards the effect of one item contributing to the cost of heavy drinking in industry – accidents at work. A study of three different plants in Wales – as reported in December 1980 [20] – showed that such accidents considerably increased in number at the beginning of new shifts and in particular after the lunch break. Drinking before the evening shift or during the lunch hour was seen as the factor responsible for the increase of industrial accidents during these periods. Alcohol consumption was estimated to lead to at least four or five times the number of accidents occurring in people who have not taken a drink.

Industry, by arranging a programme of research, prevention, early detection and (where necessary) treatment, will often preserve happiness, health and human lives – and, incidentally, save money – surely a more constructive approach than the present-day ostrich policy of 'dealing' with the problem by ignoring its existence.

References

1 'A managing director', *Brit. J. Addict.* (1957), 54, 5
2 Glatt, M M (1957), *Brit. J. Addict.*, 54, 21
3 Sir Bernard Braine, reported in *Evening Standard* (14 October 1980)
4 Glatt, M M and Hills, D R (1965), *Brit. J. Addict.*, 62, 403
5 Whitley Bulletin XLVII (1967), 71, *Brit. J. Addict.* (1967), 62, 403
6 Hawker, A *et al.* (1967), *Med. Offr.*, 118, 313
7 Gray, J (1969), *Journ. Alcoholism*, 4, 164
8 Trice, H M (1968) in *Understanding Alcoholism*, ed. Christopher D Smithers Foundation, New York, Charles Scribner's Sons
9 Trice, H M, *Alcoholism in Industry*, New York, Christopher D Smithers Foundation
10 Lederer, L G (1977), *Proc. Roy. Soc. Med.*, 70, 116
11 Ellis, J, reported in *Evening News* (15 May 1980)
12 POEU Journal, (August 1980)
13 Hore, B D (1980) in *Alcohol Problems in Employment*, eds Hore, B D and Plant, M A, London, Croom Helm, 10–17
14 Blacklaws, A F (1980) in *Alcohol Problems in Employment* (see ref. 13), 134–43
15 Plant, M A (1979), *Drinking Careers, Occupations, Drinking Habits and Drinking Problems*, London, Tavistock
16 National Council on Alcoholism (1977), *Alcohol and Work*, London
17 Jellinek, E M (1947), *Vital Speeches*, 13, 252
18 *Aspects of Alcoholism* (1963), Philadelphia, Lippinscott
19 *Doctor* (11 December 1980)
20 Christian Economic and Social Research Foundation (December 1980), London

II

Alcoholism in Doctors[1]

Size of problem and clinical aspects

It has been known for many years that doctors contribute more than their fair share to the ranks of those dependent on drugs other than alcohol. (Apart from liver cirrhosis, the two other major conditions with higher mortality rates among British doctors than the rest of the population are suicide and accidents (with risks 335 per cent and 180 per cent, respectively, as high [29]).) For example, Louis Lewin in his classic work *Phantastica* (1924) [1] stated that world-wide statistics had shown 40 per cent of morphine addicts to be doctors apparently; however, he did not refer to any special vulnerability of doctors to alcoholism. Standard mortality rates from liver cirrhosis commonly taken as a rough-and-ready indirect index of the prevalence of alcoholism (see Chapter 5) among medical practitioners in England and Wales, have gradually risen from 114 in 1911, to 185 and 183 in 1921 and 1931 respectively, 250 in 1951 and 350 in 1961 [21] (the latest published figure a decade later is 311). This would indicate, perhaps somewhat surprisingly, that doctors earlier in the century had just as high average rates with a gradual rise in more recent times. On the whole, not much attention has been paid in the past to this question of an alcohol problem among doctors [18] although in recent years some studies have been carried out in Canada and the USA, as well as in Britain.

Prevalence

Estimates of the size of the problem in certain population groups are available from Canada, the USA, Scotland and England. Vincent and his collaborators [1a] (1969) compared the proportions of doctors who had been given a primary diagnosis of alcoholism among medical men admitted for psychiatric illnesses to a private hospital in Canada [1a] the USA [2] and England [3] (1967): the proportions were 30.0 per cent (Canada), 12.2 per cent (USA) and 7.5 per cent (England) respectively. Vincent and his colleagues concluded from their comparison between these studies that emotional problems were frequent in doctors in all three countries, as were high suicide rates. Bissell and Jones (1976) [4] mentioned a number of further studies of doctors undergoing psychiatric treatment which reported alcoholism to be common.

In Britain the study by A'Brook and his collaborators [3a] (1967) found that among sixty-three addicted doctors twenty-four were dependent on alcohol alone, thirty on other drugs, and nine on alcohol and other drugs. Studies by Murray (1976) showed that:

(a) Among 144 doctors discharged from the joint Maudsley and Bethlem Royal Hospitals in the period 1964–73, 29 per cent (five women, thirty-six men) had received a primary diagnosis of alcoholism or alcoholic psychosis [5];

(b) among male doctors admitted to all psychiatric hospitals in Scotland, 39 per cent were alcoholics; first admission rates for alcoholism to these hospitals for four years (1963, 1965, 1968, 1972) were 2.7 times higher amongst male doctors than amongst non-medical social class I men [6].

The relatively higher proportion of alcoholic doctors in Scotland is ascribed by Murray to the well known higher rates of alcoholism in Scotland (see Chapter 5); and various observers (A'Brook *et al.* [3], Murray [5]) as well as the present writer [7] have found relatively high proportions of Irish and Scottish doctors among their alcoholic medical patients. Among our own male alcoholic patients over the past twenty-five years doctors have consistently formed a percentage varying from 2–3.5 per cent [7]: for example, among approximately 290 male alcoholic in-patients treated at Warlingham Park Hospital (1952–7), eleven (3.8 per cent) were doctors [8]; there were nineteen doctors (3 per cent) among approximately 640 male alcoholics admitted to the St Bernard's Hospital Alcohol Unit between 1963–7 [8], and seventeen doctors (2.4 per cent) among approximately 700 male alcoholics in the 1968–74 period [7]. Among approximately 1700 male alcoholic patients seen at an out-patient clinic or privately in the 1970–6 period, 41 (2.4 per cent) were doctors [9, 13]. Among our patients the ratio between male and female alcoholic doctors was lower than the one (thirty-six men to five women) reported by Murray. Out of 450 women alcoholics admitted to St Bernard's Hospital in the decade 1958–67 there were three alcoholic doctors (0.7 per cent) (and incidentally three other alcoholics were wives of doctors, as were five who were dependent on amphetamines and/or barbiturates – out of a total of 120 female addicts aged over twenty years). Among 784 female alcoholics who were admitted to the Spelthorne St Mary Nursing Home [10] (for dependent women) in the period 1964–73 there was a 'minimum' of two doctors (and a number of inquiries about others), and also four wives of doctors. The tendency for alcoholic doctors to develop emotional illnesses including alcoholism and drug dependence has often been reported in the literature in this country [3, 5] as well as in Canada [1a] and in the USA [4]. Of our eleven male alcoholic doctors at Warlingham Park Hospital (1952–7), five also took amphetamines and/or barbiturates; of the nineteen alcoholic doctors treated at St Bernard's Hospital (1963–.'), seven also took barbiturates and one took glutethimide [8].

From the various statistics cited it is clear that the number of doctors with drink problems in this country, as in others, is considerable.[2] Exact figures cannot be given. In view of the finding of a 3½ times as high a cirrhosis mortality rate among doctors in this country as among the general population (who may have alcoholism rates of, say, 1–2½ per cent) a very rough guess would put the number of alcoholic doctors into the region of 2000–3000. What may be much more important is that the number of medical men who are alcohol misusers (without as yet being alcoholics) must be considerably higher. The number of enquiries that over the past twenty-five years or so have been coming from partners of drinking doctors bears out the existence of a real problem in the medical profession, and one wonders how and why the profession has been able to ignore it for so long.

Causation

Factors frequently mentioned by alcoholic doctors themselves include those given by Murray [6] i.e. emotional problems, overwork, and marital problems. Among our doctor patients the most commonly named emotional factors were feelings of anxiety, tension and of (subjective) inadequacy in their undergraduate days when they learned to 'treat' such unpleasant feelings with alcohol so successfully that habitual repeat doses (on lesser and lesser provocation by anxiety-producing circumstances) seemed justified and indicated. Overwork among medical men, coupled with the high responsibility attending such work, and the emotional stress it engenders, is often a very real factor, at times again stemming from the anxiety before, and the stress of, examinations in undergraduate days. Later on, overwork may sometimes in itself be a symptom of emotional stress, including the need to work harder in the face of difficulties and the slowing down caused by heavy drinking. Marital and family problems are common among doctors [1a] with their concentration on their stressful work, irregular hours and meals, insufficient holiday etc., or as D Le Vay (1967) [4a] put it, '[doctor] work does make physical and emotional demands that tend to leave their wives and children with the dregs at the end of the day'. The finding that alcoholism among doctors' wives, too, is not uncommon among our patients (a finding consistent with a standard mortality rate (SMR) of 200 among doctors' wives [21]) can thus cause little surprise. In turn unhappy home atmosphere, and emotional disturbances among wife and children, may drive the drinking doctor even further towards alcoholism. This may contribute in a special way to the 'role strain' which, in the view of Vincent *et al.* [1a], is an important factor responsible for many doctors' emotional breakdowns, including alcoholism – the doctor's experience of constant failure and inadequacy in the face of disease and death.

A rather surprising finding in Murray's study [5] was that their heavy drinking 'usually had started . . . in the wake of well-established drug dependence (in seven cases) or other psychiatric disorder (in five cases)'. This was especially so among the women doctors: out of a total of five women, three had been drug dependent and one depressed at the onset of their heavy drinking. In fifteen of Murray's forty-one cases, conditions other than alcoholism had been diagnosed by psychiatrists. (Mainly depression, anxiety states, and personality disorder underlay the alcoholism, in particular among those whose alcoholism had been diagnosed before the age of forty.) Murray's sample in these aspects seems to be completely different from those alcoholic doctors treated in our units since the early 1950s or encountered or treated by us elsewhere. As stated above, the great majority among our doctors were males, and, as in Murray's sample the pre-alcoholic personality make-up was, by-and-large, emotionally more unstable among our female than among our male alcoholic doctors. Before the onset of heavy alcoholism most of our alcoholic doctors had done professionally quite (or often very) well (as indeed did some of Murray's doctors) and many did so again after recovery from their alcoholism; definite (pre-alcoholics) psychiatric abnormalities were uncommon, and personality disorders rare.

One has to keep in mind diagnostic difficulties, and the different views in applying diagnostic labels in this context. For example, depressive episodes are very common among alcoholics and may often be regarded and treated as the primary condition by some, as reactive and secondary to the alcoholic condition by others (see Chapter 15). Similarly, many 'practising' alcoholics behave and act out, as if they were suffering from a psychopathic personality disorder, and it is often extremely difficult to obtain a reliable history as to how they had behaved before they became heavy drinkers. However, the majority of the alcoholic doctors seen by us co-operated well and actively with treatment during their in-patient treatment. They were often extremely helpful to other patients; quite a few recovered alcoholic doctors (both in Britain and elsewhere) have been in the forefront of activities designed to assist alcoholics; and most have done well both as regards drinking habits and their continuation with, or return to, medical practice. For example, out of thirteen doctors treated at St Bernard's Hospital Alcohol Unit during the past four years, nine are sober and back in their practice; of the remaining four, two had been diagnosed in hospital as 'personality disorder' (psychopaths), one of them had left hospital after a stay of three days; one man (a consultant radiologist) died of cirrhosis; and a lady doctor (an anaesthetist) having stayed off drink for several months relapsed (temporarily) at Christmas. Similarly out of the 120 alcoholic doctors who early in 1978 were in touch with the Alcoholic Doctors' Group in the UK, almost all were doing quite well as regards their drinking and were at work professionally.

All this seems so different from Murray's findings [5] that one wonders about the reasons for this discrepancy. His lengthy follow-up (ranging from 6–132 [mean 63] months) showed that apart from five who had either killed themselves and four who had died from cirrhosis, nine had continued to drink most of the time, ten had occasional relapses and seven completely overcame their alcohol problem. Of these, five had remained totally abstinent and 'two returned to apparently normal drinking'; and of twenty-nine doctors alive at the time of follow-up only eight were practising satisfactorily; eight appeared unemployable.

Admittedly the observation period among our follow-up alcoholic doctors has frequently been relatively short – certainly much shorter than in Murray's sample. But on the other hand it has repeatedly been shown [11] that alcoholics who have stayed off drink for a minimum of six months, tend to do well in the future. More likely, the difference in the outcome might be ascribed to the different composition of the samples. It seems reasonable to suggest that a high proportion of the doctors treated at the Maudsley (Teaching Hospital) were in fact referred there because of the greater seriousness of their psychiatric and personality disorder. Murray's sample therefore would not be representative of a random selection of alcoholic doctors. In this case it could be this rather 'negative' selection in Murray's sample, with the high proportion of pre-alcoholic psychiatric abnormalities, that would be responsible for the relatively poor outcome, rather than their superimposed alcoholism.

In our experience, the 'host' (the underlying personality make-up,) in the average alcoholic doctor is not fundamentally different from that of other doctors (apart possibly from a somewhat greater disposition or tendency to suffer from anxiety and tension under stress). As among the rest of the population, so also among medical men, anyone – including those with no more than their fair share of personality difficulties – can develop alcoholism under sufficiently unfavourable circumstances and the great majority of alcoholic doctors can recover. Alcoholism among doctors seems to arise not from a very high 'host' vulnerability and abnormality, but largely from factors pertaining to the environment – risks attached both to undergraduate as well as to the postgraduate professional life [13]. It would thus seem that it is 'environment', rather than the 'host' factor, which is responsible for the great majority of cases of alcoholism among doctors; and therefore as alcoholic doctors are 'made' rather than 'born', there ought to be good chances for prevention in the first instance, and for recovery (with adequate treatment) in the case of the established alcoholic doctor.

Delay in diagnosis

While in theory the outlook for recovery in the case of alcoholic doctors should be quite good, there are factors working in the opposite direction. Most alcoholic doctors come forward at a relatively late phase of their alcoholism, commonly in the late crucial phase or sometimes even already in the chronic phase with evidence of definite physical (polyneuropathy, liver damage) or mental complications (Korsakoff, etc.). Indeed, unwilling to ask for help, they may often attempt to 'cure' themselves by means of drugs (with the risk of a superimposed dependence on other drugs) or seek final oblivion in suicide. Thus Edwards' remark (1975) [14] that 'Alcoholism is not a subject particularly well understood by the medical profession', merely understates the position. Until very recently most doctors understood very little about alcoholism and alcoholics because in their student days they had learnt nothing about alcoholism – apart from a little about its late (and uncommon but clinically interesting) complications; liver cirrhosis, polyneuropathy, Korsakoff, etc. [12, 13]. The disease concept of alcoholism has only of late come to be grudgingly accepted by the medical profession, and most doctors feel ashamed of their alcoholism. It is only the threat of his despairing partners to exclude him from the partnership that finally forces the alcoholic doctor to accept treatment still very much under protest and without any acceptance of its necessity. On the other hand, latterly, we have come across medical men asking for advice while still in their prodromal phase – welcome evidence of the effect of recent publicity. Another sign that recent publicity is finally reaching to medical students is that, over the past few years, our students at four London medical schools have begun spontaneously to remark about the high alcoholism rates in the medical profession. In the former ten–twenty years of teaching medical students such information seemed quite unknown. Unfortunately, at the same time, there often still appears to be the traditional heavy drinking among many groups of medical students, but one might hope that increasing knowledge will markedly reduce their intake, and also later the likelihood of habitual or relief, heavy drinking after those students have qualified.

Clinical aspects

At present the great majority of alcoholic doctors are seen in their late crucial phase. Typical, however, is also their tendency, before starting treatment to deny, or grossly minimise, their symptoms, and without the doctor's wife present at the interview a diagnosis is often not possible. The appearance of definite physical or mental complications occasionally puts the diagnosis beyond doubt. As in the case of their alcoholic non-medical fellow-travellers, so also alcoholic doctors often protest vehemently that they could not possibly be alcoholics or even have a serious alcoholic problem, as they were sometimes able to abstain from alcoholic drink altogether for some days, or to interrupt a drinking session in order to attend to their patients during surgery hours.

Treatment and rehabilitation

The usual therapeutic techniques (see Chapter 16) can be as helpful to alcoholic doctors as to other alcoholic patients, including, for example, group psychotherapy, alcohol-sensitising drugs (disulfiram, CCC), and Alcoholics Anonymous. Many medical men have found great help from AA (Chapter 16) and there is a flourishing International Doctors in AA association, particularly strong in the USA. Initially, however, many doctors may be reluctant to join a layman's society, and in such cases the Alcoholic Doctors' Group in the UK has proved extremely helpful [16]. In this group, as among any other larger cross-section of alcoholic doctors, a sceptical newcomer will find all medical specialities represented as well as GPs; he will soon gain a feeling of belonging and lose his initial feelings of shame when finding his predicament shared by so many obviously very able, intelligent, and often highly successful, colleagues. The British Doctors' Group started in 1974 with regular meetings in London only, but enthusiastic members have now begun to establish groups and regular meetings elsewhere, such as Newcastle and Dublin; and the group is so popular that it can only be a matter of time before such groups will also be formed in other cities. By making doctors and others aware that medical men and women, too, are by no means immune from alcoholism, and can recover from it, in time the existence of this group should help in spreading awareness of such a risk among medical students and doctors, on the one hand, and of reducing the stigma attached to alcoholism among the general population, on the other hand. In both ways this group thus-serves the goal of primary prevention – quite apart from its obvious benefits in terms of earlier diagnosis, therapy and rehabilitation.

Another risk to keep in mind in the treatment of alcoholic doctors is that of misuse of, and dependence on, other drugs. This is a danger not only to alcoholic doctors who continue to drink, but even to those who have successfully overcome their alcohol problem. We have come across cases of dependence among doctors on practically any one of the various addictive drugs.

Prognosis

For the great majority of alcoholic doctors the prognosis, in view of their relatively good personality and social stability is good, once they face up to the situation and accept the need for help and for continued support well beyond the acute phase. One of the best doctors to work in the Alcoholism and Drug Dependence Unit at St Bernard's was an Irish psychiatrist who had started his come-back 'career' at St Bernard's as a patient in the Alcohol Unit, in a state of considerable physical deterioration and after having lost several jobs as a consequence of his drinking habits. With the consent of his alcoholic co-patients, after having been a patient in the unit for three months, he was appointed initially as a Locum Registrar in the unit – after it became clear that in view of his alcoholism he was experiencing great difficulties in finding a job elsewhere. As far as his work and his alcoholism were concerned, during the subsequent five years he never looked back.

There are quite a number of examples of recovered alcoholic doctors who subsequently have rendered (and still do) great service to their fellow sufferers. In America, Dr Claire Bissell (formerly Chief of the Alcoholism Center at the Roosevelt Hospital, NY, and herself a recovered alcoholic) and the sociologist R W Jones [4] (1976) recently presented an interesting analysis of interviews with ninety-eight recovered alcoholic doctors (psychiatrists were over-represented in this group) all of whom had been totally abstinent from alcohol for at least one year. Originally over half had done exceedingly well in their Medical School – which hardly speaks for a specially inadequate or disturbed 'host' personality: of the group ninety-one were working full-time in medical practice; five were semi-retired (for health reasons); one had retired completely (he was in his seventies, and had been abstinent for over twenty years as incidentally have a number of doctors in this country); and one had left medical practice and had become a medical writer. Twenty-one held teaching appointments in medical schools. The average period of total abstinence among these doctors was 7.4 years, with a range of 1–29 years.

Prevention

As in alcoholism generally there is an overriding need for prevention. In the case of doctors there seems to be a special opportunity
to minimise greatly the risks of alcohol misuse by making medical
students aware that doctors form a specially vulnerable, high-risk
group to alcoholism as well as other forms of drug dependence [7,
8, 12]. Such specific education directed at target groups [12] in our
view seems to hold out greater chances for success in at least a
certain proportion of students than the usual 'shot-gun' approaches of advice and health warnings to the entire population
[12, 22]. Special education of medical students about the risks of
alcohol misuse and alcohol dependence will also assist them to
gain a much better understanding of the problems faced by alcoholics and their families and thereby indirectly also be of the
greatest benefit to them after qualifying, from the point of view of
early diagnosis and early institution of therapeutic measures on
their alcohol-misusing patients. Medical students in our experience over the past few years in a number of London teaching
hospitals soon become greatly interested when given the chance
to meet various types of alcoholic patients including recovered
alcoholics [15, 16]. Our findings in this area seem very similar to
the observations in North Carolina by Ewing (1976) [13].

The negative attitudes among medical undergraduates and
doctors towards alcoholics [17] must of course greatly contribute
in perpetuating the stigma attached to alcoholism. It is therefore
interesting to note that an American study (Fisher *et al.*) [19] in
1976 has found that after completion of an alcoholism education
course the training programme had been successful not only in
providing the participating doctors with greater knowledge about
alcoholism but also in 'positively modifying the participants'
attitudes'.

One important factor which has greatly contributed for nearly
fifteen years to the interest in the problems of alcohol misuse and
alcoholism has been the work of the Medical Council (see Chapter
21). Of special interest was a Symposium in January 1977, jointly
arranged with the Society for the Study of Addiction [25] and
dealing with the theme: 'Abuse of Alcohol amongst Medical
Practitioners'. As among other occupational groups in the past
there was in the medical profession a conspiracy of silence
although there are cogent reasons why doctors should take a
leading role in educating in this field. When the idea of a sym-

posium and a special publication on the theme of alcoholic doctors was first discussed in the MCA, some felt that it was wrong to publicise the fact that doctors contribute more than their fair share to the ranks of those misusing alcohol because the bad publicity might undermine public confidence in the profession. However, ignoring an undoubtedly present and serious problem is unwise, especially because more than in other occupational groups doctors suffering from alcoholism not only harm themselves but also constitute a grave risk to others. An appreciation of the fact that doctors feel it necessary to come to grips with the problem in their own ranks – by indicating the seriousness with which they regard the problem may set an example to the other sections of the community. The MCA felt that there was a need to expedite steps which should be taken to minimise the risk of alcoholism development in future doctors, to help those who are already affected and to safeguard the public who might be placed at risk [26]. Among papers read at the Symposium, apart from medical aspects [27] there were also others dealing with ethical and disciplinary aspects [25] and legal aspects [28].

Steps aimed at helping sick doctors, in particular those suffering from drink, drug, or psychiatric problems, to remain, or become again, fit to practise, have since been adopted (November 1980) by the General Medical Council. Previously doctors affected by such conditions, to an extent that they might be a threat to patients, were not liable to suspension until they had first been convicted by a court for a crime, or suspected of serious professional misconduct. Under the new scheme such a doctor could be asked by the Council to submit himself to an examination by two specialists who might suggest treatment. Should he refuse to co-operate he risks having to appear before a health committee which has the power to suspend him. What the new scheme obviously aims at is a preventive, deterrent, and supportive effect rather than punishment. It would constitute yet another example of the procedure of 'constructive coercion or confrontation' [30] originally introduced in some American industrial firms for the benefit of their employees as well as the firms concerned. Similarly, one might hope that these steps will assist many ambivalent medical men towards taking preventive or therapeutic action years before they reach a physically and mentally almost irreversible condition. Cases were mentioned at the General Medical Council deliberations of alcoholic doctors who had practised for more than twenty years (although such cases are by no means very rare); out of the cases of forty-five doctors coming before the disciplinary committee of the Council the preceding years over 50 per cent involved drink or drug cases [31].

Notes

1   Extended from a talk given at a symposium of the Society for the Study of Addiction and the Medical Council on Alcoholism, London, 26 January 1977.

2   It is of course a matter of regret and no consolation that members of other medical professions are also vulnerable to alcohol [13]. For example, among 450 women alcoholics admitted to the St Bernard's Hospital Unit in the decade 1958–67 twenty-one (4.7 per cent) were trained *nurses* and fourteen untrained nurses; of 113 women dependent on drugs other than alcohol and over twenty years of age, fourteen (including three who also drank excessively) were trained nurses (12 per cent) and twelve (including five who were also excessive drinkers) were assistant nurses. The twelve drugs involved were mainly amphetamines and barbiturates (often misused at that time by women), rarely chlorodyne and non-barbiturate hypnotics (which then gradually began to compete with the barbiturates, the more the risk of barbiturate misuse and dependence was becoming more widely known [12, 23]. Among the 560 women alcoholics and addicts over twenty years of age, there were three alcoholic doctors and eight wives of doctors. Among the latter, three were alcoholics, five dependent on amphetemines and/or barbiturates. Similarly among women admitted to Spelthorne St Mary's Nursing Home in the period 1965–7, of eighty-seven alcoholics, nine (4.4 per cent) were nurses, of sixty addicts aged over twenty years, seven (11.7 per cent) [8, 13].

References

1   Lewis, L (1964), *Phantastica*, London, Routledge and Kegan Paul
1a Vincent, M O, Robinson, E A and Latt, L (1969), *Canad. Med. Ass. J.*, 100, 403
2   Pearson, M M and Strecker, E A (1960), *Amer. J. Psychiat.*, 116, 915
3   A'Brook, M F, Hailstone, J D and McLauchlan, I E J (1967), *Brit. J. Psychiat.*, 113, 1013
4   Bissell, C and Jones, R W (1976), *Amer. J. Psychiat.*, 133, 10, 1142
4a Le Vay, D (1967), *Scenes from Surgical Life*, London, Peter Owen
5   Murray, R M (1976), *The Lancet*, ii. 729 (a)
6   Murray, R M (1976), *Brit. med. J.*, 4, 1537 (b)
7   Glatt, M M (1974), *The Lancet*, ii, 342 (a)
8   Glatt, M M (1968), *Brit. med. J.*, 1, 380
9   Glatt, M M (1976), *The Lancet*, i, 196 (a)

10 Sister Stella Mary (1974), personal communication
11 Glatt, M M (1961), *Acta Psychiat. Scand.*, 37, 143
12 Glatt, M M (1974), *A Guide to Addiction and its Treatment – Drugs, Society and Man*, Lancaster, MTP
13 Glatt, M M (1976), *Journal of Alcoholism*, 11, 85 (b)
14 Edwards, G (1975), *The Lancet*, ii, 1297
14a Horney, K (1951), *Neurosis and Human Growth*, London, Routledge and Kegan Paul, 64–85
15 Glatt, M M (1975), *Brit. med. J.*, 2, 157 (a)
16 Glatt, M M (1975), *The Lancet*, i, 219
17 Macdonald, E B and Patel, A R (1975), *Brit. med. J.*, 1, 430
18 Rolleston, J D (1933), *Brit. J. Inebriety*, 31, 33
19 Fisher, J V, Fisher, J C and Mason, R L (1976), *J. Stud. Alc.*, 37, 1686
20 Vernon, H M (1928), *The Alcohol Problem*, London, Bailliere, Tindall and Cox
21 Registrar General (1971), *Decennial Suppl. on Occupational Mortality*, London, HMSO
22 *The Lancet* (1973), Annotation, ii, 1135
23 Glatt, M M (1962) *Narcot. Bull* (UN), 14 (2), 19
24 Quoted from Simpson, M A, *World Medicine*, 24 September
25 Sir Denish Hill (1977) in *Abuse of Alcohol amongst Medical Practitioners*, London, Med. Council on Alcoholism, and Soc. Study, Addict., 9–17
26 Glatt, M M (1977), Introduction, *ibid*, 2–3
27 Glatt, M M (1977), *ibid*, 4–8
28 Butcher, C H H (1977), *ibid*, 18–21
29 Murray, R M (1980), *Hosp. Update*, 143
30 Trice, H M and Roman R M (1972), *Spirits and Demons at Work*, New York, Cornell University
31 Rodes, P (1980), Medical Council on Alcoholism General Meeting, London

12

The Problem Drinker at the Steering Wheel[1]

In the 1920s 4000 people were killed annually on the roads in Great Britain, by 1968 the number had risen to nearly 7000, with almost 90,000 severely, and a quarter of a million slightly, injured [2]. In the two decades 1960–79 the number of those killed was 143,000, the seriously injured, 1,750,000.

Alcohol is only one of several factors which – often in interaction with each other – cause accidents on the road. However, alcohol has been found to be the largest single factor responsible for fatal road crashes.[2]

About 12,000 deaths a year are the result of drunken driving. Three out of four drivers killed on an average Saturday night in road accidents have excess alcohol in their blood, as has almost every second driver in his teens and twenties who dies in any road accident on any day or night of the week [3]. In 1979 a third of all drivers killed on the road were over the legal blood alcohol level; among these were 52 per cent of those aged 20–24 years, and 41 per cent of those aged 17–19 years. Two out of every three road deaths at night are caused by drinking. The cost of drunken driving is now estimated to amount to £100 million a year (including items varying from ambulances, hospital treatment, police inquiries, loss of earnings of the injured etc.).

The higher the blood alcohol concentration the greater the risk of a severe or fatal crash, and it has been shown repeatedly that very high blood alcohol concentrations are unlikely to be reached by other than alcoholic drivers. However, significant impairment of performance – brought about by factors such as interference with judgement and concentration, increased recklessness, etc. – has been noted at levels as low as 50mg/100ml. Most countries have fixed by law a blood alcohol level beyond which it is an offence to drive, varying for example from 50mg/100ml in Norway and Sweden to 80mg/100ml in Great Britain and West Germany and 150mg/100ml in Belgium and Luxembourg.

In Britain the Road Safety Act of 1967 aimed at ensuring that a driver found to have a blood alcohol concentration above 80mg/100ml would be convicted, whereas before the introduction of this Act he usually stood a good chance of being acquitted. The introduction of this Act was followed by a significant reduction in the number of people seriously injured or killed on the roads, as has been well described by J D J Havard in the 18th Ernest Winterton Memorial Lecture (1969) [4].

The year before the introduction of the Act road accident fatalities reached a figure of nearly 8000 and approximately 100,000 more were seriously injured. The following year saw a reduction of 15 per cent in deaths (a saving of 1552 lives) and a 10 per cent reduction in total casualties, a saving of over 40,000. The role of the drinking driver is reflected in the fact that the greatest reduction of casualties occurred during those periods of the day when the alcohol effects can be expected to be most pronounced, i.e. the time between 10 p.m. and 4 a.m., and during Saturday nights and Sunday mornings.

Havard describes the reduction in road accident morbidity and mortality which followed the introduction of the Road Safety Act as 'one of the most remarkable success stories of the century', even though it was soon discovered that the Act was 'riddled with loopholes' tending to bring it into discredit and necessitating new High Court rulings.

The contribution made by heavy drinking to road fatalities is illustrated by the findings that in the first year after the introduction of the Road Safety Act the blood alcohol level in 15 per cent of drivers killed in road accidents was found to have been in excess of 80 mg/100 ml, in 11 per cent in excess of 150 mg.

In the course of time the introduction of the breathalyser (in 1967) lost its initial impact (largely because the risk of being caught turned out to be fairly remote). This is reflected, for example, in the observation that, compared to the 15 per cent with excess blood alcohol killed in the first year after the breathalyser introduction, thirteen years later, their proportion has more than doubled. Proceedings against motorists for drunken driving offences in England and Wales gradually rose from approximately 22,750 in 1968, to 31,835 in 1970, 55,600 in 1972 and 70,400 in 1975. (Corresponding figures for Scotland were 5600 (1968), 8400 (1970), 10,160 (1972), and approximately 11,700 in 1975.) In view of the failure of the 1967 Road Safety Act to maintain its initial impact in reducing deaths and serious injuries, the Blennerhassett Report [5] (1976) recommended a considerable strengthening and tightening up of procedures. What is of special interest is that quite a few suggestions dealt with the procedure to be adopted for the 'high-risk offenders' (i.e. those with over 200 mg/100 ml, or second offenders convicted twice within ten years for drinking and driving) whose number was established to amount to about 15,000 cases a year. These people were regarded as 'a more serious threat to road safety than other potential offenders', and the Blennerhassett Committee was keen to find ways to 'provide . . . those who have drinking problems with a strong incentive to change their drinking habits'. Among steps suggested was a requirement that the convicted driver, in order to have his disqualification removed, would have to provide evidence that he had 'sought help and as a result effected a change in his drinking habits'. (Some of the obvious difficulties involved will be discussed later in this chapter.) So far, however, despite the generally favourable reception of the Blennerhassett proposals, the Government has failed to implement them. Meanwhile the drunk driving problem has continued to increase. For example, the number of persons (as reported by the Chief Inspector of Constabulary [6]) required to provide an initial breath sample has risen from 133,700 in 1975, to 144,800 in 1978 and 163,580 in 1979. Although (or because) such a rise has been demonstrated, some experts in this field, such as Dr John Havard [7] feel strongly that the number of breath tests should be stepped up. (The number of breath tests carried out in this country amounts to 150,000–200,000 per year, compared with over a million tests in France; and Havard points to the lessons to be derived from a campaign undertaken in Cheshire in 1975 when ten times more breath tests were taken than under ordinary circumstances: the number of convictions doubled and the number of those killed or seriously injured on the roads during drinking hours fell by 60 per cent.)

The proportion of traffic accidents in this country caused by 'alcoholic' drivers is not known. Additionally the risk from the behaviour of the alcoholic *pedestrian* must not be overlooked either. In a recent survey 28 per cent of pedestrians involved in road accidents had a blood alcohol level beyond the legal limit for driving [8]. A few years ago (1976), a pedestrian killed in a road accident when trying to thumb a lift was found to have had a blood alcohol level of 656 mg/100 ml – said by the pathologist to be the highest ever seen in the department. This pedestrian surely had every right to have been dead (or at least severely comatose) even before being hit by a car but he was 'not in a deep coma' and had been 'laughing and joking' shortly before the accident.

Estimates in other countries about the contribution of alcoholics to drunken driving vary. In the 1960s, Swedish studies [9] found 35–48 per cent of drunken drivers to be problem drinkers or alcoholics whereas Canadian investigators [10] concluded that 28 per cent of all drivers convicted for impaired or drunken driving were alcoholics. As alcoholism in this country seems less prevalent than in Sweden and Canada, the proportion of alcoholics among drunken drivers may not be quite as high though probably on the increase.

Since the 1950s – when enquiries carried out by the Hulton Research team showed that one third of adults in this country were abstainers and most 'social drinkers' probably drank no more often than once a week – consumption of drink by social drinkers has greatly gone up. An investigation carried out in 1979 by Taylor [11] – making use of a National Opinion Poll (a 'random omnibus survey') – showed that 'a great deal of regular and heavy drinking is going on in most age groups'. Among 'regular drinkers' in the age groups 18–34 over 40 per cent, and in the age groups 35–64, over 30 per cent, drank at least two or three times a week; and there were many people in all age groups who fell in the 'heavy drinkers' categories (defined as those who drank at least 5–6 pints or 5–6 measures of spirits), with the highest percentages in the 18–24 years age groups. Nevertheless, alcoholics – while making up no more than one or two per cent of those who drink – drink much more regularly and heavily, and in their later phases they drink to excess not only in the evenings but also in the afternoon and, finally, in the mornings, including, for example, the time of going (and driving) to and coming from work.

In Sweden some years ago, Goldberg [12] found that the consumption of alcoholics surpassed that of moderate drinkers by up to forty times, not only in regard to total amounts but also in regard to the number of drinking occasions and to the average amounts taken on a single occasion. Moreover, a considerable proportion of alcoholics in this country belong to occupations and professions requiring the regular use of a car. Thus, alcoholics over here may be expected to contribute to the ranks of drunken drivers considerably more than their fair share, and a guess of 10 per cent may not be an over-estimate. In this country, as in others, alcohol-impaired and drunken driving is not only – as formerly generally assumed – a 'problem of alcohol' and thus of the moderate drinker who only occasionally may drink more than is good for him – and for other road users – but also one of the 'problems of alcoholism'.

The highest alcohol level in the blood which, according to the British Medical Association Special Committee (1960), may be 'entirely consistent with the safety of other road users' is 50 mg/100 ml, a level which is very often greatly exceeded in the case of alcoholics, as is the 80 mg/100 ml level laid down by the Road Safety Act 1967. For example, routine testing of urine alcohol levels of female alcoholics at the time of their admission to St Bernard's Hospital (1964–7) showed that of 108 patients – who had taken drink on the day of admission – eighty-seven had a urine alcohol concentration of at least 100 mg/100 ml (roughly corresponding to a blood alcohol level of at least 75 ml/100 ml), among them 37 women with urine alcohol level of at least 300 mg (corresponding to an alcohol level of at least 225 mg/100 ml) [13]. How far the alcohol levels observed on admission reflect those which such alcoholics commonly reached when drinking is doubtful, but they may give some indication of the order of magnitude of blood alcohol concentration of (female) alcoholics.

Although some authorities have found no great difference in acquired increase of alcohol tolerance between moderate and fairly heavy drinkers, habituation in alcoholics has been experimentally and clinically shown to lead to a lessened response to alcohol. On the other hand, Bjerver and Goldberg [14] found impairment of performance even in heavy drinkers when the level surpassed 100 mg/100 ml. Moreover, despite their heightened tolerance (which, in later stages may, in many alcoholics, be followed by a decrease in tolerance) alcoholics are much more frequently intoxicated than ordinary drinkers, because the goal of their drinking is different from that of the social drinker and because in practice they drink much larger amounts.

Experimentally, Goldberg [15] has demonstrated that the 'critical blood alcohol level' (i.e. the concentration at which significant behaviour changes first occur) of moderate drinkers is lower than that of alcoholics; but as moderate drinkers consume much less alcohol, they usually do not even attain their own relatively low critical level, whereas alcoholics often drink much more than even their relatively high critical level would allow, and thereby become intoxicated. The alcoholic driver must therefore be regarded as a special risk – and often as a real menace – on the road for a period commonly varying from five to fifteen years [16] – i.e. starting with the pre-alcoholic or prodromal phase till he may ask for, or be pushed into, treatment. Not infrequently alcoholics report having driven in a state of 'blackout' over long distances: they may wake up in the morning wondering how they had come home and where they had left the car, only to find it safe in the garage. Minor 'scrapes' are quite common and are freely admitted by many alcoholics who often confess openly – after having given up drinking – that for years they had taken 'fantastic' or 'appalling' risks.

Not only is impaired and drunken driving a fairly regular occurrence among alcoholic car drivers, but it also occurs fairly early in their drinking career – in our experience, in their late twenties, or early thirties – i.e. in the pre-alcoholic and prodromal phases [16] (see Chart pp. 74–5, and Tables 2 and 7, pp. 78, 99). Thus, recurrent alcohol-impaired driving may be an important, 'objective' prodromal sign, which often allows suspicion and detection of incipient alcoholism quite a few years earlier than is generally the case [16].

The danger in alcoholic drivers is not limited to the time shortly after heavy drinking. Often alcoholics remark spontaneously that they themselves feel the greatest danger to be on 'the morning after', in the hangover stage, i.e. at a time when outside observers could not smell alcohol in their breath.

The risk of driving in an unfit condition is heightened in many alcoholics who so often also habitually take other (sedative, tranquillising or stimulating) drugs to excess. Most common in the middle-class 'loss of control' addict in this country in former years was the misuse of barbiturates (mainly by women) [17]. Nowadays many (especially female) alcoholics take tranquillisers, though in Britain in general in the ordinary dosage prescribed by their doctor. (Habitual misuse of tranquillisers – mainly benzodiazepines – is much more common in North America than here.) One must always remember that alcohol and other CNS-depressing drugs such as tranquillisers and (even) the non-barbiturate hypnotics have at least an additive, and possibly a synergistic, effect when taken concurrently. This is a danger in particular when it comes to driving [17]. The risk of additional dependence on other drugs as well seems particularly great among this country's alcoholics in the middle-class drinker, i.e. the individual who is most likely also to be a car driver.

The very great danger stemming from the alcoholic car driver is illustrated by the finding that among 250 male alcoholics observed in the Warlingham Park Hospital unit in the 1950s, eight admitted to having been involved in fatal traffic accidents. Sometimes it was only the fear of punishment after an accident that had occurred which motivated these people to ask for treatment. It is interesting to report that quite a few alcoholics who readily admitted that they had been drinking at the time of the accident had not been convicted for driving under the influence and occasionally not even charged with it. This finding supports the impression that official figures at the time (1950s and 1960s) probably grossly under-estimated the contribution of alcohol to traffic accidents.

. Alcoholics, thus, do not only harm their family but – by their habitual alcohol-impaired driving over many years – they are an immediate danger to the wider community. The question arises whether, in such circumstances, more pressure could or should be brought to bear on car drivers who are repeatedly charged with alcohol-impaired driving to undergo examination, observation and possibly treatment. Their willingness to co-operate in this procedure might, perhaps, be taken into consideration by magis-trates when pronouncing sentence. Among the middle-aged al-coholic car drivers there must be many with a basically fairly good type of personality, in whom treatment, especially when instituted early, may have a considerable chance of success.

Unfortunately, at present, many alcoholics come for treatment only in relatively late phases after years of inflicting misery and suffering on their family and themselves. Caught up in the chains of their alcoholic affliction they are not really 'free' to make a rational decision to undergo or to refuse treatment.

That alcohol-impaired driving is an early and regular feature in alcoholic car drivers offers doctors, magistrates and other agencies an opportunity to suspect and detect the condition in an earlier phase, and to collaborate in prophylactic measures designed at one and the same time to arrest the further downhill path of the alcoholic driver and thereby also to diminish the considerable risk coming from one important source of traffic accidents. It also implies that the important social problem of drunken driving is a matter of great concern to the medical as well as to the legal profession.

The finding that there are many different types of drinking drivers who are responsible for road accidents explains why dif-ferent approaches are needed and why one and the same tech-nique – such as the threat of punishment – may not be the panacea. The latter approach may be sufficient to deter the social and the self-indulgent heavy drinker; the alcoholic driver, however, may often require measures such as a period of treatment and loss of his driving licence until there is reasonable hope that his alcoholism has been successfully arrested.

The present-day situation

The research for this chapter was undertaken in the main in 1960 (though obviously corrected for the purpose of the present edition). In 1979, three years after the Blennerhassett Committee submitted its proposals, the Government in a 'Consultative document on drinking and driving' published by the Department of Transport [18], suggested reforms which are mostly those recommended by Blennerhassett. A single 'impairment' offence – an excess blood alcohol level providing irrebuttable presumption of impairment – would replace the present-day offences of driving while impaired, and driving with an alcohol concentration above the prescribed limit. The proposed new legislation would greatly simplify procedures and should close the many existing loopholes. The breath test would be the normal means of providing evidence of impairment: the suggested legal limit would be 40 mg alcohol/ 100 ml breath.

When discussing the problem of very heavy drinkers the Government's document recommends a disqualification of no less than three years with a proviso that the licence should not be restored until the driver produces evidence that he no longer constitutes a 'risk'. The number of such heavily drinking offenders is estimated to be about 15,000 per year [5, 19]. Such very heavy drinkers would obviously require considerable assistance to overcome their drinking and, at present, facilities to assist them do not exist. Moreover, what would be the 'evidence' regarded as sufficient to greatly minimise (rather than ruling it out completely which in practice is not possible) the risk of such an offender being an 'undue risk on the road'? Would this, for example, mean no drink at all for some years (as very likely it should) or merely an absence of any drinking excesses? Who would be responsible for deciding on this issue? A great deal of responsibility would fall on the drinker's therapist who will often be in a considerable quandary. Presumably such a drinking offender may have to show evidence that he himself has decided to keep off drink altogether, for example by steps such as joining, and regularly attending AA and, where indicated, taking alcohol-deterrent medication under the regular supervision of an experienced GP or treatment agency. In view of problem drinkers contributing much more than their fair share to this group of high-risk offenders, answers to such questions are extremely important but introducing legislation on this issue is urgent, and there is little to be said in favour of what a leading article in the *British Medical Journal* [20] called the Government's 'leisurely approach' to drinking and driving.

The same article also poses once more the question of giving the police the right to exercise discretion to carry out breath testing (in situations where there is a strong probability of drunken driving, rather than indiscriminate random testing). The article argues that in the absence of any radical changes in public attitudes towards drunken driving 'There will be no substitute for a law that is enforced and seen to be enforced', as otherwise the risk of 'being found out' is too small to provide an effective deterrent.

Thus, as Havard [7] has pointed out, difficulties existing in the attempts to control the drinking driver do not arise solely from the state of mind of the driver but also from the public attitudes that fail to appreciate that it is the highly atypical, heavily drinking, high risk driver who attains the high blood alcohol levels, who is the real danger on the road and who is at risk of repeated offences. Only very tolerant, habitual or dependent drinkers can drink large amounts of alcohol leading to more than double the statutory blood alcohol level without feeling very ill. In his discussion of measures which could be taken in an attempt to control the drinking driver, Havard mentions:

1 *Publicity campaigns*: (Which however, would fail to reach the habitual heavy drinkers most likely to be involved in serious accidents, and would thus have little impact);

2 *Lowering the 80 mg/100 ml blood alcohol limit*: This is a measure proposed in many quarters. Havard, however, regards it as 'counter-productive': such measures would be of no significance to the priority group in terms of accident-risks, and he sees 'no justification for singling [the ordinary, social drinkers] out for special treatment before tackling the far more important problem of the very high-risk drivers'. A reduction to a 50 mg/100 ml statutory limit would threaten with prosecution many ordinary, social drinkers 'many of whom incur a relative low risk of accident'.

3   *Random testing*: This has sometimes been suggested but, in Havard's view, it would not be cost-effective considering the relatively small proportion of drivers then detected to be above the statutory limit.

4   *Raising the enforcement level* of the existing law *on a selective basis:* would, in Havard's view, have the best chance of success as it would raise the drinking driver's perception to be detected. Selective testing would, for example, include testing on roads where there is a high likelihood of the occurrence of alcohol-related accidents. It would, however, be necessary for police, the courts and the general public fully to recognise that such measures are public health steps taken in order to reduce the habit of drinking driving.

5   *Need for further research*: Adequate data are required in order to institute appropriate control measures; for example, information about the distribution of blood-alcohol concentrations in a representative sample of the drinking population, as different from the unrepresentative groups of drivers killed in road accidents, and among the breathalysed. Such information could be obtained from voluntary roadside surveys as carried out in some other countries in the past.

6   *Need for legislation*: This would, in Havard's view, not be required except to legislate the Blennerhassett proposals that high-risk convicted drivers have their licence no longer automatically restored at the end of one year but would have to show that their driving is no longer risky to themselves and others.

In Havard's opinion public opposition to control measures directed at controlling the drinking driver arises mainly from misunderstanding the role of alcohol as a drug and the kind of driver (i.e. the often habitually heavy drinker) most likely to be involved in alcohol-related accidents.

Proceeding from a brief consideration of the required publicity or information campaigns, as regards Havard's second point, the ordinary driver (including the 'casual roisterer') is not in a position to reach the high blood alcohol levels such as 200mg/100ml and still to be able to drive a car. 200mg/100ml means taking about 11–15 pints of beer or 11–15 doubles of spirits [19]. People still able to drive at this level are usually alcoholics; and obviously it is in their own interest as well as that of the public that they should give up driving until they have overcome their drinking problem.

Alcoholics, after having received treatment, almost always openly admit that they had been taking 'shocking risks' when driving. In this way the proposed tightening up procedures against high-risk drivers surely do not constitute an unwarranted interference with personal liberty and would reduce a great danger to the life and health of other road users.

Notes

[1] In some ways a more fitting title might have been 'Alcohol at the steering wheel'. With higher blood alcohol concentrations (such as those often achieved by alcoholics) it seems increasingly the agent alcohol that is taking over the rein from the person who is supposed to be the driver. The alcoholic, with his belief of what he can do greatly at variance with what he actually can do [1], may fancy himself as being in control – he may be sitting in the driver's seat but he is not in charge.

[2] Significant effects of alcohol in car drivers include deterioration of intellectual, motor functions and performance, and a marked lengthening of reaction time [21]; in particular removal of inhibitions, dulling of higher mental processes, marked impairment of judgement, attention, self-discipline, co-ordinating skills, visual acuity and a decreasing sensitivity to sensory stimuli [22]. All such effects are greater with higher and usually with rising blood alcohol concentrations.

References

1 Cohen, J (1963) in *Alcohol and Road Traffic*, ed. Havard, J D J, London, BMA, 14–19

2 Ministry of Transport (1968), *Road Accidents*, London, HMSO

3 Minister of Transport (1980), quoted from *Daily Telegraph*, October 1980

4 Havard, J D J (1969), *Alcohol and Road Safety – a Review of United Kingdom Legislation*, London, United Kingdom Temperance Alliance

5 Department of the Environment (1976), *Drinking and Driving*, Report of the Departmental Committee (Blennerhassett Report), London, HMSO

6 Chief Inspector of Constabulary, quoted from *Alliance News* November/December 1980, 18

7 Havard, J D J (1978), *Brit. med. J.*, 2, 1595

8 *Brit. med. J.* (1979), 3, 371

9a Andreason, R (1963) in *Alcohol and Road Traffic*, ed. Havard, J D J, London, BMA, 66–78

9b Klotte, H (1963), *ibid* 332–5

10   Schmidt, W S, Smart, R G and Popham, R F, *ibid*, 90–98
11   Taylor, L, *New Statesman*, 22 June 1979, 906
12   Goldberg, L (1951), European Seminar and Lecture Course, Copenhagen, 26
13   Glatt, M M (1967), Selected Papers, 13th Internat. Inst. Prev. & Treatm. Alcoholism, Zagreb, 43
14   Bjerver, K and Goldberg, L (1951) in *Alcohol and Road Traffic*, Proceed. First Internat. Confer., Stockholm, 132
15   Goldberg, L (1962), *Arbeitstagung über Alkoholismus*, Wien, xiii
16   Glatt, M M (1964), *The Lancet*, i, 161
17   Glatt, M M (1962), *Bull. Narcot.* (UN), 14(2), 19
18   Department of Transport (1979), *Consultative Document on Drinking and Driving*, London, Department of Transport
19   *Brit. med. J.* (L.A.) 1976, 2, 1103
20   *Brit. med. J.* (L.A.) 1980, 1, 135
21   Mackie, J (1979), *Practitioner*, 222, 662
22   (Irish) Commission on Driving while under the Influence of Drink or a Drug (1963), *Report*, Dublin, Station. Off., 26–31

13

Suicide and Crime [1]

1 Aggression against oneself

Both 'failed' suicide attempts as well as 'successful' suicidal acts
are common in alcoholics, although these two groups are usually
regarded as being in many ways quite different from each other
[2]. All terms used for the suicidal attempt have come in for
criticism, including 'unsuccessful' or 'suicidal gesture' or 'self-
poisoning'. Whereas suicide is more common in men and among
elderly women, *attempted* suicide is in general more common in
(younger) women – the most popular method being drug over-
dosage, and very often taken in such a way that there is no real risk
to life. In alcoholic women the risk, however, is considerably
increased because usually tablets are swallowed with, or after,
heavy drinking, carrying additional risks such as potentiation of
the effects of drink and drugs, and of being unable to keep the
number of tablets and drink down to a relatively 'safe' level.
Among the 'attempted suicides' severe depression and alcoholism
are described as being less common than among suicides [3], and
they often may want to register some form of protest or demon-
stration to those around them; whereas the lonely friendless
suicide wants to die. Again, alcoholics may often, after years of
heavy drinking, end up in a state of utter isolation and emotional
as well as financial bankruptcy and, having realised by then that
alcohol no longer gives them the required relief ('pharmacothymic
crisis'), and that their attempt at the alcoholic 'solution' to their
problem has completely failed [4], they may then decide to make
an end of it all. It may thus cause little surprise that, alongside
people suffering from endogenous depression, alcoholics are
regarded as the highest at-risk groups, estimated to be fifty times
as high as among the general population [5]. Most studies found
rates among alcoholics between six and twenty-five times that of

the average population; but an interesting investigation by Kessel and Grossman (1961) [6] in London, in two groups of alcoholics totalling 212 people, found no suicide among forty-six alcoholic women during a follow-up lasting up to eleven years, whereas among the male alcoholics 7–8 per cent committed suicide, a rate .75–86 times as high as the rates for men of similar age among London's general population. Of those who later (i.e. some time after hospitalisation) committed suicide, all but one had reverted to heavy drinking.

Similarly, suicidal ideas and actual *attempts* are quite common in alcoholics. Ritson and Hassall (1970) [7] found in Edinburgh that 20 per cent of their alcoholic patients had taken overdoses. Among our alcoholic patients at Warlingham Park Hospital in the 1950s [8], nearly half of the men, and more than one-third of the women, admitted that when drinking they had behaved aggressively or endangered others or themselves. In the light of histories obtained from the relatives of these patients, the real proportions are undoubtedly much higher.

Estimates, on the one hand, as to the proportion of alcoholics among persons attempting suicide and, on the other hand, of the frequency of suicidal attempts amongst alcoholics vary a great deal. Thus, in a number of statistical studies, the percentage of alcoholics among suicidal men varied between 25 and 40 per cent, and among women between 3 and 12 per cent.

Looking at the problem from another angle, approximately 25 per cent of the male Warlingham Park alcoholics and 15 per cent of the women had attempted suicide. Suicide attempts were more common among middle-class than among working-class alcoholics and somewhat less common among down-and-out drinkers and among alcoholics admitted to an observation ward than among the alcoholics admitted to Warlingham [18]. This corresponds to the findings of a recent American study in which Palola and his colleagues [9] found that of their alcoholc men 17.1 per cent had attempted suicide, and that such attempts were more common among Alcoholics Anonymous members than among alcoholics coming from the lower socioeconomic strata.

Although would-be ('failed') suicides are described as forming a different group from the ones who succeed in committing suicide [2], quite a few alcoholics ultimately kill themselves in such an attempt. Upton Sinclair [10], in his book *The Cup of Fury* – written in support of his thesis that 'alcohol is perhaps our most persistent purveyor of agony and of premature death' – described the cases of twenty-five outstanding people, mainly brilliant writers, who went to their death through excessive drinking; nearly half of them by suicide.

In the light of modern theories, according to which the loss of foothold within their community is an important causative factor in many suicides, the relative frequency of suicidal attempts among alcoholics becomes readily understandable. In the course of his drinking career the alcoholic becomes more and more isolated and often finally ends up a social outcast.

Some psychoanalysts, like Menninger [11], see in alcoholism, drug misuse, etc. a gradual act of self-destruction, a slow way of avoiding a more rapid and threatening self-destructive impulse. This latter, caused by guilt due to feelings of hostility, the individual is unable to cope with, and the 'need to be punished' led to suicidal feelings. One meets many alcoholics who, when asked the reasons for their heavy drinking, immediately mention a wish of self-destruction. There are many alcoholics who feel that life is so devoid of meaning and purpose, or mentally painful and oppressive, that they come to prefer the punishment following heavy drinking and even the danger of sudden death to the continual discomfort and pain of living. Even those, however, who seem sincere when saying that they do not care whether they live or die, usually have a notion of a quick, relatively painful death and do not seem to cherish the prospect of a long, lingering death from a condition like liver cirrhosis.

Among non-alcoholic wives of alcoholics the statement 'I just cannot take it any longer,' is of course heard quite frequently. There may be suicide attempts in such cases, as a kind of 'cry for help' or in order to show their drinking husband how desperate they feel but, as in other cases, such preceding suicidal attempts or the threat of suicide by no means exclude the possibility that eventually the final step may be taken, and such statements coming from the alcoholic's wife have usually to be taken very seriously.

Both among alcoholics as well as among their spouses states of often severe reactive depression are naturally very common (see Chapter 15). Endogenous depression, a common cause of suicides, is much less frequent among alcoholics, although it does of course occur. A much more common cause for suicide attempts, gestures, and even more frequently threats, in some younger alcoholic patients is an underlying psychopathic personality disorder [8]; among the total of 268 male and female patients at Warlingham Park Hospital the percentage of patients who had attempted suicide was considerably greater among the psychopaths (32.6 per cent of the eighty-six patients) than among the non-psychopaths (20.8 per cent of 182 patients), although the difference was statistically significant only among the females.

As in other aspects of alcoholics' behaviour, for example in the alcoholic marriage, alcoholism is thus by no means the only or main factor to play a role in alcoholics' suicidal attempts and suicides. Often the underlying personality may play a relatively more significant role than the superimposed alcoholism. Underlying personality factors may also come into play: some alcoholics (as well as non-alcoholics) 'gamble' with death, apparently leaving it to chance whether they survive or not when they swallow whatever tablets there may be around, together with a half or a full bottle of vodka. (This curiosity or 'gambling' inclination is, incidentally, also a factor to be kept in mind when prescribing alcohol-deterrent medication, such as disulfiram; most alcoholics will certainly not touch alcohol afterwards but a few may be prepared to take the plunge just to experience what might happen.)

The connection of attempted suicide with alcoholic drink is not only a problem of alcoholism but also a problem of alcohol: i.e. occurring in non-alcoholics but caused by drinking. For example, two Scottish studies [11a, 12], found among men and women committing acts of self-poisoning a high proportion who had done so immediately after frequently, heavy drinking. In many similar cases – especially those with a fatal outcome but also with survivors unwilling or unable to give a clear account – it may often be difficult or impossible to distinguish between an accident and suicide-bid; this would apply to alcoholics as well as to non-alcoholics. Not uncommonly, for example, one is told by women alcoholics that they had not been drinking more than their usual (though admittedly large) amounts, had gone to bed and taken their sleeping tablets; they are found comatose next morning and later maintain that they do not remember having emptied the bottle with the sleeping tablets. Often such acts take place when these women are very depressed, but they maintain that they had no intention of killing themselves. In some such cases, what seems to have happened is that, waking up during the night in a state befuddled by the mixture of drink and two sleeping tablets taken earlier, they did not recall having taken the medication and, in a state of 'automatism',* may have taken more and more of them. Obviously the question of 'automatic behaviour' and the extent to which certain actions have been determined mainly consciously or unconsciously, may become of great forensic significance in the case of antisocial and aggressive acts directed against others, and may sometimes be extremely difficult to answer, even with prolonged investigations and hospital observation.

2   Aggression against others

Drinking and antisocial behaviour

This question has been well reviewed by Hore (1976) in his book *Alcoholic Dependence* [13]. Alcohol has often been claimed to be involved in criminal or antisocial behaviour involving assault, violence (including homicide, sex crimes [14], and drunken driving), and sometimes the victim as well as the attacker has been drinking. Reference has been made to the possible relationship between alcohol and murder in Chapter 5. Among 400 Scots charged with murder between 1953–74, a high proportion both of accused men and women and of their victims had been drinking. Various studies carried out in Australia [15], Britain (the reduction of drunkenness offences following the legislative steps taken during the First World War [16]), and the USA (where serious crimes and drinking both increase during weekends [17]), vaguely point to an association between alcohol intake and antisocial behaviour. Attempts to find a *definite* link between drinking and criminal actions – involving crimes of violence and sex crimes in individual cases – have, in Hore's view, not been convincing, so that, in spite of the popular assumption linking drink and crime, he concludes much further work is needed 'on differing samples of offenders using chemical tests of alcohol levels and careful assessment of degree of intoxication'. There is, of course, no doubt as regards, for example, the influence of alcohol in driving ability, drunkenness offences and traffic accidents.

(a)   *How great is the proportion of 'criminals' among alcoholics?*
Of – mainly middle-class – male alcoholics admitted to Warlingham Park [8] approximately 20 per cent had been in prison, chiefly for minor offences; one-third had been before the courts. Of male

---

* 'Automatism': a dissociation between behaviour and consciousness [3].

homeless alcoholics and 'excess drinkers' admitted to a London observation ward [18] at about the same period (mid-1950s) 40 per cent had been in court or in prison; of a group of male homeless alcoholics and 'excess drinkers' living in a London reception centre [18] – mainly social classes V and IV – approximately 45 per cent (mainly inadequate psychopaths) had been in prison. Similarly, of a group of male alcoholics admitted to a London observation ward [19] – with a home of their own and mostly belonging to social class III – one-third had been before the courts.

Thus, in samples of alcoholics drawn from different sections of the population, the majority had never been in prison, despite a history of excessive drinking over many years. Although inebriety by releasing aggressive tendencies is a contributing factor to crime, the great majority of alcoholics never get into serious conflict with the law.

(b)   *How great is the proportion of 'alcoholics' among criminals?* Prior to the 1940s, often up to 60 per cent of all criminal offences were attributed directly or indirectly to alcoholic intoxication. However, Banay's [20] study in Sing Sing prison (1945) – which Jellinek called 'the first truly relevant investigation of the role of alcohol in crime causation' – showed that inebriates did not form more than 22 per cent of the prison population. Taking into consideration the nature of the crimes committed by the alcoholic prisoners, the findings that assaults – the main crime among in-ebriates – were more in the nature of 'brawls' and that among the sex crimes exhibitionism was more prevalent than rape among alcoholic prisoners, Banay concluded that 'the contribution of alcoholism is greater in the minor than in the major crimes'. The discrepancy between the earlier and Banay's findings of 60 and 25 per cent respectively may have been due to failure of earlier investigators to differentiate between the criminal who is also a heavy drinker and the heavy drinker who becomes a criminal, between 'alcoholic criminals' (individuals whose antisocial activities clearly preceded the onset of their heavy drinking) and 'criminal alcoholics' (alcoholics whose excessive drinking clearly antedated – and may have greatly contributed to – their anti-social actions).

In this country Norris (1941) [21] found that of approximately 1000 receptions to an English provincial prison in 1939, drink had been actually responsible for the crime in 10 per cent; and among

1000 male admissions to Broadmoor a history of excessive drink-ing was detected in 121, in approximately half of whom 'alcohol was the main, if not the only, causative factor' [22]. Among homeless men admitted to the London observation ward (1956), 40 per cent of the forty excess drinkers had been before the court or in prison, as against only 17.5 per cent of 90 men who were not excessive drinkers, but the drinkers' crimes were generally of a petty nature, those of the rest were more in the nature of cal-culated frauds [18]. Heavy drinking – as the *Buckmaster Report* [23] pointed out in 1931 – is obviously a hindrance to the pro-fessional criminal as it hampers his preparations and coolness.

It has to be admitted that in the last four paragraphs the term 'alcoholics' has been used very vaguely, often including 'excess drinkers' and non-dependent · problem drinkers. In the past, writers often failed to define too clearly the type of drinker concerned in antisocial activities. Hore refers to a number of more recent investigations. An Australian study (1962–3) [15] found that over a three year period, among murders, 26 per cent, of those committing assault and robbery, 54 per cent, of those in-volved in breaking-in and stealing, 49 per cent, and of sex of-fenders against the female, 25 per cent, were 'alcohol addicts' – a term apparently used very loosely in this study, applying to the 'heavy drinker' in AA classification [13]. Such a distinction of course makes a great deal of difference when it comes to discussing the connection between alcoholism in the stricter meaning of the term, and crime. A Northern Ireland study (1965) [24] found a history of 'alcoholism' in 55.6 per cent of successive offenders admitted to prison during a period in 1963; the term 'alcoholism' however, was not defined. A London investigation by Gibbens and Silberman (1970) [25] found among 404 prisoners and ex-prisoners of three prisons sentenced for longer than a month and thus practically excluding those sentenced merely for drunken-ness, 18 per cent with a history of excessive drinking to a degree seriously interfering with their social adjustment (which would make them 'alcoholics' according to the 1952 definition (see Chapter 1) but not necessarily people dependent on alcohol). In another study of London prisoners, Edwards and his co-workers (1971) [26] found among 312 long-term prisoners, 11 per cent to be 'severely' dependent on alcohol and serving sentences for drunkenness whereas another 19 per cent were severely depen-dent and serving non-drunkenness offences. In terms of 'heavy drinking' (10 pints of beer per day, or more), rather than 'dependence', 73 per cent of eighty-eight short-term drunkenness offenders and 14 per cent of the 312 long-term prisoners were considered 'heavy drinkers'.

Thus such recent studies confirm the generally held opinion that both non-dependent and alcohol-dependent heavy drinkers contribute a significant proportion to the ranks of those committing crimes and to the prison population. The situation has been less well studied among women, but here too from our own observations in prisons and of offenders seen in court, alcoholics contribute a certain percentage, likely to be greater than their proportion among the general population. Woodside (1961) [27], studying women with drinking problems admitted to a London prison in 1960, found the majority coming from the lowest two social classes and having a history of unskilled work records, and many with a very high number of convictions. Middle-class women are obviously mainly involved in drink-driving offences, however, in the present author's experience. According to the 1979 R.C. Psych. Report [28] half to two-thirds of male and 15 per cent of female prisoners had a serious drinking problem, most of them being petty recidivists.

In the complex interaction between drinking and antisocial behaviour drink is usually only one of a number of factors involved, naturally much more significant in some cases than in others. In some cases the main factor is the disordered personality whose emotional instability is heightened by even relatively small amounts of drink; in other cases, a large amount of alcohol has pharmacologically 'taken over' an otherwise relatively stable personality, making him act in a manner that is completely alien to his ordinary personality. Sometimes such offences are carried out by alcoholics in a state of 'blackout' or during fugues where they are away from home for certain periods, unable to recall (or sometimes only partly so) what they had been doing in such 'lost weekends'.

Sometimes of course much more serious offences are involved. However in a series of murder cases, investigated by the present author, committed by men who had been drinking, none of them turned out to be an alcoholic in the usual sense of the term. Usually the men concerned were self-indulgent or habitual heavy drinkers who came out of the pub in an intoxicated state and got involved in what seemed initially a minor row with an innocent bystander – for example someone waiting at a bus stop – or such a man felt offended and 'provoked' by a word which his wife had uttered after he finally reached home. Such 'provocations' then led to an impulsive action – often with the drinker claiming later that he had no clear idea what had been happening.

Among problem drinkers who commit criminal offences [29] one finds, apart from psychotic and 'stupid' drinkers (namely, mentally subnormal), individuals who commit crimes 'under the influence of alcohol', or after their habitual intemperance continued over years has brought about a weakening of moral and ethical sense so that such people give way to a compelling urge to get drink at any cost; passing dud cheques under these circumstances is quite common.

However, among male alcoholics seen at Warlingham Park [30] the great majority of those who had shown asocial or antisocial conduct had not done so until after a decade of excessive drinking, frequent drunkenness had set in at an average age of twenty-four years, asocial and antisocial acts at thirty-four years. Such asocial tendencies in the majority of drinkers were thus clearly a consequence of heavy drinking and cannot have been responsible for having caused excess drinking in the first place. This impression is also supported by the finding that there was no recurrence of such asocial or antisocial conduct after discharge from hospital in those (non-psychopathic) ex-patients who maintained sobriety.

Often the borderline between the various types of criminal excessive drinkers is not very clear, but just as in the case of industry 'sacking' the alcoholic from one job after the other, so a 'policy' of subjecting alcoholic offenders to moralising exhortations and perorations, repeated fines or prison sentences is economically wasteful, inhuman to the individual and unlikely to halt the drinker's downward path. The replacement of such a punitive approach by a constructive, long-term socio-medical one would seem to hold out much more hope, i.e. by an attempt to screen and observe such people in order to arrive at a more definite diagnosis and, on the basis of these preliminary investigations, to formulate a long-term programme of treatment and rehabilitation [1].

By and large, in the case of many alcoholic inebriates, one will often have to be contented with more modest expectations, more limited results – because of the presence in a higher proportion of these people of greater personality disturbance and social instability – than, for example, in the case of alcoholics in industry. But, as our own experiences have shown, quite a few alcoholics referred from court or prison have, in fact, improved greatly.

Sometimes a difference has been made between so-called 'direct' alcohol-related criminal behaviour (often violent acts) carried out in a state of alcohol intoxication, frequently by people who in the strict sense of the term would not be called 'alcoholics', and the 'indirect' alcohol criminality as seen in a proportion of alcoholics not intoxicated at the time of the offence [1]. However, the borderline between the various types is often not very clear.

Intoxication and crime

The question of an individual's medical and legal responsibility for acts committed in a state of intoxication is complex – perhaps even more so in the case of a state of intoxication in alcoholics: to what extent is such intoxication a wilful act and to what extent does it reflect his 'dependence' or compulsion? Some aspects of an individual's responsibility for a crime committed in a state of intoxication were discussed in an interesting 'Medico-legal' contribution in the *British Medical Journal* in 1976 [30]. A jury in English law can convict a person of most serious crimes only when satisfied that the accused – apart from carrying out the action he has been charged with – also *intended* to do the act. The case coming before the Law Lords involved a decision as to whether a man could be convicted of assault although he had made himself sufficiently intoxicated beforehand not to have intended the act said to constitute the assault. The seven Law Lords confirmed that 'in cases of manslaughter, assault, and unlawful wounding the accused will not be acquitted, because, having knowingly and willingly taken drink or drugs, he had deprived himself of the ability to exercise self-control, to realise the possible consequences of what he was doing or even to be conscious that he was doing it'.

In the view of the BMJ's medico-legal writer the Lords' decision that juries must ignore drink and drugs as defences in cases of basic intention, does not affect the position of an accused committing a crime while (for example, because of arteriosclerosis or hypoglycaemia) he is involuntarily unable to form any intention. But, Lord Edmond Davies commented, a considerably different attitude was adopted to states such as automatism which is brought about by voluntary acts of the accused.

However, the BMJ also comments on the risk to the public interest arising from the acquittal of the intoxicated who, 'perhaps repeatedly', commits crimes of specific intention. The Butler

Committee in its 'Report on Mentally Abnormal Offenders' [32] recommended the creation of a new offence of 'dangerous intoxication' committed when a person who is voluntarily intoxicated 'did or failed to do an act which would amount to a dangerous offence if it were done with the requisite state of mind for such an offence'.

How, then, does the alcohol-dependent individual stand as regards the question whether his intoxication is a 'voluntary' act and thus would not negate intent, or 'involuntary', thereby negating intent? If alcoholism is regarded as a disease logically he should not really be held responsible for his state of intoxication – that is unless one argues that his 'disease' strictly speaking, may start only after his first drink for which he might be held responsible. Therefore, it may matter a lot as to whether one feels the 'disease' of alcoholism – i.e. the loss, or lack, of control – already sets in before the first drink (as, for example, Keller thinks [33]) or not (see Chapter 4). Moreover if, even after the first few drinks, there is only a relative lack of control of varying degree, the question arises whether such an individual accused of a crime could not, by a special effort, have halted the increasing process of intoxication, provided his degree of dependence permitted him to do so. One might also ask whether in such rare cases where, unbeknown to the drinker, someone had slipped him a very strong drink at a party that might have triggered off a bout, the ensuing 'intoxication' should be regarded as 'involuntary', which, logically, it surely should be.

Another question often arising in alcoholics is whether whilst in a state of 'alcoholic amnesia' they are able to form an intent [1] (see Chapter 3). In a number of such cases, where the present writer was asked by defending counsel to appear as a witness, the courts usually accepted that the amnesia was genuine; this was then followed by frequently lengthy discussions as to whether there was 'intent' or not. In the present writer's view, 'in so far as alcoholics in such a state often carry out very complex activities – for example opening the car door, starting, driving a car for long distances without an accident – it would seem from the medical point of view that to a certain extent they can form such intent. However, their behaviour in such a "blackout" (the term used by AA) is often so completely alien to their ordinary behaviour, that it would seem that such intent has not been formed by the alcoholic's ordinary or conscious personality but by a personality whose standards and attitudes have been completely (though only temporarily) altered under the influence of alcohol' [1].

Special examples of 'criminal' drinkers or alcoholics are the chronic (habitual) drunkenness offenders. Among them are many emotionally very inadequate, unstable and vulnerable personalities in whom alcohol could be expected to release asocial personality tendencies. However, a high proportion are in fact 'loss of control' alcoholics. Instead of subjecting these people to innumerable fines or prison sentences, the provision of special hostels as centres of comprehensive rehabilitation programmes has been suggested and would seem to be not only a more humane but also a much more constructive and hopeful approach [34, 35, 36] (see Chapter 18).

The problems of habitual drunkenness offenders are often only to a minor extent caused by their drinking. Frequently their background is one of deprivation and poor emotional and economic upbringing. Often they are extremely inadequate, schizoid or even more openly disturbed personalities, living in a hopeless environment, who may have found in drinking their only escape route from a life which they have been quite unable to cope with. The longer they lead such a life the more they tend to become used to and even value it so that they may actively resist well meant attempts to move them into 'better' types of environment. In addition, their often heavy drinking removes even further any hope that in future they may learn to cope better than they did in the past.

Drinking, the lack of belongings and of any steady income, or their general life-style may lead to petty crime which in turn is yet another bar against rehabilitation. Extreme poverty, neglect of personal hygiene and nutrition, exposure to bad weather all tend to further undermine physical resistance. Among such offenders, there may be, on the one hand, psychotics such as overt schizophrenics, but there may also be people who once had known better days and who, as a consequence of their dependence on alcohol, have drifted down the socio-occupational scale. Most of the skid-row inhabitants are men but a few are women. Drink problems are common among them – of a sample investigated by us at the Camberwell Reception Centre twenty-five years ago, 49 per cent had problems with drinking [18]. Some drink surgical spirit; cheap wine or cider are among the favourites – all such drinks probably chosen for economic reasons and not for preference. Almost all lack family attachments; some have never been married, others – like the high percentages of Scots and

Irishmen among them (amounting to 21 per cent and 37 per cent respectively among one London sample of fifty-one skid-row drinkers) – have lost any contact with the families they left behind. 58 per cent of these men had experienced separation from parents in their childhood, an experience of childhood deprivation which, as Bowlby showed many years ago, may have a profound effect on their further development [37].

'Criminal alcoholics' are outweighed numerically by criminals showing criminal tendencies before they become inebriates [29]. Yet an attempt to treat even hardened alcoholic criminals is well worth while, as excessive drinking makes it practically impossible to reform the criminal. Indeed, favourable results were obtained by Hansen and Teilmann with a well-planned therapeutic programme at a Danish institution in 'severely alcoholic-damaged criminals' (who were serving long sentences) 'in spite of the additional handicaps of deviating personalities and criminal careers' [38].

Certainly alcoholics falling foul of the law must not be forgotten in the organisation of the comprehensive rehabilitation programme for alcoholics. But possibly more dangerous in the long run than the influence of alcoholism on the drinker himself may be the indirect effect on his offspring [39]. Juvenile delinquency may be not infrequent among these consequences. The circle of anxiety, aggression, guilt, set up by a child's insecurity, has been described as being undoubtedly one of the most constant psychological forces for crime, and especially for juvenile delinquency. Bovet, in his WHO monograph on *Juvenile Delinquency* [40], added that alcoholism has a well-established reputation for causing delinquency. Factors, which were found by the American criminologist S Glueck [41] to be much more numerous in the families of delinquents than in control groups, are often present in families of alcoholics; for example, 'faulty emotional parent–child relationships of the first few years, such as the lack of parental affection, hostile or erratic disciplinary practices, lack of supervision, family disunity'.

Medico-legally, alcoholism may become an issue in conditions such as alcoholic amnesias, *delirium tremens*, alcoholic hallucinosis, Korsakoff's psychosis, dementia, pathological intoxication (which is a 'problem of alcohol' rather than of alcoholism), etc. But the connection between alcoholism, crime and juvenile delinquency is to a large extent a challenge to medicine rather than the law.

The subjects discussed in Chapter 10 and the present chapter of the roles of alcoholism in industry and crime respectively seem to be poles apart in many aspects. For one thing, the first has been widely ignored and the second has perhaps received its unfair share of the limelight. Nevertheless, they have several points in common. In both, the approach has been largely that of rejecting and 'punishing' the 'offender' – in industry by sacking him, in the case of the criminal inebriate by measures such as sending him to prison. Neither drinker nor society benefit by this negative approach; in its place a preventive and therapeutic approach should be adopted.

For example, the early detection of a problem drinker at work or in court would provide the personnel manager and the magistrate alike with an opportunity to refer such a person to the proper medical authorities and appropriate special facilities (which in most instances will first have to be established) with a view to assessment, early diagnosis and rehabilitation. Personnel manager and manager and magistrate would thus be integrated into the multidisciplinary therapeutic 'team' that is needed to deal successfully with these important socio-medical problems.

References

1   Glatt, M M (1968) in Gradwohl's *Legal Medicine* (2nd ed.), Camps, F E, Bristol, John Wright, 584–95
2   Stengel, E (1964), *Suicide and Attempted Suicide*, London, Penguin
3   *Encyclopaedia of Psychiatry for General Practitioners* (1972) A–B, eds Leigh, D, Pare, C, Pare, M B, Marks, J, London, Roche, 53–5, 57
4   Rado, S (1953), *Psychoanalyt. Quart.*, 2, 1
5   *Encyclop. Psychiat. for GPs* (1972) Ph-Z, eds Leigh, D *et al.*, London, Roche, 378–80
6   Kessel, N and Grossman, G (1961), *Brit. med. J.*, 2, 1671
7   Ritson, B and Hassall, C (1970), *Management of Alcoholism*, Edinburgh, Livingstone, 85, 93–8
8   Glatt, M M (1961), *Acta psychiat. Scand.*, 37, 88
9   Palola, E G, Dorpat, T L and Larson, W R (1962) in *Society, Culture and Drinking Patterns*, eds Pittman D J and Snyder, C R, New York, London, John Wiley & Sons, 511
10 Sinclair, Upton (1957), *The Cup of Fury*, London, Arco Publ. Ltd.
11 Menninger, K (1938), *Man against Himself*, New York, Harcourt, Brace
11a Kessel, N (1965), *Brit. med. J.*, 2, 1265
12 Patel, A R *et al.* (1975), *The Lancet*, 2, 1099
12a Glatt, M M (1974), *A Guide to Addiction and its Treatment*, Lancas-

ter, MTP, 108–20 (Compulsive-Pathological-Gambling)

13 Hore, B D (1976), *Alcohol Dependence*, London, Butterworths, 99–101

14 Amir, M (1967), *Brit. J. Addict.*, 62, 219

15 McGeorge, J (1962–3), *Medicine, Science, Law*, 3, 27

16 Glatt, M M (1958), *Brit. J. Addict.*, 54, 51

17 Wolfgang, M E and Strohm, R B (1956), *Quart. J. Stud. Alc.*, 17, 411

18 Glatt, M M and Whiteley, J S (1956), *Mschr. Psychiat. Neurol.* (Basel), 132, 1

19 Fleminger, J J and Glatt, M M quoted from Glatt, M M (1955), *Brit. med. J.*, 2, 1029

20 Banay, R S (1945) in *Alcohol, Science & Society*, New Haven, *Quart. J. Stud. Alc.*, 143

21 Norris, F E (1941), *Brit. J. Inebr.*, 38, 112

22 Hopwood, J S and Milner, J O (1940), *Brit. J. Inebr.*, 38, 51

23 Buckmaster Report (1931), *The Social and Economic Aspects of the Drink Problem*, London, 155

24 Robinson, C B *et al.* (1965), *Med., Science, Law*, 5, 140

25 Gibbens, T and Silberman, M (1970), *Psychol. Med.*, 1, 73

26 Edwards, G *et al.* (1971), *Psychol. Med.*, 5, 388

27 Woodside, M (1961), *Brit. J. Criminol*, 1, 221

28 Royal College of Psychiatrists' Special Committee (1979), *Alcohol and Alcoholism*, London, Tavistock, 63–6

29 Haggard, H W and Jellinek, E M (1950), *Alcohol Explored*, New York, Doubleday & Co.

30 *Brit. med. J.* (Medico-legal), 1976, 2, 1286

31 Freeman, J C (1976) in Gradwohl's *Legal Medicine* (Third ed.), eds Camps, F E *et al.*, Bristol, John Wright & Sons, 15–49

32 *Report on Mentally Abnormal Offenders* (1975), London, HMSO cmnd, 6244

33 Keller, M (1972), *Brit. J. Addict.* 67, 153

34 Gath, D (1969) in *The Drunkenness Offence*, eds Cooke, T, Gath, D and Hensman, C, Oxford, Pergamon, 9

35 D'Orban, C (1969), *ibid.*, 51

36 Hensman, C (1969), *ibid.*, 35

37 Bowlby, J (1951), *Maternal Care and Mental Health*, Geneva, WHO

38 Hansen, A J and Teilman, K (1954), *Quart. J. Stud. Alc.*, 15, 246

39 Glatt, M M (1958), *Brit. J. Delinq.*, 9, 84

40 Bovet, L (1951), *Psychiatric Aspects of Juvenile Delinquency*, Geneva, WHO

41 Glueck, S quoted from Glatt, M M (1958), *Brit. J. Delinq.*, 9, 88 (Glueck, E and S (1930), 500 Criminal Careers, New York)

14

Alcohol-Induced Physical Disorders*

The term 'chronic alcoholism' was formerly used to denote cases of alcoholism with physical or mental complications [1]. Because of the ambiguity of the term [2] Jellinek later replaced it by the term 'alcoholism with complications'. Some of the complications of alcoholism are well known, but it must be stressed that they occur in a minority of alcoholics only and then only very late (e.g. cirrhosis of the liver like definite alcoholic psychosis occurs in no more than 1 in 10). Diagnosis of alcoholism must not be delayed until the appearance of such complications.

Until very recently, these 'complications' seem, however, to have been regarded as the illness itself, comparable, for example, to an attitude of considering intestinal perforation as the essential feature of typhoid fever (and to wait with treatment until perforation has taken place!). Alcoholism often may have existed for ten to fifteen years before there is evidence of definite liver damage or psychosis in the final, chronic phase.

Some of the complications of alcoholism are nowadays ascribed to malnutrition and deficiency of vitamins and proteins rather than to a toxic action of alcohol itself. The latter, however, is regarded as directly responsible for some complications – for example, it seems to be the main culprit in liver complications. Acetaldehyde, the first metabolite of alcohol, is seen by some as an important possible contributor to certain alcohol-induced disorders (for example, cardiac complications). Sudden or too rapid withdrawal of alcohol in dependent drinkers may also cause severe physical and mental abstinence signs and symptoms. Thus the catalogue of disorders caused by alcohol, directly or indirectly, is a long one affecting various systems and organs in the body. Some complica-

* This chapter will be of particular interest to the medical professions.

tions have been well known for centuries and are relatively common, others are very little known and may be quite rare.

In theory obviously the best way of tackling alcohol-related problems (including alcoholism) would be to prevent them in the first place. However good any measures at primary prevention may be in the future, clearly in practice a great deal will still have to depend on 'secondary prevention', i.e. early detection, which will then have to be followed up by motivating such people towards taking steps towards cutting down or giving up drinking. It is especially important to improve on methods of early diagnosis. For medical practitioners the most important aspect in this connection is to raise their level of suspicion: with increasing prevalence and misuse of alcohol more and more drinkers will for some reason or other present themselves at their GP's surgery, or in general hospitals (especially at casualty). Many alcoholics are admitted to general hospital wards for various illnesses or complications of their drinking without the underlying diagnosis of problem drinking being suspected. This has been acknowledged for some years in American [3, 4, 5] and Australian [6] publications. More recently British studies have confirmed this phenomenon. For example, in 1979 nearly one in five people admitted to a London teaching hospital was detected to have a drinking problem [7]; in the same year, in 27 per cent of acute general medical admissions to a Manchester hospital, drink was the immediate or contributing factor [8]; and a study in 1979 at the Royal Infirmary, Edinburgh [9], showed that 40 per cent of patients attending the accident and emergency department during the evening had consumed alcohol, and 32 per cent had a blood alcohol concentration exceeding 80mg/100ml (the legally permitted level for driving a car). Thus in hospitals as well as in general practice the prevalence of problem drinking as a significant underlying factor is much more common than generally suspected. In view of the failure to suspect or to diagnose this, such patients typically receive treatment for their secondary complications only and continue their heavy drinking without the likelihood of preventing further complications stemming from this course. It is therefore important for practitioners to keep the possibility of an underlying alcohol problem in mind, to look for clinical clues (in particular in members of 'high-risk' populations) and, where indicated, screening and special laboratory tests may prove very helpful [10].

Table 11
Physical complications of alcoholism*

1 *Liver*
  (a) Fatty Liver;
  (b) Alcoholic Hepatitis;
  (c) Cirrhosis of the liver;
  (d) Zieve Syndrome: Hyperlipaemia, haeomolytic anaemia, jaundice.

2 *Pancreas*
  (a) Acute pancreatitis (mostly an excarbation of a chronic pancreatitis);
  (b) Chronic pancreatitis;
  (c) Cancer of pancreas (often a complication of chronic pancreatitis).

3 *Gastro-intestinal tract*
  (a) Atrophy of mucosa of mouth, hypopharynx and oesophagus and larynx;
  (b) Cheilosis;
  (c) Smooth tongue;
  (d) Cancer of pharynx and oesophagus;
  (e) Acute gastritis;
  (f) Mallory-Weiss Syndrome;
  (g) Peptic ulcer;
  (h) High incidence of gastrectomy.

4 *Heart*
Cardiomyopathy.

5 *Hypertension*

6 *Disturbance of fat metabolism*
  (a) Hyperlipaemia;
  (b) Hyper-triglyceridaemia.

7 *Blood*
  (a) Thrombocytopenia;
  (b) Leucopenia;
  (c) Anaemia, haemolytic;
  (d) Macrocytic sideroblastic anaemia.

8 *Vitamin deficiency*
B1, B2, B6
e.g. wet Beri Beri (B1), Wernicke-Korsakoff (B complex, esp. B_1).

9 *Endocrines*
  (a) Cushing syndrome;
  (b) (?) Thyroid;

(c) (?) Pituitary;
(d) Hypoglycaemia.

10 *Respiratory system*
  (a) Lowered resistance to intermittent infection (including formerly
       pulmonary TB);
  (b) Cancer of larynx (especially supraglottic growth).

11 *Skeletal muscle*
  (a) Acute myopathy;
  (b) Chronic myopathy.

12 *Skin*
  (a) Hyperaemia;
  (b) Telangectases;
  (c) Rhinophyma;
  (d) Erythema of palms and feet;
  (e) Spider naevi;
  (f) Porphyria cutanea tarda.

13 *Genital system*
  (a) Testicular atrophy;
  (b) Gynaecomastia;
  (c) Impotence.

14 *Dupuytren's contractures*

15 *Neurogenic oesteoarthropathy*

16 *Perinatal*
  (a) Alcohol foetal syndrome;
  (b) Spontaneous abortion.

17 *Nervous system*
  (a) Cerebral atrophy (widened sulci and Sylvian fissure, dilatation
       of ventricles);
  (b) Wernicke-Korsakoff;
  (c) Cerebellar cortical atrophy;
  (d) Polyneuropathy;
  (e) Alcoholic tremor;
  (f) Marchiafava-Bignami Syndrome;
  (g) Laminar-cortical sclerosis;
  (h) Central pontine myelinolysis;
  (i) Nicotine deficiency encephalopathy;
  (j) Alcoholic myelopathy;
  (k) Retrobulbar neuritis;
  (l) Epileptiform attacks;
  (m) Subdural haematoma.

---

* adapted from W. Feuerlein [15]

Physical symptoms and signs of alcohol misuse

While alcoholics are not usually recognised at first glance, there are a number of physical features which could at least arouse suspicion. An excellent review of physical symptoms pointing to the possibility of alcohol misuse has recently been presented by Dr Michael Davis [11], King's College Hospital, London's Liver Unit.

Sometimes such a patient, though not in a state of alcohol intoxication, may be stuporous or comatose, or may present with epileptiform convulsions, progressive dementia, encephalopathy, loss of vision or ataxia, or there may be features such as upper abdominal pain, acute hepatitis, haematemesis, melaena or anaemia. Causes, in the alcoholic, of stupor or coma (other than the obvious one of being drunk), may be hypoglycaemia (which may follow a heavy drinking bout within a few to thirty-six hours). Epileptiform fits, which also occur in the alcoholic withdrawal phase, could be a feature of hypoglycaemia. Increasing drowsiness and coma in an alcoholic could also be caused by subdural haematoma following the head injuries common in drunken alcoholics. Altering levels of consciousness and localising neurological signs might also indicate alcoholism and is made easier by computerised axial tomography (CAT).

Loss of vision may be due to alcoholic amblyopia (though obviously much more common in methyl alcohol poisoning, or when drinking is associated, as it commonly is, with heavy smoking). *Ataxia* (when not due to acute intoxication) may be caused by cerebellar degeneration, or by Wernicke's Syndrome, which may also manifest itself by confusion, nystagmus and paralysis of eye muscles.

All degrees of *dementia* may occur in alcoholics.

Upper abdominal pain in alcoholics may have various causes. Commonly it may be due to gastritis (when it may be associated with nausea and retching which may more often be due to an accompanying smoking habit). Such pain may also be caused by the liver enlargement or disease; occasionally excruciating pain may be due to pancreatitis.

Features such as *vomiting blood* (haematemesis) or *passing it by rectum* (melaena), or *encephalopathy* (neuropsychiatric symptoms) may be due to liver cirrhosis. The dangerous complication of encephalopathy may supervene in patients suffering from cirrhosis when they are given sedatives or tranquillisers; it may also follow when such patients, suffering from fluid retention, common in cirrhotics, are given large doses of diuretics which suddenly upset the fluid balance of the body.

Many alcoholics suffer from *anaemia*, even in the absence of cirrhosis which in itself could cause anaemia. Anaemia in alcoholics could be due to toxic damage to the bone marrow, or to the folate deficiency which may in turn have been caused by undernutrition.

Macrocytosis of the red blood cells is a very characteristic feature in alcoholism, and may occur in as many as 50–85 per cent of alcoholics. Bleeding may be due to various factors, including deficiency of vitamin K or throbocytopenia; reduced synthesis of clotting factors may lead to prolonged prothrombin time, which may become important in sometimes excluding a liver biopsy that had been necessary for diagnostic reasons.

Laboratory tests which may assist in diagnosing misuse of alcohol after some of the preceding physical features have aroused suspicion, include a number of liver function tests, such as Aspartate Transaminase (AST) and Alanine Transaminase (ALT) (which among our hospitalised alcoholic patients were found elevated in 30–50 per cent of cases), and in particular the Serum Gamma-Glutamyl-Transpeptidase (GGTP), found positive in 70–80 per cent [12, 13]. It must be remembered that GGTP is raised not only in alcoholics but in otherwise healthy people who drink heavily; and it has become an accepted screening test during routine health checks. A very helpful laboratory finding, already mentioned, is macrocytosis.

Practising alcoholics are highly skilled in drawing 'smoke-screens' over their drinking behaviour. However, even the most indignant denial can hardly be maintained if the patient is confronted with the results of the examination of his blood sample showing a high concentration of alcohol.

Physical features and laboratory tests apart, there are other possibilities for suspecting excessive drinking and of obtaining support for such a diagnosis, which include interviewing family or close friends, and isolating certain high risk occupations (see Chapter 2). *Questionnaires* have also been drawn up that have been found helpful in pointing to the likelihood of people being habitual misusers of alcohol. In a recent review (November 1980) of the all-important task of early detection (also known as, and later discussed under the heading of, 'secondary prevention') Murray and Bernadt [14] mention three such questionnaires: the *24-Item Michigan Alcoholism Screening Test* (MAST); an abbreviated *Short Michigan Screening Test*, which contains thirteen questions, and, finally a four question questionnaire making up a CAGE serving as a mnemonic:

1 Have you ever felt you ought to *cut* down on
   your drinking? (C)
2 Have people *annoyed* you by criticising your drinking? (A)
3 Have you ever felt bad or *guilty* about your drinking? (G)
4 Have you ever had a drink first thing in the morning
   to steady your nerves or get rid of a hangover
   (*eyeopener*)? (E)

It has been claimed that two or more positive answers may distinguish alcoholics from non-alcoholics and may serve as a useful initial quick screening test among samples of hospital patients and similar groups. 'Confirmed' alcoholics, who may never miss a single morning without the 'hair-of-the-dog' drink but who do so unbeknown to their family – might proudly and definitely say 'no' to all such questions. But in such alcoholics, often in the late 'crucial' phases of their alcoholism, the diagnosis may anyway be easier, whereas such questionnaires might help in the early diagnosis of drinkers less dependent and therefore not having the same vested interest in denying their heavy drinking.

A similar questionnaire-test has been developed in Germany, the *Münchener Alkoholismus Test*, (MALT) [15, 16] consisting of two parts: Part I (Malt-F) with seven questions is filled in by the doctor or other therapists; Part II (Malt-S) with twenty-four questions is filled in by the patient. This method thus seems to be a shortened and simplified way of combining Dr Wilkins' longer list for the doctor (see Chapter 1) with the Selinger Questionnaire (see Chapter 1).

The acute withdrawal syndrome

The mechanism of the *withdrawal symptoms* is not clear but the most commonly accepted hypothesis rests on the principle of *homoeostatis*. A strong influence changing bodily functions in one direction induces the operation of mechanisms which bring about influences counteracting them [17] which are intended to restore the original status. The excessive intake of alcohol leads to depression of the various functions of the central nervous system, and to a general slowing down. Sudden or too quick withdrawal of alcohol leads to a rebound phenomenon: the various functions kept down by the depressant-sedating action of alcohol are suddenly released when the alcohol-brake is removed and leap back into a counter-reaction greatly overshooting their normal level with mental and physical overactivity. Thus instead of drowsiness there is suddenly restlessness, shakiness and even convulsion; in place of sleep there is insomnia.

As in the case of other sedative drugs capable of producing physical and psychological dependence, sudden withdrawal of alcohol (or even too rapid reduction) in the regular heavy drinker may lead to the emergence of more or less marked withdrawal (or abstinence) symptoms within a few hours or days.

In recent years the alcohol withdrawal syndrome has been thoroughly investigated by (the late) Milton M Gross and his colleagues at the Downstate Medical Center, New York [18] who have divided the syndrome into two main phases – most drinkers experience only the early 'minor withdrawal syndrome', whereas a minority also shows the features of the 'major withdrawal syndrome'.

(a)   *The 'minor withdrawal syndrome'*, extremely common, shows itself in features such as tremor (particularly in the morning) and sweating (particularly at night) which may appear within six to eight hours of giving up drink; loss of appetite; insomnia; anxiety or depression; sometimes a mild confusion and disorientation; a feeling of weakness, etc. In most cases drinkers recover from these symptoms within two to three days of giving up drink.

In more severe cases the morning tremor may be more marked, and there may be such features as epileptiform convulsions, mostly within twelve to thirty-six hours of giving up drink; or auditory hallucinations.

(b)   *The 'major withdrawal syndrome'*, with *delirium tremens* as the main feature, is seen in only a small proportion of heavy drinkers. It usually arises gradually out of the minor syndrome when such drinkers, instead of quickly improving, become increasingly anxious, agitated and extremely restless and may complain of an obstinate insomnia. Within approximately two to four days of giving up alcohol such people may become increasingly disorientated and confused (though characteristically the lucidity of their mental state and their degree of insight may vary a great deal and change rapidly). Gross misinterpretations (illusions) and misidentifications may be present. In about one third of cases *delirium tremens* may be preceded by a fit (or rarely by a series of fits) but no further fits are seen after the DT has developed. There is marked over-activity of the autonomous nervous system, as reflected in severe sweating, tachycardia and fever, with great restlessness and vivid hallucinations. (See mental complications, p. 315.)

Alcohol withdrawal fits

The risk of epileptiform convulsions, though well documented for over twenty-five years, seems still not fully appreciated. One often reads of a series of cases where not a single such fit was seen and where the need to keep this possibility in mind is greatly played down. In our own experience, in the case of heavy drinkers, withdrawal fits are not uncommon [19] and may be a sometimes dangerous complication, with a rare possibility of even leading to an epileptic status consisting of a series of such fits following in rapid succession. Not infrequently of course alcoholics have also taken other CNS-depressing drugs which on sudden discontinuation alongside alcohol withdrawal, may in their own right also lead to withdrawal fits and later to an abstinence-DT. Depending on the varying duration of effectiveness of the given drugs, in some such cases epileptiform convulsions can supervene suddenly much later than within the first two days as is usually the case.

The withdrawal 'alcohol-epilepsy' is regarded as a condition completely different from idipathic epilepsy [18]. Among a sample of 100 American alcoholics [20] only 12 per cent showed abnormal EEC tracing (and among approximately 150 patients of ours with withdrawal fits, there was only one, and he was found to have another brain lesion) in contrast to a control group of 150 non-alcoholic epileptics.

1   Liver disease

The relationship between heavy drinking and liver disease has been known for many years. Jellinek's famous formula published in 1951 [21], based on this connection, allowed an approximate estimate to be made of the numbers of 'chronic alcoholics' (defined at the time as those alcoholics with definite physical or mental complications) in various countries. Liver mortality rates are still generally regarded – in spite of many theoretical objections – as the most reliable among the various indirect indices employed to estimate the prevalence of problem drinking.

Until quite recently it was assumed that both the toxic action of alcohol itself as well as nutritional deficiency may, in interaction, contribute to liver disease in excessive drinkers. However, the previously held view that heavy drinkers should try to minimise the risk of developing liver disease by eating well, appears now to be more than doubtful. This change of opinion arises mainly from the work of Professor Charles Lieber [22] in the USA who has shown that the primary effects of heavy drinking on the liver are directly due to the toxic action of alcohol itself or to its breakdown products. It seems that it is only secondarily that such ill effects may be even further enhanced by the harm caused by inadequate nutrition.

The role of alcohol itself in causing liver disease is reflected in findings that increasingly severe liver disease has been found to be correlated with the amount of daily alcohol intake and the duration of drinking by French [23] and German [24] researchers. For example, alcohol intake for longer than fifteen years above a daily amount of 180g was shown to carry a 51 per cent incidence of cirrhosis; a slightly smaller amount, i.e. 160g/day, taken for 6 to 10 years, has an 8 per cent incidence of cirrhosis, rising to 21 per cent after 11–15 years' intake of the same amount. It seems to make little difference in the relationship between alcohol consumption and liver disease whether the alcohol has been taken in the form of spirits, wine or beer. The direct toxic effect of alcohol on the liver has been demonstrated experimentally by Lieber in baboons who developed liver damage even when given a full diet. Possibly there is a difference in individuals' susceptibility to liver damage; and women may be more susceptible than men, even though the condition is found to be more common in men, probably because of men's much heavier drinking.

There are three complications of heavy drinking affecting the liver: the reversible fatty liver, the irreversible liver cirrhosis, and between them, in regard to severity of illness and prognosis, alcoholic hepatitis.

(a)   *Alcoholic fatty liver (fatty infiltration)*
This is a reversible condition very common in alcoholics. Histologically, fat is deposited within the liver cells, probably because alcohol interferes with the liver metabolism of fats (triglycerides) [27]. Clinically, such an individual may show no abnormal symptoms whatsoever though at other times (rarely) symptoms may be severe or even fatal, as a result of liver (hepatocellular) failure.

Even in the patients who have no (or very mild) complaints, such as general malaise, the liver may be enlarged though smooth and usually not tender to pressure. Usually such a liver diminishes in size under treatment. LFT (Liver Function Tests) show these reversible changes and as a rule such patients recover, unless they resume drinking.

In treatment of the fatty liver, abstinence is essential, and a diet that contains sufficient protein (75–100g/day) and calories (at least 2000 kcal/day) [22]. Under such circumstances, symptoms that may have developed after months of excessive drinking (upper abdominal pain, sickness, vomiting, and more rarely elevated temperature and even jaundice) may improve rapidly. Repeated liver biopsies – which are carried out in some centres as a matter of routine in such cases – reveal a rapid disappearance of fat from the liver cells. However, in the rare cases of fatty liver, where the dangerous complication of a liver encephalopathy develops, it is necessary to limit the protein intake and take steps to suppress the production of ammonia.

As regards the question whether fatty liver can directly progress to the much more dangerous cirrhosis, most observers are sceptical, believing that alcoholic hepatitis is a necessary stage in the development of cirrhosis, although Lieber has experimentally demonstrated such direct progress from fatty to cirrhotic liver in baboons.

(b)   *Alcoholic hepatitis*

Histologically there is a death (necrosis) of liver cells and inflammation. 'Alcoholic hyalin' is found in the liver cells, a manifestation of necrosis, and is described as being characteristic, though not unique, in alcoholic hepatitis. As a rule people have to drink heavily for several years before developing hepatitis. The condition may reveal itself by much more severe symptoms than those common in the fatty liver patients. On top of a general malaise and pyrexia, patients may complain of loss of appetite (which however is common in alcoholics even in the absence of such a complication), vomiting and upper abdominal pain, and may often be mildly or severely jaundiced. Liver (and occasionally also the spleen) may be enlarged and tender. Even where there is no clinical jaundice, the serum bilirubin may be raised, and the serum transaminases may be high, SGOP (serum glutamic oxaloacetic transaminase) more so than the SGPT (serum glumatic pyruvate transaminase). Alcoholic hepatitis can be an extremely serious condition which may end fatally in perhaps up to 30 per cent, although in other cases there may be no severe symptoms at all. Alcoholic encephalopathy and protal hypertension (with ascites and bleeding from varicose veins in the oesophagus) may be serious complications. Treatment of uncomplicated alcoholic hepatitis, as in fatty liver, consists in total abstinence (and a full diet) which often leads to a full recovery but may not always prevent the development of liver cirrhosis.

(c) *Alcoholic cirrhosis*
In this condition cell destruction and death (necrosis) and attempts at regeneration of cells and healing by scarring proceed hand in hand. The architecture of the liver lobules is greatly affected throughout the liver, fibrous septa are formed, such bands of connective tissue extending from the portal tracts to the central veins and destruction (cellular necrosis) goes hand in hand with regeneration of new nodules of parencymal cells, which are often yellow in colour because of the presence of fat. The so-called micronodular type of cirrhosis – with the liver finely nodular – is the common type of cirrhosis in alcoholism.

The prevalence of alcoholic cirrhosis seems to vary greatly between different countries. It is extremely common in France and has been estimated to make up 60 per cent of the cases of cirrhosis in the USA.

In Britain estimates of its prevalence were formerly fairly low, varying between 5–25 per cent. According to figures published by the Ministry of Health, alcoholism contributed to death from liver cirrhosis in the period 1932–6 more than 15 per cent, 20 years later, less than 10 per cent; in these latter statistics, alcoholism was relatively more often mentioned as a factor contributing to cirrhosis deaths in men than in women, although clinically women alcoholics often present themselves in a worse physical condition of health than male alcoholics.[2] According to a review by Silk [28] (1977) alcohol in this country may be the cause of 25–35 per cent of cases of cirrhosis, whereas in 40 per cent of cases, cirrhosis may be 'cryptogenic' (i.e. the cause is not known). Probably with increasing 'alcoholisation' (a term coined by Dr Pierre Fouquet [29] in France several years ago) in this country the incidence of alcoholic cirrhosis (as of pancreatitis and other complications) is likely to go up, though with today's higher level of suspicion the possible alcoholic origin of such conditions may contribute to raising of such figures.

Views as to whether one can talk of amounts of alcoholic drink that can be safely imbibed without fear of liver damage vary greatly. In 1971 a French estimate [30] regarded a daily consumption of 80g or less of alcohol (i.e. five pints of beer, or one-third of a bottle of spirits) as relatively harmless; the regular drinking of double that amount (160g) as being very dangerous in regard to developing cirrhosis. This is higher than the safe upper limits recently proposed in Britain by the College of Psychiatrists and by experts in liver disease. In Germany the leading organisation in this field, the Deutsche Haupstelle gegen die Suchtgefahren, has come out strongly against publishing such estimates [31, 32]. There are wide variations in individual susceptibility, and the dynamic interaction of a variety of factors. What may be safe for the liver may be unsafe for the nervous system or for the development of physical dependence – the more so as obviously other factors such as the duration and regularity of alcohol intake, the pace of drinking (gulping versus sipping) are probably important. The susceptibility to cirrhosis, particularly in younger women [33], has been ascribed by some to the possible influence of immunological mechanisms in the aetiology of alcoholic liver disorders [37]. An elevated level of the total globulins in the blood serum (hyperglobulinaemia) occurs in most types of liver disease, probably forming part of an immunological reaction as the levels of gammaglobulins largely reflect the levels of the antibody-like protein. Thus the raised levels of gammaglobulins may signify increased levels of serum antibody caused by the failure of the diseased liver to rid itself of the antigen. A high incidence of serum antibodies has recently been detected in women.

Apart from immunological mechanisms, genetic factors, too, may be important in affecting the susceptibility of the individual to the toxic effects of alcohol on the liver.

Clinically, cirrhosis may show up gradually or suddenly. Symptoms may be similar to other alcoholic liver disorders with which cirrhosis may sometimes coexist such as fever, anorexia, dyspepsia and jaundice, but there may also be loss of weight, and, depending on the development of complications, ascites, oedema in the periphery, and bleeding from mouth or rectum, or encephalopathy (such as drowsiness or coma). Stigmata on the skin may indicate chronic liver disorder, such as recently formed 'arterial spiders' or 'spider naevi' caused by the liation of capillaries radiating out from an arteriole, small in size, occurring always on the upper part of the body; persistently reddened palms (palmar erythema) and white nails. Sometimes one also finds clubbing of the fingers and contractures of the hands (Dupuytren's contracture).

Occasionally one also encounters sexual changes in chronic liver disease mainly in form of feminisation in men. There may be atrophy of the testicles, enlargement of breasts ('gynaecomastia'), loss of pubic hair, but also a very welcome feature in the delay of appearance of hypertrophy of the prostate gland. Corresponding changes in women are less common though they may suffer from amenorrhoea etc. The origin of such sexual changes is not clear.

Not uncommon in cirrhosis is anaemia which may be due to increased production or increased destruction of red blood cells. Occasionally an alcoholic fatty or cirrhotic liver is associated with a haemolytic anaemia, hyperlipaemia (increase of fats in the blood) and at times also pancreatitis – the whole picture being known as 'Zieve's Syndrome'.

The liver, which may be enlarged and fatty in earlier phases, may become hard, shrunken and nodular in later stages. Portal hypertension may develop, due to raised resistance to the blood flow in the portal. Thus such an individual may also develop an enlargement of the spleen and ascites, and may vomit blood as a result of the formation of oesophageal varicose veins. Similarly enlarged vessels in the rectum may lead to the formation of haemorrhoids, and on the anterior abdominal wall to the picture of the 'caput Medusae'.

Liver failure may supervene, sometimes as a consequence of an alcoholic bout but often for other reasons. Such failure may manifest itself mainly in mental and neurological signs and symptoms, such as irritability, confusion, increasing drowsiness, coma, delirium, convulsions, or a coarse flapping tremor of the outstretched hands. Such encephalopthic features may change in intensity and may sometimes improve greatly.

There may be many laboratory test abnormalities, such as raised red serum bilirubin, a decrease of prothrombin and albumen but an increase of globulin in the blood, and elevation of various enzymes, such as the alkaline phosphatase, the transaminases and the GGTP.

The emphasis in treatment of liver cirrhosis, as in the fatty liver and alcoholic hepatitis lies in total abstinence and a nutritious diet. Survival rates after five years have been found to be considerably higher in those who remained abstinent than in drinkers [22].

Conclusion

Much space has been given to the discussion of the liver diseases complicating problem drinking because they are a very common occurrence, afflicting the great majority of a long-standing heavy drinkers. Although domestic and social problems occur earlier and more commonly in alcoholism than physical complications [36], many drinkers unfortunately take little notice of the former. In spite of frequent protests, quite a few drinkers are in fact concerned about their physical health and the condition of their liver, and surprisingly many alcoholics who have taken no notice of earlier warnings, give up drinking or reduce it considerably when shown the results of LFT indicating even very minor abnormalities. In this way discussion of the likely effect of a drinker's excessive consumption on the state of his liver in many cases may have a very beneficial effect.

2   Pancreatitis

The various forms of pancreatitis, whether acute, acute recurrent, chronic relapsing, or chronic, may all be caused by heavy drinking. Though for many years alcoholic pancreatitis has been a well-known and frequently seen complication in the USA (where the great majority of pancreatitis cases were considered to be due to alcohol misuse), the condition in Britain was usually regarded as rare. It is only in recent years that it apparently has become more common, to a certain extent following the increase of heavy drinking, but partly due to the greater interest taken in the association between alcohol and inflammation of the pancreas.

A recent study in Glasgow [37] found a quarter of cases of pancreatitis to be connected with alcohol: they occurred mainly in young male bout drinkers, and had a higher incidence of side-effects than the cases of pancreatitis associated with disease of the biliary tract. Both alcohol-related and other types of pancreatitis had a mortality rate of under 10 per cent, though even a first attack may prove fatal.

(a)   *Acute pancreatitis*

In the UK the majority of cases of acute pancreatitis (45–75 per cent) is ascribed to gallstone disease, in contrast to the predominance of alcohol-related cases in countries such as the USA, France and South Africa [38]. It is relatively uncommon: in England and Wales about 650 people died in both 1974 and 1975 from pancreatitis, as against nearly 5600 deaths from cancer of the pancreas in 1975 and approximately 2000 from duodenal ulcer in 1974 and in 1975 [39]. But it can be an extremely painful and serious condition.

Clinically the condition may start with often very severe, sudden epigastric pain which irradiates to the back, and with tachycardia; the upper abdomen may be very tender, and is rigid or guarded. The laboratory finding, possibly most helpful in distinguishing from other possible causes of such condition, may be raised serum amylase. The intensity of pain may vary greatly, from milder attacks in relapsing acute pancreatitis to very severe pain in other cases. Patients suffering from recurrent pain usually lack appetite and may lose weight. The outlook is somewhat better in acute alcoholic pancreatitis cases which has a mortality of about 10 per cent than in acute gallstone-pancreatitis cases. In treatment, apart from intravenous fluid administration (no oral feeding), pain relief may require the injection of pethidine.

(b) *Chronic pancreatitis*
In the UK, the main causes of this (uncommon) condition are alcoholism and gallstones, as in acute pancreatitis. Whether due to increasing alcohol misuse or because of better diagnostic techniques [40] it is gradually becoming more common in the UK. It commonly manifests itself with upper abdominal pain which may be recurrent or chronic in nature, loss of weight which may be more pronounced in alcoholic patients, and there may be various complications including a high proportion of cases of diabetes mellitus. A number of other causative factors apart from 'idiopathic' cases have been mentioned; one interesting hypothesis assumes an hereditary predisposition so that chronic calcifying pancreatitis may follow even relatively moderate continuous drinking or a dietary imbalance [40].

In treatment, relief of pain by analgesics in sufficiently high doses is important, such as paracetamol and distalgesic; often, however, they do not bring sufficient relief and one finds oneself in a quandary as narcotic analgesics in such patients may carry a considerable risk of dependence. The need for total abstinence in pancreatitis is stressed by all specialists, some recommending such a course also for the non-alcoholic cases: 'Continued indulgence [in alcohol] can be expected to aggravate existing lesions and create new ones . . . Abstinence . . . commonly reduces the severity and frequency of attacks (though not necessarily so) . . . continuous drinking ensures further trouble [40]'.

3   Alcohol and cancer

The relationship between the consumption of alcohol and the development of cancer – obvious in certain instances, doubtful in others – has recently (1979) been well reviewed by the American surgeon, A B Lowenfels [42].

In comparison with abstainers or light drinkers, alcoholics develop cancer much more frequently: one American observer [43] estimated that heavy drinkers run a 30 per cent greater risk of developing cancer. A particularly dangerous combination is that of drinking and smoking in the development of tumours of *oropharynx, larynx and oesophagus*. The alcohol-tobacco combination has been held to be responsible for as many as three-quarters of such cancer cases in American men. In the case of such cancers (as in related cases) the risk of the unexpected development of post-operative withdrawal (abstinence) symptoms after operations for conditions with a high incidence in heavy drinkers, has been emphasised. Thus Holmus and Spahn [44] reported (1974) a high incidence of such complications in head and neck surgery, due to the high rates of alcohol-related cancer of the laryngopharyngeal area and the oral cavity. In nine such patients *delirium tremens* usually set in two to four days after sudden alcohol withdrawal (the operation usually having been carried out the day following admission). There is the obvious risk that the early symptoms, such as agitation, confusion and restlessness, might easily be attributed to the anaesthetic or alternatively to the effects of the prescribed drugs, and it may thus take another twenty-four hours or so before features such as marked tremor, hallucinations or convulsions make the diagnosis clear. At this stage complications such as dehydration and hyperpyrexia make for a much more serious situation. Nursing care may be extremely difficult in the delirious patient prone to remove dressings, rush out of bed, and so on. Surgeons therefore should be aware of such possible complications supervening in the 'high-risk' patients in regard to the possibility of heavy drinking, and postpone surgery, wherever possible, for several days till the danger period for the development of a serious alcohol-withdrawal syndrome has passed or has been dealt with.

Heavy drinking (in particular of spirits), may increase the risk of cancer of the larynx by over ten times and of cancer of the oesophagus by twenty-five times. Most often affected by these cancers are those areas with direct and prolonged contact with alcohol, i.e. the floor of the mouth and the tongue. In regard to laryngeal cancer, smoking is regarded as a more important aetiological factor than drinking though supraglottic growths have been found to occur most often in the heaviest drinkers. Oesophageal cancer is much more common in men than women and has been found to be associated with excessive drinking in many parts of the world.

Primary carcinoma of the liver develops in many alcoholics suffering from liver cirrhosis; such complication is said to supervene in 8–30 per cent of cirrhosis cases and may raise a marked clinical deterioration of the patient's condition.

Reports about the incidence of cancer of the pancreas and excessive drinking are conflicting (the present writer has seen a few such cases) although there appears to be some correlation between heavy smoking (itself of course very common among heavy drinkers) and carcinoma of the pancreas.

Views also differ as to the incidence of carcinoma of the stomach in heavy drinkers, though there appears to be some correlation between oesophageal and gastric cancer; the cardia would appear to be the most likely site for a stomach growth caused by heavy drinking. Kissin and Begleiter's authoritative book [45] regards the connection between drinking and cancer of the cardia as 'at best suggestive' and clearly requiring further exploration.

Cancer of the rectum has been found to show a significant statistical association with the drinking of beer.

Of some interests in this connection is the finding that patients suffering from Hodgkin's Syndrome (and rarely also from other tumours) may exhibit intolerance of alcohol, manifesting itself by the experience of pain or discomfort within 5–10 minutes of taking even a very small amount of alcoholic drink – such pain usually being felt at the site of the tumour.

Heavy drinking, commonly in association with smoking, has also been reported as having caused multiple primary tumours, occurring either at the same time or shortly after each other, at sites where alcohol-induced cancer is common, such as the oropharyngeal region.

The mechanisms involved in the connection between certain cancers and heavy drinking are not clear. Various mechanisms seem to involved [45], among them possibly direct toxic effects of alcohol congeners,[3] the augmentation by alcohol of the effects of other carcinogenic agents such as smoking.

4   Alcohol and the stomach

Alcoholics very frequently complain of anorexia, nausea, vomiting, abdominal discomfort or severe pain, and haematemesis. Sometimes these complaints may be associated with disease of the stomach (such as acute and possibly chronic atrophic gastritis or ulcerations of stomach or duodenum) but often they may be due to other causes, and in fact the association between drinking and disorders such as chronic gastritis and peptic ulcer is not clear. The association between alcoholic liver (and also pancreatic) disease which can be responsible for similar symptoms, on the other hand, is a very definite one.

Acute gastritis is a common consequence of an alcoholic bout and may be responsible for some of the features (anorexia, nausea, vomiting, epigastric discomfort or pain) of the hangover; it usually clears up rapidly. Much more dangerous are two syndromes in alcoholics affecting the lower end of the oesophagus called the *Mallory-Weiss syndrome* and *Boerhave syndrome* [46] respectively: in the first a laceration at the junction of oesophagus and stomach may cause haematemesis but usually no pain; in the latter there is a rupture of the lower oesophagus causing severe pain and requires immediate surgery.

Whether alcohol can cause a chronic gastritis with atrophy of the mucosa is controversial.

Anyone seeing very large numbers of alcoholics is probably struck by the frequency of a history of a peptic ulcer and often also of a partial gastrectomy. Not all investigations, however, confirm the existence of a close association but majority opinion would probably accept that there is a higher incidence of this condition among alcoholics than among non-alcoholics, such incidence possibly exceeding 20 per cent [47]. The origin of such a relationship is far from clear, and a number of factors might contribute to it. Thus a similar personality make-up might possibly be responsible both for heavy drinking and for the formation of an ulcer, or excessive alcohol intake may, by causing small erosions ('erosive gastritis') and increased production of gastric acid, favour the development of a peptic ulcer. One meets many alcoholics who maintain that their ulcer preceded their heavy drinking by years.

The possibility of an unrecognised underlying state of alcoholism must be kept in mind in states of gastro-intestinal haemorrhage in view of the possible development of the complication of dangerous severe alcohol withdrawal symptoms.

5 Alcoholic heart muscle disease

According to a *British Medical Journal* leading article (1979) [48] the term 'cardiomyopathy' is now reserved for heart muscle disorders of unknown origin, so that the term 'alcoholic heart muscle disease' now seems more appropriate than 'alcoholic cardiomyopathy'.

So far, attempts at detecting incipient alcohol heart muscle damage by biochemical testing while still in its early, asymptomatic phase, has proved in vain. If an alcoholic continues drinking after developing acute or chronic heart muscle disease, recurrent acute episodes of myoglobinuria and irreversible congestive heart failure may supervene. However if, as usually is the case, such a patient denies heavy drinking, it is difficult to differentiate heart failure caused by drinking from that following congestive cardiomyopathy. New techniques may hold out some hope in differentiating these two conditions, as biopsy specimen of endomyocardial tissue (taken by the newly introduced biotome) has shown, for example, raised activity of certain enzymes in patients suffering from alcholic heart muscle disease [48].

Such a differentiation may be of practical importance as the outlook in the alcoholic variety on the whole may be much better than in congestive cardiomyopathy. Prognosis in alcoholic heart disease depends on degree and stage of damage and alcohol withdrawal may lead to complete remission of symptoms in early phases but not in cases where there is already severe myocardial damage. If the patient can be persuaded to give up drinking in time, pre-clinical and even acute alcoholic heart disease usually proves reversible, although complications such as permanent congestive failure or myoglobinuria may prove fatal. Possibly about 1–2 per cent of chronic alcoholics may proceed to heart failure. Continuation of high alcohol intake may eventually lead to 'irreversible myocardial damage with poor prognosis' [48].

The definite distinction between the terms 'cardiomyopathy' and heart muscle disease, as yet, does not seem to have been accepted everywhere, for example in a leading article [49] in *The Lancet* (May 1980) it is pointed out that 'alcoholic cardiomyopathy' cannot be differentiated from other types of congestive cardiomyopathy – all of them presenting a picture of biventricular heart failure. *The Lancet* leader therefore recommends that any patient suffering from heart failure of obscure origin should be investigated in regard to his drinking habits. Laboratory findings such as macrocytosis may be diagnostically helpful. It is assumed that people have to drink heavily for about ten years for serious heart damage to develop. Once heart failure develops, the outlook of course is poor but anticoagulant drugs may be of some prophylactic value in view of the dangers arising from systemic or pulmonary emboli. Occasionally, in cases where heart failure is not of long standing, it has been said that some patients giving up drink may show a marked improvement.

In recent years an interesting controversy has started as to whether wine may have different effects from other alcoholic drinks in regard to heart disease. Some feel that drinking wine does not bring any special benefits [50], but in 1979 some investigators [51] reported on the basis of international statistics 'a strong and negative association [to exist] between ischaemic heart death and . . . wine consumption'. A Seven Countries' Study [52, 53], covering over 12,000 men, aged 40–59 years, followed up for ten years, seemed to point in the same direction. Americans and Finns fared worst when it came to incidence of, and death from, coronary heart disease; Greeks and Japanese best. For Europe, an interesting marked gradient was found from north to south: from Finland to Netherlands, to Italy, Yugoslavia and Greece, the inhabitants of Crete found to be relatively as free from CHD as the Japanese. This was related to statistics according to which the Greeks and Italians in the study 'like their countrymen in general' were wine drinkers; the Dutch, 'like other Dutchmen', drank some wine but mainly beer and occasionally gin; the Finns and Americans seldom drank wine. The heaviest wine drinkers were Yugoslavs who, in the study, were found to be 'only slightly more prone to heart attacks than . . . our Greeks'. However, Keyes, who discusses these associations, appears to pour some cold water on them by pointing out that one might also claim that the Seven Countries' Study could also support a suggestion of using garlic as a possible prophylactic agent against heart attacks, as the Greeks, Italians and Yugoslavs of Dalamatia are heavy garlic users: one ought to be very cautious in drawing far-reaching conclusions from 'simple associations, such as those with the use of wine or garlic'.

The suggestion that wine may be less dangerous, than other alcoholic drink, or even mildly protective, is thus very much open to doubt. However, according to an American reviewer (1974) [54] the matter is still unclear – authorities' views differing greatly from each other. According to that review, it may be that 'although alcoholism, *per se*, does not afford protection against ischaemic heart disease [a statement surely amply borne out by the observation of any therapist who has seen sizeable numbers of alcoholics], those alcoholics with cirrhosis have a smaller risk than non-cirrhotic ethanolics and than their other contemporaries in the general population'. The finding that elevated levels of uric acid in the blood (hyperuricaemia) often accompany the elevated fat levels (hyperlipidaemia) of alcoholism suggest in the opinion of the reviewer (R W Hillman) that 'whatever the mechanism, it probably shows common features with that responsible for similar patterns observed in relation to coronary heart disease', but he quotes as one main reason 'for the less than satisfactory understanding of the relationship of alcoholism to hyperlipidaemia (with its relevance to CHD)' [54], a well known fact: 'Alcohol is the only substance in medicine which has both a nutrient value and a drug effect' [55].

Heavy bouts of drinking may be followed by arrhythmias which may be responsible for the 'holiday heart syndrome' [49]. Possibly arryhthmias are responsible for the finding that sudden death occurs relatively frequently in alcoholics.

Fifteen years ago Brigden and Robinson [56] described two main ways in which alcoholic heart disease may present (i.e. apart from the rare Beri Beri Heart Disease caused by thiamine [vitamin B1] deficiency in malnourished alcoholics), either with (usually atrial) arrhythmias, or alternatively with congestive heart failure (with symptoms such as breathlessness, fatigue, etc.). Cardiac arrhythmias may often be the first sign of alcoholic heart disease. However, the 'dimpled' T wave in the electrocardiogram – formerly held to be specific of alcoholic cardiomyopathy – is probably not specific.

What is the mechanism of alcoholic heart damage? The main culprit may not be ethanol itself but its first metabolite, acetaldehyde. In the concentration which acetaldehyde reaches in the blood of alcoholics, acetaldehyde is a strong depressant of myocardial function. The disulfiram – or CCC – approach of treating alcholics (see Chapter 16) is probably based on interrupting the ethanol breakdown at the acetaldehyde stage and the accumulation of blood acetaldehyde. Such disulfiram-ethanol reactions should therefore be avoided and the method should *not* be employed in order to create an aversion [57] by repetition of giving disulfiram-ethanol tests.

In regard to treatment of alcoholic heart muscle disease, a 1977 review [58] by two American authors of the influence of biochemical, physiological, clinical and morphological features of alcohol effects on the heart, concludes that abstinence from alcohol remains 'the most important therapeutic consideration'. In a similar vein *The Lancet* [49] in 1980 concludes from its deliberations that in alcohol depressed myocardial function, probably through its metabolite acetaldehyde, heart damage may be followed by permanent heart failure if the drinker continues to imbibe 'sufficient quantities for long enough'. Whether alcohol may induce damage to the heart more rapidly in patients suffering from other conditions, such as hypertension or viral hepatitis, is doubtful. But *The Lancet* emphasises that 'existing evidence makes a case for advising abstinence for patients with myocarditis'.

6   Hypertension

A raised blood pressure has frequently been found in regular heavy drinkers [15, 59, 60] with a positive correlation between amount of daily consumption and elevation of systolic and diastolic pressure [15]. In any individual case it may be difficult to determine whether it was the heavy drinking that led to the hypertension or whether the same type of factors may have been responsible for both heavy drinking and raised blood pressure – such as prolonged strain and stress from difficult psychosocial conditions.

7   Fat metabolism

A great deal of research has been carried out in recent years on the relationship or otherwise between hypertension, atherosclerosis, coronary artery disease and fat metabolism. Increased mortality from cerebrovascular lesions and coronary heart disease among alcoholics has been reported by Canadian [66] and Norwegian [94] investigators. Hypertriglyceridaemia is the main disturbance of fat metabolism in alcoholics [60a] and is regarded as a risk factor in regard to ischaemic heart disease and peripheral vascular disease. Conflicting findings have recently been reported on the effects of drinking on coronary heart disease [60b]. Alcoholics' 'binges' were shown, in an American study based on examination of coronary angiograms, often to be harmful to coronary arteries; but regular moderate drinkers were found to have a *lower* degree of coronary obstruction than people who did not take alcohol regularly. Degree of coronary occlusion was however found to be

40 per cent greater in infrequent but excessive binge drinkers than in the regular moderate drinkers. Another study showed that alcohol increases the blood levels of high density lipoprotein (HDL)[4] which has been found to lower the risk of arterial disease [60c], and lowers the level of the low-density-lipoproteins (which heighten the risk). Clearly, many questions remain unanswered but a recent editorial in *World Medicine* concludes that 'most cardiologists stressed that the dangers of excessive alcohol intake far outweighed the theoretical advantage to the coronary arteries' [60b].

8 Blood disorders due to alcohol

Changes in the blood occur in the majority of alcoholic patients [27], with *macrocytosis* the most characteristic and the most common feature. A recent study at the Northwick Park Hospital, London, showed 85 per cent of patients drinking more than 80g of ethanol per day, to have an increased mean corpuscular volume (MCV). As most of these patients had a normal level of folic acid in serum and liver, it is probably the toxic effect of alcohol on the bone marrow that leads to the macrocytosis [27]. Correspondingly, drinking is sometimes associated with a decline in the number of platelets, and giving up drinking may be followed by a rise in their number.

Chronic alcoholics often suffer from *anaemia* which may be due to a number of interacting factors [61, 62], such as poor nutrition causing restriction of folic acid in the diet and leading to its deficiency in the blood; poor absorption of food; liver disease; and suppression of red blood cell formation. Among such factors folate deficiency following dietary restriction, with megaloblastic erhythropoiesis and macrocytic anaemia, is probably one of the most significant; gastro-intestinal dysfunction with poor iron absorption may be another. The diet of chronic alcoholics often contains less than the minimum requirement of 50m folate per day. Excess alcohol can affect blood production in the bone marrow, suppress the formation of red blood cells, granulocytes and platelets; and if a drinker's diet contains very little folic acid, alcohol may inhibit an adequate response of bone marrow haemopoiesis to such minimal amounts of folic acid.

The disturbed formation of platelets (with resulting thrombocytopenia) and of white blood cells may be important factors in alcoholics' tendency to bruise readily, to bleed internally and to exhibit a poor resistance to infections. However, after hospital admission, alcoholics' anaemia often improves remarkably quickly – possibly because hospital diet provides the formerly missing nutritional constituents, so that normal blood formation can start again, and because alcohol consumption has ended. Under such circumstances in hospital bone marrow haemopoiesis is able to respond to the larger folic acid amounts in the ordinary hospital diet; there is reticulosis with an increase in haemoglobin in the numbers of leucocytes and thrombocytes.

Alcoholics very frequently present with multiple bruises and often maintain that they have no idea where they have come from. In many drinkers the increased tendency to bruise and bleed, following the thrombocytopenia, may present yet another hazard with his proneness to accidents at home, work and on the road, to head injuries with the risk of a subdural haematoma, his liability to bleed from peptic ulceration and oesophageal and rectal varicose veins, and his being a frequent candidate for emergency operations causing further loss of blood.

9   Alcohol effects on the endocrine system

This important subject has received relatively scant attention in literature but was recently well reviewed by Vincent Marks of the University of Surrey [63]. Effects of alcohol on the endocrine glands depend on whether small or very large amounts have been drunk, and how often and for how long and regularly.

Hypoglycaemia is an important and dangerous complication of consumption of alcohol. Such patients, when first seen, may be in a coma, and most such patients (but not all) are alcoholics, sometimes poorly nourished with their liver depleted of glycogen. Such hypoglycaemia may usually occur a few (up to thirty-six) hours after drinking moderate to large amounts of alcohol. Suspicion may be aroused in cases of unduly prolonged or somewhat atypical 'alcoholic intoxication'. Whereas, however, alcohol under certain circumstances can produce hypoglycaemia, Marks rejects the formerly popular hypothesis, proposed about thirty years ago, that inadequate adrenocortical function, by being responsible for hypoglycaemia, might lead to alcoholism (i.e. the drinker trying to raise his blood sugar) [64, 65]. No impairment of function of the adrenal glands has been found in heavy drinkers in spite of changes in urinary steroids.

Small amounts of alcohol (i.e. 50g) have been found greatly to increase the hypoglycaemic rebound effect that occurs in normal healthy individuals after taking a sugary drink. The implications of this recently described syndrome of a reactive hypoglycaemia induced or potentiated by alcohol are not clear [63].

In clinical practice the combination of alcoholism and diabetes mellitus is by no means rare; alcoholics have been found to have an increased mortality from diabetes [66].

Alcohol in large amounts has been found to affect adrenocortical function, and to activate cortisol release, chiefly as an indirect effect of intoxication. A small number of alcoholics have been found to show *Cushing's Syndrome* of adrenocortical hyperfunction. Such alcohol-induced Cushing's Syndrome disappears after alcohol has been withdrawn [63].

In general, no evidence of dysfunction of the thyroid is found among alcoholics so that, in Marks' view 'thyroid function, almost uniquely among endocrine functions, is neither disturbed by chronic alcohol abuse nor a contribution to its pathogenesis' [63].

A proportion of chronic alcoholics have been found to have raised levels of prolactin (secreted by the pituitary gland) which might be associated with sexual changes in alcoholics (see p. 285).

Hypothalamic-pituitary function may be impaired more often than generally thought, but may improve following prolonged abstinence [63]. The relationship of hypothalamic-pituitary-gonadal activity on the often observed sexual dysfunction of alcoholics is not clear. According to Marks [63], long continued heavy drinking may depress testicular production and secretion of testosterone, with possibly an initial rise in hypothalamic-pituitary LH secretion by way of compensation; later, however, the directly depressing effect of alcohol on hypothalamic centres may result in a depressing of LH secretion and hypogonadism. American observers ascribe the hypogonadism in alcoholic liver disease – frequently occurring in male alcoholics – to the failure of the hypothalamic-pituitary axis to ensure a sufficient production of gonadotrophins [63a].

The functioning of the sympathetic nervous system and of the adrenal medulla is stimulated by intoxicating amounts of alcohol. Both alcoholic intoxication and withdrawal of alcohol raise the production of catecholamines. In some alcoholics however, the activity of the autonomous system is lessened and may therefore be endangered when under stress. A similar suppression by alcohol of sympathetic-adrenomedulla function can also be dangerous to non-alcoholic healthy volunteers, when for example, drinking after exercise in cold weather can induce hypoglycaemia [63]. Even small amounts of alcohol, taken without food, can be risky after exercise which has reduced the carbohydrate stores. Ethanol, by reducing tissue pyruvate, diminishes gluconeogenesis [68], so that exercising after having taken alcohol may lead to hypoglycaemia [69]. Hypoglycaemia may develop when alcohol is taken while fasting or where there is a low carbohydrate intake [67].

Thus when trying to get an overview of the effect of alcohol on the endocrine system it would seem that alcohol can sometimes disturb the pituitary and other organs may temporarily malfunction but on the whole the system functions fairly well without too many mishaps. It may seem more likely, however, that future research may reveal that, as in other better researched areas, alcohol may be found to play a much more profound and disturbing role than believed at present.

10   Skeletal muscle disease – alcoholic myopathy

Although alcoholic skeletal muscle involvement does not usually attract much attention, it is interesting to note that an American writer nearly 150 years ago described 'a progressive weakness of the limbs' as a complication of the use of 'ardent spirit' which leads to 'some affection of the muscles' [70]. Very recently close examination of muscle biopsy specimens taken in non-alcoholic volunteers after drinking, have indicated similar changes to those noted in patients suffering from alcoholic heart muscle disease [71]. Clinical and laboratory features of the condition were described in the late 1960s [72] and it has been said that 'alcoholic myopathy is intimately related to [and] possibly an integral component of, the neurological complications of alcoholism' [54].

Subclinical, acute, and chronic forms of alcoholic myopathy have been distinguished. The only evidence of the clinically symptomless 'subclinical form' is an elevation in the serum of the enzyme creatine phosphokinase (CPK).

(a)   *Acute alcoholic myopathy*

This may start with weakness of limbs, sudden muscular pain or progression of previously existing myopathy. Muscles may be very tender to touch and swollen. The weakness may affect one limb only or a group of muscles, or may be more diffuse. Proximal muscles tend to be more affected than distal ones. Usually there is electromyographic evidence of myopathy. Like the subclinical variety, acute myopathy may be reversible, with signs and symptoms disappearing and function completely restored if the alcoholic stops drinking. However, there may be complications such as renal failure or myoglobinuria and the condition may prove fatal.

(b) *Chronic alcoholic myopathy*
This manifests itself by a gradually developing, incapacitating muscle weakness. This is usually symmetrical and most frequently affects the proximal muscles of the lower limbs. There may be no clinical symptoms at all but in other cases tenderness and weakness of muscles may be considerable, and acute drinking bouts may precipitate attacks of acute myopathy. As Geller and Rubin [73] state in their 1977 review of alcoholic myopathy, stopping alcohol intake may lead to improvement also of the chronic form.

The causation of alcoholic myopathy is obscure but it has been speculated that the muscle changes sometimes seen in chronic alcoholism might be due to one or both of two mechanisms [73]: a direct effect of ethanol on the muscle and/or an ethanol-induced neuropathy.

11a   The alcohol foetal syndrome

In ancient Carthage [74] married couples were strongly warned against drinking alcohol on their wedding night lest it might adversely affect the offspring; while the Talmud refers to the risk of death of the embryo carried by a woman drinking undiluted wine [75] in very large amounts, it may seem less surprising that alcohol, causing so much harm to the tissues of the adult can also do considerable damage to the immature tissues of the foetus, than that such harmful effects have only been demonstrated recently. What has been termed the *alcohol foetal syndrome*, is a combination of abnormalities (physical, mental and behavioural) seen in newborn babies whose mothers drank fairly heavily during their pregnancy. Evidence, first published in the early 1970s [76, 77], has indicated that heavy drinking by pregnant women can lead to congenital anomalies and retardation of foetal growth. All degrees of severity of the syndrome may be seen but in its fully developed form the undersized baby is born with a very small head (microcephaly) and multiple deformities of face (short palpebral fissures, epicanthal folds, facial hypoplasia and, more rarely, abnormalities of the ears), limbs (including abnormal palmar creases) and joints; heart defects (such as auricular or ventricular septal defects), and poor motor co-ordination [78]. Mental retardation is common, as is overactivity, nervousness and poor attention.

After birth, these infants grow and put on weight only slowly and show no improvement of intelligence.

The mechanism of development of the syndrome is not clear; however alcohol, having crossed the placenta barrier and reaching the same level in the unborn baby's blood as in the mother's, exercises a much greater effect on its immature liver tissue.

The amount of alcohol which a mother can drink during pregnancy without the risk of her baby developing the alcohol foetal syndrome is unknown.

Many questions about the syndrome remain open. Among various possible causes is a direct action of alcohol on the foetus, or some indirect nutritional disturbance. At any rate it is difficult to explain that in spite of the fact that some women may drink more or less regularly throughout pregnancy, the syndrome is seen (and diagnosed) so rarely. Dunn and his colleagues [79], in 1979 quoted Hungarian research work indicating that the alcohol metabolite acetaldehyde (a possible culprit in alcoholic heart disease) may be involved; this substance is said to be 'highly cytotoxic and teratogenic' at levels which, though not present in healthy people, may be reached in others suffering from an inherited (or acquired) defect of aldehyde dehydrogenase in the mitochondria of liver cells. (Alcohol dehydrogenase is an enzyme present in the cytoplasm and mitochondria of liver cells involved in the oxidation of acetaldehyde to acetate, so that in the case of deficient action of this enzyme an excess of acetaldehyde could be left. Almost all the acetaldehyde resulting from ethanol breakdown is metabolised in the liver [80].) The Hungarians also warn against the use of disulfiram in pregnant women.

As far as is known, the type of alcoholic drink taken is not important, what seems to matter is the *quantity* taken chronically. The effect of bout drinking in the development of the syndrome is unknown [81].

Summing up the position in November 1977, Gordis and Kreek [82] concluded that mental impairment in offspring seemed more commonly associated with material drinking than the physical malformations of the alcohol foetal syndrome. 'It was not possible to state with confidence' whether alcohol was a teratogen in man, but until the outstanding scientific issues are resolved, these authors felt 'the wisest recommendation [to be] total abstinence during pregnancy'.

11b Spontaneous abortion

The fears of ill consequences of women drinking during pregnancy which ancient nations often appear to have harboured have now, thousands of years later, been confirmed from recent evidence. Following a few years later than the description of the alcohol foetal syndrome, two papers [83, 84] in the same issue of *The Lancet* by American observers claim to have shown that alcohol intake during pregnancy may be followed by spontaneous abortion; moreover, according to one of these studies, spontaneous abortion can result even if there was only moderate drinking.

In one study, by Kline and her associates [83], in New York, among 657 women who had had a spontaneous abortion, a higher proportion reported to have taken alcoholic drink at least twice a week than an age-matched control group of pregnant women who had not had a spontaneous abortion. An annotation in the same issue of *The Lancet* [85], however, raises the question whether there may not also have been other significant differences between these two groups, so that there is some doubt about the conclusion made by the authors, that spontaneous abortion may follow even moderate drinking.

Some of the shortcomings of this study criticised by *The Lancet* were not attached to the (prospective) study by Harlay and Shiono [84] in California. These workers analysed questionnaires computed by 32,019 women early in pregnancy. The women who regularly (i.e. daily) imbibed alcohol during pregnancy, subsequently experienced higher spontaneous abortion rates (especially in the second trimester) than non-drinkers. Such differences persisted even if adjustment had been made for factors such as smoking, age, race, parity and previous abortion. However, no significantly raised incidence was found among the more moderate drinkers (i.e. women who drank less often than daily).

The Lancet annotation [85] concludes that both studies indicated a raised incidence of spontaneous abortion among women who, during pregnancy, drank every day. When it comes to drinking 2–6 times a week, there was no evidence from the more reliable study but only from the one regarded as less reliable. *The Lancet* therefore comes to the conclusion that on the basis of 'existing evidence' pregnant women should avoid drinking daily during pregnancy (but apparently *The Lancet* here is considering only the risk of spontaneous abortion and not the alcohol foetal syndrome where there seems to be no reliable data as to the association between frequency of drinking and the risk of the syndrome). There is an obvious need for further studies to determine the risks which might follow drinking during pregnancy less frequently than each day. 'Many women [comments *The Lancet*] chose to take a conservative attitude to drugs in pregnancy – and they should remember that alcohol, too, is a "drug".' Under such circumstances one might well think that it would surely be best to avoid *all* drugs during pregnancy that are not absolutely necessary. Whatever other doubts may exist in regard to alcohol, no reliable evidence has been forthcoming that alcohol is necessary for the well-being of pregnant women or their unborn babies; as, moreover, there is some doubt, and although it is the 'less reliable' study only that indicates some risk even from moderate drinking, it might be just as well to err on the side of caution. Perhaps it might be even more important to discuss such matters in Britain than in the USA. Whereas 42–52 per cent of the American mothers studied drank no alcohol during pregnancy, a prospective study under way at the Charing Cross obstetric unit in West London found only 7 per cent (fourteen out of the first 200 pregnant women seen) teetotal. Of these 200 women, Murray-Lyon and his colleagues [85a] found that 5 per cent were taking one or two drinks (10–20g alcohol) daily during pregnancy, and a further 6 per cent were consuming 30–40g daily. As these doctors point out, drinking in pregnancy seems to 'represent a significant problem, at least in this selected area of UK'.

12 Nervous System (Neurological and Neuropsychiatric Complications)

Common N.S. complications of heavy drinking include

1 *Epileptiform fits:* These may be precipitated in susceptible drinkers by acute alcoholic intoxication, hypoglycaemia, or alcohol withdrawal.

2 *Subdural haematoma*: This is not uncommon in alcoholics (many patients presenting themselves at accident and emergency

departments show a positive blood alcohol test e.g. 42 per cent in a recent Belfast study [86a]). Sudden alterations in the patient's mental state without obvious cause might arouse suspicion.

3 *Alcoholic polyneuropathy (polyneuritis)*: This condition may affect up to 20 per cent of chronic alcoholics, and may be of very varying degrees of severity. Often it is present in a very mild form only and rather stationary, with features such as tender calf muscles, painful cramps or discomfort in walking, and numbness, tingling and paraesthesias in the feet and hands. Legs are much more frequently affected than arms. Sensory disturbances are usually more pronounced than motor ones, and the extremities are affected symmetrically and chiefly at the periphery. Patients in more advanced stages may suffer from weakness of the legs, footdrop, wasting of leg muscles, weakness of the hand muscles, and wristdrop (tendon jerks may be absent) and blunting of all forms of sensibility. Ultimately, the legs may be almost paralysed and contractures may develop. The skin of the extremities may be sweating and oedematous or, less often, dry and atrophic.

Rarely one may also find cranial nerve palsies. Often patients with peripheral neuritis are also confused, and show memory defects; in our experience the combination of peripheral neuritis with a mild confusional state and memory defects is not uncommon, especially amongst women alcoholics, whereas classic Korsakoff's psychosis with confabulations seems very rare.

There may, however, be all kinds of combinations of the various 'syndromes' depending on the localisations of the pathological process in the various parts of nervous system. Thus in practice one may often come across such combinations of the different syndromes in the individual alcoholic patient.

In general the outlook in alcoholic polyneuritis is good, especially if treatment is begun early. On a regime of complete bed rest, a full diet supplemented by vitamins parenterally and orally (as alcoholics usually suffer from multiple vitamin deficiency, multi-vitamin preparations should be given additionally to vitamin B1) with passive movements from the start, most patients may be expected to recover, although the process may sometimes take a few months.

4 *Wernicke's encephalopathy*: (Because of its common association with Korsakoff's psychosis (see Chapter 15) this is often known as the *Wernicke-Korsakoff Syndrome.*) This

syndrome may start as an acute or sub-acute illness, an organic confusional state. The classic features of Wernicke's triad: clouding of consciousness, ataxia (on walking or standing), and ophthalmoplegia, in general, are not always present; therefore the condition, usually considered rare, may be more common than suspected [86]. Early diagnosis is important because immediate intravenous thiamine administration can lead to full recovery. The condition is caused by an affection of the brain stem and is probably due to acute thiamin (B1) deficiency. In some cases it may respond rapidly to treatment with large amounts of vitamin B1 given parenterally supplemented by another member of the B complex. It may often occur in association with other evidence of chronic alcoholism, and may, on clearing up, leave a Korsakoff's syndrome. Like the latter, Wernicke's syndrome may be due to causes other than alcoholism, as, for example, gastro-intestinal disorders.

5   *Cortical atrophy (brain damage)*:   Such changes have been shown since the introduction of CAT (computerised axial tomography) to be much more common and to occur earlier than formerly suspected – even in young drinkers (although apparently CAT changes do not necessarily indicate irreversible clinical deterioration). Cortical atrophy is probably the cause for the earlier mild intellectual deterioration and for the progressive dementia (see Chapter 15) seen in a number of alcoholics. However, Lemere [80] had already stated that 'for each alcoholic with demonstrable pathology, there must be thousands in intermediate stages of danger'.

Characteristic symptoms of irreversible brain damage are memory disturbances (usually in a setting of clear consciousness) amounting in severe cases to the Korsakoff phenomenon. However, visual-motor and visual-spatial functions may also be affected [87] – an important consideration in certain skilled occupations and professions [88].

The amount of alcohol and the duration of intake which may bring about brain damage are unknown. Individual susceptibility obviously must play a role, nutritional factors may also be involved. Air encephalography, EEG, psychometric studies, and recently the non-invasive CAT techniques, have all been employed to study existence and extent of brain damage in alcoholics. For example, in an earlier investigation by Brewer and Perrett [89] 77 per cent of male alcoholics and heavy drinkers (in Australia) showed radiological evidence of cortical atrophy; corresponding findings were obtained at the same time in Yugoslavia by Vladimar and Vishna Hudolin [90].

As mentioned above, CAT techniques have made such studies easier and have shown brain changes to occur earlier and more commonly, without (as yet) being able to answer the question to what extent such changes may be reversible. In London, the findings of Alwyn Lishman and his team [91] indicated marked differences between the brain scans of 100 alcoholics and forty-one controls. The drinkers, aged 22–67 years, had been imbibing on average eight pints per day (150g alcohol) over an average period of seventeen years. Enlargement of the Sylvian Fissures and the third ventricle and widening of sulci were seen in more than half of the alcoholics, and the average ratio between the size of the ventricles and the brain was twice that of the controls. However, most of these alcoholics also showed intellectual impairment on psychometric testing.

How far can such alcoholics recover or improve? Follow-up of nine alcoholics who had remained abstinent for one year showed improved sulci and Sylvian Fissures in no more than two patients, and the average size of ventricles/brain ratio, while improved, still remained abnormal.

Similar results were obtained by Bergman in Sweden [92] whose CAT scan studies showed clear brain damage in 62 per cent of his alcoholics. Among the 20–29 years age group, half were affected, and such young patients were particularly likely to show cortical atrophy leading to widening of the sulci and of the Sylvian Fissures. A quarter of these alcoholics showed intellectual impairment.

Lishman and his associates [91], while stressing the preliminary nature of their reports, conclude that alcoholics are 'decisively abnormal' both on radiographic and psychometric studies, that considerable brain shrinkage, cortical and subcortical, can be evident in even quite young alcoholics and that it can be influenced by their recent drinking history. Some changes can persist in spite of one year's abstinence from alcohol but 'a beginning improvement appears to be discernible after [a year's] abstinence and hopefully may continue for longer'. Whether such a condition is ever completely reversible, and what, in behavioural terms the effects on the individual may be, cannot be said at the present juncture and requires further studies. Of great significance, though as yet unexplained, is the 'lack of extensive and systematic

relationships between CAT scan and psychometric findings' which
indicates that there is more to cerebral functioning than the
morphological changes in the brain shown in the CAT scan. The
Swedish investigators [92] too found the correlations between
neuropsychological functioning and the cerebral morphological
status to be low.

Nutrition and the causation of alcoholic neurological complications
This question is very important, not least because of the therapeutic and prognostic implications. According to a detailed review
of the subject by Victor and Adams in 1961 [93] *delirium tremens*,
alcoholic epilepsy, and acute auditory hallucinosis are causally
related to habituation to, and withdrawal of, alcohol, and are not of
nutritional origin; on the other hand, Wernicke's Syndrome, alcoholic Korsakoff's psychosis, polyneuropathy and the neurological
manifestations of pellagra are clearly nutritional in origin; and
finally in a third group – alcoholic cerebellar degeneration,
central pontine myelinosis, and Marchafava-Bignami disease –
pathogenesis and the role of nutritional factors remain uncertain.

Mortality

Not surprisingly, in view of all these (and other) possible complications, the lifespan of the average alcoholic is considerably
shortened (see Chapter 3). A number of epidemiological studies
have shown an increased mortality among alcoholics in various
countries (Denmark, Norway, France, USA, etc.), mainly from
causes including pneumonia, cancers of the upper digestive and
respiratory tracts, heart disease, cirrhosis of the liver, accidents
and suicides. Among male and female alcoholic patients treated
between 1951–63 at the Toronto Clinic of the Addiction Research
Foundation, Schmidt and De Lint [66] found that excess mortality
(i.e. observed as against expected mortality) was particularly high
from liver cirrhosis (among men and women: 49 and 25 times
(respectively) the expected rate), accidents (2.52 and 12.40),
suicides (6.02 and 8.69), pneumonia (3.67 and 7.14), ulcer of the
stomach and duodenum (3.55 and 6.66), heart disease (1.74 and
4.10), cancer of upper digestive and respiratory tracts (2.79 and
1.88), and for vascular lesions of the central nervous system (1.14
and 2.43). The ratio of observed to expected deaths from all causes
was 2.02 for male and 3.19 for female alcoholics. Whereas the
death rates of women in the general population are lower than

men, alcoholic women are as likely to die as alcoholic men. In fact, the mortality of female alcoholics by cause was found closely to resemble the male pattern. The Canadian authors also attempted to trace the relative importance of the various factors possibly involved in such deaths, but found this task very difficult. The acute effects of drinking were involved in deaths from poisonings, falls, fire and the chronic effects of alcohol in liver cirrhosis; in suicides, relatively more important seemed to be the alcoholic's depression; in lung cancer the heavy smoking.

A detailed investigation carried out by Per Sundby [94] in Norway among over 1700 male alcoholics treated in an Oslo psychiatric clinic between 1925–40 and followed up until the closing day of the observation (at the end of 1962) showed similar results. Three-quarters of 'extra deaths' (over the expected rates) were ascribed to seven major cause groups: tuberculosis of the upper respiratory tract (18 per cent), cancer of larynx and upper digestive organs (10.9 per cent), accidents (10.6 per cent), apoplexy (8.5 per cent), suicide (8.4 per cent), other cancers (8.2 per cent), coronary heart disease (8.1 per cent). The extra mortality of alcoholics compared with the general Norwegian population amounted to 113 per cent or compared to the Oslo population, 69 per cent. In Switzerland, a study (1969) indicated life expectation among male alcoholics to be reduced by 15 per cent and of the females by 12 per cent [95].

Of some interest in this connection is the high mortality from (pulmonary) *tuberculosis* found among the Norwegian alcoholics. Formerly tuberculosis was a very significant risk for alcoholic patients in view of various factors, such as their unhygienic way of living with their exposure, vulnerability, and lack of resistance to intercurrent infections, their poor nutritional state, their inability to keep off drink and to co-operate with prescribed treatment etc. Various studies published in Canada, Australia and this country in the mid-1960s [96a–d] discuss the link between tuberculosis and alcoholism, and researchers in Hungary [96e], for example, are still greatly interested in this problem. Fortunately with the advent of modern treatment the prevalence of tuberculosis has fallen dramatically, and with it also its incidence among alcoholics. Nevertheless the possibility must be kept in mind, in particular in view of the high rates of intercurrent upper respiratory infections, and especially among the undernourished, 'down-and-out' drinkers. In his comment on the high tuberculosis mortality found in his Oslo study, Sundby [94] comments on the decline of crude mortality rates in Norway for tuberculous men from 16.4 per 10,000 in 1930 to 1.0 in 1960, the alcoholics benefiting from this favourable trend nearly as much as the non-alcoholics although their mortality from this condition at all times remained twice as high as that of the average population. Alcoholic vagrants studied by Sundby during the earlier part of the investigation had a somewhat higher mortality from (upper respiratory tract) tuberculosis than non-vagrant alcoholics – this difference, however, levelling off towards the end of the observation period.

Seeing that mortality rates and the main causes for such increased death rates are not all that different between alcoholics in Canada, Scandinavia and Britain, it might seem that the toxic action of the agent alcohol on the tissues of the host (the personality) largely determines its deleterious effect with relatively little interference from environmental factors, or that alternatively there may not be marked differences in important aspects of the life style and habits (such as nutritional patterns, smoking etc.) which might hinder or favour such toxic effect of alcohol on the drinker's tissues. It certainly would seem of great interest to carry out similar studies of mortality rates of 'alcoholics' (agreeing beforehand what, for this purpose, is understood by the term) among nations (or regions) with quite different life styles and habits, and compare and analyse the similarities and marked differences (if any). Such investigations would be time-consuming but do not appear too difficult to carry out. Toxic action of alcohol on the liver cells may not be greatly influenced by environmental customs in the various nations but sociocultural factors may have an important influence on the social and psychological manifestations of alcoholism, for example, guilt feelings among drinkers in a non-conformist environment may lead to secret drinking, perhaps bout drinking rather than the non-guilt-ridden, social drinking in France (see Chapters 2 and 3). While there must be a correlation between organic complications of habitual alcohol misuse and social complications, there might also exist important difference between them – the organic ones probably being more independent from national and regional influences than the former, although national laws and customs affect the *per capita* consumption and with it also the incidence of cirrhosis.

One more interesting point that emerges from Sundby's study [94] was that 10 per cent of the male alcoholics also showed some evidence of a syphilitic infection; the mortality from this cause was 4.57 times the Norwegian expectation. Writing about the relationship between alcohol and sex in 1938 a British medical expert [97] on questions of marriage and sex stated that in women 'the continuance of the alcoholic habit can only lead to an eventual loosening of moral control . . . and that . . . many [women] alcoholics have acquired this addiction owing to the fact that their sex relationships have never been satisfactory'. Attitudes have changed greatly since; but there is of course a relationship between sex problems and alcohol (and alcoholism) (see p. 321) and heavy drinking probably contributes its share to a higher incidence of 'sexually transmitted disease' [98] (although, as in the case of tuberculosis so also in VD, mortality from improperly treated infection is largely a thing of the past).

Nowadays, late complications of alcoholism – such as cirrhosis, polyneuropathy or dementia – are unfortunately still regarded by some medical men as constituting the disorder alcoholism, the diagnosis not being suspected until such complications (may or may not) appear late in the process. No doctor would dream of never suspecting a syphilitic infection until the possible (nowadays very rare) appearance of GPI or Tabes, and likewise in the interest of early detection valuable time must not be lost in suspecting the possibility of alcoholism in the absence of its late (and rare) complications.

Notes

1 Of mainly psychogenic or sociogenic alcoholics admitted to alcoholic units primarily for psychological or social complications, as many as 70 per cent are found to show some pathological changes of liver function tests – such as the serum transaminases and in the main nowadays of the Gamma Glutamyl Transpeptidase (GGTP) – which usually return towards normal within the next few weeks with total abstinence [25, 26].

2 In 1971 the official figure in this country of 5.1 per cent deaths from cirrhosis contrasted sharply with over 5000 such deaths per 100,000 of the population in France, Portugal and Italy [27].

3 Produced during the process of fermentation congeners are found in varying combinations and very small amounts in the various alcoholic beverages. There are a very great number of congeners – among them 'fusel oil' (the isoamyl alcohols), acetaldehyde, etc. They provide aroma and flavour to the drinks and some congeners are toxic (and have been blamed occasionally for contributing to the hangover) but

are in general thought to be present in too small amounts to exercise any harmful [2] effects.

4   Blood lipids (cholesterol, triglyceride, phospholipid) are carried in the plasma in the form of lipoproteins, i.e. complexes of lipids and proteins. There are various types of lipoproteins; by ultracentrifugation they can be divided into chylomicrons, low density lipoproteins (LDL) and high density lipoprotein [60d]. A very recent Leading Article in *The Lancet* [60e] describes the evidence that 'susceptibility to the clinical complications of coronary artery disease is inversely related to the plasma HDL cholestrerol concentration' as very consistent and concludes 'that at least part of any alteration of coronary risk associated with moderate alcohol consumption, regular exercise, gonadal hormone usage, obesity, and cigarette smoking (seems) probably related, directly or indirectly, to changes in HDL metabolism'.

References

1   World Health Organisation (1951), *Expert Committee on Mental Health*, World Hlth Org. Techn. Rep. Ser. 42, 19
1a   Castelli, W P *et al*. (1977), *The Lancet*, ii, 153
2   Keller, M and McCormick, M (1968), *A Dictionary of Words about Alcohol*, New Brunswick, NY, Rutgers Center for Alcohol Studies, 16, 62
3   Nolan, J P (1965), *Am. J. med. Sci.*, 249, 135
4   McCusker, J *et al*. (1971), *NY State J. Med.* 3, 751
5   Moore, R A (1971), *Am. J. Psychiat.*, 128, 638
6   Green, J R (1965), *Med. J. Austral.*, 1, 465
7   Jarman, C M B and Kellett, J (1979), *Brit. med. J.*, ii, 469
8   Jariwalla, A G *et al*. (1979), *Health Trends*, 11, 95
9   Holt, S *et al*. (1980), *Brit. med. J.*, 281, 638
10   Wilkins, R H (1974), *The Hidden Alcoholic in General Practice*, London, Elek Science, 132–6
11   Davis, M (1979), *General Practitioner*, 29
12   Rosalki, S B *et al*. (1970), *Ann. Clin. Biochem.*, 7, 143
13   Spencer-Peet, J *et al*. (1972), *The Lancet* i, 1122
14   Murray, R M and Bernadt, M (1980), *Medicine*, 35, 1811
15   Feuerlein, W (1979), *Alkoholismus-Missbrauch und Abhangigkeit*, 2nd ed., Stuttgart, Thieme, 93, 117
16   *Deutsche Hauptstelle gegen die Suchtgefahren* (1980), Hamm, DHS., 19
17   *Encyclop. Psychiatry for GPs* (1972), ed. Leigh D, *et al*., London, Roche
18   Gross, M M *et al*. (1974) in *The Biology of Alcoholism* ed. Kissin, B and Begleiter, H, NY, London, Plenum Press, Vol. 3, 191–263
19   Glatt, M M (1955), *Brit. med. J.*, 2, 737

20   Victor, M and Brausch, J (1967), *Epilepsia*, 8, 1
21   Jellinek, E M (1951), World Hlth Org. Techn. Rep. Ser. 42, 19–23
22a Lieber, C S and DeCarli, L M (1977) in *Metabolic Aspects of Alcoholism* ed. Lieber, C S, Lancaster, MTP, 31–79
22b Feinman, L and Lieber, C S (1974) in *The Biology of Alcoholism*, ed. Kissin, B and Begleiter, H, NY, London, Plenum, Vol. 3, 303–38
23   Pequignot, G (1962), *Munch. med. Wchschr.*, 103, 1464
24   von Lelbach, W K (1971), *ibid.*, 46, 1549
25   Kay, W W, Murfit, K W and Glatt, M M (1959), *J. Ment. Sci.*, 105, 784
26   Spencer-Peet, J *et al.* (1975), *Brit. J. Addict.*, 70, 359
27   Silk, D B A (1979), *Med. News*, 8 November
28   Silk, D B A (1977), *Gen. Pract.*, 17 June, 28, 29
29   Fouquet, P (1951), Europ. Seminar and Lect. Course on Alcoholism (Copenhagen), Geneva, WHO, 40
30   Pequignot, G *et al.* (1974), *Rev. Alc*, 20, 191
31   *Deutsche Hauptstelle gegen die Suchtgefahren,* Wissenschaftliches Kuratorium, Pressemitteilung, 15 April 1980
32   May, B, 4th Wissenschaftliches Symposium, Deutsche Hauptstelle gegen Scuhtgefahren, Tutzing, 15 April 1980
33   Krasner, N *et al.* (1977), *Brit. med. J.*, 1, 1497
34   Sherlock, S (1977), *Proceed. RSM*, 70, 851
35   Swain, F (1980), *Hosp. Update*, 1139
36a Glatt, M M (1964), 27th Internat. Congress against Alcoholism, Frankfurt
36b Glatt, M M (1967), *Brit. J. Addict.*, 62, 35
37   Imrie, C W *et al.* (1977), quoted from *Alcoholism – New Knowledge and New Responses*, ed. Edwards, G, and Grant, M, London, Croom Helm, 1977, 201
38   Bouchier, A D, (June 1979), *Medicine*, 18, 938
39   Hermon-Taylor, J (December 1977), *Brit. J. Hosp. Med.*, 546
40   Mallinson, C, *ibid*, 553
41   Glatt, M M (1977), *Brit. J. Addict.*, 72, 253
42   Lowenfels, A B (1979), *Brit. J. Alcohol and Alcoholism*, 14(3), 148
43   Rothman, K J (1975), *Alcohol* in *Persons at High Risk from Cancer*, ed. Fraumeni, J F, New York, Academic Press, 139–50
44   Holmus, C and Spahn, J G (1974), *Laryngoscope* 9, 1497
45   Kissin, B and Kaley, M M (1974) in *The Biology of Alcoholism*, eds Kissin, B and Begleiter, H, New York, Plenum Press, Vol. 3, 481–511
46   Fenster, L F (1977) in *Alcoholism* eds Estes, N J and Heinemann, M E, St Louis, C V Mosby
47   Edwards, G *et al.* (1967), *Social Psychiat.* (Ger.), 1, 15
48   *Brit. med. J.* (L.A.) 1979, 4, 1457
49   *The Lancet* (L.A.) 1980, i, 961
50   Levi, G F *et al.* (1977), *Brit. Heart J.*, 39, 35

51   St Leger *et al*. (1979), *The Lancet*, i, 1017, 1294
52   Keyes, A (ed) (1970), *Coronary Heart Disease in Seven Countries*, Amer. Heart Assoc. Monograph, No. 29
53   Keyes, A (1980), *The Lancet*, i
54   Hillman, R W (1974) in *The Biology of Alcoholism*, eds Kissin, B and Begleiter, H, vol. 3, 513–86
55   Galambos, J T (1968), *S. Med. J.*, 61, 129
56   Brigden, W W and Robinson, J (1964), *Brit. med. J.*, 2, 1283
57   World Health Organisation Alcoholism Subcommittee (1952), World Hlth Org. Techn. Rep. Ser., 48, 11
58   Bing, B R and Tillmanns, H (1977) in *Metabolic Aspects of Liver Disease*, ed. Lieber, C S, 117–30
59   Klatsky, A L *et al*. (1974), *Ann. int. Med.*, 81, 294
60   Klatsky, A L *et al*. (1977), *N. Engl. J. Med.*, 296, 1194
60a Chait, A M *et al*. (1972), *The Lancet*, ii, 62
60b *World Med*. (Edit.) 1980, 13 December
60c Newspaper report December 1980
60d West, R and Shaw, A (1981), *Hosp. Update*, 7, 379
60e *The Lancet* (L.A.), 1981, i, 478
61   *The Lancet* (L.A.), 1967, ii, 675
62   Glatt, M M (1971) in *Progress in Clinical Medicine* ed. Daley, R and Miller, H, Edinburgh, London, Churchill, 6th ed. 522–42
63   Marks, V (1980) in *Addiction and Brain Damage* ed. Richter, D, London, Croom Helm, 153–67
63a Van Thiel, D H *et al*. (1973), *Gastroenterology*, 65, 574
64   Tintera, J W and Lovell, H W (1949), *Geriatrics*, 4, 274
65   Glatt, M M (1955), *Brit. med. J.*, 1, 973
66   Schmidt, W S and De Lint, J (1972), *Quart. J. Stud. Alc.*, 33, 171
67   Krebs, H (1980) in *Addiction and Brain Damage*, 11–16
68   Krebs, H (1969), *Biochem. J.*, 112, 1171
69   *Brit. med. J.* (1968), 1, 634
70   Jackson, J (1837) quoted from Geller, S E and Rubin, E (ref. 73), 196
71   *Brit. med. J.* (L.A.) 1979, 4
72   Perkoff, G T *et al*. (1967) *Ann. Int. Med.*, 67, 481
73   Geller, S E and Rubin, E (1977) in *Metabolic Aspects of Alcoholism*, 187–213
74   Haggard, H W and Jellinek, E M (1950), *Alcohol Explained*, New York, Doubleday, Dore & Co
75   Abbaye (300) Niddah 24b
76   Jones, K C *et al*. (1973), *The Lancet*, i, 1267
77   Jones, K C and Smith, D W (1973), *The Lancet*, ii, 989
78   Hanson, J W *et al*. (1976), *J.A.M.A.*, 235, 1458
79   Dunn, P M *et al*. (1979), *The Lancet*, ii, 144
80   Lundquist, K (1971) in *Biological Basis of Alcoholism*, ed. Israel, Y, and Mardones, J, New York, London, Wiley Interscience, 1–52
81   Smith, D W (1977) in *Alcoholism* ed. Estes, N J and Heinemann, M E, 144–149

82   Gordis, E and Kreek, M J (1977), *Current Problems in Obstetrics and Gynaecology*, 1(3), 27–30
83   Kline, J *et al*. (1980), *The Lancet*, ii, 176
84   Harlay, S and Shiono, P H (1980), *The Lancet*, ii. 173
85   *The Lancet* (Annot.) 1980, ii, 188
85a Murray-Lyon, I M *et al*. (1980) *The Lancet*, ii, 1382
86   *Brit. med. J.* (L.A.) 1979, 3, 291
86a Rutherford, W H (1977) *The Lancet*, ii, 1021
86b Lemere, F (1956–7), *Amer. J. Psychiat.*, 113, 361
87   Clarke, J (1976), *Irish med. J.*, 69, 29
88   *Brit. med. J.* (L.A.) 1976, 2, 1168
89   Brewer, C and Perrett, L (1971), *Brit. J. Addict.*, 66, 170
90   Hudolin, V (1980) in *Addiction and Brain Damage*, 168–200
91   Lishman, W A, Ron, M and Acker, W (1980), *ibid*, 215–27
92   Bergman, H, Borg, S, Hindmarsh, T, Idestrom, C M, and Mutzell, S (1980), *ibid*, 201–214
93   Victor, M and Adams, D R (1961), *Amer. J. Clin. Nutrit.*, 9, 379
94   Sundby, Per (1967), *Alcoholism and Mortality*, Oslo, Universitatsforlaget
95   Ciompi, L and Eisert, M (1969), *Soc. Psychiat.*, 4, 159
96a Pincock, T A (1964), *Can. med. Ass. J.*, 91, 851
96b Olin, J S and Grzybowski, S (1966), *ibid.*, 94, 999
96c Green, J R (1965), *Med. Austral.*, 1, 465
96d Lewis, J G and Chamberlain, D A (1963), *Brit. J. prev. soc. Med.*, 17, 149
96e Levendel, L (1966), 12th Internat. Inst. Prev. and Treatm. of Alcoholism, Prague, June 13–24, ICCA, Selected Papers, 83–90
96f Caplin, M and Rehahn, M (1978) *Alcoholism and Tuberculosis*, RCPsych., Topics in Therapy, London, Pitman
97   Griffith, E F (1938), *Brit. J. Inebr.*, 36, 57
98   *On Call*, 11 December, 1980

15

Alcohol-Induced Mental Disorders

1 Neurotic reactions

The distinction between those (on the whole) milder complications and the usually more severe complications ('psychoses') is occasionally difficult though very obvious in many cases. It is often said that psychoneurotics have insight and live in the world of reality, whereas psychotics lack insight and live in a world of fantasy (see Chapter 19). The psychotic paranoid patient, for example, believes in the reality of his delusions (of persecution) and fights 'for' them, the neurotic obsessional patient, on the other hand, realises that his obsessions are irrational and fights 'against' them. But often the dividing line is not all that clear. Behaviours in alcoholics who suffer from superimposed neurotic reactions can be markedly affected by their general anxiety or special phobias, vague, irrational fears that may occasionally develop into panic, hysterical attack, or reactive depression.

A great many alcoholics (probably the great majority) are often very depressed, agitated, anxious and tense, and the chicken-or-egg question may present an almost insuperable problem: did their anxious personality type or greatly upsetting environmental circumstances originally lead them to relief drinking and from there to secondary alcoholism? Or were anxiety and depression essentially a reaction to the life circumstances which the excessive drinking had landed them in? The more severe 'affective psychoses' – whether manifesting themselves in recurrent ('unipolar') depressions only, or in their 'bipolar' form – with depressed and manic (elated, excitable) phases present at different times, or as the involutional melancholia at the time of the menopause, can all lead to heavy drinking (the manic phases of the manic-depressive psychosis, too, can provoke people to drink heavily, for example, in order to experience an even more intensive 'high'). Probably much more commonly, however, the depressive states which lead people to heavy relief drinking are reactive and exogenous (rather than endogenous) in origin, in response to untoward painful experiences. Women alcoholics relatively more often than men started their heavy drinking because of a more definite traumatic event or experience. Once, however, occasional relief drinking has increasingly led to 'constant relief' drinking and increase of tolerance (see Chart pp. 74–5) instead of alleviating the individual's worries and depression, such drinking in turn creates its own problems.

In cases where depression or severe anxiety occur, most doctors (certainly in the past, but probably also today) would regard the underlying depression and anxiety state as primary and treat the condition in the hope that after relief of such 'underlying' conditions the reason for the excessive drinking and with it the latter itself, would fall by the wayside. (Indeed, in cases of a severe, possibly suicidal, endogenous depression, and whenever people threaten suicide, the condition has to be taken very seriously. Lithium, a drug ordinarily used for prophylaxis and treatment of manic-depressive psychosis, has also been recommended by some therapists [1] for the treatment of depression in alcoholics.) Often the drinker himself would ask the doctor to concentrate on his 'underlying' depressed state as the alcoholic may play down, or even hardly mention, his drinking.

On the other hand, in many such cases of reactive depression and 'anxiety states', most therapists with experience in the treatment of alcoholics would feel that it is useless to treat such a patient's depression and anxiety while he proceeds to drown his worries in further drinking. Under such circumstances tranquillisers and antidepressants may potentiate the effect of alcohol, and, in particular, the tranquillisers may confuse the clinical picture. However, once such a patient can be helped with his drinking, he will often be in a mentally more alert and physically healthier state to try to analyse and face the underlying problems.

While it is necessary to investigate closely every case individually, where an alcoholic presents himself in a state of depression or anxiety, in most cases the heavy drinking has secondarily given rise to a reactive depression or anxiety rather than the other way round. Therapy should primarily be directed at relieving the drink problem or at least persuading the drinker to give a period of sobriety a fair trial, before tackling the depression. Obviously where, in spite of giving up drinking, depression and anxiety remain and interfere with the patient's ability to co-operate with the treatment for his alcoholism, antidepressants and tranquillisers may be required.

A not uncommon way in which a reactive (neurotic) depression may affect a problem drinker is by upsetting the delicate balance that sometimes exists between opposing forces in the 'lack of control' phenomenon (see Chapter 4). And clearly, in alcoholics who tend to experience episodes of depression or anxiety they must not be ignored. Quite a few alcoholics may require help for such conditions after their immediate drinking problem has been dealt with. Although, as a rule, the prescribing of CNS-affecting drugs for alcoholics should be kept to a minimum because of dangers such as potentiation of alcohol and, in particular, added drug dependence, in certain cases (such as endogenous depression) antidepressant drugs may of course be vitally necessary.

2   Alcoholic psychoses

The more severe mental complications (alcoholic psychoses) are said to occur in no more than 10 per cent of alcoholics. Often mental and physical complications of alcoholism occur side by side, such as the Wernicke-Korsakoff's syndrome, and in Korsakoff's syndrome the amnesia syndrome is usually combined with a polyneuropathy.

Alcoholic psychoses are defined in the ninth revision of the *International Classification of Diseases* as 'Organic psychotic states due to consumption of alcohol; defects of nutrition are thought to play an important role. In some of these states (i.e. DT and the Alcoholic Withdrawal Syndrome) withdrawal of alcohol can be of aetiological significance'.

The Classification lists the following 'psychoses':

1   DT;
2   Alcoholic Korsakoff's psychosis;
3   Non-hallucinatory alcoholic dementia (without the features of DT or Korsakoff);
4   Alcoholic hallucinosis;
5   Pathological drunkenness;
6   Alcoholic jealousy;
7   'Unspecified' (such as alcoholic mania etc.).

1 *Delirium tremens*

This is serious and, in its fully developed form, a dramatic condition. Its incidence seems to vary in various countries as does its severity. In Britain one seems to see in general less severe cases than often described elsewhere. It has been estimated to occur in up to 5 per cent of alcoholics with complications requiring hospitalisation.

It is now generally regarded as a severe form of alcohol withdrawal syndrome (see Chapter 14). An interesting history is attached to the concept of 'withdrawal' *delirium tremens*. Half a century ago a violent controversy existed between those believing in the withdrawal origin of DT and others who hotly denied it [3]. Later on, for a period, DT was then ascribed to the sudden, complete withdrawal of alcohol, until a few decades ago when the pendulum swung the other way and the withdrawal theory was generally abandoned. Following recent experiments, carried out in the United States, the withdrawal theory has again come into its own, so much so that an editorial in the *British Medical Journal* a few years ago suggested that all cases of DT may be due to alcohol withdrawal [22]. Clinical experience and inquiries amongst observers in many countries seem, however, to indicate that DT may be caused in some alcoholics by other precipitating factors which operate while the alcoholic still keeps on drinking his usual (or diminishing) amounts.

The delirium may start abruptly or be heralded by prodromal signs, such as occasionally an epileptiform fit. To start with, the alcoholic may be flushed, nauseated, unable to sleep, agitated, and shaky. Subsequently – often three to four days after his last drink – during the delirious stage the patient's whole body (including face, tongue and hands) may be extremely shaky, and he is restless, over-active, sleepless, suggestible; he sweats profusely and his pulse is rapid. The 'shakes' are followed by the 'horrors', i.e. the often terrifying, though sometimes grotesque, visual hallucinations in which the drinker 'sees' strange animals, distorted human faces and figures, etc. The delirium commonly ends suddenly after a few days but – in the absence of adequate treatment – there is a risk of complications (e.g. pneumonia) and of a fatal outcome (which, however, with treatment is nowadays rare).

2 *Korsakoff's psychosis*

This sometimes follows DT and is frequently but not always due to alcoholism. Severe memory loss of recent events and confabulations (when, for example, the patient may relate in detail how he spent the previous day shopping in Rome although he never left the hospital bed) are associated with polyneuropathy. Prognosis in the individual case is not good, though some degree of improvement may occur.

3 Alcoholic dementia
This neuropsychiatric complication (often with progressive intellectual and ethical deterioration, emotional instability etc.) has been described under 'Physical Complications' (see Chapter 14).

4 Auditory alcoholic hallucinosis
The 'hearing' of unpleasant, derogatory voices occurs usually in the post-intoxication or withdrawal phase and may last a few days or longer. The patient's state of consciousness and insight is commonly not impaired, but very occasionally the illness may be schizophrenic in origin.

The *International Classification* defines the condition as: 'A psychosis usually of less than six months' duration, with slight or no clouding of consciousness and much anxious restlessness in which auditory hallucinations, mostly of voices uttering insults and threats, predominate.' On the basis of two important investigations by Victor and Hope (1958) [2] and by Benedetti (1952) [3] Hore's [4] recent review (1976) concludes that in most cases the hallucinosis is acute and clears up in a few days, only a few cases becoming chronic which may resemble schizophrenia: however, available evidence does *not* indicate that such cases are due to a 'release' by alcohol of schizophrenic illness in genetically-prone individuals. Acute auditory hallucinosis may also exhibit 'organic' features, and may represent an early part of an alcohol withdrawal syndrome.

Such patients require hospitalisation, and (if the hallucinations do not disappear very soon), phenothiazines, followed by the treatment and rehabilitation régime ordinarily employed in alcoholism.

5 Pathological drunkenness
This is defined by the *International Classification* as: 'Acute psychotic episodes induced by relatively small amounts of alcohol [and] regarded as individual idiosyncratic reactions to alcohol, not due to excessive consumption and without conspicuous neurologi-

cal signs of intoxication.' It was formerly often described as a very severe pathological reaction to alcohol leading to severe anxiety, disorientation and possible senseless destructive acts [5,6] possibly following exhaustion, great strain, hypoglycaemia etc. [7] and it was sometimes distinguished from 'alcoholic intolerance', a state of intoxication following moderate drinking on the given occasion and seen, for example, among children, after brain injury, or after simultaneous consumption of alcohol and other drugs [8].

6 Alcoholic jealousy

This is described in the *International Classification* as a 'Chronic paranoid psychosis characterised by delusional jealousy and associated with alcoholism': Alcoholic paranoia. Obviously delusions of persecution, a paranoid state, or more often milder ideas of reference, may occur in alcoholics independently of jealousy, and are often readily explained on the basis of their own behaviour with inadequacy and guilt feelings which they then (often unconsciously) project onto others, mainly those close to them. However in alcoholics a paranoid state most often occurs in relation to *sexual jealousy* with delusions of the spouse's unfaithfulness, and is also known as the 'Othello Syndrome'. There may be all degrees between a vague suspicion of the partner's infidelity where the alcoholic may have considerable insight when in a sober state and where one cannot then speak strictly of 'delusion' (which is a fixed false belief that cannot be shaken by any evidence to the contrary) but rather of a neurotic 'obsession' which they try to fight against, though usually without much success, and which gets worse the more their drinking and their alienation from reality tend to progress. Moreover, there are examples of the wife, utterly disillusioned and frustrated by the drinking husband's behaviour, who does in fact find herself another partner, the alcoholic husband then becoming suspicious but trying hard to put such suspicions out of his mind in the knowledge that alcoholics often harbour such (usually) unwarranted delusional notions. Thus, there is often in such cases a vague borderland between neurotic 'obsessions' (with insight) and psychotic 'delusions', the psychotic element obviously coming to the fore when the alcoholic is intoxicated, which may then lead to violence. When drunk, the alcoholic may literally have taken leave of his senses and become psychotic (living in a fantasy world) but in less severe cases he may regain a sense of reality and insight the next morning, with extreme guilt and remorse.

'The core of the syndrome,' as described by M D Enoch [9], '[is] the delusion of infidelity and the patient's false belief that the sexual partner is actually unfaithful.' According to Enoch, men are affected three times as often as women; this refers to all cases of sexual or 'morbid jealousy', which of course also occurs in non-alcoholics, such as in individuals suffering from paranoid schizophrenia or endogenous depression, epilepsy, dementia, etc., or exhibiting no abnormal features other than the 'pure' form of a sexual paranoia. In alcoholic women, perhaps more often than in other female sufferers from pathological jealousy, there may sometimes be a factual reason for their suspicions, moreover they often realise quite well that by neglecting their personal appearance and hygiene they are driving their husband away. In other cases, however, there may be no cause for their suspicions and as in the more common cases of the male alcoholic, such a jealous alcoholic woman can make her spouse's life an unmitigated misery. The jealous drinker thinks and talks of little else to his spouse, trying continually to prove his suspicions are well founded, finding 'definite' clues by ingenious misinterpretations, following the partner or having her watched, occasionally attacking her and not infrequently, the husband too is assaulted by his jealous alcoholic wife.

The male alcoholic's impotence, his feelings of inadequacy, or his common extra-marital excursions 'feed' his delusions of infidelity, as does his wife's aversion to sleeping with an over-demanding or bullying husband strongly smelling of stale alcohol.

Enoch discussing sexual jealousy in general emphasises the danger both of homicide and suicide. In alcoholic cases the prognosis in the long run obviously depends largely on the degree of recovery from the alcoholism (though even after recovery some men may make life difficult for their wives, indicating that, in such cases, alcohol to a certain extent released underlying suspicious or paranoid character traits). But in alcoholics, probably even more than in non-alcoholic 'Othellos', such pathological jealousy may carry the risk of senseless acts of violence directed against the innocent partner (and possibly other members of the household) and illustrates once more how the drinker's family often bears the brunt of the condition even more so than the alcoholic himself.

7   Sex difficulties in alcoholics

It may appear somewhat incongruous to include this topic under the general heading of 'Mental Complications'. However, the subject of sexual problems in alcoholism illustrates how difficult, or indeed impossible, it often is to separate physical and the mental manifestations; emotions play a significant role in inducing physical disturbances, and such psychosomatic disturbances are very common in the typical psychosexual difficulties of alcoholics. Sometimes it may be psychological disturbances that come first, which in turn may lead to 'psychosomatic' symptoms; or somatic (physical) complaints may secondarily cause psychological symptoms, such as anxiety or depression which upset sexual and other functions. Impotence, for example, mentioned as an important factor in inducing jealousy in alcoholics, commonly may be psychological in origin but in alcoholics often suffering from alcoholic liver disease: under such circumstances, as described by Madden [10] 'hypogonadism is common . . . leading to testicular atrophy, reduced libido and impaired potency'. A recent American study carried out at Harvard medical school [11] discovered evidence of hormonal dysfunction in over one-third of men suffering from impotence so that they recommend the screening of all such cases with a single estimation of serum testosterone. However, even with primary organic disturbances, in such cases there will usually be a psychological overlay greatly worsening the condition. There is therefore usually a close interplay between primary physical and primary psychological factors. Sexual problems, so common in alcoholics though usually very complex and ignored, well illustrate the importance of the view of Meyer, the founder of the psychobiological school in psychiatry: in illness, the individual's psychological, biological and environmental situation must be considered; and the therapist should try to render assistance to the individual's psychological, medical and social environment [12]. Sex difficulties in alcoholics may create domestic, social, physical and mental complications, and, in turn, can be caused by domestic, social, physical and psychological upsets.

The amount that has been written about the effect of alcohol on sexual behaviour indicates that not everyone agrees with Gantt's [13] statement, made thirty years ago, according to which 'Shakespeare is still the chief authority for the effect of alcohol on sexual activity'.* Animal experiments have been carried out to add to Shakespeare's concise teaching, but most people would

---

* In *Macbeth*, in the discussion between MacDuff and the porter: 'It provokes the desire, but it takes away the performance.'

probably agree with the point made in a recent review by Car-penter and Armenti [14]: 'There is more to sexual behaviour, even in the male, than is covered by [animal] experiments.' Carpenter and Armenti conclude from their review of papers dealing with alcohol and sexual expression in human beings that it is the varia-tion in response that accompanies drinking which constitutes the main difficulty in deciding the effect of alcohol. Factors such as mood, personality and environment may all influence the effect of alcohol on sexual behaviour which therefore may vary greatly even in the same individual and obviously even more so between different individuals. As so often in our discussions of the various aspects of alcohol problems, the members of the triad [15] – host, environment and the type, concentration etc. of the agent (the alcoholic drink) – will also make their contribution to this issue. The circumstances of drinking, Carpenter and Armenti conclude, may produce greater changes in [sexual and aggressive] behaviour than the alcohol does. Alcohol may modify 'the expression of sexual or aggressive behaviour if either or both are appropriate to a particular set of stimulating conditions'.

It seems apparent that experiments made under artificial con-ditions can teach very little about complex spontaneous social or sex activities. Sex activity is influenced at many levels: nervous system (the erection and ejaculation reflexes); endocrine glands and hypothalamus; social and emotional factors; and there are too, innumerable permutations of interaction between the hormones, nervous system, environmental factors and alcohol. The alcoholic's guilt, anxiety, depression, fear of rejection, and failure, emotional factors under the control of the hypothalamus (which is also the controlling centre for the autonomic nervous system) may all contribute more to his impotence than the terse truth enunciated by Shakespeare's porter. Unfortunately all too often sexual difficulties do not disappear as soon as the drinker gives up alcohol, and often much tolerance, patience and mutual understanding of the difficulties experienced by both the drinker and his partner are needed for some time. The wife's emotional problems and frigidity – caused (or worsened) by her husband's drinking behaviour – may greatly contribute to her alcoholic husband's problems after he has given up drink. He may expect that all problems may be over once he has foresworn alcohol. But though his wife may forgive she cannot so easily forget even though she may want to, and her conditioned aversion against sex may be reflected in frigidity, vaginismus and non-orgasm. Nor does all this have to be a one-way traffic; similar difficulties may be at work, and perhaps even more so when the wife has been the alcoholic. Her appearance may have been repulsive to her husband and even if it did not affect him physically it may have induced in him a psychogenic impotence. Such impotence may have been present only *vis-à-vis* his wife, but under these circumstances great emotional obstacles have to be overcome after the wife has given up drink and in the sexual and other aspects of adjustment, giving up drink is only a beginning – a necessary means for further efforts and progress. Lack of communication and disturbance of sexual relationship, which may have started during the alcoholic marriage (though of course both may have been pre-existent factors which were responsible for husband or wife having started to drink) may sometimes also hinder the immediate return to a happy marriage after the alcoholic has stopped drinking. At the same time, it should be stressed that in spite of occasional sexual and other problems, in the great majority of cases the quality of the marriage improves greatly, often beyond recognition, once the drinker has finally foresworn alcohol.

An interesting and instructive study of 'Sexual customs and dysfunction in alcoholics' was recently undertaken by Soren Buus Jensen [16]. During a three-month period in 1974 he investigated the sex lives of 100 male alcoholics who were receiving treatment at an alcoholic treatment centre. The men, aged 30–45 years, had all undergone treatment with disulfiram for periods varying from four to eight weeks. They were interviewed about their sexual behaviour and sexual dysfunctions by means of a combined questionnaire and interview technique. Their mean age was 37.6 years; with one exception they had been drinking addictively before starting treatment. Forty-eight had steady sex-partners but only twenty were living with them; and fifty-two were single, without steady sex-partners.

As regards sexual difficulties the study showed that sixty-three patients did have sexual problems. Most common were impotence (69.8 per cent), 20.6 per cent experienced what Jensen calls 'non-specific impotence', 'lack of capacity despite presence of desire'. Reduced libido was present in 57.1 per cent, premature ejaculation in 15.9 per cent, and erection difficulties in 25.4 per cent. Many men experienced a combination of these problems. All men over forty years of age had experienced a significant decrease in intercourse frequency (and this was most pronounced in those lacking a steady partner).

No correlation was found between occurrence of sexual problems and early occurrence or duration of alcoholism. Forty-five men stated that they became sexually aroused by alcohol, thirty-five did not and the remainder felt stimulated by a certain number of drinks with the interest waning with further drinking. Half of the men claimed that they performed better sexually after alcohol stimulation (there seems to be no direct reference in the paper as to whether the female partner agreed with this estimate of the drinker's sexual prowess, other than the oblique reply implied in the statement by 80 per cent that their partners preferred them sober during intercourse). Two-thirds of the men alleged that their sexual difficulties arose at the start of alcoholism treatment which the author ascribes to the abstinence symptoms at that time. Jensen ascribes most of the alcoholic's sexual problems to psychological and interpersonal factors, and feels that sex therapy for alcoholic couples might aid the treatment usually given for alcoholism.

Therapy and rehabilitation in alcoholic psychosexual dysfunction

The view that sex therapy could be or indeed should often be an important addition to the therapy of alcoholism, is also held by two American workers specialising in this field: Dr Bruno Franek, a psychiatrist, and his wife Marliese, a sex-therapist.[1] Involved in an on-going longitudinal clinical study, they have – up to 1980 – treated 200 recovering alcoholics with various coexisting psychosexual disorders. Most patients initially denied having any sexual problems, admitting them only after more systematic and specific inquiries. The alcoholic's spouse or sexual partner likewise, to start with, denied sexual difficulties, again only to come out with often a plethora of complaints after further questioning. Not surprisingly the regular practice of denial over many years by alcoholics also extends to such a sensitive area as sexual problems; but the Franeks believe that such sexual dysfunction should constitute just as valuable early diagnostic criteria of alcoholism as other social dysfunctions. Nearly 70 per cent of recovering alcoholic patients were found to suffer from sexual disorders, mainly in the inhibited sexual desire phase. Of these, more than 30 per cent experienced additional transitory dysfunctions in terms of inhibited sexual excitement and inhibited orgasm. A 'surprisingly high 14 per cent' of patients admitted to occasional paraphilic practices during their drinking career: sadism, voyeurism, exhibitionism and masochism were reported in that order of incidence. In these researchers' view, alcoholism seemed to catalyse respective latent tendencies into overtness – such behaviour disappearing with prolonged abstinence. An obvious exception was the smaller number of individuals in whom such practices had already been well established *before* the onset of alcoholism.

Degree of sexual pathology was clearly correlated with the severity of alcoholism dependence in the given individual, and was reflected mainly by the degree of resistance to treatment. Severe sexual dysfunction often occurred in alcoholics suffering from frequent alcoholic amnesias, alcoholic peripheral neuropathy and myopathy. Approximately 10 per cent of patients presented dysfunction in all three sexual phases (see above).

In the Franeks' view two points need stressing in regard to treatment: systematic, structured sex therapy is inadvisable during the first recovery month; and sex therapy for the recovering alcoholic stands no chance of success unless the ground has been prepared by intensive sex counselling of the spouse as well as the recovering alcoholic. Often the spouse's psychosexual dysfunction may have arisen quite independently, rather than as a reaction to, the alcoholic's problems.

Treatment of psychosexual problems started with intensive sexual counselling, warning the alcoholic and his partner against the detrimental premature engagement in sexual activities before, with therapeutic help, underlying disabling attitudes have been resolved. Too early resumption of sexual activity, encouraged by the general physical improvement during the first few weeks of treatment and abstinence from alcohol, may all too easily end in failure intensifying negative emotions, such as mutual hostility or depression.

In their therapeutic approach, the Franeks distinguish three phases of sex therapy: the first *motivational phase* (1–2 weeks after detoxification) followed by the second, *intensive intermediate phase* (intensive counselling in regard to sexual problems for 2–3 weeks); and, finally, the third phase of *conjoint sex therapy*.

Obviously the co-existence of serious sexual problems and severe alcoholism makes for more complications, requiring greater psychotherapeutic endeavour and support, which the Franeks provide mainly by group therapy. Pending further elucidation from their on-going longitudinal study at this juncture their observations lead them to the belief that 'providing adequate care of co-existing sexual needs greatly promotes and enhances the overall alcoholism recovery process'.

Many other issues and problems are involved in the possible association between alcohol and sex. Many women, for example, report heavier drinking during episodes of severe premenstrual tension or during their menopause which some of them in later years consider to have been possible contributing factors to the development of their alcoholism (see Chapter 6). It stands to reason that such special problems may frequently exercise a greater impact on drinking behaviour than merely playing the same role in precipitating drinking as any other less specific disturbing or painful experience. On the other hand, the influence of homosexual tendencies (which often would be latent only – not being expressed in overt homosexual activity) on the development of alcoholism (stressed in the past by psychoanalysts) is now widely regarded as only one of many possible predisposing factors in alcoholism. Tendencies towards deviant sexual behaviour which may find expression only when such people are intoxicated, may sometimes lead to intermittent or continual relief-drinking, ending up in alcoholism.[2]

Notes

[1] I am extremely grateful to Dr Bruno and Marliese Franek [17] for their kind permission to quote extensively from their interesting paper presented at the International Conference on Alcoholism, at Bath, September 1980. I am also grateful for permission by the Conference Organisers (Broadway Lodge, Weston-Super-Mare).

[2] Cases are not infrequently seen, such as the one reported by Anthony Storr [18], of a middle-aged homosexual who though never otherwise in trouble with the law had been apprehended by the Police on two occasions, separated by a long interval, for soliciting. This man's ordinary self-control was able to keep his inclinations in check except on very rare occasions when alcohol reduced control and allowed him to give vent to his pent-up emotions. In treating such an individual Storr would primarily concentrate on helping him to stop drinking, and only secondarily on the sexual deviation for which, in this case, this man had not been searching help anyway. However, one encounters secondary alcoholics who act out underlying sexual tendencies and deviations much more regularly, so that urgent treatment would be required for both the drinking (which in such cases should take priority) but also for the underlying tendencies – a very daunting therapeutic proposition.

References

1a Kline, N S *et al.* (1974), *Am. J. Med. Sci.*, 268, 15
1b Merry, J *et al.* (1976), *The Lancet* 1976, ii, 481
2   Victor, M and Hope, J M (1958), *J. nerv. ment. Dis.*, 126, 451
3   Benedetti, G (1952), *Die Alkohol Halluzinosen*, Stuttgart, Thieme
4   Hore, B D (1976), *Alcohol Dependence*, London, Butterworths, 90
5   Binder, H (1935), *Schweizer Arch. Neurol. Psychiat.*, 35, 1
6   Steinbrecher, W (1975) in *Sucht und Missbrauch*, eds Steinbrecher, W, und Solms, H, 2, Auflage, Stuttgart, Thieme, IV, 32
7   Keller, M and McCormick, M (1968), *A Dictionary of Words about Alcohol*, New Brunswick, NY, 150
8   Glatt, M M (1976) in Gradwohl's *Legal Medicine*, 3rd ed., eds Camps, F E, Robinson, A E and Lucas, B G B, Bristol, John Wright, 547–55
9   Enoch, M D (1980), *Brit. J. Sex. Med.*, 7 (Jan.), 30
10   Madden, J S (1979), *A Guide to Alcohol and Drug Dependence*, Bristol, John Wright, 66
11   Spark, R F *et al.* (1980), *J.A.M.A.*, 243, 750
12   *Encyclop. of Psychiatry for GPs* (1972), Vol. Ph-Z, 339
13   Gantt, H W (1952), *Psychosom. Med.*, 14, 174
14   Carpenter, J A and Armenti, N P (1972), *The Biology of Alcoholism*, Vol. 2, 509–43
15   Glatt, M M (1974), *A Guide to Addiction and its Treatment – Drugs, Society and Man*, Lancaster, MTP
16   Jensen, S B (1979), *Brit. J. Sex. Med.*, 6 (Oct.), 29; 6 (Nov.), 30
17   Franek, B and M (1980), *Sexual Rehabilitation in Alcoholism Recovery*, Paper presented at the Internat. Confer. on Alcoholism, Bath, England, 22 September, 1980
18   Storr, A (1964), *Sexual Deviation*, London, Penguin, 111

Part III

Treatment, Rehabilitation and Prevention

Short- and Long-Term Treatment

It is likely that in the individual patient suffering from alcoholism a number of interacting predisposing and precipitating factors have been at work to produce the condition, which itself in turn produces physical, psychological and social change. For these reasons it is highly unlikely that one and the same method of treatment should be the best for every individual case. Rather might one expect that every patient requires careful individual study to determine which combination of the available forms of therapy is best suited in the case concerned.

Furthermore, treatment of alcoholism is not the prerogative – or the responsibility – of one profession. Workers coming from various disciplines have to share in the common task of helping to rehabilitate the alcoholic. Doctor, nurse, social worker, priest, probation officer, the alcoholic's family and friends, his boss and workmates, recovered alcoholics, counsellors, are all members of the therapeutic team who have to work in close co-operation, without mutual jealousy, to achieve the best possible results.

The need for treatment? Ability to help oneself

No wonder-drug which would enable alcohol addicts to drink safely once more in moderation has as yet been discovered, and, according to majority view, the alcohol dependent drinker should refrain from taking alcoholic drinks altogether for the rest of his life. This obviously is a very bitter pill to swallow for individuals who for so long have used alcohol as a means of adjusting to life, and whose whole life for many years may have centred on drinking; and one of the many invaluable ways in which Alcoholics Anonymous has been helpful to the alcoholic is in giving the advice to stick to a twenty-four hour programme, taking one day at a time.

Alcoholics are very often highly intolerant of frustration and desire immediate relief without giving a great deal of thought to the morrow. But by sticking to the immediate goal, 'today I shall be sober' – allowing tomorrow to take care of itself when it comes along – the alcoholic's sober days mount up to weeks, the weeks to months, the months to years, until the alcoholic has realised that it is, after all, possible for him not only to live without alcohol, but also to do so happily and contentedly. However, in recent years it has been suggested that in the case of some drinkers merely obtaining advice may be as helpful as receiving conventional treatment (Chapter 22, p. 511) and that 'the capacity of the individual' with a drinking problem to help himself and modify his own drinking behaviour needs to be much more heavily emphasised [1]. Undoubtedly some drinkers can modify their behaviour 'without professional or organised help' [1] in this way (p. 511). Yet one must not forget that at present all too many problem drinkers are doing just that, i.e. maintaining that they are perfectly able to handle their drink problem themselves in spite of desperate entreaties by family and friends. Too much emphasis on the possibility of self-help encourages such problem drinkers with complete lack of insight. Not infrequently when a patient is first seen, with his spouse present, and is told there is no 'magic cure' a 'lot depends on yourself', he will turn triumphantly to his spouse stating 'There you see – I told you. It's all up to me. Thank you doctor, goodbye!' Personal responsibility must of course be strongly stressed and encouraged from the start, but while there are undoubtedly a great many early problem drinkers who *could* help themselves, they are at the present time not often seen by helping or treatment agencies. Those whom one does come across are often those drinkers who need active encouragement to accept help rather than to go it alone. In most cases they have probably tried overcoming their problem alone with singular lack of success. Among the total number of heavy drinkers in the community the majority are probably in the very early stages, and very likely they could indeed improve with encouragement and 'advice'. But these seem to be only a minority among those who actually present themselves to treatment agencies, or professional workers. Thus those problem drinkers requiring very active help may constitute a minority among the total of such drinkers who exist within the community but they are probably among the great majority who are being seen by agencies and professional workers [2].

Thus, while many heavy drinkers are not dependent on alcohol and could cut down their drinking even without assistance or, in somewhat later phases or under different circumstances, may be greatly helped by informed 'advice', others will need more active help and support. This does not, however, usually mean residential care (which may be necessary for those more strongly dependent on alcohol and under certain other circumstances). Many more could receive support and treatment while remaining in the community [2]. It is in this field that a non-professional body has successfully pioneered community help for forty-five years: Alcoholics Anonymous.

There have been major developments in the pattern of general psychiatric services in Britain since the 1960s, emphasis on such treatment gradually moving away from long-term residential hospital care to shorter stay, and expansion of community services, such as day-hospital facilities, day-centres, hostels, homes, domiciliary services, and out-patient units. The concept was developed of providing a comprehensive district psychiatric service, as outlined in two government publications *Hospital Services for the Mentally Ill* and *Better Services for the Mentally Ill* [3]. The aim of such proposals is to provide as far as possible, a comprehensive service within a certain area which would include hospital (in-patient, day-patient, care), local authority, and general practitioner services. The district general hospital's department for the mentally ill would provide the hospital care to residential, day- or out-patients; the local authorities would be responsible for community services, such as support and care by the social work services and facilities for residential care if required. It is hoped that there would be close liaison between hospital, local authority and the GP service.

A similar development has also been proposed for the services for problem drinkers although the involvement of a pharmacological agent may sometimes complicate the situation in the case of drinkers or drug takers. The Advisory Council on Alcoholism in a report on services for such drinkers (1978) [3a] suggested demoting the role of the existing thirty-two Alcoholic (Treatment) Units in the sense that they should no longer provide a regional service but merely cater for the needs of the area or district in which they are located; no further regional units should be established. Such units, it was argued, with no more than perhaps

1000 beds between them, could provide a service (meaning presumably an in-patient service only) to no more than 20,000 alcohol misusers per year. This is obviously not enough, considering that there are approximately 750,000–1,000,000 problem drinkers in Britain. Furthermore the Advisory Council proposed that all problem drinkers and their families should receive adequate help.

Moreover the Council quite rightly criticised the patchy and poorly co-ordinated distribution of the existing units. The Advisory Council [3a] thus proposed a better, 'flexible and comprehensive community response', based essentially on assistance at the primary level by GPs, social workers, probation officers, and voluntary workers. They would be supported by 'secondary level' specially trained professional and voluntary workers, provided by statutory bodies and voluntary organisations: wherever necessary they would provide advice and help with more active training, specialist care, social support and residential accommodation.

In principle, such a planned comprehensive service provided as near to the drinker's home ground (although in the past many alcoholics preferred to receive treatment not too close to their friends and places of employment) by a primary care team and closely supported by voluntary and professional 'specialists' sounds fine. Why then was this never thought of before? Why indeed did alcoholics in the past waste their time travelling often long distances to consult therapists living miles away? or enter (often private) units long distances from home, rather than going for help locally? Is it possible that both problem drinkers, and in particular their families, as well as professionals interested in the subject and voluntary organisations, in the past have been trying to enlist interest of primary care workers, Government and local authorities to provide not only better but sometimes 'any' services at all for alcoholics? The fact, of course, is that such requests have been made urgently and continually, for many years, both abroad (mainly in the USA) but also in Britain for example, since the late 1940s by Dr John Y Dent, Dr H Pullar-Strecker, and somewhat later, Dr Lincoln Williams, and bodies such as the Society for the Study of Addiction and the Alcoholism Steering Group of the Rowntree Trust, as well as the Temperance Organisations. Will the proposed new service be able to cope (where, quite rightly, the Advisory Council feels the units would be unable to do) if the majority of this country's problem drinkers suddenly clamoured for help? The urgent need for GPs to play a key role in assisting alcoholics has been emphasised by many observers for over thirty years [6, 7], and in general the other professional groups mentioned by the Advisory Council likewise in the past did not evince any particular keenness for this type of work. In fact, the Advisory Council is aware of this difficulty, acknowledging that hitherto GPs and social workers failed to diagnose alcoholics and were not particularly interested in their problems. This the Advisory Council ascribed to their lack of 'the necessary confidence, training and resources'. Undoubtedly there has been a deplorable lack of special training in this field of knowledge and information. Here again continual requests have been made towards providing the necessary education [4, 6]. But even if this were now to change rapidly and such professional education were provided, what cannot be provided all that quickly and what the Advisory Council has hardly taken into consideration, is the necessary motivation by professionals to want to work with problem drinkers [5]. Wherever attitudes of professionals were investigated towards this type of patient, doctors in particular showed little interest [8]. Thus attempts to change such professional attitudes would probably take many years, although it should be tried and will indeed be necessary if at least a small proportion of the growing number of problem drinkers are to receive help within the community.

Everyone would agree with the Advisory Council as to the advisability, or rather, urgency, of GPs and other members of the primary care team familiarising themselves with the problems of heavy drinkers, detecting them as early as possible, and providing help and treatment. However, one has to be realistic about the difficulties involved in changing their attitudes to this problem and the unwillingness of the great majority to become involved with problem drinkers. Thus, to expect the primary care team to cope with the possibility of an influx of drinkers is as unrealistic and as doubtful, as it is in the case of the Alcoholic Units where the Advisory Council expressed such doubts quite clearly. (This subject will be discussed more fully in Chapter 18.) Surely there is a need for both?: the primary care teams to assist the great majority within the community, and the units with their out-patient, domiciliary, day care, detoxification, training and other services for the more specialised and difficult tasks. To restrict the units in their work before the primary care teams have shown not only that they have the necessary knowledge and skill but also that they are motivated to carry out this task might lead to a dangerous vacuum. Meanwhile it has been decided that one of the three existing tiers in the NHS will disappear; and it seems unlikely that there will be a sufficiently large number of alcoholics requiring hospitalisation to justify units to cater for the smaller districts. One might wonder why, at a time when the Advisory Council recommends demotion of the role of regional units in favour of primary care teams with secondary level specialist support, American business organisations feel that the time is ripe to establish private alcoholism units in the UK. As Dr I Moyes recently remarked with regard to a different subject ('The psychiatry of old age') [9], 'the most important component of any service is the enthusiasm of the members of the team and their realisation that although the problems are formidable, the rewards are great'. Whatever may be said against alcoholic units, no one who has worked in one can doubt the enthusiasm and the dedication of their staff. Rather than demoting the role of the units, the experience and professional knowledge of the staff should be harnessed towards teaching and training primary care workers and perhaps imbuing them with a fraction of their own enthusiasm [5]. The units themselves would be excellent training grounds for primary and secondary level workers (as acknowledged by the Advisory Council) and, after finishing their training, the secondary level workers, by then working in their local communities, could remain in contact with the regional 'mother' unit. In such (or similar) ways the units could greatly contribute to the necessary provision of skilled and motivated workers in the community.

Phases of treatment

Many alcoholics when first coming for treatment are more or less intoxicated and in a poor state of general health, after having neglected their food intake, their personal hygiene, etc., for weeks, months or even years. Treatment, therefore, has generally to start with a programme of sobering up, detoxification and physical rebuilding.

It is, however, essential to keep in mind that sobering up is no more than a preliminary step in therapy which has to be followed up by long-term methods aiming at full rehabilitation and resocialisation. If treatment were to stop short at the step of sobering up the drunken alcoholic – as, unfortunately, has so often been the case in the past – it would have achieved no more than rendering him fit again to resume his drinking career.

Therefore, this first phase of the therapeutic programme has to be followed up in the second long-term treatment phase by a diagnostic evaluation of the factors which were of prime import-ance in the patient concerned, and by carrying out the combina-tion of psychological, physical and social therapeutic methods best suited for his needs. In the final, rehabilitation, phase the alcoholic has to learn to live a happy and useful life without recourse to drink (and for that matter to other dependence-producing drugs as well). It is in this very important last phase of the overall therapeutic programme that Alcoholics Anonymous can often make its most valuable contribution, whatever other methods had been employed before.

Long-range plans for rehabilitation and continual support for a considerable time after discharge are absolutely essential in the care of many alcoholics. Not only the alcoholic's physical and mental state of health, but also environmental problems, such as his relationships at home, difficulties at work, his financial and economic situation, perhaps spiritual conflicts, etc., may all re-quire attention and sometimes expert help.

1   The treatment of acute intoxication – 'first aid'

Abrupt, complete withdrawal of alcohol, rather than gradual tapering off, is the method now almost universally employed for the great majority of alcoholics, with the exception of the very old or the very ill. The possibility of severe withdrawal symptoms in a small minority of cases (epileptiform convulsions, DT) will, how-ever, need to be kept in mind, and prophylactically anticonvulsant drugs (e.g. Phenytoin) and tranquillisers may be advisable for several days in order to reduce such risks.

When first seen, the alcoholic is generally starved, not only of food – in particular, vitamins, minerals and proteins – but also of fluids, rest and sleep. Malnutrition, dehydration, salt depletion, restlessness and insomnia may thus require first-aid measures. Liberal administration of fluids and salt by mouth and parenter-ally, intravenous injection of vitamins (particularly of the B com-plex), tranquillisers and (for a few days following admission) hypnotics are more or less routine measures in this phase, in addition to providing the patient with a well-balanced diet sup-plemented by vitamins.

Although the rationale is still doubtful, vitamins are usually given in much higher doses than required to make good any existing deficiency and to supply the dietary requirement. A popular proprietary preparation of this type for intravenous and intramuscular administration contains: 100 to 250 mg B1, in addition to nicotinamide, riboflavine, pyridoxine and 500 mg ascorbic acid 'Parentrovite'.

Insomnia is often a long-standing and troublesome complaint in alcoholics, some of whom blame it for their having started to drink to excess in the first place. Hypnotics may thus be necessary, but should be used sparingly, and discontinued as soon as possible. Many alcoholics – in our experience particularly those belonging to the higher social strata, and especially women – are very prone to develop the habit of taking other drugs to excess. ('If one tablet helps me, surely four tablets will do me four times as much good!')

It could almost be said that alcoholics serve spontaneously, and in spite of the greatest discouragement, the function of guinea pigs in testing out, and in more or less rapidly disproving, the claims of manufacturers that their latest hypnotic or stimulant drugs newly brought onto the market are not habit-forming. Sooner or later, probably any such drug with an action on the central nervous system will be abused by some unstable personalities, including a certain proportion of alcoholics. Advertisements for such new sedative or stimulant drugs, instead of claiming that they are not habit-forming, should thus rather read: 'have not yet been found out to be habit-forming'! The question with all such drugs brought onto the market is not 'do they lend themselves to misuse and dependence or not?' but rather whether the misuse by a minority of people justifies or necessitates the imposing of restrictions also affecting the great majority who are able to use such drugs sensibly and in moderation.

As far as alcoholics are concerned, barbiturates should be avoided because of the risk of psychological and physical dependence [11, 14]. The same applies to such stimulating drugs as amphetamines and phenmetrazine, which may produce strong psychological dependence [14]. Alcoholics should also be warned against proprietary sedative or stimulant preparations which may be bought freely over the counter.

In many alcoholics the use of such unrestricted drugs has later led to the resumption of uncontrolled drinking. *Vice versa*, the attempted substitution of a barbiturate hypnotic in an attempt to wean the alcoholic off drinking has often been responsible for creating a state of barbiturate dependence.

As so many alcoholics also tend to take hypnotic or tranquillising drugs regularly, they must be specially questioned about it, as sudden withdrawal of such CNS–depressants in individuals accustomed to their regular use may produce a severe 'alcohol or barbiturate-type abstinence syndrome' with epileptiform convulsions and a DT-like state. Non-barbiturate hypnotics are greatly preferable to barbiturates (certainly in the case of alcoholics) which, as stated above, should be avoided. Some non-barbiturates may not be quite as effective hypnotics as the barbiturates, but in general the risk of dependence seems less, although probably no effective hypnotic is quite free from it [10, 11].

Tranquillisers are nowadays widely employed in the treatment of both the acute and later stages of alcoholism. They include drugs such as the phenothiazines for example.[1]

Recent guidelines published by the Committee on the Review of Medicines [15] state that the dependence potential of benzodiazepines is low but that especially after high doses given for a long time, withdrawal symptoms may occur 1–10 days after stopping their administration. Given concurrently with alcohol they may be risky. Short-acting benzodiazepines are regarded by the CRM as suitable therapy for insomnia unaccompanied by anxiety. In view of frequent misunderstanding it is stressed that the benzodiazepines are not antidepressant drugs. The CRM also emphasises that there is no evidence that these drugs are effective in anxiety after four months' continuous treatment (clearly in alcoholics such long-term treatment should be avoided if at all possible).

Over the past fifteen years a substance somewhat different from ordinary tranquillisers has been used successfully with alcoholics on the Continent and in this country, i.e. chlormethiazole (Heminevrin) [16, 17, 18] (4g on the first day and in slowly decreasing doses on the following days), a substance which is closely related to the B1 vitamin but which through a change in its molecule has acquired different properties. Like other central nervous system-affecting drugs chlormethiazole may lead to psychological and, rarely, physical dependence, and should therefore not be given (except in DT) for longer than six to seven days. It should not be suddenly stopped but the dosage slowly reduced in order to avoid the risk of chlormethiazole withdrawal fits.

In the treatment of DT, apart from high intravenous vitamin medication, the tranquillisers (parenterally in high doses) are nowadays probably at present the most popular drugs, although paraldehyde, injected intramuscularly, is still often used. Chlormethiazole is regarded by many Swedish and German experts as the best drug currently available in DT. For prophylaxis as well as for therapy chlormethiazole and the benzodiazepines are the commonly used drugs for (more severe) alcohol withdrawal syndromes in this country, the benzodiazepines in the USA [19] (where chlormethiazole is not available). In addition to sedation, the therapy of DT, like that of alcoholic intoxication, aims at correcting dehydration and malnutrition.

With all the drugs employed, including the tranquillisers, the possibility of side-effects must, of course, be kept in mind; such as synergism with alcohol, over-dosage, dependence; and also jaundice in the case of chlorpromazine which, however, has proved to be less of a risk than one might have theoretically expected in view of the relative frequency of damaged livers in alcoholics.

The risk of interaction between alcohol and other drugs

There is clearly a risk of synergism (potentiation) and not only mere summation between alcohol and other CNS-depressant drugs, such as sedative-hypnotics, tranquillisers, opiates, but also with antidepressants. The possibility that problem drinkers – especially those who started on alcohol misuse mainly in order to obtain psychological relief from tension, anxieties etc. – may also soon come to rely on other drugs or as a substitute after alcohol's withdrawal, has always to be kept in mind. The GP treating a problem drinker on an ambulant basis may find himself in a quandary: trying to persuade the drinker to keep off alcohol he may feel that he ought to assist the drinker over physical or psychological withdrawal symptoms by prescribing tranquillisers or non-barbiturate hypnotics. In this way, however, there may be a risk of his patient taking such drugs while continuing with alcohol. This is one of the dangers existing, for example, with drugs such as the benzodiazepines, and especially chlormethiazole [20] and excluding the use of this valuable drug to ambulant alcoholic patients in general practice [21] although it is regarded as safe and valuable in the non-alcoholic elderly patient [21].

Naturally there is also a risk of complex interaction between alcohol and other types of drugs – a subject discussed recently in a leading article in the *British Medical Journal* [22]. The acute effect of alcohol prolongs the action of other drugs as alcohol inhibits the metabolism of drugs. Alcohol produces this effect as intoxication leads to pylorospasm which delays the absorption of drugs (although moderate amounts of alcohol increase gastric absorption). Moreover alcohol inhibits microsomal enzymes which are responsible for drug metabolism. On the other hand, repeated drinking or cigarette smoking induces the formation of enzymes that metabolise drugs, and alcoholics in early stages – when there is no serious liver damage – may thereby be less sensitive to other drugs.

(a)   Among the long list of drugs whose action is prolonged [22] by *acute alcohol* effect are tranquillisers (such as meprobamate and, significantly, diazepam, stated to have strong synergistic interaction with alcohol so that other benazodiazepines may be safer in certain circumstances), antidepressants and antipsychotic drugs. Drugs such as barbiturates, beta-blocking agents and antihistamines impair psychomotor performances when taken with even a little alcohol. Diabetics receiving the oral antidiabetic agents containing sulphonylureas (such as tolbutamide) may develop hypoglycaemia, flushing of the face, and other side effects. There is anecdotal evidence that drugs such as barbiturates, opiates, diazepam, chlormethiazole, paracetamol dextropropoxyphene (which combined with paracetamol forms the popular *Distalgesic*) when combined with alcohol may lead to serious and occasional fatal effects.

(b)   In the *chronic alcoholic*, on the other hand, as the result of enzyme induction, the effects of drugs, metabolised in an undamaged liver, are reduced. Drugs affected in this manner are phenytoin, meprobamate, diazepam, warfarin and tolbutamide (i.e. the same drugs whose action is intensified when taken concurrently with heavy drinking). In the *BMJ* leader writer's view, the fact that treatment of the alcohol withdrawal stage in the alcoholic sometimes requires high doses of sedatives (cross-tolerance), may also be due to enzyme induction.

The interaction between alcohol and other drugs is obviously not a one-way traffic. Just as alcohol alters the effect of these drugs, they in turn affect the actions of alcoholic drinks. Other drugs can alter absorption of alcohol in the stomach ordinarily increased by moderate drinking and its free distribution in the body water, and inhibit its metabolism. The enzyme alcohol dehydrogenase which is largely responsible for metabolising alcohol to acetaldehyde in the liver is affected by the major tranquilliser chlorpromazine, by chloral hydrate, and by disulfiram.

The oral antidiabetic drug chlorpropamide and the antitrichonomas agent metronidazole, when combined with alcohol intake, induce flushing: this antabuse action led a few years ago to the recommendation to use metronidazole in the treatment of alcoholics. The narcotic antagonist naloxone has been successfully employed in reversing a state of coma caused by ethyl alcohol [22a], an effect possibly linked to the action of the drug on central receptors in the brain.

Of the greatest importance, and always to be kept in mind, is the necessity to distinguish alcoholic coma from states of unconsciousness produced by other conditions, such as cerebral haemorrhage, head injury and diabetic (or also hypoglycaemic) coma. Clearly, an alcoholic odour in the breath is not diagnostic, and full clinical and laboratory investigations (including estimation of blood alcohol level) may be necessary.

Detoxification centres

As a rule the sobering-up process and detoxification do not present a difficult task in the case of the great majority of alcoholics but problems often arise in the case of the 'down-and-out' drinker or 'chronic drunkenness offender' (see Chapter 18). This may be due to a combination of factors, such as his complete lack of insight and motivation which in turn may be connected with marked personality disorder and almost insuperable environmental difficulties. In the past such people have often been dealt with by a 'revolving door' policy: drunkenness-arrest-court appearance - prison - discharge - drunkenness - court - appearance - prison. Everyone is agreed that this method is counter-productive and should be replaced by a more constructive policy. There is no point in well-meaning magistrates lecturing alcoholics about the foolishness of their drinking, predicting a sticky end and admonishing them gravely to pull themselves together. Alcoholics – including many down-and-out drinkers – very often know that they should not continue with their drinking pattern and behaviour but they cannot change without active help, in particular if they are rootless and know of no other allies than the bottle and their fellow travellers on skid-row. Magistrates as a rule are well aware of the position but find themselves in a dilemma as there are very few places where such drinkers can be referred to. Under the circumstances, well planned and well run detoxification centres could be a great help [23].

The idea of special detoxification centres came to the USA and Western Europe from Prague and Warsaw. It was at an International ICCA Congress in Warsaw in 1962 that many Western delegates first saw the working of such a centre, most coming away very impressed with its possibilities. Professor David Pittman and his associates were the first to open such a centre in the West (in St Louis) in the mid-sixties. Pittman was among those giving evidence before the Home Office Working Party in the late sixties. In its Report in 1971 this Home Office Working Party on Habitual Drunken Offenders [23] concluded that 'some form of special arrangement for detoxification will be indispensable to any future system which attempts to deal comprehensively with public drunkenness'.

Three basic questions posed by the Report were:

(i) Whether admission to a detoxification unit should be voluntary or compulsory;
(ii) Whether only habitual drunken offenders should be admitted or anyone found drunk in the streets (including casual roisterers);
(iii) Whether such centres should function merely as sobering-up stations or play a more constructive role in treatment.

In our view, it would clearly often be a missed opportunity if the chance were not made use of, to establish a relationship with such 'problem drinkers', and after assessment, to try to induce motivation in at least some of them in order to prevent further similar episodes. In those who have not yet reached the stage of 'alcoholism' or dependence this may possibly amount to no more than simple advice and counselling; in others it may mean referral to AA, a hostel or possibly residential treatment. In fact the experience of Arroyave and his colleagues [24] at the Oxford Detoxification Unit showed the feasibility of such an approach. These workers strongly favoured a voluntary approach as far as possible, and they feared that contamination by admitting certain drunks compulsorily might disturb the atmosphere. Similarly, Hamilton and his colleagues [25] in the Glasgow Detoxification

Centre saw no need for compulsory detentions as contact with a Detoxification Unit, even in the absence of special treatment, may lead to an increasing insight and altered drinking behaviour. However, while voluntary entry to such a centre is clearly to be preferred, the question still remains whether for those who were on no account willing to avail themselves of such opportunities and who continued to inflict harm on themselves, might not also benefit by such contact once they had been compulsorily sobered up and thus possibly brought – temporarily at least – on to another emotional wave length.

According to a Government statement (June 1979) [26] there were then in England three detoxification centres (though obviously these did not include the ones attached to alcohol units such as Oxford or Warlingham Park): an experimental centre set up in Leeds in May 1976 by a voluntary agency in association with the local health and social services authorities; a second centre set up in Manchester in November 1977 by the local Health and Social Service Authorities; and a centre in London run by the Salvation Army in Tower Hamlets, in September 1975. All three received financial help from the DHSS.

A detoxification centre could be an important part of a comprehensive alcohol unit. Such detoxification centres associated with alcohol units have been established, for example, in Manchester, Warlingham Park Hospital, and St Bernard's Hospital. The setting-up of one such detoxification centre, in 1975, in association with the Oxford Regional Alcoholism Unit was fully described by Arroyave and his colleagues [24]. Six beds were taken from the treatment unit, and as the nursing staff of the main unit were also looking after the detoxification beds a special advantage was that the detoxification service made no additional demand on resources. The annual intake to the Oxford Detoxification Unit was 300, two-thirds of whom had not previously been known to any treatment centre, and were often drinkers who were not alcoholics in the usual meaning of the term. Thus such a detoxification centre would be attached to a treatment unit, with (as in the Oxford unit) no limitation imposed on admission, no minimum length of stay, and no initial motivation required and, encouraged by the ready availability of the service and the possibility of immediate admission, problem drinkers, once admitted, would be given an opportunity for a brief period of assessment and/or therapy and possibly admission to the main unit. In the Oxford unit, such a process was made easier by the opportunity presented to the staff and also to the patients and ex-patients of the unit to form relationships with the 'Detox' patients and to motivate those drinkers who might require and might benefit from treatment, to transfer to the main unit. At the same time, those patients who suffered from problems other than 'alcoholism' might benefit from counselling and advice, and from being put in touch with the appropriate local authority and voluntary welfare services.

One further advantage is that among such 'Detox' patients, there may in fact be 'budding' alcoholics who thus may come to attention much earlier than would have been the case otherwise. Physical examination on admission would be followed within the next few days by psychiatric and social assessment. The lack of motivation to undergo long-term therapy at the time they were admitted to the Detoxification Unit would probably present no bar against possible long-term improvement; the Oxford workers [27] had found the outcome of the treatment related not to 'insight on admission' but to 'insight on discharge', *change* in insight during treatment being the important factor. This is very much in conformity with our own views that one important function of community therapy consists in the induction of (the initially usually lacking) insight and motivation [28, 29].

In the view of their positive experiences over the period 1975–8 with a total of over 800 patients, the Oxford workers feel that detoxification centres should be closely associated with existing treatment units and not function merely as independent 'sobering-up' units. They regard such arrangements as economically effective.

When starting their Detoxification Unit in 1975, the Oxford workers felt that among those who would have to be admitted (and perhaps repeatedly re-admitted) would be drinkers 'written off' by treatment units as 'untreatable' because of their repeated failures, either because of brain damage or emotional instability with progressive social deterioration (i.e. they envisaged a 'safety net' function of providing emergency short-term palliative treatment for controlling withdrawal symptoms). The Detoxification and the Treatment Units together were expected to combine detoxification assessment and crisis intervention, with the aim of improving the patients' motivation but also serving as back-up facilities to casualty departments, psychiatric admission wards and social agencies. In this way, patients felt they would have a chance to develop insight at a time when they were more receptive as they were at their psychologically 'lowest'. The same consultant psychiatrist was in charge of both the combined units. Admissions initially were only from doctors and hospitals, but later also from AA, the Samaritans and probation officers. After physical examination on admission, drugs used where necessary were chlormethiazole or other tranquillisers, and vitamins. Five days later followed a psychiatric and social assessment. Patients seen included women who comprised a quarter to a fifth of the total. In each of the three years surveyed the average length of stay was less than a week. A substantial number were drinkers previously admitted to the treatment programme but found unsuitable, and of those admitted for the first time for detoxification, not much less than half (167) were accepted for the treatment programme. Of the total admitted only one-third had previously been in touch with any treatment agency. Anyone was allowed to come in – including self-referrals. Only voluntary patients were admitted as otherwise additional staff and security would have necessitated certain changes in the regime and the atmosphere. (Each detoxification bed in this unit serves fifty admissions a year.)

As regards the possibility of 'symptom substitution' the problem of the dependency from ('addictive) personality' [14] comes to mind. In such a person (in contrast to the majority discussed above) the gap left by giving up drinking is readily filled by other CNS-affecting drugs, mainly sedatives or tranquillisers; often the alcoholic giving up drinking may also increase his smoking (this frequently happens in the immediate withdrawal period while in hospital), or his food intake, often discovering for the first time a desire for sweets and chocolate [14]. That alcoholics on giving up drinking start consuming vast amounts of tea and coffee is well known. Alcoholics have to be clearly warned against filling the 'gap' by merely changing one chemical for another.

The Oxford work certainly indicates that a detoxification unit as an additional part of a comprehensive unit provides a very valuable service; not only do many drinkers with problems other than alcoholism receive a first aid and emergency service but an additional population of such drinkers is reached who, at present, do not receive any such help; and the detoxification unit also provides an opportunity to establish contact with such problem drinkers and motivates a high proportion towards accepting further treatment in the main ('treatment') unit.

Naturally since their conception, all alcohol units have carried out detoxification on the great majority of their patients who were usually admitted in some state of intoxification and often with very high blood alcohol levels. However, in the main this was seen as no more than the first phase of their hospital stay; most units stipulated that alcoholics would have to agree to a stay of several weeks beyond detoxification. This, though legally not binding, was intended to illustrate to the drinker the need to think beyond sobering up and put him on the road to rehabilitation. On the other hand, the establishment of definite 'detoxification units' attached to 'alcoholic units' as described by the Oxford workers gives more (initially unmotivated) drinkers a chance to undergo a change of heart while coming into contact with nurses who understand, and are experienced in, helping alcoholics. However it is probably preferable to attach the detoxification unit only loosely to the alcoholic unit, as otherwise the knowledge that so many drinkers could and would leave after a few days is likely to have an unsettling effect on the majority who had agreed to stay on longer in order to start their long-term rehabilitation process.

Similarly, if the main treatment unit itself contains a high proportion of patients with little motivation, care has to be taken that the influx of many more patients with missing motivation may not greatly upset the balance and, thus, exercise a counter-productive, unsettling effect on the rest of the patients. Often it may be better to make use of the best motivated patients in the unit to attend the detoxification unit regularly in order to have lengthy, informative discussions with the detoxification patients.

A third point to be kept in mind is that a spreading knowledge that the regional treatment unit has a high proportion of very difficult patients, may militate against more motivated alcoholics agreeing to admission and thus have a counter-productive effect. Clearly while the idea of a detoxification unit attached to the main unit seems very promising, care has to be exercised, and the situation kept under continued review.

Long-term treatment

The question of treatment goals

In recent years a great deal has been said about the need for 'alternative goals' – i.e. alternatives to the goal of total abstinence in alcoholics. But neither abstinence nor controlled drinking are goals of treatment; what is important is to find ways to assist the drinker (and his family) towards achieving as satisfying and contented a life as possible. Abstinence, as Pattison [39] rightly said, is an inadequate criterion of health or of successful treatment in alcoholism but so of course is the 'achievement' of controlled drinking. The point that abstinence or controlled drinking can only be means to the goal and not the goal itself, must be kept in mind during the following review of recent arguments for and against abstinence and controlled drinking respectively.

Abstinence or controlled drinking?

It must be stressed again that many alcoholics can occasionally have a drink or two without having to continue drinking. This by no means implies that they are not alcoholics or that they may not yet suffer from 'loss of control' and that they can safely continue controlled drinking.

1   *Abstinence approach*
While the drinker continues to take alcohol it seems impossible to evaluate any underlying personality factors that may predispose or indeed could possibly assist him to get over his drinking problem [31]. Claims that deterioration in total health and personality functioning not infrequently follow abstinence [32] already put forward many years ago and refuted by Hobson in his paper [33] to the Society for the Study of Addiction in 1952 are certainly not supported by the present author's experience in intermittently ob-serving a great many recovered alcoholics and their families over periods lasting up to thirty years – although naturally such cases are bound to occur. 'A careful search for symptom substitution and evidence of impairment in a sample abstinent for several years [carried out in Oxford by Letemendia and his colleagues [34] (1973)] showed the opposite – a clear-cut improvement in pre-vious neurotic symptoms and in social and economic functioning following abstinence.' This study found 'no evidence to support' Orford's [35] (1973) claim that abstinence delays presentation by the patient for treatment. Here again our own experience agrees with the view of the Oxford workers.

Of course, many alcoholics start on abstinence without im-mediately beginning to feel 'great' or they may occasionally have 'bad patches' even though resisting the temptation to drink. There is the familiar 'Dry-Drunk Syndrome', Wellman's 'Delayed Absti-nence Syndrome', where the former drinker, from time to time, relapses into a similar uncomfortable, emotionally shaky, or re-sentful, self-pitying state which he had usually exhibited in his drinking days.

There are probably a number of emotional conditions which may present with such a state. Commonly, for example, the drinker may not really have 'surrendered' but merely, as Tiebout [36] termed it 'complied' under some protest. The drinker may have hoped, too, that abstinence may immediately present him with everything that he formerly had tried to obtain by drinking, such as euphoria, freedom from anxieties and fear, and he may be bitterly disappointed that this has not happened. Or he may become 'dry' (though not emotionally 'sober') under protest in deference to his spouse's wishes, and at least unconsciously he may have a vested interest in 'proving' that although he is now 'off' drink he remains unhappy, and, full of (psychosomatic) symptoms – thus indicating to his spouse that it was *not* drink that had been the cause of his symptoms and of his aggressive behaviour.

Such experiences only go to show that by itself giving up drinking in such (though not in all) drinkers is only the first step – to be followed up by finding out more about oneself. The gap left by giving up drinking has to be filled by enjoyable and constructive experiences. All this, however, is not an inevitable consequence of his abstinence – it occurs because he just has reluctantly 'given up' something that was precious and valuable to him without searching for, and finding, something positive to put in its place. For example he may not have altered his immature attitude of wanting immediate reward for any effort he may make. In this case he wants immediate reward for having made the 'great sacrifice', for the family's sake, of giving up something that at least previously had brought him immediate satisfaction.

According to a publication from Hazelden (a famous American treatment centre [37]) the 'dry-drunk' state implies intoxication without alcohol. But it is a state of feeling 'low' and not 'high', though it may also imply an unsatisfied, yearning, unfulfilled state, partly induced by the greed (or need) for alcohol in the hope that it would disappear miraculously and that the state of 'missing' or 'needing' something could be ended immediately by a drink. (Possibly this expectation keeps up a state of tension maintained as long as there is a chance of ultimately achieving the objective of drinking.) It thus may be sometimes a state of yearning, inducing a condition of semi-intoxication without alcohol but with the goal of intoxication by alcohol. Hazelden also rightly state that 'dry-drunk' implies a state of mind and a mode of behaviour that are poisonous to the alcoholic's well being. It obviously spells out clearly a necessity for the drinker to do something about his emotional state and (like the suicide bid) may serve as a signal that should alert the therapist to the presence of danger.

2   Controlled drinking approaches

Among the main proponents of the notion that there should be various possible goals available for alcoholics, and not only total abstinence, are E Mansell Pattison, Mark B Sobell and Linda C Sobell who set forth their ideas in *Emerging Concepts of Alcohol Dependence* (1977) [39]. They point to probable implications of recent research evidence: for example, 'recovery from alcohol dependence bears no necessary relation to abstinence, although such a concurrence is frequently the case'; and that 'the consumption of a small amount of alcohol by an individual once labelled an "alcoholic" does not initiate either physical dependence or a physiological need for more alcohol by that individual.' And, in view of the fact that 'the population of persons with alcohol problems is multivariant . . . treatment services should be diverse, emphasising the development of a variety of services, with determination of which treatments, delivered in which contexts, are most effective for which persons and which types of problems'.

Stressing that 'the empirical evidence suggests that alcohol problems are reversible,' they conclude that 'theoretically, except in irreversible cellular damage, it might be possible to reverse any drinking patterns'. In practice, in their view, for certain individuals with alcohol problems 'abstinence would be both an easier and a more appropriate treatment goal, with less danger to their ongoing stability. For others, it may be more judicious and appropriate to change their patterns of alcohol use rather than to insist on abstinence'. They emphasise the need for further clinical research on drinking goals, 'to clarify the most efficacious and appropriate long-term clinical options'.

In these and other authors' views, scientific clinical research indicates that 'some traditional beliefs' (held in this field) are in need of modification, including those concerning the ability of some individuals with drinking problems to become 'normal or controlled drinkers' [40]. According to Sobell [40], by 1978, 'at least' eighty-two studies had reported that 'some individuals have recovered from drinking problems without being totally abstinent' – most of these having been identified as 'alcohol addicts'. Sobell criticises studies which come to different results, such as those by Pittman and Tate (1972) [41] who found in a follow-up of

255 alcoholic patients no one who had returned to 'normal social drinking'; and by Ewing and Rouse (1976) [42] who, in a (non-controlled) investigation had failed to inculcate controlled drinking in alcoholics.

Are there any possible predictors of successful non-abstinent results? In Sobell's view [40], among pre-treatment variables, one such predictor is the individual with less serious drinking problems at the time he enters treatment (as reflected by less heavy drinking, less abnormal symptomatology, and a short history of drinking problems). Among variables related to treatment, therapeutic procedures aiming specifically at a non-abstinent outcome, is another predictor; and among post-treatment variables, are factors such as overcoming drinking problems which followed shortly after treatment, improvements in other areas of life and health, and possibly a significant positive change in life circumstances.

Regarding certain criticisms of non-abstinent, non-problem drinking outcomes, proponents of the controlled drinking approaches [40] argue that a patient who achieves controlled drinking in spite of abstinence-oriented treatment is unlikely to maintain contact with such clinics and may therefore be regarded as either very rare or non-existent; that the arguments that drinkers who achieve 'controlled drinking' are not 'true alcoholics', represent no more than 'circular logic'; that relapses into uncontrolled drinking occur not only in non-problem drinking programmes but also in abstinence-oriented therapies; and that much of the possibly dangerous 'newsworthiness' of such approaches must be laid at the door of their overreacting opponents, who thereby alerted the curiosity of the media.

In view of all this Sobell [40] suggests evaluating the outcome of treatment programmes as reflecting 'degrees of improvement or recovery', and that all of them adopt 'a single treatment goal, i.e. a reduction in drinking to a non-problem level' which 'for many, and perhaps most . . . might only be achieved through total abstinence', for others, however, by non-problem drinking. Research is needed to help predict what therapeutic procedures are most appropriate with which type of individual in order to achieve 'which kinds of outcome', although according to current evidence those with less chronic alcohol problems are more likely to abstain successfully.

Abstinence versus controlled drinking: advantages and disadvantages

From the standpoint of psychiatrists supporting the abstinence approach to alcoholism, a detailed and reasoned review has recently been presented by Arroyave and McKeown [31] who are critical of the 'haphazard nature of existing research and the confusion of approaches and terminology'. While the 'challenging questioning of traditional, sometimes dogmatic concepts has always been essential to progress, and clinicians must welcome such approaches [one has to keep] in mind, the danger of exciting research suggestions leading to premature ill-judged changes in clinical practice'. Drinkers themselves, as well as sociologists, psychologists and others relatively new to the field will often be very keen to substitute the much more palatable suggestion for controlled drinking in place of abstinence.

Other professions 'make important contributions to [the management of] alcoholism'. In recent years some representatives of such professions have at times gone out of their way to criticise the alleged desire of doctors to keep a kind of medical prerogative and exclusiveness in the field of alcoholism by propagating the 'disease concept' and the 'medical model' (see Chapter 4) [43, 44]. Far from such an alleged 'take-over' by the medical profession the great majority of medical men unfortunately have always ignored problems of excessive drinking including alcoholism [45, 46]. The above authors comment that 'however, the final clinical responsibility under current legislation rests with the medical profession which therefore must make its position clear concerning all those forms of human behaviour that may have organic and other repercussions'. This is the more so as, at the present state of lack of definite knowledge, the extent of the contribution made by biological, constitutional, possibly genetic factors is not clear; and as even relatively small amounts of alcohol (say, four to five pints of beer taken regularly) may bring about pathological changes in the liver and the brain (see Chapter 14).

Another point stressed by the Oxford workers is that 'before considering whether controlled drinking is possible it is essential to define precisely what it is'. Attempts made at defining it on the basis of quantity, while obviously preferable to those papers advocating controlled drinking without any definition, 'suffer from fundamental difficulties . . . unwieldy, and relying on self-reporting they take no account of variations in body weight, blood alcohol level changes and differences in tolerance to alcohol both between individuals and in the same individual at different times'. Such variations have been recognised for many years [48, 49]. The Oxford workers refer to 'the concept of an individual blood alcohol level threshold for "loss of control" [which] has been put forward by Glatt (1965)' [50].

Thus 'the same quantity of alcohol may have wide variations of effect [so that] even in small quantities it might have very different effects on those with a history of dependence, but it has not been established whether intellectual or physical damage is more likely or appears earlier in this group'.

As to the possible interchangeability of the variety of terms and definitions used, do 'controlled drinking, social drinking, moderate drinking, disciplined drinking and normal drinking' all mean the same thing? Normal drinking, social drinking and moderate drinking are imprecise terms because of cultural differences. Quoting our own strictures (1965) [50] on strictly self-rationed unpleasant, risky ('not normal') drinking, the Oxford workers state that 'if the model of critical blood level alcohol threshold is accepted then controlled drinking ("the drinking of self-monitored amounts of alcohol in non-clinical settings to an extent that it does not interfere with functioning in any area and retaining the ability to stop at will or when external circumstances render it appropriate") of ex-alcoholics will always have to remain below the self-determined threshold – a different problem in itself.'

Is controlled drinking a realistic treatment goal for some alcoholics? Behaviour of alcoholics outside treatment settings may not match their drinking patterns in hospital [51], but successful controlled drinking studies frequently relied on small groups of patients taught normal drinking in treatment settings and followed up for short-term periods only.

The authors deplore as 'dangerous' the custom of making unsupported assertions in favour of treatment directed at controlled drinking, or statements that could be taken as such, for example that 'controlled drinking is increasingly being accepted as a goal for some alcoholics'. Abstinence concepts – they state – are now made to appear 'old fashioned, punitive, prejudiced, harsh and unsupportive'; in contrast, controlled drinking therapies appear 'warm, humanitarian, progressive and attractive' in the sense that they could remove many of the tensions between the alcoholic and his helpers. However this may largely be due to the 'colluding' of the therapist with the alcoholic's denial of his compulsion, or, as the authors put it, 'denying the negative alcoholic effect on his life'. The alcoholic becomes 'motivated' to constructive action only after a breakdown of all his alibis but the controlled drinking therapies support his alibis and thereby often delay constructive action.

The Oxford workers' criticism of controlled drinking – which in their view is 'far from proven as a workable alternative – is:

(a)   Uncritical sponsors may project their unwillingness to consider the necessity for abstinence.
(b)   Much evidence is anecdotal and rests on results based on consumption data relating to periods of time and not to people.
(c)   Controlled drinking as yet should remain in the realm of research as no previous identification is possible as to whom can be helped, and it has not been demonstrated that the final outcome can be as effective, in terms of quality of life, as existing treatments aimed at abstinence. (In our own experience the reports of frequent occurrence of deterioration after abstinence has been achieved, often sound remote from clinical reality, as frequently testified by many alcoholics and their spouses.)
(d)   The advantages of controlled drinking would also have to outweigh the problem of such people being unable to benefit from AA.
(e)   Costing of personnel and training needs of controlled drinking programmes are also important.

Meanwhile the authors conclude it would be sensible to avoid creating illusory hopes and weakening the resolve of many alcoholics currently attempting abstinence. The non-specialist should keep a balanced view of both the medical and non-medical aspects of alcoholism so as to consider all potential areas of damage resulting from alcohol abuse. One could perhaps add that of all the members of the therapeutic team it is only the doctor who can fully appreciate the organic as well as the psycho-social implications of excessive drinking.

Some principles recently enunciated by Dr Anthony Clare in regard to [52] a completely different area, the controversial subject of psychosurgery, may apply also to controlled drinking. They refer to ethical difficulties arising out of 'the conflict between the patients' interest and research aims'. Obviously a full understanding of the circumstances surrounding and affecting the LoC is vital for the elucidation of causative factors in alcoholism. But it is in the patient's interest to be encouraged in his hope of safe con- trolled drinking. Even those who believe in controlled drinking feel that this applies mainly to relatively early stage drinkers and not to those strongly dependent; and it is often the latter, with a strong vested interest in continuing their drinking, who are anxious to get an 'official' stamp of approval on their continued drinking. In most cases this may be no more than prolonging the agony. There may thus exist a strong possibility of conflict between the patient's real interest and research aims. The way here is open to all kinds of rationalisations. A claim often made in favour of the controlled drinking approach is that this is what the patient really wants but what he wants may not necessarily be the best for him or feasible, and falling in with, or encouraging, such wishes may only serve to bolster up his rationalisations. One possible approach may be that suggested by Clare in the case of psychosurgery, that controlled drinking approaches could be 'confined to a few units with extensive experience, with limited and defined criteria for selection and with established methods of evaluation'. In the case of controlled drinking, patients selected for participation should only be those who want to participate and, if at all possible, with the approval of their family, without whose co-operation success anyway would seem highly unlikely. This would minimise the obvious risk that all drinkers who have done well with abstinence would feel encouraged to try 'controlled drinking' contrary to what therapists in favour of 'controlled drinking' would want them to do.

The state and degree of dependence – and their influence on the choice of treatment approaches

According to the R.C. Psych. Report not only the dependent drinker but the person who is drinking excessively without having contracted dependence may also be having genuine difficulty in controlling his behaviour. Some such non-dependent 'problem drinkers' may need little specialised treatment for their drinking problems. For example, the main problem in such cases may be the underlying personality, such as habitual relief drinking by hedon- istic, self-indulgent, inadequate, psychopathic, anxious person- alities or in other cases drinking behaviour following that of the 'crowd' or one's peers. In the non-dependent problem drinker attention to the personality and the human and/or material environment may often be sufficient; but whereas such attention to personality and environment are also needed in the dependent drinker, the super-added factor of dependence usually requires social attention in its own right, and as a rule before (or at least alongside) concentrating therapeutic efforts on personality and environmental factors.

Thus, in our view, dependent drinkers are often qualitatively different from non-dependent heavy drinkers and more than just the extreme degrees of the ordinary excessive drinkers – the superimposed LoC has created special circumstances – even though, as we have seen, the LoC and dependence develop gradually and there is therefore no sharp demarcation line (see Chapters 3 and 4). The difficulty in controlling behaviour in the non-dependent drinker stems chiefly from himself or from his environment, but in the dependent drinker mainly from the (multifactorial) LoC which often forces him into behaviour alien to his personality. Naturally, as we have seen, personality and environmental (social) factors also influence the LoC – and even in marked 'dependency' states the influence of the agent can often still be controlled to a major or lesser extent by personality and environmental factors (see Chapter 4). On the other hand, as discussed elsewhere, such (partial, impaired) control is usually in a precarious state. It constitutes a type of 'latent', 'dormant' or 'compensated' alcoholism with a risk of decompensation in compensated heart disease. In the case of the 'stabilised', moderate drinking alcoholic such decompensation may, for example, arise from unavoidable stress; moreover immature and insecure alcoholics are prone to experience (subjective feelings of) stress even without what outsiders would consider 'adequate' reason.

Just as sufferers from compensated heart disorder or stabilised diabetics should try to keep out of the way of avoidable stress, one might think that alcoholics too should try to avoid taking unnecessary risks, which are greater, the greater the degree of dependence and the greater the 'lack of control'. However, the greater the degree of dependence the greater, often, is their difficulty in refraining from having the first drink, and from following up the first few with many more. Thus those most at risk are also those more likely to take such risks, to rationalise their risk-taking and, when offered a choice between abstinence-oriented and non-abstinence (non-problem-drinking) directed approaches, to plump for the latter.

Can different types of problem drinkers (dependent and non-dependent) be treated within the same group? In 1959 at St Bernard's hospital Dr Clifford Judge and the present author [53] started what was described then as a 'widening of the scope of the group'. An alcoholic group had been set up for female patients in the female admission ward, and another consultant's male patients with a possible drink problem (the writer at the time had only female beds in the hospital but no male beds) were invited to attend. 'Initially the male drinkers admitted to the hospital vigorously denied any suggestion that they were alcoholics. To encourage them to give the group a trial, the method subsequently adopted consisted of naming it a "drinking problem" group, leaving it open to the participants to discover more about themselves during the discussions'. In fact, quite a few patients who attended were not alcoholics, but seemed to obtain some measure of insight and help from the meetings, with the result that in some cases an excessive intake was reduced. It thus proved quite feasible to treat alcoholics who naturally had to learn that alcohol in the future was not for them, alongside other heavy drinkers who had not yet crossed the line of no return and were still in a position to decrease their alcohol intake.

Reports such as these show clearly that before alcoholics reach the point of no return – which is of course no clear demarcation line but a vast, vague, ill defined or indefinable borderland [54, 55] they can, in principle, reduce their drink intake, but the question that arouses controvery is whether some can still do so after having developed early or even late dependence.

The problem of choosing the appropriate treatment goal for the right patient was also discussed in a study carried out by R G Popham and W Schmidt [56]. They found in an out-patients' clinical study with a programme aimed at a goal of moderate drinking that 'moderate drinking may be the orientation of choice for patients with comparatively low pre-treatment consumptions levels and that of total abstinence for heavier consumers'. In the authors' view in regard to treatment outcome, in contrast to social and personal characteristics of alcoholic patients, the predictive value of the individual's pre-treatment alcohol consumption has been ignored. This view implies that the agent-host-environment triad would also be significant in the assessment of probable treatment outcome, and possibly for the choice of the appropriate treatment goal.

Another conclusion arrived at in this study was that a moderate drinking treatment in contrast to abstinence orientation with un-

selected alcoholic patients 'in an otherwise conventional programme is likely to result in a lower rate of total abstinence and a
higher rate of moderate drinking than the total abstinence orientation, but not in a better overall recovery rate'. They feel, however, that a combination of the moderate drinking orientation,
not as in their own programme with conventional therapy, but
with appropriate behaviour therapy [57] will produce better
results.

The 'counter-productivity' issue [58][2]

The protagonists of such 'new' (controlled drinking) approaches
have claimed the abstinence approach to be 'counter-productive'
in several aspects. For example, the abstinence approach has been
said to be concerned with the goal of abstinence only, without
taking notice of necessary improvements in other health areas
[59]. Moreover, abstinence has been said to leave many alcoholics
dissatisfied and unhappy [60]. However, abstinence-oriented
approaches, as a rule, have never regarded abstinence as *the*
ultimate goal, but merely as the necessary condition on the basis of
which improvement in other areas of health functioning was
possible and could be helped along. It is of course true that some
alcoholics who stop short at the stage of total abstinence remain
dissatisfied and unhappy; in our experience, however, the great
majority soon come to feel very much happier in most aspects, and
their families as a rule feel much more relaxed [61]. All such
programmes should naturally stress the necessity to fill the void
left by giving up something, i.e. alcohol, by alternative, constructive activities and leisure-time pursuits.

'Self-fulfilling prophecy' is another criticism directed at the
abstinence-oriented approach: if doctors would not teach alcoholics that their loss of control makes a relapse inevitable, the
drinkers possibly would not have relapsed [59]. But it was not
doctors who taught alcoholics about loss of control; it was alcoholics' experiences as related by AA that taught doctors and not
the other way round [61]. Unfortunately, even today many
doctors have been taught so little in their undergraduate days
about alcoholism that there is hardly anything that they can teach
habitual drinkers. Many medical men – even today – know next
to nothing about loss of control [61] and have unfortunately
always taken little interest in alcoholics.

One generally acknowledged positive consequence of the disease concept has been the gradual abandoning of former views that alcoholism was a crime, sin, weakness, or a character disorder. Doctors' and medical students' interest will certainly not be stimulated if the disease concept were to be abandoned. The general public still largely takes its cue from doctors' attitudes. Acceptance of alcoholics as genuine sufferers from an illness is probably one of the most valuable means to reduce the stigma still attached to alcoholics and militating against early diagnosis and therapeutic intervention. This stigma (and the resulting fear of rejection by the doctor) is probably a much more important factor preventing drinkers from presenting themselves early at their doctor's surgery, than the fear that the doctor would prescribe total abstinence – the latter argument being another criticism levelled at the abstinence-oriented approach [59, 62]. Yet this argument does not explain why alcoholics' families likewise delay coming forward at an early stage – and certainly the alcoholic's long suffering spouse, as a rule, has prayed for years that the alcoholic husband or wife would finally give up drinking. On the other hand, holding out at this early juncture of research into the 'new' approach the hope of moderate drinking would certainly seem to be counter-productive in the prophylactic field: a great many alcoholics will thereby feel encouraged to continue their attempts to learn moderate drinking, although they as a rule may have tried (and failed) to do so for many years. Incidentally, one wonders what the great majority of alcoholics' spouses feel about the 'new' approaches. In our experience their predominant reaction is: 'We have heard all this before too often – and it has never worked!' [61] i.e. the promise that 'this time it will be different, this time I will stop after a few drinks!' Not all wives of alcoholics could be expected to be as confident as a behaviour therapist that 'the use of procedurally established methods of learning' will make all the difference in the case of their alcoholic husbands who in the past have 'tried social drinking without success' [63].

The 'new' approaches might also be 'counter-productive' in some other aspects, for example:

1 By encouraging the alcoholic to put up his 'fight' not before the first drink (when there is no real craving and no pharmacological 'agent' at work) but only after a few drinks (when the interaction between 'agent' and 'host' may have made the task much more difficult);

2   By undermining the work of AA, hitherto the most successful
     single therapeutic approach in this field;
3   By possibly once more arousing the drinker's guilt feelings – if
     he fails to control his drinking as he is no longer regarded as
     suffering from an illness – which thus could become motiva-
     tions for further drinking;
4   And whereas the disease concept helped many a wife to attain
     a different outlook and more constructive attitude towards her
     alcoholic husband as she understood that he was not just a
     wilful, self-indulgent or 'bloody-minded boozer' – and this
     change of attitude on her part in time often had positive
     repercussions on the drinking husband's behaviour – aban-
     doning the disease concept might once more rekindle the
     spouse's former doubts and difficulties in understanding her
     husband's 'learnt' drinking behaviour.

It has often been said against the abstinence-oriented approaches that strong social pressures arising from the wide acceptance of drinking makes life difficult for the abstaining alcoholic
[59, 62, 63]. This may undoubtedly be true although those abstinent alcoholic patients of ours, once they had fully accepted the
necessity for abstinence, hardly ever experienced difficulties on
that score. As a rule heavy social drinkers are mainly interested in
obtaining drink for themselves and do not bother unduly whether
others drink or not. At any rate, the alcoholic who tries to
drink moderately would likewise experience social pressure (and
possibly even greater difficulties) if he insists on stopping
after three glasses when his drinking companions continue their
drinking.

Finally, in a discussion of abstinence or 'controlled drinking' the
importance of the physical complications of alcoholism – even
though they usually appear relatively late – should not be completely ignored. No one can be sure what effect continued
drinking (even if it stayed at the moderate level) would exert on
the already damaged tissues and organs of an alcoholic (in whose
case, moreover, an underlying biological vulnerability of such
organs may be indicated by such complications arising in the first
instance). The extreme need for caution on this score is well
illustrated in *The Journal of Studies on Alcohol* (April 1975). A
quick glance at the abstracts showed the necessity for abstinence
urged by the case of various alcoholic complications by authors
from four different countries in four separate articles. A German

author considered abstinence 'mandatory in chronic pancreatitis, hepatitis, porphyria, and liver cirrhosis' [60]. French authors found mesenchymal inflammation of the liver reversed by abstinence, whereas inflammation (as reflected in certain blood serum tests) seemed to increase in those alcoholics who continued to drink [64]; a Swedish author reported that in the case of cardiomyopathy full recovery was possible with treatment and abstinence from alcohol [65], and Austrian doctors – who found that convulsive seizures had occurred in about 5 per cent of their approximately 4000 alcoholic patients – conclude that total abstinence is 'indicated in all alcoholics who have seizures' [66]. More recently improvement was noted after abstinence in the brain changes (of alcoholics) by the new technique of computerised axia tomography [67] and the need for abstinence was emphasised by specialist physicians (cardiologists, gastroenterologists, neurologists, etc.) in various physical complications (see Chapter 14). The possible harmful effect of continued alcohol intake in tissues which might already have been affected by excessive drinking, should certainly not be overlooked in discussions as to whether the abstinence or the 'controlled drinking' goal carried the relatively greater risk of 'counter-productivity'.

Methods

The preliminary tasks of sobering-up and detoxicating the alcoholic have often to be followed up by long-term methods. Most clinicians (like AA) believe a 'cure' in the sense that alcoholics can learn safely to drink in moderation is – certainly for the great majority – not possible at least with the methods available at present (although obviously one ought to keep an open mind and await the results of research going on at various centres).

What alcoholics can hope for, and what has been achieved by many thousands of alcoholics the world over, is 'recovery' brought about by an 'arrest' of the disorder. To achieve this goal the alcoholic must develop some motivation. It is usually said that in order to have a chance to recover the alcoholic must have already to start with the sincere desire to give up drinking, but such expectations would often seem unrealistic. What the alcoholic usually wants is to get out of the mess into which his excessive drinking has plunged him; he may want to learn to drink without suffering so many ill-effects. It will only be in the course of treatment that it gradually dawns on him that he can recover only through complete abstinence. Thus, an initial motivation to abstain completely is not a prerequisite of success as is so often believed; it is surely one of the tasks of the therapeutic programme to induce an understanding of his condition in the alcoholic and with it the motivation to give up drinking.

In the hands of various therapists methods which vary a great deal from each other have achieved success in the treatment of alcoholics. It has sometimes been stated that what all these different techniques may have in common is the disruption of the patient's personality and the breakdown of old-established and long-cherished attitudes, thus preparing the way for implanting new and possibly diametrically opposed attitudes in their place [68, 69]. One might, in this connection, think, for example, of the physical debility and exhaustion following aversion treatment, the often very severe consequences of the alcohol-disulfiram reaction, or also of the 'rock-bottom' concept of Alcoholics Anonymous with the 'conversion-like' experience of some Alcoholics Anonymous members.

It may, however, also be argued that even more important than the methods employed may be the basic attitude of the therapist towards the alcoholic patient [70], and his ability to establish a helpful relationship. Nobody is likely to have much success in treating alcoholics approaching them with a censoring, moralistic or even ridiculing attitude, and in a 'holier-than-thou' spirit. On the other hand, an approach based on understanding and genuine emotional acceptance (which implies much more than just paying lip-service to the disease concept of alcoholism) will often go a long way. Alcoholics are very sensitive and on the look-out for real or imagined rejection, whereas an approach based rather on an attitude of 'There but for the grace of God go I' may very often find them very accessible and easy to 'reach' once they have sobered up.

The crying need of the alcoholic is for acceptance, as an American psychiatrist put it a few years ago. This necessity to adopt a basically accepting attitude applies to all members of the therapeutic team, nurses, social workers, probation officers, just as well as to general practitioners and psychiatrists.

Dr J Y Dent [6], who in the 1940s and 1950s did so much for the cause of alcoholics in this country, achieved remarkable successes with his parenteral injection and oral apomorphine techniques. Few other therapists using apomorphine have had the same measure of success. Dent had great understanding of, and empathy with, alcoholics, which the latter were undoubtedly very quick to appreciate. Dent himself attributed his success in full measure to his tool – apomorphine – but there are many who would agree with a view put forward a few years ago that 'Dent without apomorphine would still be much more successful than apomorphine without Dent!'

It seems essential to stress the importance of the basic attitude towards the alcoholic because it may so often decide between success and failure. For many years alcoholics had been said to be extremely difficult patients, and few hospitals – general or psychiatric – were (or still are) keen to receive them. But within the accepting atmosphere of a therapeutic community formed by alcoholics, they will, as a rule, be found to be extremely co-operative patients [2, 4].

A welcome reversal of formerly widely held official and government attitudes towards the alcoholic was shown in a Ministry of Health Memorandum (1962) recommending the establishment of regional alcohol units. It is vitally important not to open such units indiscriminately without having staff available who emotionally 'accept' the alcoholic patient. Special education and training of staff called upon to work in these units is a vital necessity if they are to succeed.

The most recent and fascinating discussion of the question of what successful alcoholism treatment programmes have in common, comes from Dr G E Vaillant [71] of the Harvard Medical School. The four programmes chosen by Vaillant were:

(i) The Shadel Clinic's emetine aversion;
(ii) The Menninger Clinic's antabuse and group therapy approach;
(iii) Beaubrun's combination (in the West Indies of 'indigenous para-professionals and medically sanctioned AA', and
(iv) Sobell's 'behaviour modification'.

Vaillant refers to the comment of Professor Jerome Frank [72] on the apparent paradox that at a time 'of mounting complaint that . . . therapy may represent expensive fraud [nonetheless] demand for therapy may seem increasingly insatiable'. In Frank's view 'what feeds such demand is not the patient's need for cure as such as a need to elevate morale'. This may, in particular, apply to patients such as alcoholics who 'feel defeated, helpless, unable to change', requiring hope as much as relief of symptoms; and, in order to enter an 'ingrained, maladaptive habit' one 'must change [their] belief system and then maintain that change . . . If you can win their hearts and minds, their habits will follow'. Combining the 'best placebo effects of Lourdes with the best attitude-change inherent in the evangelical conversion of experience' may put one on the 'way to an effective alcohol programme'.

What, in Vaillant's view, the four named successful treatment programmes had in common was that 'they all maximised the placebo effect of medical treatment and effected significant attitude change'. All these therapists, as 'sanctioned powerful healers' brought hope to the patients, all four programmes indoctrinated patients 'into a coherent – if differing – ideology', maximising attitude changes in an emotionally charged setting; and each prescribed some form of daily ritual; comradeship developed among the patients, all programmes altered patients' attitudes by affecting their self-esteem and so on.

As Vaillant emphasises, there are many roads leading to recovery in alcoholism, and one needs to understand what is common to all of them. Vaillant's own programme had as its aim to encourage the use of AA, and the programme succeeded in that. He now feels able to resolve the 'dilemma' which confronts the doctor, who is now both treating alcoholism and engaged in research. Much of the evidence required to support his treatment is not there. But how can a doctor possibly ignore a chronic malady as painful, damaging and destructive as alcoholism? As the result of his searching study, Vaillant is happy to 'return to the treatment of alcoholism both with hope and confidence'.

The different forms of therapy employed in alcoholism are, of course, not mutually exclusive, in fact it may as a rule be desirable to combine several of them in an individual case. Thus detoxification and physical building-up might be followed by a course of injections of apomorphine or emetine, and then by the administration of disulfiram; some form of psychotherapy, individually or in groups, should be carried out at the same time and the patient encouraged to join Alcoholics Anonymous. The question should not be one of either 'Freud or Pavlov' to be determined by the therapist's bias even before he has seen the patient concerned. Rather, techniques based on analytical and behaviouristic theories could be carried out side by side, approaching alcoholism both from its 'symptomatic' and from its 'disease' angles [73].

A comprehensive multidisciplinary method of treating alcoholics is nowadays regarded by many as the most promising approach; it has certainly been found to be a very feasible method, acceptable to, and popular with, patients of alcohol units in this country during the past three decades [74].

Physical therapies

More or less widespread use is made of three types of drugs:

(i)   *Alcohol-sensitising drugs (disulfiram or* ccc [75]*)*
Acting as deterrents against drinking (e.g. disulfiram *Antabuse*), if followed by drinking within three or four days may produce very severe, unpleasant, rarely even life-threatening symptoms although the intensity of the action is unpredictable. The drinker's face and body become flushed, his heart may begin to race, he may become very breathless – this may be the most disturbing and frightening experience and not infrequently he may feel to be at death's door. He may feel very faint and sick, he may suffer from severe headaches and he may vomit, his blood pressure may fall; and he may collapse. (The alcoholic who is treated with such alcohol-sensitising drugs should carry a card with him indicating this fact so that, in case of accidents, etc. sympathetic bystanders do not give him alcohol.) The disulfiram-alcohol reaction is, in general, ascribed to the accumulation in the blood of acetaldehyde, the first intermediate alcohol breakdown product in the body, as disulfiram interrupts alcohol metabolism at the acetaldehyde stage.

Once the (suitable) patient has been clearly informed about the consequences of the disulfiram-alcohol reaction described, he will, as a rule, abstain from drinking. He should be told that even in the absence of a clinical reaction there may be (usually reversible) changes in the electrocardiogram. The formerly practised method of a preliminary disulfiram-alcohol test in hospital is no longer in common use – probably because of the unpredictability of the intensity of the reaction. Incidentally, in view of such unpredictability, patients should not be told that drinking on top of the tablet within the next three to four days will lead to a severe reaction but merely that this is likely; otherwise a relatively mild reaction on the first occasion (perhaps no more than the *malaise rouge* – flushing of face and body – which of course might give the drinking away to the suspicious spouse) might leave the drinker with a false sense of the relative harmlessness of such a reaction. In reality, on a subsequent occasion, the reaction might be more painful and dangerous.

It is clear that this method (like any other form of treatment of alcoholism) presupposes some motivation on the part of the patient, who otherwise could risk drinking 'on top of' disulfiram or, more commonly (but less dangerously), may 'forget' to take the maintenance dose of the drug regularly as he should do.

Psychopathic patients, or those with a very unreliable memory, should not be prescribed disulfiram because of the risk that they may genuinely forget and drink on top of the tablets; similarly, in those with 'gambling' propensities, who may risk taking drinks on top of the tablets because they are curious to find out whether 'it works', should not be given them because of the possibility of severe reactions, although in view of the smaller dosage nowadays used (the tablet used in the UK has 200 mg, as against the former 500 mg) fatal reactions – which rarely occurred in the past – are now fortunately highly unlikely.

Side effects of disulfiram medication include the relatively common drowsiness – so that, in general, the tablet should be taken last thing at night – and, more rarely, impairment of libido and potency, skin rashes, polyneuropathy, convulsions and psychotic reactions. Because of the latter possibility, the tablets are unsuitable for drinkers with a history of psychosis.

Value of alcohol-sensitising drugs

1 Deterrent effect of knowledge of likely painful and dangerous consequences of the reaction if alcohol is taken within a certain time.

    This is the main desired effect and usually the only one mentioned, even by the manufacturers. But there are other valuable effects if these tablets are taken regularly.

2 Alcoholics are not only compulsive but often also very impulsive drinkers. The fear of the reaction (unlike the long-term consequences of heavy drinking, the reaction is likely to be an *immediately* punishing one and therefore apparently a more effective deterrent) usually prevents the impulsive drinking. In this way the drinker is given a breathing space of up to 36 and 80 hours in the case of CCC and of disulfiram respectively; during this period the constructive part within the drinker's ambivalent self (i.e. the one realising that contented useful living is impossible when continuing with drink), is given a chance to reassert itself.

3   These tablets can provide peace of mind both to the drinker and his family. As to the drinker himself, the question after having taken the tablets is no longer 'Shall I or shan't I drink?'; it is now the knowledge 'I cannot' and there is no longer a conflict.

Similarly the drinker's wife, so often worried, for example, whether her husband, as regularly in the past, was at the steering wheel of a powerful car in an intoxicated state, is no longer suffering such fear.

4   For the same reason these tablets in many drinkers actually greatly minimise the drinker's desire to drink. Most relapses are, in our experience, not due to an overwhelming craving or great stress but to a feeling of 'surely after all this time of sobriety one little drink won't do me any harm'. Passing a pub and feeling like having 'just one drink', many drinkers told us that they immediately realised that 'it is no use your even thinking of a drink; you know you cannot have a drink'. In this way many drinkers felt strongly that by such feedback-mechanism, the alcohol deterrent tablets often greatly reduced or even removed 'craving'.

This is an interesting point as so often patients ask for something that would remove their 'craving', and one has to tell them that there is no definite way of achieving it. Apomorphine has been claimed by Dent [74] to bring this about in many alcoholics but in spite of a recent resurgence of interest in this therapeutic method few therapists currently use this technique [79, 80].

5   Instead of possibly having, intermittently during the next twenty-four hours, to fight against their desire to have a drink, taking these tablets means condensing this decision or conflict into just a few seconds. There is then no more conflict for (and even beyond) the next day.

6   Alcoholics often claim that they unwittingly (possibly in an unguarded moment) passively relapsed into their first drink. Having agreed and having started regularly to take alcoholic-deterrent tablets, on the other hand, usually means that they have to take an active decision *not* to take these tablets – and only after this active decision and step is their way free to drink. They can then no longer argue, as is so often done: 'I have not the slightest idea how I came to have my first drink again . . . I just don't remember . . . it just happened.' With disulfiram it does not 'happen' – the drinker has to prepare the ground

for the next drink actively, which frequently happens within one day (in the case of ccc) or two to three days (in the case of disulfiram) of forgetting to take the tablets. In the case of genuinely forgetting, there is thus ample time to resume the tablets on subsequent days.

'How long have I to take these tablets?' is a question commonly asked, when the method is first suggested.

Most drinkers who often are only too keen to try out any pill around, and often in excessive doses, remember their 'dislike of drugs' when advised to take disulfiram or ccc – forgetting that alcohol is just as good or bad a drug as other drugs which they do not care to take. As a rule they tend to give up disulfiram within a relatively short period. They ought to be warned that if they feel they are now safe to leave off disulfiram (without having discussed this matter with their doctor), the only safe way for them is to take double the dose for the next few days – until they have seen the therapist. All too often a resumption of 'craving', or at least temptation, 'happens' to set in within a few days of having stopped the tablets.

Obviously the length of time these tablets should be taken depends on many factors to be assessed and reviewed in the individual drinker from time to time. Perhaps as a rather rough-and-ready safe, general rule, the drinker should continue taking them as long as he is bothered by, or preoccupied with, the thought of having to take the tablets. As soon as he no longer cares whether he has to take them or not, this may be a sign that he no longer really bothers about drinking either and he may then perhaps fairly safely stop them.

Because of the possible risks attached (in particular) to disulfiram medication one should aim at the minimal dose (in general 200 mg, i.e. one tablet, best taken at night). Like ccc (one tablet (100 mg) twice a day), on no account must disulfiram be given to the alcoholic unbeknown to him – for example, putting these tablets into his tea or coffee, as well-intentioned wives have been known to do. Patients must be strongly warned *not* to have any alcoholic drink for at least 3½ days after having taken disulfiram, or for 1½ days after having taken ccc. If they have taken alcohol, patients should wait at least twenty-four hours before taking disulfiram or ccc can resume.

Disulfiram (Antabuse) or CCC (citrated calcium carbanide-Abstem)?

Which of these two tablets should be chosen in a given individual patient?

Disulfiram is the more potent, the effect lasts longer; it has more side effects. Disulfiram should not be used in cases of any cardiovascular disease and CCC only with caution.

CCC effect sets in much more quickly.

In principle these somewhat different actions determine the choice in the given individual. Having used alcohol-deterrent drugs over the past thirty years the present writer still adheres to the same views formed after the trial of CCC carried out at Warlingham Park Hospital in 1957; interested readers are referred to the article in question [75] describing the trial and the conclusions.

Clearly the alcohol-sensitising tablets are not a 'cure' for alcoholism; but used in the right way, in proper indications they can be of great assistance to many alcoholics as a 'crutch'. Moreover they provide the drinker with a 'breather', allowing him time to experience the positive 'rewards' obtained when abstaining, and also enabling him to attend therapy meetings without his mind befuddled with drink and so to understand and assimilate what is going on and what is being said.

The tablets are obviously not an alternative but in some people they may be a very helpful or even necessary complement to AA and psychosocial therapy.

Again, many alcoholics refuse to take disulfiram because they want to succeed without a 'crutch'. Here again, the important thing for a drinker who has in the past, and in spite of many attempts, failed to stay sober is to make use of any available methods that might help him.

One device that has proved helpful to such patients is to ask them to write down on each occasion when they feel they would like to stop taking these alcohol-deterrent tablets, why they wanted to do so, and discuss this with the therapist on the next visit. Frequently this agreement seems greatly to reduce the likelihood of such patients stopping the tablets. It makes them think twice.

Disulfiram implant

An obvious drawback with prescribing disulfiram or CCC orally is that the drinker may more readily forget to take the tablets rather than forgetting to take the drink; and the idea of an implant may therefore sound logical and attractive. In fact sometimes alcoholics themselves, who in the past have failed to stay the course with disulfiram tablets, ask whether implants would not help them. One meets alcoholics who report that such implants have helped a great deal as they now know that they cannot have a drink; but unfortunately most observers and investigators have found [76, 77] that the disulfiram blood levels obtained by such implants are so low that if the alcoholic risks taking a drink, there is no disulfiram-alcohol reaction, and thereby the whole deterrent effect of the operation is lost. This means that such an implant only works as long as the drinker believes in it, and the therapist finds himself in an ethically difficult situation: on the one hand, an alcoholic who in the past has relapsed again and again and seems convinced from Press reports that an implant would, in his case, be a powerful and effective deterrent, enquires about it and one's honest remark that, in the light of the majority view, such an implant is little more than a placebo and would rob such a drinker of possible valuable help. Nevertheless, one might feel that one could not really recommend such a method if one feels that it is no more than a placebo. Possibly, however, if the method has so far worked with an individual patient because he has believed in it and still does so now, one could possibly still evade a scientific explanation, in the sense that as this method helped in the past, there seems no good reason why it should not do so in the future: after all, not all investigators believe the implant to be merely a placebo. However, under the circumstances, one would probably not recommend the implant method to an alcoholic who enquires about it, not having tried it in the past.

(ii) *Aversion therapy with emetine*
Unlike the consciously deterrent disulfiram method, emetine aversion treatment depends on the creation of a conditioned reflex by means of classic (Pavlovian) conditioning, so that the alcoholic feels sick and vomits at the sight, smell or taste of alcoholic drinks.

This is achieved by a number of sessions (with rest periods in between) – one session per day – when emetine injections are given followed by the alcoholic drink. Usually five to seven treatments are given.

As in all other physical therapies, thorough physical and laboratory examination before starting treatment is necessary as they all have their contra-indications. The method is well described by the late Dr Lincoln Williams [69], like Dr J Y Dent [6], one of the most outstanding pioneers in Britain of the disease concept of alcoholism, who used it extensively and successfully in this country.

As the treatment is sometimes successful even when no true aversion has been induced, Lincoln Williams and others believe that personality disruption brought about by this method may be at least as important a factor as the aversion.

(iii) *Apomorphine*

Apomorphine is now believed to act on dopaminergic receptors in the brain. The majority of therapists using apomorphine for alcoholics think of it as 'aversion treatment'. However, Dr Dent, the main protagonist of apomorphine therapy, felt that the main factor was the reduction of anxiety and craving. In later years he therefore introduced an oral method by which apomorphine was taken sublingually, and which he found useful for ambulant patients; no alcohol is given at all in this (oral) method.

In the injection method apomorphine doses (intramuscularly) followed shortly afterwards by alcohol are given every two hours for about twenty-four to thirty-six hours, followed for two days by injections of subemetic apomorphine doses without subsequent alcohol administration. During the intensive phase of the first twenty-four to thirty-six hours the alcoholic is given no food (other than alcohol). Physical examinations, electrocardiogram, liver function tests and urine analysis should be carried out before the treatment is started; and, as with the emetine treatment, the patient should have had no drink for a few days and should be in physically fair shape.

With emetine as well as with apomorphine therapy, nurses should be well trained and experienced in these special methods as a lot depends on close observation and skilled supervision.

In the 1940s and early 1950s the apomorphine method was very popular, for example among private doctors (who often were members of the SSA) but markedly lost popularity in later years. The present author has used it occasionally as an adjunct to other, psychosocial methods, in particular among patients who had previously been successfully treated with it and had themselves asked for it. In Eastern Europe the apomorphine injection method is still employed as an aversion technique, but the oral apomorphine method has been taken up in recent years again by a number of psychiatrists in Scandinavia and Germany who claim considerable success with it [78, 79, 81].

In the USA a trial of Dent's oral apomorphine method was carried out by Schlatter and Lat (1972) [80]. A significant proportion of their alcoholic patients experienced a decrease of craving for alcohol compared with controls; but reliance on the patient to resume self-treatment or to seek medical aid in the event of a return of a craving – which is important in Dent's method – was unsuccessful as these patients did not return. The American authors, finding that at a six months' follow-up only three of thirty-five patients were abstinent, therefore suggested that a maintenance dose of apomorphine may be necessary. It is only fair, however, as an anecdotal afterthought, to mention that not infrequently even twenty years after Dent's death ex-patients of his are convinced that it was his oral apomorphine therapy that had helped them for all that time, and urgently asked for such treatment (often for an alcoholic friend or relative), and are bitterly disappointed that in Britain (unlike Scandinavia) these tablets are no longer available.

Other physical treatments

Many other physical therapies (including drug therapies) were proposed over the years but, after an initial wave of uncritical enthusiasm, abandoned. The field of alcoholism (as generally in medicine) is littered with the corpses of many 'wonder drugs' that once and for all would 'cure' alcoholics. A healthy scepticism thus appears whenever new therapies come on the market.

Among methods proposed in recent years is *acupuncture* (based originally on Chinese experiences, and in recent years employed by a few therapists in the withdrawal treatment of drug-dependence, including alcoholism [81]). Another suggestion concerned the *beta-adrenergic-blocking drugs* ('beta-blockers'): they act by competing with the catecholamines for the occupation of beta-adrenergic sites, thus blocking the transmission of the neurotransmitter noradrenaline at these sites. It was therefore hoped that they might be useful in the therapy of alcohol withdrawal by reducing tachycardia, palpitations, anxiety, tremor etc. and that, perhaps similar to the action of the narcotic antagonist naloxone in the case of opiate dependence, beta-blockers (such as propanol) might prove helpful in alcohol-related disorders. However, clinical trials indicated that these substances do not antagonise the effects of high doses of alcohol [82].

For long-term treatment, it has been claimed that the occasional judicious administration of tranquillisers – occasionally in combination with antidepressants (but not stimulating) drugs – by reducing the alcoholic's tension and anxieties may thereby decrease the likelihood of his resuming drinking, and that by making him less anxious and tense these drugs may keep him in a more co-operative frame of mind and thus more likely to participate actively in psychotherapy. However, apart from certain hazards such as potentiation when taken alongside alcohol, and the possibility of dependence, another important question must be kept in mind.

The aim of treating an alcoholic should surely be not only to enable him to give up alcohol but, as far as possible, to get rid of the need to seek refuge in drink or drugs. Rather than reducing tension and anxiety by artificial means, alcoholics should practise trying to – and in time (one may hope) learn to – overcome frustration and to cope with tension by a constructive effort on their own part. But sometimes this may prove to be too perfectionist an advice and goal.

Very likely in the first few precarious weeks of sobriety tranquillisers may occasionally be helpful to tide alcoholics over emergency situations during which their sobriety is threatened, and when – though still sober – they are jittery, tremulous and restless, behaving, as Alcoholics Anonymous members call it, like 'dry drunks'. In the individual case it may occasionally be difficult to decide whether there is so much tension present as to endanger the patient's sobriety and to hinder progress, thus requiring alleviation by drugs; or whether his state may be sufficiently bearable that, when endured, it may act as a spur to arouse and develop the patient's own adaptive potentialities [84].

Certainly the tranquillisers cannot be regarded as a short cut towards the alcoholic's goal of 'contented sobriety'. The late Dr Richard Asher's statement that 'despair is best treated with hope not dope' [38] certainly also holds good for alcoholics whose sober and happy future rests on the foundations of re-education and emotional reorientation rather than on chemical tranquillisation, sedation or stimulation [84].

Tranquillisers, like non-addictive hypnotics, may at times be valuable adjuncts in the overall therapeutic programme; therefore the therapist need not practise total abstinence in regard to prescribing tranquillisers in the alcoholic's rehabilitation period, but he should handle them with great care and as much moderation as possible.

Psychological methods and considerations

Dynamic psychotherapy

Whether, in the individual alcoholic, to start with, physical or psychological, social or economic problems may have been the most important ones, clearly during the drinking career many secondary psychological reactions have left their mark on the alcoholic's personality. Feelings of guilt, remorse or inadequacy, depression, hostility, self-pity, etc., as well as the habitual excessive use of such mental defence mechanisms as denial, projection, rationalisation and over-compensation, often help to produce the deceptive picture of a fairly uniform 'alcoholic personality'.

Thus in certain (e.g. the more alcohol-dependent, or the more neurotic, and the more 'psychogenic') alcoholics a process of re-education and emotional reorientation may be needed, so that such an individual, after gaining some insight into his problems, into his personality defects and his emotional conflicts, learns to cope with his inner tensions and environmental difficulties in a more mature and less destructive manner than by seeking refuge and oblivion in drink or drugs.

For many years this type of alcoholic has used alcohol as a means of alleviating his anxieties, of satisfying some 'needs', of adjusting to life. Since adolescence, he may have formed the habit of by-passing the necessity of having to face up to problems realistically by taking a drink; in this way he has missed the opportunity to grow up emotionally by facing up to difficulties as a challenge to be overcome, so that emotional immaturity has become one of the commonest features seen in alcoholics.

If the alcoholic is now required to give up his old way of trying to 'get by' and 'by-passing' problems, he must learn something about the nature of the needs which in the past he has attempted to satisfy by taking alcohol, about the emotional conflicts which he attempted to solve in this self-destructive way, and he must be helped to find alternative and more constructive ways of adjustment.

A change of feelings, attitudes, of his mode, aim and philosophy of living, will be necessary if the alcoholic wants to find not merely a more or less miserable and disgruntled, though alcohol-free, existence but a happy and contented state of sobriety. He will have to correct his personality defects, as far as possible to learn to live with those defects which he cannot alter, and to accept himself with his limitations, or, to use the terminology of the psychoanalyst Karen Horney [85], he will have to gain his satisfactions from working towards the realisation of his 'real self' rather than hoping, in vain, to realise the far too high ambitions of becoming his 'glorified self'.

When first coming for treatment, at best the alcoholic will have no more than an ambivalent attitude towards the question of giving up drinking. More often than not the alcoholic is a 'voluntary patient' in name only brought along by his spouse, who is on the verge of leaving him, or by the threat of losing his job, some part within him may indeed be anxious to do something about his drinking, whereas another part tells him that he could not possibly live without his old standby – alcohol.

He might be able to conjure up some vision of being able to exist and 'vegetate' without the help of alcohol, but he will find it quite impossible to visualise an alcohol-free future as anything but very drab and miserable.

Under these circumstances the alcoholic would have to be a superhuman being if at this stage he were expected to have a sincere desire to give up drinking. After all, for all these years alcohol has been his main interest in life, and whilst he may vaguely realise that he cannot go on like this much longer, neither does he see any way of living without alcohol.

All that the alcoholic at this stage may vaguely be hoping to achieve with the therapist's help is to learn to drink without getting into trouble and without perpetually landing in a mess. But although mere 'compliance' (Tiebout [86]), is, in the long run, not enough, even this half-hearted ambivalent attempt offers some glimmer of hope: initially merely falling in (under protest) with, and appeasing, the wishes of his wife, friends and employer, he may gradually progress towards a desire to come to real grips with his problems, and he may learn finally that the only way to do so is by giving up drinking altogether.

There are many obstacles which, at the start, interfere with any real progress. The patient usually has no idea what an alcoholic is, and the more he shares with the family and the general public all the common misconceptions about alcoholism, the more he will dread the idea of being counted among this bunch of 'spineless', 'weak-willed' and despised people. (Initially the therapist ought to employ the term 'problem drinking' rather than alcoholism in order not to frighten the new patient away.) When asked whether he had ever thought of attending Alcoholics Anonymous meetings, he may become quite indignant: 'Alcoholics Anonymous may be good company for drunks, but not for me!' Thus, one of the alcoholic's early tasks is to learn to appreciate what alcoholism is, that the down-and-out and the surgical-spirit drinkers constitute only a small minority among alcoholics and that the great majority still have a foothold at home and at work.

The concept of alcoholism as an illness may help him a great deal to allow his defences to come down; to enable him to admit that he may, after all, be an alcoholic without such admission bringing with it the loss of the last shreds of self-respect and self-confidence.

The explanation of the disease concept of alcoholism (which, of course, does not imply condoning wilful drunkenness) in itself may often come as an eye-opener to the alcoholic and also to his family; it may help them to understand many puzzling aspects of his behaviour in the past; it may alter the alcoholic's defensive attitude as well as the attitude of his relatives, and it may provide a ray of hope, helping to establish a motivation to co-operate with treatment.

A therapist's most important task during the first interview is to establish a positive relationship. His understanding, non-condemning, non-judging attitude, his acceptance of the alcoholic patient, will in time aid the latter to accept himself, in spite of his guilt feelings, of his self-hate and his self-destructive tendencies. Once the alcoholic really feels accepted, it will be relatively easy for him to discuss freely personal shortcomings and defects, the mere mention of which would previously have been sufficient to produce fits of rage and to pave the way for a quick return to the comforting bottle.

Accepting the alcoholic does not mean – and this is stressed here because it so often seems to be the basis for misunderstandings – that everything he has done is condoned and excused; but, on the contrary, it enables the alcoholic in time to drop his façade and his defences, so that instead of just denying any defects and problems, or projecting them on to somebody else, he becomes able to admit and discuss them, and to try to find better ways of handling his difficulties.

It is sometimes asked whether sympathetic understanding shown to the alcoholic would not in fact harden and consolidate his drinking behaviour. However, it is the fear of social ostracism and rejection which prevents the alcoholic from coming forward and asking for help and, thus, perpetuates his drinking, and when he finally comes for help he does so in spite of the ostracism and not because of it. In their later stages many alcoholics hate themselves and their drinking but, by stigmatising alcoholics, society effectively bars any early rehabilitation attempts which the alcoholic might have tried. The problem is, of course, quite different in the case of the compulsive alcoholic as compared to the wilful self-indulgent drunkard. The latter might be deterred from continuing his drinking excesses by punishment, whereas the compulsively drinking alcoholic has to be shown that – and how – he can continue living without drinking.

From merely grudgingly admitting to having a drinking problem, and later on, to being an alcoholic, to the emotional acceptance of this fact is still a big step which may take a long time. The drinker must also remember that he cannot accept the fact that he is an alcoholic, as one often hears, 'once and for all'. Throughout his rehabilitation phase, and indeed throughout his life, this attitude will be challenged again and again; the strength of his 'acceptance' will be tested and re-tested on numerous occasions so that one might almost say that day by day the alcoholic will have to take Alcoholics Anonymous' First Step again and again; the admission of being powerless over alcohol, and of one's life just not being manageable as long as alcohol enters into it.

Alcoholics often disagree strongly with each other as to whether it is necessary or advisable for the alcoholic to try to find out what has driven him to drink in the first place.

There are many different personality types among alcoholics, and the more in an individual case alcoholism has arisen on a 'symptomatic' basis, the more it will be necessary for him to know something about the underlying reasons.

In many relatively stable personalities, alcoholism may have arisen primarily in an accidental way, possibly depending largely on environmental factors and not on the basis of an underlying neurosis. In such a person it may indeed be enough to give up drinking – which may have been the main cause of all his later difficulties. But in many other alcoholics, underlying personality defects may have been largely responsible for causing excessive drinking; and for such neurotic or psychopathic alcoholics giving up drinking may frequently not prove enough, although it will have to precede any real psychotherapeutic endeavours.

After giving up drinking, many secondary psychological and social consequences of alcoholism may disappear. Beyond that, certain originally important pre-alcoholic difficulties may now no longer be the problem for the alcoholic that they had been years ago, or they may have become greatly modified during the many years which have elapsed since the alcoholic had started drinking to excess. Moreover, for a certain length of time – often called the 'honeymoon period' – immediately after giving up drinking the feeling of having 'finally' found a solution to his baffling problem, the glow of having discovered what might appear to him as a new world – formerly hidden from him by his alcoholic haze – the alcoholic may feel indeed that giving up drinking is all that is necessary.

However, when he is again faced by difficulties this 'inspiration' of the novelty may gradually fade, and frustrations, old personality defects, etc., may once more come to the foreground and threaten his sobriety – factors such as shyness, feelings of inferiority and inadequacy, resentments, fears, emotional conflicts, inability to handle his feelings of aggression and hostility, or difficulties in the sphere of sexual adjustment. Apart from the necessary essentially 'negative' step of not taking drink, many alcoholics must therefore also be helped to acquire some insight into their difficulties and learn constructive ways and techniques of coping with them. For example, such a patient may never have learnt to handle his emotional conflicts because of a habit – possibly acquired in his early childhood through difficulties experienced in an unstable home – of running away from reality; or his protracted drinking may have led to a 'disuse atrophy' of his ability to cope with tension or frustration. Moreover, as a rule, insight by itself is not sufficient, and factors such as moral courage, faith, the realisation of spiritual values, perseverance in spite of setbacks may also be needed.

Very often alcoholics are emotionally immature people who have grown up physically and intellectually but who, emotionally, often still react like children. Thus, many an alcoholic cannot tolerate frustration and disappointments; he must have relief immediately whatever the price that may have to be paid tomorrow – and about which he could not care less at the moment. The average non-alcoholic individual is more likely to consider the long-term consequences of his actions, whereas many alcoholics want relief and satisfaction of their needs and desires here and now without thinking of tomorrow. Many alcoholics will therefore gradually have to learn to curb this tendency and to shelve immediate relief and gratification in favour of long-term satisfaction; to work towards a more distant goal, even if it may entail temporary suffering and deprivation. The fact that alcoholics are so often concerned with the moment and the present may explain to some extent the success of Alcoholics Anonymous's 'Twenty-Four Hours' programme, requesting the alcoholic to make up his mind to stay sober 'just for today' and not to worry over problems which tomorrow may or may not bring.

One of the difficulties in treating alcoholics arises from the different viewpoints towards the alcoholic's drinking adopted by himself and by society. As already mentioned, the outsider sees only what alcohol does *to* the alcoholic, the latter's actions are determined by the feelings that alcohol does something *for* him. The alcoholic's family and friends see his increasing misery and ruin. Obviously the alcoholic also must surely be aware of this, in spite of his attempts to hide its full extent from himself by ingenious rationalisations. If he persists, in spite of this realisation, with his excessive drinking, it would seem that he is vaguely but desperately searching for something whilst persisting with this seemingly purposeless and self-destructive behaviour, even if he himself may not be aware of it. It is in this field that psychological theories abound.

Does the alcoholic look for satisfaction of his masochistic and self-destructive tendencies (gradual suicide) [87]? Is he trying to get away from deep-seated, and possibly extreme, psychological or physical discomfort? Do certain alcoholics yearn for an abnormally high degree of gratification and satisfaction, for 'Nirvana'? (As expressed during a group session by some patients: 'I got bored with ordinary life.' 'I try to get away from it, from the ordinary humdrum of low-plane living.' 'Once you were on the crest of the wave and you want to get back up there where you were when "under the influence", and you need a "shot in the arm".' 'That is the feeling when one is "flat" and when "all one's nerves are screaming for it".' 'One is not at a party all the time, and you want to be at the top of excitement, you are not satisfied with a life that is all grey!')

This latter type of personality – who may often be young or psychopathetic and may also tend habitually to take stimulating drugs to excess – wants his gratification immediately without laborious constructive efforts. He has to learn that having to put in such effort may ultimately bring its rewards, not immediately and not so excitingly maybe, but more satisfying and enduring in the long run.

Does the alcoholic drink in order to enable him to give expression to his repressed homosexual, or to his aggressive, tendencies? Does he hanker for 'mother's milk', or for the freedom from responsibility as in his infancy, or for some way 'out of' the prison-house of reality back to the Golden Age [88]? Is he attempting to become a more 'complete' or better integrated personality by trying to make up for some deficit in his mental or bodily make-up? Clearly the reasons will be different from person to person, but these are all questions which may have to be tackled from time to time in certain alcoholics, although in-depth psychotherapy may be needed in a very small number of alcoholics only.

One initial difficulty often arising in the treatment of alcoholics is their expectation that the therapist will do everything for them, that somehow he will be able to work a magical cure on them, while they, the alcoholic patients, can passively lean back in their armchairs possibly without being called upon to make any effort themselves. It often comes as a shock to the patient that there is no such miracle cure, and that in fact he himself is expected to carry out the most important part of the treatment programme, though naturally he will get support and help from staff and other patients. 'Recovery is a continuing effort not sudden magic,' as one patient put it.

The alcoholic shares his disappointment that there is no rapid wonder cure with the patient suffering from a neurosis (i.e. hysteria), with whom the alcoholic also has another feature in common. Both, while outwardly professing their willingness to be 'cured', are, underneath, quite unwilling to part with their illness. After all, their alcoholism or their neurosis represents an attempt at a self-cure, an effort to adapt themselves to reality and environment, and to cope with difficulties besetting them from within and without. Their alcoholic or neurotic 'solution' may be an attempt dictated by their unconscious, so that they are hardly aware of its nature; it is certainly not an ideal solution, and the 'cure' may in many ways be more painful than the original problems which it was designed to relieve, but anyhow by the use of this pseudo-solution they have managed to survive – to 'hang on'.

Alcoholics may not have sufficient trust in the therapist's ability to provide them with a better solution, and they may be afraid to throw away their old crutch, alcohol, treacherous though it may be, until the therapist can show them that he has a better crutch available for them. The alcoholic may feel that he might be able to endure sobriety but not to enjoy it. Thus, at the beginning of his treatment he may often say, 'Yes' on the surface only, and 'No' underneath; as Tiebout [86] has put it, he may outwardly 'comply' but he has not yet 'surrendered' to the need for treatment.

Understanding some of these difficulties may be of great value to the therapist as well as to the patient, who will have to learn that he cannot hope for a 'blitz-cure'. On the other hand, he will derive some consolation from the experience that after a few months' sobriety alcoholics generally begin to find it easier to stay sober. In the first few months, they often have to fight temptation, craving and nagging doubt whether, after all, they might not be able to drink in moderation – but later on 'craving' seems to assert itself less and less.

First relapses become progressively rarer after the alcoholic has successfully overcome the hurdles of the first six 'dry' months [89] and if an alcoholic breaks down for the first time months or years after having received treatment, the reason is usually no longer giving into an 'overwhelming' desire for drink (as he may often have done in the past) but rather overconfidence that 'surely after all these years of sobriety a drink won't do me any harm!'

Alcoholics themselves frequently are worried about their imagined 'lack' or 'loss' of willpower and think it a matter of honour to show they have regained it, by being able to drink in moderation. Thus, they squander all their energies in a vain attempt to overcome the subjectively often 'intolerable' hurdle of their 'lack of control' [90]. On the other hand, once he has accepted the necessity to live without alcohol, the alcoholic seems to be able to direct his energies and 'willpower', now freed, along with his abilities and assets, into constructive channels and become possibly more successful in his profession than he had ever been before. By itself, a combination of psychotherapy and just giving up drinking cannot have provided the recovered alcoholic with something that was not latent within him all the time; all that can have happened is that he has been helped to make use of some inner forces, some sources of strength within himself which, formerly, he had been unable to tap.

Related to the vain, energy-consuming struggle to regain their 'lost willpower' is the finding that frequently alcoholics feel much better once they have finally given up the effort to become moderate drinkers and have accepted the fact that drink for them is out of the question – as if they have been released from a heavy burden. The struggle being over, the way has now become free for them to channel their energies in the pursuit of attainable and more constructive goals than battling in vain with an adversary they could never beat. However, it is the great difficulty in accepting this fact – AA's First Step – that constitutes such a great hurdle for the alcoholic.

Among causes of relapse into drinking after a period of sobriety (more often 'dryness' rather than a state of emotional 'sobriety') may be states of tension or anxiety; in fact states of vague discomfort tension, and dissatisfaction are sometimes termed 'dry drunk' by AA members (see p. 349).

Many alcoholics seek instant solutions and cures; but they also want instant relief – here and now. They have no difficulty in promising to give up drink tomorrow. It is this tendency which, to some extent, the AA approach tries to counteract; but it is also for this reason that in many alcoholics disulfiram or Abstem are so helpful. However, many alcoholics object to taking it for this reason, fearing that should on a future occasion their need for relief prove 'overwhelming' the option is closed. Alcoholics often lack 'tolerance and impulse control'. *Antabuse* in such cases can often provide an exogenous aid. This knowledge, by a feedback mechanism (in the reverse manner from that described above), may often reduce or sometimes even remove that desire to drink.

The often heard cry 'I have given up drinking and nothing has changed' has to be forestalled by discussing with such people that it will take time before they begin to appreciate the long-term rewards of sobriety in contrast to the immediate reward of drinking. Additionally, many alcoholics proclaiming that death holds no fear for them, change their tune when they learn of the suffering caused by cirrhosis just as they may have justifiable aversion to the immediacy of the 'punishment' meted out by disulfiram-alcohol reaction. A combination of *Antabuse* (substituting for the lacking impulse-control), and the 'one day at a time' AA philosophy may help such drinkers initially to stay dry until they learn to control their impulses and to appreciate the positive rewards accruing from emotional 'sobriety'.

Alcoholics are not passive recipients at the mercy of their cravings, and should not adopt a passive, defeatist attitude, bolstered up by resentments, as a perfect alibi and a rationalisation to return to drinking. Resentment and self-pity, the 'poor me' syndrome as AA members call it, can be powerful feeders of rationalisations allowing relapses with less bad conscience. In treatment an analysis of the causes for relapse is usually much more important than that of causes for starting drinking. On analysing the cause for relapse, not only discussions but also psychodramatically acting-out of likely trigger or danger situations (the 'cues') in group sessions may often be helpful.

One important and often very helpful technique both in coping with and avoiding feelings of resentment – is that of trying to put oneself into the other person's shoes. 'My husband makes me very nervous – he drives me back to drink,' said one woman who had just left hospital. 'He follows me around everywhere I go – he wants to hold my handbag when I go to the "ladies"; he smells my breath when [in the theatre] I have come back from the "ladies" to my seat. Surely he should show me trust and encouragement?' But should she not realise that he could not possibly trust her so quickly? 'Practising' alcoholics (in very marked contrast from the no longer drinking 'retired' ones) are also highly practised and skilled liars. She has so often made promises and consistently broken them in the past that her husband could not possibly trust her immediately. She has to regain this lost trust by proving to herself (and thereby to her husband and to others) that this time she really will 'see it through'. By putting herself in the husband's shoes, she may avoid feelings of resentment because – though she may not yet agree with him – she can nevertheless understand how the position may look from his standpoint.

Alcoholism unfortunately, like other forms of drug dependence, has to be regarded as a relapsing disorder. This does not mean that from the start relapses are assumed to be inevitable, moreover they are not the end of the road if (not when) they occur. As we have seen conditions and situations which might possibly threaten an individual's peace of mind can sometimes be 'rehearsed' so that later on he should not be taken by surprise. However, in our experience, the most common cause of relapses – apart from not having accepted the necessity for total abstinence in the first place – is 'curiosity' (I would like to find out whether I can have one or two drinks). He may 'get away' with one or two drinks on the first occasion, only to increase the number until he has arrived, one or two weeks later, at the original situation of uncontrolled (or very inadequately controlled) heavy drinking.

There are a number of simple arguments which may prove helpful to such alcoholics. Many (quite wrongly) believe that the aim of treatment is never to experience a 'craving' again. They need to learn that feeling like a drink does not mean they have to have one; and that it is possible to keep off drink in spite of 'cravings'. They will then find it progressively easier to continue saying 'no' and possibly, in time, become deconditioned. It is obviously much easier to say 'no' to the desire before the first drink has been taken (psychological dependence) than after the first drink (when the physical dependence becomes an additional factor and with it the fear of, and desire to avoid the painfully remembered physical abstinence symptoms). It is important again to emphasise that, as alcoholism is a multifactorial disease, psychological factors have to be considered even when the alcoholic unwittingly has taken a drink; in other words, he need not hand himself over passively to the desires raised by the pharmacological effects of alcohol and his wish to 'feel' these effects having once again tasted the first drink. Such a drinker needs to keep foremost in his mind that the immediate but merely temporary rewards are outlasted and negated by long-term negative rewards. It is in this respect that more mature personalities who can think of the tomorrow start off with a strong initial advantage over the more impulsive, young problem drinkers. The range of psychotherapeutic techniques is very wide, and they all have been employed in the case of alcoholics. Thus, the therapist may adopt a very active, authoritative and supportive role, giving advice, reassurance, guidance; or he may, on the other hand, remain passive, being in the main a listener, giving occasional interpretations only; often he may change his roles from time to time, depending on the situation, the patient etc.

The methods employed will vary accordingly between those techniques which aim chiefly at supporting and reassuring the patient and those with the more ambitious goal to help the patient to get insight into the nature of his problems and conflicts and to undergo a change of attitudes and possibly of 'personality' functioning.

Three basic methods of psychotherapy are often combined. These were described seventy years ago by Bernard Hart [90] as persuasion based on logical reasoning; suggestion, an acceptance of ideas, etc. based on 'faith', 'in the absence of logically adequate grounds for their acceptance'; and, finally, analysis (including determination, rearrangement and readjustment of responsible causes).[3]

In an amusing article ('Which kind of psychotherapy?') Sarah Corrick [91] relates that she was taught as an undergraduate that there were three main schools of psychotherapy (Freud, Adler, Jung); 'a bewildering variety of psychotherapists' who for over forty years have been arguing which 'school' was the most effective. However, her own research has taught her that things were perhaps not as complicated as all that and that patients in southern England are usually treated 'by one of four main methods', i.e. behaviour therapists (see p. 388), traditional psychoanalysts; client-centred therapists (building up a secure relationship with patients who thereby feel encouraged freely to explore their feelings and attitudes); and cognitive reconstructing (where no emphasis is put on the unconscious, and the therapist is rather active). The one common active ingredient Miss Corrick found between all therapies was the 'therapeutic relationship', crucial to the success of treatment. Certainly trying to establish a therapeutic relationship is probably the most important task for anyone befriending, counselling, 'treating' or rehabilitating problem drinkers.

Group psychotherapy
The large number of alcoholics requiring and referred for treatment make it impossible in practice to treat by individual psychotherapy all those who may be in need of psychotherapeutic help. Partly for this reason, but partly also because of special factors, such as the urgent need of many alcoholics for resocialisation, group psychotherapy has found increasing recognition as a very valuable tool in the treatment of alcoholism [92].

Group therapy in some form or other must have taken place since time immemorial, for example whenever a leader or teacher was exercising his influence on followers or pupils. Yet it is only during the past thirty years or so that group psychotherapy has graduated into a fully recognised and consciously used method of treating patients.

Apart from its obvious economic advantage, group psychotherapy offers certain therapeutic prospects which cannot be realised in the more artificial atmosphere of individual therapy. It enables a more realistic 'living through' in the 'here and now' atmosphere of a more life-like setting, and it offers a more suitable background for the treatment of individuals whose chief defect centres on their 'social personality' and who experience marked difficulties in establishing or maintaining interpersonal relationships. As in individual psychotherapy, so also in group psychotherapy the goals may be limited or more ambitious, varying, for example, from practical guidance and intellectual stimulation at one end of the scale to emotional reorientation, insight and personality modification at the other.

In recent years, group therapy with alcoholics has been widely employed, both in hospitals and hostels as well as in an out-patient setting, and all types have been used, directive and non-directive techniques, didactic and suggestive, repressive-inspirational approaches, as well as analytical group therapy [93, 94].

For several reasons group therapy appears to be a very suitable means for treating alcoholics. Though there are many different personality types among them, they share a common overriding problem and their drinking past shows many similarities and many common experiences. Thus, patients may often see their own difficulties reflected in the experiences of others; a bond is easily established between them, and each group member readily finds a number of others with whom he can identify.

Furthermore, although no specific type of 'alcoholic personality' has been found to be responsible for causing alcoholism, character traits such as selfishness, intolerance, sensitivity, a low capacity to establish social relationships, to participate in social activities, defiance and feelings of grandiosity have frequently been described as occurring in a great many alcoholics. Group activities seem to form an antithesis and a suitable antidote to many of these qualities.

In groups formed by alcoholics, the alcoholic becomes an accepted member of a group of people who all 'speak the same language', he gets the feeling of 'belonging', he learns the need to contribute and to give just as well as to take, he participates in striving for a common goal, he helps others by, and while, trying to help himself. Where group therapy takes place as part of the treatment programme of a unit for alcoholics he learns to adapt himself to the dictates of reality in a community setting, and continual corrective emotional experiences while rubbing shoulders with each other all day long, day-in day-out, facilitate the growth of these often immature people in emotional stature [92].

Often the alcoholic may have started to drink in the first place as a passport to social acceptance and popularity and because he felt unable to form relationships without the help of a social lubricant. Group activities carried out within a therapeutic community in an alcohol unit – such as communal living, discussion, occupation, recreation, followed up by group sessions and AA meetings during rehabilitation after discharge – help the alcoholic in finding his way back to the community from which not only his personality problems but, often much more so, his drinking conduct has estranged him.

Compared to physical methods of treatment, group therapy has the advantage that the alcoholic himself gradually becomes a more and more active participant. To start with he may be silent and contented to sit back and listen, or be too inhibited to participate in the discussions, but gradually he takes a more and more active part. Group psychotherapy is thus a form of treatment carried out with, and to a large extent by, the patient, rather than treatment meted out to him. It seems to prepare him well for the task so helpful to him after discharge – to take an increasingly active interest in the welfare of fellow alcoholics and in the work of AA. The ability of establishing relationships, of tolerating frustration, of looking more objectively at their own motives and seeing the other person's point of view, often improves gradually in alcoholics whilst undergoing group therapy.

All groups in time develop what Slavson [95] calls their 'group code'. Group members not only give each other mutual support, but also help each other towards encouraging a feeling of responsibility for each other and the development of self-discipline, or at least by adhering to the unwritten laws of the group, rather than due to obedience to the rules laid down by the hospital authorities.

Among a group of alcoholics in an alcoholic community this group code and the 'brother's keeper' feeling are often very strong, and probably responsible for the fact that breaches of discipline, in spite of, or perhaps because of, a very permissive atmosphere, are the exception and not the rule as is the case when only one or two alcoholics are treated in a hospital. Thus such a group constituted predominantly by non-psychopathic alcoholics may even be able to 'carry' a few psychopaths and contribute to some slight – though perhaps only temporary – change in the latter's social attitudes and values.

However, it is probably more advisable to form separate groups of predominantly psychopathic and non-psychopathic alcoholics respectively with somewhat different therapeutic approaches and with a much more modest and less ambitious aim in the case of psychopaths.

The approach by group therapy as compared to individual psychotherapy seems to engender less anxiety and also comes less into conflict with the alcoholic's common attitude of distrusting and rejecting authority. For these reasons the alcoholic may be able to tolerate the group approach better than individual psychotherapy. Supported by the feeling of belonging to a group of people with similar problems the alcoholic may be better able to face the 'uncovering' process.

In psychotherapeutic groups of alcoholics, it is possible to approach alcoholism as a 'symptom' and as a 'disease' at one and the same time. The subjects discussed at such meetings may include personality conflicts and difficulties possibly originally responsible for the onset of excessive drinking as well as conflicts created *by* drinking, and problems arising out of the drinking behaviour. Difficulties in relationships emerging and observed in the patient's daily life in hospital form another set of subjects which patients will bring up at such meetings.

In general, the main emphasis of group psychotherapy, as for example carried out in the setting of an alcohol unit, should probably be more on the pre-alcoholic personality difficulties, leaving the task of coping with the drinking conduct problems more to AA, provided that there is close co-operation between such a unit and AA.

One incidental bonus attached to group therapy and the therapeutic community approach is the free flow of information and communication. Patients in an ordinary hospital frequently complain that they were told so little about their illness, its causation, treatment and prognosis. They are very resentful at not being treated like adults – a theme regarded as sufficiently important to warrant a recent discussion by a Nuffield Working Party on Communications with Patients [96]. Instead of being given instructions from the omniscient therapist, in group therapy patients may often find themselves in the role of therapist, encouraging others to work towards their own recovery as well as their own – communications taking place in an informal atmosphere. Patients when treated within this framework often develop a great deal of interest in all aspects of the problem, and express a wish to participate actively in the task of assisting fellow sufferers long after their own period of formal treatment has ended. Medical and other professional under- and postgraduate visitors are often surprised at the willingness of patients treated in a unit to discuss openly any aspects of their history and condition with such audiences.

Behavioural treatment
Although behavioural therapies, aimed at creating aversion have been in use in alcoholism for many years, such therapies (see p.

390) have greatly lost popularity recently. During the past decade, however, renewed attention has been given to behavioural therapies of alcoholism. The main reason for this is the conclusion that, as in the view of behaviourists, alcoholism is a *learned* disorder, and what has been learned can also be unlearned. According to this view, total abstinence is not necessarily the only approach in the treatment but there are alternative approaches, based on the possibility that at least some alcoholics can become 'controlled drinkers' (see p. 513). Among the more popular behavioural techniques (which may also appeal to common sense) are techniques such as teaching the drinker to become aware of conditions and situations which might act as trigger points or cues for relapses: for example, not to become overawed and too ashamed to ask for 'soft drinks' in company of beer and spirit drinkers; or teaching the drinker techniques to cope with anxiety and tension, which he could use instead of alcohol and other drugs; or for him to learn to tolerate withdrawal symptoms without automatically regarding them as necessitating drinking; or for the drinker to learn to estimate his own blood alcohol level and thus to keep his drinking down to moderate amounts; obviously some techniques are also very useful to therapists believing in the total abstinence goal.

In the view of Nathan and Briddell (1977) [97] the majority of behavioural researchers would probably agree with a 'Social learning theory'[3] as the best explanation of the development and the maintenance of excessive drinking, as put forward by Miller and Eisler (1975) [100]. They view alcohol and drug abuse as 'socially acquired behaviour patterns'; such behaviour patterns are maintained by a great number of 'antecedent cues and consequence reinforcers' – psychological, sociological or physiological in nature. Excessive drinking may be maintained not only by the ability of alcohol to reduce anxiety but also by the assistance it provides in gaining 'increased social recognition and peer approval', enhanced ability to exhibit more varied spontaneous social behaviour, and moreover because alcohol may be used to avoid the onset of the feared physiological abstinence symptoms following in the wake of alcohol withdrawal.

Nathan and Briddell present the following classification of the currently employed behavioural techniques in the treatment of alcoholism:

Table 12
*Behavioural techniques used in the treatment of
alcoholism*[4]

I Modifying the drinking response by:
    1 *Aversive conditioning* (see pp. 365–74)
       Electrical aversion
       Chemical aversion
       'Covert aversion' (or 'covert sensitisation' making use of aversive
       images and aversive scenes which the therapist provides or sets
       up for the patient)
    2 Operant methods
    3 Blood alcohol level discrimination training
II Modifying associated behavioural problems by:
       Systematic desensitisation (e.g. to reduce anxiety)
III Modifying the drinking response and associated behavioural problems
   by:
       Broad spectrum and multi-faceted therapies (aiming at combat-
       ing the various problems related to the drinker's problems)
IV Modifying the natural environment by:
    1 Community reinforcement counselling and contingency
       management (i.e. attempting to modify directly the drinker's
       interpersonal and environmental support systems, (e.g. by help-
       ing him to find a job, improve marital or social relationships,
       etc.))
    2 Management of behavioural contingencies by 'significant
       others' (as different from professional therapists) such as in-
       terested and helpful peers or wives

Nathan and Briddell's review gave the following answers to three
questions:

1 Is controlled drinking a viable goal for some alcoholics?
   Perhaps.
2 Is continued research on controlled drinking a legitimate
   pursuit for the behavioural researcher?
   Certainly.
3 Do we know enough to select patients for abstinence-
   oriented or controlled drinking-oriented treatment programmes on a national basis?
   No.

They add, however, that, in their view, controlled drinking
'may be almost the only viable treatment goal for some alcoholics'
(those who have tried and failed to achieve abstinence on repeated
occasions); but that, on the other hand, alcoholics who have

achieved abstinence 'should certainly not attempt to become social drinkers with these techniques as their therapeutic efficacy in this context has not been established'. They make a plea for continued support for research into treatment approaches to alcoholism from every possible angle, so that the resultant data becomes 'the final arbiter of the matter' and in passionate dispute between those who maintain that the 'disease alcoholism' can never be 'cured' in the sense that alcoholics can ever drink again, and others who believe that controlled drinking may well be within the grasp of quite a few or many alcoholics.

The family's attitude is very important to the success of a controlled drinking programme (as of any therapeutic plan): the family, too, must be deconditioned if the method is to have any chance of success.

Deconditioning would help to explain the (occasionally) better chances of drinkers succeeding if they change their circumstances: for example divorce from a spouse who has become conditioned to the drinker's failure; moving from an area where the drinker had become conditioned to drinking associations. However in the majority of such cases of 'geographic escape' much more is usually required than merely changing wife or home, a change of emotional attitude is needed, otherwise the drinker's (unchanged) attitudes – which had probably made a contribution to the development of his alcoholism in the past – are only too likely to exercise a negative influence in a new marriage and in new surroundings. Significant steps in growth in emotional maturity and social stabilisation of a drinker's personality are necessary to overcome the proneness to misuse of alcohol and to the development of dependence.

Combined behavioural and psychodynamic techniques

There are many features of the psychological management of alcoholics in which behavioural and psychodynamic approaches agree. The patient should be helped to discover what, for him, are the most dangerous internal and external cues which in the past have proved trigger points inducing him to resume heavy drinking; and to prepare him, as much as possible, to be forewarned. Possibly the most common reason given by alcoholics for their relapse is over-confidence leading to the belief that they can now resume moderate drinking with impunity. Another important point alcoholics need to remember is that they cannot rely on never again wanting a drink (which is a common experience in hospital). What they have to realise is that feeling like a drink is not synonymous with having one. People who have habitually relied on drink in all possible situations cannot realistically expect never again to want another, but provided they realise this, it is not an insurmountable hurdle.

Behavioural approaches deal with problems such as trying to overcome the urge to have a drink – for example, by learning to overcome impulsive drinking (often of course best avoided by alcohol-deterrent drugs), by concentrating on the long-term negative effects of drinking; discovering previous causes of relapses into drinking, and overcoming them by more constructive means, (i.e. finding preferable alternatives); avoiding (or minimising) contact with heavy drinkers and drinking haunts; asking the spouse to slow down her (or his) own heavy drinking, avoiding having drinks at home; among techniques recommended by behaviourists to those alcoholics aspiring to become controlled drinkers are avoiding pubs at lunchtime, going home late in the evenings etc., sipping (rather than gulping) and spacing drinks over a time, diluting drinks, avoiding spirits, setting a low target for a drinking session, carrying little money around, etc [101].

Some of the methods used by us over a number of years with such objects in mind, frequently (though not always), with (at least) partial success, include the following:

(a) `Disulfiram (or* ccc)` ,
1 Psychologically removes immediate availability of alcohol (the German 'Griffnähe').
2 Allows breathing space so that the positive part within the ambivalent self may reassert itself, or at least make its voice heard again.
3 Indirectly reduces the 'craving' because of the knowledge that immediate oblivion is only possible at the price of likely possibly severe distress.

(b) *The use of a diary*
Recording each time the drinker feels like a drink, or even only like giving up his disulfiram (without his doctor's advice). The advantage of such a diary is that, as a rule, when an alcoholic is asked how he came to have his first drink again, in spite of all his 'resolutions' (to himself) and promises (to others), he says: 'I do not know' or 'I can't remember'. Keeping a diary may prevent the alcoholic having a drink (or may delay resumption of drinking).

(c)   *Associating drinking with long-term punishment*
Instead of immediate positive rewards, in the long run this may often work in spite of initial failures.

(d)   *Balance sheet*
One such method was indicated by a recovered alcoholic doctor, at the 'International Doctors in AA' meeting of the New Jersey Chapter (Morristown, 1979). His speech was entitled 'Two hours of oblivion – This is what I obtained from drinking':
    the loss of wife and children,
    loss of home,
    loss of a number of excellent jobs,
    loss of friends,
    utter loss of self-respect,
    crashing several cars,
    and finally the loss of one eye in a car crash.

(e)   *Tranquillisers*
Although their use must be restricted in certain cases it may prove helpful in tense, anxious people. Having one tablet in one's pocket may psychologically help such a person to cope with a 'cue' that threatens to trigger a relapse. It should be possible, after a relatively short period, to discontinue these tablets once the drinker has learnt to regard an anxiety-inducing situation as something to be weathered without the help of drink.

(f)   *The 'so what' approach*
A girl afraid of blushing who is telling herself 'I must on no account blush', may find that this is the best way of inducing blushing. If she could learn to adopt the approach: 'so what does it matter if I do blush, it will not do me or anyone else any harm' – she may soon learn not to blush, as the *fear* of blushing was probably an important accessory factor in inducing the blushing.

Similarly the executive's fear of being tongue-tied in a meeting with his superiors, or his anxiety of performing well etc. (which leads him to drink) may be greatly reduced if he could envisage the consequences of not performing at his best, as not quite as earth-shattering as he fears.

(g)   *Very simple relaxation (including breathing exercises)*
These will, at the very least, remove the momentary preoccupa-

tion with his stress and direct it to mentally performing the exercises, while for example, sitting in the chair at a meeting.

The smoking drinker

Psychodynamic and behavioural techniques may be combined in the alcoholic who expresses a desire to receive help to rid himself from his concomitant dependence on smoking. Many alcoholics are also heavy smokers, and many continue or even increase their smoking after giving up drink. AA meetings are often shrouded in a haze of smoke while drinkers describe how they have learnt successfully to cope with their dependence on drink – continuing to ignore their dependence on nicotine. In alcohol units the question of doing something about smoking while grappling with drink problems is often discussed. Usually there is a divergence of opinion. Many alcoholics and their therapists feel that it is unfair to expect an alcoholic trying to overcome attachment to one addictive drug to attempt the same difficult task with an equally powerful addictive drug. A (usually) small minority of alcoholics feel that perhaps this is the time simultaneously to attack smoking dependence – but in group discussions they are usually outvoted by those who feel that smoking helps them concentrate on subjects discussed in the sessions, to endure their withdrawal pains, tensions and depression, and that outlawing smoking would force them to leave, which they did not want to do. In alcohol units compassionate therapists and therapeutic communities, shying away from an authoritarian approach, find it difficult arbitrarily to impose a 'no smoking' order on nicotine-dependent alcoholics.

Leaving the decision to forbid smoking in the unit, or at least at certain times or in certain rooms to the group itself may result in indecisive action (or no action). An alternative approach is to introduce gradually a code of 'smoking unwanted' because of its effect on fellow patients. Certainly, ignoring the problem does not seem the best method.

The finding that during their stay at a residential unit or during out-patient sessions, quite a number of alcoholic patients increase their smoking [14], only serves to underline their need to face up to this type of problem with more urgency than in the past.

(c) Alcoholics Anonymous – the understanding 'pal'

In many ways the dynamic uncovering approach of psychotherapy groups – aimed at giving the alcoholic some measure of insight into his personality conflicts and defects – is quite different but nevertheless complementary to the predominantly supportive and repressive-inspirational approach used by AA.

The latter aims at providing the alcoholic with an inspiration to adopt a way of life which is more acceptable to society and not destructive to himself; it is based on faith and suggestion. In Bernard Hart's words [90], 'the essential process in suggestion is an inhibition of conflicting ideas'. In theory the AA approach of keeping 'repressed' emotional conflicts out of consciousness sharply contrasts with the technique of analytical methods of encouraging free ventilation of any problem. However, provided the alcoholic patients are made aware of this essential difference between these two approaches, no great difficulty need arise from it.

In practice the analytically oriented hospital group therapy has often enabled alcoholics to accept the AA programme, though they had previously failed to do so, by clarifying problems which, in the first place, prevented their acceptance of AA. There may have been various factors at work. Such persons may have had many additional marked neurotic problems so that they were unable to see their way clear from obstacles by merely stopping drinking. They may have been 'individualists' or there may have been an 'intellectual' distrust of emotions and of what they may regard as 'exhibitionism' – and a desire to know more about the 'why' of their condition – an attitude which prevented them from taking to a predominantly suggestive approach.

In practice there is much overlapping between the two types of approach. Suggestion and support are obviously also at work when such patients undergo group therapy in hospital or a unit. On the other hand, the programme of AA based on its Twelve Steps includes, in the words of its co-founder, 'personality analysis and adjustment of personal relations', and aims at emotional growth and a modification of personality.

The continued support after discharge obtained from attending local AA groups is certainly of the greatest value in the rehabilitation phase. There can be no doubt that, whatever method may be preferred by the therapist in the treatment of his alcoholic patient, the most important and the most difficult part of the programme is this rehabilitation phase.

To sober up the drunk is not usually a very difficult task. To keep the alcoholic off drink whilst he is in a nursing home or in an open hospital ward is again relatively easy, even if he is frequently allowed out to his home during this period. It is much more difficult for the alcoholic to maintain sobriety once the active treatment has finished. A comprehensive therapeutic programme for alcoholism must, therefore, include provision for adequate after-care helping the alcoholic to maintain sobriety.

It is chiefly in the rehabilitation phase where anybody who is first called upon to help an individual alcoholic – whether he is a doctor, a clergyman, a social worker, a magistrate, a probation officer or a relative – can find an invaluable ally in AA. Of course, AA has helped – without any assistance from the 'professional' – a great number of alcoholics right from the time when they were in an acute bout of drinking, through the acute phase until, and throughout, the later rehabilitation period.

The recent upsurge of interest, concern and sympathy for the fate of the alcoholic is to a large extent due to the spectacular success achieved by this fellowship of laymen, themselves sufferers from alcoholism. In many cases they succeeded when all other agencies had lamentably failed.

In the past many alcoholics may have recovered, but as a rule they kept quiet about their past history, and so the popular picture of the alcoholic was of the one who failed to make the grade and went downhill. AA members, on the other hand, though not divulging their names, proclaim to the world at 'open' and 'public' meetings (which are often open to relatives, friends and the public at large) to what depths they had formerly sunk (indeed, in the view of some, they overdo this at times) and how AA had helped them to make a comeback. AA has thus provided the astonished professional and lay public with many thousands of visual demonstrations that alcoholics in their thousands want to recover and are able to achieve, and to maintain, sobriety. They thus have given the lie to the notion of doom and gloom which so long has clung to the fate of alcoholics.

Setting out without any special qualifications and without any special professional knowledge often ignored, rejected, or despised, these alcoholic lay people, observing themselves and their friends closely, found that they had one vital asset which, to alcoholics, seemed to be more important in many respects than advantages which might be brought to them through professional knowledge and skill.

The alcoholic's asset was in fact the very thing that had previously been his downfall: he had been 'there' himself, he spoke the same language as those whom he was trying to help. He could, therefore, be instrumental in bridging the gap which for so long had prevented the alcoholic from making contact with his neighbour and the world with which he has lost touch.

In AA the alcoholic could, once again, get the feeling of belonging, the knowledge that he was not a unique phenomenon, not an outcast but an individual struck by disease like many others. He would find that by sticking to other alcoholics they could help him, and that he could assist them, to stay sober.

From observations such as these, within a few years the Programme of Recovery was born, as laid down in the Twelve Steps. Out of the experience gained by the first few alcoholics who were successful in this way, there gradually evolved all the 'prescriptions' and slogans handed out by AA to any alcoholic willing to avail himself of them, such as the 'twenty-four-hours programme', 'first things first', 'live and let live', 'easy does it', etc., the practice of an experienced AA member acting as a 'sponsor' for the newcomer, the 'twelve stepping' practice by which the AA man helps the still-struggling alcoholic, and thereby also helps himself to stay sober.

AA has its main following in North America where it started. The USA and Canada had by 1969 over 10,000 groups, apart from approximately 650 hospital and 900 prison groups. Outside North America, AA then had approximately 3350 groups. Ten years later the USA had nearly 19,000 groups with an estimated membership of over 350,000. Canada had over 3150 groups with over 50,000 members. Outside America there were almost 8750 groups with 150,000 members, including 1250 groups in Great Britain with an estimated membership of 18–20,000. The total membership worldwide in Spring 1979, was estimated to be over 560,000, belonging to approximately 31,000 groups – excluding hospital and prison groups.

As AA has no membership lists (a great many drinkers just 'float in' occasionally, and so on), any estimates of membership of AA may be as impossible to give with any degree of accuracy as, say, the cost of alcoholism in industry.

In 1969, England and Wales had approximately 250 groups, plus eighteen hospital groups and forty-two groups in prisons, and new groups were founded continually. Scotland by 1968 had eighty-four groups, Northern Ireland twenty-two and the Republic of

Twelve Suggested Steps of Alcoholics Anonymous

1 We admitted we were powerless over alcohol—that our lives had become unmanageable.

2 Came to believe that a Power greater than ourselves could restore us to sanity.

3 Made a decision to turn our will and our lives over to the care of God *as we understood Him*.

4 Made a searching and fearless moral inventory of ourselves.

5 Admitted to God, to ourselves and to another human being the exact nature of our wrongs.

6 Were entirely ready to have God remove all these defects of character.

7 Humbly asked Him to remove our shortcomings.

8 Made a list of all persons we had harmed, and became willing to make amends to them all.

9 Made direct amends to such people wherever possible, except when to do so would injure them or others.

10 Continued to take personal inventory and, when we were wrong, promptly admitted it.

11 Sought through prayer and meditation to improve our conscious contact with God *as we understood Him*, praying only for knowledge of His will for us and the power to carry that out.

12 Having had a spiritual awakening as the result of these steps we tried to carry this message to alcoholics and practise these principles in all our affairs.

The Twelve Traditions of Alcoholics Anonymous

1 Our common welfare should come first; personal recovery depends upon AA unity.

2 For our group purpose there is but one ultimate authority—a loving God as He may express himself in our group conscience. Our leaders are but trusted servants—they do not govern.

3 The only requirements for AA membership is a desire to stop drinking.

4 Each group should be autonomous, except in matters affecting other groups or AA as a whole.

5 Each group has but one primary purpose—to carry its message to the alcoholic who still suffers.

6 An AA group ought never endorse, finance or lend the AA name to any related facility or outside enterprise lest problems of money, property and prestige divert us from our primary spiritual aim.

7 Every AA group ought to be fully self-supporting, declining outside contributions.

8 Alcoholics Anonymous should remain forever non-professional, but our service may employ special workers.

9 AA, as such, ought never to be organised; but we may create service boards or committees directly responsible to those they serve.

10 Alcoholics Anonymous has no opinion on outside issues; hence the AA name ought never to be drawn into public controversy.

11 Our public relations policy is based on attraction rather than promotion; we need always to maintain personal anonymity at the level of press, radio and films.

12 Anonymity is the spiritual foundation of all our Traditions, ever reminding us to place principles above personalities.

Ireland sixty-five groups.

In the British Isles, after thirty years' experience, AA has approximately 20,000 members of whom one-third are women (compared with one-fifth in 1972) – the proportion of female members is steadily increasing. By 1978 there were 1250 groups in Great Britain and AA meetings were held in 130 hospitals and 101 prisons and penal establishments in England, Scotland and Wales. The average age of members had fallen between 1971–8 from forty-seven to forty-four – those aged under twenty-five were reported to make up 1 per cent of the membership. This seems to be much smaller than might be expected from the considerable rise of alcohol use and misuse among relatively younger age groups. It would seem, therefore, that AA does not attract an equally high proportion of younger people as among the older problem drinkers, and research in this area is surely indicated (see below). Could this perhaps be partly due to the emphasis in AA literature and at AA meetings on the fairly advanced alcoholic with well established patterns of alcohol dependence, to the relative neglect of the early stages? On the other hand women are joining AA in increasing numbers – perhaps in the proportion of 4:10.

A survey (1978) carried out in 400 American AA groups showed that of its women members one-third were in sales, secretarial and clerical jobs; 28 per cent were housewives and 2 per cent managers. Others, including unskilled workers, totalled 6 per cent. To what extent such proportions reflect the proportions among women alcoholics in general is unknown, since many factors determine why and when certain female alcoholics join AA whereas others fail to do so.

Interesting findings were obtained by a number of surveys of the active membership of AA (i.e. of members who attend meetings frequently), carried out since 1968 by the General Service Office of AA in New York. The most recent of these surveys, carried out in 1977, was of over 1500 alcoholics in the USA and Canada and was regarded by the organisers as 'representative of the entire AA population', similar questionnaires having been submitted to six other countries (three in South America and three in Europe). Average length of sobriety ranged from forty months (Finland) to forty-nine months in the Hispano-American countries.

There was evidence for changes of certain characteristics of the AA membership from trends shown over the nine year period of the four surveys. The percentage of female members in North

America rose from 22–29 per cent; the percentage of newer female members (joining since 1974) being one in three. Similarly, the percentage of younger people (thirty years or less) in North America increased from 7.6 per cent (1974) – 11.3 per cent (1977). In the other countries the increase in younger members between 1974–7 was from 11–13 per cent.

The survey indicated that 18 per cent of members responded positively to the question of having been addicted to other drugs. Corresponding to our own impressions in Britain [89], twice as many women (28 per cent) as men and more than twice as many young people aged thirty years and less (43 per cent were among the 'other drug' addiction group). About 50 per cent of newcomers to AA who attend meetings regularly for a period of three months are believed to stay sober for the next year. Attending a few meetings only, in the view of AA, is not regarded as having 'tried' AA.

In Britain alcoholics interested in joining AA should have no difficulty in finding groups wherever they live; anyone requiring any information about their work can easily get it from the Central Service Office, London (p. 535).

In the London area 'closed' meetings (which unlike the 'open' and 'public' meetings are open to alcoholics only) are held every day. There are many meetings at daytime and weekends as well as the regular evening meetings. Interested people should 'shop around' various meetings till they find the type of group most congenial to them (for example, some may prefer meetings where there is greater emphasis on a free-floating discussion, others prefer groups where there is less interaction, etc.).

Al-anon

What AA is for the alcoholic, Al-Anon is for his family. Al-Anon provides help for families of problem drinkers [103]. According to a recent article [104] Al-Anon started in Britain in 1960 with ten groups. Among the first such groups was one started at Warlingham Park Hospital in the mid-sixties by spouses of patients treated in the alcohol unit at the hospital; nowadays the world fellowship numbers 15,000 groups. There are about 500 groups in the UK and Eire; and – as in the case of AA – 'loners' finding themselves in an area where there is no group can be put in touch with the members of the fellowship, after getting in touch with the London office (see p. 532). Like AA, Al-Anon is financed by voluntary contributions and profits from sale of their literature. Seven books and over forty pamphlets have been published by Al-Anon and translated into many languages.

Though naturally there is close co-operation between Al-Anon and AA they form quite separate organisations. Alateen is described as being 'a part of Al-Anon' designed to assist young people in the age groups 12–20 who have an alcoholic relative.

The aim of Al-Anon is to assist 'families, friends and working colleagues' of the alcoholic 'to come to terms with the problem as it affects them'. Al-Anon members often tell no one that in the past their alcoholic relative had usually made them angry, bitter, putting them into a retaliatory mood involving them in sterile, bitter, fruitless arguments; they had allowed themselves to be goaded into rows and hostile language which could then be used by the alcoholic to rationalise his own behaviour (which usually may have started these arguments in the first place) and his return to further drinking. 'Practising' alcoholics are indeed past masters in the art of manipulation.

It is in such situations that Al-Anon can be of the greatest help to a long-suffering spouse. They realise that their own reactions and their feelings of utter helplessness and bewilderment are shared by countless others – all equally baffled by the alcoholic relative's behaviour, all have arrived at a stage of doubting their own sanity and all are at a complete loss to know where to go next. As members explain, Al-Anon teaches them to detach themselves from the problem though not from the alcoholic relative; and rather than concentrating on 'curing' the alcoholic they learn not to have their own lives ruined by fruitless arguments and daily confrontations with the drinker.

In the group meetings of Al-Anon, 'members learn through the mutual exchange of experience, and receive comfort and understanding, strength and hope. The sharing of problems binds individuals and groups together in a bond that is protected by a policy of anonymity' [103]. In all these aspects the process is identical with the dynamics of AA meetings.

Over the past few years, the concept of problem drinkers as people in need of understanding and help has gained ground. In contrast, however, although lip-service is commonly paid to the notion of alcoholism being an illness of the family (and not merely of the drinker alone) in practice the state of the alcoholic's spouse is often ignored partly because they have no idea who possibly is in a position to advise and assist them. People who have not actually experienced, or witnessed the emotional and behavioural turmoil arising from the unpredictable behaviour of alcoholics, find it impossible to appreciate fully the quandary in which the alcoholic's family finds itself. Often the statements made by alcoholics' spouses seem so unbelievable that outsiders suspect them to be grossly exaggerated. Not uncommonly even parents of the alcoholic do not believe the description which their frantic and despairing daughter-in-law gives about the behaviour of her husband: they only know him as a sober, usually well-behaved, son who would not harm a fly.

Al-Anon has pioneered a vital, constructive, humane and understanding approach to the problems of the alcoholic's family. In Al-Anon, the family is freed from the feelings of isolation, helplessness and guilt and gains instead the feeling of belonging to a sharing, understanding fellowship that provides strength to endure the painful present, and means of coping with it in a constructive manner, and hope for a better future. As necessary as AA has proved for hundreds of thousands of alcoholics the world over, so Al-Anon is needed to provide support for their families.

Alateen

A full description of the work of Alateen has been given in Edith Lynn Hornik's book *You and your Alcoholic Parent* (1974) [105].

Before the existence of Alateen, teenage children of alcoholics often accompanied their non-alcoholic parent to Al-Anon meetings. The teenagers' inhibitions of discussing problems in front of one (i.e. the non-drinking) parent gave rise, in 1957, to the formation of Alateen, which aims at assisting those who have to live with an alcoholic parent 'to regain their inner strength and stability'. The methods used and the 'dynamisms' at work closely resemble those of AA and Al-Anon. Such youngsters, who are bewildered and torn between conflicting loyalties, no longer feel alone but find emotional and active support by sharing their experiences with others. Alateen also makes use of the 'Twelve Steps', and the 'one day at a time' approaches.

Social therapy

The alcoholic does not live in a vacuum. His family is closely affected; his wife may require help; and after the alcoholic leaves hospital he needs the assistance of an understanding family. His relatives have to learn to adjust to the changed and still changing person.

He will – if he stays sober – keep on changing for months and years to come as the rehabilitation process is long and there may be pitfalls and relapses. Difficulties have usually arisen at work, and help may be needed with negotiations with the alcoholic's old or prospective employer. Often the alcoholic will want to take unsuitable employment, e.g. as a barman. Debts may have accumulated, or the alcoholic may have nowhere to live after leaving hospital.

Just as social factors may contribute their share to pushing the drinker on the road to alcoholism, so their handling later may either hinder or contribute to his rehabilitation. The main share will fall to the social worker, but other members of the therapeutic team can assist a great deal. For example, the nurse in her conversation with visiting relatives can do a lot to help change their own often grossly misconceived notions and prejudices about the nature of alcoholism. This is an extremely important task, as to alcoholics the attitude of their human environment matters more than the state of the material environment.

Environmental manipulation

In treatment the primary and main factor is, naturally, the attempt to induce in the alcoholic an earnest and sincere desire to come to grips with his drinking and other problems. More often than not, it will be difficult to change the environment. The alcoholic will, therefore, have to learn to cope with the inevitable difficulties and to learn to live with those conditions which he will find it impossible to alter.

He may, in the past, have tried the method of 'geographic escape', changing domicile, jobs, friends, perhaps even his wife, only to find that, even under the altered circumstances and in new surroundings, his old difficulties kept cropping up again, provoked by his own attitudes and behaviour, and by his own impulsive and irresponsible reactions to problems. On the other hand, he may often find to his surprise that family, friends and boss – all the 'significant others' who not so long ago were 'quite impossible' – seem to have changed a great deal – to have grown more understanding, more sympathetic and more helpful than in the past – once he has given up drinking and once he has acquired some measure of insight into his tendency to rationalise and to project.

The alcoholic, having decided to give up drinking, needs help and understanding from those around him, from his family, his friends, his boss and fellow employees, as well as the community at large. Better education of the public about difficulties facing the alcoholic will thus be a very important part of the task of environmental manipulation in the programme of the alcoholic's rehabilitation. Then, the emotional climate in which the alcoholic will live and work will become a much more favourable one than the generally non-understanding, hostile and rejecting one which he so often meets nowadays.

To help family or employer appreciate the alcoholic's problems is, from among the members of the therapeutic team, chiefly the task of the social worker. Personnel officers, once they have some information and understanding of the problems involved, often become very interested in the problem and may take a personal interest in alcoholic employees. Once a firm has had good experience with an alcoholic engaged by them through the offices of the social worker, it may not be too difficult to place other patients. In time, having established good relationships with a number of firms, the unit's or clinic's social worker may be able to find employment for quite a number of patients, and the personnel officer may turn out to be personally interested in their fate. However, the man who advertised in a national newpaper to the effect that he was an alcoholic and a member of AA may appear to be unduly over-optimistic in his expectation that this fact would make it easier for him to find a job!

The fear of encountering difficulties in finding a suitable job is one which rests heavily on the minds of alcoholics who are undergoing treatment. In general, these patients themselves feel that it may be better not to volunteer the fact that they are alcoholics, if only because the prospective employer has little idea what this term means. When asked directly, however, the alcoholic would have to admit the fact, hoping that the employer will be like the one who told one alcoholic ex-patient of ours: 'I do not mind the alcoholic who knows he is one; what I am afraid of is the alcoholic who does not know it!' It has been the experience of a great many alcoholics that once they had held their job for a period of months or years it did not matter any more when employers then learned the fact that they had an alcoholic on their payroll. On the contrary, at the time it often seemed to produce some measure of admiration.

In many cases a psychologist's evaluation of the alcoholic's intellectual, education and performance assets, perhaps with a view to vocational guidance and a training course in a rehabilitation centre, may be called for.

Generally, it will be preferable for the alcoholic to try to find a new circle of friends, instead of returning to his old drinking companions and his old haunts. Sometimes a change of employment may be needed – for example, with jobs such as waiter, barman or merchant seaman, independent of whether the alcoholic had originally chosen these jobs because he liked the surroundings and opportunities to drink, or whether he had been tempted and encouraged to drink to excess only after finding himself in such jobs.

Often alcoholics are only too keen to look again for such occupations or have a yearning to return to those places overseas where they had been drinking formerly, and where drink is still the European's main pastime. Sometimes, indeed, for example in the case of a publican, it may be impossible for the alcoholic to avoid returning to the same old circumstances in spite of the difficulties and obstacles they present to his sobriety. Yet there are many publicans who since accepting the need for keeping off drink have managed to do so without great difficulties.

Anyway, the alcoholic cannot expect the whole world to change to his liking, and he will have to learn to live with reality and the world as it is. Two hundred years ago Dr Benjamin Rush wrote: '"Taste not, handle not, touch not", should be inscribed upon every vessel that contains spirits in the house of a man who wishes to be cured of habits of intemperance.' However, in general, the great majority of alcoholics who have managed to remain sober prefer their wives and friends to go on drinking if they have done so in the past, to keep drink in their homes for the entertainment of their friends, and to pour out these drinks themelves. The alcoholic has to realise that he cannot expect the whole world to stop drinking, he has to learn to live in, and with, a world in which drinking is socially accepted, and to adjust himself to living contentedly in this world rather than asking his family and all his friends to adapt and make allowances for his vulnerability by their also becoming teetotallers.

'Retired' alcoholics who have years of sobriety behind them may often be called upon to help 'practising' alcoholics who have got into difficulties in pubs while drinking, and they may then enter public houses without it, apparently, presenting any special problems for them. But there is a difference between an alcoholic who is still struggling and still ambivalent and the man who has remained sober for years. On the whole, it seems very much better for the alcoholic to attempt to find hobbies, entertainments and some way of spending his leisure time other than frequenting bars and pubs.

The question of whether it is safe or advisable for an alcoholic to visit public houses is often brought up in discussion. Many alcoholics claim that they like going to public houses, not because of the drink, but because of the 'atmosphere'. This is, of course, the same argument with which alcoholics, at the beginning of their drinking career, deceive themselves that it is the place and the environment in which they drink that attract them, and not any special virtues that they see in imbibing alcohol. The general opinion seems to be that it is much wiser for the alcoholic who has just started his sobriety to keep away from places and social occasions which may centre chiefly on drinking, where he can avoid it. Some, of course, will have to attend such functions and public houses in the course of their duties. But otherwise it seems preferable for alcoholics not to go out of their way to invite temptation.

In women alcoholics where, possibly, exogenous precipitating factors are often more important than in men, manipulation of environmental conditions may assume an important role. Merely to give up drinking may not be sufficient, leaving a woman with all the dissatisfactions, tension and loneliness which had driven her to drink. Assisting in finding her a congenial job, a suitable place to live, and friends – all this may make a lot of difference in her future life. This is necessary in particular as the alcoholic woman may find the way back more difficult, and many more doors barred to her, than her male counterpart, due to society's less tolerant attitude towards women alcoholics.

When the alcoholic first comes for treatment, a change of environmental circumstances is usually all he thinks necessary for him to alter his drinking pattern. 'Everything would have been all right if only my wife had stopped nagging', or 'if I had not been single', 'if my boss would not be so unfair and burden me with so much (or give me so little) responsibility', 'if I did not have to work so hard', or 'if I did not have so much spare time on my hands'.

One of the aims of psychotherapy in alcoholics consists in making them realise that what may often matter much more than their material circumstances and environment is the reaction and attitude they adopt towards them. Without such a change of heart, change of environmental conditions will do little good for them.

Two hundred years ago Dr Rush wrote about the treatment of alcoholics: '. . . some men drink only in the morning, some at noon, and some at night. Some . . . only on market day, some at one tavern only, and some only in one kind of company. Now, by finding a new and interesting employment or subject of conversation for drunkards at the usual times in which they have been accustomed to drink, and by restraining them by the same means from those places and companions which suggested to them the idea of ardent spirits, their habits of intemperance may be completely destroyed.'

In the case of alcoholics such hopes may often seem to be unduly optimistic and unrealistic. These methods may be of some help to the self-indulgent, heavy drinker who drinks from choice, but by themselves such measures will usually not be sufficient in the case of the compulsive alcoholic. Even so, however, as an additional measure to psychological and physical treatments in a comprehensive programme for the alcoholic, the advisability of attempts at changing the alcoholic's environmental conditions, at home and work, both in its human and in its material aspects, has to be considered in each case as an integral part.

Evaluation of treatment programmes

In spite of the understandable desire by therapists and patients alike to see further facilities established on the model of those which have had initial success and have found acceptance and popularity with patients, it is obviously necessary to have programmes – and, in particular, outcome-evaluation studies – carried out before declaring any one method as 'the' (or even as one likely) answer. Questions are important as to whether the programme and the methods – or which of its components – contributed to the final result [106]; and what in fact are the results. Apart from the components in a treatment programme regarded as important by the therapist, many other factors influencing the outcome; such as the therapist's own vested interest in the success of 'his' method, his relationship with the patient, the 'atmosphere' of the facility, the pervasive therapeutic (or non-therapeutic) *milieu*, the types of patient and their 'motivation', the support (or otherwise) which such patients receive from their families. Ethical questions are obviously closely involved, for example, in the case of controlled trials of drugs, the information given to patients about the nature of the trials, placebo administration, and so on. Questions relating to evaluation of alcoholism programmes were well discussed in detail in 1976 by Rossi and Filstead [106] and Schuckitt and Cahalan [107] in 1976.

Notes

[1] The 'major tranquillisers' (i.e. mainly the phenothiazines) do not lead to dependence, and the benzodiazepines ('minor tranquillisers') only rarely so. Tranquillisers with a definite risk of dependence (and therefore best avoided in alcoholics [14] include methaqualone (*Mandrax*), meprobamate (*Equanil, Miltown*), gutethimide (*Doriden*), chloropromazine (*Largactil*), promazine (*Sparine*), thiodazine (*Melleri*), chlormethiazole (*Heminevrin*) and the benzodiazepines. Among the latter chlordiazepoxide (*Librium*) and diazepam (*Valium*) are the most popular, but the list of available preparations has now greatly lengthened. Recently a difference has been made between long-acting (plasma half-life of drug and active metabolites lasting longer than ten hours) and short-acting benzodiazepines [15]. Chlordiazepoxide, diazepam, chlorazepate (*Tranxene Frisium*), flurazepam (*Dalmane*), medazepam (*Nobrium*) and nitrazepam (*Mogodon*), are long-acting; lorazepam (*Ativan*), oxazepam (*Serenid*), temazepam (*Normison*), and triazolam (*Hacion*) are short-acting. They are undoubtedly of great value in the acute phases. In severe cases and DT parenteral therapy may be required and often leads to rapid amelioration of the symptoms [12, 13].

[2] This section is based on a talk given at the twenty-first International Institute on the Prevention and Treatment of Alcoholism in Helsinki, June 1975, and reproduced here by kind permission of the ICCA (and the Editor of the *British Journal of Addiction*).

[3] Transactional analysis in some ways resembles psychoanalytic therapy. TA analyses relationships between people as 'games that people play' and in which 'sick' people and alcoholics often lose out. Greater awareness through TA should help people to play less harmful games.

[4] The Australian sociologist Dr Margaret Sargent [98], also includes social control as a cause of a social learning process and thus as among the cases of deviant behaviour, similar to the 'amplification of deviance' theory of American and British authors [99] including alcoholism. According to her 'Power Relations Theory', powerful political groups' social pressures on subordinate groups make the latter drink heavily, thus helping maintain the *status quo* of society with its inequality between dominant and subordinate groups. She defines

alcoholism as the 'role into which socially disapproved heavy drinkers are thrust by more powerful persons who use the term so as to justify the exercise of social control such as jailing, hospitalising or firing'.

5   This table is based on the description given by Peter E Nathan and Dan W Briddell in their chapter 'Behavioural Assessment and Treatment of Alcoholism', in *The Biology of Alcoholism* (ed. Benjamin Kissin and Henri Beglieter), vol. 5, pp. 301–49, New York, London, Plenum Press, 1977.

References

1   *Alcohol and Alcoholism* (1979), Report of a Special Committee of the Royal College of Psychiatrists, London, Tavistock, 117, 145
2   Glatt, M M (1955), *Brit. J. Addict*, 52, 55
3   Department of Health and Social Security (1975), *Better Services for the Mentally Ill*, London, HMSO
3a   Advisory Council on Alcoholism (1978), *The Pattern and Range of Services for Problem Drinkers*, London, DHSS and Welsh Office
4   Glatt, M M (1967), 'Alcoholism in Britain', in *New Aspects of the Mental Health Services* eds Freeman, H and Farndale, J, Oxford, Pergamon, 115–48
5   Glatt, M M (1979), *The Lancet*, i, 814
6   Dent J Y (1947), *Anxiety and its Treatment*, Belfast, Mullan
7   Glatt, M M (1960), *J. Coll. Gen. Pract.*, 3, 292
8a   Macdonald, A B and Patel, A R (1975), *Brit. med. J.* 1, 430
8b   Barber, J H *et al.* (1975), *ibid*, 1, 431
9   Moyes, I (1980), SK & F Publications, 3 (2), 10
10a Glatt, M M (1959), *Brit. med. J.*, 1, 50
10b Glatt, M M (1959), *ibid* 2, 1100
11   Glatt, M M (1962), *Bull. Narcot.* (UN) 14, 19
12   Blair, D (1963), *Modern Drugs for the Treatment of Mental Illness*, London, Staples Press
13   Dally, P (1967), *Chemotherapy of Psychiatric Disorders*, London, Logos Press
14   Glatt, M M (1974), *A Guide to Addiction and its Treatment*, Lancaster, MTP
15   Committee on the Review of Medicines (1980), *Brit. med. J.*, 280, 910
16   Glatt, M M, George, H R and Frisch, E P (1965), *Brit. med. J.*, 2, 401
17   Chlormethiazole (1966), ed. Frisch, E P, *Acta psychiat. Scand.*, 42, suppl. 192
18   Glatt, M M (1976), 22nd Internat. Inst. Prev. and Treatm. of Alcoholism, ICCA, Vigo, Spain
19   Gross, M M, Lewis, E and Hastey, J (1974) in *The Biology of*

Alcoholism, ed. Kissin, B and Begleiter, H, New York, London, Plenum, 191–264

20   Keup, W (1977), Dtsch. Arztebl., 74, 30, 1903

21   Glatt, M M (1980), *Fortschritte der Medizin*, 98, 784

22   *Brit. med. J.* (L.A.) 1980, 281, 507

22a Jefferys, D B *et al.* (1980), *The Lancet*, i, 308

23   Home Office (1971), *Habitual Drunken Offenders*, London, HMSO

24   Arroyave, E *et al.* (1980), *Health Trends*, DHSS and Welsh Office, 12, 36

25   Hamilton, J R, *et al.* (1977) *Health Bull.*, Edinburgh, 35, 146

26   Sir George Young, 11 June, 1979

27   Willems, J P A *et al.* (1973), *Brit. J. Psychiat.*, 122, 637

28   Glatt, M M (1955), *Brit. J. Addict.*, 52, 55

29   Glatt, M M (1976), *Nursing Mirror* (15 January), 59

30   Glatt, M M (1967), *Brit. J. Addict.*, 62, 35

31   Arroyave, F and McKeown, S (1979), *Brit. J. Hosp. Med.*, 604

32   Pattison, E M (1966), *Quart. J. Study. Alc.*, 27, 49

33   Hobson, J A (1952), *Brit. J. Addict.*, 49, 5

34   Letemendia, F J J *et al.* (1973), *World Psychiatric Assoc. Sympos.*, Madrid

35   Orford, J (1973), *Behav. Res. and Therapy*, 11, 565

36   Tiebout, H M (1954), *Quart. J. Stud. Alc.*, 15, 610

37   Hazelden Publication, *The Dry-Drunk Syndrome*, Minnesota, Hazelden Foundation

38   Asher, R (1958), *The Lancet*, i, 954

39   Pattison, E M, Sobell, M B and Sobell, L C (1977), *Emerging Concepts of Alcohol Dependence*, New York, Springer, 4

40   Sobell, M B (1978), *Amer. J. Drug and Alcohol Abuse*, 5(3), 286

41   Pittman, D J and Tate, R J (1972), *Internat. J. Social Psychiat.*, 18, 189

42   Ewing, J A and Rouse, B A (1976), *Brit. J. Addict.*, 71, 123

43   Robinson, D (1972), *Quart. J. Stud. Alc.*, 33, 1028

44   Robinson, D (1976), *From Drinking to Alcoholism: A Sociological Commentary*, *Brit. J. Addict.*

45   Glatt, M M (1957), *ibid*, 54, 47

46   Moss, E C and Davies, E B (1967), *A Survey of Alcoholism in an English County*, Cambridge, Geigy (UK)

47   Shaw, S (1979), *Brit. J. Addict.*, 74, 339.

48   Jellinek, E M (1960), *The Disease Concept of Alcoholism*, Connect., Hillhouse Press

49   Brit. med. Assoc. (1965), *The Drinking Driver*, London, BMA

50   Glatt, M M (1965), 11th Europ. Inst. Prev. Treatm. of Alcoholism, Selected Papers, Oslo, 14–25 June; ICAA 59–65; (*Brit. J. Addict.* 1967), 62, 35

51   Saunders, B and Richards, G (1978), *Brit. J. Addict.*, 73, 375

52   Clare, A (1980), *Proceed. Roy. Soc. Med.*, 73, 526

53a Glatt, M M and Judge, C G (1961), *Med. J. Australia*, 24, 590

53b Glatt, M M and Judge, C G (1961), *ibid.*, 24, 686

54 Glatt, M M (1972) in 30th Internat. Congress Alcoholism, Abstracts Amsterdam

55 Glatt, M M (1974) in Proceed. First Internat. Med. Confer. Alcoholism (eds N. Kessel *et al.*), London, B Edsall & Co., 122–32

56 Popham, R G and Schmidt, W S (1978), *Alcoholism* (Zagreb-Lausanne), 14(1), 3

57 Sobell, M B and Sobell, J (1975), *Alcoholism*, 10(1), 5

58 Glatt, M M (1976), *Brit. J. Addict.*, 71, 135

59 *The Lancet* (L.A.) 1975, i, 151

60 Rosch, W (1974), *Fortschritte der Medizin*, 92, 316

61 Glatt, M M (1975), *The Lancet*, i, 447

62 Drewery, J, *J. Alcoholism* (London) 9, 143

63 Miles, K C *et al.* (1971), *Behav. Ther.*, 2, 18

64 Lamy, J *et al.* (1973), *Clin. Chim. Acta*, 49, 189

65 Asnaes, S (1974), Ugeskr. Laeg., 136, 130

66 Wessely, P *et al.* (1973), Wien. Z. Nervenheilkunde, 31, 63

67 Lishman, W A *et al.* (1980), in *Addiction and Brain Damage* (ed. D Richter), 215–27

68 Sargant, W (1949), *Proceed. Roy. Soc. Med.* 42, 3

69 Williams, L (1956) London, Edinburgh, Livingstone

70 Glatt, M M (1965), *J. Irish Med. Assoc.*, 57, 67

71 Vaillant, G E (1980), in *Alcoholism Treatment in Transition* ed. G Edwards and M Grant), London, Croom Helm, 13–31

72 Frank, J D (1961), *Persuasion and Healing: A Comparative Study of Psychotherapy*, Baltimore, John Hopkins Univ. Pr.

73 Glatt, M M (1961), *The Lancet*, i, 1112

74 Glatt, M M (1977), *Brit. J. Alcohol and Alcoholism*, 13 (i), 11

75 Glatt, M M (1959), *J. Ment. Sci.*, 105, 476

76 Madden, J S (1979), *Brit. J. Alcohol and Alcoholism*, 14 (i), 7

77 Malcolm, M T *et al* (1974), *Brit. J. Psych.*, 125, 484

78 Martensen-Larsen, O C (1974), 20th Internat. Instit. on Prevention and Treatment of Alcoholism, Manchester

79 Beil, H and Trojan, A (1977), *Brit. J. Addict.*, 72, 129

80 Schlatter, E B and Lat, S. (1972), *Quart. J. Stud. Alc.*, 33, 430

81 Bowne, P G (1977) in *Drug Dependence* ed. Glatt, M M, Lancaster, MTP, 195–221

82 Mendelson, J H *et al.* (1972), Proc. 5th int. Cong. Pharmacol., 157

83 Mendelson, J H *et al* (1976) quoted from Mello, N K (1976) in *Alcohol and Alcohol Problems* (ed. Filstead, W J *et al.*), Cambridge. Mass Ballinger, 181

84 Glatt, M M (1959), *Brit. J. Addict.*, 55, 111

85 Horney, K (1951), *Neurosis and Human Growth*, London, Routledge & Kegan Paul

86 Tiebout, H M (1949), *Quart. J. Study Alc.*, 10, 48

87 Menninger, K (1938), *Man Against Himself*, New York, Harcourt

88 Trotter, W (1916), *Instincts of the Herd in Peace and War*, London

89   Glatt, M M (1961), *Acta Psychiat. Scand.*, 37, 143
90   Hart, B (1950), *Psychopathology*, Cambridge, University Press
91   Corrick, S (1980), *World Med.*, 18 October, 84
92   Glatt, M M (1958), *Brit. J. Addict.*, 55, 51
93   Foulkes, S and Anthony, E J (1957), *Group Psychotherapy*, London, Penguin
94   *Practical Approaches to Alcoholism Psychotherapy* (1978), (ed. Zimberg, S, Wallace, J and Blume, S B, New York, London, Plenum
95   Slavson, S B (ed.) (1956), *The Fields of Group Psychotherapy*, New York, Internat. Univ. Press, 247
96   Nuffield Working Party (1977), *Communication with patients*, London
97   Nathan, P E and Briddell, D W (1977) in *The Biology of Alcoholism*, vol.5, 301–349
98   Sargent, M (1979), *Drinking and Alcoholism in Australia*, Cheshire, Longman
99   Images of Deviance (1971) (ed. S. Cohen), London, Penguin
100 Miller, P M and Eisler, R M (1975), *Alcohol and Drug Abuse*, in *Behaviour Modification Principles, Issues, and Applications* (ed. Craighead, W E, Kazdin, A E and Mahoney, M J)., Boston, Houghton Mifflin
101 Thorley, A *Medicine* 1980 (Nov.), 35, 1816
102 Norris, J L (1978), 32 Internat. Congr. Alcohol and Drug Dependence, Warsaw, ICCA
103 Al-Anon Family Groups, Health Trends 1980 (Febr.), 12, 8
104 Glatt, M M (1980), *ibid* (Febr.), 12, 8
105 Hornik, E L (1974), *You and Your Alcoholic Parent*, New York, Associate Press, 114–19
106 Rossi, J J and Filstead, W J (1976) in *Alcohol and Alcohol Problems: New Thinking and New Directions* (ed. Filstead, W J, Rossi J J and Keller M), Cambridge. Mass., Ballinger, 193–228
107 Schuckitt, M A and Cahalan, D (1976) *ibid*, 229–66

17

Teamwork

The complexity of the problem of alcoholism is one of the reasons why no one single agency has been consistently successful with alcoholics. Alcoholism is a medical, psychological, social, religious, economic, political and legal problem at one and the same time. The public health worker, educational authorities and industrialists are, or should also be, vitally interested. AA, as we have seen, approaches the problem of alcoholism from several angles – as a disease of the body, mind and spirit – and is very keen to collaborate with any other agency interested in the alcoholic's welfare.

What is required is co-ordinated and integrated teamwork and there is no room for inter-departmental rivalry and jealousy between the many disciplines who have to play their part in an overall rehabilitation programme.

The agency which happens to be approached first may have to refer him, to start with or later on, to other members of the therapeutic team, not in order to escape from and to shift responsibility, but in order to share it. Thus, the clergyman when first asked for assistance may find that his primary task, apart from showing sympathy and understanding, is to arouse in the alcoholic a desire to undergo counselling or medical treatment, and to refer him later on to a doctor for physical building-up or drug treatment, or to AA.

On the other hand, doctors treating alcoholics will often come across religious conflicts and guilt feelings among the factors from which the patient seeks refuge in drinking, and where, therefore, the spiritual adviser may become the most important member of the therapeutic team.

Even AA, at present the most important single therapeutic agency in alcoholism, often requires the help of other agencies –

for example, in dealing with the physically ill individual, the psychopath, the very unstable neurotic and the suicidal alcoholic [1].

In other chapters the roles of the family, AA, magistrates, employers, the social worker, the welfare worker, sociologist and psychiatrist have been referred to. In the present chapter the functions of the medical practitioner, the nurse, the counsellor and the clergyman will be briefly discussed.

The roles of community services, out-patient clinics, day centres, day hospitals, alcoholic units, etc. will be discussed in the next chapter.

The family doctor

With increasing professional and public understanding of the problems of alcohol and alcoholism, problem drinkers can be expected to come forward at earlier stages of their drinking career so that they can be treated as ambulant patients, remaining in the community and continuing to work and to live with their families. This has always been recognised [21], and clearly only a certain proportion of alcoholics will require residential treatment. However, much greater emphasis has recently been placed on the need for increasing involvement and responsibility of 'community agents'. This is reflected, for example, in the recommendations of the Advisory Council on Alcoholism (1978) [2] that the primary care team should assume the main role in the overall care of problem drinkers. Among such 'community agents' are the GP, other professional workers (such as local authority social workers, probation officers, health visitors and voluntary workers). However, in practice, AA is likely to remain the most important single community agent for many years. The establishment of 'Community Agency Teams' as suggested by the Maudsley project [3] (1975) may still take a long time [4] (except in a few special areas where the ground has been well prepared over years by the presence of many interested professional workers, as in Camberwell). Obviously social workers and voluntary workers will (and should) play an important role, but in spite of all the arguments whether or not alcoholism is a 'disease' will still depend on the role of the family doctor, and the general public will probably continue to take its cue about attitudes to alcohol problems from the attitude of their own GP, and his willingness to become involved, provide help and enlighten not only the drinker but also his family.

The family doctor is strategically in the best position. He has the chance to 'spot' the alcoholic at an early stage [5, 6], to win his confidence and co-operation, to impress upon him the need for treatment, which he can either administer himself in certain cases or administer in collaboration with other members of the therapeutic team. He can encourage the alcoholic to join AA and he can assist and supervise the alcoholic's rehabilitation phase, and possibly play a very active part in looking after alcoholics while in a hostel.

One of his most important tasks may consist in the education of the family as to the disease nature of alcoholism and help the relatives to change their attitude from a negative, condemning one to a more positive, understanding, constructive and helpful one. Finally, by showing interest and understanding in their alcoholic patients, family doctors as a body could contribute a great deal to altering the attitude of the general public towards the acceptance of the concept of the alcoholic as a person suffering from a disorder deserving and requiring medical help.

In practice, it has proved extremely difficult to motivate GPs towards the problem. Members of the Society for the Study of Addiction, such as Drs J Y Dent and H Pullar Strecker, attempted this in the late 1940s and early 1950s. Dr D Parr's [7] questionnaire investigation among GPs in England and Wales (1957) showed that GPs knew of no more than about one tenth of the estimated number of alcoholics in the country on the basis of the Jellinek Formula. As argued at the time in the discussion at the SSA meeting, this finding only illustrated the failure of GPs to get involved in the problem, perhaps largely connected with the lack of specific training in this field [8]. This impression was later confirmed by a study of the prevalence of alcohol-related problems in the Cambridgeshire County, by Moss and Beresford Davies (1967) [9].

Alcoholism is likely to affect the drinker's psychological and social functioning long before it may strike his liver or his nervous system clinically [13]. GPs with special interest and greater clinical experience in this field learn in time to spot tell-tale symptoms in the way the drinker presents his story (answering or failing to answer certain questions, ducking questions, etc.). Not unusual, for example, is the alcoholic's emphasis on how little he drinks: for example he may say 'I have not had any drink today or yesterday' or 'It does not worry me at all not to have any drinks', when asked how much he drinks. For GPs with no special experience, Wilkins

[10] has prepared an 'At Risk Register' (see Chapter 2). The method adopted by Wilkins in compiling this consisted in handing out a questionnaire over a one year period, to selected patients who attended general practitioners at health centres in Manchester. Proceeding from a provisional list containing a total of sixty-four factors known from previous studies to be associated with alcoholism, any patient identified as having any of these factors was given a 'Spare Time Activities Questionnaire' (STAQ).

546 questionnaires were analysed and over a quarter (28.4 per cent) were diagnosed as past or present alcoholics. The previous rate for (past and present) alcoholics was estimated to amount to 1.82 per cent of the (adult) practice population (aged 15–65). Based on these findings Wilkins constructed a 'Modified Alcoholics at Risk Register (AARR) with forty-five factors. The prevalence rate for the alcoholic was at least 25 per cent for one of these factors. Validation studies of AARR showed that the proportion of alcoholics among patients who were not at risk (2.8 per cent) was significantly lower than among the 'at risk' group (28.4 per cent). Wilkins concluded that GPs, by putting questions about alcohol abuse to 'at risk' patients, could detect a considerable proportion of the hidden alcoholics.

Wilkins' Modified At Risk Register points to the significance of certain factors, including: the presence of certain physical or mental diseases; certain 'alcoholic symptoms'; particular occupations; work problems; accidents; criminal offences and family problems (see Chapter 2). The fact that someone has asked for treatment or that the patient was smelling of drink at consultation; the patient's marital status (e.g. unmarried middle-aged or older men or repeatedly married, separated, or divorced), the fact of living in a hostel for destitutes, or being known as an alcoholic (i.e. confirmed by a psychiatrist), and a family history of abnormal drinking.

Wilkins' list certainly contains the items found over the years to be useful pointers in our own experience. Other relevant physical disorders would include the history of a gastrectomy or pancreatitis, peripheral neuritis, possibly also malnutrition. (Most of these are mentioned by Wilkins in his lengthier version of the AARR [10].)

The mental illnesses mentioned in the questionnaire could be the reasons for a patient's drinking as well as the consequences. This 'chicken or egg' question is important, although as a rule helping a patient first to come to grips with his drinking problem is usually necessary in order to enable one to assess and treat the accompanying mental disorder. Other 'alcoholic symptoms' could be added as possible pointers, as of course could a number of other occupations 'at risk' (see Chapter 2). GPs should, for example, be aware of the possibility of excessive drinking among their medical colleagues (see Chapter 11).

· A team is required to deal with the manifold complexities of problem drinking. Who is to be the 'leader' of the team will largely depend on local situations and the degree of experience, involvement and commitment of the various team members. As the Royal College of Psychiatrists' Report [14] puts it 'Too narrow a specialism cannot meet the diversity of physical, social and psychological problems that relate to alcoholism'. If this pronouncement is accepted, it is clear – notwithstanding arguments about 'medical models' 'disease concepts etc.' – that medical men will have to start playing a significant role as team members in this field. For the doctor who becomes interested in the wider ramifications of the alcohol problem the growing experience in so many facets of the problem may well become a fascinating and rewarding experience, and an intriguing learning process in its own right.

What it amounts to then is that the GP – knowing that he is likely to have quite a number of problem drinkers on his list – should be on the look-out for them and raise his level of suspicion, especially among those who form a 'high risk' group.

The GP and the treatment of alcoholism

Views differ greatly as to what extent the GP – having diagnosed the problem drinker – could or should involve himself in treating him [10].

The more the treatment of problem drinkers becomes a responsibility of the primary health care team, the more important will be the role of the GP alongside the health visitor [16] and the practice nurse. As Acres [17] points out, within a group practice it is more likely that one of the partners, because of personality and enthusiasm, may develop a special interest in the task, although it may often be frustrating and time-consuming; and he has found that for those interested in such a task, giving vitamin injections may be one way of maintaining regular contact with the patient.

It is important for the GP to be aware of the need to establish and maintain a good working relationship with unspecific or more specialised official and voluntary agencies in the neighbourhood:

local detoxification facilities, AA, Al-Anon, hostels, 'walk-in' (shop front) facilities, local DRO, Government Training Centres, Industrial Rehabilitation Units, Family Welfare agencies, Information Centres of the NCA, and the community and residential facilities of the regional alcoholics unit.

The Advisory Council on Alcoholism in its 1979 recommendations [2] advises the primary care team workers not to think of themselves as merely 'referral agents' as, in the Council's view, they themselves could deal with problem drinkers. The Council 'expect GPs to play a greater role in the management of problem drinkers without its being necessary to increase their numbers'. As regards the main tasks of primary level workers, they should 'render help as it lies within their scope; know when and where to seek expert help, provide continuing care and support before, during and after any period of specialist treatment, and provide adequate follow-up'.

GPs are not included among the 'essential' members in the local team proposed by the Advisory Council to be established in each area; which 'as a minimum' would comprise a psychiatrist, nurse, social worker and voluntary counsellor – all with specialist skills. However, motivation (see Chapter 15), though hardly mentioned in the Council Report, is as important in the therapist as in the patient.

Recent studies have thrown doubt on the effectiveness of intensive treatment and the superiority, in certain cases, of 'treatment' over simple 'advice' [18, 19]. Clinicians active in the field nevertheless continue to treat their alcoholic patients – and like the majority of patients, they feel that the results, very modest as they unfortunately often turn out to be, have been well worth the effort. There is no doubt that the GP himself can do a great deal to help his alcoholic patients and their families directly, but one hopes he will not be deterred when reading such reports from referring those of his patients who he feels need further help to other professional agencies.

Even though too many alcoholics will not respond with immediate or permanent abstinence and even though doctors and other professionals may often feel like giving up, many drinkers improve greatly and may ultimately recover (albeit after many relapses). But even temporary improvement may mean a great deal to the sufferer and perhaps even more to his family who will derive a great deal of support and hope from the sympathetic assistance of their family doctor. 'There is [stated an Editorial in the official journal of the Medical Council of Alcoholism a few years ago] [20] no agreed cost evaluations of pain, anguish and guilt in an individual, nor for similar distress, emotional deprivation and social consequences to other members of the family. Nevertheless relief, or amelioration of all these categories of pain in all involved is an important benefit of treatment and this will always be an impelling case for action to doctors and some members of Parliament.'

Nor does the GP need to feel lost when confronted by somebody who he thinks is an alcoholic but who maintains that he is not. As stressed elsewhere, there is nothing to gain from a discussion with such a patient during the first few interviews. A simple way of approaching the task may be to proceed as briefly described in Chapter 4 ('the Gentleman's Agreement'). If such an individual can safely control his drinking, why not allow him to show it? In fairness, in such cases the therapist should not indicate his own doubts but point out to such a patient that there are in fact quite a number of serious, very competent research workers who feel that certain problem drinkers with a mild degree of dependence can achieve controlled drinking. The therapist may then give the drinker some such advice as briefly indicated in the 'Gentleman's Agreement' section and ask him to report back in a few weeks. As long as such a drinker manages moderate or controlled drinking, there would seem no immediate need to advise any further steps. It is, however, very important to enlist the spouse's collaboration, and this will usually be much more difficult than the initially enthusiastic consent of the patient himself.

The role of other medical practitioners

Apart from the GP's possible key role [6] in the detection and management of problem drinkers, many other medical men also play an important role. The frequency with which drinkers find themselves unrecognised in the ordinary wards of the general hospital (mostly in medical wards but often also in surgical wards) has already been discussed (see Chapter 14). The long list of complications of alcoholism indicates that all types of medical and (often) surgical specialists will often have to look after alcoholics: in the main, those specialising in diseases of the liver and pancreas, gastrointestinal disorders, neurologists, haematologists, cardiologists, sexologists, dermatologists, ophthalmologists and others. The high incidence of problem drinkers in emergency and casualty departments has already been discussed. Specialists in forensic medicine, toxicology, pharmacology, and, of course, general pathologists and biochemists are often very much involved with problems arising out of misuse of alcohol. The community physician has a very important role to play in this field, in particular in the area of prevention. Gradually more and more general hospitals will open their doors to alcoholics not only because of the definite medical or surgical complications, but also for short-term detoxification, which should enable more patients to undergo the rest of their treatment and rehabilitation within the community. Obstetricians and gynaecologists, in view of the possibility of complications such as spontaneous abortions and the alcohol foetal syndrome (Chapter 14) will also need to take a greater interest in alcohol problems.

In the past, psychiatrists were the ones to take an interest in problem drinkers, though, among these too, the great majority kept a distance and aloofness. Most alcohol units were established by psychiatrists, though in recent years other medical men have increasingly taken charge of problem drinkers. However, the psychiatrists in charge of alcohol units certainly have always seen their function as catering – as far as possible – for all the psychosomatic, social and other requirements of their patients and not only or mainly for their psychiatric state [21].

It goes without saying that the great majority of alcoholics can recover without ever having to seek psychiatric (or often indeed any other professional) help, as indicated by the success of AA. In many cases, however, emotional conflicts and personality difficulties have been responsible for the onset of excessive drinking in the first place.

Quite apart from the relatively small number of alcoholics who are basically psychotics or mentally subnormal and require expert psychiatric handling, many more are psychoneurotics or psychopaths, who may often need attention. Moreover, years of excessive drinking have produced secondary psychological difficulties (see p. 479) and changes even in many alcoholics who at the start of their drinking career were psychologically relatively normal. There are thus a great number of alcoholics who need psychiatric help, who have failed with other methods, including AA, and for whom psychotherapy or behaviour therapy in one or the other of their forms may be necessary and successful.

At any rate, many other medical specialists may have important contributions to make to the management of alcoholism. As Professor Camps put it 'unless this multidisciplined approach is adopted it may well be that one aspect such as psychiatry may be so emphasised as to conceal the facilities and the knowledge which can be offered and developed by clinical medicine, toxicology, and pharmacology' [22].

The nurse

In many aspects the nurse [23] is the most important member of the therapeutic team caring for the hospitalised alcoholic. She* is the person who welcomes the alcoholic into the clinic or the ward and from her he gets his first impressions about the prevailing attitude. She spends more time with him than any member of the team. To a large extent the all-important ward 'atmosphere' will depend on her attitude. It is the nurse who acts as the intermediary between the alcoholic and other members of the team, including the psychiatrist, as she has a much better chance to observe the patient in 'action' – in the way he relates to other patients (his 'siblings'), to authority, in the manner in which he reacts to frustrating situations, to disappointments and to happy tidings, and as to whether he habitually denies, rationalises, projects or represses. The nurse has a chance to convey something of the nature of the problems involved to visiting family members.

The nurse will come into very close contact with the patient in some physical treatments, and she needs knowledge of the procedures as the patient will turn to her for elucidation of any doubtful points that worry him.

To start with, the alcoholic may seem to the nurse a rather frightening and unpredictable patient. He has been using alcohol as an emotional 'crutch' and will be afraid to 'let go', till he has got sufficient confidence in treatment and staff to believe that he may obtain from them a better form of support. If she remembers this, the nurse will learn to tolerate better the patient's 'ambivalent' attitude to therapy.

There are many other points about the alcoholic which the nurse initially will find difficult to understand and accept. But the more she learns about him, the easier she will find him as a patient.

At the same time, as many alcoholics are immature and inclined to be overdependent, the nurse must be careful not to allow

* To simplify matters, the female gender is used here, although frequently, of course, it will be a male nurse who may look after male and nowadays also female alcoholics.

herself to be manoeuvred into the role of dispenser of direct advice. The aim should be to help the patient to grow up in emotional maturity and gradually to assume more and more initiative and responsibility, and not to make decisions on his behalf.

In her contact with alcoholics the nurse will need patience, tact and tolerance. She will have to shed her initial pessimism. Initially she will be very hurt by relapses, but in time she will learn to look on alcoholism as a relapsing illness. The relapse then becomes a challenge rather than a deeply wounding disappointment. Indeed, the nurse like every other member of the therapeutic team will have to learn to be satisfied in many alcoholic patients with improvement rather than recovery.

The alcoholic will be very grateful to a nurse with a non-rejecting, non-preaching, non-moralistic attitude. Having experienced so much rejection in the past, he may have come to hospital expecting more recriminations and 'lectures', and consciously or unconsciously he may even invite and provoke rejection by his own grandiose or aggressive attitude. The alcoholic is very often resentful of authority and the nurse's non-condemning, non-authoritarian approach will reassure him. He will then be able to allow his defences to come down and to communicate his feelings, anxieties and fears. A good nurse may do a great deal for him by just listening, as she may be the first person he has ever met to have done so.

Thus the task seems to bristle with difficulties. However, participation in group therapy sessions and meeting recovered alcoholics will gradually help the nurse towards a more understanding (yet not sentimental) attitude. She will appreciate and will feel rewarded by the knowledge that in helping the alcoholic patient she has also done a great deal for his wife and his children.

Many nurses entering work in an alcohol unit with diffidence or great scepticism very soon begin to develop a more positive outlook after getting to know alcoholic patients better [24, 25, 26]. Like all members of the alcoholic team, in our experience, nurses, in particular, often benefit a great deal emotionally from close contact with the non-drinking type of alcoholic. Not everyone is able to work well with alcoholics but long-term members of our teams with few exceptions felt that they had been greatly helped in their own emotional growth from regularly attending the group therapy sessions. Certainly, working with alcoholics is by no means a one-way traffic with all the help being extended from staff to patients. Thus two of our charge nurses (one female, one male)

who at the beginning of their work in the unit were highly authoritarian in their approach, learnt to 'let go' considerably, leaving
a lot to their patients' own initiative and responsibility; another
(female) ward sister, initially very insecure, was gradually 'nursed'
along by generations of very understanding alcoholic patients in
her ward until she had become extremely competent in coping
with even the most difficult and psychopathic alcoholic patients.
In general, members of the unit staff do more than their official
share of work and become extremely popular with the patients.
Many nurses working for some time in such units also develop into
skilled group therapists and become extremely helpful to the
visiting family members of their patients.

It is not only in hospital that nurses have an important role to
play in care, treatment and rehabilitation, and even in prevention.

Psychiatric nurses have an important role to play outside the
hospital. For example having known a patient well in hospital they
are in a good position to provide after-care and support. They may
work in hostels, day centres or out-patient clinics, and act as a link
between the members of the primary care team and the alcohol
unit. Working as a community nurse, and possibly having been
present at the first domiciliary visit by a medical or psychiatric
specialist, they are often in a position to carry out much of the
treatment needed at home enabling the patient to continue his
work, and to avoid having to enter hospital.

As regards the latter aspect, for example, health visitors are now
concerned with psychosocial aspects of family life as well as
physical health and basic hygiene [27] and are in an excellent
position to function as health educators and to inform women of
child-bearing age, and in particular those who are pregnant, about
the dangers of drinking – a good example of primary prevention.
Similarly, nurses attached to a general practice, district nurses,
and psychiatric nurses during their domiciliary visits are in a
position to assess the home 'atmosphere' and emotional climate,
especially where there is an excessive drinker who may progress to
battering his wife or children: a nurse alive to such possibilities will
often be able to suspect or to spot the cause. To what extent her
own relationship with the members of the household may be
sufficient for her to 'go it alone' by talking it over with the alcoholic
himself, or at least by advising his wife and children, will obviously
depend on the circumstances. But in such cases an alert nurse may
prevent tragedies which are only too likely to occur (see Chapter
9).

It is of some interest that, twenty years ago, health visitors and probation officers were chosen by the Rowntree steering group on alcoholism as the social agencies best situated to provide data about the incidence of alcoholism [28, 29] (see Chapter 5). The reasons for the choice, as explained by G Prys Williams, were that these two groups 'had access to the households in their administrative ambit as of right [and] that the discharge of their administrative functions required the collection of socio-economic data about the families of a kind similiar to that needed to discover chronic and obvious alcoholics'. An added important reason for choosing probation officers was that their clientele was less likely to come to the attention of GPs: 'the male alcoholic in more or less settled employment [usually has] to go to his doctor for medical certificates if his addiction leads to absence or late attendance at his work. This constraint is less effective in the case of the unemployed, the criminal, or indeed, any males to whom regular employment is not important'. To some extent a similar situation was thought to apply to women who stayed at home and who 'were essentially free from the need of certificates to cover lapses in punctuality and efficiency'. One outcome of the investigation was the conclusion that – in view of the probation officers being in a position to know a great deal about the segment of the alcoholic population unlikely to come to the attention of their GPs – periodic checks on the trend of incidence of 'advanced alcoholism' could be provided, if 'adequate samples of probation officers, and of GPs with lists of patients below about 2500, were used to supplement each other'.

Again, as regards the work in alcohol units many other staff members play an important role, including occupational therapists and physiotherapists who are in a position, during the course of their work and by bringing a great deal of relief (and relaxation) to establish helpful relationships, and to arouse and maintain a patient's motivation [32]. Physiotherapists working in a general hospital are also in an excellent position to encourage patients to embark on long-term rehabilitation programmes, rather than leaving hospital as soon as they have obtained relief from their initial pain [32].

Counsellors

Non-professionals have only recently begun to participate in counselling in Britain, but have been active for many years in the

USA. In particular, recovered alcoholics in America have often played a leading role in establishing and successfully running treatment centres. Such centres seen by the present author include Alina Lodge in New Jersey and there are many others. Counsellors form a large proportion of the staff at the well known Hazelden Foundation in Minnesota and also at Broadway Lodge, a treatment centre in Britain. In our own units we have, for many years, found the (occasional or regular) collaboration with selected alcoholic ex-patients and other recovered alcoholics (mainly members of AA) extremely helpful. Over the past few years the National Council on Alcoholism, in association with the Alcohol Education Centre, has been running a successful Alcoholism Counsellors' Training Scheme. As to what exactly the functions of such a 'counsellor' are or should be, often depend on the views and the needs of the team or the faculty that employs him; on his experience and his own inclinations.

In general, 'counselling' has been said to be concerned with educational, marital, vocational and personal difficulties. 'The Counsellor [according to the *Encyclopaedia of Psychiatry for GPs* [33]] usually a psychologist, sometimes a priest [both of course often valuable members of the team assisting problem drinkers], may advise the client as to the best course to take in order to resolve his problems, or he may be more non-directive, in the sense that sessions with the counsellor may give the client the opportunity to ventilate his anxieties and uncertainties.'

In the case of counsellors who are recovered alcoholics, they may, of course, be in a good position to render (preferably non-directive) help to the client with drink problems, with difficulties arising out of his drinking behaviour, and in his problems with his spouse and children, etc. Similarly, the wife of a recovered alcoholic who is a counsellor may be in a good position to assist other spouses of alcoholics.

A good review of 'The Alcoholism Counsellor as a Member of a Treatment Team' has been given by Dr Sheila B Blume [34]. The first requirement for certification mentioned in an American report on a 'proposed National Standard for Am Counsellors' (1974), named a minimum period of two years' freedom from alcohol or drug misuse for immediate certification. Interested, understanding, experienced and well-trained non-alcoholics could do well as counsellors, but recovered alcoholics start off with certain advantages. However, not every recovered alcoholic is suitable, although a great many alcoholics, when undergoing treatment, express a wish to help others. As Blume points out, counselling techniques 'involve listening . . . far more than talking'. To be successful, counsellors need the feeling that they have the backing, and can rely on the active help when necessary, of the professional members of the team.

Problems arising in this respect are well discussed in Blume's review. It is obviously necessary in any set-up for both the professional team members and the counsellor to keep an open mind and to discuss regularly and openly problems and difficulties. 'All too often, [as Audrey Newsome [35], Director of Appointments and Counselling Service, University of Keele says] no clear definition has been made and the counsellor himself has had to shape his role according to qualifications and predilection.' In the view of Newsome and colleagues (1973) [36], 'it is easier to say what counselling is *not* – it is not giving advice, persuading or convincing, interrogation, psychoanalysis, or a pale imitation of the practices developed by psychoanlaysts'. They quote the definition of counselling recently published by the British Association for Counselling:

> People become engaged in counselling when a person occupying, regularly or temporarily, the role of counsellor, offers or agrees explicitly to offer time, attention and respect to another person or persons temporarily in the role of client. The task of counselling is to give the client an opportunity to explore, discover and clarify ways of living more resourcefully and towards greater well-being.

This definition is, of course, a rather vague and wide one. 'Giving time, attention and respect, and even an abundance of good will and sympathy is not enough, and obviously insight into one's own limitations, one's own bias, etc., is needed as well as some training, supervision by, and collaboration with, other team members. Many AA members, for example, are only too willing to give an abundance of time and attention but often they are able to see only the part of the problem which they themselves had experienced (usually the drinking itself and not other associated problems which may have originally contributed to the emergence of the drinking problem). They may see AA as the *only* answer, and may extend their fear of psychotropic drugs to use of any drugs, whatever the circumstances, so that their advice may be dogmatic, even though well intentioned. This is not said to belittle the immense help which AA members often render, but the alcoholic counsellor has to learn to be aware of this and other pitfalls. If he is able to do so, and keep an open mind, such people can be immensely valuable members of the therapeutic team. It is of course only fair to add that just as the recovered alcoholic naturally may stress the drinking aspect in the recovery process and neglect the pre-alcoholic problems, so the professional worker, trained in considering general emotional and social problems may concentrate on these while lacking understanding and empathy for the drinking behaviour. As discussed in an earlier chapter, this consideration alone explains the immense benefit of professional workers and AA pooling their experience, skill and efforts on behalf of the problem drinker.

Role of the Church

The number of problem drinkers suffering from spiritual problems is immense. Over the usual preoccupation with the alcoholic's physical, emotional, social and economic problems, his spiritual needs must not be forgotten. In many cases it may be found that the clergyman is, at least in some phases of the disorder, the most significant member of the therapeutic team.

Over the centuries the influence of religion must have undoubtedly exerted an immeasurable influence towards abstinence or moderation. Faith and religious 'conversion' must in the past have helped a great many alcoholics to regain freedom from their slavery to drink. As things stand today many alcoholics often prefer to turn to agencies other than doctors or social workers for assistance. Among such agencies, the clergyman may take on a favoured role [37, 38, 39].

As to the spiritual aspects, the AA concepts of a 'Power greater than ourselves' and 'God as we understand Him' are directly mentioned in six of the suggested Twelve Steps (AA stresses that its programme is no more than a suggestion, not a 'must', thus by-passing the alcoholic's distrust of any authoritarian approach). Step Four suggests 'a searching and fearless moral inventory' to be taken once the alcoholic has achieved sobriety. (See Chapter 16.)

A great deal depends on the pastor's initial approach. Telling the alcoholic that he has sinned at a time when he is still drinking may have no other effect than driving him even more to the bottle. The position may be quite different once the alcoholic has stopped drinking, when his thinking begins to change, and he may then himself ask for the pastor's help.

In his book *Just One More*, J L Free [40], himself a recovered alcoholic who later on worked as a lay-therapist with alcoholics, states that what the alcoholic primarily needs in the initial stage is help to get well. He needs to be shown how to stop drinking; and what the pastor can perhaps do at this stage is to get in touch with medical men or with AA.

In Free's views it is in the later stages of the rehabilitation process – after the alcoholic has found sobriety – that the clergyman may come very much into his own by providing spiritual guidance and by teaching the alcoholic to pray.

It is one of the contradictions inherent in the problems of alcoholism and alcoholics that the latter so often at one and the same time denounce 'religion' and the failure of religion to help them, and yet are inwardly hoping and searching for spirituality, for somebody to show them the way back into their religious fold and to regain their lost faith. Certainly many alcoholics who had become estranged from their faith, after regaining sobriety gradually found their way back to their Church. For some this regained faith later becomes the cornerstone of a new way of life.

The question of 'Alcoholism – Sin or Disease' has been examined by the Rev. R B Rea [38] from the pastor's point of view. He concludes that 'alcoholism is, in most cases, the result of sin, but it represents a phase at which drinking has become a disease; to cure it, therefore, it must be treated first of all as a disease'. He commends the AA approach to alcoholism to the pastor, because 'inherent in its therapy there are many principles of deep theological significance . . . The recognition that past sins are causative factors in addiction and that getting right with God is essential to recovery, is implicit in the Twelve Steps.'

Other clergymen have expressed themselves in similar vein. The General Assembly of the Presbyterian Church in the USA has stated that 'once drinking has passed a certain point, alcoholism is a disease; that is, the drinking cannot be stopped by a mere resolution on the part of the drinker. He needs treatment, not punishment; understanding, not condemnation'.

Again, the pastor is in a position, by showing understanding and by 'acceptance', to assist not only the alcoholic but also his family, who may come for advice long before the alcoholic himself may see the need for help. The family equipped with a better understanding of the 'disease' nature of the condition may develop a different attitude towards their alcoholic family member which may make it easier for him to 'open up' and ask for help.

In our hospital units the pastor has always been a very important member of the therapeutic team, helping patients individually and during his group sessions with them; moreover, by holding regular seminars and arranging for young clergymen to participate actively in the work of the unit, a great deal has been done to educate and train these men in a vital task which will later on come their way quite often.

Vague, nameless but intensive fears (perhaps due to guilt feelings) are many alcoholics' unwanted but constant travelling companions. Directly or indirectly (via psychoanalytic symptoms) they often trigger off relapses. Faith may often prove the most effective antidote against fear [41].

References

1 Kreitman, N and Dyer, J A T (December 1980), *Medicine* 36, 1827
2 Advisory Council on Alcoholism (1978), *The Pattern and Range of Services for Problem Drinkers*, London, DHSS and Welsh Office
3 Cartwright, A K J, Shaw, S J and Spratley, T A (1975), *Designing a Comprehensive Community Response to Problems of Alcohol Abuse*, London, Maudsley Alcohol Pilot Project
4 Glatt, M M (1976), *Brit. J. Psychiat.*, Notes and News
5 Rees, T P and Glatt, M M (1954), *Med. Press*, 231, 338
6 Glatt M M (1960), *J. Coll. Gen. Pract.*, 3, 292
7 Parr, D (1957), *Brit. J. Addict.*, 54, 25
8 Glatt, M M (1957), *ibid.*, 54, 47
9 Moss, E C and Davies, Beresford E (1967), *A Survey of Alcoholism in an English County*, London, Geigy (UK)
10 Wilkins, R H (1974), *The Hidden Alcoholic in General Practice*, London, Elek Science
11 Prys Williams, G and Glatt, M M (1966), *Brit. J. Addict.*, 61, 257
12 Pollak, B (1971), *Practitioner*, 206, 531
13 Glatt, M M (1967), *Brit. J. Addict.*, 62, 35
14 *Alcohol and Alcoholism* (1979), Report of a Special Committee of the Royal College of Psychiatrists, London, Tavistock
15 Glatt, M M, Rosin, A J and Jouhar, P (1978), *Age and Ageing*, 7, Suppl., 64
16 Glatt, M M (1973), *Midwife and Health Visitor*, 9, 262
17 Acres, D I (1977), in *Alcoholism: New Knowledge and New Responses*, eds Edwards, G and Grant, M, London, Croom Helm, 321–7
18 Orford, J and Edwards, G (1977) *Alcoholism*, Oxford, Oxford Univ. Pr.
19 Glatt, M M (1977), *Lancet*, ii, 817
20 *British J. Alcohol and Alcoholism* (Edit.) 1977, 12(4), 141
21 Glatt, M M (1955), *Brit. J. Addict.*, 52, 55

22 Camps, F E (1970) in *Modern Trends in Drug Dependence and Alcoholism*, ed. Phillipson, R V, London, Butterworth

23 Glatt, M M (1964), 'The Alcoholic and his Problems', *Nursing Mirror*, January, February

24 Glatt, M M (1 May, 1975), *Nursing Times*, 680

25 Caruana, S and Buttimore, A (1974), *Nurse's Handbook on Alcohol and Alcoholism*, London, Edsall

26 Rabbitte, M and Peters, T, *Nursing Mirror*, 1975 20 February, 58

27 Clark, M C (November 1980), *Health Trends*, 12, 98

28 Steering Group on Alcoholism founded by the Joseph Rowntree Social Services Trust, 1960–3, *Chronic Alcoholics,* ed. Prys, Williams, G, London

29 Glatt, M M and Whiteley, J S (1956), *Mschr. Psychiat. Neurol.*, 132, 1

30 Home Office (1971), *Habitual Drunken Offenders*, London, HMSO

31 Glatt, M M (1977) in *Drug Dependence: Current Problems and Issues*, ed. Glatt, M M, Lancaster, MTP, 223–60

32 Glatt, M M, *Nursing Mirror*, 15 January 1976, 59

32a Hazell, S and Glatt, M M *ibid*, 62

33 *Encyclop. of Psychiat. for GPs* (1972), vol. C–D, London, Roche, 122

34 Blume, S B (1977) in *The Biology of Alcoholism*, vol.5, 553–67

35 Newsome, A (July 1980), *Bull. Roy. Coll. Psychiatr.*, 102

36 Newsome, A *et al.* (1973) quoted from Newsome, A (ref. 35)

37 Clinebell, Jr H J (1956), *Understanding and Counselling the Alcoholic through Religion and Psychiatry*, Nashville, Abingdon Press

38 Rea, R B (1956), *Alcoholism – its Psychology and Cure*, London, Epworth Press

39 Glatt, M M (1981) in *Dictionary of Medical Ethics*, ed. Duncan, A S, Dunstan, G R and Welbourn, R B, London, Darton, Longman and Todd, 14–19

40 Free, J L (1955), *Just One More*, New York, Coward-McCann

41 Bill (on) Fear, *Grapevine*, London, AA

18

Alcohol Units, Hostels, Residential and Community Services

Out-patient treatment

In theory, it should only be a minority of alcoholics who require in-patient treatment in hospitals [1]. If they are diagnosed in relatively early phases and provided that they do not suffer from complications, out-patient treatment should be sufficient and has in practice often proved successful.

Here supportive or, where necessary, more intensive psychotherapy, individually or in groups, drug treatments (such as tranquillisers, vitamins, the alcohol-deterrent drugs), help by social workers and community agencies would be available and such therapy could be carried out in collaboration with AA. Many such clinics have successfully operated in the United States since the post-war period, the staff including as a rule a psychiatrist, a physician, psychiatrically trained case workers, a psychologist and nurses. Where the alcoholic has no home or family, a stay in special hostels or halfway houses – e.g. for down-and-out drinkers or ex-prisoners – may be required without such people necessarily needing hospitalisation.

In Great Britain over the past twenty to twenty-five years a number of specialised out-patient clinics have been started – run either by voluntary organisations or under the National Health Service; in the latter case mainly OP clinics working in association with in-patient units. Until the mid-1950s there were, in the British Isles, no out-patient clinics exclusively devoted to the treatment of alcoholism. Among the reasons for this state of affairs was probably the fact that because of the lack of information among the general public and the medical profession about alcoholism and because of the stigma attached to such a diagnosis, alcoholics were not generally diagnosed until they had reached the advanced stages, when many required at least a preliminary period of in-patient treatment.

The in-patient unit

Yet until fifteen years ago specialised facilities for in-patient treatment of alcoholism were likewise very few and far between (and are not plentiful even today) under the National Health Service, although there were then quite a number of private nursing homes catering largely (and often providing excellent treatment) for the small minority among alcoholics who could afford private treatment[1]. In 1952 – as Dr H. Pullar-Strecker, the secretary of the Society for the Study of Addiction at the time, pointed out – there was in the British Isles not a single hospital which had a whole ward or unit set aside exclusively devoted to treating alcoholics.

Fortunately since then the situation has greatly improved, but to a certain extent some of the problems existing at that time are still present today and a brief sketch of the situation in the early 1950s – which was written at the time – may not be out of place [1].

Doctors in this country particularly interested in the problem of alcoholism have repeatedly stressed how woefully inadequate the present facilities were for the adequate treatment of alcoholic patients under the National Health Service. The few places which try to cater specially for the alcoholic's needs have long waiting lists.

Waiting lists in the case of alcoholics are clearly impracticable: by the time the prospective candidate's turn has arrived he is either too drunk or not sufficiently drunk to take the voluntary step of entering a hospital for treatment. But what are the alternatives?

Some alcoholics, probably a very small minority, are still lucky enough to have private means at their disposal and can receive specialised care and attention in private nursing homes. For the great majority of alcoholics in this country the only possibility seems to be admission to an observation ward (or to a Salvation Army Hostel) for a few days during the acute stages, provided they are lucky enough to find sympathetic mental welfare officers who feel that these drunks need or deserve a hospital bed; or waiting till they have acquired a 'respectable' medical complication, such as liver cirrhosis or peripheral neuritis, which allows them to enter the general hospital; or applying for admission as a voluntary patient to their regional mental hospital. Even this may be difficult as many hospital authorities have a marked reluctance to admit alcoholics.

Most alcoholics, moreover, are not very keen to go to mental hospitals, partly because of the fear of the stigma and partly because they believe – rightly or wrongly – that they are not really welcome, that they are out of place among a majority of psychotic patients, and that there is no special attempt made to deal with their particular problem.

In many ways the alcoholic's needs are different from those of the ordinary mental hospital patient. In the latter the alcoholic usually feels alone and not understood and, not seeing that any specific treatment programme is laid on for him, he quickly becomes discontented. Therefore, as soon as he is sobered up and detoxicated he takes his discharge – only to continue his rounds, attendances at other hospitals, and perhaps courts or prisons. With each subsequent hospital admission he becomes more frustrated, more lacking in hope, more bitter and resentful. Hospital authorities, on the other hand, take the alcoholic's poor hospital record as an indication that he is a very difficult, extremely unco-operative and in general an 'impossible' patient.

However, experience of doctors, not only abroad, but also in this country, who are interested in treating alcoholics, have helped to explode the misconception of the alcoholic as a particularly unco-operative patient. Given adequate special facilities (and of course the therapist's sympathetic understanding) the alcoholic can be helped and becomes a very co-operative and rewarding patient. Thus it has been shown that even when alcoholics are admitted to a mental hospital ward where there are non-alcoholic, neurotic, or early psychotic cases, they show themselves to be very pleasant and co-operative patients, provided they find other alcoholics in the place, thus taking them out of their feeling of utter isolation. Not only this, but alcoholics, due to their often high intelligence, drive and initiative, may contribute a great deal to the hospital community as a whole.

In spite of the size and the importance of the problem, however, apart from private societies, until very recently only social welfare and religious bodies seemed to be interested in taking any active steps. The official view seems to be that alcoholics in need of treatment should be scattered haphazardly throughout the country's mental hospitals. Many hundreds of testimonies of alcoholics with, between them, thousands of hospital admissions, testify that such a 'method' is worse than useless.

In contrast to the obvious deficiencies of this approach, the formation of specialised units in a few selected hospitals – each of which could take alcoholic patients from a wide (perhaps regional) catchment area – could enable the application of a combination of psychological, physical and social therapies best suited to the individual case. It would enable the alcoholic to mix with other alcoholic patients, to live, to work, and enjoy life in a therapeutic community formed by alcoholics, thus giving him the long-lost feeling of 'belonging', of being accepted, and understood by a group of people all 'speaking the same language' and having similar backgrounds and similar experiences.

Such a unit would function as a therapeutic community, and be able to provide a comprehensive physio-psychosocial therapeutic service, the central core being group therapy and community living. It would also offer unique facilities for the medical and nursing staff to acquire experience in treating alcoholics and for research work in which alcoholic patients usually are only too keen to co-operate.

Quite apart from the provision of facilities for treatment, education and research in the subject of alcoholism, such units would incorporate a form of 'residential AA' and would be ideally suited to collaborate closely with AA who now have groups in all parts of the country and are only too willing to co-operate with the State and anybody else in the task of rehabilitating the alcoholic.

Close collaboration of hospitals with AA is an important feature of many Government-sponsored programmes for the care, treatment and rehabilitation of alcoholics in the United States. There is no reason to assume that such co-operation should not also prove of the greatest benefit in this country, and, in fact, in the relatively few instances where it has been tried it has proved very feasible and successful.

Views differ as to the best place for such an alcohol unit, whether it should best be an independent unit, or attached to a general or mental hospital. There are pros and cons for each of these alternatives. Doctors associated with private nursing homes feel that alcoholics, because of the stigma, would be reluctant to enter mental hospitals; doctors who use an exclusively, or predominantly physical therapeutic approach feel that the best place would be in a general hospital. On the other hand, alcoholism is to a large extent a mental health problem, and among doctors, apart from the family doctor, it is the psychiatrist who is, or should be, particularly interested. Moreover, where special provisions have been made in mental hospitals for alcoholics there was no dearth of applicants for the few beds available and, in fact, large waiting lists became necessary . . .

In many ways the alcoholic patient proved to be a great help to non-alcoholic hospital inmates and he himself benefited from participating in the activities of the whole hospital community. The hospital also offers the opportunity to alcoholics to avail themselves of the general services, such as the very important aspect of occupational therapy.

The stigma attached to mental hospital admission may in future be confidently expected to decrease under the new Mental Health Bill. Special units for alcoholics only, situated in separate blocks in a progressive mental hospital, provided with their own entrance and given their own name, might therefore appear a good and, under present circumstances, less expensive way of achieving this end.

The foregoing comments were based on experience gained in the early 1950s at Warlingham Park Hospital in Surrey, a medium-sized public psychiatric hospital. Its Medical Superintendent at the time was Dr T P Rees, one of the foremost and earliest pioneers of the open-door policy and of a highly permissive hospital atmosphere.

As far as alcoholics were concerned, Warlingham Park had its usual trickle of patients coming from the Borough of Croydon. They came in, were sobered up, stayed on a little longer, left – and very often returned. One patient was re-admitted about twelve times during a period of about five years, eleven times in a state of DT, or bordering on it.

There were two or three alcoholics during 1951 and 1952, members of a group run for neurotic patients. These few alcoholic patients proved to be intelligent and very interested group members who contributed a great deal to the discussions during the short time they participated. It appeared therefore to be an interesting project to try to form a group consisting of alcoholics alone if a sufficient number of alcoholics should happen to be in hospital at the same time. Such an opportunity occurred in August 1952 when two patients were newly admitted in addition to two other patients who had been in hospital for some time. There was no fixed programme when this group of four male alcoholic patients met for the first time. They were just told that there existed a method of psychotherapy carried out in groups, and they were asked what they thought of the idea of having a special discussion group composed entirely of alcoholics . . . although initially everyone was sceptical . . . it became obvious very soon that patients appreciated these meetings very much and felt subjectively that they derived benefit from them. [1]

Within a few months there was a regular programme 'based chiefly on the use of group therapy in the widest sense of the word', not only in the hospital but also in the community, a local AA group had been formed in Croydon at the initiative of the hospital patients, a follow-up group, a relatives' group, a regular monthly reunion meeting of ex-patients in London[2] and a monthly magazine was published. Nowadays, over thirty years later, all these activities are still carried on by the WPH unit. There were so many applications for admission from alcoholics outside the local official 'catchment area' that it became necessary to limit the number of male alcoholic patients (at any one time) to twelve as there seemed to be a danger that WPH would soon develop into a mainly alcoholic hospital!

The favourable experience with alcoholics, who proved extremely co-operative when approached in this way, and the need manifested by the great number of applications for admission from all parts of the British Isles led logically to the recommendation to establish regional alcohol units which 'could also become centres for research, education and teaching' [3, 4].

Subsequently the advisability of establishing special clinics and units was accepted both by the combined committee of the British

Medical Association and the Magistrates' Association (1961) and by the Ministry of Health (1962, 1968). In its 1962 Memorandum on *Hospital Treatment of Alcoholism*, the Ministry recommended that as far as possible treatment for alcoholism should be given in specialised units – initially one in each region – and situated at psychiatric hospitals or psychiatric units at general hospitals. Such units were to have a size of between eight to sixteen beds – a convenient size for group therapy – regarded as often being a valuable form of treatment. 'The units will run out-patient clinics and co-operate with AA and local health authorities and other interested agencies.'

The 1968 Memorandum of the Ministry of Health on *The Treatment of Alcoholism* dealt briefly with the needs for research studies, prevention, assessment and after-care as well as with the treatment for alcohol dependence. It rightly stressed the necessity for clinical trials to investigate specific indications for in-patient and out-patient care, and the need for the specialised hospital units also to provide out-patient services. It reported that although since the time of the 1962 Memorandum progress has been made in developing hospital facilities for the treatment of alcoholism, special units are required in some regions where no units exist or where facilities comparable to those at special units are insufficient. Since the Ministry of Health memoranda over thirty new special alcohol units were formed in England (see *Helping Agencies*, pp. 531–5). The first special alcohol unit in Scotland was formed in Edinburgh in 1963 [6]. There might possibly be not quite the same need for the establishment of the proportionate number of special alcohol units in Scotland compared with England. Because of the relatively much larger number of alcoholic admissions to Scottish psychiatric hospitals it is much more likely that there will be, at any one time, in quite a few Scottish hospitals, a sufficiently large number of alcoholic patients enabling the formation of special groups (even if they do not constitute special units), in particular when encouraged to do so by a psychiatrist who is interested in the problem of alcoholism.

The 1962 Memorandum constituted a clear reversal of the former official policy and practice of scattering alcoholics haphazardly into numerous local hospitals. Thus, by 1960, only two hospitals had special units established for the treatment of alcoholism, and of just over 2000 alcoholics admitted in 1959 more than half were scattered throughout 100 different psychiatric hospitals, the numbers admitted to each hospital varying from one to nineteen [5]. In 1962, approximately one out of twelve patients admitted to psychiatric hospitals for the treatment of alcoholism or alcoholic psychosis entered a special unit, a proportion that had risen to one in six by 1964.

The principles at work in a specialised alcohol unit (i.e. the one in Edinburgh) were well described in a book on *The Management of Alcoholism* [6], written by Bruce Ritson and Christine Hassall and introduced by H J Walton, who established the Edinburgh unit. Whilst the running of various units varies from each other, for example, according to the treatment philosophy favoured by the consultant, these authors rightly stress that it should *not* be the aim of such units to discover (and to accept for treatment) the alcoholic who is suitable for group therapy (as had been alleged by some critics): 'any treatment service designed for the alcoholic should provide, in some way, although not necessarily by admission to hospital, for all the manifestations of this disease. The treatment programme should be sufficiently flexible to accommodate the differing problems of individual patients'. Not only gaps in current knowledge but also insufficient staff and inadequacy of the range of suitable treatment facilities may make it difficult to achieve this task, but the Edinburgh unit was in fact able to offer some help to all patients who were referred.

Incidentally, many factors discussed by Vaillant (1980) [7] (see Chapter 16) as being important in the role professionals play in the recovery process, are at work in an alcohol unit – the need for relief of suffering, elevation of the patient's morale, hope, 'raising the patient's expectations of "cure" and his reintegration with the group'. Stressing the possibility so pronounced among alcoholics of being of service to others, militates against the patient's morbid self-preoccupation and strengthens his self-esteem. 'Group acceptance, an emotionally charged but communally-shared ritual and a shared belief system, contribute to helpful programmes, and an important function of a medical care system consists in facilitat[ing] the transition of the isolated patient to group membership.' In order to maintain the patients' modified attitudes, group rituals and support must be maintained after clinical discharge. Attempts at changing the patients' attitudes are based not on threat or rational advice, but 'by affecting self-esteem'. Encouraging patients' group activities helps the development of comradeship among the patients. 'The opportunity to identify with helpers once equally as disabled and to help others to stay sober fits in well with J Frank's [8] general prescription for a 'therapeutic group process', from which some aspects were quoted at the beginning of this paragraph. Identification and mutual support and help are both prominent features of alcoholic units and AA.

It is of course not just the in-patient department which consti-tutes the alcohol unit. As stated at an international London ICCA Institute (1964) clearly, a hospital treatment centre can be no more than one part of an integrated service for alcoholics. A comprehensive service catering for alcoholics of all types and in all phases of their addiction must provide out-patient and community services, halfway houses and hostels, as well as in-patient facilities. The whole integrated complex of facilities should be regarded as the unit, rather than the in-patient facility by itself, and should be the responsibility of one medical director, thus allowing trasnfer of the patient from one facility to another, which may often become necessary. This unit should, of course, work in close contact with general practitioners, AA, and other voluntary and official agencies, especially the local medical officer of health, and should also have easy access to general hospitals for patients requiring sobering-up and detoxification only [9].

Thus the in-patient department is clearly only one part of an integrated service for alcoholics, which must also have its out-patient clinics and community services, such as hostels and pos-sibly social clubs, and should have links with local authorities and voluntary agencies. Detoxification centres have recently been established in some units (see Chapter 16). Several units might together have at their disposal a special after-care hostel. The more known and accepted among a community is the concept of alcoholism as a treatable illness, the less important will be the role of an in-patient facility, and the more important the role of out-patient facilities and of a service within the community. But the often posed question as to whether out-patient or in-patient facilities are more important seems to be largely academic.

There will always be those alcoholics who need in-patient therapy. There will always be others – and one may hope that in the future their proportion will rise – who do not require hospital admission, in whose case either the whole treatment programme may be carried out within the community (by the GP and the primary health care team in co-operation with local authorities and voluntary organisations, such as AA) or who perhaps only need a few days' sobering-up and detoxification either in a general hospital or in special 'drying-out' or detoxification centres –

followed by a supportive rehabilitation programme.

Undoubtedly the Ministry memoranda constitute a great step forward, but before such 'units' can be expected to be run successfully, it is clear that much more undergraduate and postgraduate medical education on alcoholism is required, and also that nurses will need to acquire greater understanding of the condition. (Likewise, later DHSS memoranda emphasising the need for the building up of community services for alcoholism (1973) and similar suggestions by the DHSS Advisory Committee on Alcoholism (1975–9) obviously require for their realisation a greatly improved training and education of professional and voluntary workers in this field.)

If medical and nursing staff are just drafted into such units without adequate understanding and experience of alcoholism, they may be unable to tolerate the relapses and difficulties confronting them, and the outcome may be a waning of any initial interest. If special clinics and units are started without doctors or nurses who are experienced in the special problems presented by alcoholics, the result may easily be mutual misunderstanding between staff and patients with the result that both might tend to walk out and abandon the whole venture. Adequate training of any staff must therefore precede the establishment of special clinics and units, which, on the other hand, are excellent training centres for doctors, nurses, social workers and other professional workers who would like to obtain first-hand information and practical experience in the field of alcoholism.

The need for hostels

Reference has repeatedly been made in previous pages to the need to cater for all types of alcoholics in all phases of their affliction. Halfway houses, as mentioned before, should form an integral part of the special alcohol unit. Such halfway houses, including day hostels, night hostels (for those who have employment but may be without home and family) and weekend hostels (for such alcoholics who may be without job, home, family, friends, etc.), would often circumvent, or at least greatly shorten, the length of the stay in hospital.

In some cases, the in-patient facility, by allowing regular attendances of out-patients or day-patients, or by arranging for patients during the latter phase of their hospital stay to go out to work from the hospital prior to their complete discharge, may also serve the functions of a day-and-night hostel and a halfway house. The main function of a halfway house in the case of patients discharged from hospital is that of providing an often very helpful, or even absolutely necessary, transitional support measure for those well enough to leave the sheltered atmosphere of the hospital but who, at the same time, are not yet fit enough to stand completely on their own feet. In the halfway house they receive continuing support from living in a therapeutic community formed by alcoholics, from group therapy and from an understanding warden (who, if at all possible, should already have got to know the alcoholic whilst he was still a patient in the hospital).

Even the best-intentioned alcoholic who may have done well whilst in hospital may break down quickly after discharge if he lacks the support and security derived from a stable home and congenial job. Friendless, homeless, not knowing how or where to spend his leisure time constructively, he may all too readily be tempted to drift back to his former drinking friends, his old bars and haunts, and to his previous drinking habits.

The abrupt change from the sheltered hospital atmosphere to living by himself in unfamiliar 'digs' without the support of stable friends may be too much for many alcoholics to cope with. For such a person, the special alcoholic hostel can act as a bridge; supported by the hostel community he will be encouraged to start work whilst still living in the hostel, before the next phase of living by himself whilst perhaps still using the hostel as a type of social centre and at weekends, etc. Thus gradually he may come to function more and more independently.

In some cases the length of hostel stay of a formerly fairly well-adjusted alcoholic may average no more than three to six months. In other alcoholics who perhaps never in their life had been 'socialised', a much longer stay may sometimes be needed; and possibly there may be a need for some very inadequate and insecure personalities to stay indefinitely in certain types of hostels geared to the needs of long-stay residents.

The (1968) Ministry of Health Memorandum recognised that 'there is a need for more hostels specifically for alcoholics, which might be provided by local authorities or by voluntary bodies'. There is as yet little evidence that local authorities have been working overtime to comply with this recommendation so that the brunt of such efforts – as so often in the field of alcoholism – has been borne by voluntary organisations, in particular the West London Mission and the 'Helping Hand' which have both established a number of hostels for various types of alcoholics in the London area.

Clearly the personality of the warden is of the greatest importance for the atmosphere and thus for the success or failure of such hostels. However, the often debated question whether it is advisable or not to have a recovered alcoholic as a warden of such hostels is of much less importance than his personality and his general attitude and approach to the residents. Having successfully overcome one's alcoholism may give a person certain assets and should obviously be taken into consideration but cannot by itself be the decisive factor when a warden for an alcoholic hostel is chosen.

Obviously a wide variety of such hostels is required providing a flexible service. Social services, local authorities, voluntary and religious organisations have provided such hostels which have been supported by a grant from the DHSS. Addresses are given in Appendix I. A Director of Projects (England and Wales) gives details of all types of accommodation and information services for the people who have drinking problems. The 1980–1 edition is available from FARE (the Federation of Alcoholic Rehabilitation Establishments) (address in Appendix I).

Special hostels

Special hostels may be required to assist down-and-outs, drinkers, chronic drunkenness offenders and ex-prisoners, all of whom may suffer from personality and environmental problems beyond those which confront the more common type of alcoholic. In the past such people have often been 'dealt with' by a revolving door policy: drunkenness-arrest-prison-discharge-drunkenness. Everyone is probably agreed that this method is fruitless and should be replaced by a more constructive policy rather than sending the drunken 'offender' to the prison cells and bringing him before the courts next morning. Recidivists could, for example, be taken to medically directed sobering-up or detoxification centres (see Chapter 16). There, if they were to stay a few days at least, attempts could be made to induce in them a measure of motivation to co-operate with long-term treatment and rehabilitation approaches, starting off, for example, by transfer to a special hostel for this type of problem drinker.

The long-term aim should be his rehabilitation or at least improvement as far as possible, not merely a more humane version of the *status quo.* One voluntary organisation which has struggled hard for years to alert the public to the needs of the skid-row alcoholic is the Simon Community, which provided shelters for these people in which they were allowed to come and go and (more or less) to do as they like, in a very permissive atmosphere. However, best intentioned as such attempts were, one may question whether such shelters do not just perpetuate these people's unfortunate plight, when possibly more active support and treatment may achieve more, at least in a proportion of these sufferers.

It was interesting to read in a 1969 newspaper report that the hard-working and idealistic founder of the Simon Community from his experience of working with crude spirit drinkers had come to the conclusion 'that with the vagrant drinker of ten or more convictions we are dealing with a person who in the interests of the greater goal and in his own interests, needs to be compulsorily detained and committed to a rural colony . . . a compulsory care centre developed on Scandinavian lines . . . offering all facilities for those wishing to accept help' [10].

However, one must surely question whether the failure of an over-permissive and perhaps somewhat unrealistic venture means that one must jump immediately to the opposite extreme; and whether it would be justified to consider these rather drastic steps without first making a determined attempt to provide a comprehensive rehabilitation programme, based on a more realistic appraisal of these people's needs rather than just giving them a roof over their head and a warm meal but otherwise leaving them to their own devices – as some of the Simon Shelters seem to have done in the past. The over-permissive approach may be more than these often inadequate personalities with the superimposed handicap of frequent intoxication can cope with.

Special hostels seem to be the most promising alternative to prison for the chronic drunkenness offender, as Lord Stonham, former Minister of State, Home Office, stated at an international symposium on *The Drunkenness Offence* held in London in 1968 [11].

Whilst there is nowadays a total of over 100,000 convictions for drunkenness per year, the number of habitual drunken offenders is relatively small. About 1000 such people are in prison at any one time, out of a rough estimate of a total of 2000 habitual drunken offenders in the community. Recent studies have shown that a high proportion of these chronic offenders are 'loss of control' alcohol addicts, people who, as we have seen, require specialised treatment and are unlikely to respond to imprisonment – even if repeated again and again. Their need is for an integrated and comprehensive, therapeutically-oriented service, probably best centred on the provision of special hostels.

If there are a number of such hostels, run by wardens who each may have a slightly different philosophy of approach – e.g. one being more permissive, the other less so – and each one perhaps catering for a slightly different type of resident, it should be possible to refer and transfer these alcoholic offenders to the hostel best suited for their individual needs and to give them a chance gradually to 'move up' into a hostel where there may be more scope for showing responsibility, initiative, etc. Naturally, with many such people one has to be satisfied with a very limited goal, but that a surprising amount can often be achieved especially where there is a dedicated warden and a very interested general practitioner has been shown, for example, by experiences of Rathcoole House in London [12].

Rathcoole House is a residential hostel established by the *Alcoholics Recovery Project* in south London. They were founded by Tim Cook, a barrister who took up prison welfare work. Cook described his experiences in *Vagrant Alcoholics* [12] which relates the help the Project had rendered to homeless alcoholics in the preceding ten years: in court, prison, lodging houses, hospitals, and by establishing hostels and 'shop-fronts' (walk-in facilities) where the drinker can meet staff and other people in a similar position to his own and where he can find understanding, friendship and more tangible assistance if necessary. In what a reviewer [13] called 'a most illuminiating chapter' the vagrant alcoholic's attitudes are described to hostels ('he is sick of places like the Sally'), methylated spirits ('when you begin drinking the jack, you have to join the rough boys'), social workers and doctors (often unprintable), Pentonville Prison ('the Dossers' Retreat') and other people and institutions.

In this review Dr Granville-Grossman says: 'The hearts of most psychiatrists and social workers sink when faced with the vagrant alcoholic or derelict skid-row drinker . . . "inadequate" with a "life-long personality disorder" and a "pathological social adjustment", "lacking in motivation", "unhelpable" . . . "incurable" . . . Not surprising(ly) . . . most vagrant alcoholics receive more attention from the courts and prisons than from social agencies and hospitals.' In spite of all these difficulties quite a few people have been trying to render help, and like Rathcoole

House, have achieved some measure of success.

Another hostel for the down-and-out in the East End, is in the Crypt, Christ Church, Spitalfields, which provides a 'refuge from the cold, poverty and methylated spirits', and the beginning of a way back for those who want to avail themselves of it [14]. Most inmates have been sleeping rough in doorways in the neighbourhood. Opened in 1965 as a hostel for alcoholics and first serving as a night shelter, it was soon found that the men wanted the security of a home, and the Crypt became a residential facility in 1974 with eighteen beds. Some people stay for weeks or even months; the 'no drinking' rule for the residents is working well. In the first decade (up to 1974) the Crypt had 888 admissions – 450 men (many admitted repeatedly) of whom two-thirds were Irish and Scots, and mainly in the over forty age group. The first medical adviser was Dr John Coleman before he returned to his medical work in Iran. He worked hard at introducing motivation in his patients and quite a few of them were referred by him to other facilities, such as the St Bernard's Alcohol Unit. For many of its residents this was not possible; as the Church Army Captain Ronnie Rooke, who helped in setting up the centre, put it: 'There is no reason [among such men] for controlling their alcoholism. Families have gone, homes have gone, money has gone and the purpose of living has gone.' Such considerations bear out the essential differences between down-and-out drinkers and the (far larger) sections of the working population who are still at home with their families, and a job, and who have ample reasons and motivation to make a come-back.

The aim of the Spitalfields workers is to assist their patients towards helping themselves to find jobs and a place to live outside the Crypt. Some men have succeeded, many have remained failures and have returned to drinking. But for those who keep trying, a nearby second-stage hostel has been established: Downham Lodge which accommodates twelve men. This was opened in 1973.

Clearly for many such people, the outlook is not good and it takes a dedicated staff to continue such work and to keep on trying. However, to an outsider watching this work, such 'limited' improvement often means a great achievement and often much more than could be hoped for considering the very limited potential illustrating the great difficulties of 'measuring' therapeutic success.

For many years it has been left to voluntary bodies to look after the homeless alcoholic, foremost among them the Salvation Army, but also the Church Army, the churches, and other voluntary organisations. A Home Office Working Party published a report on 'The treatment of the habitual drunken offender within the penal system' (1971) [15], and it was hoped that this would hasten the long overdue progress in this field. The recommendations aimed at replacing the traditional penal approach by a more constructive one of care, assessment, treatment and rehabilitation. To this purpose, it was proposed to establish a chain of detoxification centres (see Chapter 16), various types of hostels and, 'shop front' counselling facilities. Apart from a few isolated 'private enterprise' detoxification centres few of the Report's proposals have been acted upon. Alcoholics cannot, of course, be divided into those who are the special responsibility of the penal system and those who 'belong' to the National Health Service, and there is an obvious need for close co-ordination of such services. Hostels may also have an important role to play in the rehabilitation of 'criminal alcoholics'. It has rightly been said that criminal proceedings are usually an inhumane, inappropriate and ineffective response in ordinary cases of drunkenness; alternative responses will usually be more helpful, such as a number of 'low key' measures recommended by the Chief Probation Officers – cautions, fines and attendance centre orders, in the case of juvenile offenders; or detoxification with subsequent assessment procedures in detoxification centres. But there will always be a number of alcoholics to be found in prison for offences other than just public drunkenness. Apart from the necessity to provide special hostels for them after release, possibly experimental schemes of establishing special pre-release alcoholic hostels might be considered. Thus suitable 'screened' alcoholics who show evidence of progress whilst in prison might possibly be allowed to spend part of their sentence in such a hostel where, apart from therapeutic community approaches and group therapy, they might receive vocational guidance, job training and attend evening school; some might be permitted to go out to work. In time, some might be well enough to go on parole whilst still remaining under regular supervision, and possibly work with employers with whom the prison social worker has established close, regular contact [16].

Clearly, should there be any return to alcohol or of asocial behaviour, the alcoholic would have to return to prison. The knowledge that this sanction exists may – in the view of alcoholic prisoners and ex-prisoners with whom this problem has often been discussed by the present writer in group sessions – often act as a deterrent against the resumption of drinking and thus be a powerful motivating factor towards keeping off drink [16].

Quite apart from the possibility of special hostel provision, as in the case of hospitals, it may be greatly preferable to aggregate alcoholic prisoners in a certain number of prisons rather than haphazardly scattering them throughout all prisons. In this way the possibility of establishing some type of therapeutic community and of group therapy, and of forming AA groups should assist towards inducing some motivation in a proportion of alcoholic prisoners.

Vocational guidance, education schemes, meaningful and interesting occupation, etc., should of course all be part and parcel of such prison alcoholic therapeutic communities. As with all such undertakings, the personality and the attitude of the people in charge is of vital importance, and the knowledge of 'limited returns' with regard to success should not be a bar to such experimental schemes with built-in research facilities [16].

Alcohol units in prisons

Imprisonment does not constitute treatment of alcoholism, and prison is not the best place for treating alcoholics. On the other hand, the often heard statement that 'prisons are unable to deal with the treatment of alcoholics' requires some qualification. There will always be some alcoholics who find themselves in prison for criminal activities directly or indirectly connected with their behaviour arising out of their preoccupation with drink. Even under custodial circumstances, humane and constructive therapy may instil initially missing motivation, and encourage initiative and the development of new attitudes. That this is so has been shown, for example, in the therapeutic community facility for treating alcoholics (and other drug addicts and compulsive gamblers) in Wormwood Scrubs since 1972. A review [16] published after the unit had been functioning for five years came to the following preliminary conclusions:

(a) The formation of a therapeutic community for 'addicts' in prison is a feasible proposition.
(b) Many prisoner-addicts (whatever their initial notions) will develop positive 'motivation' in such a unit.

(c)   Prison (Hospital) Officers, who, because of their close contact with the inmates, are the most important members of the integrated multidisciplinary team in such a unit rapidly assume a therapeutic role completely at variance with the custodial role popularly ascribed to prison staff. The understanding, accepting (though by no means uncritical) attitude of these officers is probably the main factor in producing an atmosphere of constructive co-operation and very active participation of the patients.

(d)   Like a hospital unit, a prison addiction unit is incomplete and cannot be expected to succeed without a planned, prolonged, specialised, multidisciplinary after-care service. A special halfway house where patients can spend the last few months of their sentence before full discharge would seem highly desirable. Continuity of staff – not only within the prison unit but possibly also with the same officers working with 'their' ex-patients in the after-care period – would also seem highly desirable.

(e)   Evaluation of long-term results (after establishing an adequate after-care service) is obviously needed, in spite of the problems and difficulties involved. Nevertheless, in the view of all staff members who were involved in this work, the findings of the Wormwood Scrubs Addiction Unit would justify the establishment of similar experimental units in other prisons.

(f)   The prison addiction unit is well suited for training of Prison Officers and other professional staff, and for research.

(g)   Experiences with Prison Officers in the Wormwood Scrubs Addiction Unit strongly suggest their potential for adopting a predominantly therapeutic role: a finding which seems to deserve much wider recognition and utilisation.

Probation officers attached to the Prison's Welfare Department (like psychologists, clergymen and others) took a very active part in the work. In a written Report (1976) presented by two probation officers at the end of their period of working in the 'Annexe', they said:

Within the limits necessarily imposed by the penal system, the inmate learns that there is room for self-determination and exploration of himself and his peers. Much has yet to be learned about the effectiveness of the régime. How favourably, if at all, does it compare with other methods of treatment? Can the high cost of running such a unit, using a high staff-to-inmate ratio and use of highly trained therapists be justified? These are questions that must be asked. But from a social worker's point of view, the movement observed in a man's attitude, his growth in maturity, and awareness of his difficulties and willingness to face them, gives rise to a hope that such treatment centres should be increased in number . . . (the Annexe experiment . . . also . . . shows one way in which the Probation Service and the Penal System can work together) [17].

Incidentally, a 'Report on Drug Dependants within the Prison System in England and Wales', written by the Advisory Council on the Misuse of Drugs (December 1979), had among its recommendations that 'Further therapeutic units for dependency on the lines of those at Holloway or Wormwood Scrubs should be established'.

To end this section on a personal note, in the writer's view, the creation of a helpful, therapeutic atmosphere at the Wormwood Scrubs Annexe has been due in the main to the application, enthusiasm and dedicated work of many prison hospital officers whose great help has been acknowledged openly and spontaneously on many occasions by many prisoner-patients at the unit. I have long felt that public acknowledgement of the work of these officers is overdue, and I am grateful for this opportunity to do so.

The question of compulsory treatment

(a) *Could alcoholics be treated compulsorily?*
An old myth perpetuated from textbook to textbook is that the alcoholic must be 'ready' before he can be helped and that therefore any attempt to start treatment without his consent is doomed to fail. It is very likely true that, all other factors being equal, patients admitted voluntarily (informally) will do better than those compelled to undergo treatment. It is also true that no treatment of alcoholics can succeed unless they become 'motivated' and want to get better. But that is quite different from claiming that such 'motivation' must be present at the time treatment is instituted. We have seen quite a number of alcoholics in whom, despite a strong initial refusal to co-operate, such 'motivation' was induced when they were treated within the framework of a 'therapeutic community' alongside a great majority of other alcoholics who had a strong desire to get over their drinking problem.

The old idea that alcoholics could only recover after having reached their 'rock bottom' (in the Chart of Alcohol Dependence and Recovery) and having 'knocked their heads against a brick wall' again and again, is fortunately not true. It would seem often quite wrong to wait until the alcoholic himself acquires insight and asks for help, as not infrequently the initially missing 'motivation' can be induced in the course of therapy. Indeed, to help in bringing about such 'motivation' would seem to be one of the main goals of a treatment programme for alcoholics, and the permissive alcohol unit would often seem to be a very good place for this to happen. Clearly it is in such cases only the manner of admission that is 'compulsory'. Once in the unit it is usually possible – with the help of the 'voluntary' patients – to treat the 'compulsory' patient in more or less the same permissive way as the rest of the patients. The emphasis on the term 'compulsory treatment' should be on 'treatment' – it should certainly not mean custodial care.

(b) *Should some alcoholics be treated compulsorily?*

This question is bound to arouse strong passions. One usually hears arguments that it is quite wrong to force drinkers into a treatment situation if they themselves do not want it, and that such people should be allowed to make up their minds whether and when they would like to be treated.[3]

Impressive as such views may sound they seem completely unrealistic in the case of alcoholics. Drinking alcoholics are not free agents; they are slaves to their compulsion and are not at liberty to decide whether they want treatment or not. It is one of the characteristics of the illness alcoholism that the sufferers lack insight and are quite unable to appreciate what they are doing to themselves and their families.

One may therefore ask not only whether it is right to consider compulsory therapy in the case of an alcoholic who is obviously going downhill and who refuses all appeals to come for treatment, but whether society has the right to stand by and watch him going to his grave while debating whether or not one should intervene. Whilst drinking, such people are unable to take rational decisions. The matter may be quite different after the alcoholic has been taken into an appropriate treatment centre and has been without drink for, say, at least a month. If he then still insists on leaving hospital in order to (virtually) continue drinking himself to death, possibly one might then have to accept that this is what he really wants (even this seems very doubtful) and what he should be allowed to do.

It has often been argued that compulsory admission of alcoholics to hospitals has generally failed. For example, an Irish law allowed the compulsory admission of alcoholics to psychiatric hospitals, usually with conspicuous lack of success. But usually these people were admitted to hospitals which were not 'geared' to the admission of alcoholics and had no special treatment programmes for them. It is quite useless to consider compulsory treatment of alcoholics, unless there are an adequate number of suitable centres and of experienced staff available to provide the special therapy they require.

Incidentally, when talking of alcoholics who come for treatment voluntarily it must not be overlooked that more often than not these patients are voluntary in name only. Many come to hospital in such a sorry mental or physical state, more often than not pushed along by the threat of wives leaving or employers sacking or the police prosecuting them, that they are hardly any longer in a state to say 'no' to hospital admission.

All would agree that every attempt should be made to persuade alcoholics to come for treatment voluntarily. However, if this fails and if the alcoholic is clearly in need of treatment, it can be said that not only can alcoholics be treated with some hope of success even if such treatment is initially started without their consent, but also that sometimes such treatment is absolutely necessary in their own interest to avoid lasting physical or mental damage or even death.

One paradoxical point, often making such a decision even more difficult, is the finding that it is – as in the case of 'voluntary' treatment – the person with a relatively stable personality type – e.g. the middle-aged man who in the past may have achieved a great deal and who has seen better days even if now he may be in a very poor physical and psychosocial state – who may benefit from treatment that is started without his consent or who may be coerced into treatment by the method of 'constructive coercion', e.g. in problem drinkers in industry, among car drivers and doctors, among those with 'bitter' wives and children etc. (see Chapter 10); there seems to be as little hope of getting very far in the case of the young, psychopathic alcoholic with compulsory as with voluntary treatment, although – keeping the principle of modest, realistic goals in mind – an attempt or rather a number of attempts may yet seem worth while, and should be made.

One further point must not be forgotten in the debate on compulsory treatment of alcoholics. As we have seen, their unpredictable behaviour often harms the mental (as well as the physical) health of wife and children; in many cases the alcoholic's wife states that she herself has reached breaking point and may be on the verge of suicide. By his irresponsible behaviour, for example in traffic, the alcoholic is often a habitual menace to the community (see Chapter 12). For the sake of others as well as for his own sake – and in such cases they usually go hand in hand – it would therefore seem that the State could give more serious attention to the question of compulsory treatment of such alcoholics who are clearly in need of treatment but are in an unfit state to make a rational decision; and that society should stop hiding its uneasy conscience behind the rationalisation that liberal principles forbid interference with the liberty of habitual, compulsive drinkers to decide whether or not to drink themselves to death.

Certainly no one wants to recommend compulsion unless it is absolutely necessary, and yet the lack of clear guidance and everyone's unwillingness to take responsibility for the unpalatable step of imposing compulsory treatment often leave the alcoholic's spouse in a hopeless dilemma. This is illustrated in two examples of alcoholics' wives: one, not seeing any other way out any longer, tried to take her own life; and the other one (herself a medical practitioner), who was told by us that there were after all only two ways of dealing with her chronic alcoholic husband (incidentally also a doctor) – either voluntary or compulsory admission – replied: 'There is another solution, and that's what I've decided to do – let things take their course. I'm at the end of my tether – I've left him – he'll just go on killing himself!'

Treatment outcome

The answer to the all-important question as to the outcome of treatment and the evaluation of treatment results discussed elsewhere is beset by a great many problems. Personality and social stability of the patient are obviously decisive factors in the outcome and it is impossible to compare the results of the various treatment programmes without knowing the composition of the 'case material'. All too often this is heterogeneous in composition and makes comparison impossible, much too depends on what type of problem drinker has been treated for example, dependent or non-dependent? How long (and how much) has he been drinking to excess? Did he start to drink heavily mainly for psychological or social reasons? To rule out some of the obvious difficulties one would need controlled trials, matching the patients treated with a special régime with others equalling them in all other respects but not receiving the treatment under scrutiny.

Another great obstacle in the way of evaluating treatment results is the difficulty of obtaining truthful answers from patients. Even though other aspects of the patient's readjustment and functioning are important, improvement in drinking behaviour still remains a key factor in evaluating results. But practising alcoholics are notoriously unreliable when it comes to assessing the amount they drink. In Toronto, Orrego and his colleagues [20] investigated the 'reliability of assessment of alcohol intake [among thirty-seven patients with alcoholic liver disease who had been advised to abstain from alcohol] based on personal interviews'. Urinary alcohol was measured daily for six months, and the patients were asked every week about their drinking during the week. It was found that fewer than 17 per cent of patients who had alcohol in their urine acknowledged having taken drink, at all times when they were questioned; and as many as 25 per cent 'convincingly' denied having taken drink. The unreliability of interviewing becomes even greater the longer the interval between interviews, because alcoholics are prone to 'forget' their drinking episodes. The Ontario workers therefore suggest that 'The personal interview should not be used to separate populations of abstainers and non-abstainers in the follow-up of alcoholic patients', whilst pointing out that self-reporting has in fact been used as a major form of assessment in many alcohol treatment programmes. However, to make matters even more difficult, they point out that the alternative (or complementary) form of assessment – obtaining evidence from families or other collateral sources – has also been found of no greater value than self-reporting, as discussed by M B Sobell and his colleagues [21] and Guze and his associates [22]. Armour and his colleagues (in the controversial *Rand Report*) [23] show that observers cannot readily discover an intoxicated state in an alcoholic with a blood ethanol level under 150 mg/100 ml; collaterals in the Ontario study reported patients who consistently denied drinking as abstinent whilst in reality nearly half of them (41 per cent) had alcohol in their urine. (However Orrego and colleagues found that deniers appeared to drink less than those who admitted their drinking.)

In view of these and many other difficulties it will cause little surprise that, according to a review by Madden (1979) [24], follow-up statistics of treated alcoholics have presented abstinence rates ranging from 10 per cent to nearly 70 per cent. This compares with a spontaneous remission rate reported by Lemere (1953) [25] to amount to 11 per cent. Two follow-up studies carried out in Britain in the late 1950s and referred to by Kessel and Walton in their *Alcoholism* (1965) were those of Maudsley [27] and the Warlingham Park Hospitals [28] respectively. At the Maudsley Hospital, Davies and his colleagues [27], providing treatment in a ward admitting all types of psychiatric patients (but no group therapy) and supportive out-patient therapy, found among fifty patients, after two years, 36 per cent abstinent all or most of the time, with 42 per cent remaining socially efficient in spite of light or heavy drinking. Of our ninety-four WPH patients [29], treated by a comprehensive approach but mainly group therapy in an alcoholic unit, a third had (after 2–3½ years) remained abstinent, a third had improved, and a third were (at the time) regarded as treatment failures. Prognostically important factors among our patients at the time were a relatively stable, non-psychopathic personality, male sex, older rather than very young (but see Chapter 7), high intelligence, sustained marital relationship, and better social status [29]. Hore's more recent critical review (1976) [30], on the whole appears to confirm this, but he raises certain questions relating to the need for research in the areas of social stability and of motivation towards sobriety. It is clear that if one agrees with Hill and Blane's [31] conditions regarded as necessary to indicate a treatment's effectiveness, that patients must be randomly assigned to control or treatment groups and that outcome criteria must be measurable by reliable techniques to be applied before and after treatment, almost all the follow-up studies carried out in the past would undoubtedly fail; but it seems extremely difficult in practice to fulfil such conditions. In a review of 271 investigations of treatment results, Emrick (1974) [32] found that approximately two-thirds were improved or abstinent after having received psychological treatment. In Britain studies found a significant outcome of treatment between (small groups of) in-patients and OP [33, 34], or between groups receiving only *milieu* treatment and those receiving group or aversion therapy as well as *milieu* treatment [35], or between male groups receiving short-stay (mean twenty days) and long-stay hospital care (mean eighty-two days) [36]. However, no such study is beyond criticism.

In view of all such difficulties and disagreements one can understand that all of today's treatment approaches including the alcohol units have come under fire. However, keeping all the criticisms in mind, Madden [37] nevertheless feels that certain studies 'indicate that intensive therapy which employs a variety of techniques is worthwhile, and that [such] therapy is often provided by specialised in-patient centres'. He mentions in this context the study by Costello (1975) [38] who investigated fifty-eight publications coming from seven countries. The one-year treatment outcome was affected by various treatment factors, as indicated by cluster-analysis of the collective data. Factors used by the successful therapeutic programmes included:

(i) A stay of longer than a month;
(ii) *Milieu* therapy with ward community involvement;
(iii) Counselling of spouses, relatives and employers;
(iv) Disulfiram or a corresponding drug;
(v) Behavioural modification;
(vi) Energetic out-patient follow-up.

Although selection of patients was made by the more successful programmes, better results with such methods were also found in the case of patients with unfavourable as well as among those with favourable prognostic features.

A later study carried out by Costello [39] confirmed these findings in twenty-three investigations with post-treatment results over a two-year follow-up period; it was also found that the successful programmes made:

(vii) More effective use of AA (which thus would be another factor to be added to the six mentioned above).

Finally, Madden [37] mentions the study by Blaney and his colleagues (1975) [40] who compared two in-patient groups in the UK treated, respectively, in an alcohol unit (group therapy, educational methods, disulfiram and AA) and in an ordinary psychiatric hospital: the alcohol unit sample showed a substantially more favourable outcome.

Obviously not only the reported results of the abstinence-oriented treatment programmes but (and probably much more so) also the ones aiming to assist certain alcoholics to achieve non-problem drinking, have come in for strong criticism. The best known examples are the two *Rand Reports*). The first Report [23] received favourable comment in *The Lancet* and the *British Medical Journal* but, on the whole, had a very unfavourable press in the USA; the decision whether this was mainly for good or inadequate reasons, may have depended largely on the observer's emotional bias. The first *Rand Report* (Armour, D J *et al.* (1976) [23]) was usually reported, in Britain, as supporting a non-abstinence drinking goal in alcoholics (although apparently the authors themselves did not quite see it this way). Among the many criticising the Report in the USA were Wallace [41], Chambers [42], and Seixas. For example, Dr Frank Seixas [43] (at the time Medical Director of the National Council on Alcoholism, a nationwide organisation committed to the goal of abstinence for alcoholics), stated (1978) that the Rand study originally involved forty-four treatment centres and 17,000 people but in the end (Seixas claimed) there were only three treatment centres from which the (non-randomised samples of) patients came, on which the observation was based that the percentage of relapsers in normal drinking was the percentage of relapsers in abstinence: 'The total number [says Seixas] was 161 . . . that represents eight people who relapsed after having abstained or going into socialised normal drinking'. Seixas suggested this to be 'an invalid finding . . . [a] research [that] needs redoing . . . to find out what truly happens'.

In fact, this is what Dr Armour and his colleagues did in publishing (1978) the second *Rand Report* [44] stating that the study was based on 'a random sample of 922 males who made contact in 1973 with any one of eight Alcoholism Treatment Centres (ATCs)' funded by the National Institute on Alcohol Abuse and Alcoholism. They followed up the same cohort (which was previously interviewed after six and eighteen months) for four years, obtaining information 'from 85 per cent of the target sample'. At the four-year point 'the basic condition of the subjects was measured by the presence or absence of alcohol-related problems over the six-months' period before the follow-up interview'. Among the results were: patients 'receiving higher amounts of ATC treatment [e.g. more than five OP visits] exhibited slightly more favourable status at four years': the alcohol problem among the high-treatment group was 11 percentage points lower than that of the low-treatment group, and 21 points lower than the rate for a group of subjects who made only a single contact with the treatment facility'. The results also indicated that the drinking status after four years was not associated with the treatment setting (i.e. in- or OP). However, the treatment groups were not randomly assigned. The problem rate after four years was high but nevertheless constituted 'a substantial improvement since admission to treatment'. Alcohol dependence as shown by presence of such symptoms when starting treatment, was prognostically important in indicating an increased probability of continuing drinking problems, whereas the initial level of alcohol consumption, in the absence of dependence, did not. As regards relapse rates, at the four year follow-up, 'problem drinking rates' were found to be '30 per cent for previous long-term abstainers, 53 per cent for short-term abstainers, and 41 per cent for previous non-problem drinkers'. Similarly the mortality statistics showed rates of alcohol-related death to be 1 per cent for long-term abstainers, 9 per cent for short-term abstainers, and 3 per cent for non-problem drinkers.

Armour and his colleagues stress that their study 'does not recommend a particular treatment approach, and does not recommend that any alcoholic should resume drinking'. Many alcoholics experienced significant periods of remission after treatment: after the four year follow-up 46 per cent were in remission for at least six months: (of whom 28 per cent were abstaining, and 18 per cent were engaged in drinking without problems). Such remissions were, however, not stable in general over long periods of time. 13 per cent of the sample had been abstainers at both follow-ups, 9 per cent non-problem drinkers at both follow-ups, and an additional 6 per cent had shifted from one to the other (and *vice versa*). 'Change was [therefore regarded as] the dominant pattern of alcoholic behaviour over time', with a high probability of relapse for all types of remission. Armour and his colleagues therefore recommend measuring success by length of time spent in remission periods, rather than using long-term continuous remission, as usually used for this purpose ('the data suggest that alcoholism, once established, is unlikely to abate spontaneously'). Another important suggestion is the 'central importance' of dependence in the process of relapse: 'the greater the initial level of dependence, the higher the likelihood of relapse for non-problem drinkers'.

Services for alcoholics – recent recommendations

In contrast to past periods of inactivity and *laissez faire* attitudes recent governments have begun to take a more active and enlightened attitude to the problems of heavy drinking. A number of Reports on prevention and provision of services have been published under the auspices of the Advisory Committee of Alcoholism, including a *Report on the Pattern and Range of Services for Problem Drinkers* (Kessel Report) [47], the *Report on Education and Training* [48] and a *Report on Prevention* [49]. Recommendations have to take into consideration availability of capital and revenue, and the priority problem drinking should take compared with many other competing disorders. An important question too is the relative attention given to earlier 'problem drinkers' and to established 'alcoholics'. Important considerations are the need to co-ordinate the many services established by various organisations, to pool experiences and resources and avoid overlapping. (Local services have usually been established by interested individuals or groups who often provided such services in quite a patchy way, so that some areas may have a number of facilities, others none.) An early Ministry of Health memorandum (1962), called for the establishment of units to work with local authorities in each region. In the past directors of such units may have been liberal in their policies, and ready to help problem drinkers from outside their area. But preferably each area should have its own comprehensive and integrated range of facilities. Meanwhile (1980) the intended abolition of 'one tier' would make it more difficult to establish facilities catering for such 'areas' as envisaged by the Kessel Report.

The Kessel Report [47] while full of good intentions, seems to presuppose money and expertise and perhaps, above all, a degree of motivation among professional workers, social workers as well as medical men, that as yet does not exist, and that might take many years to develop. Previous experiences with similar demands put forward in many other parts of the world have usually shown that the majority of professionals and social workers, do not want to be involved or even committed in such work. Clearly GPs at the primary level and the secondary level should be strongly encouraged to take an active hand. Meanwhile the main body of work will fall on those who for some reason or other have become interested and committed. It would be simple and helpful to make use of their expertise and motivation, and to employ their skills to act as catalysts for spreading interest in such works [50]. This, for example, would include the interdisciplinary teams working in the community and in-patient departments of the alcohol units, or those NCA Information Centres which have also been acting as Advisory Centres, building up networks of support. In either case, the units or Regional Councils could act as centres, providing training and support for local teams working in localities somewhat remote from the main centres, building up regular counselling treatment and after-care services, and working in close contact with the primary care workers, such as GPs and social workers, general hospitals, voluntary and statutory services, community physicians, social services, AA and Al-Anon; also providing services for industry (through keeping in touch with industrial medical advisers and their personnel officers); units, perhaps working together with such Regional Information and Advisory Centres, should also be centres of education and training for professional and voluntary workers and counsellors.

Voluntary workers – including ex-patients of units who are only too keen to participate in any such work [51] – would be a great asset.

Creating facilities without expert and interested manpower invites failure; and allowing units to run down, in the hope that their place will be taken by possible future facilities again is courting disaster. Alcohol units have in the past two to three decades acted as catalysts in this field – attracting public and professional and governmental interest, training medical and other professional staff, who in turn created facilities elsewhere, providing lecturers to professional and lay groups. The mere presence of the units acts as a publicising agent, creating pressure and interest. There is certainly a need for a national strategy co-ordinating an integrated range of the available services and utilising the existing 'know-how' among their staff. Facilities such as the units or the Regional Advisory Centres of the National Council of Alcoholism should receive adequate official support to develop into always available centres, providing advice, support and, where necessary, active help immediately. At the same time professional undergraduates should be given a basic understanding of the condition so that they, in turn, would provide advice and assistance to the great many drinkers still in their early stages.

The question of 'New Directions'

No one would maintain that the results of treating alcoholics are very satisfactory. There is a great need for continuing research; first to minimise the number of future casualties by improved primary methods of prevention; then to delay progress of the disorder from early to later phases by early recognition by motivating the drinker to take stock and do something constructive about his dangerous drinking patterns; and thirdly to improve on treatment methods and to establish, if possible, what type of drinker responds best to which method. (The question of treatment goals (the need to be sometimes grateful for small mercies in very inadequate and unstable personalities), has already been touched upon.)

All these considerations are probably shared by the great majority of those engaged in this field, and, some voice their dissatisfaction much more loudly and clearly (people who are looking for 'new directions' in alcoholism treatment stated to 'stem from the sense that the old ways of looking at alcoholism treatment now, in many ways no longer serves us well' [52]).

The wish for change seems sometimes to characterise those criticisms of the traditional techniques. Whilst old treatment results are not ideal, there is little or no evidence that the 'new' techniques are any better or even as good.

The search for new directions is urgently required, but so far there is little evidence that these have shown the way to more successful treatments. While the old ways are often unsatisfactory, they do enjoy a certain degree of professional acceptance – and a high degree of patients' acceptance. In this latter way they give rise to hope, co-operation and motivation. To throw them over for largely untried new methods whose value is not yet clearly shown, seems premature. As stated in Edwards' and Grant's Introduction to *New Knowledge and New Responses* [53] there is a need to accumulate new knowledge, to continue professional education, to plan and evolve 'better services shaped in terms of all the growing understandings' but in spite of 'advances in understanding many aspects of drinking' it is equally clear that there are important gaps in knowledge [52]. Very often no real attempt has been made by either side to try to understand the differences that very often seem to exist between recent research findings on often relatively small and not always representative samples, and the clinical findings of a great many therapists the world over.

Notes

[1]   During the past two or three years, quite a few new private nursing homes for alcoholics have been established.

[2]   The first reunion meeting was held in February 1954 and the First Report (later developing into the monthly magazine), written by an ex-patient reads as follows: [2]

First Report – February 1954

'Example is the school of mankind and they will learn in no other' wrote Edmund Burke in 1795 and it was with some such idea in mind that former and present patients of WPH held their first meeting at St Martin-in-the-Fields' Assembly Rooms on Thursday evening 18 February, 1954.

There was a warm atmosphere of reunion and it was good – as Burke would have agreed – for those who are successfully rehabilitating themselves to try to be the examples, and for one and all to try and learn. Of course, a relapse is also an example from which to learn, but this was a fortuitous occasion.

The gathering was kept informal (light refreshments in steady circulation) and no one took the chair, but a little business had to be done and it was agreed (a) to hold meetings on Thursday evenings monthly, (b) to keep such meetings strictly limited to WPH people, (c) in order to keep the attendance so restricted, not to form an official AA group although those who so wish naturally continue with their own groups.

The meetings will be fortunate in having the continued advice and support of a doctor and social worker, who has kindly agreed to continue her secretarial help. On this first occasion was one guest, for whom there was a special welcome, 'Paget' the secretary of AA who, with the doctor, has done such great work in linking WPH and AA.

Discussion was initiated on the subject of rehabilitation and there was disclosed such a quest for information and such a fund of experience to supply it that there is obviously material here for many future meetings. There will always be those who have before them the major undertaking of stepping out from the protection of WPH into a new and rather fearsome looking life. The example of those who have found life not only possible but also enjoyable and full when WPH and AA teaching is applied to its problems will be an invaluable aid to them and a reward to those who can give help in any direction. There are also those former patients who still find the problems of living difficult. They should feel at home, we think, with their fellow old sweats from WPH (and let there be no wrong impression) the new meetings are for mutual help, not mutual admiration.

[3] The point that an alcoholic needs by no means to be 'ready' at the onset for treatment to be successful is well illustrated by the story in Chapter 20, p. 475. In this connection the suicide risk in alcoholics should be borne in mind – a risk stressed again in an article on suicide in December 1980 [18]. Moreover such a drinker may lose more 'status' by loss in 'human dignity' (betrayal of one's value, self-esteem) [19] than by coercion into treatment.

References

1   Glatt, M M (1955), *Brit. J. Addict.*, 52, 55
2   Whaakey-Whaakey (Warlingham Park Hospital), First Report, February 1954
3   Glatt, M M (1955), *The Lancet*, i, 1318
4   Glatt, M M (1959) *ibid*, ii, 397
5   Phillipson, R (1964), *Health Congress of Royal Society of Health*, London, 303
6   Risson, B and Hassall C (1970), *The Management of Alcoholism*, Edinburgh and London, Livingstone
7   Vaillant, G E (1980), *The Doctor's Dilemma* in *Alcoholism Treatment in Transition*, eds Edwards, G, and Grant, M, London, Croom Helm, 13–31
8   Frank, J (1961), *Persuasion and Healing*, Baltimore, John Hopkins Univ. Pr.
9   Glatt, M M (1964), 10th Europ. Inst. Prev. and Treatm. of Alcoholism, London (reprinted in: *New Aspects of the Mental Health Service*) eds Freeman, H and Farndale, J, Oxford, Pergamon, 131–48
10 *Guardian* 2 September; 1969
11 Lord Stonham (1969) in *The Drunkenness Offence* eds Cook, T, Gath, D and Hensman, C, Oxford, Pergamon, 1–8
12 Cook, T (1975), *Vagrant Alcoholics*, London, Routledge and Kegan Paul
13 Granville-Grossman, R (1975), *Brit. J. Psychiat.*, 203
14 Bramley, R, *Alliance News*, January, February, 1975
15 Home Office (1971), *Habitual Drunken Offenders*, London, HMSO
16 Glatt, M M (1977), in *Drug Dependence*, ed. Glatt, M M, Lancaster, MTP, 223–59
17 Askem, L and Breed, K (1976), *The Annexe-a Therapeutic Community within a Prison*. London
18 Kreitman, N and Dyer, J A T (1980), *Medicine*, 36, 1827
19 Gordis, E and Sereny, G (1979), *Controversies in Approach to Alcoholism* in *Controversies in Therapeutics*
20 Orrego, H *et al.* (1979), *The Lancet*, 2, 1354
21 Sobell, M B *et al* (1974), *Quart. J. Stud. Alcohol*, 35, 276
22 Guze, S B *et al* (1963), *Quart. J. Stud. Alcohol*, 24, 249
23 Armour, D J *et al.* (1976), *Alcoholism and Treatment*, The Rand Corporation
24 Madden, J S (1979), *A Guide to Alcohol and Alcohol Dependence*, Bristol, John Wright and Sons, 126–30
25 Lemere, F (1953), *Am. J. Psychiatry*, 109, 674
26 Kessel, N and Walton, H (1967), *Alcoholism*, London, Penguin Books,
27 Davies, D L *et al.* (1956), *Quart. J. Stud. Alcohol*, 17, 485
28 Glatt, M M (1959), *The Lancet*, ii, 397
29 Glatt, M M (1961), *Acta Psychiat. Scandiv.*, 37, 143

30 Hore, B D (1976), *Alcohol Dependence*, London, Butterworth, 125–30
31 Hill, M J and Blane, H T (1967), *Quart. J. Stud. Alcohol*, 28, 76
32 Emrick, C D (1974), *Quart. J. Stud. Alcohol*, 35, 523
33 Edwards, G and Guthrie, S (1966), *The Lancet*, 1, 467
34 Glatt, M M (1966), *The Lancet*, 1, 7, 91
35 McCance, C and McCance, P F (1969), *Brit. J. Psychiat.*, 115, 189
36 Willems, P J A *et al.* (1973), *Brit. J. Psychiat.*, 122, 637
37 Madden, J S (1979), *Brit. J. Addict.*, 74, 318
38 Costello, R M (1975), *Int. J. Addict.*, 10, 251–75, 857–67
39 Costello, R M (1977), in *Alcoholism and Drug Dependence*, eds Madden, J S *et al.*, New York and London, Plenum Press, 209–26
40 Blaney, R *et al.* (1975), *Brit. J. Addict.*, 70, 41
41 Wallace, J (1979), *World Alcohol Project*, 2(1), 3
42 Chambers, D K (1979), *World Alcohol Project*, 2(1), 18
43 Seixas, F A (1978), *Am. J. Drug Alcohol Abuse*, 5(3), 293
44 Armour, D J *et al.* (1978), *Alcoholism and Treatment*, New York, John Wiley and Sons
45 Roth, R, *Alcoholism – The National Magazine*, September–October 1980, 19
46 Jaffe, J (1980) in *Alcoholism Treatment in Transition*, eds Edwards, G and Grant, M, London, Croom Helm, 32–48
47 Advisory Committee on Alcoholism (1978), *The Pattern and Range of Services for Problem Drinkers*, London, DHSS and Welsh Office
48 Advisory Committee on Alcoholism (1979), *Report on Education and Training*, London, DHSS and Welsh Office
49 Advisory Committee on Alcoholism (1978), *Report on Prevention*, London, DHSS and Welsh Office
50 Glatt, M M (1979), *The Lancet*, i, 814
51 Glatt, M M (1962), *Brit. J. Addict.*, 58, 13
52 Brit. J. Addict. (Editor.), 1979, 74, 225
53 Edwards, G and Grant, M (1977) in *Alcoholism – New Knowledge and New Responses*, Introduction, London, Croom Helm, 11–13

19

Improvement and Recovery

Our introduction referred to Keller's remark that throughout history alcohol has shown itself to be a 'double-dealer' [1]. Throughout the centuries medical writers extolled its virtues and prescribed it for their patients (and often probably for themselves with equal dedication). As Andrew Poznanski tells us [2], Arnold of Villanova, physician, philosopher and alchemist (1235–1311) had this to say in his *Treatise on Wine:*

> No physician blames healthy people for the use of wine, unless he censures them for the quantity or for mixing it with water. If wine is taken in the right measure, it suits every age, every time, and every region. It is good for the old and for young children.

No wonder then that he used wine (in particular Wormwood wine) to cure all ills – for intestinal worms, jaundice, poor vision, deafness and for people going out of their mind.

But the alchemists soon discovered that newer alcoholic drinks held out even greater hope and promises than Villanova's panacea. Towards the end of the thirteenth century distilled spirits began to appear in Europe. Distilled liquor came to be regarded as the 'water of life'; *eau de vie* in France; Celtic uisquebeatha – later to become usquebaugh (said to be first manufactured about 1100 by the Irish [3]). Others soon followed: for many Scots whisky became the elixir of life, for Russians, vodka and for Scandinavians, aquavit. For an unfortunate minority these drinks rather than being the 'water of life' proved a harbinger of ill health and death: a 'double-dealer' indeed. Robbie Burns in *Tam O'Shanter* could talk of:

> Inspiring bold of John Barleycorn! What dangers thou can make us scorn!
> Wi'tippeny, we fear nae evil; Wi 'usquabae, we'll face the devil!

And Shakespeare in *Othello* (Act II, Scene 3) obviously felt he did not have to go anywhere else to face the devil:

> O though invisible spirit of wine,
> if thou hast no name to be known by,
> let us call thee devil.

In view of the hazards that threaten the problem drinker it is not surprising that, fifty years ago Pearl [5], in his *Alcohol and Length of Life* [4], an investigation of statistical records of life insurance companies, found that 'the only definite conclusion that may be reached is that excessive drinkers have a greater mortality and a shorter average life than moderate drinkers and abstainers'. A much more recent review (1975) by W Schmidt and R Popham [6] also concluded that 'chronic heavy users of alcohol . . . have a substantially elevated risk of premature death'.

There is, however, great variability in individual susceptibility. Schmidt and Popham go out of their way to echo Pearl to 'disclaim any responsibility for applying such general conclusions to the individual case: . . . a conclusion which is on the average true for a large statistical aggregate may not be so for a particular individual in that aggregate', and they refer to the well known cases of octogenarians who have been imbibing heavily all their lives. In clinical practice one finds again and again that provided alcoholics have not reached the final, irreversible stages of physical complications they often improve remarkably rapidly once they do something about their drinking (see Chapter 14). Even drinkers who look very bad at the time of admission to hospital usually make a quick physical recovery within a few days. The important point is for the drinker himself to come to grips with his problem. The great difficulty he may soon find is not giving up drink but maintaining motivation. This chapter therefore does not deal with the short-term outlook but with long-term chances for maintaining improvement and recovery.

How great are the chances that one's alcoholic husband, wife, father, friend, employee can be successfully rehabilitated? Naturally this question cannot be answered fully without an individual assessment of the factors at work in the given patient. However, some general points may serve as very broad guidelines.

To start with, it can be said that just as the alcoholic's own view of his chances is usually unduly over-optimistic, so the views of the professional and the lay public are unduly pessimistic. Probably one contributory factor to the public's scepticism is the statement that flows so freely and glibly from the alcoholic's lips: 'Of course, I will be able to stop. This time I have seen the light. After all, I *must* stop.' The doctor, the wife, the employer may be forgiven for remaining sceptical in the face of such protestations which they have so often heard in the past; it may remind them of Mark Twain's remarks: 'Of course, I can give up smoking any time I want to . . . After all, I ought to know, I have given it up hundreds of times!'

However, one of the main reasons for the prevalent pessimistic notions about the alcoholic's ability to recover is probably based on the widely advertised behaviour of the psychopathic[1] type of alcoholic whose feats attract attention in newspaper reports and bring him before the courts at regular intervals. Such misconceptions are often also derived from unwarranted generalisations from special groups, such as alcoholic criminals or psychopaths or the rare alcoholic psychotic. In all these it is the underlying personality disturbance or illness which is responsible for the often poor outlook, with alcoholism merely a superimposed factor though certainly one that must be tackled as it aggravates the condition and makes treatment of the underlying condition even more difficult.

Certainly the prognosis for the basically *psychopathic* alcoholic, for example, is poor. Such individuals – they may often be rather young, unstable, extremely self-indulgent persons with poorly developed conscience (super-ego) and a lack of 'empathy', the ability to feel deeply for and with others – will as a rule have shown poor adjustment – at home, school, at work – even before the onset of heavy drinking.

Most of them relapse quickly after treatment and they prove difficult and often troublesome members in AA. Views differ greatly how such psychopaths should be treated. With a relatively permissive therapeutic community approach – e.g. the one pioneered by Maxwell Jones [11] at (what is now called) the Henderson Hospital in Sutton, Surrey – some such inadequate and immature personalities may make certain progress, and a few alcoholic psychopaths can be 'carried' by a predominantly non-psychopathic alcoholic group. With some psychopathic drinkers, relapses may become less severe and less frequent, and there is some glimmer of hope provided by the finding that psychopaths become a rare phenomenon in middle age – possibly because of delayed, later emotional maturation.

Fortunately, however, these psychopathic alcoholics form a

minority only of the total alcoholic population. The more common, older type of alcoholic (in the past, beyond his thirties, but now quite frequently in his twenties), with a basically good personality type, in the great majority of cases will do well with treatment under appropriate conditions [9]. Very often such a man has done well in the past, having achieved success in his profession or business before being struck by alcoholism; and more often than not he may have retained a foothold at home and at work despite the severe handicap of his uncontrolled drinking. Being married and still enjoying the support of his family and the stabilising influence of a steady – though by then usually jeopardised – job are prognostically good signs.

A basically 'good' type of personality who in the past showed evidence of a fair degree of social stability (marital, residential, occupational) seems to be the most important favourable prognostic factor – such a person can often be expected to do well even if, before coming for treatment, he may have slipped down the socio-occupational scale and may be in dire straits. Relatively 'normal' personalities – e.g. people who have become excessive drinkers mainly under the impact of environmental factors – temptation, opportunity, exceedingly severe stress – and mildly neurotic individuals usually have the best prospects. In Lincoln Williams' formulation [8]: the 'good' and the 'sad' (neurotic) alcoholics will usually fare better than the 'bad' (psychopaths) and 'mad' (psychotics) ones.

It goes without saying that no alcoholic can recover who himself does not want to do something constructive about his drinking problem; this motivation is a *sine qua non* for success. However, as we have seen, fortunately an initially missing motivation can often be induced during the course of treatment.

In the past *young* alcoholics by and large did less well than the middle-aged. Partly this may have been due to their often greater degree of pre-alcoholic personality disturbance. Often, too, one hears some such comment from young alcoholics as: 'It's all very well for older alcoholics to give up drinking – they've had their fling and enjoyment out of it. I'll consider giving up drinking once I get to their age . . .' little realising that ahead there is a life of heartbreak and suffering and not of enjoyment, and that possibly they may never live to see the day when they can decide to give up drinking. Nowadays, with some young people developing alcohol dependence often for social rather than psychological reasons, prognosis for these may often be quite good (see Chapter 7).

There is no reason to give up hope in *elderly* alcoholics, who may feel that they have left it too late. Clearly it is better to diagnose alcoholism as early as possible and to institute early treatment before alcoholism has produced mental, physical, domestic, social and financial complications, all of which may interfere greatly with the sufferer's ability to co-operate in an effort-consuming rehabilitation programme. On the other hand, provided that there are no irreversible physical or mental complications, even the old alcoholic can be helped a great deal (see Chapter 8).

Two points which must not be lost sight of have already been stressed repeatedly. First, alcoholism is basically a relapsing disorder and it often takes repeated 'skids' before the alcoholic finally recovers. Secondly, depending on the potentialities of the individual alcoholic, frequently one has to be satisfied with a relatively limited goal, often falling far short of the ideal goal of a happy, useful life of contented sobriety. This may apply in particular to such alcoholics as skid-row drinkers, of whom quite a few can perhaps not be assisted further than to function fairly well in a sheltered environment for the rest of their lives. Certainly for many alcoholics even a moderate degree of improvement must be regarded as a worthwhile achievement even if – to start with – one would try to set a further-reaching goal. But a perfectionistic approach – expecting complete, lasting sobriety in practically every alcoholic – is certainly quite unrealistic, giving rise to disappointments and perhaps causing many a therapist to withdraw from all work with alcoholics.

Some alcoholics may keep on having relapses, and whilst such a result is neither satisfactory for the patient, the therapist nor for the statistician, it may mean a great deal to the sufferer himself, and to his family perhaps even more, if instead of a continual state of quarrelsome, noisy and aggressive drunkenness, separation from his family, and unemployment, the alcoholic may now have only a few minor bouts during the year, and is able to keep his job and live in relative peace with his family.

Women alcoholics (see Chapter 6) are usually said to be tougher therapeutic propositions than men – perhaps partly because of greater pre-alcoholic personality deviations, partly because of more unfavourable environmental problems. But beyond doubt most female alcoholics can improve or recover once they bring out into the open their habit of secret drinking, and come for treatment or join AA. At St Bernard's Hospital the female alcoholic ward has certainly been functioning at least as well as the male ward, and female alcoholics have contributed their fair share to the working of the whole 'mixed' unit and to after-care programmes arranged to a large extent by the ex-patients themselves.

One often reads of attempts to compare the treatment results obtained by different therapists. Without the knowledge of what type of patient was treated, such comparison is quite meaningless. Every therapist taking some interest in these patients will achieve good results if he limits himself to the treatment of good personalities who are well motivated and sincere in their desire to overcome their drinking problem. On the other hand, no one will do well if the great majority of his alcoholic patients are psychopaths. Therefore such reports should include a detailed analysis of the composition of the group of patients treated.

To start with, if one wants to keep one's interest in treating alcoholics and to maintain one's own morale and that of one's staff, one should certainly try to work mainly with non-psychopathic, well-motivated alcoholics before embarking on the more difficult therapeutic propositions. What would be needed are planned studies aiming at finding the modes of treatment, or their combination, best suited to the different types of alcoholics. However, a large sample of patients chosen at random may be expected to divide into the well-known 'three-thirds': one-third to recover, one-third to improve to a large extent, one-third to show little if any improvement [9]. Yet one may sometimes be surprised to learn that alcoholics who initially had failed to show any response to treatment have in fact much later made considerable progress, and that they themselves ascribe this to the seed laid during their treatment periods, which bore fruit much later in life.

There is, of course, no point of talking of 'recovery' in alcoholism as soon as a patient has managed to stay sober for a few weeks. Many claims put forward for wonder successes are based on such short-term results. Any form of new therapy can be expected to lead to a temporary amelioration – as it may provide new hope and inspiration, even in psychopaths. It has been said that it is best to try out a new treatment while it still works! A World Health Organisation Alcoholism Sub-committee (1951) [10] report suggests the use of the terms 'recovery' or 'successful arrest' of alcoholism only in the case of such drinkers who have managed to stay off drink for at least two years. However, a useful pointer may be obtained as early as about six months after the treatment has finished. Most individuals who have been doing well up to that time can be confidently expected to carry on this good work later [9].

This does not mean that first 'skids' cannot occur much later, but as a rule such 'late' first relapses are due to over-confidence ('Surely after all this time I should be able to have just one drink!') rather than to giving in after a bitter effort and inner struggle – the latter so often the reason for a relapse in the first few months. Nevertheless, most observers remain convinced that alcoholics must never forget that drink is out for them. The saying that 'I am just one drink away from drunkenness and disaster' remains true for the rest of the alcoholic's life. At the same time, the urge to have the first drink can be confidently expected to wane after a few (unwillingly accepted) months of sobriety – so that, from the point of reliability of performance, and the expectation of a relapse, alcoholics who have been sober for a few years are, of course, in a much better situation than the newcomer who has been off drink for a few days or weeks only.

Finally, the outlook for the individual alcoholic depends to a large extent on the after-care service and on the facilities provided, including AA; on the patients' willingness and perseverance in availing themselves of such services; and on the attitudes of their family. Thus of the three main sets of factors involved in causing his alcoholism – 'host', environment and the 'agent' alcohol – the first two also play an important role in his rehabilitation and in his hopes for recovery, but if the alcoholic wants to recover he should have no truck with the third factor involved in causing his affliction, i.e. the 'agent' alcohol.

Scientific research in the field of alcoholism is still in its early stages. For example, as to therapeutic goals, apart from (according to the majority view) total abstinence, there are other important indicators of improvement – e.g. social recovery, improved functioning at home and at work, etc. As to treatment, there is room, and indeed need, for planned controlled trials comparing the various methods and their suitability or otherwise for the various types of patients. As we have seen, there is still great divergence of views about the merits of the various therapies popularly employed in alcoholism, and all of them have had many successes and failures.

Notes

[1] The controversial term 'psychopath' is employed in this book to describe – following Henderson-Gillespie's *Textbook of Psychiatry* [7] – those persons who have been from childhood or early youth habitually abnormal in their emotional reactions and conduct . . . show no intellectual defect . . . do not benefit under prison treatment . . . whose emotional instability is largely determined by a state of psychological immaturity, which prevents them from adapting to reality and profiting from experience . . . They lack judgement, foresight and ordinary prudence . . . Such psychopaths may be predominantly aggressive, predominantly inadequate or passive, or (rarely) predominantly 'creative'.

The term '(psycho) neurotics' usually refers to individuals who tend to suffer more or less frequently from 'minor' functional (i.e. non-organic) emotional disorders (such as anxiety, phobias, obsessions and compulsive acts, hysteria), in contrast to 'psychotics' who suffer from (either functional or organic) 'major' emotional disorders. People suffering from neurosis usually have insight (i.e. they realise that they are ill), and they live in a world of reality, whereas 'psychotics' usually have no such insight and often live in a world of fantasy. Like the term 'alcoholism' itself, all these terms are frequently used by different psychiatrists in different ways. By and large, other circumstances being equal, alcoholism may arise more readily in psychopaths and neurotics than in people not so disposed.

References

1 Keller, M (1976), 'Problems with Alcohol: An Historical Perspective' in *Alcohol and Alcohol Problems: New Thinking and New Directions*, ed. Filstead, W J *et al.*, Cambridge, Mass., Ballinger, 5–28

2 Poznanski, A (1959), in *Drinking and Intoxication*, ed. McCarthy, R G, New Haven, Yale Center of Alcohol Studies, 42–3

3 Wilson, G B (1940), *Alcohol and the Nation*, London, Nicholson and Watson

4 *Quart. J. Alcohol Studies* (1941), Lay Supplements No. 6, Yale Center of Alcohol Studies, 12

5 Pearl, R (1926), *Alcohol and Longevity*, New York, Knopf

6 Schmidt, W and Popham, R (1975), *Drug and Alcohol Dependence* (ICAA), 1, 27

7 Henderson, Sir David and Gillespie, R D (1950), *A Textbook of Psychiatry*, 7th ed., London, Oxford University Press, 388

8 Williams, L (1960), *Tomorrow will be Sober*, London, Cassell

9 Glatt, M M (1961), *Acta Psychiat. Scand.*, 37, 173

10 World Health Organisation (1951), Alcoholism Subcommittee, Wrld Hlth. Org. Techn. Rep. Ser., 42, 8

11 Jones, Maxwell (1968) *Social Psychiatry in Practice*, London, Penguin

20

Alcoholics Looking Back

The following contributions are written by recovered alcoholics. In their cases, it was the therapeutic community and group therapy which they felt had helped them most. Admittedly not everyone is convinced that these methods are the best for alcoholics. Obviously similar case reports can and have been written by alcoholics who have been helped by other techniques: 'Treatment by group therapy – Blimey!' wrote an alcoholic a few years ago in a book which described his own successful 'cure' by Dr Dent's apomorphine treatment [1]. The following therefore aim not so much at illustrating the merits of one particular method of treatment but rather the fact – well known to everyone who has taken a close interest in the problem but still coming as a surprise to many doctors as well as laymen – that a great many alcoholics can and do make a successful comeback.

1   The Fleet Street man's story

I think I know the reason why I took to drink, but when, exactly, it is impossible to say. For there was no firm 'here we go', instead a slow build-up. First, why? I didn't drink much before the war – in fact I didn't and never have liked the taste of liquor. I fought in Burma during the war as a captain, flying artillery-spotting aircraft. They were defenceless but I never drank to give myself false courage nor took a flask with me flying as some of our pilots did. But what a let-down there was when I got back to England after it was all over. After the luxury of being OC of a small unit in Malaya life was very humdrum.

Moreover as the years went on I realised that the fat top job I was after wasn't going to be mine. I began to feel that Captain X, former head boy at his grammar school, cricket and football captain, was being cheated out of his rights.

Fleet Street was ready to pounce.

On newspapers you sometimes work hard for a solid forty-eight hours then have nothing to do for the next forty-eight. The hours are elastic. Lunch, if you were waiting in the office for something to happen, would begin at 12.30. You'd meet the gang in one of the local pubs and grouse about how badly you had been treated. Fleet Street men are always talking shop and usually moaning, usually over a pint or a double.

Come three o'clock you'd still not had that meal you'd promised yourself nor did you want it. Instead there'd be another round at the local club and back to the office at three-thirty. Nobody cared very much what hours you kept if the article you were doing was on time.

Gradually I found that I needed a double to get me out of bed and another before I could get into the train. I had a couple of flasks hidden around the house so I could sneak a quick one. So while some people could get good and drunk and not touch a drop for days afterwards I, like a true alcoholic (Delta alcoholism), was never really very drunk but I was living on the stuff. All the time I was kidding myself nobody was noticing, that I could do my work as well as ever . . . and nursing those grievances as another editor arrived and I wasn't appointed sports editor. 'The world is against me' period (the 'Poor Me' syndrome). Drink was the only thing that could make me forget what a poor badly treated genius I was; and I was hitting the free drink really hard ten years ago.

In the end my wife insisted I consult a doctor. His verdict: 'you're an alcoholic'. But by that time I couldn't give it up despite his warnings.

I was saved in an odd way. I think I'd taken some barbiturates as well as my usual whisky. I was clear headed enough to help my eleven-year-old youngest daughter with her mental arithmetic. I remember saying 23 times 97 is 2300 less 69, when I passed out.

My lungs filled with fluid and my temperature went up to about 106 but they saved my life at Hillingdon Hospital. But I didn't wake up there. I was in a psychiatric ward at St Bernard's when I did. I had no idea how I got there. My wife had remembered the clinic there and made sure I got there . . . I can never thank her enough.

The ward is not a home from home when you first see it. I wanted to run. But a few hours afterwards I knew that this was it.

In hours you had made friends, and friends who were all in the same boat as yourself. It was as though I was getting protection from the menace outside.

I began to enjoy the routine and listening to other men's troubles. I began to realise that I was lucky, I was only on booze and not a junkie as were many in the ward.

I dried out without any trouble and from then on made a mental promise to the nurses and the doctors that I'd make it.

After ten weeks I was discharged. That was four years ago. I've not drunk since.

The problem then was how to plan my life. For a time I took tablets which would have made me ill if I'd had a drink. But I decided that this was the weak way out.* It was like being a boozer still who was just afraid to drink. At St Bernard's we had had visits from AA. Right from the start I felt that, good a job as they were so obviously doing, they were too sorry for themselves. Anyway the constant bleat of 'I am Joe, I'm an alcoholic' wasn't for me. In St Bernard's I'd been visited by my editor. Everybody knew anyway. So I decided that my attitude was to be 'I'm X and I used to drink, but I don't any more'. It worked; instead of being reminded of my sins people were often congratulating me, some have even asked my advice. 'How do you do it?' they would ask and still ask. I felt I had achieved something.

For the first time since the war I was proud of something I had done.

Mind you the editor helped. He made sure I was given something to do which I liked doing. That is important. It is no use going back to something which bores you stiff. You have got to have plenty to do, and you've got to be trusted. A friend of mine is now dead because after much effort to give up drink he was shunted into an office of his own with nothing to do – forgotten.

As part of my work I still have to visit pubs, for you hear a lot of gossip around a bar. It's part of the job, but it's accepted now that I drink a tonic and a slice of lemon and I like to buy my round. Nobody thinks it's unusual any more.

One word of warning. When you booze you don't eat and it could have an effect upon your health. A year ago last June after worrying my doctor he decided I was anaemic and should have a chest X-ray. It showed three TB cavities. I've also had an ear drum

---

*   This view, which one hears quite often, is, in the present writer's view, quite wrong and may in fact often constitute a rationalisation, leaving the door open for a drink, should the 'need' arise.

graft operation which wasn't successful. It was a sad blow and I could have done with a drink but by this time I'd got to the stage when I believe I'm incapable of lifting a glass with alcohol in it. So, thanks to my wife, doctor and employers, I've come to terms with Fleet Street – without having to join in one of its main exercises.

2   The Civil Servant's story

Some time has elapsed since the events which led me to hospital, nevertheless much of what transpired during the three months I spent there and from then to the present will, I hope, provide encouragement to those who are working out plans for their own recovery.

My turning point came only when I realised the futility of trying to find a way by which I could control drinking. Each experiment had failed with increasingly disastrous results, latterly ending in near lethal consequences. At one time I had been told that I was suffering from an illness (alcoholism) and this may have induced me to rationalise my drinking by saying to myself 'this is all part of my illness'. A more negative view would be difficult to find and to any who may be thinking on the same lines, my advice is 'forget it for all time'.

At Warlingham Park I found a refuge both from the point of view of restoring myself physically and becoming a member of a group of people all afflicted in varying degrees with the same problem, all friendly and understanding of each other. This relationship was invaluable in the organised group discussions which were to follow. Led by the doctor, these 'seminars', known as group therapy, involved an analysis of individual experiences including their apparent causes and how in future to deal with similar situations.

By contributing and listening to other members one saw a similarity of pattern running through each history and in detail the actions and reactions were strangely identical. It was this recognition which formed a close bond and stimulated enthusiasm to derive the maximum benefit from the discussions.

Prior to this method of treatment the underlying causes of one's submissions to compulsive drinking had remained a mystery. Previously, in many cases, physical restoration with a parting warning 'you must not drink again' or 'stick to beer in moderation' merely left one no wiser and sooner or later ready to embark on another 'bender'.

With the knowledge one acquires in the course of group therapy there should be no doubt whatever that alcohol in any form or quantity has to be strictly avoided, so far as an alcoholic is concerned. There is no reprieve from this by thinking that after an abstinence period of one, five or even fifteen years it will be possible to return to the state of a controlled drinker. There is no known cure, but the disease can be arrested permanently to allow one to enjoy a normal healthy existence without discomfort and the desire to imbibe again.

Two or three weeks before leaving hospital I began to make a reassessment of my circumstances in the light of what I had to face on returning to circulation and everyday routine. The problems I had felt on coming into hospital still remained unsolved and others had accrued to make matters more difficult. The foremost question in my mind at that time was, how could I effectively and in so short a time put into practice all that I had learned in the group discussion; to pull out all the stops at any given moment, when perhaps I was in a vulnerable position, was, to say the least, too ambitious to contemplate. I kept looking for one single solution which would stand me in good stead until I was able gradually to adjust myself into a new attitude towards variable situations.

In the hospital discussions I had been impressed by the effect of the reactions which alcohol provokes in an alcoholic, in that the first drink may set up an irresistible urge for the second, third and so on, the consequences of which I knew only too well. To remember this seemed to me the safest and sensible way of coping with all contingencies. By realising what would happen, it would be easier for me to resist the momentary impulse for the first drink than to suffer the inevitable result of those which must surely follow. The solution which I had been seeking was no longer elusive – 'whatever the circumstances avoid the first drink'. With that resolution I left hospital to start life again.

I had now taken a decision which relaxed my mind to dwell less apprehensively on other matters hanging over me like the proverbial sword of Damocles. I looked at these one by one and decided to deal with first things first. The primary step was to engross myself in my work, the next to see people with whom I had to make amends and thirdly to ensure that I could usefully occupy my leisure time.

My work presented no difficulties, and greatly to my relief and surprise I found the people I had seen were friendly and understanding of my intentions to deal with matters affecting them as soon as I was able. The question of filling one's leisure time is in some respects of vital importance, for this reason. The group therapy which we receive in hospital is only the commencement in revealing the nature of our problem and its purpose is to supply the 'tools' which we are to use in furthering our recovery. To pigeon-hole that knowledge until it all but recedes from memory is to court disaster.

I could not afford to rest indefinitely on the single resolution with which I left hospital, and from my previous experience of AA I felt that there was a fellowship of people similar to those in my hospital group and in whom I would find help if necessary and an anchor. Apart from the prospects of receiving help in AA it is worthwhile to feel that one may also render help to others.*

For the first two years after discharge from hospital I spent the greater part of my leisure time in AA visiting various groups as well as my own and frequently taking part in the hospital AA groups on Sunday afternoons and evenings. One makes very good friends in AA and perhaps more than anything else one accumulates renewed encouragement in witnessing the progress and recovery in those who have had to cope with problems akin to and sometimes more difficult than one's own. The challenge 'if he or she can do it, so can I' is a great spur.

I have already referred to methods of approach towards recovery. In hospital one has a good deal of time to think over his or her 'make up' and of its corresponding reaction to self-imposed conditions. Naturally we may differ in the course we propose to follow but having found what works successfully for oneself, it is better not to change to some other line of approach.

If one is seeking a miraculous transformation in personality by the elimination of unwanted emotions which have in the past gone hand in hand with drinking, it is just as well to remember that control of emotions is not readily acquired; and to concentrate too deeply on this aspect may cause one to overlook the danger of that first drink.

Whatever I have added to my knowledge of the problems of alcoholism and the many suggested ways of dealing with them, my first warning light shall always be 'avoid the first drink'. It is

---

* The finding that, in spite of just because of one's previous experiences of 'lost weekends' and wasted years, in group therapy sessions and in AA one is not only being helped but is also an active helper to fellow-sufferers, has assisted many alcoholics to regain a measure of self-respect, badly needed to make further progress [5].

possible, as in my case, that this indelible resolution can, regardless of all other adjustments, build up a mental aversion to alcohol.

Rehabilitation is a tangible growing process and as time marches on one indulges in occasional stock-taking and never ceases to appreciate the freedom from the shackles which bound one so relentlessly in the past. One has won back the respect of friends and, in business relationships, where I was once almost invited to tender my resignation, the same authority have since my recovery given me three promotions.

The way back has not been as difficult as I thought it would be – and certainly more than worth while.

3   The wife of an alcoholic comments

I write as the wife of a recovered alcoholic.

It is especially frustrating and baffling for the non-alcoholic to understand, and perhaps no less trying for doctors to explain, why a person who is basically intelligent, industrious and concerned in the welfare of his or her family becomes addicted to alcohol. Even the person so affected can offer no reassuring reason for this compulsion. Whilst there may be in some instances evidence of strain due to worry, shock or acute depression, one may argue that other people who choose to relieve their feelings by over-indulgence are at least capable of stopping when the effect has temporarily succeeded. Unfortunately the alcoholic cannot do this.

Although my husband has sustained his recovery for the past sixteen years during which time more has become known of the problem of alcoholism, the manifestations and basic facts still remain. Given the necessary understanding and proper treatment the alcoholic can return to a normal state of well-being and the enjoyment of a contented and alert mind free from any further desire for alcohol.

The subterfuges to which an alcoholic will resort in his active periods are as unpredictable as they are unending. This is only too well known to the wives of alcoholics [6].

Times have changed since the days when one had to endure indefinitely the consequences of alcoholic behaviour and it is on this note that I will turn to the constructive side.

The first prerequisite towards recovery is that the alcoholic should be persuaded to come to terms with his difficulties and allow himself to be helped. The second is that he must want to give up drinking for his own sake.* Experience has shown that he cannot do it for anyone else and while this may appear selfish, the fact that he is willing to make the effort because he wants to is in the long term bound to restore good relationships with other people, not least those of his own family.

My husband entered a hospital ward and found himself one of a group of people beset with the same problem, and within moments he realised that he was on common ground amongst others who understood him and with whom he could speak the same language. It was, so to speak, the opening of the oyster and the release of thoughts which formerly he had been unable to communicate with other people. As the group lived and moved amongst themselves, conversation on the same theme was naturally liberal but what followed in organised discussions under the supervision of a doctor provided the key to many of their questions.

It is worth while to mention that upon conclusion of hospital treatment it would be unwise to assume that no further care is required. An ex-patient misses to some extent the security which he acquires in hospital and although full of determination and resolve he is released into a world where the old temptations still remain and the problems he left behind have very often accumulated. He has been taught how to deal with these but the process of applying this knowledge may take a little time to work smoothly. It is during this period that consideration and patience will help him tremendously. In this way he will seek some form of interest to fill the time which he hitherto spent in clubs or hotels and in this connection he would find comradeship and continued help in the fellowship of AA.

AA has groups in almost every suburb as well as in various parts of Town, each comprising members, some of whom have received hospital treatment and others recovering from alcoholism by the help and programme of AA. These meetings are both social and instructive with a common aim to help anyone who has a drinking problem. The discussions are not unlike those of the hospital group and through them a person who has recently left hospital will find an anchor and help at any time.

In the initial stages of recovery it is essential for an alcoholic to be on guard. Despite all the precautionary plans he may have

---

* Alcoholics who declare proudly that they gave up drink for the sake of their family sooner or later become resentful of the unnecessary burden and sacrifice and relapse.

made there is just the possibility that some wrong thinking or something will trigger off a sudden desire for alcohol. Obviously the reaction and remedy has to be quick and in such circumstances my husband has always remembered the danger of alcohol entering the blood stream and setting up a chain reaction of continuous drinking. He has maintained that it is easier to resist a momentary impulse by avoiding the first drink than to try and stop after a dozen or fifty. He assures me that in time this mental reaction becomes automatic and acts as a sure brake.

There is sometimes a feeling in a recovering alcoholic that he must avoid social functions where alcohol is served. This may be wise in the early stages until he is absolutely sure of his ability to decline alcohol and ask for some other drink. Later on he can usually do this with equanimity.

My last word to the wives of other alcoholics who are striving for recovery is that your help in understanding and patience will bring its reward.

Finally, it must be remembered that a recovered alcoholic is still an alcoholic. There is no cure for this illness (at present) but it can be arrested permanently. If my husband again attempted to become a social drinker he would start where he left off sixteen years ago and probably with regrettable consequences.

References

1   Riddell, P (1955), *I was an Alcoholic*, London, Gollancz, 188
2   Glatt, M M (1974), *A Guide to Addiction and its Treatment*, 279
3   Plant, M A (1979), *Drinking Careers, Occupations, Drinking Habits and Drinking Problems*, London, Tavistock
4   Glatt, M M (1970), *Health Education J.*, 29, 4
5   Glatt, M M (1955), *Brit. J. Addict*, 52, 55
6   Burton, M (1974), *An Alcoholic in the Family*, London, Faber and Faber

21

The Need for Prevention

Increasingly, alcoholism ranks among the foremost international public health problems. Although therapeutic techniques have developed in the past few decades, no more than two alcoholics in three can be expected to improve. Prevention therefore is a very urgent task, requiring an integrated approach, involving many disciplines, the State, politicians, and the general public as well as professional workers [1].

Quite apart from the public health aspect and the avoidable waste of human life, and of physical and mental health and happiness, the economic cost of alcohol abuse is staggering. This is the subject of a recent book by Berry Jr and Boland [2] which shows that in the USA the economic cost due to alcohol abuse is estimated at almost $30 billion, including the costs of low production health care, motor vehicle accidents, fire, and the cost of social responses such as the social welfare system, alcohol treatment programmes, expenditures for highway safety and fire protection, as well as the cost to the criminal justice system arising from drunkenness and drink-driving offences. In addition to this sum the authors estimate a further economic cost associated with alcohol of $2 billion to include the cost of violent crime (and with it the cost to the criminal justice system). Altogether then, in 1971, the economic cost due to alcohol abuse and associated with alcohol in the USA was estimated to amount to $31.4 billion.

Most significant was the economic cost of lost production; next came health care costs due to alcohol abuse (the most significant proportion of alcohol abusers, in the case of health care costs, being the heavy frequent drinkers who account for almost 7 per cent of all deaths; excess morbidity among frequent heavy drinkers and other alcohol abusers accounts for 10 per cent of all health care costs); and third in order of magnitude is the cost arising from motor car accidents. Losses due to fire are another important item – fire being regarded as 'particularly hazardous for chronic alcohol abusers'; the excess mortality of frequent heavy drinkers accounted for almost 40 per cent of fire fatalities. From their detailed analysis the authors conclude that 'perhaps the most obvious policy implication . . . is the need to gather additional information and seek new knowledge'; nevertheless they would answer those in decision-making on their question: 'does incomplete information have any value'?: 'Yes, definitely.'

Thus, from a purely economic viewpoint, the development of sound programmes designed to prevent and control the widespread misuse of alcohol, and to diagnose and treat casualties as early as possible will yield far-reaching benefits.

In the task of prophylaxis of alcoholism primary methods of prevention would be ideal in forestalling the development of the condition and problems in the first place. Prohibition is generally regarded as 'out' but other approaches may in time be found helpful in minimising the emergence of alcohol problems. However, there will always be a need for 'secondary prevention' that is, early detection and treatment to prevent the establishment of the fully established disorder. Success at this level has been achieved in American industry. 'Tertiary Prevention', too will always be needed for the recovery and rehabilitation of established alcoholics.

The various preventive methods and alcohol control policies generally used are legislative, fiscal, educational and sociocultural. In the future, organic biochemical techniques might also be developed that could be helpful in both primary and secondary prevention [3].

Different emphases have been laid by various programmes on the primary target for preventive programmes: professional workers, lay groups, children, the total population or special high risk groups. Prevention is everybody's business. There may also be different emphasis placed on the extent to which strategies should concentrate specifically on the prevention of alcohol problems and alcoholism, or on the underlying factors (social or psychological, etc.) which may lead to the development of alcohol problems in the first place.

Control and legislative measures

For many years legislation was the principal means of attempts at the prevention of alcoholism by limiting the opportunities for drinking (for example by prohibiting or restricting the sale of drinks and specifying the opening hours of public houses) and by punishment (fines and imprisonment) of the drunkard. In various countries where prohibition has been tried, the result has been a failure because it created new problems [4] – providing opportunities for the building up of organised crime syndicates and making it impossible for the police to enforce the law. Punishment may have some deterrent effect on the self-indulgent drinker but not on the compulsively drinking alcoholic.

However, the fact that legislation has an important role to play is evident from the great improvement in regard to drunkenness convictions, mortality from liver cirrhosis, etc., that followed in the wake of the restrictive legislation applied in the United Kingdom during the first world war, after Lloyd George had described drink as a more dangerous enemy than Germany and Austria [50]. The deadly danger of the war situation at the time clearly helped in the acceptance by the population of otherwise very unpopular measures. Since alcohol is regarded and accepted in many parts of the western world as an integral constituent of daily life, legislation that is out of step with public acceptance and understanding is bound to arouse bitter public hostility.

Availability of drink was markedly reduced as a consequence of the restrictive measures taken by the Liquor Control Board in 1915 which cut down the number of pubs' opening hours from twenty hours to five and a half per day. Another factor involved was the increased taxation. The influence of price (i.e. higher taxation) on the development and even on the type of alcoholism may to a certain extent be reflected in the greater prevalence of spirit than beer drinking among English middle classes and *vice versa* among the working classes. Again, other factors being equal (the more expensive) spirits cause drunkenness more rapidly and frequently than the (cheaper) less concentrated drinks, wine and beer. Taxation could thus influence not only the incidence of drunkenness and alcoholism but affect even the type of alcoholism seen in a given country, and 'pleas for dilution' [5] have been put forward from time to time as one of the means which may help to reduce the prevalence of alcoholism.

What is important with regard to price is – as investigators at the Ontario Alcoholism and Drug Addiction Research Center in Toronto have shown – not the absolute price of alcoholic drinks but their cost in relation to income. It is interesting to compare in this connection the poverty and misery alcoholism, seen for example among English working classes in the eighteenth and nineteenth centuries, with the 'affluence alcoholism' prevalent in Western countries. But most alcoholics do not remain 'affluent' for very long, and with progressive impoverishment the spirit drinker may have to make do with cider and later perhaps even with surgical spirit.

The fall of the real price of alcoholic drink in Britain in the 1970s very likely has been an important factor contributing to the increase in consumption (see Chapters 2 and 5). This view is supported by the findings of 'an econometric analysis of total demand for alcoholic beverages in the UK, 1956–75', undertaken by T McGuinness [6] and published in 1980. The analysis of the consumption of alcoholic drink by type of beverage, as well as by the total amount of ethanol, shows that a rise of the real price of alcoholic drink is associated with a decline in consumption; for example, an increase in price of 10 per cent is associated typically with a 2.5 per cent drop in consumption. The effect of the rise in real disposable income on the national consumption of alcohol was regarded as unimportant. On the other hand, the marked increase in the number of outlets (in particular of licensed supermarkets (see Chapters 5 and 6)), was held to contribute to the increasing consumption. (Conversely, it may be argued that a primary rise in the demand for alcoholic drink has led secondarily to a multiplication of the number of outlets in order to satisfy the demand.)

Other methods of control include *licensing* of premises for the sale of alcoholic drink and restriction of the hours in which (and also of the age of people to whom) drinks can be sold. Two recent official Committees in Britain (the Errol Committee in England (1972) and the Clayson Committee in Scotland (1973)) [53, 54] both recommended far reaching relaxation of the licensing laws. Both the Errol and the Clayson proposals met with strong opposition, as they were held completely to ignore the public health risks involved. There is a large degree of unanimity among professional agencies that there should be no further relaxation of alcohol control measures. However, while the Errol proposals were not adopted, some of the Clayson suggestions were (Licensing [Scotland] Act 1976). However, the extension of opening hours in Scottish licensed premises (a one hour extension was introduced in

1976) does not seem to have had adverse effects: i.e. no rise of average alcohol consumption, and there are reports of reduction in the 'beat the clock' drinking rush at the end of an evening [6a] but from careful review of the situation G Prys Williams [6b] concludes that 'just as we have seen easier access to drink means more rather than less drunkenness, so . . . longer time in which to drink is more likely to result in more drunkenness, whatever may have been the benefits in the reduction in accidents brought about by intoxicated drivers leaving pubs and clubs later in the evenings. Regretfully the millennium has not come to Scotland'.

The findings of McGuinness' study [6] also bear on the important question of the effect of *advertising* on alcohol consumption. As regards spirits, a decrease in expenditure on advertising of 10 per cent is typically associated with a drop of consumption of alcohol (by volume) of 1.3 per cent. Whereas McGuinness himself did not recommend extrapolating his findings greatly beyond the observed range, an Annotation in *The Lancet* (1980) [7] proceeded to do just that. *The Lancet* concludes from McGuinness' figures that a total ban on advertising might be associated with a reduction of alcohol consumption of about 13 per cent – provided that such a ban was extended to all alcoholic beverages and was applied 'efficiently'. (A partial ban on alcohol advertising a few years ago in British Columbia, far from reducing consumption, proved counter-productive [8]).

In the view of *The Lancet* [7], a 13 per cent decrease in alcohol consumption might seem modest but would actually have a considerable impact. It argues that a reduction in *per capita* consumption is reflected in an even greater fall of consumption by heavy drinkers and has been reckoned to be as high as 25 per cent.

In spite of the careful statistics assembled over the years, what may be difficult to understand however is how reduction of, or a ban on, advertising could greatly affect the drinking customs of compulsively drinking alcoholics. It makes sense that the habits of heavy drinkers, who do so mainly because they enjoy drink and the atmosphere of pubs, or because of the influence of a heavily drinking 'subculture', might be affected by a ban on advertising. For the alcoholic-dependent section, however, surely advertising has little bearing upon their consumption? And it is this section of heavy drinkers ('alcoholics') who are at greatest risk of alcohol-related harm [9]. Thus this special aspect of reasoning by *The Lancet* seems open to doubt. By and large, however, there will be a great deal of agreement with its conclusions that a marked reduction of advertising may be followed by a considerable general decrease of drinking, including the non-dependent, heavy drinkers. This should result in a considerable reduction of alcohol-induced harm – even though the more severely dependent alcoholics may not benefit from such measures.

The question of the influence of advertising on drinking habits urgently requires further research in view of the discrepancy of findings by Osborne and Smart (1980) [10], of the effect of restrictions of alcohol advertisements in Manitoba, Canada, and in the USA. They found that advertising restrictions were 'unrelated to *per capita* beer, wine or spirit consumption, to total *per capita* consumption or to alcoholism rate'.

They therefore thought 'it unlikely that restrictions on advertising will reduce *per capita* consumption in the short run but if continued over generations, some impact may be felt'. Under the circumstances they would accord such restrictions no more than 'a low priority among the possible solutions to problems of restraining *per capita* consumption'.

However, the alcoholic drinks industry in 1979, and five years after agreeing to a code of advertising practice, has published a new Alcoholic Appendix to the British Code of Advertising Practice [11]. Accordingly, advertisements:

 (i) Should not be directed at the young, and should not be based on 'dare';
 (ii) Should not emphasise the stimulant, sedative or tranquillising effects of any drink;
(iii) Should not imply that alcohol can improve physical performance;
 (iv) Should not imply that drinking is necessary to social or business success or distinction;
 (v) Should not imply that drinking contributes to sexual success or attraction;
 (vi) Should not encourage over-indulgence and repeated buying of large rounds.

Clearly, on the question of advertising, the last word has not yet been spoken. Those accepting the connection between *per capita* consumption and the rate of excessive drinking, and alcohol-related harm will continue believing that advertising does contribute, for example, by introducing newcomers to the habit, and acting as a reminder to the average drinker.

The fact that, in itself, fining or imprisoning the drunk or the alcoholic driver is unlikely to prevent a repetition of their alcohol-related activities has already been referred to. It is a forlorn hope to expect that by itself a certain period away from drink will help alcoholics to 'come to their senses'.

Thus while legislative measures are necessary and valuable,[1] and whilst for example restriction by law of unscrupulous advertising directed at the young may be beneficial, on their own they can obviously not solve the whole problem of the prevention of alcoholism.

As Dr H Halbach, Chief of the Drug Section of the WHO, put it with regard to 'dangerous drugs': 'no restriction, however severe, on the production, distribution and administration of dangerous drugs can entirely solve the problem of prevention. Or, in epidemiological language: preventive measures should not be limited to the agent, they should also deal with the host and the environment, thus aiming at the underlying causes of addiction' [12]. Few however, would today be as dogmatic as was another medical writer in the first decade of this century: 'The principle of making people good by Act of Parliament is a mistaken one. Educate, point out the evils of excess, encourage modification and self-control, and more lasting good will be effected by the arbitrary elimination of an article of diet, which has in some form or another been almost universally consumed from the commencement of history' [12a].

There is certainly another side to the question; the British restrictive approach for example, during the 1914–18 War, certainly seemed to bear fruit very rapidly, and the progress thereby achieved by legislative and fiscal means was maintained for several decades. Dr Griffith Edwards believes that 'since we are not able to manipulate personality and produce a race with no neuroses, the only realistic method of asserting a benign influence on the prevalence of chronic alcohol problems is by control of environmental conditions of drinking, and it is the availability element that remains the prime candidate for control' [12e].

Yet one might feel that in spite of cutting down on availability the individual who is not aware of the risks of misusing drink may be seeking alcoholic drink even if it is not readily available, he may follow the lead of his drinking peer group, and attach himself to a drinking subculture, or try to solve his problems by escaping to drink. By itself, cutting down on availability will still leave sufficient drink available for too many who might be prone to misuse it unless they have learnt better techniques to handle their anxieties.

Education, too, remains an important factor in a comprehensive preventive approach [12d].

The Canadian workers [14–18] feel that the approach to the prevention of alcoholism lies in an attempt to reduce *per capita* consumption. In their view, approaches aimed at lowering the intake of heavy drinkers only [16] would probably fail because:

(a) This attempts to reduce the amount of drinking in those deriving most satisfaction from it;

(b) This would 'rearrange the "who-drinks-more-than-whom" order in the society';

(c) This would probably necessitate the distribution of alcohol consumption taking on a shape that it is not known to have anywhere else in the world – a very unlikely occurrence.

In their discussions the Canadian workers contrast the unimodal with *sociocultural models* of prevention. These latter models believe social and cultural factors to be the most significant ones and recommend the setting-up of proscriptive and prescriptive norms within which controlled, integrated drinking habits would become established. This approach derives from the work of American sociologists, such as Ullman [19] and Blacker [20]. In the latter's formulation 'in any group or society in which drinking customs, values and sanctions – together with the attitudes of all segments of the group or society – are well established, known to and agreed upon by all, consistent with the rest of culture, and are characterised by prescriptions for moderate drinking and proscriptions against excessive drinking, the rate of alcoholism will be low'. Such approaches were partly based on studies about different rates of alcoholism between ethnic minorities such as Irish-Americans and Jewish-Americans with their different drinking norms. Those who favour the sociocultural model of prevention tend to recommend the development of healthy drinking practices: for example drinking wine with meals (a practice claimed in the past to explain the alleged rarity of Italian alcoholism) and the integration of drinking into a wide range of social activities with the accent on the social occasion rather than on the drinking.

Adherents of the unimodal approach [21] have, however, pointed out that proposals such as improving the acceptability of public houses as social centres, or the encouragement of drinking wine with meals, very likely leads to an increased *per capita* consumption. A similar effect might follow such proposals as those made by the Licensing Committees in Britain (of allowing parents to take their children into pubs, or recent recommendations to teach children and young adolescents 'responsible' drinking). Many such suggestions are made with reference to French 'civilised' drinking habits (in spite of the French having the highest alcoholism rates in the world [22]). In the view of De Lint [15] available data indicate a definite trend in many countries towards increasing levels of alcohol consumption – a consequence of a growing acceptance of so-called civilised, French-style drinking habits: 'to promote the use of beverage alcohol as an incidental part of daily life, to encourage the introduction of so-called civilised drinking patterns, to favour the use of wine and beer, is to support the current widespread trend toward a saturation of our life-style with alcohol use'.

Unimodal versus sociocultural models of prevention

In recent years the unimodal approach to preventing alcoholism has found increasing attention. It originated in the work of Ledermann [13] in France some twenty-five years ago, and has been developed by workers at the Ontario Research Foundation, Toronto [14, 15, 16, 17, 18]. In contrast to the sociocultural theories of the causation of alcoholism, in which the condition is seen as arising on the basis of social (or psychological) conditions, the unimodal approach regards high alcoholism rates as a consequence of a high *per capita* consumption in the population.

The unimodal or consumption model is based on research showing that the distribution of alcohol consumption in a population does not produce a 'bimodal' curve with two different clusters, (i.e. large numbers of drinkers to be found at the low end of consumption ('social drinkers') and another, smaller cluster at the opposite, high consumption end of the distribution ('problem drinkers')). In fact, the curve has been found to be unimodal, i.e. smooth with no large discontinuities. Such a curve conforms with what mathematicians call a logarithmic normal curve. The great majority of drinkers find themselves at the low end of consumption, a smaller number in the middle, and a still smaller number at the high end of the consumption distribution, so that there is no clear distinction between social, heavy, and problem drinkers. This would be different from the clinical impression of bimodal alcohol consumption with a clear cut difference in the amount of alcohol intake between social drinkers and alcoholics. As the transition from moderate to large amounts of drink is very gradual, the Canadian workers point out that to define alcoholism on the basis of consumption quantities has to be very arbitrary, but they define as alcoholics those drinkers who have an average daily consumption in excess of 150 ml of absolute alcohol. This figure was arrived at from considering the daily consumption of patients admitted to alcoholism clinics which averaged at least 150 ml of absolute alcohol, and was found to be in agreement with estimates based on mortality data of alcoholics.

The Ontario workers thus feel that there is an inextricable link between alcoholism and other levels of consumption, and that one cannot reduce the rate of alcoholism without affecting the rate of other levels of consumption. Schmidt and De Lint [17] have shown that a daily intake of 100 ml per day is associated with a risk of physical complications such as liver cirrhosis, and that there is a significant relationship between *per capita* alcohol intake and liver cirrhosis mortality in nine countries studied [18].

The proponents of the consumption model propose that to reduce *per capita* consumption the price of alcohol should be raised. According to De Lint [15], in every country (or region) studied, the effect of taxation has been found to be related to overall consumption and to prevalence of alcoholism: no country was found where alcoholism rates were high in the presence of a high, relative price. However, De Lint points out that the amount of alcohol taxation tends to reflect the degree of acceptance of alcohol use in that society so that increases in overall consumption and alcoholism cannot be solely ascribed to a fall in the relative price of drink. Nevertheless because of its importance governments should adjust alcohol taxes as often as is necessary in order to 'maintain a constant relationship between the price of beverage alcohol and average disposable income'. And later, following an intensive educational effort, governments may wish to establish a higher price to reduce further alcohol consumption and hence alcoholism. These education programmes should inform people about causes and consequences of alcoholism, including the effect of integration of alcohol into the daily life of society with consequent rise of consumption levels and alcoholism.

Would legal restrictions on availability and higher taxation penalise the many moderate drinkers for the disease or the 'weaknesses' of a few? This argument, in De Lint's view, ignores the 'social nature of the alcoholism problem', as everyone makes a contribution towards determining the extent to which alcohol use is to be part of his culture and way of life. However, other observers feel that public and governmental acceptance of a policy involving increases in price of liquor may be slow in coming [21]; may require educational campaigns for both legislators and the public; that social remedies based on the unimodal model might be 'politically unsaleable' [22]; and that preventive policies aimed at minimising alcoholism may be more effective if directed at problem drinkers rather than the general public [23].

In Britain much support has recently been voiced by both politicians and professional workers for approaches based on the unimodal model and for regarding alcoholism as essentially a political problem [24, 25]. However, the politician cannot move too far ahead of the general public [26]. At present public opinion might well support measures aimed specifically at encouraging the excessive drinker to reduce his consumption, but might be reluctant when it comes to reducing the consumption of the average, moderate drinker [27, 28].

Some critics of the unimodal approach have queried the type of mathematical fit of the alcohol consumption distribution to the log normal expectancy [21], or whether, in order to lower the mean consumption of a population, one might not (instead of greatly raising taxes) have to influence the drinking habits of the individual drinkers [29], as it is changes in individuals' drinking that change the mean, rather than the other way round.

Another question that arises is whether a marked rise in liquor price might not mainly affect the relatively poor rather than the more affluent drinker, so that the spirit drinking of the higher income groups may be less affected than the (by and large less dangerous) beer drinking of the lower income groups.

The evidence of the influence of *per capita* consumption on harm mainly refers to physical damage. In clinical practice, it is the daily, heavy (Delta) drinker who seems more likely to suffer physical damage. The more often psychogenic bout (Gamma) drinker – perhaps more prevalent in Anglo-Saxon countries – may present relatively more often with psychosocial than with physical problems (although the Gamma alcoholics seen in alcohol units in 70–80 per cent of cases show abnormal liver function tests [30, 31]).

These questions are not raised here to throw doubt on the valuable work of the Canadian researchers which must surely prove of immense practical significance in reducing the rates of alcohol-related problems. The emphasis on safe maximum levels of drinking – arising from such work – in itself should help in the reduction of the consumption of many social drinkers who may realise that their 'moderate' drinking was carrying a considerable risk. On the other hand, since their work has become known in Britain so much emphasis has been put on this approach, with the implication that there might soon be much less need for special treatment facilities than the relatively few that exist today that it is important to point out that certain questions remain, and that, moreover, other preventive measures, such as appropriate education, have to go hand in hand with the attempt to lower *per capita* consumption.

Health education: influencing social and professional attitudes

In the long run equally important as legislative and control measures, but much more difficult to plan, carry out and evaluate, are preventive public health measures aimed at influencing the attitudes of the general and the professional public.

(a)   *Public education*

According to the Royal College of Psychiatrists' Report [33] this has four important tasks:

(a)   In order to build up a climate of informed public debate it should provide sound information on key issues, such as the nature of alcohol as a drug, alcohol dependence and alcohol-induced disabilities, the relationship between national *per capita* consumption and the size of its drink problem.

(b)   It should inform the public on the risks involved if alcohol is taken for purposes such as relieving feelings of discomfort.

(c)   It should encourage public disapproval of drunkenness as informal social controls, such as public sentiments and attitudes strongly disapproving drunkenness, may be more potent than formal control.

(d)   It should warn against transgressing the upper, 'safe' levels of drinking. There is no full agreement yet as to the exact levels of relative safety which anyway will vary from person to person. What is very important is the notion of the existence of such levels; especially as they are much lower than most drinkers expect. The notion should in time greatly contribute towards reducing *per capita* drinking.

Public education should be directed at reducing the stigma still attached to alcoholism and alcoholics. Admittedly, some alcoholics fear and 'perceive' ostracisation and rejection where none is intended (just as their preoccupation with drinking often makes them think of the subject obsessively making them aware of every off-licence and of references for example, to drinking in every TV programme which a non-alcoholic would probably miss).

While developing an attitude of disapproval of drunkenness, and thereby helping to create a norm of not heavy drinking, people should come to understand that it is incongruous to treat the compulsive dependent alcoholic as a contemptible social outcast while at the same time strongly encouraging his direct predecessor, the heavy drinker, to 'drink up!'. Many alcoholics complain bitterly that everybody loves the drinker but hates the drunk. Attraction, rather than promotion, has always been the watchword of AA since its inception, but nevertheless the knowledge of its successes has gradually helped in changing the public image of the alcoholic from that of the hopeless drunk to a person who can, and often does make good. The praiseworthy example of fifty leading American men and women who at a National Committee on Alcoholism Forum in Washington DC (1976), publicly proclaimed that they were (recovered) alcoholics, has not yet been emulated in Britain, with some notable exceptions, such as that of a well-known member of the House of Lords. Recovered alcoholics can do a great deal for public and professional education.

Though it seems difficult to evaluate health education, it probably can influence attitudes. How important sociocultural attitudes of a given population towards drinking and heavy drinking can be in influencing the prevalence of alcoholism can be illustrated, for example, in the low alcoholism rates of Jews, among whom, despite the widespread custom of occasional moderate drinking, heavy drinking is frowned on, and the high alcoholism rates of the French, among whom, partly connected with economic conditions, the custom of heavy drinking is widespread and accepted. While Jewish cultural norms may have been significant contributory factors in keeping Jewish alcoholism rates down [34] modern relaxation of such norms in certain parts of the world may make Jewish alcoholics a less rare phenomenon [35]. Culture-shock in some underdeveloped nations as a result of sudden economic changes of living standards may similarly favour the development of alcoholism among a minority. In Western society social attitudes regard drink as a necessary part of ordinary life; it is incorporated into the cost-of-living standard, and politicians and governments think twice before raising the price of alcoholic beverage by taxation.

Beyond merely influencing the prevalence of alcoholism, social acceptance or rejection of heavy drinking may even have a bearing on symptomatology. Thus among the heavily drinking French the alcoholic may be free from the severe guilt feelings that beset the average Anglo-American alcoholic who lives in countries where excessive drinking is widely frowned upon; and in alcoholics guilt feelings and rejection by society – coupled with a lack of facilities to which the drinker may turn for advice and help – may drive them even further towards alcohol abuse as the only means of finding at least temporary relief. Thus, although obviously alcohol abuse should be frowned on, the alcoholic should know that he will find ears that listen, hearts that feel for him and hands that help.

Social attitudes are of great importance in influencing the stage at which the alcoholic – and his family – may seek help. Where there is a severe stigma attached to the diagnosis of alcoholism, the alcoholic may prefer to stay underground, undiagnosed and untreated; and his family may choose silent suffering rather than exposing itself to public shame.

The necessary change of social attitudes requires health education directed to the general public, and specific professional training. Public education should start at school so that the adolescent, when later confronted with the question 'Shall I take alcoholic drink?' will be able to make up his mind on the basis of sound knowledge rather than being at the mercy of biased statements and advertisements.

Such teaching would probably best be integrated into the various subjects where the question of alcohol may come up and could be fitted in easily; and it is probably advantageous in the long run that teaching should be about alcohol rather than 'for or against it' (namely for moderate drinking or for total abstinence – although both these latter viewpoints have their adherents). It is vital that teachers must therefore themselves be well informed about alcohol and alcoholism. A Teachers' Advisory Council on Drug and Alcohol Education ('Tacade') was launched in 1968 by Lord Soper (see Appendix I).

Public education should be factual and objective rather than moralistic, although ethical considerations obviously enter into the problem. Factual, objective, non-sensational presentation of the subject in mass media would seem to have an important role to play in public education in this field.

(b) *Professional education*

In a similar way, it is important that teaching on this condition should be included in the curriculum of all those whose work may bring them into professional contact with the alcoholic, such as doctors, nurses, priests, social workers, etc. Such teaching should lay stress on early phases of alcoholism rather than as hitherto emphasising the late stages. Training should start at the under-graduate level, for example in medical school where in general teaching on the essential, early phases of alcoholism is sadly neglected. Proper special training of the medical student on al-coholism would help doctors to accept alcoholism as a genuine illness and the alcoholic as a sick man in need and worthy of medical help. This would in time assist to remove the stigma as public opinion would gradually follow the lead set by doctors. It might also have the useful side-effect of toppling doctors off their positions among the occupational groups with high liver cirrhosis mortality.

Alcohol units can greatly help in the urgent task of providing education and training of professional workers. By spending short periods in such centres, getting to know alcoholics (and thus freeing themselves from the misconceptions as to what is al-coholism and who is an alcoholic), attending group sessions, etc., professional workers' emotional attitudes towards alcoholics are likely to undergo a profound change.

An additional method which has in the present author's experi-ence proved very helpful in the education of the general public and the training of students, doctors, probation officers and other professional groups is the participation of recovered alcoholics at lectures, discussions, meetings, etc. [36]. Recovered alcoholics who are prepared to talk freely and to answer any questions put to them by the audience, relating to their own past experiences, provide vivid demonstrations of the fact that many alcoholics can recover. Such discussions with recovered alcoholics seem very often to provide an eye opener, a lesson which the professional participant is not likely to forget in a hurry, and which thereby may prove very helpful to him and even more so to the alcoholic patients he may meet in the future. By assisting in the education of doctors and thereby indirectly helping other alcoholics, recovered alcoholics carry out what virtually amounts to 'thirteen-step' work complementing the 'twelve-stepping' of the alcoholic sufferer himself.

In recent years a number or organisations made important contributions to the education of professionals in this field. The Medical Council for Alcoholism has arranged one day seminars for medical students in London and in the provinces, and provides its informative quarterly *Journal of Alcohol and Alcoholism* to GPs free of charge. Whereas this journal carries both practical and scientific articles, the contributions to the official magazine of the Society for the Study of Addictions (SSA), the *British Journal of Addictions*, are scientific in nature. The Alcohol Education Centre in association with the National Council on Alcoholism has annual residential summer schools for the education of the various professional disciplines, and has arranged other courses in London and the provinces. The National Council on Alcoholism apart from its regular educational work among the general public (local information centres, the training of counsellors), has been instrumental with financial backing from the Government as well as from the NCA and many hostels run by voluntary organisations, in carrying out two large-scale educational campaigns in the North-East of England (a similar campaign in Scotland was arranged by the Scottish Alcohol Education Unit). The various alcohol units have also regularly provided teaching to professional under- and postgraduates and their staff members (like the MCA) lecture regularly to professional audiences.

Targets of prevention programmes: selectivity versus the shot-gun approach [37]

As discussed earlier, in Chapter 2, certain sections of the population run a higher risk of developing alcohol problems and alcoholism than others. Members of these susceptible groups clearly should be made fully aware of this hazard. This may seem so obvious that it appears unnecessary to single out such groups as targets for programmes of special education. Yet the continuing high incidence of alcoholism even among highly educated and well-informed professional groups [38] (including doctors and journalists), of liver cirrhosis among publicans and their wives and the general lack of interest in industry, all testify to either the lack of information or to a general indifference, and, therefore, the necessity of paying more attention to the special education of 'high-risk' groups beyond that required for other sections of the community. In 1970, the need for such a special alcohol-education programme for journalists was discussed at great length by (a fairly large number of) members of that profession who were patients (or ex-patients) of the alcohol unit at St Bernard's Hospital. They were of the unanimous opinion that in journalism opportunities and the socio-occupational pressures to drink were so plentiful that alcoholism was not so much an occupational hazard as virtually an occupational necessity. They therefore regarded a preventive educational programme making newcomers to the profession in particular aware of this risk as a probably very valuable and promising task that might help many to maintain a state of relative sobriety and health. Similarly, the increasing awareness among medical under- and postgraduates of the high incidence of liver cirrhosis among doctors, the knowledge of the existence of a special British alcoholic doctors group, and the educational work among medical men of the Medical Council on Alcoholism can be expected to bear some fruit in the future.

The knowledge of alcohol problems among certain groups provides a challenge and an opportunity for primary and secondary preventive work. For example, in industry, the Civil Service, the Armed Forces and Merchant Seamen. All should reap ample rewards if they encourage alcoholics to come forward at an early stage in the knowledge that they will find help and be assisted to have treatment. Even better, early education programmes could help at least some of these people keep their drinking within moderate levels so that no need would arise for secondary or tertiary preventive measures. Secondary prevention is now beginning to be applied in some cases.

The alternative to a selective approach, i.e. preventive methods directed at the whole population (as already discussed) include, special under- and postgraduate training of professional groups and the health education of the general public, as well as control (legislative and fiscal measures) aimed at reducing availability of alcohol. Prominent and topical are the suggested recommendations to reduce alcoholism by cutting down *per capita* consumption of alcohol. Indeed there is considerable overlapping between the 'shot-gun' and the selective approach when it comes to such very large target groups as children (who nowadays start drinking at a progressively younger age) whose own drinking greatly influences the drinking habits of their peers; adolescents and their parents (whose own attitudes and drinking habits greatly affect their children).[2] With women closing the traditional gap in numbers of alcoholics, that in the past separated them from men, they too need to be regarded as a special though very large 'target' group (see Chapter 6). It can be argued that the selective and the more general preventive approaches are complementary and that there is a need for the general approach as well as a special additional need for the high-risk groups. Research should help find the best way to 'get through' to such special target groups –the required techniques probably varying from group to group.

Unspecific measures of primary prevention

General, unspecific approaches directed at improving and stabilising 'host' and 'environment' – i.e. *mental hygiene measures and improvement of socioeconomic conditions* indirectly also contribute to the prevention of alcoholism. More mature, stable and adequate personalities are less vulnerable to the temptation of heavy ('relief') drinking than maladjusted, psychoneurotic or psychopathic individuals, and – other factors being equal – those living in socially adequate and healthy surroundings are less vulnerable than people living in squalor and slums, though material affluence (in particular when accompanied by a spiritual vacuum) by no means protects against alcoholism, which can accompany prosperity as well as poverty. Application of the principles of sound mental hygiene in childhood and the improvement of social conditions should help to diminish the risks of emotional and social insecurity and indirectly lower the need of insecure personalities to look for relief.

Earlier diagnosis (secondary prevention)

This, and earlier treatment, would be another consequence of a general improvement of public attitudes (and of professional education) as reduction of stigma would bring the alcoholic to the doctor at an earlier stage. Earlier diagnosis and treatment would prevent the sufferer from slipping down the road even further, thus forestalling further social and economic decline, mental and physical deterioration, and the infliction of further emotional and physical harm on those close to him.

Early diagnosis is usually a very difficult task in view of the alcohoholic's skill in 'covering up'. A change in character, in attitudes, neglect of personal cleanliness or of one's work, without obvious cause, might arouse vague suspicion if it happens in people who formerly behaved quite differently. When this occurs in people whose occupation brings them in close contact with alcohol or who are traditionally 'alcoholism-prone' – publicans, travellers, waiters, seamen, retired army and naval officers, journalists, etc. – one might be even more suspicious, just as in the case of sons and daughters of alcoholic fathers, of the habitual alcohol-impaired driver, the accident prone, of suicidal people, etc.

Research

Research (basic, clinical and operational) is another essential in the task of prophylaxis of alcoholism. Despite recent progress made in many centres, gaps remain in our knowledge about the causation, prevention and treatment of alcoholism. In alcoholism, the absence, or lack of, factual information, unproven hypotheses, confused attitudes, misconceptions and misunderstandings prevail. As Dr Erich Gordis [40] has emphasised, at present we do not even understand four of the basic and most widely debated clinical phenomena of alcoholism: loss of control, craving, tolerance and physical dependence.

Use-oriented research geared at finding means of curbing problem drinking and its harmful consequences was one of the main tasks discussed in the first American national symposium on research priorities in the field of alcohol studies, arranged in 1977 by the Rutgers Center of Alcohol Studies, a leading international research centre in this field. A wide range of investigations on basic research issues was proposed, but participants were mainly concerned with the immediate or ultimate applicability of research toward a better understanding of alcoholism, its treatment, and prevention. John Ewing [41] has divided 'research being done and needing to be done' into three types: Research concerned with:

(a) Aetiological factors behind the development of alcoholism.
(b) Damage (tissue or organ damage to the individual, and social damage to the family or community).
(c) The efficiency of programmes which are aimed at producing changes within society, e.g. by preventive measures, or within the individual by his taking part in a treatment programme for alcoholism.

The need for research has been stressed throughout this book in regard to the various aspects of the overall problem. One topic of special interest is that of the need for long-term *longitudinal research*, stressed in recent years by a number of American workers. In the past quite a few investigations have dealt with drinking behaviour of children at school or of college students, but hardly any studies have been concerned with drinking at home and at work. These may tell one much less about the development of drinking patterns than prospective longitudinal research carried out over many (say 25–40) years [42, 43], following the careers of pre-teenagers and young drinkers continually or intermittently every five years or so [44]. This may assist early identification of those at risk of developing into problem drinkers. Such studies should involve large numbers of people representing all social strata and should include non-alcoholic drinkers and abstainers. Such research might reveal much about the natural course; the impact on drinking habits of stresses; and of legislative control measures [42], described by Robert Straus as the 'in-and-out' pattern of alcoholic misuse (or Cahalan's 'remission phenomenon') [45] i.e. people behaving like problem drinkers for years but who may then for years drink in a non-problem-causing fashion or stay sober. Usually such occasions of problem drinking may be triggered by stress so that Straus speaks of 'situational dependence' [44]. A typical 'trigger' may be in regard to sex, leisure or work, all of which can provide many people with much satisfaction and pleasure, but may also cause severe disappointment and anxiety.

This type of study, while involving great effort in planning and execution, should teach one a great deal more about drinking careers than is known so far from retrospective case histories.

Alcohol research in this country is nowadays carried out, for example, by special research departments, such as the Addiction Research Unit at the Institute of Psychiatry, or, rarely, at some teaching hospitals or in the form of more clinically oriented research studies in the special alcohol units whose function should not only be treatment and rehabilitation but which could, and should, also be centres of research and education.

In all these fields a great deal remains to be done. However, it is only fair to state that in the past few years much thought has been given to the problems of prevention in this country both by the National Council on Alcoholism and by the Medical Council, for example by the setting up of a number of Information Centres by the National Council, and the encouragement of research by the Medical Council, which has been enabled to provide grants for research due to the generosity of a Scottish charitable trust. There is some evidence that at long last there is a beginning realisation that in the UK alcoholism constitutes, and should be tackled as, a major public health problem.

The National Council on Alcoholism

The National Council, established in 1962, originally based its programme on the very successful US National Council on Alcoholism. It is a voluntary agency with both professional and lay members. From the start its aims have been to propagate the notion of alcoholism as a public health problem and a public responsibility. Its work is carried out by local councils, with, among their chief activities, the formation of information centres. The Local Councils (numbering, in 1980, twenty-three in England and two in Wales with more to be opened in 1981) 'provide a focal point for alcoholism services in their area . . . a counselling service for people with drinking problems . . . and [should] be seen as a specialist resource to enable primary care workers and voluntary workers of other social agencies to support people with drinking problems and their families' [46, 47]. They also act as advisory centres providing counselling and after-care, and, by keeping in touch with local statutory, voluntary and NHS facilities (general hospitals, units, detoxification centres, general practitioners, social services) they could act as an immediate referral agency in cases where this is considered necessary.

Medical Council on Alcoholism

The Medical Council on Alcoholism was formed in 1967 by a group of medical practitioners after preliminary discussions among themselves and with outsiders (including for example the International Council on Alcohol and Addictions). Among the five doctors involved in the early discussions were Professor F E Camps, a forensic medicine specialist, who became the first Chairman of the Council, Dr H D Chalke, a public health physician who became the first Hon Secretary and Editor of the Council's Journal, Dr (now Sir) N H Moynihan, a GP who became Hon Treasurer, Dr R Phillipson who was a Senior Medical Officer in the Ministry of Health, and two psychiatrists, Dr A Minto, who became Assistant Secretary, and the writer of this Report, who became Vice-Chairman. The President was Sir Clement Price-Thomas, a surgeon, who took the Chair at the inaugural meeting of the Medical Council in April 1967.

All the doctors involved had been interested in alcoholism problems for some time, and felt that doctors should play a more active role than in the past in showing their concern with alcoholism, by helping to interest not only the medical profession but also the general public and the State. The venture immediately attracted attention and throughout the almost fifteen years of its existence the Council has been able to do a great deal not only to encourage and finance (initially mainly with the help of a Scottish Trust, more recently also with backing from others and the DHSS) but also by means of its Journal and regular lectures to arouse the interest of many medical men who formerly seemed to stand aloof. Initially five sub-committees were formed – for Treatment, Occupational Medicine, Research, Medical Education and Public Health. As Admiral Sir Dick Caldwell, the Executive Director appointed a few years later, said (1972) [48] the Council has undoubtedly played a large part in the growing recognition of alcoholism as a disease by the public, the government, industry and doctors themselves. A great deal of its success the Council owed to its ability to attract to its offices some of the most eminent medical men in the land, such as Lord Rosenheim, who followed Professor Camps as Chairman, Lord Porritt who succeeded Sir Clement Price-Thomas as President, Sir Thomas Holmes Sellors, who followed Lord Rosenheim as Chairman, and is now President following the retirement of Lord Porritt. Undoubtedly Sir Dick Caldwell (formerly Medical Director of the Navy) himself played a very important role during his ten years as Executive Director in popularising and furthering the Council's work. The Medical Council – while naturally mainly concerned with the education of medical students and doctors, and research – works closely with bodies with similar interest such as the National Council and FARE (Federation of Alcoholic Rehabilitation Establishments) and – as Sir Dick put it in 1972 – its members feel that it 'has a leading role to play in this challenging, complex and multi-faceted disease'. Presumably, by now, some of its members might like to alter the term 'disease' but in our, admittedly biased, view the great majority of doctors interested in the problem would leave the wording as it was written nine years ago.

The need for complementary preventive (control and education) and treatment approaches

At a time when the economic climate is unfavourable to much spending on health and research, questions have been raised whether the available resources should be spent on prevention rather than care and rehabilitation. It is hoped that research, in the long run, will lead to improvement in therapeutic methods and results. At present, however, many issues are unresolved and the findings among research workers and clinicians are often contradictory. Research is required into the reasons for the discrepancies between the findings obtained in carefully controlled studies (but with relatively very small and not always representative samples of patients) and those of clinicians, who may observe very large numbers of patients of varying backgrounds but who lack the opportunity to carry out controlled investigation. Both those who are primarily clinicians and those who are primarily interested in research need to keep an open mind and work towards much closer collaboration.

Just as, on their own, even the most effective therapeutic methods will never solve the problem of alcoholism, so the most successful preventive techniques in a non-Utopian society will never eliminate the need to help the sufferers from alcohol problems. Both prevention and treatment will always remain high priorities in a caring society.

Are alcohol problems a political or a professional problem? This question is repeatedly raised in view of the importance of *per capita* consumption for prevalence of alcohol problems. In making more often highly unpalatable control policies more acceptable the medical profession could and should play a very important part. Two well known American researchers Mark A Schuckitt (a psychiatrist) and Don Cahalan (a sociologist) made the point (1976) that 'In view of the high prestige of the medical profession, clinical practitioners will find themselves a force to be reckoned with whenever they can manage to get together in a concerted drive to bring about public policies that are conducive to preventive approaches aimed toward diminishing the present magnitude of the alcohol-troubled population within our society' [49].

Doctors could make a valuable contribution in the prevention of alcohol problems by making it clearly and widely known that alcohol, though readily available without prescription (or just because of it), has to be handled with even more caution and

504   *Alcoholism*

responsibility than other drugs for which the prescribing doctor carries a large measure of responsibility. The opportunity and the right of the public to use a drug freely also entails a higher responsibility to use it sensibly and in moderation.

In the task of prevention (as in any other aspects of drink problems) biased partisans have often emphasised the (almost exclusive) benefit of their own situation, to the detriment of alternative approaches: a point made strongly by Paul C Whitehead in Canada, and David Robinson [16] in Britain. In an attempt to combine the sociocultural and distribution of consumption models of prevention, Whitehead would like to find 'reconciling' approaches which would increase the integration of drinking practices without significantly raising *per capita* consumption (such as permitting parents to purchase alcoholic drinks for their children with meals in restaurants) or which would reduce *per capita* consumption without significantly changing the integration of drinking practices (such as lowering the alcohol content of drinks),[3] or simultaneously increasing the integration of drinking practices and reducing *per capita* consumption (which Whitehead suggests could be achieved by eliminating advertising). Robinson [25a, 52] welcomes the principle underlying Whitehead's proposals as 'the real task is to begin the process of constructing an overall preventive strategy which takes into account and inter-relates each of [the] major preventive goals', instead of continually harping back on 'the many tired arguments in favour of secondary prevention or the encouragement of healthy drinking practices or the control of overall availability'. 'The time [Robinson feels] . . . to expect research, or sweet reason, to make any impression on the problem, is well past. It [now] needs co-ordinated political action.'

A comprehensive set of *Recommendations* was proposed by the Executive Committee of the Addiction Research Foundation of Ontario [51] in February 1978: 'In an overall preventive strategy the legislative approach must be complementary to educational and treatment approaches. It would be entirely unrealistic' [and perhaps counter-productive] to rely exclusively either on attempts at control by taxation and highly restrictive control measures, or alternatively, on "education and treatment alone".' What is required is 'an integrative approach'. Among other proposals, the *Recommendations* demand:

1   No further relaxation of alcohol-control measures, and an

adoption of a health-oriented policy with respect to such measures, i.e. one directed towards preventing further rises in the prevalence of alcohol problems.

2 Adoption of a pricing policy aimed at maintaining a reasonably constant relationship between the price of alcohol and the consumer price index.

3 Increasing the legal drinking age.

4 Discouraging life-style advertising of alcoholic beverages.

5 A vigorous effort to increase public awareness of the personal hazards of heavy drinking, the economic and other consequences for society of high consumption levels, and the potential public health benefits of appropriate control measures.

Like so much other valuable work by the Ontario Research Foundation over the past thirty years these *Recommendations* appear as good as or even better than proposals coming from other sources.

Notes

1 Sociologists sometimes talk of an 'amplification of deviance' i.e. a further increase in 'deviant' behaviour brought about by (what is alleged to be) undue interference from outside bodies. (For example, by State and police in regard to individuals found in possession of cannabis.) Sociologists, however, seem to talk of 'amplification of deviance' mainly in terms of 'overactivity' of such bodies. But surely amplification of deviance could also arise from 'underactivity' and 'sins of omission'? [12c] Not taking any legislative action, for example, against drunkenness in 1914–1918 might have led to a gradual amplification of excessive drinking; and the lack of interest evinced by State and the medical profession over the years in the problems of alcohol and alcoholism has certainly not contributed to their solution [50].

The *dolce far niente* approach may sometimes be sweet but it is not necessarily masterly. As sociologists rightly say, what constitutes 'deviance' (or rather is labelled as such) depends largely on the viewpoint of the beholder. In the case of alcoholics however their behaviour is demonstrably highly dangerous to their own health and by doing nothing the majority 'amplify their deviant' self-destructive behaviour and life style. In the view of clinicians working with alcoholics, such people as a rule, are not in a position to extricate themselves from their situation without assistance, and moreover are not in a position to develop motivation to do so. Steps taken such as 'constructive confrontation' (see Chapter 10) (and even considering in certain cases the possibility of starting treatment under compulsion) far from leading to 'amplification of deviance', offers a lifeline. In such cases it is the inactivity of the State, community and the professions which permits an amplification of their self-destructive 'deviant' behaviour.

2   Adolescence may be for many ordinary youngsters (and of course even more so for the emotionally disturbed or maladjusted) a time of special strain and stress, uncertainty about their identity, their sexual role and occupation, etc. At such an intermediate stage of growing towards adulthood, and encouraged by society's gradual acceptance of even heavy drinking by teenagers as the norm, many adolescents may all too easily find in alcohol a temporary respite from nagging doubts.

3   Whitehead's second proposal of reducing *per capita* consumption without changing integration of drinking practices, by diluting alcoholic drink, would in his view circumvent the risk of boot-legging practices: these might flourish in case of marked increases in the price of drink (similar perhaps to the increasing popularity of alternative spirits after the imposition of very high taxes on gin in Britain 250 years ago [50] and thereby lessen the gain of integrating drinking practices.

References

1   Glatt, M M (1967), *WHO Chronicle*, 21, 293
2   Berry Jr, R E and Boland, J P (1977), *The Economic Cost of Alcohol Abuse*, New York, The Free Press, London, Collier, MacMillan, 187–94
3   Littleton, J M (1977), in *Alcoholism: New Knowledge and New Responses*, London, Croom Helm, 107–16
4   Seixas, F A (1974), *Preventive Medicine*, 3, 1
5   Henderson, Y (1935), *A New Deal in Liquor: A Plea for Dilution*, New York, Doubleday, Doran and Co.
6   McGuinness, T (1980), 'An econometric analysis of total demand for alcoholic beverages in the UK, 1956–75,' Edinburgh, Scottish Health Education Unit.
6a   Bruce, D (1980), *Health Bull.*, 39, 133
6b   Prys Williams, G (1980) in *Drink in Great Britain 1900–1979*, ed. Prys Williams, G and Blake, G T, 342
7   *The Lancet* (Annot.) 1980, ii, 1175
8   Smart, R G and Cullen, R (1976), *Brit. J. Addict.*, 71, 23
9   Bruun, K *et al.* (1975), *Alcohol Control Policies in Public Health Perspectives*, Helsinki, Finnish Foundation for Alcohol Studies
10   Osborne, A C and Smart, R G (1980), *Brit. J. Addict.*, 75, 293
11   National Council on Alcoholism News Service (1979), November, December, 5–7
12   Halbach, H (1959), *Brit. J. Addict.*, 56, 27

12a Hillier, S (1909), *Popular Drugs – their Use and Misuse*, London, T Werner Laurie
12b Young, S (1972), *The Drug Takers*, London, Paladin
12c Glatt, M M (1974), *A Guide to Addiction and its Treatment*, Lancaster, MTP
12d Glatt, M M (January 1974), *Brit. J. Hosp. Med.*, 111
12e Edwards, G (1971), *The Lancet*, ii, 729
13 Ledermann, S (1956) quoted from Smart, R G in *Drug Dependence – Current Problems and Issues,* ed. Glatt, M M, 263
14 Smart, R G and Whitehead, P C (1972), *Bull. Narcot. (UN)*, 24, 39
15 De Lint, J (1974), *Preventive Medicine*, 3, 24
16 Whitehead, P C (1979) in *Alcohol Problems*, ed. Robinson, D, London, Macmillan 217–26
17 Schmidt, W S and De Lint, J (1970), *Quart. J. Stud. Alc.*, 31, 957
18 De Lint, J and Schmidt, W S (1971), *Brit. J. Addict.*, 66, 97
19 Ullman, A D (1958), *Am. Acad. polit. soc. Sci.*, 135, 48
20 Blacker, E (1966), Intern. Psychiat. Clin., 3, 51
21 Smart, R G (1977), 'Social Policy and the Prevention of Drug Abuse', in *Drug Dependence*, ed. Glatt, M M, Lancaster, MTP, 263–80
22 Glatt, M M (1974), *Brit. J. Addict.*, 69, 105
23 Firth, J, *Journal* (Toronto), 1 July 1980
24 Kendell, R E (1979), *Brit. med. J.*, 1, 367
25 Sir George Young, *Ann. Gen. Meeting, Nat. Ccl. Alcoholism*, 10 July 1979
25a Robinson, D, *Alliance News* 1980 September, October, 11
26 Glatt, M M (1979), *Brit. med. J.*, 1, 684
27 *Daily Telegraph*, 30 July 1979
28 *Ibid*, 2 January 1980
29 Duffy, J C (1975), *Brit. J. Addict*, 70, 151
30 Kay, W W *et al.* (1959) *J. Ment. Sci.*, 105, 748
31 Spencer Peet, J *et al.* (1972), *The Lancet*, i, 1122
32 Whitehead, P C, *Journal* (Toronto) 1 August 1980
33 *Alcohol and Alcoholism* (1979), Report of Special Committee of R. C. Psychiatrists, 139
34 Snyder, C R (1958), *Alcohol and the Jews*, Carbondale, South. Illin. Univ. Press
35 Glatt, M M (1970), *Brit. J. Addict.*, 64, 297
36 Glatt, M M (1967) in *New Aspects of the Mental Health Services*, eds Freeman, H and Farndale, J, 115–48
37 *The Lancet* (Annot.) (1973), ii, 135
38 Plant, M A (1979), *Drinking Careers*, London, Tavistock
39 Bateson, M C (1980), *Brit. med. J.*, 281, 1472
40 Gordis, E (1976), *Ann. Intern. Med*, 85, 821
41 Ewing, J A (1980), *Internat. Confer. on Alcoholism*, Bath, England, 20–24 April
42 Bacon, S D (1976) in *Alcohol and Alcohol Problems*, eds Filstead, W J *et al.* Cambridge, Mass., Ballinger, 57–134

43 Murphree, H B (1976), *ibid*, 135–66
44 Straus, R (1976), *ibid*, 29–56
45 Cahalan, D (1970), *Problem Drinkers, a National Survey*, San Francisco, Jossey-Bass
46 National Council on Alcoholism, *Two Decades*, 16th Annual Rep., 1978–9, 14
47 National Council on Alcoholism (1980), *Counsellor's Guide on Problem Drinking*
48 Caldwell, Sir R D (1972), Annual Rep. Medical Council on Alcoholism 1972
49 Schuckitt, M A and Cahalan, D (1976) in *Alcohol and Alcohol Problems*, ed. Filstead, W J *et al.*, 229–66
50 Glatt, M M (1958), *Brit. J. Addict.* 54, 51
51 Addiction Research Foundation Ontario (1978), *Journal* (Toronto), 1 June, 178
52 Robinson, D (1979), *Alcohol Problems*, London, Macmillan, 4–7
53 Report of the Departmental Committee on Liquor Licensing (1972), London, HMSO
54 Report of the Departmental Committee on Scottish Licensing Law (1973), Scottish Health and Home Department, Edinburgh, HMSO

22

Controversial Issues in Alcoholism[1]

Alcoholism is a complex, multifactorial disorder with many inter-disciplinary aspects which have to be approached by a team of which the doctor is only one. Doctors working in this field need, therefore, to have a grasp of the way their non-medical colleagues approach the overall problem and should take an interest in all aspects (not just merely what some psychologists may like to term 'medical', i.e. drug therapy) and phases of the approach, including prevention and the long-term rehabilitation process, not in an attempt at a 'take-over' bid, but in order to share in what is an important sociomedical problem.

Is there any need for 'treatment' of alcoholics? This question must surely appear nonsensical to any clinician who has ever been faced with the problem of the heavy drinking alcoholic, but nevertheless, in view of some recent statements, a brief discussion is not out of place.

1 Prevention

Clearly, as in all other illnesses, prevention is better than cure and all attempts by all means at one's disposal (fiscal, legal, educational and research) are highly necessary. Recent pronounce-ments imply that better preventive approaches might very soon markedly reduce the need for in-patient facilities [1] and that alcoholism is a political rather than a medical problem [2]. How-ever, the preventive approaches have all been tried for many years and in many places, without unfortunately ever eliminating the occurrence of many alcoholic casualties and fatalities; to hope that even the most effective means of primary prevention (or of early diagnosis) will ever eliminate the need to have trained professional workers of various disciplines assisting alcoholics within the community and in in-patient centres, is surely Utopian [3]. The need for fiscal and legal means of prevention is obvious and most observers tend to agree with the Ontario research workers [4] that national *per capita* alcohol consumption of alcohol and the incidence of alcohol-related complications are correlated; and that therefore, in theory, reducing national *per capita* alcohol consumption would seem the surest way of cutting down the incidence of alcoholism. But does this make alcoholism mainly and primarily a political problem? Governments will not move unless backed by public opinion. It would therefore need much better and more intensive specialised education of both the professional and lay public than hitherto to mobilise opinion towards supporting significant taxation increases on alcoholic drink [5], in order to influence the decisive ratio between income and the relative price of alcohol, which largely seems to determine the incidence of heavy alcohol consumption. Until very recently, medical students have been taught so little about problem drinking [6] that few doctors have taken an enlightened interest (and this is reflected in the unfortunately high rates of alcoholism among doctors themselves the world over) [7]. Moreover, in spite of the so often minimised role of doctors in this field, the general public still probably takes its cue from doctors. Education of doctors, therefore, remains vital in any comprehensive preventive approach; it cannot be all left to the politicians – desirable as the greater interest of recent governments in this field and the recent formation of an all-party group in the House of Commons (by Sir Bernard Braine) are. In this area, as in so many others in the field of problem drinking, the question is surely *not*, as posed in a recent BMJ article ('Alcoholism – a medical *or* a political problem' [2]) one of 'either/or'. It is both a political and a socio-medical problem and has surely to be approached from both these angles [3, 8].

2   Early diagnosis

Early diagnosis of alcoholism is obviously vital and has been urged by all workers in this field. Unfortunately, it has never been widely achieved and though, with wider and better education of the professional and lay public, by reducing the stigma and with the work of local Information Centres of the National Council, this situation should improve, wider education and bringing to light many more as yet undiagnosed cases will also uncover cases of alcoholism in *later* phases in greater numbers than hitherto. Rather than reducing the need for special community and residential centres (as envisaged in the 'Services' report of the Advisory Council [1]) such improved measures of case-finding are likely to lead to a greater demand for such centres [8].

3 Treatment or advice?

A valuable research study by Edwards *et al.* [9] has shown that in a sample of 100 married men living with their wives, 'conventional' therapy did not give better results than no therapy; a finding that has been widely commented upon. However, Edwards' *et al.* 'no therapy' included a long session of intensive assessment, discussion and advice over four to five hours by a highly skilled, multidisciplinary team, followed by monthly home visits by a social worker. This type of advice, followed up by regular visits seems much more in the nature of 'therapy' than what is still done for alcoholics in most places today. Furthermore, this was a highly selective sample of male alcoholics whose wives were prepared to stay with their husbands in spite of their not having any treatment as such – all this being highly unusual and unrepresentative in the case of alcoholics and their wives seen in general clinical practice [10, 11]. Married men living with their wives, moreover, are generally better therapeutic propositions than any other alcoholic group [12], and may require less professional support and treatment, compared with other groups, such as single or divorced women or men who frequently are not motivated, or prepared to stay on for even the briefest assessment [10, 11]. Madden [12] therefore rightly warns against, 'any tendency towards therapeutic nihilism that may follow a single British study that failed to find an effect from therapy – mainly of an out-patient nature – among its subjects'. Clinical experience clearly indicates the need for the therapist to give a great deal of support and/or treatment for problem drinkers and their families if the risk of damage is to be minimised. What, however, this study once more indicates is the vital importance of a sympathetic, informed interest shown by professionals towards their clients. It has long been known that an accepting, non-judgmental relationship may be more important to the patient than the special type of therapy which the individual therapist may administer [6, 7]. As the Advisory Council Report on Services rightly points out, 'not all problem drinkers need medical care'. It fails to point out that not all such drinkers need the help of social workers or of other members of the primary care team either (although the important role of the primary team in general is quite rightly stressed in that Report). In the past, more problem drinkers have been helped by AA than by any professional workers. The earlier problem drinkers come to the fore, the less they will be in need of medical or other professional care – especially if they come before they have reached the stage of dependence. In such relatively early cases informed advice may indeed often be sufficient. In general, it is the task of the agency first approached by the drinker or his family to assess the special circumstances and then refer the drinker to that member of the team (or agency) best suited to his individual needs – not to shift the problems on to somebody else's shoulder but to share them with other team members [6]. However, assistance from the GP remains essential in all phases of the process.

Treatment goals

1   There has been in recent years a great deal of discussion about alternatives to the treatment goal of total abstinence [13, 14]. But surely neither abstinence nor controlled drinking are treatment goals? What the advocates of the abstinence approach believe is that abstinence is the best and indeed usually the only means towards giving the drinker and his family the best chance to learn to live happily, usefully and in harmony. Of course, there are parameters of success other than abstinence [13], but in clinical practice in the very great majority of cases abstinence will be, in time, accompanied by improvement in other parameters, provided the drinker realises that he cannot be satisfied with resting on his laurels having achieved abstinence.

2   There are many *problems of alcohol* other than alcoholism –as recognised by a WHO Expert Committee (1955) [15]. This has been stressed much more in recent years [14, 16] and clearly for earlier problem drinkers (those who have not yet become dependent on alcohol) there might be no necessity for total abstinence. Assessment in practice, however, may often be difficult, as alcohol-dependent drinkers are much more prone to experience and develop other alcohol-related problems (such as accidents following intoxication, or antisocial behaviour under alcohol influence). As the 'Alcohol and Alcoholism' Expert Committee [15] stressed the public health action called for by the different cate-

gories is quite different. The dividing line between other alcohol problems and essential (or true) alcoholism drawn by the 1955 Committee were the manifestations of either loss of control (later called Gamma alcoholism by Jellinek [17]) or inability to stop (better termed 'inability to abstain', Jellinek's Delta alcoholism [18]).

3   For drinkers who are not alcohol-dependent a goal of moderate drinking seems feasible. The trouble in practice, is that the majority of those seen are already well into the crucial [6, 17] Gamma or Delta phases of alcoholism.
   As reflected in the *Chart of Alcohol Dependence* [6, 7] there is usually a long interval between social drinking and the first evidence of dependence and biological changes (such as tolerance and amnesias). During this interval, drinkers can successfully cut down on their excessive drinking. The obvious difficulty is to determine *when* the dependence has set in or has reached a degree where safe, consistent, controlled drinking is beyond their reach.

4   It stands to reason that the more intensive the dependence the more remote the chance of safe, controlled drinking. The 1972 who Alcoholism Subcommittee, in its well known definition [19], calls alcoholics 'those excessive drinkers whose dependence on alcohol has reached a certain *degree*'. No one becomes an alcoholic or reaches dependence spontaneously. Thus in the long, drawn-out development of the process there must clearly be excessive drinkers who self-indulgently, or deliberately misuse alcohol and who, in their earlier drinking career, could modify their drinking. There are others, clearly dependent, who will have to remain abstinent. In between there must be many intermediate drinkers, on the brink of dependence, who might, at least in theory, still become safe, controlled drinkers.

5   *'Disease' or 'learned behaviour'?* Learning principles certainly play a role in the development of alcoholism: e.g. in the drinker's progress from occasional to constant relief drinking (Jellinek's prodromal phase [6, 17]) due to the positive rewards following drinking, and later on, after physical dependence has set in, when the drinker learns to avert (or avoid) the onset of physical withdrawal symptoms by either rapidly drinking, or more simply by *not* withdrawing from drink in the first place.
   However, biological processes appear to occur quite early in the development of the disorder. To start with, the drinker may take a

lot of alcohol (perhaps in order to relieve mental stress) but soon develops metabolic or cellular *tolerance* – a biological process which *compels* the drinker to raise his alcohol intake in order to achieve the needed effect.

Alcoholic *amnesias* also occur fairly early in the alcoholic's drinking career and though their nature is obscure they may indicate some early organic changes – even if, like tolerance, or the fatty liver, such changes may be reversible.

Thus learning processes alone are probably insufficient to explain the whole alcoholism process, as biological changes may set in early on. The occurrence of such biological changes, even though reversible would render alcoholism an illness even in the purists' sense who define a disorder as a 'disease' only when organic processes are at work. To what extent, if any, organic factors are involved in the causation of alcoholism is still unknown but they certainly cannot be excluded at least in certain of the various types of what Jellinek calls the *alcoholisms* [17]. Most doctors are interested in the whole person – with psychological as well as physical aspects of his functioning, against his total social background, and many would not equate terms such as 'disease', 'medical model', and 'loss of control' over alcohol intake, with organic changes only, but take them to include psychosomatic, psychosocial and psychopharmacological factors as well as physical ones [20].

The often heard argument that the 'disease' concept of alcoholism provides the drinker with a welcome alibi has little foundation. The abstinence-oriented approach clearly emphasises the drinker's responsibility for the first drink, and, as in other illnesses, it is up to the patient to accept and follow the therapist's advice. Again, in alcohol units, stress is laid on encouraging the drinker to take an active part in his own recovery and to assume initiative himself [21].

6 *'Lack of Control'* – *a multifactorial phenomenon* The disease concept of alcohol has usually been associated with the 'Lack of Control' (LoC) phenomenon. Clearly LoC only means that such a (Gamma) alcoholic can never be certain that he will be able to stop drinking on any given occasion; it does not mean that the first drink *inevitably* necessitates further drinking [23, 24].

Does the finding that many alcoholics can drink moderately for short periods (and a few for long periods, or even indefinitely) imply that LoC is a myth? that there is no biochemical basis for

LoC and with it no absolute necessity for alcoholics' lifelong abstinence? Theoretically, perhaps LoC could be of an intermittently active nature only, being sometimes in remission (latent) and become active under certain conditions only [25].

Many of our alcoholic patients who initially had insisted that they could drink safely in moderation if they put their mind to it, were in fact only able to do so for limited periods (weeks or, rarely, a few months). Since 1963 we often concluded a 'Gentleman's Agreement' with such drinkers [22, 23], according to which, no matter what the circumstances, they were never to drink more than an agreed amount – usually a few pints of beer or glasses of wine. Most failed after a very short period, but some managed to last longer. Their experience seemed to point to the likelihood that LoC was associated not only with the activity of the agent (such as the concentration, amount or rapidity of consumption of the alcoholic drink), but also with the environment (e.g. whether drinking alone or in one's spouse's company) and with personality (host) [20, 22, 23, 26].

These drinkers thus seemed to exhibit a *relative lack of control* [20, 26] over drinking (i.e. the 'impaired control', regarded as a characteristic of the 'alcohol dependence syndrome [16]), which seems a variable, and in many cases, progressive phenomenon, in the sense that it manifested itself increasingly often in relatively later phases of a drinking career. Given some insight, a certain degree of emotional maturation or increased social stability, considerable effort and some luck, certain alcoholics can indeed stick to 'controlled drinking' as long as the going remains good, but when faced with adverse conditions drink may, as in the past, be taken for its pharmacological, 'therapeutic' purpose; and, in this way, the balance between the opposing influences (the 'pull' of the LoC, on the one hand, and the psychosocial brakes, on the other), once more may be tipped towards a defeat of the controlling or disciplining factors [20, 26].

The alcoholic's compulsion, then, to continue drinking after one or two drinks (either immediately, as in the Gamma alcoholic, or delayed for a few hours, as in the Delta alcoholic), is not necessarily derived, as hypothesised by Jellinek [17], from biochemical processes alone, but rather 'from a dynamic interaction of factors pertaining to host and environment as well as to agent'. Psychosocial, psychopharmacological and psychosomatic factors may all influence the activation and manifestation of the LoC. Under such circumstances it is readily understandable why some alcoholics can drink in a controlled manner for shorter or longer periods. In theory, therefore, the great majority of alcoholics could do so. In practice, however, so many internal or external cues can trigger relapses that it is highly unlikely that more than a small minority can achieve a goal of safe controlled drinking. Though it seems likely that the chances are relatively greater in those with lesser degrees of dependence [16], with better social conditions, possibly with those of a shorter drinking history or with a history of not too heavy drinking [27], no one can yet say with any degree of certainty which alcoholic stands a fair chance of becoming a safe controlled drinker. Whilst alcoholics themselves may be very keen to attempt such approaches, their spouses may view such approaches with great misgivings and will require assistance and persuasion to co-operate [20, 26].

In summary therefore, whilst research in selected centres with such attempts at controlled drinking is indicated in order to learn more about the LoC phenomenon, at the present juncture to propagate such a goal generally may encourage the majority to what ultimately seems only too likely to prolong their suffering.

Venue of treatment

1   *Out-patient or in-patient treatment?*
This obviously depends on many circumstances. With earlier recognition many patients could be treated while remaining within the community; under more difficult domestic circumstances, hostel accommodation may be necessary, and certain patients – such as those with a much greater degree of psychological or physical dependence or complications – may require at least a certain amount of preliminary in-patient treatment, as may the seriously depressed or disinterested drinker. Alcoholics are at increased risk of suicide, particularly (as claimed recently) [36] when their drinking is associated with losing their employment or their spouse. Both these socio-domestic complications are common in heavy problem drinkers.

The question of out- or in-patient treatment seems therefore largely an academic one. Edwards and Guthrie (1967) [28] showed in a relatively small sample (a total of forty, twenty out-patients and twenty in-patients), that out-patient treatment gave the same results as in-patient treatment. The in-patient régime concerned was a thirty-bed general psychiatric ward in which there were only four or five alcoholics, and not a specialised unit; and whilst their paper states that the patients treated by them as out-patients were of the type 'usually treated as in-patients', in the view of most clinicians experienced in the work with alcoholics, there are many patients who possibly having tried community therapy before and failed repeatedly, for some reason or another can no longer be cared for as out-patients [29]. As Marjot [30] has pointed out, in such attempted comparisons often different types of populations are involved; for example, returning to Edwards' *et al.* [9] sample of married men living with their wives, and among thousands of alcoholic patients still living with their wives, I have come across very few wives who would agree without misgivings to an approach consisting of no more than an advice session and a visit from a social worker who was to exercise no 'therapeutic' function.

2 *The alcohol unit*

In my opinion, the recently introduced term ATU (Alcoholic Treatment Unit) is a misnomer. The alcohol unit has not been introduced to be exclusively a unit for treatment but has always been thought of as a centre for the education, training and research, as well as for treatment [21].

There are many myths about the role, function and the goal of the alcohol units [31]. It has sometimes been implied that alcohol units have been formed in order to solve the problem of alcoholism. I am sure no one concerned about such units shares any such delusion. They came into being at a time when public and professional attitudes to the problem were much less informed than they are today. At that time, when visitors to Britain were told at government level that there were no alcoholics in this country and, if there were, any medical hospital could cope with them; when industry claimed that there were hardly any alcoholics to be found; when general practitioners knew of no more than 35,000 alcoholics in England and Wales; when pioneers such as Drs Dent and Pullar-Strecker bitterly complained that, in the whole of the country; there was practically no in-patient or out-patient facility primarily concerned with helping alcoholics [37], units started off with not more than the function of helping those in urgent need of assistance.

A unit does not consist merely of a residential facility [32] with out-patient and community service, half way houses and hostels, as well as in-patient facilities. The whole, closely-integrated complex of facilities should be regarded as the unit, rather than the in-patient facility alone [32]. A detoxification centre could be integrated in such a unit [33]. The units make use of a multi-disciplinary team of workers [21] and usually employ psychological as well as physical and social treatment, although the core of the treatment is the therapeutic community and extensive group therapy. Contrary to the often heard criticism that units only take those with good prognosis, that certainly does not hold good for the great majority of them. At St Bernard's, for example, we always used to take single, homeless, often antisocial girls, referred from Holloway prison as well as those referred from court and occasional skid-row drinkers referred from the Spitalfields Crypt. In the units alcoholism is usually approached as a symptom of the underlying psychological and/or social maladjustment, as well as an illness in its own right. Good contact should be maintained with the primary care team and all agencies involved in assisting problem drinkers and with casualty departments.

3   *Primary care team*

The Report of the Advisory Committee on Alcoholism [1] rightly stresses the important role which the primary care team could play in the overall programme needed to assist problem drinkers. However, the claim made in the introduction to the Report, that the knowledge and skill required to help the majority of problem drinkers are 'relatively simple' is surely unrealistic [39]. The task would indeed be simple if such drinkers really wanted to overcome their problem, but most problem drinkers, initially, do not. Yet drinkers do not have to reach rock bottom to be ready to accept this help, such motivation to do something about the problem can be induced at a much earlier phase in quite a number of problem drinkers. The skill needed to achieve such a goal is by no means simple and may take years to acquire. It will therefore take a long time before there are a sufficient number of members of the primary care team who have the motivation and the skill and the time to help problem drinkers.[2]

The units can and should take an increasingly larger role in helping them to acquire the necessary motivation.

'Alcoholism' or 'Alcohol Dependence Syndrome?'

In line with the recommendation of a group of investigators [16] called together by the World Health Organisation in 1977, the who's *Ninth Revision of the International Classification of Diseases*, dropped the term 'Alcoholism' replacing it by 'Alcohol Dependence Syndrome'. The definition reads: 'a state, psychic and usually also physical, resulting from taking alcohol, characterised by behavioural and other responses that always include a compulsion to take alcohol on a continuous or periodic basis in order to experience its psychic effects, and sometimes to avoid the discomfort of its absence; tolerance may or may not be present'.

One immediate difficulty arising from this definition is the required presence ('always') of a 'compulsion' to take alcohol continually or periodically. In this case the definition would, for example, exclude the case of a heavily drinking publican and his wife whose regular drinking (probably often in the absence of compulsion but carried out for social, business or economic reasons) often ends in liver cirrhosis, the latter being expressly excluded from the term 'alcohol dependence syndrome'. Certain alcohol related disabilities [16] can arise in the absence of compulsion or dependence. The newly proposed term thus does not really replace the terms 'alcoholism' or 'alcoholics' as understood by the who (1952) definition [19] which clearly included mental and physical drink-induced complications. Quite apart from the notion of the alcohol dependence syndrome, the plausible equation of alcoholism with alcohol dependence has recently been proposed by various observers. The publican however who, even in the absence of dependence, ultimately dies from liver cirrhosis as a complication of his heavy drinking, has surely acquired the right, posthumously, to be diagnosed as having been an alcoholic, even though he showed no clinical or other evidence. For these reasons the substitution of alcoholism by the alcohol dependence syndrome does not seem a satisfactory step. Moreover the term is clumsy and unlikely to be accepted in common use by alcoholics themselves, their families and even possibly writers [14] about the problem. One valuable service rendered by the new term would be in helping doctors to realise fully that in treating alcoholics the emphasis has to be on coping with the dependence and not just sobering-up and treating complications.

Although other disabilities or complications can also occur in the absence of dependence (a possibility fully realised by Jellinek as seen in the description of his term 'Beta Alcoholism' [17]), the likelihood of such complications is obviously higher, the greater the intensity of dependence. This correlation between state of dependence and likelihood of resulting harm, probably explains the wording of the WHO 1952 definition [19]. Essentially this definition describes alcoholics as those excessive drinkers whose dependence on alcohol has attained such a degree that it leads to physical, mental and socioeconomic harm. Probably the higher the incidence and the more severe the intensity of such complications, the greater the likelihood of the presence of a considerable degree of dependence.

Physical treatment

Detoxification: in alcoholics the use of dependence-producing drugs should be avoided or minimised as far as possible [6, 21]. However, they cannot always be avoided. A case in point is chlormethiazole, which has proved very valuable for the withdrawal treatment of serious states of alcohol intoxication in particular in the prevention and treatment of *delirium tremens*. However, chlormethiazole should only be used in the correct indications, which means, as a rule, only for in-patients and for no longer than about six or seven days. Failing this there is a risk in ambulant patients of a potentiation of chlormethiazole and alcohol effects and of psychological and physical dependence on the drug itself. Such risks exist to a larger or lesser degree with all other central nervous system affecting drugs used in the alcohol withdrawal period.

As regards *long-term treatment* it should be emphasised that drugs such as Antabuse or CCC (Abstem) often also have the effect of reducing the craving for alcohol by putting alcohol, for a certain period, outside the reach of the patient. As regards the disulfiram implant such implants seem to work only as long as the drinker believes in their effectiveness.

Conclusion

In spite, or perhaps because of valuable recent research many aspects of problem drinking, alcoholism and alcohol dependence remain obscure and controversial. It would seem, however, that often in questions concerning alcohol problems the answer is not one of 'either . . . or' but rather '. . . and/or . . .' [5]. This aspect has been briefly touched upon in the text in reference to the 'political or medical problem?' issue but it seems important in regard to many other questions also. For example:

Alcoholism – learned behaviour or 'disease?

Alcoholism – dependence or harm?
Alcoholism – symptom or disease?
Alcoholism – a political or a medical problem?
Prevention or intervention (treatment) in alcoholism?
Social or psychological or physical approach?
Psychodynamic or behavioural therapy? (Freud or Pavlov?)
Disulfiram or AA?
Out-patient (community-based) or in-patient treatment?
Primary care or 'unit'?
Prevention control or education
Reduction of national *per capita* alcohol consumption or 'specific target-directed' approach?
Primary care team or specialists?

And even in the emotionally so highly charged debate: controlled drinking or abstinence? the answer may often appear to be a complementary one depending on the (different) target population; 'controlled drinking' may often be within reach of 'problem drinkers' who have not yet reached the stage of dependence although they may be hovering on the brink, whereas abstinence is likely to be the only *safe* approach for the clearly dependent 'alcoholic'.

Notes

1 Based on a paper read at the International Conference on Alcoholism, Bath 1980 and in part reported here by kind permission of the organisers, Broadway Lodge, Weston-Super-Mare.

2 According to a recent editorial in *Hospital Update* (January, 1981) [38] with 30,000 GPs in the NHS there is one GP to 2100 patients. The low-consulting GP will have twenty consultations a day, the high-consulting GP, sixty. A GP sees 6–10 patients per hour. Patient care may sometimes be with nurses, health visitors and social workers. Nevertheless, as the editorial points out, if the GP is also asked to undertake more preventive care (including regular medical screening for a number of conditions, more counselling, health education, social care) 'we must give the practitioner more time'. This editorial speaks of care for the general patient; certainly problem drinkers require much more time from the practitioner who, in order to be in a position to help them, will have to establish a relationship with them. The editorial's comment that 'the realities are far removed from the theories' certainly seems fully to apply to those recommendations by the Advisory

Council on Alcoholism that the often overburdened GP and his team could, on top of their other duties, take on the main responsibility of looking after problem drinkers and their families [1].

References

1 *The Pattern and Range of Services for Problem Drinkers* (1977), Report of the Advisory Council on Alcoholism, Department of Health and Social Security and the Welsh Office, HMSO.
2 Kendell, R E (1979), *Brit. med. J.*, 1, 367
3 Glatt, M M (1980), *The Lancet*, i, 982
4 De Lint, J and Schmidt, W, *Brit. J. Add.*, 66, 97
5 Glatt, M M (1979), *Brit. med. J.*, 1, 684
6 Glatt, M M (January 1974), *Brit. J. Hosp. Med.*, 111
7 Glatt, M M (1974), *A Guide to Addiction and its Treatment*, Med. & Techn. Publ., Lancaster
8 Glatt, M M (1979), *The Lancet*, i, 813
9 Edwards, G *et al.* (1977), *J. Stud. Alcohol*, 38, 1004
10 Glatt, M M (1977), *The Lancet*, 2, 817
11 Glatt, M M (1977), in *Alcohol and the Family*, 24, United Kingdom Alliance, London
12 Madden, J S (1979), *Brit. J. Addict.*, 74, 318
13 Pattison, E Mansell, Sobell, M B and Sobell, L C (1977), *Emerging Concepts of Alcohol Dependence*, New York, Springer
14 Royal College of Psychiatrists (1979), *Alcohol and Alcoholism*, Report of a Special Committee, London, Tavistock
15 World Health Organisation (1955), *Alcohol and Alcoholism*, Report of an Expert Committee, Wld Hlth Org. Techn. Rep. Ser., 94, 12
16 *Alcohol-Related Disabilities* (1977), eds Edwards, G, *et al.*, World Health Organisation
17 Jellinek, E M (1960), *The Disease Concept of Alcoholism*, Hillhouse Press, New Brunswick
18 Glatt, M M (1957), *Brit. J. Addict.*, 54, 47
19 World Health Organisation (1952), Alcoholism Subcommittee. Second Report, World Hlth Org, Techn. Rep. Ser., 48, 16
20 Glatt, M M (1976), *Brit. J. Addict.*, 71, 133
21 Glatt, M M (1955), *Brit. J. Addict.*, 52, 55
22 Glatt, M M (1965), *Quart. J. Stud. Alc.*, 26, 117
23 Glatt, M M, (1967), *Brit. J. Add.*, 62, 267
24 Keller, M (1958), *Annals American Academy Political Science*, 35, 1
25 Keller, M (1972), *Brit. J. Addict.*, 67, 153
26 Glatt, M M (1980), *Brit. J. Alcohol & Alcoholism*, 15(2), 48
27 Popham, R E and Schmidt, W (1978), *Alcoholism* (Zagreb), 14(1), 3
28 Edwards, G and Guthrie, S (1967), *The Lancet*, i, 555
29 Glatt, M M (1967), *The Lancet*, i, 791
30 Marjot, D (1980), personal communication

31   Glatt, M M (1978), *British J. Alcohol and Alcoholism*, 13(1), 11
32   Glatt, M M, (1964), Tenth European Institute on the Prevention and
     Treatment of Alcoholism (ICAA), London
33   Arroyave, F *et al.* (1980), *Health Trends*, DHSS and Welsh Office,
     12, 36
34   Holt, S *et al.* (1980), *Brit. med. J.*, 281, 638
35   Jarman, C M B and Kellett, J M (1974), *Brit. med. J.*, ii, 469
36   Kreitman, N and Dyer, A T (December 1980), *Medicine*, 36, 1827
37   Pullar-Strecker, H (1952), *Brit. J. Addict*, 49, 21
38   *Hospital Update* (Editorial) 1981, 7(1), 5
39   Glatt, M M (1979), *Brit. J. Addict.*, 74, 115

23

Conclusion

Dr Donald Gould [1, 2] once said: 'People will do what pleases them, regardless of the most painful consequences'; and this is especially true of alcoholism. People, unfortunately, are often only too confident that many drinking habits, although obviously 'painful to others', will bring nothing but pleasure to themselves. As in the case of infectious diseases, in alcoholism, too, host, environment and an agent are involved. But while no one voluntarily embraces any of the killing infectious agents, the 'double-dealing' [3] agent alcohol has an attractive face and, far from keeping away from it, the great majority of mankind seek it out and ignore its darker side. For this reason the eradication of alcoholism will not be brought about in the same way that epidemics of, for example, smallpox have been brought to an end. Nevertheless all possible steps should be taken towards the goal of primary prevention in the hope of minimising the incidence. In the past, neither prevention nor treatment of alcoholism has been very effective, however, no one knows whether today's problem would not have been even much worse, and how many of the treated alcoholics might have fared much worse without such treatment. More significant still is the shift in professional and public attitudes which have greatly changed for the better since the wide acceptance of the disease concept of alcoholism; this must have exercised some effect at least on the goal of secondary prevention. And the great majority of clinicians active in this field remain convinced that treatment often exercises an extremely valuable effect on alcoholic patients in spite of occasional relapses, accompanied by an often marked improvement in other spheres of functioning, with considerable relief to the hard-pressed families.

The cost of an efficient preventive, educational and rehabilitation programme is great but it bears no comparison with the expenditure – no less heavy and crippling because it is often hidden and ignored – in terms of human health, happiness and efficiency following in the wake of alcoholism and perpetuated by the failure of society to attack the problem in earnest. Society when making available and encouraging the widespread use of potentially as dangerous a drug as alcohol cannot shirk its responsibility and duty to try to reduce excessive consumption of alcohol, to educate the public about the nature of the risks of the alcohol habit, and to help in rehabilitating the large number of unfortunates who have become its victims.

Some years ago an American publication [4] posed the question 'What is the truth about alcoholism?' It rightly pointed out that 'many statistics, slogans, statements and ideas [are] so relentlessly repeated that they may become popularly accepted as "truths".' This undoubtedly holds good for statements uncritically accepted by many in the past and rightly challenged, but it equally applies to certain criticisms of such old 'truths': the endless repetition of the same type of criticism in itself does not prove that such criticism is necessarily true. Clearly what may be regarded as true today may in fact turn out to stand on insecure foundations; or they may all prove essentially true or false, or possibly to be half-truths. Obviously there is an urgent need for continued research in this complex matter.

The same Editorial made a number of interesting statements. 'Most alcohologists [it claims] will [probably] accept the following:

1 Some people cannot handle alcohol.
2 No one knows why.
3 No test exists to pre-determine who is at risk.
4 The only solution (for alcoholics) is total sobriety.
5 The main problem is the inability of the alcoholic to see this.
6 Any alcoholic can quit –
7 But most don't.
8 Many quit periodically but fall back.
9 Thousands have attained sobriety in Alcoholics Anonymous.
10 Others have also, with help from clergymen, doctors, lawyers, judges, boss, family, clinics, councils, and recovery houses.
11 AA does the most effective job with the most people.
12 YOU can help your alcoholic! Do it NOW . . . or when the next crisis occurs, kindly but firmly insist that they do something (admitting in the process your own inability to cope).'

If the term 'alcoholic' in this connection, means the Gamma alcoholic, our own viewpoint would agree with all the points made, given present knowledge. Most alcohologists would accept all – or almost all – the propositions made, although others would passionately object to some of these points.

Points 1–3 would probably be agreed to by everyone. There are no end of theories and hypotheses, some more plausible than others but as yet no one really knows why a minority of people cannot handle alcohol as well as the majority and there is no way to predetermine who will develop alcoholism.

As to the belief that total sobriety is the only solution for every (Gamma) alcoholic, whilst this is probably the majority view, nowadays a number of observers claim that this not so and that a minority of alcoholics can learn controlled drinking. Most Gamma alcoholics suffer from a relative lack of control and not of an absolute loss of control so that it is not a question of all or nothing on every occasion. Many alcoholics get away with controlled drinking on a number of occasions. But no Gamma alcoholic can ever be sure on what occasion he can stop, so that the viewpoint adopted in this book is that to advise Gamma alcoholics to attempt controlled drinking is to play 'Russian Roulette'. Planned research is needed with co-operative patients.

The degree of alcohol dependence involved seems an important factor but it cannot be measured, only guessed at. The risk of failure is considerable and the outcome of any one drinking bout, unpredictable. The only *safe* solution, therefore, in the case of Gamma alcoholics, is total sobriety.

Point 5 would probably also be agreed to by most observers, although there are many different reasons for the drinker's inability or unwillingness to see sense. In practice many drinkers who intellectually can see that it would be best to give up alcohol altogether, for various reasons seem to be unable to achieve this. In such individuals, therapists have to be grateful for small mercies and be satisfied with achievements more modest than total abstinence. The knowledge that in the view of some authorities total abstinence is not the only solution will confirm the hope of many drinkers that they are the exceptions to the abstinence rule.

As to point 6, practically every alcoholic can give up alcohol without danger although immediately after heavy drinking certain precautionary measures may be necessary. The difficulty is not to come off alcohol but to stay off it; and many alcoholics might indeed be helped by informed advice only, but here again, only inspired guesswork can tell for whom advice will prove sufficient and who will need treatment, rehabilitation and continuous support.

Most alcoholics do not give up alcohol (point 7), the great majority of non-dependent problem drinkers and of (established) alcoholics at present do not come to the attention of AA or any other helping agency. Intensified attempts at prevention by spreading objective information, may in time bear fruit.

Unfortunately (point 8) many of those who try to give up alcohol, experience 'skids'. Alcoholism, like other forms of drug dependence, is a relapsing condition: many alcoholics finally make it only after a number of relapses. A relapse should not be regarded by the therapist as a failure on his part and give rise to feelings of guilt or defeatism but as a challenge to try again.

Most observers would probably fully agree with points 9 to 11: no one therapeutic method is best for every alcoholic. Many different approaches carried out by professional and non-professional workers have proved successful with different individuals. Interdisciplinary teamwork may often be needed and the agency first approached should be prepared to refer a drinker, where advisable, to another agency (at least temporarily) not in order to shift the responsibility but in order to share it. Hitherto, however, the most effective single therapeutic approach has been AA, and whatever other approaches may be preferred, most alcoholics would benefit from an introduction to AA.

Point 12 is probably true in many cases in the long run. It should be remembered though that the alcoholic breaks his promises again and again after a short period. The question for the family whether it is best to stay with the drinker (and thus to protect and shelter him) or, by leaving him (temporarily) confront him with the consequences of his drinking, is one of the most difficult to answer. It varies from individual to individual and usually requires a weighing up of the probabilities after an assessment of the total situation. Expert advice is required but even then the choice will usually be a very painful one, with the outcome remaining uncertain.

Whilst this mainly applies to the Gamma alcoholic 'alcoholism' is far from being a homogeneous entity. Individuals of different psychological and physiological make-up, of different age, sex, socioecomomic, educational and vocational backgrounds, take alcoholic drinks of varying composition and concentration under widely varying environmental situations and for quite different motives. The consequences, too, vary greatly in different people. In the past, problem drinkers, whether dependent or non-dependent, were probably lumped together as 'alcoholics'; and often the therapist may have treated them all alike. In view of so many distinctions between the various types the present writer completely agrees with Jellinek's suggestion to talk of the 'alcoholisms' rather than 'alcoholism' [5]. Apart from Jellinek's five categories there are also many other subgroups and syndromes. The presence of these different forms has important therapeutic implications, but it is possible (or likely?) that there may be quite different combinations of causative factors involved in the various subgroups and types. To a certain extent this might explain so many different research findings obtained by so many highly experienced, *bona fide*, dedicated workers all prepared to swear that their methods and findings are correct. For example, constitutional susceptibility or vulnerability might be relatively more important in some species of the alcoholisms, acquired factors in others. Predisposition not only to develop dependence but damage to the various organs may vary greatly among the various subgroups. There may be a varying 'vulnerability' among the different alcoholisms towards developing 'dependency' on the one hand and damage to certain organs, on the other. All this is, of course, hypothetical and requires a great deal of research for partial or total refutation or confirmation. But it seems a pity that Jellinek's proposals in that direction made twenty years ago and which received so much acclaim should not have been followed up by research to test his hypotheses.

This is not intended to imply a complete acceptance of Jellinek's classification. In the intervening years many studies have had some bearing on his formulation. His concept of loss of control has been rejected by some observers. Most still accept it, with some modification. In our view, for example, corresponding to degrees of dependence, or relative lack of control leading to a nearly absolute loss of control; and, differing from Jellinek's hypothesis of a physiopathological, biochemical nature of LoC, there is the concept of a multifactorial lack of control – affected not only be interaction between 'agent' alcohol and the 'host' but also very much by factors pertaining to the environment. This same triad of factors (which also appear to influence causation) may be very significant for assessing prognosis, and for planning preventative and rehabilitation programmes [6].

Similar to more recent emphasis by WHO Committees on 'dependence', Jellinek's disease concept was limited to the Gamma and Delta types. Symptomatic or 'secondary' form of excessive drinking, in the absence of psychological dependence, should not be included in the term 'alcoholism'. There may be more than academic or semantic interest in this differentiation. In the absence of LoC a return to 'controlled drinking' might be possible at least in theory; the possibility of safe, controlled drinking becomes more remote, even in the absence of physical dependence the stronger the degree of psychological dependence. The presence of psychological dependence (though much less so of its degree) can be inferred with a great deal of confidence: for example, when an individual (who is not psychopathic, psychotic, or intellectually subnormal), appears unable to learn from his previous drinking experiences and continues to drink excessively in spite of the consequences. The likely diagnosis of a state of psychological dependence thus is often possible long before the advent of psychological abstinence symptoms following alcohol withdrawal, in contrast to physical dependence which can be diagnosed only by the development of physical abstinence features subsequent to abrupt (or too rapid) withdrawal of alcohol.

As different from Jellinek's and previous WHO Committees' views of Gamma and Delta types as being essentially different, largely determined by the type of alcohol drink taken, in our own clinical experience they very commonly co-exist in the same individual, their manifestation as either Gamma or Delta often depending on psychosocial factors, such as the knowledge or otherwise of the opportunity for drinking later on during the day. There is always an interplay between a more or less 'adequate' or temporarily 'motivated' host with the agent in the given situation. Thus some individuals 'must' have the next drink immediately, others go overboard only after having had a number of drinks (the question of a varying range of 'thresholds'), again others may be able to delay having to take the next drink for a few hours, at least under certain circumstances. The first two would be examples of Gamma, the third, of the Delta type.

In conclusion, one has to admit that much in the field of problem drinking and alcoholism remains unsatisfactory: a great deal remains to be done and there is much room for marked improvement in all aspects – prevention and treatment. It must be hoped that preventive measures, in time, will markedly reduce the numbers of problem drinkers and alcoholics. But what about the message to those who have become already alcohol-dependent and to their families? The present author can do no better than once more refer to the exposition of Dr George Vaillant. The clinician who is mindful of or engaged in research indeed finds himself in a dilemma: much of the evidence to support treatment has not been forthcoming, but at the same time 'the problem of alcoholism is too immense', the pain and suffering it causes not only to the drinkers but also to their families too severe and widespread, for clinicians to ignore it or hand out 'advice', and – as Vaillant puts it – to tell government bodies that it is useless to fund large-scale treatment programmes. After a lengthy review of one's clinical experiences over the years, and of the ever increasing mass of conflicting evidence the present author, like Vaillant [8], 'returns to the treatment of alcoholism both with hope and confidence'. This text – whilst directed at the professional and the general public – has been written mainly for problem drinkers and their families, and helpers and therapists. In spite of all undoubted shortcomings, in spite of the need for further research and improvements, there is no reason whatsoever to lose hope. Alcoholics and their families should come forward; they should apply to the helping and treatment agencies with hope and confidence. They will receive not only comfort, understanding and compassion but also active and effective help.

References

1   Bres, P L, (1980) World Health (November), 7
2   Gould, D *ibid.*, 1980 (November), 23
3   Keller, M (1976) in *Alcohol and Alcohol Problems*, ed. Filstead, W J *et al.*, 5–28
4   *Alcohol Affairs* (1974), Baton Rouge, Louisiana, 1, 1
5   Jellinek, E M (1960), *The Disease Concept of Alcoholism*, New Haven, Hillhouse
6   Glatt, M M (1974), *A Guide to Addiction and its Treatment – Drugs, Society and Man*, Lancaster, MTP
7   WHO Expert Committee (1980), *Problems Related to Alcohol Consumption*, Wld Health Org. techn. Rep. Ser. 650, WHO, Geneva
8   Vaillant, G E (1980) in *Alcoholism, Treatment in Transition*, eds Edwards, G and Grant, M, London, Croom Helm, 13–31

Appendix I – Helping Agencies

Medical Council on Alcoholism
3 Grosvenor Crescent,
London SW1X 7EE
Tel: 01 235 4182

**Federation of Alcohol Rehabilitation Establishments
(FARE)**
3 Grosvenor Crescent,
London SW1X 7EE
Tel: 01 235 0609/0600

Turning Point (formerly Helping Hand)
8 Strutton Ground,
London SW1P 2HP
Tel: 01 222 6862/3

Alcohol Education Centre
Maudsley Hospital,
99 Denmark Hill,
London SE5
Tel: 01 703 6333 Ext. 40
    01 703 8053

ACCEPT
Western Hospital,
Seagrave Road,
London SW6
Tel: 01 381 3155

Alcohol Counselling Service
92 Nunhead Grove,
Peckham,
London SE15
Tel: 01 639 3252/3

Aquarius
Aquarius Centre,
41 Newhall Street,
Birmingham 3
Tel: 021 233 1268

Al-Anon
61 Great Dover Street
London SE1
Tel: 01 403 0888

Alateen
c/o Al-Anon
61 Great Dover Street
London SE1
Tel: 01 403 0888

National Council on Alcoholism
3 Grosvenor Crescent,
London SW1X 7EE
Tel: 01 235 4182

Contact points
AVON Council on Alcoholism, 14, Park Row, Bristol BS1 5LJ
    Tel: (0272) 293028/9
BERKSHIRE Council on Alcoholism, Room 5, Old Town Hall,
    Blagrave Street, Reading RG1 1QM
    Tel: (0734) 598850
BIRMINGHAM Council on Alcoholism, 32 Essex Street, Birmingham
    B5 4TR
    Tel: (021) 622 2041
COVENTRY & WARWICKSHIRE Council on Alcoholism, 5a Priory
    Row, Coventry CV1 5EX
    Tel: (0203) 26619 & 26610
CUMBRIA Council on Alcoholism, (temporary address) 6 West
    Walls, Carlisle CA3 8UG
    Tel: (0228) 44140

DEVON Council on Alcoholism, 4 Wynards, Magdalen Street, Exeter EX2 4HX
Tel: (0392) 55151

EAST SUSSEX Council on Alcoholism, 190 Church Road, Hove, Brighton
Tel: (0273) 739147

GREATER MANCHESTER & LANCASHIRE Council on Alcoholism, 87 Oldham Street, Manchester M4 1LN
Tel: (061) 834 9777

HAMPSHIRE Council on Alcoholism, 18 West Park Road, Southampton SO1 0GA
Tel: (0703) 30219

HEREFORD & WORCESTER Council on Alcoholism, (temporary address) c/o Community Health Council, Severn House, 10 The Moors, Worcester WR1 3EE
Tel: (0905) 27417

HERTFORDSHIRE & BEDFORDSHIRE Council on Alcoholism, 3–5 George Street, Luton, Beds
Tel: (0582) 23434

HUMBERSIDE Council on Alcoholism, St Andrew's Information & Advisory Centre, Albion Street, Grimsby DN32 7DY
Tel: (0472) 53416

KENT Council on Alcoholism, 41 Wincheap, Canterbury
Tel: (0227) 54740

LEEDS Council on Alcoholism, 21/22 West Bar Chambers, 38 Boar Lane, Leeds LS1 5DB
Tel: (0532) 31029

LEICESTER & LEICESTERSHIRE Council on Alcoholism, 7 Pocklington's Walk, Leicester
Tel: (0533) 539538

LONDON Council on Alcoholism, 146 Queen Victoria Street, London EC4V 4BX
Tel: (01) 236 9770

MERSEYSIDE, LANCASHIRE & CHESHIRE Council on Alcoholism, 1st Floor, The Fruit Exchange, Victoria Street, Liverpool L2 6QU
Tel: (051) 236 0300 and 1372

NORFOLK Council on Alcoholism, 11 Parsonage Square, Norwich
Tel: (0603) 60070

NORTHAMPTON (County of) Council on Alcoholism, Bungalow 1, The Health Clinic, 18a Oxford Street, Wellingborough, Northants NN8 4JE
Tel: (0933) 223796

NORTH EAST Council on Alcoholism, Mea House, Ellison Place, Newcastle-on-Tyne NE1 8XS
Tel: (0632) 20797

NOTTINGHAMSHIRE Council on Alcoholism, 86, Mansfield Road, Nottingham
Tel: (0602) 582807

OXFORDSHIRE Council on Alcoholism, c/o Health Education Unit, 103 Banbury Road, Oxford
Tel: (0865) 511451

SHEFFIELD Council on Alcoholism, Lawton Tonge Centre, 8 Beech Hill Road, Sheffield S10 2SB
Tel: (0742) 666165

SOMERSET Council on Alcoholism, 3 Upper High Street, Taunton TA1 3PX
Tel: (0823) 88174

WALES

SOUTH GLAMORGAN Alcoholism and Information Service, 13 Richmond Crescent, Cardiff
Tel: (0222) 499499

WEST GLAMORGAN Council on Alcoholism, Alcohol Centre, 75 Uplands Crescent, Uplands, Swansea
Tel: (0792) 57519

CHANNEL ISLANDS

GUERNSEY Council on Alcoholism, 50 The Bordage, St. Peter Port
Tel: (0481) 23255

JERSEY Council on Alcoholism, 2 Colomberie Chambers, 1 Green Street, St. Helier
Tel: (0534) 36672

Contact Al-Anon if you have a group in your area. It is a fellowship comprising the families and friends of alcoholics who know all about it from experience and provides emotional and social support for its members.

Society for the Study of Addiction to Alcohol and Other Drugs
(Hon. Sec. Dr B Ettore)
Addiction Research Unit,
1 Denmark Hill,
London SE5 8AI

Alcoholics Anonymous (AA)

Service offices

ENGLAND & WALES General Service Office, 11 Redcliffe Gardens, London SW10 9BG *Tel:* (01) 352 9779 Monday–Friday 9.30 am–5 pm

BIRMINGHAM Today Centre, 3 Birchfields Road, Sixways, Lozells, Birmingham B19 1SU *Tel:* (021) 523 9310 every evening AFTER 7.30 pm.

BRISTOL Western Service Office, P.O. Box 42, Bristol BS99 7RJ *Tel:* (0272) 25520/25926

BOLTON East Lancs Intergroup, 2 Hulme Street *Tel:* Bolton 25566 every evening 7.00 pm–11.00 pm

LONDON London Region Telephone Service (01) 351 3344 10 am 10 pm every day, Ansaphone other times.

LUTON Lea Valley Intergroup, 4 Midland Road, Luton *Tel*: Luton 35005 after 7 pm every day, from 4.30 pm – 11.30 pm and 12.30 –11.30 pm on Saturday and Sunday

NOTTINGHAM East Midlands Intergroup *Tel:* Nottingham 47100, 7 pm–10 pm every evening

SCOTLAND Scottish Service Office, Baltic Chambers, 50 Wellington Street, Glasgow *Tel:* (041) 221 9027 Monday–Friday 9 am–5 pm.

NORTHERN IRELAND Central Service Office, 73 Lisburn Road, Belfast 9. *Tel:* Belfast 23305

EIRE Service Office, 26 Essex Quay, Dublin *Tel:* Dublin 774809

A list of NHS units can be obtained from the National Council on Alcoholism.

Appendix II – Further Reading

An enormous amount of literature concerned with problems of alcohol and alcoholism has accumulated in recent years. Only a few of the many valuable books can be mentioned here, and readers specially interested in certain aspects are advised to consult the list of references at the end of the chapter concerned. A detailed survey, *Recent Books on Alcohol Misuse and Alcoholism* (concentrating in the main on books and publications in the UK), was published recently (Glatt, M M in *British Book News*, March 1980, 133–7), with the subheadings; 'Historical and General Introductory Texts'; 'Texts on the Misuse of Other Drugs as well as Alcohol'; 'Books for Special Professional and Non-Professional Groups'; 'Treatment and Rehabilitation'; 'Prevention'; and 'Periodical Publications'.

The Disease Concept of Alcoholism, E M Jellinek, Hillhouse Press, Connect., 1960

Alcohol Dependence, B D Hore, Butterworths, London, 1976

Alcoholism, N Kessel and H Walton, Harmondsworth, Penguin, 1965

The Hidden Alcoholic in General Practice, R H Wilkins, London, Elek Science, 1974

The Management of Alcoholism, B Ritson and C Hassall, Edinburgh, Livingstone, 1970

A Guide to Alcohol and Drug Dependence, J S Madden, Bristol, Wright, 1979

A Guide to Addiction and its Treatment – Drugs, Society and Man, M M Glatt, Manchester, MTP

Alcoholism Treatment in Transition, eds G Edwards and M Grant, London, Croom Helm, 1980

The Biology of Alcoholism (five volumes), eds B Kissin and H

Begleiter, New York, Plenum, published in the 1970s

Alcohol and Alcohol Problems: New Thinking and New Directions, eds W J Filstead, J B Rossi and M Keller, Cambridge, Mass., Ballinger, 1976

Emerging Concepts of Alcohol Dependence, E Mansell Pattison, M B Sobell and L C Sobell, New York, Springer, 1977

Alcohol and Road Traffic, ed. J D J Havard, London, BMA, 1963

Alcoholism, a Medical Profile, First Internat. Med. Confer. on Alcoholism eds N Kessel, A Hawker and H Chalke, London, B Edsall, 1973

Notes on Alcohol and Alcoholism, ed. S Caruana, London, Med. Council on Alcoholism, 1975

Home Office, *Habitual Drunken Offenders*, London, HMSO, 1971

Alcohol and Alcoholism, Report of a Special Committee of the Royal College of Psychiatrists, London, Tavistock, 1980

From Drinking to Alcoholism: A Sociological Commentary, D Robinson, London, Wiley, 1976'

The Big Book, Alcoholics Anonymous, New York, AA World Services, 1939

Addiction and Brain Damage, ed. D Richter, London, Croom Helm, 1980

Metabolic Aspects of Alcoholism, ed. C S Lieber, Lancaster, MTP, 1977

Sucht und Missbrauch, eds H Steinbrecher and H Solms, Stuttgart, Thieme, 2nd ed. 1975

World Health Organisation, *Alcohol-Related Disabilities*, Geneva, WHO, 1977

World Health Organisation Expert Committee Reports (on problems of alcohol and alcoholism), Geneva, World Health Organisation Technical Report Series, 1951, 42; 1952, 48; 1954, 84; 1955, 84; 1967, 363; 1980, 650

Annual International Institutes on the Prevention and Treatment of Alcoholism, organised by the International Council on Alcohol and Addictions, Case Postale 140, 1001 Lausanne, Switzerland

Drugs, Alcohol and Tobacco in Britain, eds J Zacune and C Hensman, London, Heinemann Medical, 1971

Drug Dependence: Current Problems and Issues, ed. M M Glatt Lancaster, MTP, 1977

Journals of Studies on Alcohol, Centre of Alcohol Studies, Rutgers University, New Jersey, USA

British Journal of Addiction (Official Organ of the Society for the
    Study of Addiction), Longman
British Journal of Alcohol and Alcoholism (Official Organ of the
    Medical Council on Alcoholism), B Edsall
Series of pamphlets and Journals published by:
    International Council on Alcohol and Addictions (ICCA),
        Lausanne;
    Center of Alcohol Studies, Rutgers University, New Jersey;
    Research Foundation on Alcohol and Addictions, Toronto,
    Ontario, Canada;
    Alcoholics Anonymous;
    Al-Anon; Family Groups;
    Medical Council on Alcoholism;
    National Council on Alcoholism, London;
    United Kingdom Alliance (*Alliance News*);
    Deutsche Hauptstelle Gegen die Suchtgefahren (DHS);
International Journal of Addictions (Marcel Dekker, USA)
American Journal of Drug and Alcohol Abuse (Marcel Dekker,
    USA)
Drug and Alcohol Dependence (ICCA)
Drug Dependence, Excerpta Medica (Amsterdam)
Addictive Diseases (Spectrum, USA)
The Journal (Addiction Research Foundation, Toronto)

Index

DRUGS IN PERSPECTIVE

MARTIN A. PLANT

A lucid and non-alarmist approach to the often emotive subject of mind-altering drugs, reflecting current research and thinking and placing all drugs, whether 'social', 'illicit', or 'prescribed' in their proper perspective.

Tobacco and alcohol, tranquillisers and sleeping pills, illicit drugs – the effects, legal status and patterns of use of each are discussed, and the author identifies the social and age groups at risk in each case. He considers the underlying causes of the increase in drug consumption in the West in recent years and critically appraises treatment of drug problems.

This is a book for anyone interested in the subject of drug consumption and its social effects, and will be particularly helpful to those whose work involves contact with drug problems.

TEACH YOURSELF BOOKS

CHILDREN WITH HANDICAPS

LORNA SELFE AND LYNN STOW

This wide-ranging survey considers every aspect of children's handicaps – physical, sensory and intellectual, specific learning difficulties, language problems, social disadvantages and emotional maladjustment – giving practical advice oriented towards remedial help. The emphasis throughout is on positive achievement. Recent trends in educational practice and legislation are examined, and the findings of the Warnock Report discussed. Coming to terms with parenting a handicapped child and a comprehensive list of helping organisations are also included.

Teachers, social workers and medical staff will find this book invaluable and parents of handicapped children will appreciate its positive approach and practical advice.

Lorna Selfe is an educational psychologist who works and researches in the field of children's handicaps. Lynn Stow currently lectures and researches in educational psychology and has worked with children with learning difficulties.

TEACH YOURSELF BOOKS

USING CHILD PSYCHIATRY

DEREK STEINBERG

A lucid and thought-provoking analysis of the aims, uses and limitations of child psychiatry.

The author suggests that problems in collaboration between professionals in the child care field, misunderstanding about each other's functions, skills and difficulties, and uncertainty about both the nature of psychiatric problems and the scope of child psychiatry itself, result in too many children receiving poorly co-ordinated attention from too many professional workers. He defines the contribution of child and adolescent psychiatry, and argues that other agencies, too, should delineate their functions more precisely, with more informed and skilful consultation between professionals, and a higher priority for the supervision and training needs of individual workers.

The author is a leading child psychiatrist who works in the child and adolescent departments of the Maudsley and Bethlem Royal Hospitals.

TEACH YOURSELF BOOKS

PSYCHOLOGY FOR TODAY

ED. BILL GILLHAM

This introductory text by past and present members of Nottingham University's Department of Psychology surveys what has been described as 'the most important human science'. Each author is an expert on the subject he discusses and the book as a whole reflects, in summary, current thinking on all the major areas of psychology studied at universities and polytechnics.

The 'non-technical' language makes this book suitable for a wide readership and it will be particularly useful in sixth forms as an advanced course and at first-year undergraduate level. Each chapter is intended as an introduction to its subject and contains a comprehensive list of references for further reading.

A lively and wide-ranging collaboration, the book goes a long way towards meeting what its editor considers the greatest challenge to psychology today – 'communicating its methods and findings to people at large'.

TEACH YOURSELF BOOKS